BELONGING TO THE NATION

BELONGING TO THE NATION

Inclusion and Exclusion in the
Polish-German Borderlands
1939–1951

JOHN J. KULCZYCKI

Harvard University Press

CAMBRIDGE, MASSACHUSETTS
LONDON, ENGLAND
2016

Copyright © 2016 by the President and Fellows of Harvard College
All rights reserved
Printed in the United States of America

First printing

Library of Congress Cataloging-in-Publication Data

Kulczycki, John J., author.
Belonging to the nation : inclusion and exclusion in the
Polish-German borderlands, 1939–1951 / John J. Kulczycki.
    pages cm
Includes bibliographical references and index.
ISBN 978-0-674-65978-0
1. Oder-Neisse Line (Germany and Poland) 2. Nationalism—Germany—History—20th century. 3. Nationalism—Poland—History—20th century. 4. Germans—Poland—History—20th century. 5. Polish people—Germany (East)—History—20th century. 6. World War, 1939–1945—Territorial questions—Poland. 7. World War, 1939–1945—Territorial questions—Germany. 8. Poland—Boundaries—Germany. 9. Germany—Boundaries—Poland. I. Title.
DK4600.O3385K85 2016
305.800943'153—dc23
2015034187

In memory of my brother Al
(1926–2012)

Contents

Introduction 1

1. The Disputed Polish-German Borderlands 8
2. The German Occupation of Poland 25
3. The Creation of a New Poland 53
4. The Recovered Lands and Their Inhabitants 70
5. The Prologue to Polonizing Identities 91
6. The Initial Polish Government Nationality Measures 109
7. After the Potsdam Conference 137
8. The Central Government and Nationality Verification 168
9. The Rehabilitation of *Volksdeutsche* in 1946 205
10. A Year of Crucial Changes 217
11. Nationality Policies Following the End of Mass Expulsion 245
12. The Status of Autochthons at the End of 1949 273
13. The Last Phase of Nationality Verification and Rehabilitation . 284

Conclusion 300

Abbreviations 311
Notes 313
Acknowledgments 387
Index 389

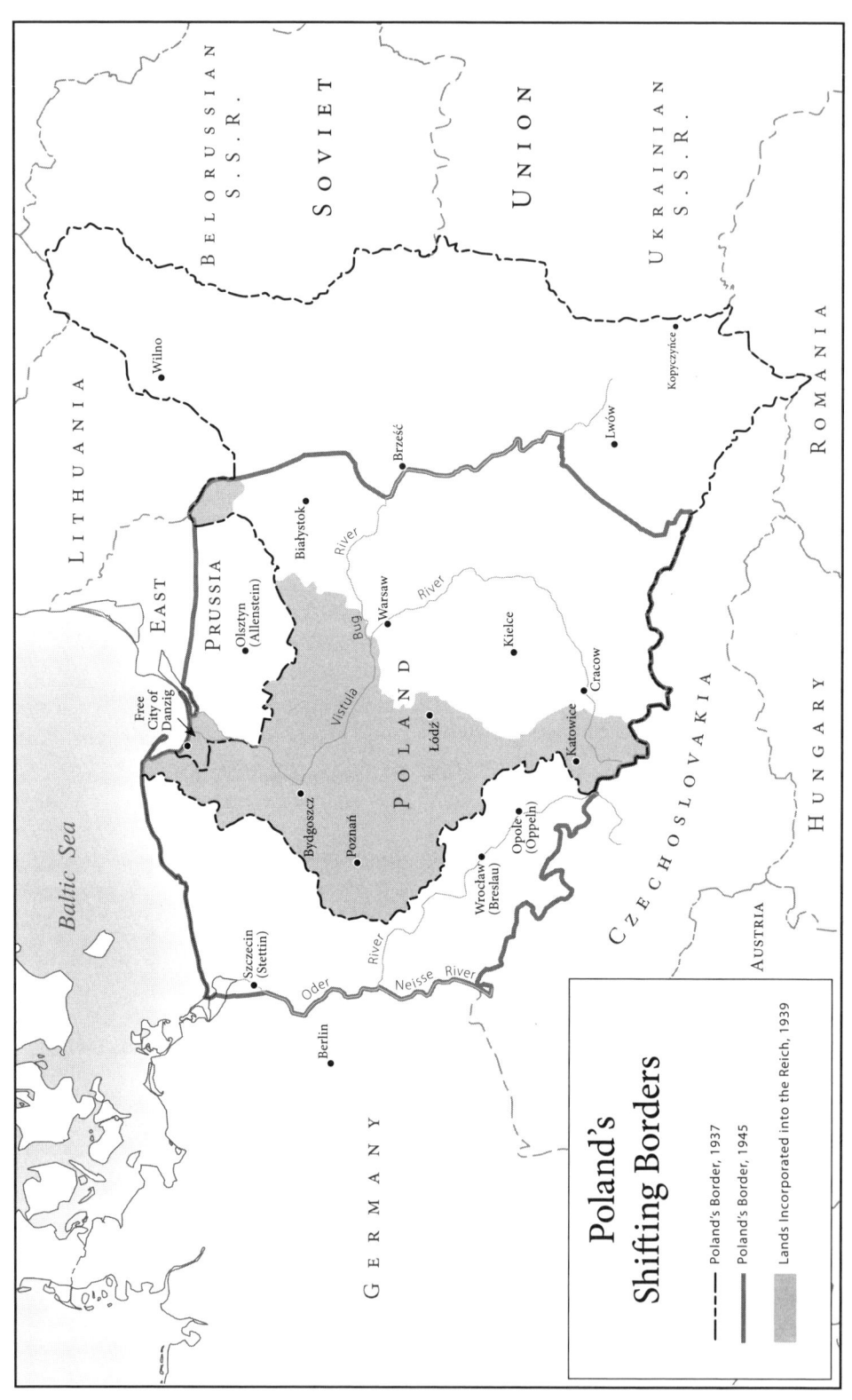

Niech my są Poloki, niech my są Niemce, niech my są Ruski, niech my są Pruski,
zeby my tylko mogli pracować, zeby był spokój, zeby było co jeść,
zeby był cukier dla dzieci.

Let us be Poles, let us be Germans, let us be Russians, let us be Prussians,
just so we can work, that there is peace, that there is something to eat,
that there is sugar for the children.

—*A seventy-year-old woman in Opole Silesia to Stanisław Ossowski, 1945*

Introduction

IN 1939, AFTER invading Poland, the Nazi regime incorporated western Poland into the German Reich and proceeded to recognize Germans with Polish citizenship as *Volksdeutsche*. With Germany's defeat, the communist-dominated Polish regime brought eastern Germany under its administration and recognized German citizens of Polish origin as belonging to the Polish nation. It also established a procedure for *Volksdeutsche* to rejoin the nation. This study focuses on the efforts of both regimes to nationalize these inhabitants of the transnational zone of the Polish-German borderlands that in the imaginations of German and Polish nationalists rightfully belonged to *their* nation. This process of inclusion and exclusion necessarily involved in the formation of an imagined national community is often marginalized in discussions of the emergence of nations.[1]

The centuries-old eastern migration of German-speaking population into Slavic-speaking lands frequently resulted in assimilation, but islands of German culture survived. With the partitioning of the Polish-Lithuanian Commonwealth in the late eighteenth century, its western territory came under Prussian rule. A majority of its inhabitants, however, continued to speak Polish and preserved other elements of Polish culture. Besides this territory, Polish nationalists claimed areas beyond the western border of the Commonwealth, citing the boundaries of territory ruled by the Polish Piast dynasty (the late tenth century to 1370) and the Polish origins of its inhabitants.

Even in the twentieth century, the creation of nation-states in Europe was a relatively recent phenomenon.[2] Yet congruence between the territory of the state and the area inhabited by the titular nation proved difficult to achieve.[3] Disputes over national boundaries and the composition of the nation continued long after the creation of putative nation-states. National minorities within these states seemed to constitute threats to domestic and international stability. Statesmen sought to promote peace by redrawing borders, sanctioning exchanges of populations, and imposing agreements protecting minorities. The treaties that concluded World War I were part of this effort.

The Treaty of Versailles of 1919, however, brought the contradictory pretensions of Polish and German nationalists to a head. It granted part of eastern Germany to the reborn Polish state and left German-speaking as well as Polish-speaking minorities on the "wrong" side of the border. Both states saw the treaty as a violation of the principle of national self-determination and pursued policies that sought to assimilate their national minorities.

The conflict over the Polish-German borderlands reached its apogee in the years 1939 to 1951 as first Germany and then Poland expanded into the borderlands. This was a period of transnational fundamental political, social, economic, and constitutional changes in Europe, with one framework of practice and belief replacing another.[4] Violent movements of population of massive proportions marked the period in Europe and beyond, with the postwar partitioning of India and Palestine and the redrawing of state boundaries. Flight, deportation, expulsion, and forced migration brought these movements about as part of a project of "people-making" and state formation. In Europe much of this displacement of population had a direct link with the war.[5] But war merely provided the occasion for the realization of a conviction that national homogeneity enhanced international peace. Winston Churchill defended an "exchange" of minorities in the House of Commons on 15 December 1944, stating, "There will be no mixture of populations to cause endless trouble. . . . A clean sweep will be made."[6]

In Europe, however, the threat of "mutual assured destruction" contributed more to peace than ethnic reorganization, and international tension and the threat of conflict in Central Europe remained. Near ethnic homogeneity hardly resulted in domestic tranquility in Poland with major social and political disruptions in 1956, 1968, 1970, and 1980–1989. Indeed, it contributed to the massive support for the Solidarity movement in opposition to the government that, along with changes in the Soviet Union, brought about the end of communist rule in Poland. Meanwhile, unassimilated ethnic minorities remain an occasional source of friction in Poland's borderlands.[7]

The Polish-German borderlands constitute an exemplary case, countering the false dichotomy between western and eastern Europe, a division of Europe that the 1989 revolutions called into question and that opened the way for an expansion of the European Union.[8] The pursuit of ethnic homogeneity in the Polish-German borderlands bears comparison with developments in the Lands of the Bohemian Crown. The Nazis killed 89 percent of the Jews in the Czech lands (90 percent in Poland) and 50 percent of the Roma (70 percent in Poland). After the war, throngs of Czechs drove out three million Germans.

As a result whereas before the war, three out of ten inhabitants were German, by 1950 nearly 94 percent were Czech.[9]

With the end of the Cold War the push for ethnic homogeneity resumed, most notably in the Yugoslav wars of the early 1990s, and the term "ethnic cleansing" gained worldwide notoriety. In the midst of those wars, the prominent Polish publicist Marcin Król cited "a country nearly without national minorities" as a positive legacy of communist rule. "I can imagine what would be happening now and during the next century" if Poland had "a compact Ukrainian, Belarusian, and Lithuanian minority."[10] He elides the price paid by these minorities as well as by Jews, Germans, Poles, and others in the "ethnic cleansing" and worse that took place in the years 1939 to 1951. In essence, he advocates one nationalism as a defense against other nationalisms.

Despite the clash between the Nazi and communist ideologies and the difference in the level of violence employed, the German and Polish policies in the years 1939–1951 bear a striking similarity, making them seem less exceptional and suggesting their grounding in wider transnational beliefs and practices. Each regime in turn laid claim to the borderlands out of imperialistic aims—economic, military, political, and strategic—not just on the basis of history or the national identity of the inhabitants. Both in principle saw national identity in biological terms, that is, as determined by descent. But neither enforced this principle universally, if only because reality proved too complicated for such a simplistic approach. Furthermore, officials at the regional and local levels determined what would be done and often acted out of material motives as well as pragmatic considerations. Some gave greater weight to cultural traits and behavior than to evidence of ethnic origin or "racial" characteristics. Both regimes made exceptions, allowing a supposedly temporary presence of national minorities for economic reasons, often under conditions equivalent to slavery. A comparison provides insights into other attempts to achieve ethnic homogeneity.

Such comparisons, however, must be made with care, and not only because of the difference in the level of violence. One must recall that the unprovoked Nazi onslaught elicited the retribution that followed. Maria Dąbrowska relates in her diary under the date 28 June 1948 how angry a Polish professor became during a visit to the United States when an American said, "Why do you complain about what the Germans did to you. After all, you are doing the same to the Germans in the western lands." Although she rejects the comparison, she adds, "If it is permissible to resettle elsewhere a population settled somewhere for centuries, in this case one cannot consider what the Germans did a crime, what the Russians did, what . . . we also are doing."[11]

For Anthony Smith, nationalism involves four elements: a vision, a culture, a solidarity, and a policy. The vision consists of humanity "naturally" divided into distinct communities of history and culture called "nations," which define the identity of their members. Nationalists base the solidarity of the nation on its historic homeland, and they preceded the Nazis and Polish communists in claiming the Polish-German borderlands. The pursuit of ethnic homogeneity involved a process of selecting who belongs and who does not.[12] This study focuses on that process.

In the past nationalist governments sought to assimilate national minorities by various means, limiting their freedom of cultural expression (language, religion, etc.) or pressuring them to adopt the culture of the titular nation. In this respect developments in the Polish-German borderlands in the years 1939–1951 did not differ except in the degree of violence, especially by the Nazis. What differed was the official effort to seek out individuals who supposedly met criteria qualifying them for membership in the nation in whose name the authorities ruled.

After incorporating western Poland into the Reich, the German authorities registered selected Polish citizens in the territory on a German nationality list (*Deutsche Volksliste* or DVL), giving them rights denied to other Polish citizens, who suffered deportation, enslavement, or death. As the Polish authorities regained control of western Poland, they initiated the legal "rehabilitation" of the *Volksdeutsche* who held Polish citizenship before the war. In the territory of eastern Germany that came under Polish administration—the so-called "Recovered Lands" (*Ziemie Odzyskane*)—the Polish authorities introduced a process of "nationality verification" of "autochthons," i.e., supposedly indigenous German citizens of Polish origin.

The "rehabilitated" or "verified" could stay—or had to stay—within the borders of the Polish state with the right of citizenship. Those who did not undergo these legal procedures or did not do so successfully were expelled, frequently under inhuman conditions that caused great suffering and in some cases death, though many were retained "temporarily" under conditions of forced labor that were only gradually alleviated. The Law on Polish Citizenship of January 1951, which eliminated the requirement of Polish nationality as a qualification for citizenship, theoretically brought this period to a close, though conflicts over national identity continued.

Rehabilitation and verification tested the Polishness of those who underwent the procedures. Although contemporary sources did not use the term "genuine Poles" (*prawdziwi Polacy*), the period initiated the questioning of the "genuine" character of various groups that marks the history of postwar Poland. Were the rulers of Stalinist Poland "genuine Poles" or merely Soviet puppets? Were the many Polish Jews who left Poland in the late 1940s, in 1956, and in 1968–1969 "genuine Poles"? Who were the "genuine Poles" in the 1980s—the members of the Solidarity Trade Union or its communist opponents? Even today some question whether those who support membership in the European Union or seek to minimize the role of the Roman Catholic Church in affairs of state are "genuine Poles."[13]

All of this presupposes the existence of nations, which some argue is a concept created by social and official institutions with no concrete reality. At best we can regard a nation as a process of becoming, never fully achieving realization other than perhaps at a fleeting moment of national tragedy or triumph. As suggested by Rogers Brubaker, I focus on "nation as a category of practice," on "nationness as a contingent event or happening" in the Polish-German borderlands in the years 1939–1951. Similarly, Geoff Eley speaks of focusing on what the "nation" signifies in terms of practices, definitions, and official actions, giving it an appearance of solidity.[14]

The *Deutsche Volksliste,* rehabilitation, and nationality verification gave national identity a salience that previously it did not necessarily possess, on the nationalist supposition that it indicated where one's supreme loyalty lay. As a further supposition, one's descent, name, the language spoken at home, the church prayed in, or other characteristics of behavior came to define one's national identity. We, however, should not assume that everyone has a national identity as ascribed by state institutions and elites—or that a national identity is stable, palpable, and homogeneous among all members of the purported nation rather than an ongoing narrative constantly redefined.[15] Indeed, many residents of the Polish-German borderlands were indifferent to nationality or without an irrevocable attachment to a nationality despite the nationalizing efforts of the interwar Polish and German governments and the German occupation, during which one's national or ethnic identity could mean the difference between life and death. Thus, my study responds to calls for a reexamination of understandings of the nation and the meaning of citizenship in Poland and for additional studies of the postwar displacements.[16] It joins other recent studies on Central Europe that question the national narrative of a natural, progressive nationalization of a people and documents that national indifference continued to exist in the mid-twentieth century.[17]

Nevertheless, in this study, I speak of Germans, Poles, and so forth, as if they belonged to a fixed category. This reflects the sources on which the study relies and serves as a convenient shorthand to distinguish one set of the population from another and indicate its dimensions and fate. Unfortunately, this can foster the illusion that the groups are fixed, internally united, and measureable.[18] Similarly, I use other terminology employed by the sources, such as "autochthons" and "Recovered Lands," without accepting their implications. The term "re-Polonization" has an especially paradoxical character, suggesting the individual subjected to the process was once Polish and therefore should be again. Similarly useful but potentially misleading is the euphemistic official identification of inhabitants of eastern Poland (*kresy* or borderlands) ceded to the Soviet Union in 1945 who emigrated to Poland within its new borders as "repatriates," even though they left their homeland for a new homeland they never knew. In the Recovered Lands they were joined by repatriates from other countries; "settlers," a term used exclusively to refer to inhabitants of prewar Poland within its postwar borders (Central Poland); and "re-emigrants," who resided abroad before the war.[19]

The literature on the subject of the Polish-German borderlands in the years 1939–1951 is vast and seems to grow daily. Since the end of communism in Poland and the unification of Germany, the expulsion of the German population from Poland has been a source of considerable controversy. "Ethnic cleansing" in Yugoslavia in the 1990s prompted proposals for the creation of a European center against expulsion, adding to the dispute.[20]

My study examines the processes involved in deciding who should *not* be expelled, whereas the expulsion itself has occupied the center stage in the controversy.[21] I give priority to primary sources with a wide array of documentation, above all the four volumes of selected documents from the Polish archives published in Polish and German.[22]

I devote far more attention to the postwar years during which the Polish authorities dealt with the consequences of Nazi nationality policies, complementing the recent scholarship on the immediate aftermath of the war in Europe, a period that long fell into the gap between studies of the war and the Holocaust on one hand and histories of the Cold War on the other.[23] This period is also much less well known, in part because most of the existing scholarship is available primarily in Polish and is narrowly focused, often on a single region or one aspect of my study.[24] A few take an essentialist approach to national identity that I call into question.

The German Nationality List, in particular, was and continues to be a source of controversy. During the period of communist rule in Poland, historians and publicists, with few exceptions, emphasized coercion in registration on the list, ignoring the differences among the various regions of the German occupation and the several hundred thousand Poles who signed voluntarily. Gerhard Wolf illuminates these differences and the question of coercion.[25]

Hardly any topic has attained the political significance that ethnic identity and "genuine" political loyalty currently enjoy. Secessionist movements bedevil states on nearly all continents, including Europe, from Scotland to Ukraine. European struggles over Muslims and Roma are echoed by concerns about undocumented immigrants in the United States. Labor migrants from earlier decades, asylum seekers, and refugees have prompted antiforeigner feelings and hostility to immigration. Even terrorism is often linked to ethnic identity. There are, then, continuities between the issues of the years 1939–1951 and the present. The emphasis of those years on ethnic or "racial" homogeneity contributed to the development of "a culture of purity."[26] In this context, my study warns of the dangers and complications associated with equating a supposed ethnic origin with a particular national loyalty and using it as the primary criterion for granting the rights of citizenship.

[1]

The Disputed Polish-German Borderlands

THE POLISH-LITHUANIAN COMMONWEALTH partitioned by Russia, Prussia, and Austria in the late eighteenth century had a ruling elite of multiethnic origin, including such elements as the Protestant German-speaking nobles and burghers of Royal Prussia, linked by "loyalty to a constitution, a common history and a common political culture." It constituted a *political* nation that identified with the state and its territory, where this social stratum enjoyed "golden liberty," a civic nation *avant la lettre*.[1]

After the destruction of the Commonwealth, political activists initially focused on its resurrection within the territory prior to 1772 and thought of the nation in terms of all its inhabitants, an extension of the civic nation. As the great Polish historian and sincere democrat Joachim Lelewel wrote in 1836, "Ukrainian, Kashub, Ruthenian, Great or Little Pole [i.e., inhabitants of Great and Little Poland], Lithuanian, Podolian, Żmudzin, Mazur, Volhynian, and the son of whatever land of the former Commonwealth is a Pole and in this name alone do we see our whole."[2]

But the modern ideology of nationalism "holds that humanity is naturally divided into nations, that nations are known by certain characteristics which can be ascertained, and that the only legitimate type of government is national self-government."[3] Moreover, "the right by people to choose their own type of governments" came to mean the right of nations to their own states.[4] In 1861 John Stuart Mill argued,

> Free institutions are next to impossible in a country made up of different nationalities. Among a people without fellow-feeling, especially if they read and speak different languages, the united public opinion, necessary to the working of representative government cannot exist. . . .
>
> For the preceding reasons, it is in general a necessary condition of free institutions that the boundaries of governments should coincide in the main with those of nationalities.[5]

This doctrine achieved its "greatest triumph" in the twentieth century, "the enshrinement of national self-determination as the organizing principle of international order."[6]

The concept of a Polish nation based on linguistic and cultural ties also gradually challenged that of a community with a shared history and political life. A growing awareness of ethnic differences contributed to this development. Moreover, a distinctly anti-Polish character marked the national movements that arose among Ukrainians and Lithuanians.[7]

Michał Bobrzyński, a leading conservative political activist, saw Poland's expansion beyond its ethnic heartland as a source of the Commonwealth's downfall. In 1879 in his classic history of Poland, he concluded:

> Civilizing and colonizing the vast Ruthenian and Lithuanian territories... absorbed our most vital forces, dissipated them in the far east instead of what one would have intensified in a narrower space, united, and awakened life more deeply but more vigorously. Let us for only a moment think that these millions of Polish people, this capital and labor, which we poured into the east, remained within our ethnographic borders, what a different route our internal development would have taken![8]

Bolesław Wysłouch, who founded an independent political movement among the peasantry of Austrian Poland, was one of the first to advocate an ethnically homogeneous Poland. In 1886 the *Przegląd Społeczny* edited by Wysłouch stated the goal unambiguously: "The Unification of all parts of ethnographic Poland in one whole—as the first point of the national program, and *the achievement within these borders of the most complete homogeneity*—as the most important task of our internal national activity—that is the task of the first rank of the nationality aspect of our program."[9]

Under the leadership of Roman Dmowski, the National Democratic Party (*Endecja,* its Polish acronym, later renamed the National Party, *Stronnictwo Narodowe*), which published its first program in 1897, also saw the future of the Polish nation in the Polish-speaking peasantry. For the party, language constituted the major component of the national culture along with a common history and racial identity. On this basis, Poland should incorporate the Polish-speaking ethnic groups of East Prussia, Pomerania, and Silesia, areas beyond the borders of the Commonwealth.[10] *Endecja* along with other right-wing nationalist parties elsewhere during this period "envisioned the creation of political communities whose values, structures, and institutions would be a direct expression of their own people's idiosyncratic character, in which the civic identity would simply function as the public expression of ethnic kinship."[11]

Some Polish socialists reflected these nationalist trends. In 1903 Leon Wasilewski defended the rights of Poles in Upper Silesia and Mazuria. The

Polish Marxist Kazimierz Kelles-Krauz, chief theoretician and ideologist of the Polish Socialist Party (*Polska Partia Socjalistyczna* or PPS) until his premature death in 1905, believed that the proletariat could achieve socialism only in a democratic nation-state without large ethnic minorities, anticipating the view of Soviet communist leaders—minus the democratic element.[12]

With the collapse of Poland's partitioners at the end of World War I, Ignacy Daszyński, the head of the Polish Social-Democratic Party in Austria, led a group that issued a manifesto on 7 November 1918.[13] It declared that the Polish People's Republic would embrace "all lands inhabited by the Polish people, with a seacoast of its own," reiterating almost verbatim the thirteenth of President Woodrow Wilson's fourteen points of January 1918. Significantly, the manifesto also proclaimed "full equality of political and civic rights for all citizens irrespective of origin, faith and nationality."[14]

Of all the Polish political camps, only *Endecja* had a coherent conception of Poland's future borders.[15] In 1917 with the Allies in mind, Dmowski published in English his proposal for the reorganization of East Central Europe. Portraying Germany as the main threat to peace, he argued the western border of Poland should run

> from the western extremity of the Carpathian Mountains to the Baltic . . . Such a line would correspond more or less to the western ethnographic frontier of Poland. . . . Such a frontier would not only be the most rational from the geographical, economic, and strategical standpoint, but would constitute a true racial frontier between the two nations. West of it there would be a German country, having small Polish minorities in certain districts: east of it a Polish country, with small German minorities.[16]

With regard to Poland's eastern border, however, Dmowski urged something other than "a strict application of the ethnographic principle."[17] Essentially, the western border was to be based on ethnicity and the eastern border on history, oddly foreshadowing the recourse to these same two arguments by Polish communists in defense of Poland's post–World War II borders, but with a reverse application.[18]

By 1914 unresolved demands for national self-determination seemed to threaten international stability and even caused the Great War itself. Each side in the war used national self-determination in its propaganda against the enemy. Before the war ended President Wilson adopted the promotion of national self-determination as his mission.[19]

Led by Wilson, the Paris Peace Conference sought to apply the principle in central and eastern Europe. There language stood for nationality. A leading German statistician arguing that language provided the only adequate indicator of nationality convinced the International Statistical Congress in 1873 that state censuses should include a question on language.[20] Some states manipulated questions about language in their censuses, as Prussia did in 1905 and 1910 to minimize the Polish-speaking population, by changing the way bilingual speakers were counted or choosing the everyday language over the mother tongue. Moreover, since the 1830s the Prussian authorities promoted the German language among the Polish-speaking population and colonized Prussian Poland with ethnic Germans.[21]

The reliance on ethnographic data in applying the principle of national self-determination to disputed areas legitimized the equation of ethnicity with nationality and favored an ethnic national identity over a civic one.[22] Despite the extreme difficulty of making clear and obvious decisions in assigning territory, Wilson continued to advocate national self-determination. Winston Churchill, minister of war during the peace conference, also took a positive view of its implementation in a book published in 1929.[23]

The Treaty of Versailles shocked the German delegation at the peace conference. Expectations aroused by Wilson's rhetoric contributed to a denunciation of the treaty by virtually all sectors of German public opinion. Contempt for the Poles heightened German resentment of the loss of territory to Poland.[24]

To offset the imperfect realization of national self-determination and to prevent secessionist movements and unilateral foreign intervention on behalf of national minorities, the victorious Allied powers turned over their protection in the new states to the League of Nations, legitimizing the creation of nation-states and the aspirations of those minorities to be part of their own nation-state. Once Germany became a permanent member of the League Council in 1926, it used the League's Minority Protection System in support of a revisionist foreign policy directed against Poland. With Germany's backing, Poland's German minority petitioned the Minority Protection System more often than any other group.[25] In the view of Christian Raitz von Frentz, this ultimately destroyed the system and "paved the way for forcible population transfers on an unprecedented scale."[26]

The permanent resettlement of a minority came into practice before World War I. An annex to the Treaty of Constantinople of 1913 between Bulgaria and the Ottoman Empire provided for an exchange of population. In 1915 the Swiss anthropologist and ethnographer George Montandon proposed the "massive transplanting" of those who were unwilling or unable to be absorbed by the national majority of a state with borders based on ethnic criteria.[27]

The Treaty of Lausanne of 1923 between the Allied powers and Turkish Nationalists set the most important precedent. The Turks insisted on a compulsory "exchange" of population with Greece, resulting in tremendous suffering. Because religion was used as the criterion (reflecting the Ottoman *millet* system), the expulsion of 1.5 million "Greeks" included some 50,000

Greek Orthodox Turks; and the expulsion of 400,000 to 500,000 "Turks" included Greek and other non-Turkish-speaking Muslims. The refugees from Anatolia spoke a different dialect than the Greeks among whom they were settled. They particularly resented being barred from returning to their ancestral homelands as well as the inadequate compensation for lost property and their exclusion from the negotiation of the agreement. Their integration proved difficult, and their housing situation and that of many of their descendants remained unsatisfactory more than a half century later.[28]

Mindful of Poland's own ethnic minorities, who constituted more than a third of its interwar inhabitants, a Polish specialist in population movements in 1931 hailed the results of the Treaty of Lausanne for Turkey as "extremely significant":

> From a multilingual, multinational state, it became a state of far advanced national consolidation. . . . A further consequence of the consistent policy with regard to migration movements is that the Turkish republic finally rid itself of irredenta of national minorities in its own country, . . . irredenta which during the period of the liquidation of the world war led Turkey to the deadly danger of nearly complete annihilation.[29]

Others later also claimed the Treaty of Lausanne successfully dealt with the problem of national minorities. Czechoslovak President Edvard Beneš had it in mind when on 15 September 1938 he sought to appease Hitler by offering a territorial concession in return for accepting the compulsory transfer of 1.5 to 2 million Sudeten Germans.[30] The achievement of nationalist goals by means of forced removal trumped the democratic content of national self-determination.

Self-Determination in the Borderlands

In setting the Polish-German border, the Allied powers made a minor concession to self-determination by mandating plebiscites in Upper Silesia and East Prussia. The assumptions that "nationality follows language" and, more fundamentally, that a cultural or ethnic identity dictated loyalty to a particular political identity proved problematic.[31] The human desire for the security and prosperity offered by a state does not necessarily depend on its congruence with the area inhabited by the ethnic group an individual identifies with.[32] But the nationalist assumption that everyone has an unalterable national identity meant that an individual can decide once and for all at a particular moment to which nation-state he wishes to belong—after all, one cannot hold "a daily plebiscite," which Ernest Renan famously suggested brings a nation into existence.[33]

Upper Silesia

Historically, neighboring states contested control of Upper Silesia. The Polish Piast kingdom that ruled the territory disintegrated into regional principalities in the twelfth century. From the end of that century, the independent Piast princes in Silesia sponsored German colonization to develop the region economically, initiating a centuries-long process of cultural Germanization. Gradually—the last Piast ruler died in 1653—the territory successively came under the Bohemian crown, the Habsburg monarchy, and, for most of Silesia, the Kingdom of Prussia, which settled Protestants in Silesia and promoted the German language, with Lower Silesia becoming overwhelmingly German-speaking by the nineteenth century.

At the turn of the nineteenth and twentieth centuries, Protestants constituted about 9 percent of Upper Silesia's population, though in Kluczbork County Protestants made up more than 65 percent of the population. On the eve of World War I the rural population and most industrial workers of Silesia spoke a Silesian-Polish dialect that included numerous German loan words. Except for counties west of the Oder River, it dominated in rural areas over the German language, which was generally more widely used in urban areas.[34]

A wide social gap divided the mostly Slavic-speaking labor force in industry and mines from the German owners and managers, so that class antagonism marked their relations as much as any ethnic antagonism. However, class ties and the overwhelmingly predominant Catholic religion linked the Slavic-speaking natives to working-class Germans. This social and ethnic structure set the region apart from neighboring regions of Austrian Galicia and Russian Poland. Only two forms of overarching loyalty enjoyed broad support: a state patriotism connected with the person of the Kaiser and a Catholic patriotism strongly identified with the region. The basic traits of the post-1989 Upper Silesian identity noted by sociologist Danuta Berlińska seem valid for earlier periods: a deep attachment to the Catholic Church and its local rituals, transcending loyalty to a particular nation; an abiding tie to the region as homeland and to its dialect; and orderliness, cleanliness, and the rule of law often perceived as "Germanic."[35]

With Germany's defeat fierce competition arose between proponents of Upper Silesia remaining with Germany or of becoming part of Poland. A separate status for Silesia, expressed in the rhetoric of self-determination, also attracted many members of the region's elite, including the influential Catholic clergy. To them it seemed to offer the best chance of preserving the region's unique culture and economic strength. But ultimately the choice came down to Poland or Germany.

The plebiscite did not take place until 20 March 1921. In the interim Polish activists organized two armed uprisings against the continued German administrative and security presence. The plebiscite campaign waged by each side further heightened national tensions, making it difficult for individual clerics to minister to both language groups. For regional and confessional activists the conflict was a fratricidal war.[36]

The 1910 census suggests about a third of the population of the plebiscite area spoke German as a mother tongue and almost two-thirds Polish. Yet 59.6 percent opted for Germany and 40.4 percent for Poland, as a substantial minority of German speakers as well as of Polish speakers chose the "wrong" nation-state, expressing national allegiances that were "mutable and conditional, oscillating between cultural connections to Poland and familiarity with the rights and obligations of German citizenship." Among Polish speakers doubts about the future of the Polish state and disillusion with activities of Polish partisans probably played a bigger role than a positive view of Germany. Among German speakers some recalled their Polish origins or reacted against the social-economic domination of German nationalists and Protestants. The propaganda in both languages highlighted the potential economic consequences of the vote, which possibly influenced the voters more than any other factor.[37]

The Treaty of Versailles mandated consideration of the communal-level results in drawing the Polish-German border. But in the industrial district, Polish-leaning rural areas and working-class suburbs surrounded German-leaning cities. Distrust of the Allies and impatience with the diplomatic negotiations led to the third and most successful of the Polish Silesian Uprisings, also the bloodiest, with fatalities in the thousands, as the German paramilitary *Freikorps* entered the fray. Finally in October 1921 the Allied Supreme Council settled on a border that ran through the industrial district.

The Geneva Convention signed by Poland and Germany on 15 May 1922 recognizing the border guaranteed the rights of the national and religious minorities on each side. Significantly, article 74 accepted a subjective definition of nationality: "The question of whether a person does or does not belong to a racial, linguistic or religious minority may not be disputed by the authorities."[38] Nevertheless, both states pressured the minorities to assimilate to the titular nation.[39]

Following the partitioning of Silesia, about 10 percent of the region's population migrated to the "right" side of the border. But the majority of those who found themselves on the "wrong" side remained where they were, some assimilating to the dominant culture, others maintaining their traditions. Bilingual practices survived in both Polish and German Upper Silesia. Even those identified as German or Polish retained elements of the regional identity and did not fully assimilate to their respective nations.[40]

In German (Opole) Upper Silesia Germanization of Slavic place names began in 1931 and of personal names a year later. Germanization intensified once the Nazis came to power in 1933. The totalitarian system sought to force those with mixed feelings or who thought of themselves as Silesians to identify unambiguously as Germans. In 1937, when the Geneva Convention expired, the authorities saw to the removal of Polish shop signs and inscriptions. Banning the Polish language from all public spheres exacerbated linguistic differences among the generations. In the census of 1939 the authorities counted as German those who indicated their language as Upper Silesian, leaving only 2,760 inhabitants regarded as Poles.[41] At the start of the war, signs appeared in Silesian villages with the slogan "Whoever speaks Polish is a traitor to Germany," making it dangerous to use the local Polish dialect even in one's own home.[42]

In Polish Silesia educated Poles, mainly from Galicia and the former Austrian (Teschen) Silesia, replaced the c. 100,000 German civil servants, engineers, teachers, employees, and merchants who left eastern Silesia for Germany, forming a new "foreign" elite.[43] Native Silesians saw themselves as the true masters of the region, and their ties to the region took priority over other links. They regarded those who migrated into the area as "foreigners," an aversion to newcomers that before 1914 applied to Polish-speaking laborers from Austrian and Russian Poland as well as to Germans. As the Silesian Emil Szramek wrote in 1934:

> Every political change in Silesia ushered in not only officials, but also newcomers from distant places.... The influx of people from areas with a different past and tradition always evoked a more or less violent reaction from the indigenous element. Antagonism between the natives and the newcomers in Silesia reaches into the very distant past and usually prevails over the national bond.[44]

Warsaw granted Silesia autonomy with its own parliament but also promoted an influx from the rest of Poland to Polonize Silesia, resulting in tensions at many levels. Alfons Górnik, a native Upper Silesian, who became the mayor of Katowice in 1922, allowed the use of both Polish and German in administration. But after 1926 when Michał Grażyński assumed the governorship of the province, ethnic antagonism rose as non-Polish-speaking civil servants were let go. The authorities also pursued a policy of Polonizing place-names and sporadically even surnames. But for a substantial portion of the native inhabitants, Polish economic and political difficulties played the key role in undermining whatever loyalty they had to Poland.[45]

Mazuria

Beginning in the fourteenth century, the ancestors of the Mazurs migrated in several waves from the Piast Duchy of Mazovia to the southern and southeastern forests of the state of the Teutonic Knights, later the Duchy of Prussia. With its secularization in 1525, they also adopted the Evangelical Lutheran religion, which along with their language (originating in the Polish of the fourteenth and fifteenth centuries) would mark their regional identity. They did not develop a Mazurian national identity, having become Prussian, with a strong sense of loyalty to the ruling house, long before the rise of modern nationalism.[46]

With the creation of a German nation-state in 1871, an alliance of the government, the Evangelical Church, and the press promoted assimilation to the German majority. The authorities Germanized Slavic place names where Mazurs had lived for centuries, supposedly because no German would live in a place with an unpronounceable name. With the Polish language driven from public life, the Mazurian language found refuge in *Gromadki* (literally, small groups), which met under lay leadership in private homes to pray in their mother tongue. A product of the spiritual awakening that affected Protestants from North America to Europe, the *Gromadki* demonstrated the attachment of Mazurs to their language and their religion. Concern about the Mazurs prompted the government in 1905 to create the Allenstein Administrative District encompassing all of the Mazurian counties except Olecko. But loyalty to the Prussian dynasty prevented any organized resistance to Germanization. World War I transformed the pre-national Prussian patriotism into an all-German one.[47]

Germanization in Mazuria triggered a reaction on the part of the Polish public. Wojciech Kętrzyński laid the foundation for Polish interest in the Mazurs with his work *O Mazurach* in 1872. His nearly half century of scholarly activity embedded the concept of the Mazur as a "Polish brother" in the consciousness of Polish society, and it would remain at the core of Polish views.[48]

The Treaty of Versailles awarded the Soldau (Działdowo) region to Poland but called for a plebiscite in southern East Prussia. The centuries-long separation from the Polish state and culture more than any other factor prevented the development of a strong movement for unification with Poland. Although a census in 1910 indicated 47.4 percent of the population of the plebiscite area spoke Polish (including bilinguals), only 2.2 percent voted in 1920 to become part of Poland.[49] Following the plebiscite, a massive German propaganda campaign turned it into a crucial experience for the future radicalization of the Mazurs, fostered their assimilation, and internalized the "Polish peril," ready to be reactivated at any time. As a result, according to the Polish consul in Allenstein (Olsztyn) in 1921, "The Mazur regards every Pole as an alien and cunning individual." Even speaking in Polish Mazurs identified themselves as Germans.[50]

Richard Blanke sees the plebiscite as evidence that Mazurs belong to the German nation by personal or historical choice, whereas other scholars posit a strong Mazurian regional identity, typical of borderlands, rather than an unambiguous German identity. Polish publicists since 1920 ignore centuries of socialization in a Prussian-German state and instead focus on the terror, massacres, and harassment of the Polish Mazurian movement to explain the plebiscite results and justify the policy of "re-Polonization" after 1945.[51]

Nevertheless, the Polish-Mazurian language remained the language of communication of the rural population. When in 1922 a pastor in Ortelsburg (Szczytno) County neglected to learn Polish, Polish-speaking community members requested his dismissal, asserting, "we [are] Mazurs of the Polish mother tongue." Germanization had its greatest success among the younger generation. Ideologically attracted to German nationalism, it saw the German language as a means of social advancement.[52]

A poor and underdeveloped area before 1914, East Prussia suffered more than most from Germany's postwar economic difficulties and crises. This underlay the political radicalization of the Mazurs. Early on the National Socialist German Workers' Party (*Nationalsocialistische Deutsche Arbeiterpartei* or NSDAP, i.e., the Nazi party) demagogically spoke out on behalf of Mazurian interests. Nazi populist-nationalist propaganda made Mazurs, particularly the highly Germanized younger generation, feel for the first time as valued members of the German nation. They joined the Nazi party in massive numbers. In the early 1930s Storm Troopers (*Sturm-Abteilung* or SA) ruled the streets of Mazuria. The success of the NSDAP in the elections of 1932 and 1933 in Mazuria outshone the party's results in the rest of the country. The economically poorest counties with a Polish-speaking majority gave the highest proportion of votes to the party.[53]

With the Nazi assumption of power in Germany in 1933, the authorities sought to eradicate the Polish-Mazurian roots of the population. At the same time, the economy of Mazuria blossomed as never before. Party membership also offered an opportunity for social advancement, filling local offices. Yet the Mazurian language remained a common language of everyday use. Though the number of religious services in Mazurian declined, some pastors maintained them out of conscientious concern for the population or out of fear that it would turn to the *Gromadki* or religious sects.[54]

In Działdowo County re-Polonization of the Mazurs based on the equation of Polish ethnicity (language, origins) with membership in the Polish nation had little success. The local population protested its inclusion in Poland. When during the Polish-Bolshevik War of 1919–1920 the Red Army entered Działdowo, locals enthusiastically greeted it as a liberator. In the first election to the Polish parliament, 74.6 percent of the voters gave their support to a German candidate, although according to a census in 1921 54.9 percent were Catholic and 65.3 percent spoke Polish as their mother tongue.[55]

Latent tension between the Polish administration and the Mazurian population marked the entire interwar period. Polish Catholics came from other regions to staff the administration. They had little understanding of the situation, regarding even Polish-speaking Mazurs as Germans because of their Protestant religion. In 1924 only 5.1 percent of officials in Działdowo were Protestants.

The overwhelming majority of Mazurs belonged to the Consistory of the Prussian Union Evangelical Church. The Consistory of the Evangelical-Augsburg Church in Warsaw, whose members were mostly German before World War I, sought to increase its Polish membership. In the plebiscite it supported the incorporation of Mazuria into Poland. With its assistance a small group of pro-Polish Mazurs around Karol Małłek sought to win over the Działdowo Mazurs. This led to a struggle with the Protestant Union for their souls, fostering a pro-German attitude among them.

Moreover, the Polish provincial authorities of Pomerania, to which Działdowo belonged until 1938, countered the efforts of the pro-Polish Mazurs. The view that re-Polonization came through conversion to Catholicism predominated. When in 1931 pro-Polish Mazurs formed the Union of Mazurs (*Związek Mazurów*), communal authorities banned it as separatist. Under Małłek's leadership, it was reestablished in 1935 with the goal of winning the Mazurs for Polishness while at the same time preserving their denominational and cultural distinctiveness. But the discrimination experienced by the Mazurs negated these efforts. The majority of Mazurs proved immune to re-Polonization. Ultimately, the Polish authorities lacked a clear, effectively realized nationality policy to win over the Mazurs for Polishness, foreshadowing the failure after World War II.[56]

The Revisionist Ideologies

The Treaty of Versailles left Germany with lingering grievances over the territorial losses to the reconstituted Polish state. Although Poland "recovered" the overwhelming majority of the territory that Prussia gained in the partitioning of the Polish-Lithuanian Commonwealth, it too had grievances concerning the border.

The territorial disputes between Germany and its neighbors gave rise to supposedly scholarly claims in support of each state's expansionist goals. In the Rhineland occupied by French troops in 1919, a propaganda campaign known as *pénétration pacifique* sought to promote a separatist movement by claiming that geography, culture, and race marked the area as part of the sphere of French civilization. German scholars countered with economic, socio-historical, and ethnographic arguments to demonstrate the "Germanic" rather than "Roman" character of settlement patterns. Whereas the French saw the Rhine River as the "natural" border of France, Germans argued that it united the region through common patterns of culture, settlement, and agriculture and that the region constituted the cultural axis of the Holy Roman Empire.[57] In the case of the Polish-German borderlands, rival claims came under the rubrics of *Ostforschung* (Research on the East) and *Polska myśl zachodnia* (Polish Western Idea).

Research on the East

The German-speaking migrants and colonists who over the centuries established communities among the Slavic majority played a crucial role in German national self-understanding.[58] By 1900 the population of Germany became aware of the so-called Germans abroad (*Auslandsdeutsche*). Nationalists idealized them as examples of German ethnicity, whereas in reality over time many had undergone various stages of assimilation, and their national identity was open to question.

Radical nationalists elaborated a vision of a German imperium stretching eastward encompassing these "Germans" as part of the national community, the *Volksgemeinschaft*.[59] This contributed to support for a new German citizenship law in 1913, which defined citizenship in terms of descent rather than residence.[60] As for the non-Germans in this projected imperium, radical nationalists advocated mass deportation during discussions of German war aims of World War I, foreshadowing developments during World War II.

But the goal of expansion to the east involved more than just an imperialist landgrab. The German myth of the east resembled the "Manifest Destiny" of the United States, with its sense of mission to populate and civilize a supposedly empty West. After 1918, popular accounts contrasting the superior level of culture of Germans abroad with that of their surroundings multiplied. Nationalist organizations concerned with the *Auslandsdeutsche*, funded and supported by the German government, dramatically expanded. The largest, the *Verein für Deutschtum im Ausland*, sharply criticized the Treaty of Versailles for violating national self-determination by turning over some fifteen million citizens of the Reich into the hands of foreign governments with their own nationalist agendas.[61]

German academics gave "scientific" legitimacy to revisionist demands. Although the term *Ostforschung* hardly appears in scholarly discussions before 1940, politically motivated historical research on eastern Europe predated World War I and came into its own after 1918 in defense of the *Heimatrecht* (right to the homeland) of the German minority in Poland and elsewhere.[62]

To underpin a belief in the indivisibility of the German people and to demonstrate the historical roots of German rights to a homeland in the east, *Ostforschung* focused particularly on German ethnographic territories (*Volksboden*), those settled at one time more or less entirely by Germans; and German cultural territories (*Kulturboden*), wider areas that individual German settlements first rescued from sociocultural backwardness through their cultural activity (*Kulturarbeit*).[63] As Michael Burleigh states, "it was not a matter of indifference whether the Germans had been in the East a thousand years before the Slavs, or whether medieval German migrants were harbingers of a higher civilization or mere 'guests' and 'strangers.'"[64] German foreign policy goals included not only revision of the Versailles Treaty but also the creation of *irredenta* in other areas supposedly influenced by German culture, such as the Baltic states.[65]

Research on Germans abroad introduced the term *"Volksdeutsche"* for members of the German nation residing outside the German state. But the islands of German-speaking population in Poland had formerly lived under German, Austrian, and Russian rule; had no contact with each other; arose under different historical circumstances; and therefore had little in common other than language, often mutually incomprehensible dialects.[66] The Polish Western Idea would encounter similar problems among the allegedly Polish residents of territory acquired from Germany in 1945.

Following President Wilson's endorsement of the principle of nationality in January 1918, a battle of maps ensued, fostering the nationalist myth of the nation dwelling in a well-defined space with borders clearly separating its homeland from that of foreigners. German geographers led by Albrecht Penck produced maps indicating the German *Volksboden* and *Kulturboden*, the latter encompassing all of western Poland.[67] The first congress of German geographers after the war in 1921 decided that patriotic duty required all maps, especially in school atlases, to show the lost territory as still belonging to Germany. The Federal Republic of Germany continued this practice after World War II with maps showing the eastern border of Germany of 1937 until Willy Brandt's *Ostpolitik* of the early 1970s.[68]

In 1926 the geographer Wilhelm Volz extended the *Volksboden* into the *Kulturboden*: "The Kashubs and Mazurs, the Upper Silesians and the Wends are German culture, branches of the German nation, Germans, even if the old idiom is not yet extinct. . . . Race does not decide nationality. . . . Rather the will and national consciousness decide."[69] Thus, *Ostforschung* promoted a new type of German, the *eigensprachiger Kulturdeutsche* (own-language-speaking cultural German). Mazurs were an indivisible part of the German nation, an essentially Germanized people in a Polish guise. Protestants who saw themselves as *Prussaks,* not *Polaks,* they expressed their inner convictions in the plebiscite of 1920. Even their language incorporated modified German verbs. Heinrich Himmler made the breakup of east European peoples an explicit goal of his nationality policy, and the *Ostforscher* would take part in the planning of *Generalplan Ost* to clear the territory of Poles and Jews and settle it with Germans.[70]

Popularly, German ancestry formed an essential basis of Germanness and took priority over a cultural definition of Germanness. The emphasis on biological descent played into the racial vision of the Nazis for whom *Volksgemeinschaft* became a key concept, but it encompassed only those who met certain racial, hereditary, behavioral, and political criteria. Nevertheless, the ambiguity of the concept allowed the Nazis to apply it in ways that suited their military, economic, and political goals and racial delusions, e.g., declaring the Mazurs a special regional variation of the *Volksgemeinschaft.* Beyond Germany's historical borders, they proved even more flexible, with so-called biological characteristics (hair and eye color) overriding a lack of supposedly German cultural traits (language, orderliness, and cleanliness), which could be acquired.[71]

The *Kulturarbeit* of German ethnographers to make the scattered islands of German population conscious of their nationality in the years 1933 to 1939 increasingly assumed the character of Nazi propaganda, preparing the ground for the population transfers during the war.[72] From 1938 *Ostforschung* legitimized and supported German policies of occupation in eastern Europe. The historian Theodor Schieder provides the clearest example with his call in that year for *"eine Neuordnung in Osten"* (a new order in the east).[73]

Polish Western Idea

The Polish Western Idea consisted of views and images of which lands should form the western territory of an ideally reconstituted Polish state. Prior to World War II it principally engaged in defending against the claims made by *Ostforschung* and after World War II in legitimizing Poland's territorial gains.[74]

Its roots reach back into the nineteenth century, when scholars of partitioned Poland felt a patriotic duty to affirm the place of Poland in Europe and Western civilization, e.g., by attempting to document the Polish origins of Veit Stoß, the creator of the famous altar in the Cracow cathedral. In 1869 the occupant of the first Polish chair in geography at the Jagiellonian University in

Cracow countered German claims by asserting that the German plain ended at the Elbe River and that the region of the Oder River marked the western border of the Polish plain.[75]

In 1914 the archeologist Józef Kostrzewski responded to German scholars who argued that Germanic tribes settled the area between the Oder and Vistula Rivers and Slavs arrived later as migrants from the East. Relying on the same archeological evidence, Kostrzewski placed the original home of the Slavs between the Oder and Vistula Rivers in the Bronze Age, linking proto-Slavs with the Lusatian culture. Except for the Goths and Getae, he excluded the presence of Germanic tribes in the area. The simplistic conclusions of both theories concerning ethnic relations in antiquity reflected the nationality of the researcher.[76]

With the outbreak of World War I, a professor of geography in Lwów Eugeniusz Romer, realizing that it would result in great territorial and political changes, published an atlas in which Poland included Upper and Lower Silesia. Criticized by German geographers and banned during the war from export by Austrian officials, the atlas was later distributed at the Paris Peace Conference, where its maps illustrating the national, linguistic, and religious affiliations of the population took on particular significance. Based on the Prussian census of 1910, the atlas portrayed the area with a Polish majority reaching into Opole Silesia and encompassing all of the Poznań region and Pomerania. Recognizing the threat to the Polish position in Pomerania and Mazuria, Romer critically analyzed the results of the 1910 census, which sought to minimize the Polish population. He counted Kashubs and Mazurs as Polish, which prompted a polemic with the German geographer Penck. Another map in the atlas relied on data from the Prussian school census of 1911, which favored Poland because of the high Polish birth rate.[77]

The Polish Western Idea went beyond defending Polish gains after World War I. Romer's most prominent student, Stanisław Pawłowski, advocated a Poland within the borders it had under the Piast dynasty and regarded the Oder and the Lusatian Neisse Rivers as the proper Polish-German border. At the University of Poznań, the most important center promoting the Western Idea, his studies of the settlement and population of Great Poland (Wielkopolska) and Pomerania sought to document the Polish character of areas questioned by *Ostforschung*. He did not conceal his view that the Versailles border did not correspond to the ethnic and economic interests of Poland. He saw East Prussia as a barrier to access to the sea. In a lecture published in 1937, he advocated the removal of the German population from the borderlands. Under his influence and leadership, work began on a multivolume lexicon of Slavic place names between Hamburg and the Polish border. Antoni Wrzosek, deputy director of the Silesian Institute established in Katowice in 1934 as another propagator of the Western Idea, expanded geographic research to include the part of German Upper Silesia that had a Polish population.[78]

The Polish Western Idea debuted in the field of linguistics at the turn of the nineteenth century in response to German scholars who disputed the existence of a Lechitic West Slavic language community and treated Kashub and the Mazurian and Silesian dialects as separate Slavic languages. Heated discussions over whether Kashub was a Polish dialect or an independent language had already taken place since 1850 with the publications of Florjan Cenôva, who in that year urged the use of Kashub: "We speak among ourselves in Kashub, the speech of our forefathers and of our own fathers, which we sucked in with our mothers' milk." In contrast, a contemporary Polish democrat, Roman Zmorski, published an article in 1861 stating, "The Kashubs are as pure a tribe of the Polish race as the Cracovians, Mazurs, Silesians [or] Great Polanders. The quite considerable differences which exist today between their speech and our written language are the result of their long withdrawal from the general Slav intellectual movement."[79]

Following World War I, the linguistic arguments of *Polska myśl zachodnia* became most closely linked with Mikołaj Rudnicki and the Western Slavic Institute he founded at the University of Poznań. Multidisciplinary research on western Slavic tribes who at the dawn of history inhabited the area from both sides of the Elbe River to the Vistula constituted its mission with the main focus, according to Rudnicki, "on the already Germanized population or their few remnants." In the popular press, he called for documenting the Polish right to the "Lost Lands."[80]

In his many articles on western Slavic linguistics, detailed onomatopoetic studies of the names found in the Oder and Vistula basin, and comparative research in Slavic and Indo-European languages, Rudnicki sought to prove that it constituted the original home of the Slavs, disputing, often in intemperate language, claims that German tribes inhabited the area in late antiquity. In 1936, referring to Poles, Czechs, Pomeranians, Sorbs, and Germanized Slavic tribes between the Elbe and the Polish and Czech borders, he claimed, "43–75% of the inhabitants of eastern Germany are such Slavs. They are admittedly Germanized, but the German tradition is not their tradition: this circumstance lays the foundation for their return to the womb of Slavdom."[81]

In 1925 two Polish historians presented images of the territory of the Piast dynasty that became the standard historical map of medieval Poland, identified with the "motherland." At about the same time, the historian Zygmunt Wojciechowski formulated the concept of Polish "motherlands" (*ziemie macierzyste*) for the territory between the Oder and Bug Rivers as the cradle of the Polish state. The "recovery" of the western lands from Germany represented the crowning achievement of Polish history.[82]

The rapid defeat of Poland in 1939 and the occupation did not destroy the belief in *Polska myśl zachodnia*. As early as 1940 a group of its proponents, including Wojciechowski and others from Poznań, met secretly in Warsaw to consider the future Polish-German border. Intense discussions in 1941–1942 led to the conclusion that the Oder and Lusatian Neisse Rivers would constitute the best border for Poland. In 1942 a group, including Wrzosek and Wojciechowski, drew up a "Memorandum Concerning the Settlement of the Territories in the West," which included a call for the interests of the Polish "autochthonous" population to be absolutely respected above those of any incoming settlers.[83]

The Polish Western Union (*Polski Związek Zachodni* or PZZ), an organization that focused on issues of the Polish-German border and the fate of the Polish minority in Germany, renewed its activity in mid-1943 and, independently of any other organization, proposed the incorporation into Poland of specific areas west of the prewar border where a significant majority of Poles were thought to reside. It estimated the number of those with a living tradition of being of Polish origin at 1.5 million and sought to influence them during the war, sending manifestoes in German and the Mazurian dialect to specific addresses in East Prussia. On 13 November 1944 activists in Lublin formed a committee to reestablish the PZZ based on three main principles: anti-Germanness, democracy, and the idea of Slavic power.[84]

The authors of an atlas prepared during the Nazi occupation in 1943–1944 claimed, "The native Polish lands, in which the Polish population was Germanized, extend up to the Oder and Lusatian Neisse. The existing German population here is only functionally German, but by race, blood, name, and tradition—Slavic-Polish." They saw a historical continuity in German aggression: "Ethnically Polish areas were included in the Prussian state, which de-nationalized them by force. It was just as unlawful as the current incorporation of native Great Poland and the creation of the German Warthegau. It was only accomplished at a slower rate."[85] The advocates of *Polska myśl zachodnia* did not accept what might well have appeared to be an anomalous brief period of Polish independence.

[2]

The German Occupation of Poland

LATE ON THE NIGHT of 23 August 1939, Germany and the Soviet Union surprised the world by signing an agreement that sealed an alliance between them. Touted as a nonaggression pact, it included "one of the most famous documents in diplomatic history."[1] The secret protocol partitioned eastern Europe into German and Soviet spheres of influence, clearing the way for the invasions of Poland by Germany on 1 September 1939 and by the Soviet Union on 17 September 1939. Few historians, however, note the significance of the subsequent German-Soviet Boundary and Friendship Treaty of 28 September 1939. It, too, had a secret protocol, one providing for an exchange of Polish territory on the Soviet side of the line of demarcation for Germany's renunciation of its claim to Lithuania as well as for an exchange of population, presaging the postwar Polish-Soviet border and the massive movement of peoples based on ethnicity.[2] On 3 October 1939 British Prime Minister Neville Chamberlain called it "a fourth partition" of Poland.[3]

Germany's war against Poland was not a "normal" war but one that targeted the civilian population from the very beginning.[4] As Adolf Hitler told senior members of the Wehrmacht on 22 August 1939, "Thus for the time being I have sent to the East only 'Death's Head Units' with the order to kill without pity or mercy all men, women, and children of Polish race or language. Only in such a way will we win the vital space [*Lebensraum*] that we need."[5] Colonel-General Fedor von Bock wrote to army commanders justifying the "otherwise uncommonly harsh measures toward the Polish population of the occupied areas" as necessary to "secure German *Lebensraum* and the solutions to ethnic political problems ordered by the Führer." For Burleigh this "regime of unrestrained terror" was "the nightmare scenario among the occupied nations of Europe."[6]

Germany followed up the "fourth partition" with its own division of Polish territory. On 30 September 1939, Hitler explained, "the new political boundary of the Reich in the East will in general encompass the former German area of settlement and in addition those areas, which are especially valuable for the military, the arms economy, and technical communications."[7] Germany already annexed the Free City of Danzig on 1 September 1939. On 8 October 1939 a decree established the territorial and administrative structure for the incorporation of western and northern Poland, nearly half of Nazi-occupied Poland, along with Danzig.[8]

The German province of East Prussia absorbed parts of the Polish provinces of Warsaw (including Działdowo County), Pomerania, and Białystok, which together formed so-called "Southeast Prussia." Most of the rest of Polish Pomerania was combined with the Free City of Danzig along with parts of Poznań and Warsaw Provinces to constitute the Reichsgau Danzig-West Prussia. The rest of Poznań Province (Wielkopolska) and much of Łódź Province along with parts of the provinces of Warsaw and Silesia formed the Reichsgau Wartheland or Warthegau, by far the largest of the new territories. German Silesia expanded, incorporating Polish Silesia along with parts of the provinces of Cracow and Kielce (including the Dąbrowa Basin), under Russian rule before 1918, and that part of formerly Teschen Silesia that Poland annexed in 1938. On 18 January 1941 the Germans divided the enlarged province of Silesia into two provinces, Upper and Lower Silesia. In extending its territory east of the 1914 border, the Reich absorbed areas that had never been part of Germany or part of Prussia after 1807.[9]

The German occupation gave national identity a new significance. Although nationality is not a fixed attribute and is subject to manipulation (such as classifying Kashubs, Mazurs, and Slavic-speaking Upper Silesians as Poles), the estimates in table 2.1 provide some orientation as to the character of the population of the Polish territory incorporated into the Reich.

The Germans designated the remaining occupied territory as the *Generalgouvernement,* a reservation and colony for exploitation. Although a customs frontier separated the *Generalgouvernement* from the incorporated lands, the

TABLE 2.1 National Identities in the Incorporated Lands

Incorporated Lands	Total Population	Poles	Germans	Jews	Ukrainians	Others
Wartheland	4,933,600	4,220,200	324,600	384,500	—	4,300
Upper Silesia	2,632,630	2,404,670	98,204	124,877	1,202	3,677
Danzig-West Prussia	1,571,215	1,393,717	158,372	14,458	1,648	3,020
Southeast Prussia	1,001,560	886,061	18,400	79,098	8,099	9,902
Totals	10,139,005	8,904,648	599,576	602,933	10,949	20,899

Data source: Czesław Madajczyk, *Polityka III Rzeszy w okupowanej Polsce,* 2 vols. (Warsaw: Państwowe Wydawnictwo Naukowe, 1970), 1:72. I have corrected a mathematical error in the total number of Jews.

1914 border served as a police or "disease-policing" border, indicating a greater significance attached to territory Prussia ruled until 1919.[10]

Home to the Reich

To build a racially pure nation within Germany's *Lebensraum*, ethnic Germans living abroad had to replace its undesirable inhabitants. In the 1930s German experts estimated that at least 10 million *Volksdeutsche* resided in eastern Europe. They had a special role to play in Nazi plans. Constituting something of a fifth column and at the same time justifying German expansion, the *Volksdeutsche* would benefit from the dispossession of Jews, Slavs, and others.[11]

In 1938 the German Chancellery defined *Volksdeutsche* as noncitizens of Germany whose "language and culture" had "German origins." But the descendants of migrants from the German heartland generations earlier varied widely in their culture and identification with Germany. Placing them in rigid categories resulted in many arbitrary decisions with serious consequences for their fate.[12]

In the Reichstag on 6 October 1939, Hitler echoed the concerns of statesmen about ethnic minorities when, concerning the "fragments of the German people" in eastern and southeastern Europe, he stated, "it is part of the task of a far-sighted ordering of European life, to effect resettlement here to eliminate in this way a part of the European sources of conflict."[13] The next day Hitler appointed Heinrich Himmler to head what became the Reich Commission for the Consolidation of German Nationhood (*Reichskommissariat für die Festigung deutschen Volkstum* or RKF) with the task of eliminating "the harmful influence of ethnically alien populations" and the resettlement of ethnic Germans from abroad to achieve the complete Germanization of western Poland.[14]

As *Reichsführer* or head of the SS (*Schutzstaffel,* NSDAP internal security) and chief of German police, Himmler could eliminate the "ethnically alien" Jews and Poles through deportation and execution. He planned vast settlements of ethnic Germans that would "surround" the local Jewish and Polish settlements and "gradually crush them to death economically and biologically."[15] He thus provided the institutional connection for the "Solution to the Jewish Question" and the policy of resettling the ethnic Germans known as *Heim ins Reich* (Home to the Reich). Before the end of the war, approximately one million *Volksdeutsche* resettled within the Greater German Reich and occupied Poland. In the incorporated lands, the resettlement focused above all on Wartheland, where as of 15 November 1944 the resettled *Volksdeutsche* numbered 536,951, 85.0 percent the total (631,485).[16]

Eradication and Deportation

At a meeting in January 1940 Reinhard Heydrich, a leading figure in the SS, estimated that some 120,000 Poles and Jews would have to be deported to make room for German resettlers. Ultimately, the Nazis drove 923,000 inhabitants of the incorporated lands from their homes.[17]

Himmler assigned the control and planning of the deportation of Jews and Poles to the Reich Central Security Office of the SS. But even before the centrally planned evacuation began, deportation got under way in October–November 1939, especially in West Prussia. Himmler ordered the expulsion of the Polish elite first. The arbitrary orders of local authorities and the denunciations and greed of local *Volksdeutsche* as well as the wholly improvised procedures seeking primarily the rapid removal of the occupants of houses, plots of land, and farms frequently distorted Himmler's general guidelines, a phenomenon that would mark expulsions under a different regime after 1945. Task forces of security personnel (*Einsatzgruppen*), local officials, or recent settlers from Danzig acted on their own. In practice the quality of an individual's housing often decided who was expelled. To make room for the mostly urban Germans from Estonia and Latvia, the task forces suddenly emptied whole housing blocks. In Pomerania the expulsion affected Kashubian and Polish farmers who inhabited the area for generations and had no connections with Polish nationalists. In the late fall of 1939 newly appointed local party officials there even expelled several thousand local *Volksdeutsche* regarded as politically unreliable or denounced by their neighbors.[18]

The *Gauleiter* (regional party leader) and *Reichsstatthalter* (governor) of Wartheland Arthur Greiser, like other Nazi leaders, believed that "the Polish element must be eradicated."[19] Shortly after being appointed, he undertook to integrate the territory into the rest of the Reich with the goal of complete Germanization within ten years. *Einsatzgruppen* initiated the process. Already in the first days of the occupation they publicly executed individuals regarded as a threat. Known as a "political cleansing of the terrain," it relied on lists of Polish social activists, artists, teachers, administrative officials, clergymen, and so on, based on information provided by the German minority. Other members of the Polish elite were sent to concentration camps—about 5,000 in April and May 1940 alone. Altogether about 10,000 Poles from Wartheland were deported to concentration camps by the end of the war; only a small percent survived. The German minority in Poland provided the names of more than 90 percent of those sent to concentration camps. Another 50,000 Poles were sent to prisons in Wartheland or to "educational work camps." The Wehrmacht also executed prisoners of war and civilians, about 10,000 by the end of October 1939. Mass executions continued in Great Poland throughout the war. One operation targeted the incurably ill and psychologically disturbed and residents of homes for the elderly, the blind, and needy children. Euphemistically referred to as euthanasia, it claimed 4,500 Polish victims in Wartheland. Such direct executions in Wartheland alone resulted in the death of some 70,000 Poles.[20]

The extermination of the Jews of Wartheland also continued throughout the war. It began in September 1939 with soldiers of the Wehrmacht executing Jews out of racial hatred and continued in October–December 1939, including several hundred community activists at the hands of various German security formations. At the same time the German authorities began to herd Jews into ghettoes and labor camps: by war's end there were 173 labor camps for Jews in Wartheland, where conditions, maltreatment, and executions resulted in the death of at least 25,000. The first ghetto was organized in Litzmannstadt (Łódź) on 8 February 1940 and became the largest in the incorporated lands, amassing about 200,000 inhabitants during the occupation. They perished in large numbers from hunger and epidemics. In July 1941 Greiser and Himmler decided to build the death camp in Chełmno for the purpose of murdering 300,000 Jews. It began operations in December 1941 with the gassing of Jews in mobile vans, prior to the Wannsee Conference on 20 January 1942, where top-ranking Nazis met to coordinate an effort to eliminate Europe's entire Jewish population. Overall about 380,000 Jews of Wartheland died at the hands of the Germans, 98.7 percent of the prewar Jewish population.[21]

Deportations from Wartheland exceeded those from any other German administrative unit of occupied Poland. The first occurred in November 1939. Selected individuals were ordered to leave, usually within twenty-four hours. Here, too, the initiative came mostly from the local authorities and local Germans, most often to acquire the property left by Jews and Poles. In the first centrally planned mass deportation to accommodate the settlement of 40,000 Baltic Germans and to diminish the number of Jewish and Polish property owners and elite, 87,838 Poles and Jews were deported to the *Generalgouvernement* in just seventeen days in December 1939. Preliminary surveys and determinations by officials and *Volksdeutsche* established lists of those to be deported, which again depended less on political or security considerations than on ownership of the most valuable farms, commercial enterprises, businesses, and practices of doctors, lawyers, and so on. A later report of the head of the Posen (Poznań) RKF Department indicated that in several thousand cases local *Volksdeutsche* "had exchanged or taken possession of estates or whole farms."[22]

This was only the first small step. There remained 450,000 individuals in Wartheland who under Himmler's guidelines had to be deported as members of the politically active elite. As late as 28 April 1944 Greiser ordered the deportation of Poles to make room for additional ethnic Germans from the Baltic states and Transnistria. A German document indicates 435,167 Poles were expelled from Wartheland by October 1944: somewhat fewer than 300,000 to the *Generalgouvernement*; 125,551 for labor or Germanization to the "Old Reich"; and 23,512 for labor to occupied France.[23] Altogether the German authorities deployed 670,000 deportees from the incorporated lands for forced labor in the Reich and France.[24]

Families were evicted, leaving their furnishings behind, to make way for offices and homes for officials or other Germans. The stenographer Ruth Toltz, who came to Poznań from the Old Reich, wrote the *Reichsstatthalter* in March 1941 requesting the removal of Poles from an apartment she desired. Stanisława Bartkiewicz, a deportee from the incorporated lands in 1944, recounts that the Nazis needed her home for Germans from the Black Sea region and that she and others were deported to Lower Silesia to work on German farms. When in January 1945 Germans fled the Soviet military, they took Bartkiewicz and other deportees with them. Her forced labor ended only when the U.S. military liberated the last place to which she had been moved.[25]

On 23 September 1940 an official of the RKF reported on the deportations in the fall of 1939 to the head of the SS and police in Danzig:

> It has been established that in the overwhelming number of cases an alarmingly large number of evacuations were ordered out of envy, personal grounds . . . Therefore only property-owning individuals were declared to be Poles; 2 witnesses were found who swore some general phrases (e.g., he hated all things German and was a fanatical Pole); and the further fate of the family was already decided. The property was divided among the inhabitants of the village; the family was evacuated to the *Generalgouvernement* with only the clothes on their backs. What is more, it was unimportant if the family was of German blood or if only one family member was an active Pole.[26]

Conflicts arose over the confiscated property as prewar residents of the territory now reclaimed property for which they had received little compensation. They competed with the local *Volksdeutsche* and those resettled from abroad as well as citizens of the Old Reich who flooded the area looking for plunder. Regional differences also divided *Volksdeutsche,* with, for example, local ethnic Germans calling those from Bukovina "gypsies" and the latter calling the former "Poles."[27] These conflicts and abuses resemble those after 1945 following the expulsion of the Germans suggesting that they are typical of all such population removals.

Despite eradication, deportation, and resettlement, the Wartheland remained predominantly Polish. In mid-1944 Germans constituted 22.9 percent of the population of the province. Ultimately, the Germanization of Wartheland ran into fundamental difficulties. The railways of the region constantly operated at full capacity, and the resistance of the *Generalgouvernement* to further deportations steadily increased. Moreover, officials came to recognize that the unwanted inhabitants constituted a necessary labor force, irreplaceable in the medium term.[28]

Nazi Nationality Policies

The Reich Citizenship Law of 15 September 1935, unlike that of 1913, required appropriate political behavior in addition to German descent. It drew a distinction between a *Staatsangehörige* (state member) and a *Reichsbürger* (Reich citizen), a state member with "German or related blood who by his behavior shows that he is willing and fit to serve the German people and Reich faithfully" and who alone enjoyed full political rights.[29]

Within days of the creation of the Protectorate of Bohemia and Moravia in March 1939 following the destruction of Czechoslovakia, the Reich Protector's Office issued a citizenship law distinguishing Reich citizens from state members, who were subject to the laws of the Protectorate. Non-Jewish Germans could apply to be recognized as citizens. The Interior Ministry in Berlin stated on 26 March 1939 that one could prove Germanness "through certain factors such as language, education, culture, and so on." Even those "with part or totally different family backgrounds" could in limited numbers become citizens, and many did. Complaints that "undesirable elements" had passed as Germans, many of them speaking only Czech, prompted officials to tighten controls.[30]

In Poland, with its small German minority, the Nazis faced the question of how to consolidate German rule without violating their ideology. The debate focused on the ethnicity of the native population, with some officials putting forward the concept of a mixed or transitional ethnicity, which identified a linguistically, culturally, and politically Polish population as inclined toward Germanness.[31]

At the beginning of October 1939, Hitler suggested the assimilation of "vast segments of the Polish population" by resettling them in purely German areas, "where they would be swallowed up" as happened in "the Ruhr valley, where the Poles have been almost entirely Germanized."[32] In Hitler's view even a small amount of German blood could overwhelm alien blood, except of course for Jewish blood.[33] Similarly, Himmler feared that "racially undesirable" children sired by German soldiers with local women in the eastern territories would strengthen the enemy with their "share of Aryan blood."[34]

Obsessed with "fishing out the racially valuable people from the [Polish] mishmash," Himmler wrote a report that Hitler marked "very good and correct" in which Himmler outlined the "racial screening" of Poles and their integration "with confidence into German life after changing their names."[35] Himmler expected that only 8 percent would qualify. The fanciful "scientific" bases of "racial screening"—eye and hair color, skull measurements (supposedly indicating intelligence)—allowed officials a great deal of flexibility, resulting in practical considerations and ideology influencing each other.[36]

The law annexing the Free City of Danzig recognized its state members as Reich state members, whereas the decree incorporating Polish territory limited state membership to "residents of German and related blood" who would become citizens in accord with the law. Before the law was formulated, the Reich Interior Ministry on 25 November 1939 provisionally recognized as state members those belonging to the German nation who had Danzig or Polish state membership on the day of incorporation. A questionnaire covered such matters as language spoken, evidence of membership in the German nation, and the "Jewish race or religion" of any grandparents. Those who were undoubtedly German received certificates of state membership.[37]

Detailed instructions from Berlin focused on the political behavior of the applicant. Race as a criterion applied only to Jews and was explicitly excluded from the selection of Christian Poles. The fundamental criterion was: *"The declaration of German nationality during the time of foreign domination,"* which as a rule meant membership in a German organization prior to the war. This resulted in acceptance in Group A, which formed the basis for the party. For Group B, political behavior along with German origin mattered. The "indifferent" and an individual who under Polish pressure did not declare his German nationality were to be carefully checked if in light of "the overall picture of his character and his behavior . . . he was acknowledged as a German." The impossibility of a concise and practical definition of who is German made the decision dependent on personal characteristics, past behavior, and political considerations.[38]

The ministry regarded a large number of former Prussian citizens as assimilable and believed that the passive collaboration of at least part of the population had decisive importance. When officials in Upper Silesia criticized the decree as too strict, the state secretary of the Reich Interior Ministry on 26 November 1939 allowed for decisions in Silesia in accord with "local relations": above all "the so-called Wasser-Poles [Upper Silesians], Schlonsaks [natives of Teschen Silesia], Mazurs . . . can be seen as members of the German nation." On 4 January 1940 he stated that it was in German interest "that also a larger part of the nationally indifferent in-between stratum, especially in East Upper Silesia and East Silesia [are] registered."[39]

Volk versus Rasse

The selection process for German state membership prompted Himmler to lodge a protest with the Interior Ministry on 13 January 1940. For Himmler it was not a question of purely external characteristics of Germanness (language, culture, education, etc.) but of German racial origin. Whereas the ministry looked above all to behavior indicating a readiness to collaborate, Himmler argued for racial attribution relying primarily on biometric characteristics. Previously, race had been used above all to exclude Jews. Himmler wanted to go further by sorting the entire non-Jewish population of the incorporated lands by means of a complex process, giving race a central significance in the selection for a German nationality list (DVL). The rest of the population, that is the overwhelming majority, was cynically recognized as "under the protection of the state" (*Schutzangehörige*), i.e., designated for expulsion. This conflict over criteria would increase in intensity throughout the war.[40]

On 12 September 1940 Himmler ordered the "Examination and Selection of the Population of the Incorporated Eastern Areas" "according to racial, health-related, and political criteria" for the "recovery of lost German blood," including up to one million "members of a foreign nationality" able to be Germanized, of related blood, and racially valuable—the basis for accepting Upper Silesians and Kashubs into the German community (*Volksgemeinschaft*). "The identification of these individuals can take place in accordance with our National-Socialist knowledge only through their racial selection." Following an example set in the Wartheland, the decree ordered that the German nationality list sort the *Volksdeutsche* and those of German origin into four categories.[41]

The DVL Ordinance of 4 March 1941

In the tussle between the Interior Ministry and Himmler, the latter won the approval of Hitler for his guidelines. Therefore on 4 March 1941 the ministry issued an ordinance concerning the DVL in the lands incorporated one and a half years earlier. In addition to DVL offices at the county, district, and central *Gau* level, it created a last instance of appeal, the Highest Court of Examination for Nationality Questions, presided over by Himmler within the RKF. Even in 1944 it still deliberated the categorization of individuals within the DVL. But it was a Pyrrhic victory as the unauthorized growth in the selection of natives in the individual provinces continued. Himmler's repeated attempts to enforce race as the decisive criterion ran into the opposition of the regional authorities, who regarded it as inadequate in differentiating Poles from Germans.[42]

Based on Himmler's decree, the ordinance as supplemented established four categories of German nationality with corresponding graduated rights of citizenship and state membership. Individuals who demonstrated their German origins through active participation in the nationality struggle constituted category I of the DVL. Category II consisted of those who had "demonstrably proven their Germanness" without being active in the nationality struggle. The members of both categories received certificates (blue IDs) of German citizenship, but primarily only those in category I could become Nazi party members. For both categories behavior had greater weight than descent. The differentiation between the categories was only for internal use: not even the recipients of the blue IDs were informed of their category.[43]

"German descent" was the primary requirement for acceptance in categories III and IV. Those with pro-German convictions but with connections to Polishness, e.g., through marriage, fell into category III (green IDs) along with, as a rule, speakers of Slavic languages "whose racial classification is not clear, but who by blood and culture are inclined toward Germanism," such as Kashubs, Mazurs, and Upper Silesians. It gave members some of the same rights and entitled them to the same rations as those in the first two categories but made them subject to Germanization (or "re-Germanization") and imposed some restrictions.[44]

After Germany invaded the Soviet Union in 1941 creating a pressing need for military recruits, DVL category III conferred citizenship but only on an individual basis. An amendment on 31 January 1942 granted citizenship automatically but revocable at any time for ten years.[45] As citizens they were now subject to conscription. In addition, the authorities in Upper Silesia demanded a change in procedures that would require "the German population of Upper Silesia" to apply to the DVL or be treated as not "belonging to the German nation." Himmler complied on 10 February 1942 with an order covering all of the incorporated lands with a registration deadline of 31 March 1942.[46] The need for recruits similarly prompted the Interior Ministry to relax citizenship requirements in Alsace, Lorraine, and Luxembourg: two German grandparents and enrollment in the Waffen-SS sufficed.[47]

A small but very diverse group, including so-called "renegades" hostile to Germany, made up category IV (red IDs) with revocable state membership. On 16 February 1942 Himmler cited individuals of German origin in mixed marriages who lived with foreign ethnic groups and the children of such marriages or who came under Polish influence through the Catholic Church or the Polish Evangelical-Augsburg Church and individuals who gave up their German identity to attain a social advance or to live in a purely Polish environment. As Polonized Germans they were regarded with suspicion and therefore came under special police surveillance, and their rights in other respects were restricted. But they were exempt from the 15 percent tax imposed on Poles and were entitled to the same wages as Germans. Therefore, in some areas category IV, which included people who could not speak German, was referred to as the *Lebensmittel Liste* (foodstuffs list).[48]

Thus, much depended on the category in which one was registered. The higher categories received the best of the property that the Nazis confiscated from Jews, Poles, and others. Those in categories I and II were linked with the Nazi authorities, and in the Polish environment many played the role of masters. They could fill high-level positions in the administration and economy. Those in category III could marry Germans or others in category III but not Poles. They could not be a civil service official (*Beamte*) or hold an executive position as a state employee. Men were often registered primarily to supply the military, particularly in Pomerania and Upper Silesia. The revocability of their citizenship made clear their vulnerability akin to that of the rest of the population, which lived in constant fear of being deported or executed. Those of German origin who refused to register were threatened with being sent to concentration camps, as happened in a number of cases.[49] When found to be "infected" with Polish patriotism, the category III *Volksdeutscher* Theodor Kühn from Sichelberg (Sierpc) County, who declared, "still today I feel profoundly loyal to and proud of the Polish flag . . . therefore I cannot swear an oath to the Führer," was sentenced to a concentration camp in March 1942.[50]

Chaos reigned in the DVL registration process among the civil authorities. On 28 October 1941 the Kattowitz (Katowice) County *Landrat* thought completion of the process could take seven years. Delays made the regulation of social benefits, particularly for families of Wehrmacht conscripts, and the ownership of confiscated property among the most pressing issues for the German administration.[51] The protracted postwar process of nationality verification and rehabilitation faced similar issues.

The DVL served as the main instrument of Germanization of Polish citizens and one of the most important tools for segregating the population of Nazi-occupied Poland. Analogous programs existed in other Nazi-occupied countries. Following his appointment as Reich Protector of Bohemia and Moravia in September 1941, Heydrich set out to Germanize the Protectorate. But the importance of industry meant Germanizing the mainly Czech workforce. Heydrich foresaw about half of the Czech population becoming German. Instead of individuals deciding their nationality, the security police would register all Czechs according to "national" and "tribal/biological" features. The criteria, however, remained vague and "racial" concepts murky. Outward behavior and appearance dictated who had "German blood," allowing Czechs to influence the selection process by providing the appropriate information to racial examiners. But the assassination of Heydrich at the end of May 1942 cut the project short.[52]

Local Implementation of Nationality Policies

Even prior to orders from Berlin, security considerations and the deportations prompted local authorities to identify Germans. The *Gauleiter* had very decided ideas concerning the selection of *Volksdeutsche* in their regions. Himmler's insistence on the strict application of regulations concerning DVL categories did not suit all of his lieutenants.[53] The variety of standards used in recognizing individuals as Germans would complicate their rehabilitation by the Polish authorities after 1945.

Category III became the main point of contention. The vagueness of terms such as "German origin" or "racial suitability" invited wide interpretation. *Gauleiter* and *Reichsstatthalter* Albert Forster of Danzig-West Prussia and *Gauleiter* and *Oberpräsident* Fritz Bracht of Upper Silesia pursued their own policies, particularly in relation to the so-called nationally "in-between" strata, resulting in category III comprising the overwhelming majority in the DVL. In his study of nationality policy in the incorporated lands, Wolf concludes that in effect Forster and Bracht pursued a policy of assimilation unprecedented in German history and more akin to pre-1918 Prussian Germanization of the population than to Nazi race-based Germanization of the territory. In contrast, Greiser wanted to Germanize Wartheland solely by resettling *Volksdeutsche* from abroad and removing Poles and Jews.[54]

Wartheland

The importance that Greiser attached to verifying Germanness according to strict standards, excluding individuals of Polish or ambiguous nationality, prompted him to act before other *Gauleiter*. On 28 October 1939 he set up a new authority in Poznań to create a German nationality list with special commissions to examine the validity of the declarations of applicants. A positive decision required continuous membership in the German nation, an active role in the political life of the German minority in Poland, the use of the German language in everyday life, the enrollment of children in German schools, and the German origin of at least one parent. On 8 November 1939 the Poznań DVL office began to distribute a questionnaire to 6,648 individuals who impressed officials as being "German" while rejecting some 3,000 other applicants. But the Reich Interior Ministry halted the procedure as too exclusive and unauthorized.[55]

Following the November 1939 decree of the Interior Ministry, the creation of the German nationality list in Wartheland began on 1 February 1940. As it became known that Hitler favored the Germanization of about a million inhabitants of the incorporated territory and that Himmler wanted to Germanize racially suitable inhabitants, officials sorted successful applicants into five categories ranging from group A for active Germans to group E for Polonized individuals of German origin hostile toward Germany, so-called "renegades," based on a differentiated list of criteria that combined a *"nationality* judgment" with a *"political* judgment." Only those in groups A and B received certificates of membership in the DVL.⁵⁶ Other incorporated lands did not differentiate among *Volksdeutsche* until the spring of 1941.

Greiser also sought to segregate Germans and Poles by their names. On 14 September and 11 October 1940 he directed registries not to record German names for newborns of Polish origin. With the introduction into the incorporated lands of registry regulations from the Old Reich, in May 1941 Greiser proposed the creation of a list of typical Polish names analogous to an already existing list of Jewish names. Those in the DVL were required to change Polish names to German ones. Unsuccessful applicants with a decidedly German surname would be required to adopt a Polish surname. On 1 November 1941 Greiser directed administrative districts to implement immediately a proposal restricting the choice of given names of children both of whose parents were Polish to a long list of Polish names from "Bądzimierz" to "Żytomir" and requiring the additional name of "Kazimierz" or "Kazimiera," just as Jews in Germany were required to add "Israel" and "Sara." Children with one German parent were prohibited from receiving Polish names.⁵⁷

The 1941 DVL ordinance had little effect in Wartheland. Greiser ordered a review, with group A automatically entered into category I and generally groups B and C into II and III and groups D and E into IV. The review overwhelmed officials, who often simply followed procedures mechanically. Only in Litzmannstadt District did the review result in a significant difference, with c. 20,000 previously rejected applicants now accepted. After the review, new applicants had to be at least 50 percent of German origin, though for categories I and II this had less significance than a demonstration of Germanness.⁵⁸

On 28 February 1942 Greiser issued an ultimatum to the population of German origin to apply to the DVL or be treated as a Pole, but in contrast to elsewhere, this did not greatly increase the membership of the DVL so much as the number of rejections. To meet the needs of the military, on 8 April 1943 his deputy instructed district offices to transfer all category IV males born in 1923 or later to category III.⁵⁹

The case of Bruno C. in Wollstein (Wolsztyn) County illustrates the priority given to behavior. Initially, he was denied German state membership because he was a Pole. With the reorganization into five categories, he was entered into category C. In April 1942 he received a category III ID. His persistent protests resulted in his advancement to category II: he had married an ethnic German before the war, joined a German organization, and in addition received a positive evaluation from his German employer.⁶⁰

Officials who favored a policy of re-Germanization were ready to accept race as a criterion. Only after Hitler expressed support did Greiser agree to

Himmler's plan to carry out a racial examination of the Polish population in three locations as a test in early 1942, resulting in about 7 percent of the population classed as "able to be re-Germanized" (*wiedereindeutschbar*).⁶¹ By November 1944 "racial screening" in Litzmannstadt sent 17,423 such individuals from Wartheland to the Old Reich for Germanization.⁶²

Viewing high productivity as evidence of susceptibility to Germanization, Greiser proposed special rights for particularly productive workers, but Himmler only approved the creation in Wartheland in 1943 of an Association of Productive Poles (*Verband der Leistungspolen*) with the same pay and food rations as Germans and the right to remain in their homes. For most, registration was compulsory, though refusal apparently did not result in repression. Altogether the *Verband* included not more than 2 percent of the Polish workforce, which nevertheless meant some 40,000 *Leistungspolen*. Greiser later claimed that the goal was to disrupt Polish unity and fully exploit the lowest population before its disappearance.⁶³

Despite public warnings that applications to the DVL from Poles would be rejected, several hundred applied. By 1 March 1941 125 such applications were rejected. After March 1941 Greiser made an exception for the offspring of German-Polish marriages and those with two German grandparents. Other exceptions included individuals related to Nazi officials or high-ranking Wehrmacht officers. Greiser's strictures and the pressure of Polish society resulted in DVL registration of relatively few who before the war identified themselves as Poles, primarily in categories III and IV. Coercion played a role in a small number of cases, mainly of individuals with German-sounding names who sought to get married or had a spouse who was German or were registered in the years 1942–1944, when refusal met with the threat of being sent to a concentration camp. An analysis of the distribution of *Volksdeutsche* within Wartheland indicates that most resided in counties with a large German minority along the prewar border and in the city of Poznań.⁶⁴

Upper Silesia

Beginning in November 1939 inhabitants of the territory incorporated into German Silesia had to register to obtain a personal ID, the so-called *"palcówka"* because of the fingerprint required on the document.⁶⁵ Significantly, the instructions concerning nationality differed in German and Polish. Whereas in German the registrant was to declare "the people [Volk] to which the individual inwardly feels bound," in Polish he was to declare "that nation to which the registrant feels *most inclined.*" Both versions required certain characteristics, such as language, upbringing, and culture, to confirm the nationality. For language, the registrant was directed not to write "local" but a specific language, e.g., "slonzakisch" (*Ślązacki*).[66]

Out of fear of deportation and repression, many bilingual speakers declared knowing solely German (77.8 percent of all inhabitants—only 11.9 percent indicated Polish to be their mother tongue). Others indicated Silesian as their native language and some as their nationality.[67] In all of Polish Silesia 94.97 percent declared German nationality. For example, in Pleß (Pszczyna) County, where during the 1921 plebiscite 25.8 percent voted for Germany, 96 percent now registered as German. Significantly, where there was less official pressure, as in the incorporated counties of Cracow and Kielce Provinces, only 0.69 percent gave their nationality as German, which may also illustrate the fluid and contingent nature of the nationality of many Upper Silesians, among other factors.[68]

Just prior to the war, on 28 August 1939, Bishop Stanisław Adamski of Katowice issued a letter to the clergy and the faithful pointing out that a foreign occupation does not change the citizenship of the local population. On 7 September 1939 he affirmed this to the clergy and directed them to instruct the faithful. When the German authorities began to issue IDs, he advocated "masking oneself" to avoid mass expulsion. Privately, he recommended that members of his diocese declare themselves as "inclined toward Germanness," though he declared himself to be a Pole. On 25 May 1940 the vicar general of the diocese also recommended that the clergy register as "inclined toward Germanness" and appeal any contrary decision to the highest German authorities. Interestingly, the clergy of the Żory (Sohrau) Deaconate, unaware of the stand taken by Adamski, also advised the faithful to follow the same strategy, which suggests something more profound about attitudes in Upper Silesia.[69]

As the first results of the questionnaire ordered by the Interior Ministry reached the Kattowitz District president, he intensified his criticism of the time-consuming procedure. In Pleß County alone, the *Landrat* expected some 160,000 applicants but could not handle more than 100 per day. The District president favored a more inclusive selection because of the decisive importance of a massive integration of what he saw as an extraordinarily large stratum of Upper Silesians, "who in the last 20 years for various reasons have taken an undecided and neutral stance toward Germanness and hence are often described as an unstable floating stratum [*Schwemmschicht*]."[70]

Finally, the demand for soldiers for the Wehrmacht provided the occasion for less restrictive criteria. On 7 March 1940 the Interior Ministry issued guidelines for the mustering of German state members born in the years 1913 to 1920. Whereas officials in Wartheland and Danzig-West Prussia summoned only a very small portion of the local population, on 26 March 1940 the Kattowitz District deputy president instructed officials, "The national-political goal with regard to the Upper Silesian mixed population is its complete Germanization. The Slonsaks [Schlonsaks], who in the census... described themselves as Silesians, German-Silesians, or Slonsaks, are to be treated in exactly the same way."[71] Some of those called up in 1940 declared themselves to be Poles, but refusal to serve risked confinement in a concentration camp. According to the memoirs a German official in Teschen Silesia, a district commissioner in Skoczów reported on 8 April 1941 that 186 potential draftees requested that their nationality be changed from "Silesian" to "Polish" and 72 from "Polish" to "Silesian" or "German," illustrating the contingent nature of their national identity.[72]

Responding to the call to muster was taken as sufficient evidence that the individual "has a feeling of belonging to the German nation." Officials had only to check for any certificate confirming membership—the word *Volksdeutscher* sufficed—and if in the census the individual indicated "German, Silesian, German-Silesian, or Slonsak." Even if he indicated he was Polish, he was not to be excluded if he "credibly" affirmed he had done so in error. Finally, he had to attest to no previous convictions or membership in a radical Polish nationalist organization. He could then immediately fill out the questionnaire for registration as a state member and receive provisional approval on the spot. Problems did not arise until 4 February 1943 when the deputy chief of staff inquired why in 1940 and 1941 at least 40,000 men were inducted into the Wehrmacht prior to a decision concerning their nationality.[73]

Bracht announced the DVL on 10 April 1941, addressing "all those Upper Silesians who profess to be German or are of German origin." The social and political behavior of applicants played an even more significant role in Upper Silesia for categories I and II than ordered by the Interior Ministry. Thus, individuals who in the census identified themselves as German and then in 1940 and 1941 declared themselves to be Polish to avoid conscription were excluded from category I. But Bracht ignored the requirements for category III and included the so-called in-between strata.[74]

Following Himmler's order obligating all Germans to register, Bracht's nationality expert advised the DVL central office that belonging to Polish economic and cultural organizations was "often unavoidable" and therefore their members could absolutely be registered in category II. But above all he urged liberality in the selection for category III of the "mixed population with a Slavic mother tongue [*Haussprache*]," even some members of radically anti-German organizations. In a meeting on 17 November 1942, Bracht himself stated, "The Upper Silesian... who behaved with indifference and whose national emotions are at all roused only since 1870... is to be admitted to the DVL as a German, even if under Polish rule he made... certain concessions." Indeed, active participants in the third Silesian Uprising were not to be excluded if Germanization was anticipated, leaving officials little basis for rejecting anyone unless persistent in his Polishness. Bracht also persuaded Himmler to extend the deadline. As a result, in Upper Silesia 80 percent of those in the DVL at the end of the war registered in 1942.[75]

The Gabor family illustrates how officials dealt with the ambiguous background of many Upper Silesians. After the lower offices rejected the family's application, the central office confirmed that Gabor had strong Polish ties, participated in the anti-German uprising after World War I, and later was a member of Polish radical nationalist organizations. He also received several decorations from the Polish state. Nevertheless, he fought on the German side in the war; was awarded the Iron Cross, 2nd class; and, according to his own testimony, always identified himself as a German. In addition, he subscribed to a German newspaper and since 1936 belonged to the professional organization for owners of German shepherds. Decisive was that both of his parents were of Upper Silesian origin and that he had relatives in the Old Reich and in categories I and II in Upper Silesia. On 14 August 1944 the authorities placed Gabor in category IV and the rest of the family in category III.[76]

Bracht, however, restricted these inclusive policies to areas formerly under Prussian rule after 1815 and Teschen Silesia. Thus, implementation of the DVL varied greatly within Upper Silesia. Officials in Kattowitz County considered 300,000 of 387,000 inhabitants for acceptance in the DVL. In Bielitz (Bielsko) County German opposition to mass Germanization resulted in more than 68 percent of inhabitants recorded as Poles, according to German statistics on 10 October 1943. Counties that had not been part of Prussian Poland after 1815 had higher proportions of Poles: 95.5 percent in Ilkenau (Olkusz) County on 10 October 1943 and 89.1 percent in Saybusch (Żywiec) County in January 1944. In Warthenau (Zawiercie) County officials halted the process after handling 600 applications, excluding the rest of the 120,000 inhabitants from consideration.[77]

The belief widespread in formerly Polish Upper Silesia that the leadership of the Catholic Church and the Polish authorities in London approved of the "masquerade" of Poles identifying themselves as Germans was of fundamental significance. Circles close to the *Delegatura,* which represented the government-in-exile in the underground, regarded the lack of a clear stand on the part of the government led by Premier General Władysław Sikorski along with rumors of the supposed approval of registration by Sikorski as among the most important reasons for the extensive accession to the DVL in the incorporated lands.[78] Supposedly, the government-in-exile approved of Adamski's strategy in a Polish broadcast on British radio: "The military is waging an active struggle for Poland at the fronts, while you in the homeland have the task of defending the internal front—with all [your] strength and all means—remain in place—do not allow yourself to be removed from Silesia and defend our labor establishment."[79] When the government-in-exile passed a resolution on the question, it did so with circumspection and ambiguity, warning that Polish citizens who declared their nationality to be German would suffer consequences after the war unless they could prove "that they really acted under absolute coercion, having in this consideration for the national public interest." In any case the resolution reached the occupied territory only on 21 December 1941 when DVL registration was already well under way.[80]

Following Adamski's deportation to the *Generalgouvernement* on 28 February 1941, the majority of the clergy of the Katowice Diocese applied for registration in the DVL, which usually placed them in category III. In mid-1943 almost half of the clergy of the diocese was in categories I–III of the DVL.[81] Adamski later argued: "It was a question of the Silesian people not losing their priests, whom they knew and who knew them as well as to protect the diocese and people from dispatched German priests, who already because they did not know Polish would have a negative effect on the national consciousness of parishioners." After the war he claimed unequivocally that the Polish government-in-exile approved of the "masquerade," but no evidence of the approval has been found in the records of the London government. Quite possibly the bishop acted on his own.[82]

The *Delegatura* softened a negative opinion of Adamski's stand over time. The leadership of the Home Army (*Armia Krajowa* or AK), loyal to the government-in-exile, initially criticized his tactics as ineffective and regarded him as a "good faith opportunist" who made a concession to the Germans to protect the Church and the people of Silesia. But by mid-1941 political leaders recognized that the situation in Silesia and Pomerania was complicated and could not be assessed unequivocally.[83]

Within the territory of former Polish Upper Silesia nearly 1,290,000 individuals were registered in the DVL by 10 October 1943, i.e., about 95 percent of the population. Some older inhabitants, who were German citizens before 1922, sought the highest DVL category, while the younger generation was passive, perhaps to avoid conscription. Enrollment in the DVL, however, usually took place without an individual's direct participation.[84] Thus, most in category III had the status imposed on them, which they were generally not unhappy to accept in light of the privileges it offered. Many Upper Silesians, however, willingly applied for categories I–III, attracted by the rights and protections that came with them, particularly as Germany moved from success to success in 1939–1941, but also even as late as 1944.[85]

A report in 1943 by a member of the Polish underground illustrates the casual attitude toward nationality of many.[86] On a tram on the Bielski line, three soldiers in German uniforms openly conversed in Polish. When a

German civilian objected, they loudly advised him to learn Polish, "because things will turn out badly for whoever does not know Polish." When a gendarme chimed in, the soldiers asked him, "Where will you hide that uniform when the time comes? You should learn Polish, too." The gendarme responded in Polish, which he spoke well, and they parted in a friendly manner at a tram stop.[87]

Reichsgau Danzig-West Prussia

When the killings and deportations began in West Prussia, local party leaders early on granted requests for a *Volksdeutsche* ID. The first census in the Reichsgau 3–6 December 1939 sorted the population into four categories, partly based on political behavior: *Volksdeutsche,* Jews, native Poles (i.e., resident since before 1918), and immigrant Poles. Those "who *openly declared themselves to be German and supported their Germanness*" qualified as *Volksdeutsche,* whereas those natives who "took an active part in combating Germanness" were classified with the immigrants.[88]

Forster resisted the Interior Ministry's November 1939 decree primarily as an attack on his authority granted by Hitler to Germanize the incorporated lands. The civil authorities were to issue questionnaires only to individuals whom party leaders already designated as *Volksdeutsche*. Officials were explicitly prohibited from denying the questionnaire to applicants with a Polish name or to Catholics. Although evaluation of the questionnaires was based on the behavior of the applicant, the significance attached to attendance at a German school even before 1918 allowed the inclusion of nearly all former German citizens.[89]

In response to the controversy over race as a criterion, Forster invited the most famous National-Socialist racial expert to tour the *Gau* in September 1940. He concluded that the population represented "an inextricable racial mixture" and "that about $4/5$ of the Polish population there is racially not distant from the German nation of East Middle Germany." With this blessing for an inclusive nationality policy, Forster on 14 December 1940 ordered a "re-Germanization operation," particularly aimed at "formerly German families" who in the last thirty to forty years established bonds with Polishness or were Polonized—in his view constituting a large part of the native population.[90]

In contrast to Warthegau, where the initiative lay with the DVL applicant, in Danzig-West Prussia it resided with the authorities. The lack of a fixed formula as to whether a family could be Germanized allowed for a wider inclusion than the previous selection. If all desired conditions were met, re-Germanization was mandated even in doubtful cases without proof of German origins. Moreover, it expediently encompassed those on whom the local economy depended, a factor of increasing importance throughout the incorporated lands after a year of German occupation. Only if a decision was fundamentally flawed did the case come before Forster. Additionally, the results of the operation were decided in advance: the registration of 30,000 families capable of being re-Germanized and the establishment of German rule on a broad socio-economic foundation. The sole concession to the anticipated introduction of uniform DVL regulations was the denial of any possibility of equality of rights for those families placed in the third category, allowing for coercive measures directed against them.[91]

Following the DVL ordinance of March 1941 Forster continued the "re-Germanization" of natives with a specific quota for each county. When Forster finally announced the introduction of the DVL on 21 May 1941, he refrained from defining what excluded one from being considered of German origin. Even individuals with Polish names could qualify. A surname might have been Polonized under economic or political pressure, a "Kowalski" could have been a "Schmidt." Similarly, membership in a Polish political organization might have been compulsory. Categories I and II required an ability to speak German but not category III.[92]

Locally, Forster could rely on party members such as the Thorn (Toruń) County leader: "The population residing here ... externally appear[s] Polish, the core alone is German, and it is only for the National Socialist educational work to make of these individuals, who in part themselves do not know where they belong, worthwhile German individuals."[93] After 1945 some local officials also decided the nationality of individuals who did not know "where they belong."

In executing Himmler's order that Germans register on the DVL, Forster instructed officials to evaluate applications summarily. As in Upper Silesia, the number entered into the DVL grew rapidly. In December 1941 it was made up of more than 31,000 individuals; ten months later they numbered almost 800,000. To a lesser degree there was also a geographic differentiation similar to Upper Silesia, with only 17 percent of the native population registered in formerly Russian-ruled Rippin (Rypin) and Leipe (Lipno) Counties at the end of March 1943 compared with 58 percent in the rest of the province.[94]

A German woman stationed in a village in Danzig-West Prussia reported in 1942 that those in category III "do not stand out in any way from the Poles and speak just as much or as little German as the Poles."[95] A Pole vividly described the situation:

> Meanwhile the Germans went mad. In the freezing winter of 1942 the registration on the *Volksliste* began by order of Forster, voluntary, if anyone wants to, but

who does not sign will be regarded as an enemy and treated like a Jew. A blind panic and utter despair overcame the inhabitants. Sign and you have to go to the German army and what's more risk your life for such gangsters; not sign, go to Dachau, *till the end of the war I'll survive like a bump on a log,* the bolder decided. *Oh God, let loose a bolt from heaven at such scoundrels*—the women lamented— *For God's sake, don't talk so loud, because they can eavesdrop at the window and shoot all of us here. What is happening, for whose sins did we live to see such times.*[96]

East Prussia

The DVL had only marginal significance in East Prussia except for Działdowo, where Mazurs were registered in the higher DVL categories. According to the Polish resistance on 10 December 1942, no more than 2 percent of the Polish population of Zichenau (Ciechanów) District was registered on the DVL, at times without strict regard for racial or nationality criteria. As proof of German origin it often sufficed that they migrated from formerly Prussian Pomerania or Great Poland.[97]

The *Gauleiter* and *Oberpräsident* Erich Koch saw "Southeast Prussia" as a place for the landless sons of East Prussian farmers to colonize and play the role of masters. The tendency was to exploit the area for the benefit of the "homeland," in particular through the recruitment of Polish agricultural workers. Like Greiser, Koch sought to Germanize this area through the resettlement of Germans and the elimination of Jews and Poles.[98]

The Mazurs, however, were subjected to intensive Germanization as the authorities now abandoned all restraint in their effort to eliminate the population's Polish-Mazurian roots. On 24 November 1939 the president of Allenstein (Olsztyn) District banned the use of Polish in religious services, which had been prohibited in the Diocese of Warmia since July 1939. Many Polish Mazurian officials were arrested, the majority accused of high treason and sent to concentration camps and prisons. The brother of Karol Małłek, Robert, was shot near Działdowo. In February 1940 the authorities transformed former barracks in Działdowo into a transit, detention, and extermination camp for pro-Polish Mazurs, dependents of Polish intellectuals, Jews, and mentally ill East Prussians—some with the sole symptom of anti-German feelings. The 83-year-old Archbishop Antoni Julian Nowowiejski of Płock was among those murdered. Of approximately 200,000 individuals who passed through the Działdowo camp, about 10,000 were killed.[99]

In spite of such measures, officials reported a revival of the Polish-Mazurian language in 1940. The annexation of the Zichenau District and the presence of Polish forced laborers and POWs threatened the national character of the

Mazurs. A witness in Lyck (Ełk) County complained that villagers speak "Polish in the street and at the inn." On 21 February 1941, the chief administrative officer of Ortelsburg confirmed that the introduction of 2,000 Polish workers into the county had resulted in an increase in the use of the Mazurian language. There were other consequences. By the beginning of 1940 a large number of East Prussian women had received severe prison sentences for forbidden contact with prisoners of war. Official reports made frequent references to the "un-German" behavior of sentries and the civilian population in showing hospitality to Polish prisoners, with whom they often had positive relations. To break the tie between Poles and Mazurs, officials demanded an increase in Belgian and French prisoners of war.[100]

In 1943 a high-ranking SS officer warned against settling Mazurs as colonizers in Zichenau District because of their susceptibility to Polonization:

> One could also often notice during the current war that the Mazur with great pleasure and linguistic ability dug out of memory and used in Poland his Mazurian dialect, which in general can be very well understood by Poles. Admittedly, every Mazur speaks flawless German, but precisely among agricultural workers, fishermen, small landholders, petty craftsmen, one converses in family circles in Mazurian. At least parents and grandparents speak Mazurian among themselves, and one often speaks Mazurian to children and certainly to cattle. Also, the attitude toward work, the condition of the farmyard, the type of entertainment, and many other phenomena of everyday life have a character that dissociates it still very clearly from German traits. From a national-political point of view they nevertheless at times lack absolutely a certain instinct, an absolutely clear feeling that the Mazovian or Pole is something foreign, which should be treated with reserve.[101]

Admitting the failure of Germanization, officials replaced the characterization "Mazurian" with "Polish" to emphasize its anti-German aspect and increasingly resorted to pressure to assimilate. The Mazurs, a loyal and extremely pro-German population, were not trusted in wartime.[102]

The DVL Total in the Incorporated Lands

Most estimates put the total number of natives of the incorporated lands registered in the DVL at about 2.8 million.[103] As the statistics for January 1944 in table 2.2 indicate, there was considerable variation in the proportions of the DVL categories from one incorporated land to another. But even within each category, not all *Volksdeutsche* were alike.

The predominance of categories I and II, which depended on more or less definable behavior, in Wartheland and Southeast Prussia and of category III,

TABLE 2.2 DVL Categories in the Incorporated Lands

Incorporated Lands	DVL I	%	DVL II	%	DVL III	%	DVL IV	%	DVL Total
Wartheland	218,000	45.1	192,000	39.8	64,000	13.2	9,000	1.9	483,000
Danzig-West Prussia (without Danzig)	113,000	12.0	97,000	10.3	726,000	77.4	2,000	0.2	938,000
Upper Silesia	97,000	7.2	211,000	15.8	976,000	72.9	54,000	4.0	1,338,000
Southeast Prussia	9,000	19.6	22,500	48.9	13,500	29.3	1,000	2.2	46,000
Total	437,000	15.6	522,500	18.6	1,779,500	63.4	66,000	2.4	2,805,000

Data source: Trials of War Criminals before the Nuernberg Military Tribunals under Control Council Law no. 10: Nuernberg Oct. 1946–April 1949, 15 vols. (Washington, DC: U.S. Government Printing Office, 1949–1953), vol. 4, "The Einsatzgruppen Case." "*The RuSHA Case*" (1950), 937–938. The source gives a total of 493,000 for Wartheland and 1,420,000 for Upper Silesia. DVL statistics vary by date, category, and *Gau*, but the proportions in various sources remain approximately the same.

which depended on the much vaguer requirement of German origin, in Danzig-West Prussia and Upper Silesia reflects the respective exclusive and inclusive approaches of the authorities in these lands.

German officials turned down the applications of more than 400,000 Polish citizens to the DVL: 269,000 from Pomerania, 82,000 from Upper Silesia, 50,000 from Wartheland, and 1,000 from the Zichenau District.[104] The reasons for the rejections varied and were in some cases purely technical.

Fear as well as a desire to protect their families from persecution or deportation and their property from confiscation motivated many who applied. The *Delegatura* reported in September 1943: "In the Ciechanów [Zichenau] District registrations on the [D]VL recently increased, all of the registrations have a material basis, people tired of persecution, economic difficulties, hope to improve their standard of living. They are mainly hired hands and small farmers, the latter out of fear of deportation."[105] The Western Section of the Department of Information and Press of the *Delegatura* reported: "VD [*Volksdeutsche*], those are mostly middle-class and merchant circles, they are in the DVL for profit. Materialism plays the basic role for them." In rural areas some registered primarily to keep their farms. In Litzmannstadt District some even Germanized their Polish-sounding names, suggesting a belief in the longevity of the Third Reich, which in light of Poland's brief interlude of independence and its rapid defeat as well as Germany's early military successes seemed reasonable.[106]

Some who registered voluntarily sought to portray it as a patriotic act. A report from Bydgoszcz (Bromberg) in 1941 to the *Delegatura* sarcastically noted: "They had to agree to register on the DVL because otherwise the Germans will prepare inevitable ruin, and they after all will be indispensable for the new Poland, without them Poland will not survive, they have to preserve their great talents and then put them at the disposition of the fatherland." In some instances, individuals registered on the DVL at the direction of the Polish underground. A report of the *Delegatura* on the mood of the Polish population in 1943 emphasized that in Pomerania and Silesia conspiratorial activity and the resistance movement relied in large part on individuals registered on the DVL.[107]

In the *Generalgouvernement* the authorities introduced an ID for Germans on 26 January 1940. Because of the limited number of residents who truly felt German, on 29 October 1941 the authorities formally recognized individuals of German origin (*deutschstämmig*), which required at least one German grandfather, but in practice a German-sounding surname sufficed. On 20 May 1942 an order allowed the authorities to treat even an individual who professed to be Polish as *deutschstämmig* if a "race judgment" resulted in "25% proven *Deutschstämmigkeit*." At the turn of 1944–1945 an estimated 90,000 *Volksdeutsche* resided in the *Generalgouvernement*.[108]

In his memoirs Stanisław Drygas, who worked as a translator in a county office in the *Generalgouvernement*, characterized *Volksdeutsche* of Polish origin as "opportunist pigs [*świn koniunkturowych*]." "The difficult times induced pusillanimous individuals to sell themselves and their children—whom the Germans were most interested in—for porridge, flour, sugar, and the like." One explained why he registered: "Man, all is lost. The Germans won't any more move out of here. One must grab a chance to live and to live well. We have a lot of years ahead of us. I want to live in affluence and not starve."[109]

The image of *Volksdeutsche* as "opportunist pigs" had the greatest influence on the attitude of the Polish population—even currently—toward *Volksdeutsche*, but their largely voluntary status in the *Generalgouvernement* gave it a different significance than in Upper Silesia and Danzig-West Prussia. In Wartheland, however, Poles serving the Germans were thought of as worse than "real Germans." The Poznań worker Irena Nieznaniec wrote in her memoir concerning lower-level Polish supervisors who harassed workers to please their bosses: "These scoundrels literally shove past each other to kiss the rear end of these krauts [*w tyłki tym szwabom włażą*]."[110]

When on 9 September 1939 the German army entered Litzmannstadt, German inhabitants greeted it with applause, flowers, alcohol, and cigarettes and decorated the parade route with Nazi flags and welcome signs. Some *Volksdeutsche* played a more nefarious role. German intelligence may well have used some ethnic Germans. A widespread belief that the German minority as a whole acted as a fifth column of the invading German army imposed a heavy burden on the image of the German minority and justified its expulsion after the war, though the accusation is controversial.[111]

On 3 September 1939 retreating Polish troops in Bydgoszcz reacted to what they believed were shots fired by the town's ethnic Germans, murdering many of them. German propaganda exploited the so-called "Polish September murders" and "Bromberg Bloody Sunday" to promote aggressive anti-Polish feelings and charge the Polish nation with collective guilt. In Bydgoszcz itself ethnic Germans assisted in the murder of hundreds by identifying alleged Polish perpetrators.[112]

Volksdeutsche joined "self-defense" (*Selbstschutz*) militias—not as benign as the name—in droves to assist the German police. Membership in Upper Silesia reached 452,000, 228,000 in Kattowitz District alone. In West Prussia the 17,000 who joined by October 1939 identified Jews and Polish suspects for the police and SS, served as guards at forced labor camps, and assisted the task forces in eliminating political and racial enemies until Himmler disbanded the *Selbstschutz* in August 1940. By that time the militias may have assisted in the killing of as many as 20,000 individuals and the transfer of 10,000 others to concentration camps.[113] Doris L. Bergen concludes, "Both as an abstract category and as real people, the *Volksdeutschen* occupied the cutting edge of German racial warfare."[114] A systemic study of core constituencies of Nazi perpetrators found that they were overrepresented in the population of Upper Silesia and East Prussia and among the German minority in Poland generally.[115]

Other *Volksdeutsche*, however, sought to protect Polish neighbors despite the possible consequences. Because the chairman of a town council in Danzig-West Prussia intervened too often on behalf of Poles, he was sent to the eastern front where he died under mysterious circumstances.[116] Where generations-long strong relations existed between Germans and Poles, the Gestapo had difficulty breaking them. The Gestapo even printed special warnings against Germans assisting Poles during mass arrests. The threat of draconian punishments did not prevent intimate relations between Germans and Poles: the prohibition of interethnic sexual relations proved impossible to enforce.[117]

As the end of the war approached, even the Highest Court of Examination for Nationality Questions took into account the need for cannon fodder and ignored questions of "purity of blood."[118] To prevent a further deterioration in security, on 14 December 1944 the Kattowitz Oberpräsidium demanded that the Interior Ministry recognize the "courageous attitude" of numerous young Poles in the Wehrmacht, withdraw restrictions on the Polish population, such as the higher legal marital age (to stifle the birth rate) and lower wages, and register in DVL category III without a determination of nationality the tens of thousands of individuals called up for the Wehrmacht or at least treat them the same as Germans in economic matters. The Oberpräsidium saw this as perhaps the last opportunity to convince the "thus far loyal . . . overwhelming part of the Polish population of the wish of the German Reich to recognize it as a part of the European cultural nation."[119]

Inevitably, many inhabitants of the incorporated lands took a different view as the war turned against Germany. In West Prussia and Upper Silesia the number of individuals returning their DVL IDs or refusing to accept them, above all to avoid serving in the German army, began to increase. The Gestapo sought to counter this trend with warnings and then with detention and transfers to concentration camps. The SS in Danzig in April 1943 reported that category III *Volksdeutsche* in West Prussia frequently behaved in public as Poles despite the prohibition on the use of the Polish language and went to great lengths to avoid work and military duties. In Graudenz the call-up of recruits from category III resulted in open demonstrations of pro-Polish feelings, with conscripts waving Polish flags as their train departed and singing "Boże coś Polskę" (God Protect Poland). In 1943, to prevent the frequent desertions of Poles from Pomerania to the Red Army, the inspector of the military prohibited sending them to the eastern front. Where loyalty to the Nazis was tenuous, the authorities feared losing control. In Danzig-West Prussia Forster reacted with conciliatory gestures. Himmler, however, at the end of 1944 ordered the execution of those who refused to accept their DVL IDs.[120]

Masses of prewar Polish citizens served not only in the German army but also, not in large numbers, in the Waffen SS. Service in the Wehrmacht had a universal character in the incorporated lands, but because of the fragmentary nature of the evidence and the fluid nature of national identity, it is impossible to determine how many ethnically Polish natives it encompassed. Polish estimates commonly put the number at 250,000.[121] Based on the existing and analogous evidence, Ryszard Kaczmarek concludes that at least 295,000 inhabitants of the incorporated lands served in the German army: 195,000 from category III, of whom no fewer than 75,000 died in the war, and 100,000 from categories I and II. But he sees these figures as extremely low estimates and is inclined to accept that mobilization of those in category III was similar to that of males in the Old Reich, i.e., a maximum of 500,000. This figure finds some support in reports of the Polish underground of 400,000 to 450,000 Poles from Silesia and Danzig-West Prussia in the German military in early 1944. These estimates presume that DVL category III consisted mostly of ethnically Polish natives. The leadership of the Wehrmacht made the same assumption when in 1943 it directed that the military passes of soldiers from category III be inscribed with the word "Pole" to warn commanders of possible desertion.[122]

The participation of non-German Polish citizens in the Wehrmacht resulted from a combination of factors. Nazi racial authorities justified the acceptance of groups such as Silesians and Kashubs in the *Volksgemeinschaft*. German citizenship, which had its attractions, carried with it the obligation of military service. In a memoir a former soldier from Kattowitz County saw joining the German army as simply an obligation. The early German military successes glamorized the uniform. The spectrum of attitudes included opportunism and adaptation to a situation that frequently changed; they cannot be simply identified with collaboration.[123]

The Polish Underground and the DVL

The radical faction of the national camp ONR-Szaniec went the furthest in demanding retribution: the one million Polish dead require the death of three million Germans. "Therefore the basest of the base so-called *Volksdeutsche* must perish" along with other Germans, including children.[124] Nevertheless, the complexity of Nazi practices called for a more nuanced approach.

The communist-dominated Polish Workers' Party (*Polska Partia Robotnicza* or PPR), formed in German-occupied Poland in January 1942, stated in its program of November 1943 that special courts would deal with traitors and agents of Hitler as well as those hostile to the Polish nation.[125] Significantly, PPR activists in Silesia regarded registration on the DVL as coerced.[126] Initially, the underground loyal to the government-in-exile sharply condemned voluntary registration on the DVL, but in developing proposals for dealing with *Volksdeutsche* after the war, it took into account the conditions under the occupation. Members of a conspiratorial organization *Ojczyzna* (Fatherland), which focused on the problem of the DVL more than any other organization, played a significant role in this and continued to do so after the war.[127]

In June 1942 *Ojczyzna*'s publication *Be-zet* distinguished among *Volksdeutsche*, advocating different treatment of *Volksdeutsche* in the *Generalgouvernement*, where registration was voluntary, and in the incorporated lands, where it was coerced and the character of the population was typical of a borderland with shifting state sovereignty. Articles in *Be-zet* also saw the DVL category as significant. Concerning those in category III, an article in July 1942 flatly stated: "These are not Volksdeutsche—these are Poles forcedly enrolled in Germanness." A year later an article emphasized that those in categories I and II were undoubted Germans. A Pole was in this category "only at the price of performing a special service and therefore from our point of view, a traitor."[128] Influenced by *Ojczyzna*, the Western Section of the Department of Information and Press developed a detailed draft of a law in the second half of 1943 that recognized the distinctions among *Volksdeutsche* to be taken into account in deciding whether to return Polish citizenship.[129]

On 1 August 1944 as the Warsaw Uprising began, the Homeland Council of Ministers deprived Polish citizens of German nationality of their citizenship and obligated them to leave the territory of the Polish state. It defined as German those who belonged to a German organization, spoke German at home, observed German customs, raised their progeny in the German spirit, or renounced their citizenship to Polish officials or institutions or in other ways indicated they belonged to the German nation. In addition, the decree recognized as German whoever was registered on the DVL or received an identity card or German citizenship as a German or as of German origin. The non-German wife of a German deprived of citizenship did not automatically lose her Polish citizenship unless she left the country with him. Polish citizens of German nationality could apply to the minister of internal affairs for an exemption by proving that they displayed loyalty to the Polish state in a special way during the war.[130] Similarly, on 27 September 1944 the government-in-exile stated, "The experience of the 'fifth column' and the methods of occupation applied by the Germans in this war render the coexistence of the Polish and German population within the territory of one state impossible."[131]

At first, the communist-dominated Polish Committee of National Liberation (*Polski Komitet Wyzwolenia Narodowego* or PKWN) paid no attention to differences among *Volksdeutsche*. On 30 October 1944 the Director of the Department of Public Security Stanisław Radkiewicz ordered the detention in forced labor camps of "traitors of the Nation, the so-called 'Volksdeutsche,'" without addressing the complexity of the matter in the incorporated lands.[132]

Nazi nationality policies in Poland led to the destruction of millions of Jewish and other Polish citizens. In addition, ethnic redistribution displaced 1.71 million residents of Poland from their homes during the war.[133] *Heim ins Reich* also brought about the resettlement of ethnic Germans, not all of whom left their homes willingly for their putative "homeland." With the advance of the Soviet forces, vast numbers of *Volksdeutsche* and Reich Germans fled. When the Western Allies, accepting the demands of Joseph Stalin, set the borders of postwar Poland, and approved the removal of the German population, Nazi nationality policies provided a justification as well as a model for Polish policies. The stage was set for the postwar Polish authorities to complete the resettlement of Germans to their much reduced "homeland," deal with Polish citizens registered as *Volksdeutsche*, and identify the Poles among the remaining German citizens. This, however, constituted only part of the effort to create an ethnically homogeneous Poland that included the "repatriation" of Poles from territory annexed by the Soviet Union and of Ukrainians and others from Poland to their respective Soviet Socialist Republics, part of the vast movement of peoples after the war affecting more than 31 million.[134]

[3]

The Creation of a New Poland

THE SOVIET UNION was the main protagonist in the creation of a new Poland. The first act unfolded already in the years 1939 to 1941. But Britain and the United States played supporting roles in the drama. In the end, they approved the new borders and accepted the forced migration advocated by Stalin that was supposed to result in an ethnically homogeneous Poland. Other actors also had bit parts.

The German attack on Poland on 1 September 1939 followed by the Soviet invasion on 17 September 1939 did not dispel Polish hopes for a re-created Poland with more favorable borders. In October 1939 the National Party became the first in occupied Poland to spell out its proposal for a Polish-German border on the Oder and Lusatian Neisse Rivers with Stettin (Szczecin) on the Polish side, marshaling ethnic, historical, and moral arguments and emphasizing economic considerations, Slavic solidarity, and the strategic argument with the Oder-Neisse line as "the military backbone of Europe."[1]

Polish official circles also envisioned revision of the Polish-German border. Shortly after Poland's defeat, the Polish government-in-exile led by Sikorski suggested that Poland should receive territory from Germany that would give it a strategically more favorable border in the north and in the west. (Apparently fearful that Poland would not regain the territory occupied by the Soviet Union, Sikorski early on also thought of German territorial concessions as compensation.[2]) In a memorandum on 20 November 1940 to the British Foreign Office, the Polish government-in-exile justified claims to East Prussia, Pomerania, German Upper Silesia, and territory east of the Oder River not only on strategic grounds but on an ethnic basis as well, arguing that the population included a large number of Polish-speaking and "racially Polish" (i.e., Germanized) inhabitants.[3]

The Great Powers and the Reconstruction of Poland

Along with Poland's demand for a border revision, the Great Powers came to accept the necessity of the removal of the German population. The radical nationality policies of the Nazis and the participation therein of Poland's German minority led the Great Powers to conclude that it would be impossible for Poles and Germans to live together in one state.[4]

A negative view of the results of minority treaties accompanied a positive evaluation of the "exchange of population" sanctioned by the Treaty of Lausanne of 1923. On 12 December 1940 Prime Minister Churchill told his private secretary, "Exchanges of population would have to take place on the lines of that so successfully achieved by Greece and Turkey after the First World War." In a conversation in mid-September 1941 British Foreign Secretary Anthony Eden and his private secretary Oliver Harvey both agreed that the "minority treaties had been a curse" and that "next time there should be no minorities. They must opt between exchange and absorption." Harvey, who earlier expressed some doubts about the removal of Germans, noted in October 1941, "Anyway we have Hitler's authority for mass deportation and it may be a solution."[5]

Unwilling to alienate a potential ally, the Western Powers sought to mitigate the Soviet invasion of Poland. Despite Britain's alliance with Poland, Foreign Secretary Viscount Halifax ominously noted in the House of Lords on 26 October 1939 "that the action of the Soviet Government has been to advance the Russian boundary to what was substantially the boundary recommended at the time of the Versailles Conference by ... Lord Curzon, who was then Foreign Secretary."[6] Following the Soviet-German treaty of 28 September 1939, the U.S. ambassador in Moscow noted, "The line establishing the frontier between the Soviet Union and Germany is clearly drawn according to ethnological lines."[7] In recognizing the Polish government-in-exile on 7 October 1939, U.S. Secretary of State Cordell Hull omitted a passage from an earlier draft asserting that the United States would never recognize territory gained through aggression.[8]

All this confronted Poland itself with an "ethnographic danger," as Polish Foreign Minister August Zaleski put it, referring to the Polish-Soviet border. On 16 April 1940 before the National Council, a representative body of political parties, he noted that "there are a lot of people who continue to maintain that the political organization of Europe should be based on ethnographic premises."[9]

The German attack on the Soviet Union on 22 June 1941 brought the Soviet "entry" into the war against Germany hoped for by the Western Allies. But it did not alter Soviet claims to Polish territory. As Eden informed Sikorski on 4 July 1941, "Soviet policy was to favour the establishment of an independent national Polish State. The boundaries of this State would correspond with ethnographical Poland." Although an agreement with Poland reached on 30 July 1941 recognized that the Soviet-German treaties "lost their validity," the Soviets continued to insist on ethnographic considerations in demarcating the Polish-Soviet border.[10]

When President Franklin Roosevelt and Churchill agreed on the principles enshrined in the Atlantic Charter on 12 August 1941, they stated their "desire to see no territorial changes that do not accord with the freely expressed wishes of the peoples concerned." In signing the Declaration of United Nations on 1 January 1942, the Soviet Union also subscribed to the charter.[11] The Polish authorities, who saw the charter as endangering their demands for East Prussia and Danzig, responded with arguments that strategic and economic, not just ethnic, considerations must be taken into account.[12]

In mid-December 1941, with Eden in Moscow, Stalin linked three proposals that the Western Allies ultimately accepted: retention of the 1941 Polish-Soviet border with possible minor changes in Poland's favor, Poland's incorporation of "all the lands up to the Oder," and the transfer of the "German population of those regions" to Germany.[13]

Sikorski increasingly saw the necessity of a compromise regarding the Polish-Soviet border. Polish demands for German territory and the expulsion of its German inhabitants expanded in parallel with the negotiations leading to the loss of the eastern lands.[14] On 9 January 1942 Sikorski's intelligence chief Leon Mitkiewicz noted in his diary that during a briefing session Sikorski referred to Poland's national minorities as "a weak spot" and hinted at reaching an understanding with the Soviet Union based on "rebuilding Poland as an ethnically pure state, a national state."[15] In a report to the Polish Council of Ministers, Sikorski favored expansion westward: "It is history that pushes us in this direction," providing an opportunity to build a strong Poland "by regaining old Slav territories, with wide access to the sea, and secure from a military point of view." Nevertheless, "The Polish-Russian frontier must remain what it has been for centuries, a frontier of Western and Christian civilization."[16]

In July 1942 the British War Cabinet agreed in principle to the transfer of German population from Poland and Czechoslovakia and so informed their governments.[17] But the territory that Poland would receive had not yet been delineated. On 1 December 1942, the Polish government presented the Foreign Office with its demand for the annexation of Danzig, East Prussia, and German (Opole) Upper Silesia based on strategic, economic, ethnic, and historical grounds. It argued that an emigration westward of Germans since the nineteenth century, the return to Polishness of the only superficially Germanized Slavs, and the freely chosen emigration of Germans in reaction to Poland's takeover would facilitate the Polonization of this territory. Part of the German population would have to be resettled by force so that it could not constitute a "fifth column." Hitler's policies indicated Germany's acceptance of population transfers.[18]

Western leaders favored Polish territorial gains at Germany's expense but turned them into compensation for Soviet gains at Poland's expense. At a meeting in Washington on 15 March 1943, Eden and Roosevelt acquiesced to the Soviet tactic of using territorial gains in the west to pressure Poland to accept losses in the east. To "help maintain peace," the president thought that the allies "should make some arrangement to move the Prussians out of East Prussia the same way the Greeks were moved out of Turkey after the war."[19]

In December 1943 Stalin advised Beneš, who led the Czechoslovak government-in-exile, to get rid of all his Germans.[20] Stalin wanted to minimize the ethnic conflicts within his sphere of influence and increase its dependence on Soviet protection from German revanchism. In the eighteenth century when Russia chose Poland's rulers, Poland similarly became dependent on Russian (and Austrian) support against Prussia.[21]

No statesman seems to have considered a critique of creating ethnically homogeneous states published in the British periodical *Political Quarterly* in 1943, pointing out, "Migration or any free movement of people would have to be prohibited lest it should lead to the gradual creation of new unwanted and irritating minorities.... The 'New [postwar] World' would be inaugurated by the suppression of an old freedom."[22] Indeed, the postwar Polish government would seek to prevent the departure of Poles.

Events in 1943 further complicated Poland's situation. In mid-April 1943 Germany reported the discovery of a mass grave of Polish military in the Katyn Forest and accused the Soviet Union of responsibility. The Polish government's request for an investigation by the International Committee of the Red Cross gave the Soviets a pretext to sever relations with the Polish government-in-exile. The Western Allies knew the truth about the Soviet massacre but concealed it to prevent public opinion from turning against their Soviet ally.[23] Then in early July 1943 Sikorski died in a plane crash.

In mid-August 1943 the Foreign Office concluded that the Curzon Line should form the basis of Poland's eastern border and that Poland should receive Danzig, East Prussia, and Opole Silesia.[24] At meetings with Sikorski's successor, Premier Stanisław Mikołajczyk, Eden presented the territorial gains in the west as compensation for losses in the east. When the Poles objected, Eden testily responded, "Do you think you will be able to get those valuable acquisitions and at the same time keep your eastern frontier? That is not possible."[25]

At the conference of the Big Three in Tehran, Churchill meeting alone with Stalin on 28 November 1943 proposed, "Poland might move westward, like soldiers taking two steps 'left close'" and demonstrated this with three match sticks.[26] On 1 December 1943 Roosevelt met with Stalin and expressed his support for moving Poland's eastern border west and its western border to the Oder River, but asked for Stalin's understanding for his inability to take part in the decision for fear of alienating six to seven million Polish-American voters.[27] This violation of no territorial deals during the war and lack of tactical savvy "dismayed" Charles Bohlen, the president's interpreter.[28] Thus, by the end of 1943, the signatories of the Atlantic Charter signaled their consent to the proposals Stalin made to Eden in December 1941.

The Soviet Union and National Self-Determination

In Marxist theory, workers have no country; their liberation as a class has priority over national liberation. In the Leninist-Stalinist version, the interests of the nation coincide with that of the Communist Party, the vanguard of the proletariat. Where the vanguard achieved power, the right of national self-determination was realized.[29] In actual practice, however, the Soviet Union "was the world's first state to institutionalize ethnoterritorial federalism, classify all citizens according to their biological nationalities and formally prescribe preferential treatment of certain ethnically defined populations."[30] Enabling the major ethnographic groups to realize self-determination within separate territories seemed a necessary step on the road to socialism and ultimately communism.[31]

Moreover, Soviet views shifted from a portrayal of nations as products of capitalism to a conception of national identity with a life of its own deeply rooted in the distant past. The elimination of class antagonisms supposedly reconstituted nations as "socialist nations" that no longer seemed destined to wither away.[32] By 1939 the Soviet Union had officially become a federation of nation-states. The right of national self-determination evolved from a right of a people to decide its fate to the state determining which people received an ethno-national territory and where it would lie. Voluntary resettlement became forced deportation. The use of repressive and violent means in the application of the right of national self-determination illustrated the primacy of Soviet *raison d'état*.

The Soviets "nationalized" individuals as well as territory by making nationality the standard category of identity. Beginning in 1928 official documents requested the nationality with which an individual identified.[33] But fears that "suspect" nationalities might register as members of other nationalities led the

People's Commissariat of Internal Affairs (*Narodnyj Komissariat Vnutrennych Del* or NKVD, the security police) to require documents such as birth certificates and family records to confirm one's nationality.³⁴ "By the end of the 1930s every Soviet child inherited his nationality at birth: individual ethnicity had become a biological category impervious to cultural, linguistic, or geographical change."³⁵ The official registration of nationality in internal passports introduced in 1932 became "a cornerstone of the political management of ethnic processes."³⁶

Just as elsewhere in Europe, the Soviet authorities linked loyalty with ethnicity. The Great Terror of 1937–1938 targeted not only kulaks (exploitive farm owners) but also national groups, particularly the approximately 600,000 Soviet Poles. A special operation, second in size only to the one against kulaks, focused on Poles as an ethnic group. Attachment to elements of Polish culture or Roman Catholicism sufficed to be considered a part of international anti-Soviet espionage. The operation against kulaks also disproportionally affected the ethnically Polish. Once arrested Poles were somewhat more likely to be executed than sent to a gulag. A conservative estimate puts the number of Poles killed in 1937–1938 at some 85,000, one-eighth of all fatalities of the Terror, though they constituted less than 0.4 percent of the population. The operation became a model for dealing with "enemy nations."³⁷

Nevertheless, the Soviet authorities thought of extending "ethnoterritorial federalism" to the Poles of Soviet-occupied eastern Poland. Along with the goal of "the destruction of the existing [Polish] bourgeois-state authorities," the Soviet War Council of the Belorussian Front on 16 September 1939 called for the creation of a "Polish People's Assembly—of representatives chosen from provinces with a predominance of Polish population" to proclaim "unanimously" the creation of a "Polish Federal Soviet Republic" and to petition for inclusion in the Soviet Union.³⁸ But Stalin thought better of it, apparently fearing that Poles would seek to unite their partitioned lands. He therefore proposed a revision of the German-Soviet division of East Central Europe, exchanging territory inhabited predominantly by ethnically Polish population for Germany's renunciation of Lithuania, a revision confirmed in the German-Soviet agreement of 28 September 1939.³⁹

The German attack on the Soviet Union on 22 June 1941 initiated what is known as the Great Fatherland War, with its appeal to patriotism rather than to socialist ideology. Furthermore, Soviet propaganda invoked pan-Slavism, making appeals to Polish nationalism acceptable.⁴⁰

Polish Communists and a Polish Nation-State

To execute his will in Poland, Stalin had a more pliable alternative to the government-in-exile in Polish communists. In accord with the interests of their Soviet sponsor, Polish communists conceded the necessity of changes in the Polish-Soviet border and became advocates of an ethnically homogeneous Polish nation-state.

The Communist Workers' Party of Poland, later renamed the Communist Party of Poland (*Komunistyczna Partia Polski* or KPP), came into existence in December 1918 with the goal of a worldwide proletarian revolution opposed to Polish independence. When attempts to spark a socialist revolution in Poland failed, the party had no choice but to accept the existence of a Polish state. The Communist International (Comintern) organized in March 1919 also significantly affected the stance toward the national question by declaring that nation-states had a powerful incentive to develop capitalism, a necessary stage for the development of socialism.[41]

Nevertheless, Polish communists wavered in their support for Polish independence. Moreover, as elsewhere in eastern Europe, the internationalist orientation of the party attracted ethnic minorities. Jews, Belarusians, and Ukrainians together outnumbered ethnic Poles in the party. Jews constituted about 22 to 26 percent of the membership and played a pivotal role in the leadership of the party, though the overwhelming majority of Poland's Jewish minority remained indifferent or hostile toward the party.[42]

The party focused mainly on the right of oppressed nations to self-determination. The Sixth Congress in October 1932 accepted a draft program that recognized the right of self-determination of Upper Silesia and Polish Pomerania, including the right of secession, and the right of the Free City of Danzig to reunite with Germany, a declaration that a little more than a decade later Polish communists would turn on its head. The party also attempted to establish separate national identities for Silesians and Kashubs. Borders based on ethnicity also meant a Polish state minus its eastern borderlands.[43] This vision violated what most of Poland's population regarded as in its national interest. In particular, "Polish society viewed the attitude towards the Eastern Borderland as the touchstone of patriotism."[44]

Once Hitler came to power, the Soviet Union and the Comintern targeted fascism rather than capitalism as the main enemy. Under pressure from the Comintern, the KPP in February 1937 recognized Nazi Germany as the sole enemy of Poland and gave priority to defending Polish independence and Polish Upper Silesia.[45]

Despite this reversal, the Comintern dissolved the KPP in 1938, a time of heightened repression of "enemy nations" within the Soviet Union. Arrests of Polish communist activists began as early as 1933 and peaked in 1937. Out of a hundred members of the KPP's Central Committee (*Komitet Centralny* or KC), some sixty-nine were executed.[46] On 3 July 1938 the Executive Committee of the Comintern decided to arrest former leaders of the KPP as "enemies of the people."[47]

Opposition to Polish independence stigmatized the party as an agent of a foreign enemy. The high proportion and prominence of ethnic minorities compounded its identification with alien aspirations. Germany's attack on the Soviet Union in June 1941 provided the opportunity for Polish communists to resume their activities as Polish patriots. Dependence on Soviet support also increased the relevance of the Soviet model of national self-determination. As Krystyna Kersten observes, "The word nation, rarely present in the documents and publications of the KPP, became the word most often used and supplanted all others with social and class content."[48]

Alfred Lampe, a leading member of the KPP and co-founder of the Union of Polish Patriots (*Związek Patriotów Polskich* or ZPP) in the Soviet Union in March 1943 and its primary ideologist until his death at the end of 1943, sketched a strategy for Polish communists at the turn of 1942–1943. Under "New Idea," he wrote "reconstruction acc. to *a national plan*" and a democracy "*without national antagonism.*" Under "Polit[ical] Specificity," he noted "patriotism" as one of the characteristics of the PPR: "The linking of the principles of a great reconstruction with *the principles of national solidarity.*" He foresaw "the domination of so-called *general-national* matters" in postwar Poland and therefore proposed "a strategic plan of socio-political transformation" that included "Preventing the restitution of the condition of big-capitalist possession and influences (national slogans)." The possibility of a peaceful transformation could be "the foundation of a new strategy and tactic of the proletariat," but he feared its disclosure would result in the view "that the communists were only lying in wait and feigning their patriotism." Dismissing the possibility of a Russian-style social revolution, he asserted, "Poland needs *its own road of development*—not painting models from the West or the East."[49] Polish communists should appeal to widespread Polish nationalist sentiments as a means to achieve their goals.[50]

Although initially avoiding specifics about Poland's future borders, on 1 March 1943 the PPR press claimed that Sikorski's defense of Poland's prewar eastern border "undermined the confidence in us of fraternal nations." In its view, the right of every nation "to unite its lands within the framework of a national state [*państwa narodowego*] can be the right to self-determination of every nation. In mixed areas the right of the majority decides."[51]

A turning point came following a dispatch from Georgi Dimitrov on behalf of the Comintern to the KC PPR on 2 April 1943, stating that the future Polish state should be a strong national state based on friendly relations with fraternal Slavic nations, above all the Soviet Union. Therefore it should expand westward, incorporating lands to which Poland had ethnographic and historical rights. Moreover, "The question of the joining to Poland of the indicated lands proposed by us has enormous political significance for us because it will ward off the accusation against us that we desire to diminish the territory of Poland and undermine its independence."[52]

In an article in April 1943 Lampe stated unequivocally, "The rebuilt Polish state will be a nation-state."[53] In Moscow in June 1943 the first congress of the ZPP delineated the territorial changes. Harkening back "to the glorious traditions of the great architects of the Polish state," the Piasts, the ZPP called for "the strengthening of Poland in the west and on the Baltic." "After the victorious conclusion of the war in Silesia, Polishness should be restored. The Polish ethnic masses in Silesia must again be united with the core of the motherland."[54]

In November 1943 the PPR program of Communists in German-occupied Poland "What Are We Fighting For?" was less explicit: "In the west and on the Baltic we must recover the ethnographically Polish lands, de-nationalized and Germanized by force." The demand for all "Polish lands" found reflection in later documents, such as the announcement on 15 December 1943 of a National Council of the Homeland (*Krajowa Rada Narodowa* or KRN) as a representative body of the nation and its declaration at its first plenary session on 1 January 1944, which demanded the return of all formerly Polish areas that had been Germanized.[55] In the first months of 1944 the PPR press specifically mentioned Warmia and Mazuria, Gdańsk, Pomerania, and Silesia.[56]

As for the inhabitants of these "Polish lands," Hilary Minc, an organizer of the ZPP, asserted in an article titled "To the West" in *Wolna Polska* on 8 February 1944:

> So that after this war Poland could achieve security, the Germans must be driven out of East Prussia, Silesia, Western Pomerania, those territories, which were always the staging area for German aggression against the East. The return to Polishness of the local Polish population Germanized by force must be facilitated. The immigrant German population must be gotten rid of.[57]

The Soviet Offensive of January 1944

Decisive, however, was the advance of the Red Army, which crossed the Polish-Soviet border on 4 January 1944 for the second time in the war. On 11 January the Soviet government again asserted claims to a revised border "approximately along the so-called Curzon Line." At the same time it insisted, "Poland's Western borders must be extended through the incorporation in Poland of ancient Polish land previously wrested by Germany and, without which it is impossible to unite the whole Polish people in its State."[58]

The British now joined the Soviets in promoting the idea of an ethnically homogeneous Poland, invoking "ethnographic premises" in their arguments to persuade the Polish government to accept the Curzon Line. During a meeting on 6 February 1944 Eden asked the Polish government to state publicly "that they wished to be a homogeneous State." On 16 February Churchill offered to work to secure the Poles "a prospect of a homogeneous home," explaining that "Europe could not be plunged into endless wars arising out of the intermingling of ten million persons of different race. They must be disentangled as had been done in the Greco-Turkish exchange."[59]

Secret negotiations in London between the Soviet Union and the Polish authorities in May and June 1944 came to naught when the Soviets insisted on the nomination of several Polish communists as ministers in the government-in-exile.[60] Stalin turned instead to Polish communists. As the Red Army and Polish troops under Soviet command approached the Curzon Line in the second half of July 1944, Stalin authorized the KRN to set up an administration in the liberated areas.[61]

Polski Komitet Wyzwolenia Narodowego

The PKWN held its first meeting in the headquarters of the ZPP on 22 July 1944. The composition of the PKWN and its manifesto reflected the predominance of the ZPP and its pro-Moscow orientation.[62] The manifesto spoke specifically of the fight "for the return to the Mother-Fatherland [*Matki-Ojczyzny*] of old Polish Pomerania and Opole Silesia, for East Prussia, for wide access to the sea, for Polish border posts at the Oder." But with regard to the eastern border, it spoke more generally, stating, "it should be regulated in keeping with the principle: Polish lands—Poland, Ukrainian, Belorussian and Lithuanian lands—Soviet Ukraine, Belorussia, and Lithuania."[63]

Officially, the PKWN issued the manifesto in Chełm, the first liberated town within the territory Stalin assigned to Poland, before moving to Lublin. As one of its first acts, the PKWN signed a secret agreement with the Soviet government on 27 July 1944 designating the Curzon Line with minor changes in Poland's favor as its border. The agreement obligated the Soviets to support and assist Poland in obtaining a western border on the Oder and Lusatian Neisse Rivers, the same western border advocated by Polish nationalists in October 1939. In September 1944 the PKWN signed agreements with representatives of the Ukrainian, Belorussian, and Lithuanian Soviet Republics for an exchange of population to promote ethnic homogeneity in their respective territories. The Polish and Soviet governments did not officially confirm their border until an agreement signed on 16 August 1945.[64]

Unaware of the secret agreements, Mikołajczyk went to Moscow at the urging of Roosevelt and Churchill for direct talks with Stalin at the beginning of August 1944. When Stalin proposed the Curzon Line and the Oder and

Neisse Rivers as Poland's borders, Mikołajczyk made a plea for Lwów and Wilno. Stalin countered that Wrocław (Breslau) was better than Lwów. When Mikołajczyk objected that it was a purely German town, Stalin replied that "in olden times Wrocław was a Slav city and nothing prevents it from returning to its former historical tradition."[65]

In October 1944 pressed by Churchill, who was in Moscow, Mikołajczyk once again journeyed to the Soviet capital and met with Stalin together with Churchill and Eden on 13 October 1944. There he learned that Poland's eastern border had been set nearly a year earlier at the Tehran conference.[66] The next day Churchill urged Mikołajczyk and the Polish delegation "to settle upon the frontier question. . . . It means compensation in the west and the disentanglement of populations."[67]

Back in London the British government cast doubt on how much German territory Poland would receive in compensation. As a British official disingenuously explained to Mikołajczyk, the British government had always officially maintained that all territorial changes awaited the peace settlement unless agreed upon by the parties involved. Unlike the agreement between the PKWN and the Soviet Union, the British asked the Polish government to accept losses to the Soviet Union without specifying the allocation of German territory. On 6 November 1944 Eden told Mikołajczyk that he regarded it as "sheer madness" for Poland to claim the territory up to Oder River, including Stettin. The Polish premier replied that Poland needed this territory to house the expected four to five million Poles and Catholic Belarusians and Ukrainians from the eastern lands lost to the Soviet Union. The Polish government also asked for a British guarantee of the assignment of this German territory. A British official objected that the German expellees would impose an intolerable burden on Germany's economy and agitate for the return of their homeland, making Polish security entirely dependent on the Soviet Union.[68]

Mikołajczyk looked to Roosevelt for a clarification of the American position, but Roosevelt, on the eve of an election in which he was counting on the Polish-American vote, put off replying until 17 November 1944. Then promising not to object to any agreement reached with the Soviets and the British, Roosevelt invoked the American policy of not guaranteeing any specific borders. He did, however, offer to have the American ambassador intervene with Stalin on behalf of Lwów. Although Mikołajczyk favored taking up this offer, a majority of his cabinet did not, fearing it would lead to the loss of other territories east of the Curzon Line. In these circumstances, Mikołajczyk resigned as premier on 24 November 1944.[69]

Mikołajczyk defended his decision to accept the Curzon Line in a dispatch to the *Delegatura* and the Council of National Unity of the underground on 28 November 1944. Putting his faith in the promises of the Western Allies and a belief in the inability of the communists to dominate Polish society, he argued that territorial compensation on the Oder River and economic assistance could enable Poland to be "non-Communist." "Such a Poland would undoubtedly have a hard existence, but the national substance preserved, with its demographic and great economic potential, nationally homogeneous, without minorities—that is the foundation for a strong Poland in the future and a quite acceptable place for the development of the nation."[70]

Stanisław Grabski, chairman of the National Council in London and associated with the National Party, also resigned. In December 1944 he published *Nil desperandum,* in which he firmly supported shifting Poland westward to its territory at the time of King Bolesław III the Wrymouth (1086–1138) and ensuring its new international standing through an alliance with Slavic nations, particularly Russia, which reflected the traditional position of the National Democrats and Dmowski.[71]

On 18 December 1944 *Pravda* published an article by the head of the PKWN Department of Information and Propaganda Stefan Jędrychowski, advocating that Poland receive Stettin and that the border run from there south down the Oder and western Neisse to the Czechoslovak border, the first public claim by the PKWN for what became the Polish-German border. George F. Kennan, minister-counselor in the American embassy in Moscow, commented, "It makes unrealistic the idea of a free and independent Poland."[72]

On 1 January 1945 the PKWN declared itself to be the Provisional Government of the Polish Republic, and the Soviet Union recognized it on 5 January 1945. On 22 January 1945 Eden argued in a memorandum to the War Cabinet that because the Lublin government already recognized the Curzon Line as Poland's eastern border, the British government no longer had to support Poland's annexation of more German territory than seemed appropriate. In the debate over the transfer of Germans, questions came up about how many Poland would recognize as Germans and how many with Polish-speaking parents would choose Polonization over expulsion, questions that did not arise in connection with the population transfer from the territory lost by Poland.[73]

The Big Three at Yalta

The leaders of the three Great Powers met again, at Yalta in the Crimea. According to a briefing paper for the U.S. delegation, Polish gains should be limited to "the bulk of East Prussia," "a small strip of Pomerania... and Upper Silesia which is predominantly Polish in population and is particularly important from an industrial point of view." Although this would considerably reduce Poland's size, "it would include only areas which are predominantly Polish," create an economically viable state, and reduce to a minimum the transfer of minority groups. The goal was to "minimize future points of friction, possible Irredentism . . . in order that the solution would contribute to the fullest possible extent to the peace and future tranquility of Europe." As for the eastern border, a memorandum proposed accepting the Curzon Line with Lwów inside Poland.[74]

The final declaration at Yalta accepted the Curzon Line, with Lwów on the Soviet side of the border, and stated that Poland "must receive substantial accessions of territory in the north and west," but left the determination to the peace conference.[75] The Polish government-in-exile called the declaration "a fifth partition of Poland." The Council of National Unity in Poland proved more delusional. It passed a resolution on 22 February 1945 declaring that the Polish-Soviet border would be settled by direct negotiations or at the peace conference but that Poland would extend in the north to East Prussia and in the west to the Oder and Neisse Rivers—the opposite of the decisions taken at Yalta.[76]

On 27 February 1945 Churchill placed a motion before the House of Commons to approve the "joint policy agreed to by the Three Great Powers at the Crimea Conference." He asserted, "The three powers are agreed that acceptance by the Poles of the provisions on the Eastern frontiers and, so far as can now be ascertained, on the Western frontiers, is an essential condition of the establishment and future welfare and security of a strong, independent, homogeneous Polish State."[77]

The Big Three, however, faced a major test in forming a Polish government recognized by all. The Western Allies put forward Mikołajczyk, who explicitly accepted "the Curzon Line with the possibility of small rectifications" as Poland's eastern border, while expressing his view that at least Lwów and the neighboring oil district should remain Polish and making clear that "an absolute demand on the Soviet side" motivated his declaration.[78] Finally, on 23 June 1945 a commission made up of Soviet Commissar of Foreign Affairs Vyacheslav Molotov and the British and American ambassadors to Moscow agreed on the composition of a Polish Provisional Government of National Unity that included Mikołajczyk but gave an overwhelming majority to members and supporters of the Provisional Government recognized by Stalin.[79]

The Big Three at Potsdam

As the Big Three prepared to meet at Potsdam, the Provisional Government of National Unity marshaled a wide range of arguments—moral, economic, demographic, strategic, historical, and ethnic—to back up its claims to the lands east of the Oder and western Neisse Rivers, reflecting the views of the Polish Western Idea. A memo that the Polish ambassador in Moscow gave to his British and American colleagues on 10 July 1945 argued, "The Polish territory ought to form a natural and compact geographical unit, as she did at the time of the reign of the Piast dynasty (X–XIV centuries), when she was a homogeneous state spreading over the systems of the Odra [Oder] and the Vistula." Since Poland was about to lose 47.5 percent of its territory in the east and even the proposed annexation of German territory would leave Poland 22 percent smaller than before the war, the memo characterized Poland's territorial demands as "moderate."[80]

A section on Polish historical rights claimed the prehistoric peoples who inhabited the Oder and Vistula river basins in about 2000 BC "show traits in common with the Slavonic races" and "formed the demographic foundation of the Polish nation. Thus the lands between the Odra and Vistula may be considered the primordial territories of the Polish State." Only in the thirteenth century did Poland begin to retreat east under German pressure. The Teutonic Knights as "active exponents of German imperialism" for the next 200 years pursued "the extermination of Slavonic peoples living on the shores of the Baltic Sea."[81] In the eighteenth century "German imperialism" brought about "the downfall of Poland. Poland's history shows the need for Poland's return to the Odra territories, out of which she had been ousted by force and subterfuge to which she has rights well grounded in history."[82]

The memo also made ethnic claims. "Fairly large territories with a preponderating Polish element were not included within the boundaries of Poland in the years 1918–1939," citing southern East Prussia and Opole Silesia. "Poland has to be an independent state, she has to return to her primordial lands, and to continue the old political tradition of her Piast rulers as a national state, in harmony with the democratic ideas."[83]

The leaders of the three Great Powers met in Potsdam 17 July–2 August 1945, with President Harry Truman as Roosevelt's successor and Clement Attlee replacing Churchill during the conference. Truman raised the matter of the Polish border at the plenary session on 21 July 1945, saying that the Soviet Union violated an agreement on the occupation of Germany by giving eastern Germany over to the Poles.[84]

Privately, Mikołajczyk warned British officials that the communists would use the resistance of the Western democracies to the Oder-Neisse border to attack him and to portray Molotov as the only friend and protector of Poland.[85] In a secret memorandum to the American delegation Mikołajczyk based his entire argument on the need for territory to settle Poles from the former eastern borderlands of Poland, Western Europe, and the overpopulated central provinces so that elections could be held soon.[86]

Despite Truman's insistence that a peace conference must determine the future border of Poland, on 30 July 1945 U.S. Secretary of State James F. Byrnes informed Molotov that he agreed to Polish administration of the formerly German territory up to the Oder and western Neisse Rivers. The final communiqué confirmed this concession but at the same time reiterated the stricture that "the final delimitation of the western frontier of Poland should await the peace settlement." Yet it was rendered meaningless by the provision recognizing the necessity of "the transfer to Germany of German populations," which "should be effected in an orderly and humane manner," cavalierly presuming this was possible. But concern over "the influx of a large number of Germans into Germany" rather than over the "humane" manner of the expulsion resulted in its temporary suspension.[87] The Big Three updated Hitler's *Heim ins Reich* policy, bringing Germans "home" with no regard to the guilt or innocence of those who thus lost the right to remain in their homelands. International diplomacy set the borders of the new Poland in keeping with Stalin's wishes with the goal of creating an ethnically homogeneous state. What remained was to align the population within these borders with this goal.

"Not a Single German in Poland"

English-language and German literature usually characterizes the displacement of the German population simply as "expulsion" (*Vertreibung*). Until recently, Polish scholars rarely used this term (*wypędzenie*). The communist authorities used "resettlement" and "repatriation," also for the displacement of Poles from territory annexed by the Soviet Union. Typically, Polish scholars see three stages in de-Germanization: the evacuation and flight before the Soviet Red Army in the first half of 1945, a "wild" expulsion from the end of the war until Potsdam, and an organized resettlement in conjunction with the Potsdam agreement.[88]

The use of "expulsion" as a catchword ignores the complexity of the process, oversimplifies the motivation of the displaced, and implies a moral condemnation that ignores the decision of the Big Three and the reasons for it. Breaking the process down into phases reveals more about the process but exaggerates the differences from the point of view of the victims. Kersten regards *"przymus sytuacyny"*—the force of circumstances, if not direct force—as always marking any resettlement based on nationality.[89]

Anthony Richmond argues that in any population movement "the distinction between 'free' and 'forced' or 'voluntary' and 'involuntary'" is misleading. "All human behavior is constrained." Instead, he offers a nuanced paradigm for the motivation behind population movements based on particular circumstances. Of relevance for a discussion of autochthons and *Volksdeutsche* is his category of "defectors," whom he regards as those who exercise the most autonomy in deciding to migrate.[90] The expulsion, evacuation and flight, or resettlement directly or indirectly affected them and ultimately influenced which nationality they would claim.

For Poles, the ferocity of the German occupation, the precedent set by Hitler's "ethnic redistribution," and doubts about the loyalty of Polish citizens of German origin justified their expulsion and validated the popular rhyme dating from the seventeenth century, "As long as the world is no other, a German will never be a Pole's brother" (*Jak świat światem, nie będzie Niemiec Polakowi bratem*). Mass public meetings met under the slogan "Not a single German in Poland."[91] Most did not need anti-German demagoguery to hold the German nation collectively responsible for the crimes committed during the war. A sense of grievance and a desire for revenge added emotional punch to the rational calculation of the advantages of ridding the Polish state of the German minority.[92] By associating themselves with such feelings, the PPR and its allies gained a measure of social acceptance that they generally lacked.[93]

As in other formerly German-occupied territories, *Volksdeutsche* in Poland were terrorized, beaten, raped, robbed, and murdered in revenge for the years of occupation and persecution, especially where no coercion to register on the DVL existed.[94] The *starosta* (county executive) in Oborniki on 22 August 1945 reported that "in the first moments of liberation of this county from the occupier, the reaction of society against the so-called *Volksdeutsche* manifested itself in a very strong way, intensified still more by the orders of the Soviet military authorities."[95] As the Red Army advanced on Łódź, the flight of a large portion of the German population left behind primarily women, children, and the elderly. The Polish population took revenge on these remaining Germans, often robbing them of their property and subjecting them to forced labor, according to a report of the Provincial Socio-Political Department (*Wydział Społeczno-Polityczny* or WS-P) on 13 February 1948. In the first months of 1945 Germans were forbidden to leave urban areas. Stores put up signs prohibiting the entry of Germans. The situation resulted in a wave of German suicides.[96] Despite the ambiguities of the categories of the DVL, it resulted in a rigid identity that could prove fatal.[97]

Few spoke out against the violence. A leading Marxist economist, Witold Kula, a participant in the 1944 Warsaw Uprising, stood in defense of humanism, denying the existence of "gangster nations" in a polemic with a professor who so branded the German nation. Kula saw it as racism, a crime of the Nazis.[98]

In Mogilno County, where Germans constituted 9 percent of the population in 1939, Poles sought to intercede on behalf of Germans who assisted them during the occupation. The *starosta* wrote to the Poznań Provincial Office (*Urząd Wojewódzki* or UW) on 17 May 1945: "Some Germans were very hostile to Nazism and treated the Polish population favorably, helped it materially, gave it their radios to use, often hid Poles pursued by the Gestapo, sent Poles food packages, and the like, by which these Germans often risked harassment and persecution by the German authorities." The *starosta* added that better treatment of these Germans would split the unity of Germans, provoking disagreements among them. As "better treatment," however, he suggested, for example, that women be put to work solely as servants in Polish homes, not given the rights of a Polish citizen.[99]

Ultimately, the Polish authorities recognized that not all of the Polish citizens registered on the DVL were alike and had to be considered on a case-by-case basis. By means of a process termed "rehabilitation," *Volksdeutsche* could retain their Polish citizenship and avoid expulsion. But misunderstandings of the significance of registration on the DVL often had tragic consequences.

[4]

The Recovered Lands and Their Inhabitants

POLISH COMMUNISTS INVOKED the principle of national self-determination to justify Poland's new eastern border, making a virtue out of necessity while ignoring the historical ties of the *kresy* to Poland since the fourteenth century. Although the new eastern border furthered the ethnic homogeneity of Poland, the new western border immensely complicated it. Polish communists laid claim to the formerly German territory and the Free City of Danzig on several bases, but historical grounds received the most prominence and proved the most enduring. The first most important monuments built or projected in Poland after 1945, at Góra św. Anny in Silesia and Grunwald in Mazuria, emphasized the Polish and Slavic character of the so-called Recovered Lands, which constituted a third of the Polish state.[1] The constant repetition of the term "Recovered Lands" in government publications, speeches, and so forth, made it an unconscious part of the ordinary speech of the Polish population.[2]

Although most of the territory had at one point been under the rule of the Piasts, some of the territory had been part of the Polish state only briefly and scarcely any of it following the fragmentation of the Polish kingdom in the twelfth century. The last of the Piast kings, Casimir, the only Polish ruler to receive the appellation "the Great," formally recognized the crown's loss of the Silesian duchies and extended the eastern border deep into areas that Polish communists recognized as belonging to Soviet Ukraine, which prompted them to direct that he be referred to as Casimir III, not as Casimir the Great. Nevertheless, they characterized the territorial reconfiguration as a return to an ethnically homogeneous Piast Poland.[3]

In this, the new administration adopted a program developed most thoroughly by political forces hostile to communism, the National Party and advocates of the *Polska myśl zachodnia*. Like these forerunners, Polish communists portrayed the Germans as the greatest threat to the nation. In the postwar years, historical research concentrated mostly on German terror during the war, the martyrdom of the Polish nation, and the struggle against the German occupation, which reflected the experiences of the overwhelming majority of Poles during the war.[4]

Although the term "Recovered Lands" may suggest they constituted a single unit, administrative restructuring fragmented them. The northwestern part became the District (*okręg*) of Western Pomerania and, in the administrative reform of 1946, Szczecin Province (*województwo*). "Western Pomerania" implicitly denied the existence of a German Pomerania west of the Oder River, giving the impression that as the indigenous land of the Slavic Pomeranians and part of Piast Poland, it was historically and geographically always linked with Poland.[5]

Elsewhere, the new Polish authorities showed a notable disregard for history. In re-creating a separate Pomerania Province in 1946, they included less than half the territory of its medieval eponym without a seacoast though the Polish name "Pomorze" derives from the Slavic *po morju* or *po morze*, "on the sea."[6] The northern part of prewar Polish Pomerania along with the Free City of Danzig, part of East Prussia, and Lębork County of prewar German Pomerania formed Gdańsk Province. Another part of East Prussia joined Białystok Province. The Polish authorities tried to invoke a historical claim to the remainder of East Prussia by initially naming it the District of Warmia-Mazuria, a hybrid term without any basis in history. Commonly referred to it as Mazuria, it became Olsztyn Province.[7]

South of Western Pomerania the early medieval Piast kingdom extended west of the Oder River, including today's German city of Lebus (Lubusz), formerly a diocesan seat, which gave its name to a region in Poland still known as Lubusz Land (*Ziemia Lubuska*) in an attempt at historical legitimization despite the absence of its eponym. Warsaw assigned most of the area to the Polish prewar Poznań Province, but with the special status of a Regional Branch (*Ekspozytura*) centered in Gorzów Wielkopolski.

The District of Lower Silesia became Wrocław Province in 1946. German Upper Silesia initially constituted a separate District of Opole Silesia, but in practice came under the authority of the governor (*wojewoda*) of Silesia and formally part of the province in 1946. The inclusion of the Dąbrowa Basin surrounding Dąbrowa Górnicza validated the 1939 German administrative decision incorporating it into Silesia.

The Polish Western Idea after World War II

Ostforschung and *Polska myśl zachodnia* supported the respective political goals of West Germany and Poland in the latest chapter of their conflict.

While West German scholars emphasized legal entitlement to the lost territory, Warsaw embraced the ideology of the Polish Western Idea, endowing its claims to the Recovered Lands with a historical dimension and dignity. Over the long run, it raised the Polish Western Idea to a science in support of the state, which financed it accordingly.[8]

Faced with the need to win over public opinion by proving the Slavic and Polish character of the Recovered Lands, Polish scholars responded with gusto. Patriotism and anti-fascism along with a feeling of national defeat after Yalta, the delay in international recognition of the western border, and the need to defend the national existence from Soviet domination spurred Polish scholarly activity, independently of directives from above. With restrictions on research on the *kresy*, research on the Recovered Lands provided psychological compensation that scholars exploited as much as possible.[9]

As the frontline of two hostile Cold War blocs, the confrontation between *Ostforschung* and *Polska myśl zachodnia* took on a new quality and particular bitterness, constituting literally the foremost lines of resistance and legitimization. The Polish Western Idea contributed not insignificantly to the communist hold on power as *Ostforschung* encouraged the revisionist tendencies of the Federal Republic of Germany (FRG). Although superficially the issues did not change much, the conflict was in essence also an ideological proxy war over a divided Europe. Thus, the Polish Western Idea functioned within a defense system in the Soviet Union, the German Democratic Republic (GDR), and Czechoslovakia as well as in Poland, mobilizing against the "falsifications" of a West German revanchist *Ostforschung*.

The Uses of the Recovered Lands

The Recovered Lands served the Polish communists well by diverting attention from the loss of the *kresy*. Severed from the eastern roots of their historical existence, the public as well as the intellectual and cultural elite searched intensively for the slightest traces of Polishness in the western lands and stubbornly sought to eliminate evidence of Germanness.[10]

Furthermore, Polish communists saw the "recovery" of this territory as an important asset in their efforts to win the support of the Polish population. In mid-November 1944 a PZZ activist, Szymon Żołna, submitted a memorandum to the Bureau of the KRN Presidium, proposing a strategy and identifying potential allies.

> After a long period of a political fast, the masses of the Right of the middle class are ripe for inflaming with a clear, vivid national idea. The Right has long been interested in German affairs, the lands of the former Prussian occupation zone

constituted its domain, and, after all, these lands were of an especially strong anti-German attitude.... In the displaced intelligentsia of Wielkopolska and Silesia and to a certain extent also the intelligentsia from the *kresy,* we have a ready cadre for work in the recovered western areas and their management.... They can stir up the middle classes by means of propaganda work without being restrained by local reactionary groups ... The attractiveness of the slogans and vividness of the propaganda forms will awaken a strong emotional current, opposing which should mean a loss of support. Resistant activists of the National Party will have the choice of either risking decisive discrimination or swimming with the current while hiding false honor. With the current, that is, with our constructive work, and therefore not against us.[11]

Indeed, partisans of the Polish Western Idea would become the main allies of the PPR in rallying the public around the Recovered Lands.

An Organizational Committee of the PZZ sent a letter to President Bolesław Bierut of the KRN on 10 January 1945 explicitly stating that the organization stood with the government's "western policy, based on the alliance with the Soviet Union as opposed to the noble-landowning eastern policy."[12] The PZZ manifesto published in 1945 declared that "the first and invariable chief task of the PZZ remains always: the struggle against Germanness."[13] Its leaders included Zenon Kliszko as vice chairman: a member of the Secretariat of the KC PPR and chairman of the PPR in the KRN. Although its goals harmonized with those of the government, the PZZ sought to act as an independent organization. At a plenum of the KC 20–21 May 1945, Kliszko complained that the PZZ was in certain areas behaving as a separate political party over which the PPR had to maintain control.[14] Nevertheless, the PZZ had an enormous influence on the formation of the government's nationality policies.

At that plenary meeting, in an atmosphere of crisis for the party and in the face of British opposition to the Oder-Neisse border, First Secretary (General Secretary from 12 December 1945) of the party and vice premier of the Provisional Government Władysław Gomułka stated in his opening speech, "The matter of the western lands is one of the reasons for the support of the government in society. It neutralizes various elements and binds them. The westward expansion of lands and agrarian reform bind the nation to the system. Retreat weakens our position in the country." The western expansion and the removal of the Germans would provide land for the landless and deportees, presumably tying them to the party. At the same meeting PPR Politburo member and undersecretary of state in the Presidium of the Council of Ministers (*Prezydium Rady Ministrów* or PRM) Jakub Berman asserted, "The Neisse and the Oder—that is a legend that will live for hundreds of years. The AK will disappear."[15]

Although the AK did "disappear" as an armed force, the memory of it and particularly its ultimate act, the Warsaw Uprising of 1944, would haunt Polish communists until the end of their dominance of Polish politics. Nevertheless, relations with the Germans and the acquisition of new western territory were the two questions on which Polish communists and loyalists of the government-in-exile agreed.[16]

In a letter to London on 18 July 1945, Grabski—now a vice president of the KRN—expressed cautious optimism:

> Of course full "civil freedom" will not return at once nor will control of the NKVD cease. But it is coming to that. And for it to come as quickly and as fast as possible—there is only one way: the entry of all good patriots into all self-governing organizations—social, cultural, and administrative authorities. The PPR does not have the people to control the whole administration.

In a letter on 15 August 1945, he prophetically foresaw the alternative to "good patriots": "If honest people drag their feet, the riffraff will seize control of public life."[17]

Non-communists in the underground also backed the efforts of the government. On 12 February 1945 Wojciechowski, a National Democrat by conviction, presented a memorandum to Premier Edward Osóbka-Morawski, in which he offered to cooperate with the government and proposed the creation of the Western Institute, which the government agreed to just fifteen days later. With the consent of the *Delegatura*, *Ojczyzna* handed over many of its proposals and projects to the government, and its members participated in the Western Institute and the PZZ.[18] In July 1945 the government created the Research Council for Issues of the Recovered Lands (*Rada Naukowa dla Zagadnień Ziem Odzyskanych* or Research Council) as an advisory body consisting of eminent Polish scholars—economists, demographers, historians—many of whom had worked on these issues in the underground.

German Citizens of Polish Nationality: The Autochthons

A tenet of Polish nationalism maintains that Poles living under German rule successfully resisted centuries of German imperialism and oppression, preserving their Polish identity.[19] A Union of Poles in Germany (*Związek Polaków w Niemczech* or ZPwN) existed before the war.[20] But all Polish political camps believed that the inhabitants of the Recovered Lands included far more individuals of Polish nationality.[21] In 1942 a periodical that expressed the views of the *Delegatura* stated:

> The recovery of these hundreds of thousands of people whose Polish blood has been absorbed by the German organism will be one of Poland's most important national tasks. The theft of blood perpetrated together with the theft of land has

caused us irreparable losses throughout the centuries. The victory of the Polish cause in the current war must be not only a day of territorial reckoning, but also the day of recovery of the most valuable loss: Polish blood.[22]

A pamphlet published in 1945 by the Polish Army under Soviet command claimed that "2 million brothers" lived in the territory.[23] Estimates of the number of Germanized inhabitants lacking "full consciousness of belonging to the Polish nation and without Polish national ambitions" fluctuated between 720,000 and 6,000,000 (sic!).[24] The higher estimates assumed that prewar German inhabitants were Germanized Poles. Thus, in 1945 the historian Józef Mitkowski argued that the Germans should be won over and re-Polonized rather than driven out.[25]

The Polish authorities and publicists used the term "autochthon" exclusively for the inhabitants of the Recovered Lands presumed to be Polish, stressing that the Poles were the original inhabitants of the area and justifying Polish territorial claims. The widespread use of the term fostered the acceptance of this view as axiomatic. The German inhabitants were by implication aliens.

Polish *raison d'état* and social consensus required the broadest retention of individuals of Polish origin and yet the strictest exclusion of all Germans. In the words of a slogan that Silesian Governor Aleksander Zawadzki coined in 1945, "We don't want a single German, and we won't give up a single Polish soul."[26] This simplistic slogan, widely repeated in various versions, became in the popular imagination the guiding principle of official nationality policy.

Complications arose because of the nationalist assumptions on which this goal was based, that everyone possesses a durable national identity; that this national identity is stable, palpable, and homogeneous among all who belonged to the nation; and that they give their primary loyalty to their nation. This left no room for individuals who identified themselves as neither Polish nor German, though the PZZ recognized that inhabitants of borderlands have difficulty in deciding their national identity, but this posed no obstacle to counting the ethnically Polish as part of the Polish nation.[27] Because Germanization did not destroy one's essential Polishness, re-Polonization, a *return* to the Polish nation, not a de-nationalization of Germans, aimed at bringing about this redemption.[28]

But how to distinguish Germans from Germanized Poles? As a writer from Silesia put it a half century later, "A person born here can with equal ease invoke Polish tradition and roots as well as German."[29] Some delegates at a meeting of the PZZ Silesian District on 28 April 1946 highlighted the problem when they objected that instead of decisively battling Germanness, the organization was ignoring it by re-Polonizing the inhabitants of the Recovered

Lands.³⁰ In practice many officials assumed the attitude of Deputy Eugeniusz Kembrowski expressed at a meeting of the Denomination and Nationality Commission of the KRN on 13 March 1946: "better to resettle too many than too few."³¹

The Polish authorities and their allies had to decide on criteria and procedures for separating the wheat from the chaff, on those ethnic traits that supposedly distinguished a Pole from a German. The Nazi DVL provided a model. During the war the Bureau of the Western Lands of the *Delegatura* proposed sorting the population of the territory in three categories: nationally conscious Poles, Poles who spoke Polish but lacked national consciousness, and Germans of Polish origin who did not know Polish but retained an awareness of their origin as indicated by their surname or family history. The proposal presumed that the last group would include the remaining inhabitants of the territory with the exception of German colonists (since the thirteenth century!) and government officials from outside the territory who were clearly of German nationality.³²

It was generally assumed that the autochthons would willingly accept "re-Polonization" and identify themselves as Poles.³³ The 1945 Polish Army pamphlet predicted that the "veneer of Germanness" that coated some of the population would in many cases "disappear when the superficially Germanized population finds itself within the borders of Poland."³⁴ Because Germanization had not penetrated to the Polish "essence" of the natives, they could be "cured" relatively easily, as one drains an abscess of its pus. In 1945 the Catholic writer Władysław Grabski proposed that the Polish nation had the mission of liberating "the Slavic blood flowing in the veins of Germanized Silesians and Pomeranians, making them abhor the foul poison of Germanness, disinfecting them and returning them to health by teaching them the native tongue in order to incorporate them back into the mother country, not as prodigal sons but as victims rescued from the ultimate outrage."³⁵ The recovery of "stolen [Germanized] souls" would also be rapid. De-nationalizing susceptible Germans suitable for verification as Poles was also considered.³⁶

There were, however, disagreements over what constituted Polishness. Significantly, Władysław Grabski, who believed that "the Polishness of the recovered lands is inseparably linked with Catholicism," did not mention Mazurs among those in whose veins "Slavic blood" flowed. As a member of the Research Council and an advisor of the Ministry of Recovered Lands (*Ministerstwo Ziem Odzyskanych* or MZO), he represented a widely held point of view that had negative consequences for the "re-Polonization" of Mazuria, where Catholic priests participated in the process of nationality verification of the Protestant population.³⁷

The Uses of the Autochthons

In staking a claim to formerly German territory, Polish official circles gave a higher prominence to Polish historical rights and also, particularly for foreign audiences, the security of Europe from further German aggression than to the ethnic argument, which Polish authorities invoked more frequently in propaganda addressed to the Poles themselves.[38] As a scholar of nationalism concludes: "Those who have successfully mobilized nations have understood that at the core of ethnopsychology is the sense of shared blood."[39] Polish communists needed to mobilize support if they were to maintain and strengthen their tenuous hold on power. A lack of "shared blood" also served as a justification for the loss of the eastern borderlands.

Following the war every European government sought to recover from its losses of dead soldiers and civilians and secure the labor power needed for postwar reconstruction. In Poland some saw the Polish population of the Recovered Lands as a necessary supplement. At the first session of the Research Council in the summer of 1945, a member saw the need to replenish the Polish nation after the enormous losses during the occupation. In a memorandum on 6 April 1946, the plenipotentiary of Mazuria claimed that the population of Poland had decreased by twelve million since 1939 and therefore the state could not afford additional losses.[40]

The authorities thought it necessary to develop the Recovered Lands as quickly as possible if Poland were to retain them. To advocates of the autochthons, no one seemed better placed for this task. An article in *Przegląd Zachodni* (a publication of the Western Institute) at the end of 1946 asserted that "only on the basis of the resident population can a lasting and profound union ensue of the Recovered Lands with the Motherland."[41]

Communist party leaders also viewed the autochthons as potential supporters. The party's press claimed that it was precisely the poorer elements among the native population of the Recovered Lands, the peasants and workers, who most successfully resisted Germanization and preserved their Polish identity, the very same classes that the PPR looked to for support. Reports in April 1945 of the degree of Germanization of industrial towns such as Bytom, Gliwice, and Zabrze caused particular concern, both because of the class origin of the population and its economic importance. Before World War I Bytom and Gliwice already had a disproportionately high share of Upper Silesia's bilingual population—partially Germanized inhabitants of Polish origin—and all three towns remained part of Germany after the partitioning of Silesia.[42]

The Recovered Lands and their inhabitants had considerable significance for postwar Poland. The German population had to be removed and the "essentially" Polish element retained and if necessary "re-Polonized." Success depended in part on the character of the population of the Recovered Lands and their experiences in the final phase of the war and in the immediate postwar years.

A Diverse Population

Significant differences among the native inhabitants of the Recovered Lands hampered development of consistent nationality policies. Those who did not identify themselves as German did not necessarily see themselves as Poles. Many identified primarily with their religion, customs, region, language, or dialect of their ancestors rather than with a particular nation. The Polish and German linguistic and cultural elements that pervaded their identities did not clearly mark them as belonging to either nation. The region and the community connected with it, regardless of linguistic and ethnic differences, constituted the fundamental value.[43]

Opole Silesia

Significantly, Warsaw united Germanized Opole Silesia with Polonized Polish Silesia and the non-Silesian Dąbrowa Basin in one province, throwing together inhabitants with very different historical, cultural, and administrative traditions, which hindered integration.[44]

A pamphlet published in London in 1941 claimed that 60 percent of the population of Opole Silesia consisted of Poles.[45] On a trip 20–29 April 1945 to survey the situation, 2nd Lt. Benjamin Zylberberg of the Propaganda Unit of the Polish Army's Political-Educational Agency found that the state of Polishness "went beyond all expectations. The village is today completely Polish. . . . Everywhere in rural areas one hears Polish. Older women often don't know German at all. Even some Germans residing in the countryside underwent Polonization. Children raised in the terrible conditions of Hitler's anti-Polish terror are the most Germanized, but these also speak mostly Polish among themselves." In Zylberberg's view, however, the urban areas of Opole Silesia were significantly Germanized and the national consciousness of the residents of the city of Opole weak, "the mood not so much anti-German as anti-Nazi." "Of enormous significance is . . . the cleric, who although he speaks Polish is still in principle German." But a number of former activists of the ZPwN occupied lower positions such as village heads. Many natives who emigrated to Poland before the war also filled positions in the county and urban administrations. In Polish Upper Silesia, he found "unquestionable, obvious patriotism" in conversations with inhabitants, particularly workers. Yet he also met several cases of "manifestations of regional distinctiveness and machination [*lawirowania*] (nationality—Silesian)."[46]

During an investigation of identity among the inhabitants of one of the largest villages of the Opole region in August 1945, sociologist Stanisław Ossowski encountered a concept of national identity that differed from the one accepted by the Polish authorities and the Polish public. A significant majority regarded nationality as something akin to membership in a political party or acceptance of a political ideology, which depended on circumstances beyond the control of an individual. Nationality was not a permanent trait. Only the regional Upper Silesian identity that marked one from birth had a permanent character, and it took precedence over any transitory national identity.[47]

Ossowski's interviewees applied the term "Pole" either to someone from prewar Poland or to local "great Poles" (*wielkie Poloki*), that minority of local residents who chose to be active in the ZPwN or otherwise manifest Polishness. In most cases only the more prosperous individuals could risk taking such a stand in a hostile environment. For the majority their "Polishness" lay solely in their customs, traditions, and language, which they cultivated not because these were in any sense Polish but as elements of their local Upper Silesian culture. It distinguished them from the Germans without at the same time linking them to the Polish nation. Aware of the similarity of the Silesian dialect to literary Polish, they nevertheless mixed their dialect with German in their daily speech in various proportions depending on circumstances and the age of the speaker. They did not share the general Polish hostility to all things German, and some even regarded the use of German as a sign of refinement.[48]

In a report in June 1945, journalists Stanisław Sokołowski and Edmund Osmańczyk, the latter an activist in the ZPwN and leader of the PZZ in Silesia, claimed that the Poles of Opole Silesia had preserved their language and in large part their national consciousness. But they also noted how some natives regarded the question of one's nationality as a relatively trivial matter, dictated by circumstances: "In Bodzanowice, a village in Olesno County, blank cards were returned during the nationality census with the explanation that they did not know who is going to rule here—Poles, Russians, or Germans."[49] Similarly, a seventy-year-old woman told Ossowski in 1945, "Let us be Poles, let us be Germans, let us be Russians, let us be Prussians, just so we can work, that there is peace, that there is something to eat, that there is sugar for the children."[50]

For the Silesian playwright and publicist Stanisław Bieniasz, "nationality indifference" (*indyferentyzm narodowościowy*) typical of historical borderlands prevented many Upper Silesians from identifying strongly with either the German or the Polish nation.[51] Sociologist Maria Szmeja takes the same view: "Because Silesians live in a cultural borderland area, they are tied to the Polish as well as the German nation. They, however, differ from both of these nations unquestionably. Nevertheless, they always lived in frameworks of one of them, therefore ambivalence or simply national indifference became a universal trait of Silesians."[52] Officials often described this "national indifference" as an "undeveloped feeling of nationality" based on the teleological assumption that a fully developed human being naturally has a strong sense of nationality.[53] Yet, many Silesians regarded as Polish or even verified as Polish in the immediate postwar years later opted for Germany.

Mazuria

The war strengthened anti-Polish attitudes among Mazurs. Military service as well as Germany's early successes in the war increased the identification with the Reich. Even publications in the Polish underground recognized that Mazurs lacked a consciousness of their connections with Poland and of their prospects for development in a Polish state. But Mazurs continued to use their version of the Polish language in daily life and in contact with Polish prisoners of war and forced laborers, with whom they often had positive relations. Still, for Poles performing forced labor or making forced deliveries, Mazurs who served as overseers or translators represented the hated occupying authorities. Polish inhabitants of the area south of East Prussia who resettled to the north in 1945 regarded the Mazurs as Germans who had persecuted them during the war. Indeed, East Prussians were greatly overrepresented among Nazi perpetrators.[54]

In the last months of 1944 the PKWN received two proposals illustrating the major disagreements over the formulation of nationality policy toward the Mazurs. Mieczysław Rogalski, a former diplomat in consulates in East Prussia, presented a memorandum to the PKWN on 24 August 1944. Highly critical of past policies toward East Prussia, he nevertheless expressed optimism about the prospects for re-Polonizing Mazurs:

> This does not mean these are Poles, patriots, molded people and nationally and politically sophisticated, but 75 percent of material unconditionally Polish.... Within [this population] we will have mostly a Polish element forcibly Germanized. We must Polonize these elements ... not hostile to Poland and not participants in criminal agitation or anti-Polish activity, so-called indifferent, neutral, apolitical, forcibly incorporated into the German cadre. We have to give

them time and the possibility of finding themselves, and we must rely on the clearly Polish local element.[55]

Yet he criticized this "Polish local element" for its local rivalries, narrow provincialism, and lack of objectivity and therefore opposed entrusting it with executive positions or a decisive role.

He assured his audience that permanently linking East Prussia with Poland could be accomplished quickly and effectively. The first step should be a careful sorting of the population, though he did not indicate by which criteria, as if it were obvious. Following the removal of the Germans, the remaining population must be convinced of the advantages of Poland. The Nazis won over the ethnically non-German element by bestowing benefits on it. "We must in this regard even outdo, outbid the Germans. We must do this better and intelligently.... We must resuscitate Prussia, elevate it culturally." Because the population "was constantly frightened by Polish poverty, we must inspire confidence that we do not intend to fleece, starve, and humiliate it, but that we desire to restore it."[56] The betrayal of any such confidence had an enormous impact on Mazurian identity.

Rogalski advocated the immediate return of Polish place names and surnames forcibly changed in the late 1930s. He insisted that teaching Polish posed no problem since everyone spoke Polish, supposedly even the most anti-Polish Hitler youth, contrary to other reports. "Of course this Polish language is somewhat different, archaic, contaminated with Germanisms, but it is Polish." He dismissed the results of the plebiscite in 1920 as marked by bribery and fraud. Still, he suggested a delay in the introduction of local self-government until the area was cleansed of foreign and hostile influences to avoid power falling into the hands of undesirable elements.[57] Thus, Rogalski regarded the population with a mixture of excessive optimism and an underlying political distrust, which one historian considers "the original sin" of postwar policy toward the Mazurs.[58]

Rogalski criticized pro-Polish Mazurian activists, but they had a deeper understanding of the need for a special status for Mazurs. On 18 March 1943 former members of the Union of Mazurs in Działdowo created a conspiratorial Mazurian Institute (*Instytut Mazurski*) under the leadership of Karol and Edward Małłek. They developed a program that called for autonomy for East Prussia within Poland and proposed that Mazurs from the Ruhr region—migrants from East Prussia and their descendants capable of being "re-Polonized"—replace the expelled Germans, reinforcing the Mazurian character of the province.

Deeply disappointed by the treatment of the Mazurs of Działdowo by the prewar Polish government and faced with a new geo-political reality, these activists looked to the PKWN rather than to the government-in-exile. On 27 October 1944 a member of the Mazurian Institute Jerzy Burski, who was already working with the PKWN, brought it a memorandum with proposals for the takeover of East Prussia prepared mainly by Karol Małłek. Małłek and other members of the Union of Mazurs met with Bierut on 22 November 1944.[59]

The memorandum began with an historical survey of the Mazurs in East Prussia that had less to do with reality than a desire to document a "centuries-old struggle for Polishness." It even placed the start of the migration of Polish peasants into the territory in the twelfth century, that is, before the arrival of the Teutonic Knights, the basis for characterizing Poles as the autochthons of the area. The memorandum mentioned the plebiscite only to point out that Mazurian activists did not give up the struggle and went into exile rather than accept German rule. The rest of the memorandum consisted of thirty propositions in nine topical sections covering organizational, demographic, linguistic, economic, cultural, and denominational issues.[60]

On ethnic, historical, and geographic grounds, the memorandum called for recasting East Prussia as the province of Mazuria, including only those counties, such as Działdowo, with the same character. The proposal showed more confidence in the population than Rogalski by advocating the immediate introduction of local self-government and the appointment to local positions of above all suitable Polish elements from among the autochthonous population. "Knowledge of the Polish literary language cannot be the decisive measure of evaluation. The sole indispensable condition will be the possession of a certificate of membership in the Polish nation."[61] A special commission would certify this membership. "A Pole in the Mazurian land is: a) someone who has a Polish surname. b) someone whose Polish surname (or that of his ancestors) was Germanized. c) someone with a non-Polish surname who knows the Polish language and uses it, if he is counted as part of Polish society d) a spouse of a mixed marriage, in which the other side is of Polish origin or their offspring." Germans had to be removed, but "attention should be paid that not even one drop of Polish blood accidently slipped into this group."[62]

The memorandum stoutly defended Protestantism in Mazuria as Polish, strongly warning against attempts at re-Catholicizing the 95.6 percent of the population that it claimed belonged to the Evangelical Church. In places inhabited by Protestants, all Catholic processions and field Masses were to be avoided for they would have a negative influence on national rebirth.

The activists proposed that the Mazurian province be closed to outsiders except officials and the military so that undesirable elements not hinder the political, economic, and social transformation of the province, which proved to be a realistic fear. The state should provisionally control property abandoned by the local native inhabitants until they returned. The memorandum closed with an appeal that all propaganda reflect the main idea, "the National Rebirth of the Mazurian people," and therefore avoid anything that would offend the feelings of Mazurs.[63] Significantly, the emphasis was on the Mazurian, not the Polish, character of the population.

The PKWN placed more confidence in Rogalski than in the members of the Union of Mazurs with its emphasis on Mazurian separatism. On 1 December 1944 the PKWN denied the ideologically suspect Union the right to exist "in actual fact and legally," but did not exclude the appointment of individual members for "administrative and social work."[64] Several initially received positions of local importance, and Burski was appointed to the KRN.

At a session of the KRN on 2 January 1945, Burski roundly condemned the policy of the prewar Polish government toward Działdowo's Mazurs, blaming it for the Germanization of 18,000 Mazurs, thereby denying the Mazurian identity an independent existence. "What the Germans were not able to do in the course of 700 years—that the *sanacja* [the prewar government] achieved in the course of several years. Shame and eternal dishonor on them—flunkies of Hitler!"—a charge that would soon be leveled against the postwar communist government. Despite the plea of the Union of Mazurs on behalf of a Mazurian identity, Burski emphasized national unity: "We demand protection and a physician for those sick brothers of ours who, subjected to cruel Germanization, in part were Germanized. Indeed, we are one people, and one blood unites us."[65]

Nevertheless, the Protestant religion distinguished the Mazurs sharply from the majority of Poles. A document emanating from the circle of the government-in-exile expressed a deep distrust of the religion of the Mazurs as an avenue of future German influence.[66] Such views persisted. In 1947 the official bulletin of the Ministry of Public Security (*Ministerstwo Bezpieczeństwa Publicznego* or MBP) claimed that only Protestant natives had given in to Germanization. In November 1948 the hostile relations between Mazurs and Poles prompted PZZ General Secretary Czesław Pilichowski to call for breaking with the stereotype, "every Protestant is a kraut."[67]

During the interwar years, the Evangelical-Augsburg Church unsuccessfully sought to win over the Mazurs of Działdowo for the Polish state. As the Germans invaded Poland in 1939, 120 out of 210 pastors of the Church declared themselves to be Polish. The Nazi authorities imprisoned Polish members of the Evangelical-Augsburg Church and sent many of its pastors, including its leader Bishop Juliusz Bursche, to concentration camps or executed them as "renegades" or "Polonizers."[68]

On 9 March 1945 the Ministry of Public Administration (*Ministerstwo Administracji Publicznej* or MAP) sent a decree to governors certifying the Evangelical-Augsburg Church as a legally recognized denomination. Nevertheless, the Church ran into opposition locally, including from officials who refused to ensure the return of its property and even prevented it from holding services in Polish.[69]

Like the central state authorities, the leaders of the Evangelical-Augsburg Church saw the Mazurs as tragic victims of forced Germanization who needed to be re-Polonized. There was no suggestion of recognizing a separate Mazurian identity. The first pastors of the Church faced a difficult task. Mostly survivors of Nazi concentration camps, they entered a formerly German territory where a majority of inhabitants had enthusiastically supported the Nazi regime. At the same time, the Mazurs had a deep-seated suspicion of Poland as overwhelmingly Catholic. For many of them, the Polish pastors were covert Catholics. When the clergy of the Evangelical-Augsburg Church sought to introduce services exclusively in Polish, attendance fell significantly.[70]

Szczecin Province: Kashubs and Polish-Speaking Inhabitants

Among the residents of the Western Pomerania District, autochthons of Slavic origin constituted only 1.8 percent of the population at the end of the war. Concentrated in the eastern counties, their self-identification was local rather than national. Most were of Kashubian origin. Their representatives, often self-appointed, regarded themselves first of all as Kashubs. Under Prussian rule, the influence of German culture was strong and long-lasting, fostering assimilation. The Evangelical Church reinforced this as the territory became almost exclusively Protestant.

The national identity of the Kashubian population was not always unambiguous and stable. Most Kashubs who preserved their culture and ethnic identity resided in the region further east that had been under the influence of Royal Prussia and the Roman Catholic Church and became part of Poland in 1919.[71] Bytów County had the largest percentage of Kashubs in Western Pomerania, constituting an estimated 20 percent of the population, residing in concentrated groups primarily in the southeast of the county. Kashubs made up a much smaller percent of the inhabitants of Słupsk, Miastko, Człuchów, and Lębork Counties. Some were former citizens of the Free City of Danzig. As in other formerly German counties along the prewar border, migrants flooded in from neighboring Polish counties after the war. Of great ethno-cultural significance in this case, the first migrants were Kashubs, many of whom had maintained contact with relatives and friends across the border and in many areas became the dominant element in the Kashubian population, contributing to the re-Kashubization of the area and a change in the geography of Kashubian settlement.[72]

Szczecin Province also had a Polish-speaking population in Złotów County, where the Polish school strike of 1906–1907 against Germanization had an echo.⁷³ But one researcher maintains that since the beginning of the twentieth century the Polish-speaking and the German-speaking inhabitants identified above all with their own place of residence, distinct from neighboring communities, that a local cultural identity had more significance than a regional or national identity.⁷⁴

The PPS Szczecin Provincial Committee (*Komitet Wojewódzki* or KW) reported on 12 September 1945 that Poles who wanted to resettle within the borders of Poland after 1919 were told to remain in Złotów County so that Poland could lay claim to the territory. It categorized the local Polish population in three groups: the "enlightened," who consisted of members of the ZPwN, which before the war had 1,500 members in Złotów, including Rev. Bolesław Domański, who led the ZPwN, 1931–1939; the "unenlightened," those outside of the ZPwN who did not belong because of their economic vulnerability—mostly merchants, craftsmen, pensioners, and office workers; and "renegades," individuals of Polish origin "who not only publicly renounced their Polishness but even harmed and persecuted Poles. These last ones we must exclude from their society."⁷⁵

Regional Differences

An article published in *Przegląd Zachodni* at the end of 1946 maintained the illusion of the autochthons as part of a uniform primordial Polish nation. The author saw in their folk traditions all the traits of a universal Polish folk culture. One only had to activate its various regional forms. Where Polish folk culture no longer existed, as in Pomerania, ethnographic research needed to find the traces of the culture of the legitimate inhabitants of the "Slavic land." If no such traces were likely to be found, as in Lower Silesia, the indigenous Polish folk culture of neighboring regions would do. She claimed that mobilizing Polish folk culture would give "the new settlers who came here . . . the possibility of cordially coming together with the local, autochthonous population, becoming acquainted with their culture and quickly establishing fraternal relations."⁷⁶

The regionalism that marked the work of some Polish writers came in for criticism after 1945. A history of Polish literature published in 1949 asserted that regionalism diverted attention from more important matters, gave birth to separatism, and contributed to the infiltration of reactionism, i.e., opposition to communism. Seeing the same threat in the differences among autochthons, officials argued that the acceptance of other national types, like Silesians or Mazurs, created by historical processes different from those of the majority of the Polish nation, would signal the triumph of German machinations. In March 1945 Governor Zawadzki criticized the prewar autonomy of Polish

Silesia as harmful to the interests of Poland. In May 1945, at the inaugural session of the Provincial National Council (*Wojewódzka Rada Narodowa* or WRN) in Katowice, he declared, "the period of separating Silesians from the rest of Poland, the period of treating Silesians as a separate nation in between the Polish and German nations has come to an end."[77] In insisting on the unity of the Polish nation and denying autonomy to Silesia or Mazuria, Polish communists laid the foundation for a highly centralized state over which they sought a monopoly of power.

"Re-Polonizing" the Recovered Lands

In a memorandum dated 14 February 1945, a Polish sociologist argued that only a migration of Polish population to the territory claimed from Germany "will constitute a true victory of our State in the current war concerning the resolution of the centuries-old Polish-German dispute." As for the natives of the territory, he harbored some doubts: "The population of Polish origin, even if partly Germanized, can and should remain in the lands of the Polish state, with only the reservation of a possible limitation on their rights until their complete re-Polonization."[78] The migration, a Polish version of *Heim ins Reich*, would profoundly affect the success of re-Polonization.

Poland had a powerful practical argument for claiming Germany's eastern lands and expelling the Germans in the 2.1 million homeless people to be resettled following the war, a task that the PKWN and its successors proved ill prepared to accomplish. The PKWN created the State Repatriation Office (*Państwowy Urząd Repatriacyjny* or PUR) on 7 October 1944, following agreements for an exchange of population with Soviet republics in September 1944.[79] Already in the last quarter of 1944, 117,212 "evacuees" left Soviet Ukraine for Poland. Their resettlement in the Recovered Lands and the removal of the Germans were linked, with the latter providing "living space"—and farms and places of employment.[80] Yet not until 1945 did the PUR also receive the task of resettling the German population.

Although the Yalta conference ended without delineating Poland's western border, the need to populate the formerly German territory with Poles and prepare for spring planting prompted the Council of Ministers (*Rada Ministrów* or RM) on 13 February 1945 to approve proposals by Władysław Wolski, head of the PUR, "to enter immediately upon a massive repatriation of the Polish population without regard for the difficulties connected with the destruction of the country by the war."[81] A month later on 16 March 1945 the RM voted to give repatriates priority in the resettlement of the formerly

German territory despite Wolski's report of serious inadequacies in the resettlement process, particularly in transportation, resulting in sickness and even death of so-called repatriates due to exposure to the elements and disease during their journeys, which usually lasted for several weeks.[82] On 30 April 1945 the PUR directed its regional offices to send all transports of "repatriates" to the "newly recovered territory" until further notice.[83] The first transports of repatriates appeared in Silesia already in March 1945, and on 23 April 1945 a transport of a thousand repatriates arrived in Opole Silesia.[84] According to one study, ultimately 1,235,148 of the repatriates from Poland's former eastern territories (81.4 percent of the total) resettled in the formerly German territory, constituting about 18 percent of its population.[85]

The authorities also recruited settlers from Central Poland. In mid-April 1945 the PPR and allied parties called on Poles to "Go West" (*Na Zachód*):

> The ancient Piast lands, torn away by the partitioning Teutonic order, trampled on and oppressed by the Prussian barbarians, are returning to the motherland.... Not even one Prussian *Junker* will remain, not even one Teutonic rapist.... The German will no longer spit in our face and Germanize our children[86] ... Immense wealth falls to our lot! Go west—the Polish Army is pursuing victory. Go west—in the footsteps of the soldiers—we are all going, the whole of society, model farmers, wise organizers. Our hands and brains are needed to wipe away the remnants of Germanness from our land.[87]

Even earlier, beginning in February 1945, migrants from prewar Poland occupied abandoned farms in Upper Silesia, and in March a spontaneous flood of people came looking for anything of value and appropriating the best farms whether abandoned or not with little regard for their ownership. They assumed it was German property and could hardly conceive of German citizens of Polish origin. The Silesian Provincial PUR estimated that by the end of June 1945 138,000 settled in the province without the intervention of any government agency. In November 1945 they numbered 171,500. In Warmia and Mazuria settlers occupied a large number of farms in March and April 1945, months before the district authorities set up an office of settlement.[88]

Gomułka emphasized the urgency of resettling the Recovered Lands at the plenum of the KC PPR in Warsaw in May 1945:

> International pressure is one of the symptoms of British policy. If we do not Polonize the formerly German lands, we will not have a basis to reclaim that which they already do not want to return to us.... If there is no Polish population in the western lands, the administration will lie in the hands of the Red Army. Connected with this is the problem of the return of the Germans who fled before the Red Army. We have to throw them out because all countries are built on national principles and not multinational ones.[89]

Removal of the Germans would provide housing and employment for incoming Poles. A resolution of the KC on 26 May 1945 spoke not only of removing Germans from the Recovered Lands by the end of the year, but also of resettling 3.5 million Poles there, 2.5 million in time to carry out the harvest so that crops would not go to waste, goals that would take much longer to achieve.[90]

The authorities also sought to lure back to Poland those who emigrated before the war and their descendants. Ultimately, 250,000 so-called re-emigrants from several countries returned between 1946 and 1949, nearly three-fourths of them settling in the Recovered Lands, adding to the area's heterogeneity.[91]

With repatriates and settlers arriving in the Recovered Lands inhabited by autochthons, problems of integration arose reminiscent of those faced by the Nazis in the incorporated lands.[92] Political leaders sought to integrate the various groups into a cohesive, homogeneous society. Members of the Research Council at its first meeting in the summer of 1945 argued that the Poles settled in particular regions should be of a similar culture and civilization as the local population so as to minimize conflicts.[93] "A New Type of Pole, a New Polish Culture Will Arise in the Recovered Lands," an article in the Polish press optimistically declared in July 1946.[94]

Repatriates and settlers came to the Recovered Lands conscious of their rights as Poles to the territory.[95] From the moment of first contacts with natives, unexpected differences in spoken language, customs, and traditions prompted newcomers to the Recovered Lands, including the newly appointed officials, to regard all natives as Germans. Germanisms sprinkled in the speech of Slavic-speaking Silesians and the "German" faith of the Protestant Mazurs seemingly confirmed their German nationality.[96]

Upper Silesia became the new home for 262,000 repatriates from the Polish East. In addition, by June 1947 220,000 settlers from Central Poland and 56,000 repatriates from western Europe and Germany had to be accommodated in the all too few homes and farms fit for immediate occupation abandoned by or taken from their German owners. The Roman Catholic faith shared by the overwhelming majority of inhabitants in Opole Silesia and the incoming population did not necessarily smooth intergroup relations. Ossowski found that for most residents of Opole Silesia, Catholicism served as a regional link, not a national one.[97] The natives of Silesia had a long history of regarding newcomers, whether Polish-speaking or not, as "foreigners." The influx of population intensified the polarization between "one's own" (*swoi*) and "foreigners" (*obcy*) that existed before the war and affected the attitude of the natives toward the new political and social reality.[98]

The migrants from the territory of prewar Poland did not take into account the historical experiences of the local inhabitants who exhibited many of the externals of German culture and whose Slavic customs and traditions underwent a different evolution than in prewar and partitioned Poland. Newcomers to the Recovered Lands found the very speech of many natives, infested with Germanisms, repugnant.[99] The German Silesian composer and journalist Joachim Georg Görlich, who witnessed postwar developments in Silesia, later observed, "The relevant authorities ... completely ignored that even Poles born here were educated in German culture and in this connection absorbed German influences. One could even conclude that this offended the administration and the incoming population."[100] The anti-German obsession of newcomers to the Recovered Lands hindered the acceptance by locals of a Polish identity. The cultural clash resulted in their glorifying the interwar period under German rule and in diminishing the distance between their culture and German culture.[101]

According to the PUR in Prudnik County in February 1947,

> The deportee [from the East] saw in every autochthon a German or a Nazi. This attitude in any case dates from the beginning, from the takeover of these territories by our authorities. The first colonists of these lands did not always live up to their obligations and often, not because of ill will but out of ignorance, treated these territories as an occupied country inhabited by Germans. Once committed an evil cannot today be corrected so quickly, and a wrong done, especially to a Silesian accustomed to the rule of law, is not so quickly forgotten.[102]

One of the early settlers voiced a typical reaction upon encountering the natives: "What kind of Poles are these who do not speak Polish, know nothing of Polish history, culture, literature? Again it is that Silesian opportunism. They favor whoever is in power." Stereotypes deepened the gulf. The natives repeated a verse, "Lord, why did you send us so much poverty, that Polacks [*Gorole* (pejorative)] and Kikes [*Żydi* (pejorative)] are pushing their way into Silesia." Among Silesians one frequently heard comments such as, "People from Lwów and also from Central Poland are not to be seen in mines and factories. They are with the railroad or in offices, they won't take up hard work. And even if such a one goes to a factory, he looks for easy work, wants to take it easy and earn well. Sometimes ... he prefers to earn less, skimp on food, but not work hard." Again, "Repatriates are people who occupy themselves with everything but not decent work."[103]

The inhabitants of lands that had not been part of a Polish state for centuries did not share in such Polish myths as the so-called "Miracle Myth" or "Insurrection Myth" so important in the development of Polish national consciousness. Polish romanticism, Messianism, and Martyrology were alien to the autochthons, nor did the myth that they had resisted Germanization like the schoolchildren in Września ring true for the overwhelming majority. Even the Silesian Uprisings that the authorities celebrated as an example of a Polish insurrection were for a majority of natives more of a tragedy, a fratricide stimulated by outsiders, than a triumph of the Polish spirit.[104]

Thus, the Political-Educational Department of the 7th Łużycki Infantry Division on 21 May 1946 reported a dispute among autochthons in Koźle County, a battleground during the Silesian Uprisings. The local inhabitants were divided between those who, on one hand, long felt themselves to be Poles and belonged to the ZPwN and, on the other, former members of the Nazi party recently verified as Polish. The report took it as characteristic of the county that the graves of Poles and Russians who fell in the war were neglected and vandalized whereas those of fallen Germans were kept in the best order with flowers and wreaths. Similar developments were reported in Nysa County.[105]

Significantly, sociological research in the 1980s in two urban areas of prewar Polish Upper Silesia found a persistent gulf based on mutual stereotypes and objective cultural differences between newcomers, who continued to note the "Germanness" of Silesians, and native Silesians, who remained firmly attached to their regional identity, which as in the past generally prevailed over any national ideological connection.[106]

Despite the diversity among autochthons of the Recovered Lands, the Polish authorities refused to recognize regional differences in formulating nationality policies and instead held to a rigid concept of the Polish national identity. Similarly, the repatriates and settlers generally did not consider the inhabitants they encountered to be compatriots. This together with other developments in the last phase of the war and its immediate aftermath had a great impact on the national identity of the inhabitants.

[5]

The Prologue to Polonizing Identities

ON THE EVE of the Soviet offensive of 12 January 1945, Lavrenty Beria, head of the NKVD, directed it to "cleanse" the hinterland of the front of all "hostile elements."[1] Although the Big Three at Yalta did not define Poland's western border, on 20 February 1945 the Soviet State Defense Committee recognized the Oder-Neisse line as the western border of Poland until the peace conference. The Soviet forces controlled all the territory east of the line by the end of April 1945, and it remained under the authority of the local Soviet military commandants for several months thereafter.

Soviet military authorities posted a sign on the border between the *Generalgouvernement* and the Polish territory incorporated into the Reich that read: "This is them, the accursed Germans."[2] A study of the terror of the first postwar years found that the scale of plundering was greatest and the feeling of security of Poles lowest in the Recovered Lands because the Soviet military regarded it as conquered territory.[3] Minister of Public Administration Edward Ochab claimed in a report for February 1945 that Pomerania and Poznań Province suffered the most because the soldiers who marched through East Prussia, the first part of Germany that the Red Army entered, were probably given "more freedom in relation to the population and in this connection were more difficult to bring under control."[4]

The passing of the front in any war, particularly one as brutal as World War II, inevitably brings with it violence, chaos, and revenge at the expense of a civilian population identified with the enemy.[5] But the unsettled loyalties in the borderlands gave it greater significance. Already in July 1943 a bilingual doggerel identified category I and II *Volksdeutsche* with the enemy whereas those in III and IV were safe:

>   *Ein, zwei—uciekaj* [flee],
>   *Drei, vier—bleiben hier* [stay here][6]

In a memorandum on 25 August 1944 pro-Polish Mazurian activists Fryderyk Leyk, Burski, and Rev. Ewald Lodwich called on "the military and civilian authorities of the Allied states, in their justified anger in punishing German jackals, also active in our Mazurian misery, to treat our fellow countrymen residing in their native land with the greatest understanding."[7] Their fears proved justified.

Although individual Soviet soldiers treated the population humanely, wanton violence, pillage, rape, murder, and arson on a massive scale characterized the order of the day and remained widespread even toward the end of 1945.[8] The demographic structure of the population of the borderlands made it particularly vulnerable: 63 percent was female; overall 36.5 percent was below the age of eighteen and 15.8 percent above the age of sixty. Conscription left few young men behind.[9]

A palliative report on 18 February 1945 of the future historian Captain Juliusz Bardach hardly concealed the horror.

> THE BEHAVIOR [sic] of individual officers of the Red Army leaves much to be desired. The fact that the front line passes through Poznań and that the attitude in the army is that everything is permitted in relation to Germans results in some less disciplined units, in the face of a lack of Germans, to treat Poles in a way that harms the matter of Polish-Soviet friendship and weakens the feeling of gratitude and sympathy with which the population of Poznań regards its liberator—the Red Army. The order of the day is a matter of taking watches, rings, jewelry—simply on the street or in homes and shelters. We have thousands of such cases. Instances of the rape of Polish women—often in the presence of parents and husbands are also very common. . . . In connection with robberies and rapes there are also instances of the killing of Polish civilians.[10]

In Działdowo County the Allied armies acted as if the territory were German, exacting revenge; raping most of the women, including children and the elderly; shooting many of the inhabitants, including the parents of a KRN deputy and a family that during the occupation hid Poles who escaped from forced labor; and confiscating livestock and other belongings, leaving the population practically naked, according to a memorandum that Karol Małłek, Bohdan Wilamowski, and Walter Późny sent to the Provisional Government on 26 February 1945.[11]

The passing of the front gave Polish activists in the Recovered Lands their first shock, but not their last. Expecting liberation, not indiscriminate violence, they did not feel the need to flee and thought that a ZPwN membership card would protect them. Others thought a knowledge of Polish would suffice. In some cases it did save one's life. In Nidzica County two Mazurian women avoided being shot by convincing Soviet soldiers that they were Poles. Another woman succeeded in preventing Soviet soldiers from shooting her grandchild by pleading with them in Mazurian.¹² But, in general, Soviet soldiers made no distinction as to nationality.¹³ At the end of January 1945 in Boguszyce near Opole, where a majority spoke the Polish Silesian dialect, the Soviet military killed 273 civilians, mostly women, children, and the elderly.¹⁴

Following a three-day tour of northwestern East Prussia, the chairman of the Olsztyn Land Office (*Urząd Ziemski* or UZ) reported on 19 March 1945 that he found the Soviet military exacting forced labor from hundreds of Poles—both locals and Poles deported to the region by the Nazis. All had the same complaint: "unceasing raping of women carried out by the Soviets."

> I was told disgusting and horrible things with the names of witnesses. Hardly any woman remained untouched no matter what nationality, beginning with 10-year-olds and ending with 70-year-old elderly ladies. . . . There were cases of simultaneous rapes in one house of a mother, grandmother, daughter, and granddaughter. These rapes were carried out in turn. The raped women were used by at least a dozen soldiers, and it happened that their number on one woman reached thirty. Of course such a woman paid for this with her life. Such things still continue to occur.¹⁵

On 16 July 1945 the director of the Terrain Organizational Department of the Ministry of Information and Propaganda (*Ministerstwo Informacji i Propagandy* or MIiP) reported on the situation in Western Pomerania:

> Polish women are constantly in danger of being raped by soldiers of the Red Army. The command, especially the military commanding officers, take a not at all equivocal stand in this matter, asserting that their soldiers have already been away from their families for a long time, and with the lack of German women—Polish women should satisfy their needs.¹⁶

When Milovan Djilas complained about the behavior of the Red Army in Yugoslavia. Stalin responded, "Does Djilas, who is himself a writer, not know what human suffering and the human heart are? Can't he understand it if a soldier who has crossed thousands of kilometers through blood and fire and death has fun with a woman or takes some trifle?"¹⁷

All this had political consequences. According to 2nd Lt. Zylberberg, in Opole Silesia it evoked spontaneous hope in England and America, whose propaganda reached the region and which were in a position to "drive out" the Russians. In Zylberberg's view, because national consciousness there was weak, the important question was whether one looked to Poland or to Germany.¹⁸

On 12 February 1945 a Civic Committee of Poles of Opole Silesia submitted a memorandum to Governor Zawadzki supplemented with a draft proclamation for the Red Army and a placard, which Zawadzki forwarded to the commander of the 1st Ukrainian Front Marshal Ivan Konev on 14 February 1945.

His headquarters responded that he "issued an order of protection by the Red Army of everyone who proves his Polish origin," an order that was mostly ignored.[19]

Zawadzki's action prompted the Main Directorate (*Zarząd Główny* or ZG) of the PZZ on 26 February 1945 to call on the government to ensure the safety of the Polish element in areas occupied by Allied armies by appointing plenipotentiaries who, together with selected local activists, could identify those of Polish nationality based on their role in the defense of Polishness or membership in Polish organizations; knowledge and use in everyday life of the Polish language; or their Polish origin as attested to by their surname, ties, or family traditions. The PZZ urged quick action and attached a questionnaire for the resident population as a basis for awarding Polish citizenship.[20]

Plenipotentiary of the District of Mazuria Colonel Jakub Prawin, following conversations with the Soviet military authorities, reported on 23 March 1945 that the question "of Polish autochthons, Mazurs, and Kashubs has not yet been clarified." On 13 May 1945, he reported that, although the Soviets had a negative attitude toward the local Polish population, following conversations concerning forced labor, the Soviets formally recognized the existence of a Polish population and placed it under the care of the Polish authorities.[21]

A situation report on 4 April 1945 of the municipal government in Gliwice stated,

> The attitude of the Red Army toward the population is in general ruthless; according to the declaration of the commanding officer of the Military Command of the Red Army, they cannot distinguish between the German and the Polish population and use one and the other equally for work and services for the army because all were citizens of the Reich and all fought against the Red Army.

Unable to secure the release of Polish detainees, the Opole Civic Committee reported that the attitude of the Polish population "is not what it should be because so far it does not feel defended and treated differently" than the German population.[22]

At the plenum of the KC PPR on 20–21 May 1945, Zawadzki warned, "Anti-Soviet feelings, growing as a result of marauding, favor the development of the sabotage operations of the AK bands." Ochab suggested that, with the war over, the Red Army should leave Polish territory, except for some important points of communication on the coast. Gomułka, however, recognized that the party needed the presence of the Red Army in Poland. He meekly proposed that it might be advisable to ask the Command of the Red Army to take tougher measures against marauding so that Poles would know that the Red Army opposed it.[23]

As problems continued, on 10 January 1946 Gomułka complained in a letter to Soviet Marshals Georgy Zhukov and Konstantin Rokossovsky and the Soviet ambassador:

> The attitude of units of the Red Army toward the Polish population of the territory of the Recovered Lands often tends to be unfriendly [sic!], which evokes feelings of bitterness and discouragement in Polish society. The behavior of some units of the Red Army, committing acts of violence, robbery, plunder, and murder, hamper Polish activity in the area of the Recovered Lands.

He suggested "the application of the most severe penalties to soldiers of the Red Army caught plundering, robbing, or raping women."[24]

On 20 June 1946 the MZO inspector for Słupsk, Sławno, and Miastko Counties (Szczecin Province) reported that the main cause of confusion and fear among the population "continues to be the improper behavior of units of the Red Army stationed here," which ignored orders from superiors. Also, Red Army deserters formed their own gangs. "The murder of inhabitants is carried out by Soviet soldiers mainly for the purpose of robbery. Unfortunately, Poles became participants in the attacks, including functionaries of the MO [*Milicja Obywatelska,* Civic Militia] and UB [*Urząd Bezpieczeństwa,* Office of Security]." The inspector concluded that the sole solution was the departure of the Soviet military, since all attempts to negotiate were in vain and complaints should be sent where they belong, from the top.[25] In November 1946, with the approach of the parliamentary election in January 1947, the MO deputy commander in Świdnica County (Wrocław Province) reported that a section of the population completely lacked confidence in the government because of attacks by the Red Army.[26]

The Soviet military constituted the ultimate defender of the Polish communists' hold on power, which prevented them from effectively addressing abuses. In October 1946 the Soviet Minister of Internal Affairs reported to Beria that when he discussed the withdrawal from Poland of sixty-four divisions of the military with Bierut, the Polish president stated that they were indispensable in the current situation and requested that they remain until 1 March 1947, i.e., after the election.[27]

Detention and Deportation to the Soviet Union

Marauding troops were not the only threat to the inhabitants of the Polish-German borderlands. On 7 February 1945 the Soviet commandant of the 1st Belorussian Front ordered the mobilization of all males seventeen through fifty years of age to repair roads and rail lines destroyed by the German army.[28] Thousands were interned in labor camps and in March–April 1945 deported for forced labor in the Soviet Union. Of those who survived, the last returned from the Soviet Union in the fall of 1947 following a recommendation of the Soviet Council of Ministers on 26 July 1947 to release individuals of Polish nationality who had been mobilized for labor during the war, unless suspected of serious crimes against the Soviet Union.[29]

Incomplete data of the Polish administration indicate that some 15,000 were deported from Pomerania, mostly "ethnographically Polish" elements coerced into registering on the DVL.[30] In June 1945 the governor wrote:

> A serious complaint of the people of Pomerania is . . . the lack of resolution so far of the matter of the individuals arrested and deported by the Soviet authorities. If those arrested were to return, the population here would see the return of the arrested as an effective effort of the Government on behalf of Pomerania, and the actions of the party and the authorities would then be much more effective.

The first returnees, emaciated and ailing, arrived in August 1945, and with them came news of those who died, which inclined many of the remaining *Volksdeutsche* of the province to leave for Germany voluntarily.[31]

The number of autochthons deported from East Prussia was estimated at 60,000 to 100,000.[32] The Soviets sent about 15,000 Silesian miners to the Donets coal basin in the first months of 1945, 8,000 from Bytom alone in February 1945.[33] Soviet data indicate that in the territory east of the Oder-Neisse line by mid-April 1945, 215,500 individuals were detained: 138,200 Germans, 39,000 Poles, and more than 27,000 Soviet citizens.[34] In addition, the Soviet Union held 1,373,027 German POWs as of 1 October 1946, according to a report of the Soviet Minister of Internal Affairs on 23 November 1946.[35] Presumably, they too included many German citizens of Polish origin.

Although Stalin agreed in June 1945 to the return of Upper Silesians, in 1946 Polish authorities estimated that 10,000 to 25,000 had not yet returned.[36] On 10 July 1946 the Silesian UW laconically reported, "In June several thousand Poles returned who last year were regarded as Germans and were removed to Ukraine."[37] Many did not return until 1955.[38]

The Soviet military authorities also maintained forced labor camps within Poland. In 1946 the Soviets transferred "German prisoners of Polish nationality" to forced labor camps in Jaworzno and Złotów, among them 5,492 miners deported to the USSR the previous year.[39] The Soviets shortly handed over some labor camps to the Polish authorities while other camps long remained under Soviet control.[40]

Poles returning from forced labor in the Reich with German documents aroused the suspicions of the Soviet military, which executed some as "German spies." On 17 May 1945 the PZZ called for issuing Polish documents to such individuals.[41] In mid-June 1945 Governor Zawadzki demanded the intervention of Warsaw on behalf of Poles returning from Germany detained in Soviet labor camps, including veterans of the Polish Silesian Uprisings. After meeting on 30 July 1945 with Marshal Rokossovsky, who had jurisdiction over the Red Army in Poland, Zawadzki together with Soviet officers visited several camps, and on 5 August the NKVD ordered the release of detained Poles. A Soviet-Polish commission was created to secure their release. Zawadzki sent a commission to the formerly German camp—now Soviet—at Auschwitz to investigate a report that it held a large number of Poles. It met with the Soviet commander of the camp on 21 August 1945 and secured the release of 4,156 Poles, more than half of the camp's prisoners. A Selection-Control Commission formed in August interviewed 18,400 prisoners in Silesia, of whom 7,000 qualified for release as did 1,047 Silesians imprisoned in camps in Pomerania.[42] On 13 August 1945 the Strzelce *starosta* obtained the release of 1,200 Silesians from the Łabędy camp awaiting deportation to the Soviet Union after dismantling the Hermann Göring Steel Mill for shipping to the Soviet Union.[43]

The "Wild" Expulsion by the Polish Military

In Czechoslovakia immediately following liberation, many Czechs took revenge on Germans who had not yet fled even though they were underrepresented among Nazi perpetrators.[44] Between April and the Potsdam Conference at the end of July 1945, 600,000 Germans left the country and an estimated 19,000 to 30,000 died, 6,000 of them as a result of violence, 5,000 by suicide.[45] All this took place within the pre-1938 borders of Czechoslovakia.

In Poland the Polish military took up the task of cleansing prewar German territory, triggered in part by a change in Soviet tactics. On 15 April 1945 the Red Army directed the military to treat rank-and-file members of the Nazi party humanely, arresting only their leaders, and to introduce German administration in towns and counties. No longer were Germans to suffer collective punishment.[46] In a letter to Stalin on 22 April 1945, Beria cited the example of the Western Allies relying on the local German police, courts, and institutions of self-government in areas that they occupied.[47]

Gomułka reacted at the plenum of the KC PPR in May 1945: "The Red Army's hard line on Germany has changed so as not to push Germany into Britain's embrace. The matter is of special interest to us in view of the western territories."[48] Also, in May and June 1945 at least one million refugees from the borderlands returned to their homes east of the Oder-Neisse line.[49] On 26 May 1945 the KC PPR directed that the 2nd Polish Army expel Germans from a zone along the Oder-Neisse border.[50] Brutality and retaliation against Germans marked the expulsion.

On 22 June 1945 the 7th Infantry Division began to clear inhabitants from the border zone and from several counties in Western Pomerania and Lower Silesia.[51] The head of its Political-Educational Department reported on 26 June 1945 that 40,000 to 45,000 people were "evacuated" daily for a total of 160,000 since the operation began. To prevent refugees from returning, on 10 June 1945 the head of the Polish Army Marshal Michał Żymierski ordered the 12th Infantry Division to secure the border. Though the flow of individuals eastward subsided, some still managed to return. On 23 June 1945 the 3rd Infantry Division on 23 June 1945 reported that thirty individuals of Polish nationality crossed the border into Polish territory. Commanding officers issued additional orders on 24 and 25 June 1945.[52]

Expulsions also occurred far from the new western border. In Bytom the Internal Security Corps initiated the expulsion of Germans in early July 1945, according to a report on 30 July 1945 of the propaganda inspector of the 13th Infantry Division. The operation, however, was suspended after two days because of the resulting chaos. The Polish Army resumed the expulsion in a more orderly manner on 15 July 1945. Significantly, among the difficulties encountered, the inspector listed a lack of criteria for determining nationality, "which during the operation resulted in a whole array of ambiguities and misunderstandings." Nevertheless, he reported the expulsion of 4,000 "Germans" with 8,000 remaining under the order of expulsion.[53]

The protests of the Western Allies, whose good will Poland needed for the recognition of its western border, prompted a discontinuation of the expulsions in the border zone in mid-July. In all, the operation in June and July 1945 resulted in the forced removal of at least 250,000 inhabitants of the Recovered Lands.[54]

Despite the ban, forced expulsions continued until the end of 1945. In a report for November 1945, the *starosta* of Nowy Tomyśl County, Poznań Province, complained about the improper actions of the security organs in removing German citizens of Polish nationality and *Volksdeutsche* in categories II–IV in the process of being rehabilitated.[55]

Too late did the Poznań UW send a memo to General Karol Świerczewski on 21 August 1945 requesting that he order his subordinate officers not to deport German citizens of Polish nationality. The governor described the operation in a report to the MAP on 1 March 1946:

> The Soviet and Polish military displaced whole villages and towns, often plundering the possessions left behind. With spring this operation took on greater dimensions ... The [ethnic] origins of the displaced Germans were then not

rigorously investigated, nor were the documents submitted closely examined. The designation "Reichsdeutsche" or "Volksdeutsche" sufficed as a reason for displacement. In the face of such a procedure, there was in this mass operation a certain slight percent of displaced Polish autochthonous population residing in the territory of the Recovered Lands and possessing German citizenship.[56]

One can safely assume that the "wild" expulsions included far more than this "slight percent" of individuals qualified to seek Polish citizenship.

Forced Labor and Detention in Poland

Forced labor for Germans had wide support in Polish society. "Work awaits them. They must rebuild everything that their foul hands destroyed," asserted the *Głos Ludu* on 7 March 1945.[57] Ambiguity marked the legal status of *Volksdeutsche* and German citizens. Local officials decided their treatment, detention, and the conditions of forced labor. The central authorities did not regulate their pay and working conditions until the spring of 1946.[58]

In Poznań Province already on 29 January 1945 a local High Provisional Committee in Śrem ordered the detention of all male *Volksdeutsche* between the ages of sixteen and sixty. On 26 February 1945 a report to the provincial commander of the MO stated, "The militia carried out work mainly within the scope of the administrative authorities: liquidation of Germans and *Volksdeutsche*." In Wieleń on 6 February 1945, the mayor ordered "all German inhabitants of the town, that is, *Reichsdeutsche* and *Volksdeutsche* of all three [sic] categories, men as well as women 15 to 60 years of age will report today at 10 o'clock in the Market Square" under threat of the death penalty by court martial. In Szamotuły County the mobilization announced on 20 February 1945 included those males "of German nationality with personal identification as *Reichsdeutsche,* categories I, II, and III *Volksdeutsche* . . . or those without any personal identification from German times," who were simply assumed to be German. On 17 April 1945 the Poznań County *starosta* ordered all Germans, including *Volksdeutsche,* from the age of twelve to register for employment for no less than sixty hours per week.[59]

Local residents at times aided the round-ups. Denunciations resulted in detention without due process. At a meeting of the Poznań WRN on 15 May 1945, the governor noted, "there are cases in which individuals finding themselves in camps were fingered by Poles to settle personal scores."[60]

Not everyone accepted collective German guilt. On 1 March 1945 the Nowy Tomyśl *starosta* threatened with prosecution officials who did not mobilize all Germans and *Volksdeutsche*.[61] The mayor of Kościan similarly threatened to treat those who hid Germans "as Germans." In the last ten days of May 1945 alone the MO arrested seventy-eight individuals in Poznań Province on charges of hiding Germans. The Gniezno County National Council (*Powiatowa Rada Narodowa* or PRN) voted unanimously on 1 March 1945 to brand publicly those who supported the applications of *Volksdeutsche* to retain Polish citizenship as "Defenders of *Volksdeutsche*."[62]

In Silesia on 9 February 1945 Governor Zawadzki became the first to introduce forced labor throughout a province, ordering "all Germans, that is, citizens of the German Reich" along with *Volksdeutsche* in categories I and II to register for work.[63] On 7 June 1945 Zawadzki standardized their obligation to work and labor conditions with 75 percent of the pay Poles received for the same work and a 25 percent deduction for a fund to aid victims of the Nazis.[64]

In Działdowo the MO, which consisted mainly of newcomers, indiscriminately identified Protestants as Germans and detained them in camps where, after being beaten, they were kept hungry and ragged and forced to work while their property was plundered, according to the memorandum that Mazurian activists addressed to the Provisional Government on 26 February 1945. In the camps children were deprived of milk and some women were systematically raped, sometimes protected only by a Soviet military commandant. The memorandum accused Catholics, some of whom were also *Volksdeutsche*, of abetting the military in abusing Mazurs. It called on the government to order an immediate end to executions, terror, and detention; a reorganization of the MO and the recruitment of commanding officers familiar with the situation and in contact with the PRN; and the creation of Population Commissions by the PRN to identify Germans.[65]

During a tour of Działdowo County and southern East Prussia commissioned by the RM, Warsaw Governor Stanisław Mazur found the same conditions in detention centers. On 9 March 1945 he confirmed that officials were totally ignorant of particular local problems and dealt with them in ways that furthered their own interests. Detainees clamed that the Nazis had placed them on the DVL but contemptuously called them "Polacken" and now Poles called them Germans.

The governor could not learn what crimes the detainees committed. A deputy commanding officer of the MO asserted that they should be "annihilated" for accepting the status of *Volksdeutsche,* which he claimed he had refused, though a document he produced indicated he had applied for German citizenship but was denied. Others simply claimed that the detained were Germans and should be treated as such. The report above all blamed those who simply wished to obtain German property and therefore instigated soldiers to kill, rape, and plunder and local officials who sanctioned this state of affairs, often exploiting it to their own personal advantage. Following the governor's report, the legal bureau of the PRM recognized the need for an immediate dissolution of camps for those in the three lower DVL categories, the return of their property, and the assurance of their personal security.[66]

Local officials in the Recovered Lands often assumed that all who fled the advancing front were Germans. In largely Protestant Kluczbork County, the German army forced the evacuation of most inhabitants of several villages as the Red Army approached. When they returned in June 1945, officials prevented them from reoccupying their property, of which often nothing remained. On 4 July 1945 the *starosta* ordered those who returned after 15 May 1945 to be transferred immediately to farms to perform labor services. Some who evaded the evacuation also had their small properties confiscated. Psychologically and emotionally tied to their properties, they refused another property in exchange.[67] In Wojciechów, Olesno County, from May to November 1945 local officials interned about 300 individuals returning from Germany, of whom half were later verified as Poles.[68]

As the borderlands came under Polish administration, the number of prisons and forced labor camps multiplied. In response to what was often a chaotic and haphazard process, in June 1945 the MBP and the Ministry of Justice directed the release of those against whom the sole accusation was membership in DVL categories III and IV. Local courts took up complicated cases, including those of individuals in category II. Nevertheless, *Volksdeutsche* would remain the largest single group of inmates in forced labor camps throughout the 1940s. Suspicion of being a *Volksdeutsche* or a German citizen sufficed for detention.[69]

The punishment of Germans and "national traitors" had popular support. But leaving the identification of Germans to local officials opened the door to abuse. The possibility of free or cheap labor for state enterprises and farms favored the creation of labor camps and the retention of those detained. In Grodków, Silesia, the County Office of Information and Propaganda (*Powiatowy Urząd Informacji i Propagandy* or PUIiP) reported on 8 November 1945, "Difficulties are encountered here because nearly all not yet verified Poles are for unknown reasons isolated in 'camps,' their property plundered, and they continue to be treated as germans [sic]. Despite our intervention these Poles continue to be wronged. Expulsion occurred without the notification of the *starosta*."[70] The Olsztyn District Nationality Committee sought the release from the Jawor camp in February 1946 of three Warmiaks of Polish origin who served in the German army. Following a thorough investigation of their Polish origins, the matter was referred to the Ministry of National Defense (*Ministerstwo Obrony Narodowej* or MON). Not yet released as of 28 August 1946, they were transferred to the dangerous work of clearing land mines.[71]

On 16 May 1945 the deputy director of the 4th Department of the Cracow Provincial Office of Public Security (*Wojewódzki Urząd Bezpieczeństwa*

Publicznego or WUBP) reported that about half of the prisoners in the Jaworzno camp died because of cutbacks in their food supply, part of which the prison administration sold to cover other expenses. He also found that the commanding officer allowed guards to take *Volksdeutsche* home to work for them and that at night guards took female *Volksdeutsche* to their quarters and raped them. On 5 September 1945 its detainees included 640 *Volksdeutsche* in category II, 264 in category III, 27 in category IV, and 223 *Leistungspolen*.[72]

The records of the camp in Świętochłowice indicate that 1,855 of 3,265 prisoners died between March and November 1945. The camp commandant Salomon Morel took revenge on inmates for the murder of his family in the Holocaust. He was removed in November 1945, only to be reassigned to run a prison and later another labor camp. After the fall of communism, Polish prosecutors charged him with responsibility for the deaths of at least 1,583 prisoners, but Israel, to which he fled in 1994, refused two requests for his extradition.[73]

More than 6,000 individuals, including residents of the surrounding villages, passed through the camp at Łambinowice (Lamsdorf).[74] Following a fact-finding tour of Niemodlin County, a PPR-MBP commission issued a report on 22 February 1946:

> This camp exists without any legal basis and is not maintained or used by any higher authorities. . . . The guards live off of robbing the prisoners and the local population, which lives in fear. Drinking sprees and violence are on the daily agenda in the camp. . . .
> The director at that time was a certain Czesław Gemborski [Gęborski] who cruelly abused prisoners. He is also guilty of murdering 46 Poles in the camp in October [1945] and with his own hands shot an activist of the Union of Poles in Germany well-known in the county.
> The population of the county is convinced that the leadership of the camp is allowed to commit this murder out of hatred for the native population, which [the camp's leadership] regards as German, and a desire for plunder.

Twenty-one-year-old Gęborski ran the camp on the model of the Nazi concentration camp in which he had been a prisoner. He was arrested on 4 October 1945 but was released by the end of the year and returned to duty in the MBP in Katowice, thanks to his connections and a relative who was deputy commander of the county militia.[75]

At a briefing for subordinates 8–9 April 1945, the director of the MBP Department of Prisons and Camps denied that the labor camps were modeled on those of the Nazis. Rather, the law required the indefinite detention of traitors to the Polish nation. But abuses continued. On 27 February 1946 the director of the camp in Złotów wrote to the Pomeranian WUBP, "I request attention to the matter of the personnel of my camp because in the face of inordinate difficulties and burdens as a result of ill will of the State Treasury employees of the Camp, I have no desire to work. Here one has to shoot on the spot and beat or resign from the function of director." Common criminals imprisoned with *Volksdeutsche* proved no less hostile, denouncing them and even physically attacking them. In effect the camps often did resemble German concentration camps.[76]

On 18 March 1946 the governor of Gdańsk Province ordered the creation of a Provincial Verification Commission to visit every county to correct errors made by local verification commissions.[77] Following visits to the labor camps of Potulice and Rudak near Toruń, the commission concluded that there were hundreds if not thousands of prisoners in these camps who were imprisoned by the Soviet and Polish military merely because they were German citizens whose claims to be Polish were not believed. In addition, hundreds of Mazurs who spoke Polish were forced to work on farms controlled by the Soviet military and not allowed to undergo verification of their nationality.[78]

The commission continued its investigations in 1947. On 7 May 1947 a delegate reported that individuals of Polish origin were detained in forty-six camps. But MBP officials believed that too many individuals had already been verified as Poles and that natives who served in the Wehrmacht and did not desert did not deserve to be verified.[79]

Most camps ceased to exist by mid-1947, but the remainder were not liquidated until 1950. In February 1948 the forced labor camp of Potulice had 422 inmates with German citizenship and 4,710 *Volksdeutsche*, including 1,402 children without parents, elderly individuals, and other family members of inmates. Another 3,200 German citizens and 12,347 *Volksdeutsche* under the camp's jurisdiction worked outside the camp. Between 1945 and 1949 nearly 4,500 prisoners died.[80]

In Silesia the high mortality rate in the camps drew the attention of the central authorities. Service in the German army and widespread DVL registration branded inhabitants of Polish Silesia as "renegades" and "traitors." In a report on 15 March 1946 MBP inspectors noted serious conflicts between "Silesians" and personnel from outside of the area, mainly from the Dąbrowa Basin, where DVL registration was voluntary.[81] Ossowski reported that some from the Basin sought revenge for wrongs suffered during the occupation at the hands of gendarmes from Silesia speaking the Silesian dialect.[82] On 2 April 1946 the central authorities distributed the report "Our Attitude toward Silesians" to camp staffs explaining that Silesians are also Poles and that DVL registration in Upper Silesia was coerced; even category II did not necessarily mean membership in the German nation. It called on the personnel to "actively cooperate in the struggle for the soul of the Silesian, remembering that he is a brother who suffered much and if he offends us with some shortcomings, it is mainly not his fault—and that besides these, he has valuable virtues."[83]

Looters

Autochthons and *Volksdeutsche* faced not only depredation and summary expulsion or forced labor at the hands of the Soviet and Polish military, the local administration, and security services. They also faced looters (*szabrownicy*) who followed in the wake of the front, with the areas formerly under German control among the worst hit. In much of the Recovered Lands, the first Poles from Poland to make contact with natives, even before the arrival of officials, were looters. Heightened nationalism among Poles from Central Poland who filled positions in the official apparatus inclined them to overlook all but the worst abuses in the formerly German territory.[84]

Nearly six years of the brutal Nazi occupation necessarily had a demoralizing effect. In a study of Polish society in the *Generalgouvernement,* Jan Tomasz Gross concluded, "The overwhelming picture is one of social disorganization and breakdown of social bonds. Constant fear for one's life, the unpredictability of German terror, and finally, anarchy . . . contributed to the disintegration of social life." He quotes an underground newspaper from 19 March 1944: "Demoralization, resulting from prolonged war and acts committed on purpose by the occupier, is reaching deep into society. Banditry and blackmail are plaguing the population of cities and countryside. Unfortunately, banditry often appears in the disguise of work motivated by high ideals." Czesław Miłosz observed, "The killing of a man presents no great moral problem . . . The nearness of death destroys shame." In an article published in August 1945, Kazimierz Wyka claimed that no one could survive on the rationing system that the Nazis imposed on the population without bribery. Amoral economic activities even became a patriotic duty. Looking for opportunities for plunder, chasing after loot, replaced ordinary commerce. In March 1945 Wyka predicted that people from the *Generalgouvernement,* used to morally corrupt trade practices, would in the coming months "infect the Western lands."[85]

The brutality of the German occupation fed a desire for revenge to satisfy a primitive sense of justice. Looting frequently assumed the patriotic cloak of retaliation against the Germans. A widespread belief in the right to compensation for material losses during the war justified plundering German property. The concept of law and order of Polish security forces often did not differ from that of the looters.[86]

Not all who decided to "go west" intended to stay. Instead, they joined the ranks of the looters, even dismantling whole houses brick by brick to take back to their home villages. Some settled temporarily in the Recovered Lands to "legalize" their activity and establish a base for their operations. Officials hesitated to act against them, not wanting to discourage settlement or to be accused of defending "Germans."⁸⁷ When the PUR suggested that settlers in the Recovered Lands transfer the farm they left behind to the state, the MAP overruled it on 27 April 1945. The MAP sought the quickest, widest settlement of the Recovered Lands and opposed any measure that might discourage settlers. One result reported by an MZO inspector in September 1946 was that some returned to their original farms after harvesting crops on farms in the Recovered Lands, leaving the area bereft of all food.⁸⁸

As the head of the Provisional State Agency for Gdańsk Province reported on 24 May 1945,

> The creation of the province of Gdańsk fomented a "gold fever" in society, so everyone from all parts of Poland by all roads and means of communication are rushing to this Klondike, and with the sole goal not of work but of a desire to rob and loot. Simply, a pathological condition of lawlessness arose in this terrain because almost everyone regards the property in homes, factories, enterprises as his property and that he can quietly take as much as possible. . . . Searches carried out in trains, on roads and in planes yield such results that it is a disgrace not only to speak about such things but even to write about them. They are taking away pictures cut out of frames, sheets, linen, things of historical value, in general whatever is possible. Counteraction through prohibitions of removal, controls, have so far had little effect because of a lack of professional organs of Civic Militia trained for this purpose.⁸⁹

"The first looters appeared in Olsztyn already in March [1945]," according to a prewar ZPwN activist.

> They loaded everything they could onto trucks and drove away. They went from house to house, looking for treasures. They took the best carpets, china, glass, and pictures from the houses—everything that fell into their hands. Their greed was so great that sometimes they took things that they then discarded in the street, looking for other things.⁹⁰

They made no distinction among the locals, whether Germans, Mazurs, or Warmiaks.⁹¹

After touring Mazuria in mid-August 1945, the Protestant minister Rev. Feliks Gloeh reported that he found his trip by train unbearable: "The overwhelming majority of passengers were common 'looters'—thieves of abandoned property, constantly traveling between Warsaw and the newly attached provinces, there and back with the goal of achieving personal gain in a vile way."⁹²

All this hindered natives from identifying themselves as Poles. In June 1945 *Gazeta Robotnicza* reported that the population of Opole Silesia "currently is beginning to disparage Polishness and to request in filling out forms to be listed as Germans. They don't want anything to do with those Poles who bring with them the greatest disgrace—looting—to the heroic name of Pole."⁹³

Looting long remained a troubling issue. Following complaints by Mazurs, the Węgorzewo County UZ reported on 14 January 1946 that many instances of robbery went unpunished. "Recently audacious looters plunder Mazurian and German homes even during the day, taking the remaining food, grain, peas, potatoes, clothes, dishes, and the like." Yet the head of the commune did not inform the *starosta*. The lack of elementary concern over crimes committed against Mazurs negatively affected their willingness to register as Poles. In one village, where the majority spoke Polish, the inhabitants had delayed registering until recently.[94] When in April 1946 a District Nationality Committee sought to gather data on robberies of natives, the chairman of the County Nationality Committee in Lidzbark, Warmia, replied, "There is no family in the whole county which in the past year was not robbed. . . . To detail the foregoing data is simply something impossible."[95]

To bring a halt to the activities of looters, on 22 February 1946 the Ministry of Recovered Lands prohibited the removal of goods from the entire territory under its jurisdiction. In May 1946 the governor of Olsztyn Province met with the governors of Warsaw and Białystok Provinces to agree on a common effort to halt the invasion of looters, but a month later he reported that the situation had not changed.[96]

The Confiscation of German Property

The PKWN Manifesto dated 22 July 1944 declared the confiscation of German property.[97] On 6 September 1944 the PKWN expropriated the property of Germans, traitors, and collaborators.[98] On 2 March 1945 a decree "Concerning Deserted and Abandoned Property," freed "German" farms for settlement, especially by deportees from the East. Passed by the KRN on 6 May 1945, Article 2 of Part 1 declared "the property of German citizens or individuals who fled to the enemy is abandoned property in the understanding of this decree."[99] It made no exception for property of German citizens of Polish origin.

Flight, evacuation, and the casualties of war resulted in the abandonment of more than half the farms in regions like Opole Silesia. They needed to be secured from plundering and prepared for spring planting. On 29 January 1945 Governor Zawadzki ordered the confiscation of all abandoned farms and the property of German citizens. On 22 February 1945 a provincial Liquidation-Control Commission assumed jurisdiction over these properties and those of category I and II *Volksdeutsche*. Individuals who appropriated such properties rarely notified the administrative authorities as required. As late as 12 July

1946 the Poznań District Office of Liquidation (*Urząd Likwidacyjny* or UL) reminded the population of this obligation.[100]

Repatriates from the *kresy* ceded to the Soviet Union began to arrive in large numbers in the borderlands in April 1945. As a railhead of the wide-gauge tracks used by the Soviets, Kluczbork County was overrun from the very beginning. Rather than wait days or weeks to be transported further west, repatriates occupied whatever farm appealed to them, whether the owner was present or not, disregarding even natives who spoke pure Polish, treating the local population, part of which was Protestant, as "Germans and krauts."[101]

To accelerate the Polonization of the Recovered Lands, the Provisional Government decreed on 12 June 1945 that all property in the territory that belonged to the German state or administration, Nazi organizations or its members, or citizens of the Reich of German nationality to be the property of the Polish state. German citizens of Polish nationality on property that came under the decree had only the right to manage and use the property until their Polish citizenship was confirmed.[102] On 18 June 1945 Governor Zawadzki ordered officials in Opole Silesia to remove Germans "unconditionally" from their farms and expel them or put the whole family in detention when a repatriate or settler arrived to take over the farm. In no case were officials to allow Germans who were returning from beyond the Oder-Neisse line to reoccupy their homes and farms. Instead, they were to be sent back to Germany or arrested if they resisted.[103] In the first half of 1945 the newly installed Polish officials at all levels typically identified these returnees as German.[104]

In September 1945 the inspector for settlement in Miastko County, Western Pomerania, issued similar instructions concerning the appropriation by Poles of a German farm or dwelling.[105] The Settlement Committee of Warsaw Province, which included Działdowo, issued guidelines for the new territories on 12 June 1945, flatly stating, "The German population loses all rights. It is treated as criminal, which is temporarily free. It is to be used for work," without any mention of *Volksdeutsche* or German citizens of Polish origin.[106]

During the German occupation Polish farmers in areas incorporated into the Reich whose property was confiscated often ended up working as farm hands on their own farms. Now the natives in many areas of the Recovered Lands had a similar experience. Deportees from the *kresy* were quartered on farms or laid claim to farms still inhabited by their owners, forcibly moving in with them with the expectation that eventually the owners would be expelled as Germans. In some villages every single farm housed two families. Conflicts were even worse in urban areas where a significant portion of the town population could claim to be of Polish origin: whole families were sent to detention camps as Germans, and newcomers took over their homes and businesses.

As Liah Greenfield concludes,

> No individual and no group of people are genetically bound to define themselves in one or another fashion, and as the original interests which gave rise to particular national identities disappear, a change of national identity is not impossible. Apart from deep changes in the economy, other structural changes—for instance ones brought on by the outcome of a war and occupation—may result in the redefinition of a particular identity.[107]

Because national identity is mutable, the maltreatment that autochthons and *Volksdeutsche* encountered as the war ended inclined many of them to conclude that their primary loyalty lay elsewhere than with the Polish nation.

[6]
The Initial Polish Government Nationality Measures

AT FIRST POLISH officials, particularly at the local level, shared the view of the general public that Polish citizens registered on the DVL were traitors and collaborators.[1] Crucial in the establishment of Polish administration, operational groups dispatched by the PPR consisted of members of the party and its PPS ally who often had little knowledge of local conditions. Antoni Alster, who led the operational group in Pomerania, regarded its inhabitants as politically unreliable because they had "besmirched" themselves through registration in DVL category III. Such officials sought above all to strengthen the position of the new political regime. As a result many *Volksdeutsche* suffered mistreatment and lived in constant fear of being declared German. Security organs, which had a decisive voice in the "rehabilitation" of *Volksdeutsche,* also took little interest in where and when registration on the DVL was mandatory.[2]

Party leaders, however, split over the fate of the *Volksdeutsche*. Berman thought they should be excluded from of the national community. Some thought that each case should undergo a judicial inquiry. Regional activists from Silesia advocated a rapid expulsion of category I *Volksdeutsche,* the possibility of rehabilitation of those in category II through individual judicial procedures, and a legislative act recognizing the Polish citizenship of those in categories III and IV. The belief that the German authorities had coerced registration on the DVL as well as the importance of maintaining the integrity of the workforce in Silesia lay behind this view, largely realized under Governor Zawadzki.[3]

Ultimately, Warsaw focused on the question of coercion in DVL registration in a particular region as the decisive factor. Still, liquidating the legal repercussions of the DVL would take more than five years. The process may have contributed significantly to the integration into Polish society of many of the *Volksdeutsche* in Silesia.[4] But the conflict engendered by the issue and the countless errors and abuses that marked the process alienated others.

Because in Wartheland, which encompassed Poznań Province, registration on the DVL had generally been voluntary and was perceived as such by the population, it took a harsher view of *Volksdeutsche* than in other areas incorporated into Reich. Moreover, a significant number of *Volksdeutsche* in the province aided the German occupier in various ways. To many this appeared to be an escalation of the historic conflict when *Ostforschung* and Prussian attempts at Germanization centered on the region. Indeed, many advocates of the *Polska myśl zachodnia* were based in Poznań before and after the war, including the Western Institute and the PZZ. Thus, officials treated *Volksdeutsche* as Germans. When on 12 February 1945 the Kościan County *starosta* directed Germans to register, he included "Poles with red and green German listings," i.e., categories III and IV. Similarly, the order of the provincial plenipotentiary on 14 April 1945 to register all Germans included both *Reichsdeutsche* and *Volksdeutsche*.[5]

The question of *Volksdeutsche* posed particular problems in Działdowo County, with its ties to Mazuria, its troubled history in interwar Poland, and the predominantly Protestant faith of its population. In 1939 the Nazis reincorporated the county into East Prussia but placed much of the rest of Warsaw Province within the *Generalgouvernement*. As a memorandum of the Presidium of the Działdowo PRN to the PRM in February 1945 pointed out, "The problem of the *Volksdeutsche* in Działdowo County presents itself fundamentally differently than that of the *Volksdeutsche* in the other counties of Warsaw Province." The Nazis recognized all inhabitants of the county who were German citizens before 1920 as *Volksdeutsche*—simply a resumption of German citizenship. Mazurs who identified themselves as Polish faced the threat of death, imprisonment, or denial of all means of livelihood. The memorandum warned, in prosecuting all *Volksdeutsche,* the Polish authorities would, like the Germans, deny that Mazurs are Polish; and more than half a million Mazurs in East Prussia and 300,000 Mazurian migrants in the Ruhr were watching to see what happens in Działdowo County.[6] The prominent pro-Polish Mazurs who addressed the Provisional Government on 26 February 1945 also claimed that the Nazis registered inhabitants of the Działdowo County in category II "without their consent."[7] Indeed, they included some members of the Małłek family.[8]

During a discussion in the RM on 23 February 1945, Bierut politicized the issue by declaring the necessity of "attracting precisely the German population to combat our political opponents." Michał Kaczorowski raised two points that did not always receive the attention they deserved: it was wrong to recognize as German all those on the DVL, and "the whole problem today boils down to who will decide who is a Pole and who is not."⁹ A decree on 28 February 1945 provided for the recognition of the rights of citizenship or "rehabilitation" for *Leistungspolen* and *Volksdeutsche* in categories II, III, and IV residing in the lands incorporated by Nazi Germany who did not voluntarily register on the DVL and whose behavior displayed "Polish national distinctiveness."¹⁰

The decree drew the criticism of Warsaw Governor Mazur. In his report on 9 March 1945, following his tour of Działdowo County and southern East Prussia, he advocated recognizing the Polish citizenship of Mazurs, Warmiaks, and Silesians in categories III and IV without closing the door for those in category II, calling to account only those who collaborated with the Germans. He believed registration on the DVL in Działdowo was coerced. German military needs dictated registering draft-age sons as Germans while their parents received Polish identity cards. Mrs. Rycicka from a village in Działdowo County was registered as a Pole and deprived of her farm, but her three sons were registered as category III *Volksdeutsche*. When as a German soldier the eldest son's protest brought no result, he requested to be removed from the DVL and discharged. Released from the military after a half year, he disappeared within two weeks of returning home. The governor thought that natives, not wanting to abandon their homeland, demonstrated some ignorance regarding nationality in registering as Germans. He cited their divergent self-identification—"we be Mazurs" *(my som Mazurzy)*—but emphasized "the necessity of rescuing this population, which despite six hundred years of Germanization did not lose its Polish speech."¹¹

Zylberberg also reacted to the February decree in his report on 2 May 1945 following his tour of Silesia, noting that all Silesians, except Polish activists, were automatically inscribed in the DVL, most independently of their will. Furthermore, Silesians considered strict acceptance of DVL categories improper: some in category II were less guilty than many in categories III and IV.¹²

Hastily prepared, the decree of 28 February 1945 was superseded by the law passed by the KRN "Concerning the Exclusion of Hostile Elements from Polish Society" on 6 May 1945. It did not prejudge the mere fact of registration on the DVL, except for those in category I. Like the decree, the law provided for the rehabilitation of *Leistungspolen* and *Volksdeutsche* in categories III and IV of the DVL who were registered against their will and whose behavior manifested "Polish national distinctiveness." Following a declaration of "loyalty to the Polish Nation and democratic State," they retained full rights of citizenship, and the administrative authorities publicized the declaration and issued a provisional certificate. In areas where the MAP determined DVL registration was not universally mandatory, applicants also had to show that registration took place against their will or under constraint. Whoever had information about the applicant freely registering on the DVL or not behaving in accord with "Polish national distinctiveness" was obliged to report this to the offices of public security or special prosecutor, which decided whether to refer the case to a magistrate's court for a public hearing. The applicant received a permanent certificate if within six months no official raised any objections. Most rehabilitations took place in this manner.[13]

Those in category II and the few in category III who received irrevocable membership in the German state had to seek rehabilitation by a more difficult judicial route. At the cost of the applicant, the local magistrate's court published an announcement of the hearing and invited those who knew of activities of the applicant harmful to the Polish nation to inform the court. The Office of Revenue took over all property of the applicant. If the court recognized the applicant's defense as valid, it confirmed the applicant's full rights of citizenship and the right to the sequestered property. Those whose applications were rejected were interned for an unspecified period, stripped of all civil rights, and deprived of their property.[14] Even if they successfully completed the rehabilitation process, a decree of 30 October 1945 legalized the de facto ownership of their property as of 1 August 1945, and instead the state treasury would assign a property of equal value and quality in place of seized property.[15] This decree did not apply to category III and IV *Volksdeutsche,* who retained title to their property unless denied rehabilitation.

The law of 6 May 1945 perpetuated Nazi nationality practices, which blurred the distinction between perpetrator and victim, forcing even those coerced into DVL registration to confirm their loyalty to the Polish nation. "Rehabilitation" implied guilt. The law also accepted the Nazi classification of *Volksdeutsche.* Those in category I had no possibility of rehabilitation though exceptions occurred, particularly in Rybnik County.[16]

Regulations for implementation of the law issued on 25 May 1945 empowered governors to set the deadline for declarations of loyalty but no later than 31 August 1945 (subsequently 31 October 1945). Deported individuals had until one month after their return but no later than one year after the end of the war.[17] These deadlines greatly underestimated the task. A decree on 6 June 1945 also created a financial obstacle by setting the application fee for rehabilitation at 500 złoty. In addition, the return of sequestered property required payment of 100 to 5,000 złoty to cover costs.[18]

Volksdeutsche denied rehabilitation had a right to appeal, though expulsion often ensued immediately following the revocation of Polish citizenship or even before.[19] On 5 November 1947 the *starosta* of Gostynin County, Warsaw Province, reported that 20 percent of "germans" [sic] deprived of Polish citizenship in October 1947 appealed to the District Court.[20]

Volksdeutsche could also apply to President Bierut for a pardon or a commutation of their sentences. Nevertheless, a commutation could be harsh. On

1 August 1946 the Ministry of Justice appealed the sentence of indefinite detention imposed by the Łódź County court on Waleria Leokadia Benke (née Nowak). Her husband declared his membership in the German nation in 1940, after which he was drafted into the Wehrmacht and had not yet returned; she was registered in DVL category III in 1941. She did not speak German and, moreover, raised her children "in a Polish spirit" and maintained close relations with her Polish family and Polish society. Also, her four small children and her ailing elderly Polish mother required her care. The ministry recommended that she be released from detention but not that the confiscation of her property be reversed.[21]

Calls for leniency were rare. The director of the Nowy Tomyśl Office of the Treasury on 30 June 1945 observed, "Doubtless there are among them many good poles [sic], who nevertheless went astray because of the huge propaganda of the occupier and submitted an application."[22] The stigma of their status would long mark all *Volksdeutsche* without exception. They were barred from benefiting from agricultural reform. Official bureaus noted their past in their individual records, to which security agencies had access. References required for promotions to all positions in government service and the party or social organizations included this information as did the certificates issued by the local administration to those applying for admission to higher education. Nearly all letters of reference issued between 1945 and 1950 included a statement whether the candidate or parents had applied to the DVL.[23]

The law did not resolve all of the complex issues posed by the DVL. Some local officials long did not distinguish between ethnic Germans and *Volksdeutsche* of Polish origin, simply classifying them all as Germans.[24] The issue of whether registration on the DVL involved coercion continued to be the main source of controversy and conflict. Obviously, the pressure that Nazi officials exerted as well as an individual's perception of the threat posed could vary widely. On 12 June 1945 the governor of Pomerania decided that compulsory registration on the DVL began only with Forster's decree on 22 February 1942.[25] On 20 July 1945 the Poznań governor published a proclamation flatly stating that DVL registration had not been universally coerced in the province and declaring in bold letters the obligation to report immediately information concerning *Volksdeutsche* in categories III and IV who registered voluntarily or whose behavior "could not be reconciled with Polish national distinctiveness."[26]

In some cases the authorities acted solely on the basis of denunciations. On 2 July 1945 the Poznań Provincial Office of Information and Propaganda (*Wojewódzki Urząd Informacji i Propagandy* or WUIiP) directed the chairmen of national councils in towns with more than 10,000 inhabitants to organize neighborhood committees (reminiscent of similar committees organized by the Nazis) to assist administrative organs "in the detection of enemies and traitors to the Polish nation, actively cooperating with the occupier." The Western Institute collected the evidence.[27]

In Czechoslovakia a presidential decree on 19 May 1945 classified as German above all those who declared German nationality in a census after 1929 and, secondarily, individuals who after 1929 declared themselves to be German or joined a German national group, organization, or political party, except for victims of the Nazis who demonstrated loyalty to the state.[28] In Poland the law of 6 May 1945 gave officials more latitude in defining who was German, though changes in both countries soon altered the number of individuals affected.

Rehabilitation in Cracow Province

The nearly automatic administrative rehabilitation of category III and IV *Volksdeutsche* where registration had been compulsory prompted widespread protests claiming that registration had actually been voluntary. That the Reich incorporated only part of Cracow Province complicated the dispute.

In late May 1945 representative bodies in several communities passed resolutions similar to the one passed in Alwernia:

> We express our regret at the release of *Volksdeutsche* as the main culprits in the people's misfortune. The Communal National Council appeals to the responsible elements for a change in the decree regarding the release of *Volksdeutsche* and an immediate halt to the further releases from the labor camp Jaworzno, bearing in mind that those criminals of humanity should suffer appropriately severe punishment for their deeds.[29]

Even a PPR meeting in Trzebinia, Chrzanów County, on 27 May 1945 protested, claiming that out of 3,500 Poles in the community only the 600 *Volksdeutsche* cooperated in oppressing the population. "We demand the immediate isolation of these deliberate traitors of the fatherland."[30]

In response the Cracow governor on 6 June 1945 notified the public prosecutor of the Special Court in Cracow that, although a third of Chrzanów County had been part of the *Generalgouvernement,* where DVL registration was not mandatory, *Volksdeutsche* from both parts of the county were released from detention. Since merely 7 percent of the county's population was on the DVL, he requested that Chrzanów along with Biała, Wadowice, and Żywiec Counties, which were divided during the occupation, come under the decree of 4 November 1944, which made traitors subject to criminal prosecution, instead of the law concerning *Volksdeutsche*.[31]

The dispute reached its apogee in Biała County. In Wilamowice, which originated in the early medieval period as a settlement of migrants from

Flanders, Friesland, and Scotland, and whose inhabitants spoke a unique Germanic language, the Provisional National Council already on 18 March 1945 declared that registration had been compulsory and on 30 June 1945 requested that the governor so classify the community. The council conveniently claimed that inhabitants, three-fourths of whom were on the DVL, mostly in categories III and IV, were of English or Dutch (not German) origin, had remained faithful to the Polish nation and that the Nazis resorted to terror and harassment.[32] But some were not so loyal. The MO compiled a list of members of the SA and arrested them. Others—mostly members of the SS and SA—fled with the German army.[33]

As if in response, on 9 July 1945 the national council of neighboring Wilkowice declared that compulsory registration did not occur there or in most of the rest of Biała County.[34] Other communities in the county similarly denied coercion in DVL registration. The governor later claimed that, aside from any patriotic motivation, envy of the model farms of Wilamowice accounted for the intense campaign against it.[35] Perhaps with Wilamowice in mind, in July 1945 he identified Biała County as the only one where coercion had occurred and directed that there *Volksdeutsche* submit a declaration of loyalty by 20 August 1945.[36] Yet, on 1 September 1945 the Biała County *starosta* reported that only 3,562 out of 6,000 eligible *Volksdeutsche* made the declaration. He conjectured that some had been hostile toward Poles and Polishness during the war and feared being investigated. Others lost or destroyed their German identity cards, and fees for replacement cards ran as high as 10,000 złoty because of abuses. An extension of the deadline to 30 October 1945 yielded only 395 additional declarations.[37]

Rehabilitation in Silesia

Disputes over the culpability of *Volksdeutsche* arose in Silesia as well. In preparation for the expulsion of Germans, Governor Zawadzki on 2 July 1945 directed officials in prewar Polish Silesia to register all *Reichsdeutsche* and category I *Volksdeutsche* as well as category II *Volksdeutsche* with "no prospect of their rehabilitation" by 20 July 1945 and to forbid their residence in that part the province after 24 July 1945.[38]

Concerned that Poles were being classified as Germans, Bishop Adamski had complained to Minister of Public Administration Ochab on 14 June 1945.[39] Although on 10 July 1945 the governor ordered resettlement commissions to ensure that only indubitable Germans were expelled, Adamski complained to Zawadzki that his order of 2 July 1945 resulted in injustices. At a meeting of the WRN, Rev. Rudolf Adamczyk, seen as a pro-Polish "zealous defender of

Silesians" and a representative of the bishop, accused the administration of incompetence and ignorance of the historical realities of Upper Silesia.[40] He appealed for a simplification of the rehabilitation process, the abolition of fees, and an end to the repressive measures directed against category II *Volksdeutsche*. The diocesan newspaper *Gość Niedzielny* published a report on the meeting despite the opposition of the authorities.

Addressing the KRN on 22 July 1945, Zawadzki seemingly accepted the criticism: "One cannot regard the *Volksdeutsche* in Silesia as traitors of the type of *Volksdeutsche* from Warsaw. This is an element that speaks Polish. There, 70 percent [of the population] consists of such people. The operation, which is undertaken for the purpose of rehabilitation, does not suffice. The innocent should be turned into Poles."

Furthermore, he referred specifically to Adamski's recommendation during the war that the inhabitants of Upper Silesia register on the DVL. A speaker from the PZZ enthusiastically endorsed the governor's stand, particularly his public recognition that the bishop acted in conjunction with the government-in-exile.[41] The attitude toward Adamski changed once Polish communists were firmly in power and battled the Catholic Church. On 14 March 1949 Minister of Public Administration Wolski referred to Adamski and other bishops "who disgracefully distinguished themselves during the period of occupation not only by conciliatory but plainly servile relations with the Nazi occupier."[42]

Still, officials encountered difficulties. On 10 August 1945 the Rybnik *starosta* reported:

> The directive of the Silesia-Dąbrowa governor of 2 July of this year began the operation of the resettlement of Germans. It seemed that the matter was clear. Nevertheless, practice showed that here many serious problems emerged, above all, whom to regard as a person of German nationality. . . . The problem was not easy to solve because—especially in the county's rural areas—many communal documents were completely destroyed and the communal authorities often did not know what group a given citizen belonged to. The cooperation of social circles in this operation proved very positive.

Of 1,345 individuals placed in camps, only 290 were expelled. The Provincial Verification Commission freed the rest, wrongly in his view. "I hear that local society received this large number of freed Germans with murmurs raising the issue that Germans are freed but not the Poles taken by the Red Army. The current operation to free Poles from [Soviet] labor camps will have the positive effect of calming minds."[43]

Local security officials in particular were unhappy with alleged lenient treatment of category II *Volksdeutsche*. On 31 July 1945 the MO in Ustroń expressed his dissatisfaction to the Cieszyn PUIiP with the release of 163 category II *Volksdeutsche* designated for expulsion. "Naturally, each of them professed to be a 100-percent Pole, forgetting about their actions during the German occupation and their bowing down to Hitler and his co-workers." They returned to their homes and tried to throw out the repatriates who occupied their property. The PUR, however, ordered that the repatriates should continue to reside on these properties.[44]

Problems with the Law of 6 May 1945

In Działdowo County only 878 of 12,000 *Volksdeutsche* applied for rehabilitation. In Łódź Province only a relatively small portion of those in category III applied. Local officials in Warsaw Province blamed the meager results on costs imposed on applicants. But other factors also played a role. Many *Volksdeutsche* were poorly educated, even illiterate. Some applied after the deadline, claiming a lack of information. The negative reaction of the Polish population also discouraged some from applying. The enormous number of cases that came before the courts made the prospect of a quick decision unlikely. In Upper Silesia, where solely those in category II had to petition the courts, only 3,618 cases out of some 100,000 were decided by the end of 1945, 3,213 positively and 405 negatively.[45]

In addition, during the war many lost documents attesting to their Polishness, and local archives were often destroyed. The Biała County *starosta* charged that many *Volksdeutsche* destroyed their documents to claim a lower category. Because of a lack of instructions, he did not issue new certificates or, as of mid-June 1945, initiate the process of rehabilitation.[46] The Żywiec *starosta* reported on 24 July 1945 that a whole series of individuals without the required identity papers applied for rehabilitation as *Volksdeutsche* in categories III and IV.[47]

Nazi files that alone distinguished between those in categories I and II and included rejected DVL applications were crucial. In Biała County security officials seized the files from the administration by force. On 14 June 1945 the *starosta* claimed that in some cases security officials altered the categories of *Volksdeutsche* "for purposes of intelligence"—security officials frequently forced *Volksdeutsche* to cooperate in return for their freedom.[48] A similar conflict occurred in Wągrowiec County. Ultimately, on 4 April 1947, the Poznań governor instructed all subordinate offices to search for DVL files, treat them as secret, and send them immediately to the WUBP. In 1948, during a verification of PPR members, the party excluded individuals accused of destroying

DVL files—the Chodzież County *starosta* allegedly burned 2,000 DVL applications.[49]

Already in May 1945 the public began to demand sanctions against individuals whose applications to the DVL were rejected. But after consulting prosecutors, the Poznań governor stated on 10 October 1945 that the law did not require such individuals to undergo rehabilitation nor did they come under any political sanction unless their applications indicated "a strong current of ill will."[50] Chrzanów County, where the German authorities rejected 2,000 applications, illustrates the dimensions of the problem. Thus, those registered on the DVL against their will suffered more consequences than those who sought to register but failed. In 1946 a commission examining the policy toward *Volksdeutsche* in Poznań Province concluded that the law of 6 May 1945 erred in focusing on registration rather than on applications to the DVL.[51]

Frequent violations occurred in the treatment of *Volksdeutsche*. Prior to any court judgment, officials removed *Volksdeutsche* from their farms, placed them in labor camps, and distributed their property to repatriates or even to local Poles, resulting in conflicts when rehabilitated *Volksdeutsche* sought the return of their property. At least initially, the PUR made little distinction among the categories of *Volksdeutsche* in allocating their farms. In mid-June 1945, a report at a meeting of *starostowie* of Poznań Province indicated that in some counties repatriates were driving masses of *Volksdeutsche* in categories III and IV from their farms, an operation at times unpleasantly reminiscent of the infamous German "round-ups."[52] Carried out by elements of the MBP, they did not spare the rehabilitated. Whole families, including children, were detained and their personal property confiscated. Some were sent to labor camps where their labor was sold by the camp administration. The round-ups caused considerable consternation, with youths fleeing to the forests. Even the *starosta* was not informed about the basis for the operation.[53] Employers, not wanting to lose free or cheap labor, prevented *Volksdeutsche* from seeking rehabilitation. The Poznań municipal president intervened on 24 August 1945 to facilitate this for those employed in villages in Poznań County.[54]

Some administrators charged exorbitant fees for accepting declarations of loyalty from *Volksdeutsche* in categories III and IV, in Poznań Province as much as 6,000 złoty. On 13 August 1945 the Ministry of Justice ruled that such fees had no legal basis. In the WRN on 5 September 1945, the governor commented that this was an unacceptable means for communities to raise money. But one councilor favored high fees as a means of impeding the majority of *Volksdeutsche* from rejoining Polish society.[55]

As a result of their treatment in this initial period and other factors, more *Volksdeutsche* requested permission to leave the country than applied for rehabilitation.[56]

The Verification of Autochthons in the First Half of 1945

To accommodate quickly the masses of repatriates and settlers arriving in the Recovered Lands, local officials expelled German citizens on their own authority, often with little or no inquiry into their nationality. Also, the predominance of women, children, and the elderly in the Recovered Lands seemed an unnecessary burden in rebuilding the country.[57] This created an urgent need for the establishment of criteria and procedures for identifying German citizens of Polish nationality. But an incessant drumbeat called for the expulsion of all Germans, which often took priority over verification of their nationality. Moreover, officials had difficulty distinguishing among individuals of German nationality, *Volksdeutsche* in various categories, and German citizens of Polish origin, often making it impossible to know precisely whom their references to "Germans" comprise.[58]

Bernadetta Nitschke attributes the enormous difficulties that nationality verification encountered from the very beginning to a lack of knowledge on the part of Polish officials concerning the state of national conscousness among the inhabitants of the Recovered Lands and a lack of understanding on the part of the inhabitants of the significance of the verification process, which in most cases officials made no effort to explain. Moreover, official actions in many areas undermined the trust required for a greater effort to lay out the basis and purpose of verification to make a significant difference.[59] Nitschke does not question the feasibility of a verification process achieving its goal of sorting Poles from Germans in the borderlands.[60]

Piotr Madajczyk regards the lack of a verification process that took into account the regional and historic differences between the population from Central Poland and the autochthons of the Recovered Lands as a lost last chance to peacefully create an open and resilient society as opposed to the Soviet plan of secluding Poland within narrow ethnic boundaries.[61] "Recognition of [Silesians] as Poles, however, would have required a decided broadening of the concept of Polishness, which the nation, severely affected by occupation, was not completely capable of before the war, and all the less after the painful experiences of the second world war," as Silesian writer Bieniasz observed after the fall of communism.[62]

Nationalist assumptions led the authorities to underestimate the difficulty of identifying supposedly Polish German citizens. Germanization meant that not all alleged Poles, particularly the younger generations, spoke Polish. Others spoke a regional dialect, which outsiders often took as evidence that they were not Polish. Also, many Germans knew at least some Polish and might pass for Poles. A traveler between Poznań and Szczecin reported on

27 August 1945 that the German population was intensively learning Polish and looking for every possible way of establishing a connection with Polishness.[63] Thus, Governor Zawadzki argued, Germanization "made it necessary to separate the Polish population from the Germans by way of individual verification."[64]

The authorities invested national identity with just as much or even more significance than origins, which meant, as Piotr Madajczyk suggests, that they pursued not so much ethnic cleansing as nationality cleansing. One had to declare one's national loyalty to Poland, not just exhibit Polish ethnic characteristics. This is what the creation of a nation-state, with all its assumptions about the value of a common nationality as an integrative force, implied. But the depredation suffered prior to nationality verification together with its actual implementation hindered many natives, particularly those ambivalent or indifferent to nationality, from committing unalterably to a Polish national identity. Of those who did for a variety of reasons, only a minority felt to some degree Polish.[65]

Although official propaganda, particularly for internal consumption, made much of the existence of Polish inhabitants in the Recovered Lands, Warsaw did not initially concern itself with this population.[66] When in February 1945 PPR leader Gomułka spoke of tasks connected with the Recovered Lands, he left no doubt about an early forced removal of the Germans but did not mention the supposedly Polish population.[67] His speech at the party plenum in May 1945 emphasizing the urgency of resettlement similarly omitted any reference to that population.

A detailed proposal of criteria to be used in sorting the inhabitants of the Recovered Lands came not from the government but from that organization of enthusiasts of westward expansion, the PZZ. In a memorandum to the central authorities on 19 February 1945, it called for the application of a variety of criteria: a history of active participation in the struggle for Polishness and membership in a Polish organization, a knowledge of the Polish language and its usage in daily life, and evidence of Polish origin, such as a Polish-sounding surname and Polish family ties and traditions.[68]

In the absence of guidelines from the central government, the regional authorities pursued their own improvised approaches, much as had happened in the Reich's incorporated lands during the war, which hindered Warsaw from developing and pursuing an appropriate policy.[69]

In Silesia Governor Zawadzki initially made no distinction among German citizens. But on 22 March 1945 he directed local officials to protect "Polish souls" by issuing provisional affidavits of Polishness to applicants in the Opole region who "unquestionably belong to the Polish nationality."[70] These "Polish souls" had to present a document certifying membership in a

Polish organization active in the Opole region or the testimony of three individuals of unquestioned Polish nationality. A further directive on 7 April 1945 added the criteria of the use of Polish in the home and in prayers as well as the ability to read and write in Polish and ordered the formation of special commissions in every community consisting of trusted local individuals "of undoubtedly Polish nationality" to decide who should receive Polish citizenship.[71]

In Mazuria Plenipotentiary Prawin issued a proclamation on 24 April 1945 calling on Poles of local origin to register for provisional affidavits of membership in the Polish nation.[72] On 26 May 1945 Deputy Plenipotentiary Burski instructed local officials that a lack of documentation of Polish origin, such as a Polish-sounding surname, or an absence of Polish national consciousness, as when applicants declared themselves to be Warmiaks or Mazurs, was not to prevent certification as belonging to the Polish nation. The basic criterion of a minimal knowledge of Polish could also be waived in exceptional cases for individuals who had a connection with the Polish nation. Nevertheless, officials were to examine the past of each applicant carefully so as not to protect "foreign elements, enemies of the Polish Nation, or those encumbered with anti-Polish activity."[73] If approved by a local Polish Nationality Committee, the applicant received a permanent affidavit of Polishness.

In effect, whereas the initial directives in Silesia meant that whoever is not Polish is German, in Mazuria the authorities defined as Polish all who were not German, two different approaches to nationality verification. In Silesia the approach required the autochthons to prove their Polishness. In Mazuria, little more than a declaration of loyalty was required.

The Nazis regarded Mazurs as "racial Germans" without individual verification. Leading elements in Mazuria debated the possibility of a preemptive recognition of Mazurs collectively as Poles and Polish citizens, excluding solely those individuals unquestionably of German nationality. In May 1945 Karol Małłek warned against individual verification:

> Because first we robbed this local Polish population of its livestock, then of its equipment, its furniture, clothes, sheets, linen, shoes, food, and then we chased it from its homes and farms and placed it in isolation—in camps, raped, infected with various diseases, in a word—deprived it of all honor and human dignity, we treated it just like Nazi murderers and thugs, and now you demand of it that it voluntarily declare in favor of Poland, for this new fatherland, which acted as its most torturous judge and not as its own and brother. In other words, you are holding a plebiscite. Who is demanding this? The Germans?[74]

Because of a rigid definition of Polishness as well as the perception of Mazurs as Germans, local officials balked at carrying out the directives allowing for their acceptance as Poles. On 7 June 1945 Prawin threatened officials with sanctions, admonishing them:

> Let the Polish citizen remember that the Kashub, Pomeranian, Warmiak, Mazur—we all, despite these or other religious, political, or social beliefs, are children of one blood of fraternal clans and Polish tribes, and this without regard to whether our closer or more distant compatriots are today conscious of their Polish origin or not. . . . I categorically direct you to register as Poles . . . all individuals identifying themselves as Kashubs, Pomeranians, Warmiaks, Mazurs without demanding of them additional declarations in this regard and to recognize those so registered as Polish citizens.

Prawin allowed for the revocation of citizenship only after its bestowal: if "it is proven in an administrative and legal way that someone himself consciously of his own criminal instinct acted against Poles and Poland, then of course the Polish citizenship granted him will be withdrawn."[75]

On 11 June 1945 Prawin reported that only about 350 Mazurs had applied for recognition of their Polish nationality, and the rate of new applications had somewhat declined, which he blamed on a campaign by the German population to keep Mazurs tied to Germanness. On 16 June 1945 Prawin created the District Polish Nationality Committee (*Okręgowy Polski Komitet Narodowościowy* or OPKN) consisting of Mazurian and Warmian activists with Burski as chairman to establish local committees and to advise on the distribution of certificates of membership in the Polish nation.[76]

The governor of Poznań, whose jurisdiction included Lubusz Land, imposed stringent conditions for the recognition of Polishness. He delineated the criteria in a memorandum on 27 April 1945 and directed that applicants for Polish citizenship receive a certificate simply stating their application was in process. As proof of Polish origin, an individual had to show that an ancestor had resided permanently in that part of the former Polish state and had "demonstrated unambiguously that he belonged to the Polish nationality by using the Polish language in everyday speech, observing Polish customs and traditions, raising progeny in the Polish spirit, etc." Furthermore, the applicant had to have belonged to Polish organizations and "unambiguously used the Polish language externally within the limits of possibility, observed Polish customs and traditions, and so forth."[77]

The Polish authorities estimated that only about 10 percent of Lubusz Land inhabitants (8,000 to 10,000) were of Slavic origin, widely dispersed throughout the territory. As a result, some officials did not thoroughly check the origins of individuals. Concerned about such a large German majority, they resorted to expulsion even before the war ended. A hasty operation in Gorzów on 5 May 1945 to remove as many Germans as possible resulted in the inclusion of individuals of Polish origin. The expulsion of a dozen Polish families from Międzyrzecz County received wide publicity, which prompted not only protests from the local community but also demands from organizations such as the PZZ for a suspension of expulsions until nationality verification could be carried out, which finally began in July 1945.[78]

In Lower Silesia the recognition of the native population as Polish was even more circumspect. In fact few could claim Polish origin. Before the war, they resided in concentrated groups only in three northeastern counties. In a directive on 2 April 1945, the plenipotentiary expressed his doubts: "With regard to individuals of Slavic origin who underwent Germanization, until specific directives are issued, you should act sympathetically but without making any commitment concerning the future."[79] He did not issue any instructions concerning autochthons until 10 October 1945.[80]

The Central Authorities and Nationality Verification

Concerned over the lack of uniformity in identifying German citizens of Polish nationality, the PZZ addressed a plea to the KRN Presidium on 25 April 1945, requesting a law to protect "the rights of the Polish autochthonous population" by establishing "the procedure for proving Polishness, the method of granting Polish citizenship, and the rights of this Polish group."[81]

When Warsaw addressed the issue on 20 June 1945, Minister Ochab stated only that the required regulations were being prepared. In the meantime, he authorized governors and plenipotentiaries to issue provisional three-month affidavits granting the rights of citizenship pending verification to those who inhabited the territory before the war and "belong to the Polish nationality" following a declaration of loyalty to the Polish Nation. But Ochab did not define the criteria for membership in the Polish nation, except for specifically excluding former members of the Nazi party and "fascist-Nazi criminals." On 23 June 1945 the director of the Legal Department of the KRN Presidium argued that the criteria should be left to administrative and public security organs, which had the necessary information to differentiate Poles from Germans, and any regulation should await the provisions of the peace treaty between Germany and the Allied powers.[82]

The explicit exclusion of Nazi party members proved controversial. In the summer of 1945 the Ministry of Justice took the view that even membership in Nazi youth and social organizations sufficed for detention in a labor camp. But on the same day as the MAP memorandum, 20 June 1945, the Opole *starosta* raised this very issue with the UW. Agents appointed in various communities to evaluate applications for verification found cases hard to resolve: individuals who belonged to the Nazi party or Germanized their names but never hid their membership in the Polish nation, always spoke Polish, and so forth. Because of the lack of instructions, some received certificates of Polish nationality. Women concerning whom the officials had the highest opinion but whose husbands were active members of the Nazi party, the SA, or the SS posed similar difficulties.[83] A provincial commission justified certifying a Gliwice shopkeeper as Polish: "As a merchant forced to belong to the NSDAP from 1935–1936. Thrown out of the party for selling to Jews. Wife verified [as Polish]. Comes from a Polish family. Children raised in a Polish spirit." Others, including veterans of the Polish Silesian Uprisings, maintained that they joined the party to keep their jobs or to receive a disability pension.[84]

In August 1945 Ossowski found that inhabitants in the Opole region did not condemn all Nazi party members, particularly those who joined after the war began. Instead of seeking revenge, they tended to recall good Germans with whom one could live in harmony. They regarded only the "true" Nazi as their enemy. Other than a few enthusiasts, of whom one had to be wary, people joined the party to maintain their positions or to advance to better ones, or they were simply too afraid or did not know how to resist the pressure to join, which greatly increased after 1939. Some party members even assisted their neighbors, for example, by warning them about the plans of the German police.[85]

The Silesian Provincial Verification Commission noted that in Zabrze the local population "reluctantly, or not at all, points out who is a German, who belonged to the [Nazi] party—and only under great pressure did the Verification Commission identify several people who belonged to the party."[86] But at a conference of local officials on 26 October 1945, some maintained that because of pressure to join, not every Nazi party member "must be treated as an enemy of Polishness." This should be taken into account, they believed, to avoid the expulsion of many individuals of Polish origin.[87]

Ties between autochthons and Germans also aroused the suspicions of Polish officials. On 28 August 1945 the *starosta* of Sztum, Gdańsk Province, lamented:

> The local Polish population is very close to and connected with the German population and, not being appropriately enlightened, hide the local German population, facilitate their obtaining provisional certificates [of Polishness], testifying on their behalf. Good opinions are issued for former Pole-haters. Lately members of the NSDAP have been caught with provisional certificates.... Local Germans and Poles are hostile to the arriving Polish population, calling them . . . colonists and the like. One can notice antagonism from one side as well as the other.[88]

Ossowski saw a strengthening of local ties among natives as a defense against the cultural differences with newcomers and their ignorance of local conditions, especially among newly arrived Polish officials.[89]

Implementation of the MAP Directive

On 5 July 1945 the Lębork County plenipotentiary issued a directive stating that the Polish government regarded German citizens of Kashubian origin as Poles and citizens of Poland, and he provided a bilingual Polish-German form to be used in registering the population in the second half of July. Applicants had to present evidence of their Kashubian origins, including the names of two individuals able to confirm their origins. Those who did not register during this period would lose all rights based on their Kashubian origins.[90]

The plenipotentiary of Western Pomerania issued his first instructions concerning verification on 10 July 1945. In Gdańsk Province verification began on 16 July 1945, mainly in Gdańsk and Sopot. Many other counties had no verification commissions until 1946.[91]

Silesia

The most extensive responses to the MAP memorandum came in the two areas with the most autochthons, Silesia and Mazuria. Governor Zawadzki had already ordered the creation of communal commissions to identify German citizens of Polish nationality. To oversee their work, on 10 July 1945 he ordered the creation of verification commissions at the county and municipal levels consisting of local administrative and security officials; representatives of local teachers, political parties, and the PZZ; and three to five representatives of the local population recognized as Polish. In August 1945 the Opole municipal commission had nine prewar residents among its nineteen members.[92]

The governor optimistically set 14 August 1945 as the application deadline.[93] But with uncertainly about the future border and ill treatment at the hands of officials, many natives hesitated to apply. A report that an MO officer searching a home in Czarnowąsy, allegedly to confiscate an accordion, stated, "Wait until the Russians get out of here, then you will learn what the Poles mean," which drew a reaction at an organizational meeting in Opole on 13 July 1945: "If the Polish authorities are going to be like the Civic Militia, then all citizens will refrain from filling out questionnaires, particularly with regard to nationality."[94]

Doubts about those applying for verification persisted. On 17 July 1945 the Opole PUIiP expressed alarm: "Lots of locals are applying for verification and don't speak a word of Polish." Unaware of the pressures applied under the Nazis, the official cited examples of applicants whose husbands or sons were in the German army; women who belonged to the leading organization for women in the German Reich; a woman who Germanized her Polish name, probably in the 1930s; and individuals who belonged to the Nazi party. "These are facts that do not need interpretation!" He attributed their applications to German influence and propaganda.

> In the future if we do not put a stop to this, there will be unpleasant fruit for us Poles. After all, the Silesian uprising went in a similar way. History teaches us how to eradicate one's enemy with arms and this lesson should now be applied to the fullest extent, all the more that now is the most appropriate time to cut out this German ulcer quietly.[95]

In the latter half of July 1945 the MO also reported that Germans, sometimes not even knowing a word of Polish, were desperately seeking recognition as Poles. In a report on 4 June 1945, the Prudnik PUIiP doubted the claim of a local official in Biała that about 80 percent of the inhabitants of the environs spoke Polish and that most identified themselves as Polish. Although 60 percent of the inhabitants of Biała spoke Polish, the author of the report regarded their nationality as "nevertheless unclear."[96] Such doubts gave rise to the characterization "a provisional Pole for 25 złoty," the fee for filing for verification.[97]

Initially, officials in Opole Silesia considered applications for verification of Polishness from spouses separately, which raised the possibility of the wife of an absent Wehrmacht veteran being verified as Polish and her husband being declared German. Although both may well have been nationally indifferent or ambivalent, it created the conundrum of not losing a Pole while not allowing a single German to stay without dividing families. Appeals, however, took into account the situation of the whole family. On 11 September 1945 Zawadzki tried to prevent supposedly ethnically mixed marriages by ordering Polish citizens and those with provisional certificates of Polish nationality to obtain his permission to marry Germans.[98] In Czechoslovakia officials punished "amorous relations" with Germans after the war as an offense against national honor as late as 1947. But in Opole Silesia natives commonly placed religion above nationality, marrying within their religion with little regard to a fluid or ambiguous nationality, which outsiders might well regard as treason.[99]

Mazuria

Like the Silesian governor, Plenipotentiary Prawin began to create a structure for nationality verification prior to the MAP memorandum. On 9 July 1945 he directed *starostowie* and municipal presidents immediately to instruct the local Polish inhabitants to apply for provisional certificates with the rights of citizenship. The sole requirements were that they resided in the district on 31 August 1939, were not members of the Nazi Party nor guilty of fascist-Nazi crimes, and submitted declarations of loyalty.[100]

The verification process, however, ran into difficulties according to the report for July 1945 of the Mazurian WS-P. A lack of qualified county officials required frequent intervention by the department, but it did not have the transportation to visit rural areas, resulting in a great deal of arbitrariness and diversity in practice. Nevertheless, Prawin reported on 13 August 1945 that an increasing number of Warmiaks and Mazurs were applying for recognition of their Polish origin. In the town of Olsztyn the authorities received 1,028 applications and issued 553 certificates confirming Polish origin. Security officials, however, subjected applications to greater scrutiny than the OPKN. On 21 August 1945 the director of the Pisz County Office of Public Security (*Powiatowy Urząd Bezpieczeństwa Publicznego* or PUBP) sent a memorandum to the county office stating that Mazurs could submit their applications solely to the PUBP. "The application should include a detailed biography and social origin as well as one's activity during the period of Hitler."[101]

The memoirs of Warmian folk poet Michał Lengowski illuminate the verification process. As secretary of the Olsztyn County Polish Nationality Committee, Lengowski regarded nearly all the rural inhabitants, mostly the elderly and mothers with children, as Poles. To those who established contact with a husband or son in Germany, he provided certificates, with which family members could apply to a Polish consulate, initially enabling many to return home.

But Lengowski also encountered "ignorance of understanding the difference between nationality and citizenship [that] begat many errors in the first years of uniting Warmia and Mazuria with its rightful fatherland." When an official claimed a whole village was German, Lengowski surmised that the villagers said that they were Germans "because the unenlightened people thought to themselves like this: if we say Poles, then he says to us that we are lying because we were born and resided in Germany." A woman accused of insulting the Polish flag hoisted on her home by throwing it on the ground mistook it for a sign of expropriation of her farm. When asked, "Are you a Pole?" only after reflecting for a moment did she reply that she was a Warmiak, which Lengowski again attributed to a lack of understanding.[102]

Another Warmian cultural activist, Władysław Gębik, who served on the same committee, states that Lengowski intervened whenever Poles were wronged. "Nevertheless, the influence of these committees on the course of public affairs was minimal. The local representatives of the people's authorities [appointed by Warsaw] disregarded its [sic] presence."[103]

Other problems arose in the East Prussian counties incorporated into Białystok Province, where they were marginalized and officials favored settlers over natives. The Ełk *starosta* reported on 10 July 1945 that because Mazurs fled the advance of the Red Army, he gave priority to settlers who took over and cultivated their farms. Similarly, the governor frequently criticized the practice in Olsztyn Province of restoring farms to Mazurs with certificates of Polish nationality, discouraging new settlers.[104]

Thus, the verification process ultimately depended on provincial and local officials, who mostly came from prewar Poland and had no knowledge of conditions under German rule. Furthermore, the quality of officials—their competence and integrity—frequently declined the lower one went down the administrative hierarchy. Many officials simply regarded the autochthons as Germans and often targeted those with homes and farms. Years later a responsible public security functionary admitted, "We did not know how to make proper use of the Union of Poles in Germany. If we did not treat activists of the Union as Germans, then as [DVL] 'twos.'"[105]

The question of Polish autochthons often came before the Research Council, and opinions varied, sometimes causing confusion and distrust of autochthons. At the first session, 30 July–1 August 1945, the vice chairman of the council, Rajmund Buławski, who during the war was connected with the *Delegatura*'s Bureau of Western Lands, called for "far reaching caution" in relation to the Germanized Polish population.

> If someone already betrayed his nationality once, he can do it a second time. One should not deceive oneself about it, that Germanized Poles are Germans in spirit and—as happens with renegades—they are often more zealous German patriots than native-born Germans, and if today they manifest a desire to return to the bosom of the Polish Nation, this is probably explained by opportunistic considerations.

Some simply wanted, "under the cloak of Polish origin," to rescue their property, particularly farms, which decreased the amount of surplus land available for repatriates and settlers. To avoid the problem of national minorities that caused so many difficulties before the war and greatly weakened Poland's internal cohesiveness, in general "Germans of Polish origin" like other Germans should be expelled from Poland or allowed to stay only under certain conditions, most importantly, the loss of their landed property.[106]

At the same session of the council, Professor Kazimierz Dobrowolski of the Jagiellonian University disagreed, emphasizing the necessity of compensating for the nation's enormous losses in the war. He regarded Silesians as "one of the most valuable ethnic groups, thanks to their sobriety, diligence, frugality, high social sense, and wonderful military virtues"—qualities that he might have characterized as Germanic! He believed that Germanized Poles could be brought back to Polishness through appropriate efforts, a view adopted by the authorities, though the Research Council had little influence on official policy.[107]

Views advocating a wider verification of German citizens as Poles found expression mainly prior to the Potsdam Conference. Thereafter, the concept prevailed of expelling all Germans except for a limited number of specialists temporarily needed for industry and the local economy as well as for state farms.[108]

The Catholic and Protestant Churches

The Polish hierarchy of the Catholic Church unequivocally supported the government's goal of Polonizing the Recovered Lands. Most active in this regard was Bishop Adamski, who before the war had promoted the national and cultural integration of Polish migrants and the German minority in his diocese and during the war headed a committee of the *Delegatura*'s Western Bureau.[109] Already in mid-May 1945 Adamski vigorously intervened on behalf of the Polish takeover of the Church's administration in Wrocław.[110] In a letter to the MAP on 27 July 1945, he related that he informed the Wrocław curia of the government's decision not to allow any Germans to remain in Poland, not even opponents of the Nazis. Adamski, however, protested the methods used in the "resettlement." The minister replied on 5 August 1945 acknowledging shortcomings but also complaining that many settlers in the western territory had no Polish clergy and instead "German priests often known for their close cooperation with the Nazi regime and even for their criminal activity in relation to Polish citizens during the war."[111] Warsaw feared that the overwhelmingly Catholic settlers would not stay without Polish clergy, endangering Polonization of the Recovered Lands. But removal of the local clergy risked alienating autochthons.[112]

Adamski's actions anticipated those of the Polish Primate August Cardinal Hlond after he received extraordinary plenipotentiary authority from Pope Pius XII in Rome on 8 July 1945, which he used to appoint five Polish apostolic administrators in the Recovered Lands to replace German bishops, an action some argue exceeded the authority granted him.[113]

The appointed clerics had views compatible with Warsaw's goals in the Recovered Lands. Rev. Teodor Bensch, the apostolic administrator of Warmia, taught in the underground during the war, including with the Secret University of the Western Lands. Rev. Dr. Karol Milik, the apostolic administrator of Lower Silesia, shortly before the war took part in the distribution of anti-German postcards at an international fair in Poznań that bore a map with the formerly Piast lands stamped "Drang nach Osten."[114] To an apostolic administration in Opole carved out of the archdiocese of Wrocław, Hlond appointed the native Silesian Rev. Bolesław Kominek.

The support of the Polish Catholic hierarchy provided the government with an additional argument for the Polishness of the territory, and the party could invoke its support for Hlond's actions as proof of its Polishness.[115] At the same time, the Church reinforced the policy of the government directed against minorities and thereby assisted its manipulation of social anger, diverting it away from the regime and the Soviet Union.[116] The identification of Catholicism with Polishness became a source of the strength of the Church as it resisted repressive measures. It would haunt the authorities of the Polish People's Republic throughout its existence.

The hostility of the Vatican toward the Polish regime had the paradoxical effect of forcing the Polish hierarchy to maintain its autonomous stance. The pope's Christmas message in 1945, critical of the injuries inflicted on Germans after the war, and his message on 2 June 1946 demanding the closure of camps for Germans compelled the Polish Church to emphasize its Polishness.[117] On 1 March 1948 the pope wrote a letter to German bishops in which he expressed the hope of a retreat from the resettlement of Germans "to the degree to which it can still be reversed."[118] Warsaw portrayed the letter as an attack on the Oder-Neisse border and instituted an anti-Catholic campaign to weaken the Church. Hlond responded on 24 May 1948 with an open letter, asserting: "There are no grounds on which the Church would desire to diminish the territory of the Republic. Statements as if the Church supports the idea of revision of the borders of the Polish State are baseless," misleadingly implying Vatican recognition of the Oder-Neisse border.[119] On 27 June 1948 *Nowiny Opolskie* retorted: "The Population of the Land of Opole Condemns the anti-Polish Policy of the Vatican."[120] A poster printed for the International Day of Peace on 21 September 1949 read "Vatican—ally of American imperialists—protector of German retaliatory forces—enemy of Poland and peace."[121]

Protestants, a minority lacking the unity of the Catholic Church, faced greater difficulties in organizing autochthons. In Mazuria on 26 June 1945 Prawin proclaimed the immediate appropriation of the property of Protestant Churches by the Evangelical-Augsburg Church acting through its consistory in Warsaw with the task of "awakening, propagating, and nurturing of the Polish spirit and civil life among believers." But on 28 August 1945 Mazurian activists persuaded Prawin to authorize the creation of a separate Council of the Evangelical Church. Because of the pressing need to re-Polonize and minister spiritually to Mazurs of the Prussian Union Evangelical Church, he transferred its property to the council. In fact the council's request to the MAP on 13 September 1945 to take over the Union's property delayed the rebuilding of the framework of the Church in Mazuria.[122]

Rev. Gloeh of the Evangelical-Augsburg Consistory, who toured Mazuria in August 1945 to organize Protestant parishes in the area, in his report on

10 September 1945 to the MAP Department of Religion likened the actions of the Mazurian activists to those of the Prussian authorities in imposing the Prussian Union Evangelical Church to separate Mazurs from the Consistory in Warsaw. In his view, Polish social and official elements who continually set Mazurs apart contributed to their lack of a proper national consciousness. Catholic elements took advantage of this, refusing to accept them as Poles because they were Protestant. Germans called them Mazurs or Prussian Mazurs to separate them from the Poles, but for Rev. Gloeh the Mazurs, who used a Polish bible and hymnal, could not be German.

To overcome Mazurian separatism, Rev. Gloeh advocated a government decree abolishing the Prussian Union Church and the assumption of authority over its churches by the Consistory of the Evangelical-Augsburg Church.[123] In fact in September 1946 the Evangelical-Augsburg Church of Poland officially absorbed the leadership of the Evangelical Church.

The Administration of the Recovered Lands

Rev. Gloeh likewise called for the removal of all borders between the Mazurian District and the rest of the country and the distribution of Mazurian counties among neighboring provinces, so that Prussian Mazuria as a separate entity would cease to play a role "and preoccupy incompetent melomaniacs [sic]." In particular, he urged that Działdowo County remain in Warsaw Province as before the war, when he claimed the county lost many of its Prussian-Mazurian characteristics, its sectional separateness. "And ultimately we would face a dilemma, before which actually no Pole should for a moment think twice: whether to Polonize Prussianized Mazurs, or to Mazurianize Polonized Mazurs? Whether to distinguish Poland by region, or to level differences, smooth out and unite the whole of Poland?"[124]

In 1905 the Prussian government combined most of Polish-speaking East Prussia in one administrative district. Mazurian activists now wanted no less. What Gloeh regarded as separatism, they saw as the recognition of the different character and history of the Mazurs required to win their loyalty. On 20 August 1945 the OPKN as "representatives of the Polish population settled for centuries in Warmia and Prussian Mazovia" decided to send a delegation to President Bierut with a memorandum requesting the realization of "the centuries-old dream and goal of our people" to become a province of the Polish Republic encompassing all of the lands and people "which common misery and struggle linked together, and therefore also our brothers" in the counties of Elbląg, Kwidzyń, Malbork, and Sztum in the west; Ełk, Gołdap, and Olecko in the east; and Działdowo in the south.[125]

On 28 August 1945 the delegation reported that complaints about existing conditions, which caused some natives to prefer to leave for the collective farms of Russia or as Germans to the Reich, deeply moved the president, who vowed to look into the matter.[126] In fact Warsaw firmly opposed any form of regionalism that threatened its goals of the formation of a highly centralized state and monolithic control over it. A decree of the RM on 29 May 1946 provisionally assigned the four western counties to Gdańsk Province and the three eastern counties to Białystok Province. Działdowo remained in Warsaw Province until 1950, the only change prior to 1975.[127]

At the same meeting of the OPKN on 28 August 1945, Burski raised the matter of filling positions with "our people." Several members proposed choosing Burski as governor, as if the OPKN had the power to do so. Burski resisted, pointing out that Prawin, though not a Mazur, was not responsible for the area's problems. Nevertheless, the OPKN appointed a committee to explore the matter, arguing that Prawin did not symbolize the advancement of Mazurs, who needed to know "that the era of lords is over."[128]

Despite Rev. Gloeh's differences with Mazurian activists and a low opinion of some of them, he agreed with the demand for the appointment of local inhabitants to positions in the new administration, specifically naming Karol Małłek, Fryderyk Leyk, and Gustaw Leyding. He found most administrators to be schemers and others seeking personal enrichment. In Szczytno the director of the PUIiP had two months of training in the Soviet Union and focused on promoting the PPR and the allied Peasant Party.

Gloeh thought the security agencies too incompetent to counter German propaganda, which along with a lack of confidence in the Polish government, resulted in whole villages whose inhabitants spoke only Polish identifying themselves as German. Newcomers eyeing Mazurian farms constantly accused Mazurs of being German so that they would leave or be expelled. Gloeh claimed that the militia, for whom Mazurs were Germans and Protestants were Mazurs, not only did not intervene to protect Mazurs but instead terrorized them.[129] In general, the personnel policy of the security agencies placed primary emphasis on loyalty to the new authorities rather than experience in police work. In 1945 18 percent of functionaries in the security services were under twenty-two years of age, 47.5 percent between twenty-two and thirty. The uneducated predominated, especially at the local level.[130]

In Działdowo Gloeh found the PUBP "decorated with a portrait of the head of a foreign power"—presumably Stalin—and none of the highest Polish authorities. The director agreed with Gloeh that religious denomination should not be confused with nationality. In the midst of their conversation a Soviet colonel walked into the office without knocking. The director introduced him in a loud voice, "'This is my *sowietnik*,'" and added in a louder voice, "'I do not believe in anyone but Stalin. Stalin is my god.'" Gloeh commented: "A Polish official made such a declaration in an office that remained Polish while carrying out the duties of his office. I do not formulate the conclusion that emerges on this subject."[131]

Gloeh did, however, draw some conclusions: "Fill the more important state and self-government positions with appropriate people, in so far as possible with local people. Reorganize and train the department of security and Civic Militia and change their relations to Protestant Mazurs." "To the commission for the reform of legal rules concerning activity harmful to the Polish State, beyond the team of officials, appoint Mazurian social activists."[132]

Some pro-Polish Mazurian activists received positions under the new authorities. Burski became a deputy district plenipotentiary on 14 March 1945. Edward Małłek and Późny served as *starostowie*. Późny remained in office until 1949, but Edward Małłek gave up his position after he concluded that he could not do enough for the remaining Mazurs. His brother Karol was also briefly *starosta* in Działdowo. But in total, prewar activists received few positions in the new administration and then usually only subordinate ones with little influence. Even at the local level few positions in administration or national councils or as communal heads were held by Mazurs and Warmiaks in mid-1946.[133]

The autonomy of the OPKN also did not last, apparently a victim of political conflict. MZO Deputy Minister Józef Dubiel criticized the OPKN for its constant complaints, which he blamed on the opposition Polish Peasant Party (*Polskie Stronnictwo Ludowe* or PSL), which drew the support of Burski and other activists by promising to respect Mazurian interests. Prawin's successor as governor Zygmunt Robel in effect paralyzed the work of the OPKN at the end of June 1946 by placing the verification operation under the authority of the PZZ district directorate. On 1 April 1947 Robel liquidated the OPKN and incorporated some of its members into the local PZZ.[134]

Whereas the government divided historic Mazuria, it added the historically unrelated Dąbrowa Basin to Silesia. Reliance on individuals from the Basin, where Governor Zawadzki originated, in filling local offices exacerbated a sectional conflict. Often ignorant of the conditions in Silesia, they brought with them their prewar prejudices against Silesians, particularly their dialect. Natives often responded with xenophobia and their own prejudices. Touring Silesia in April 1945, 2nd Lt. Zylberberg noted, "There is a certain antagonism, . . . especially between Silesians and individuals from the Dąbrowa Basin."[135]

Officers of the WUBP came mainly from the Dąbrowa Basin, some of them Jews. The first commandant came from an Orthodox Jewish family. His deputy and the head of the Silesian Department of Prisons and Camps were also of Jewish origin and came from the same town in the Dąbrowa Basin.[136] Although in 1945 only 438 out of 25,600 in the Office of Public Security (*Urząd Bezpieczeństwa Publicznego* or UBP) were Jews, they held 13 percent of the executive positions, and historians generally agree that they were overrepresented in some sections of the UBP.[137] As for the quality of the security forces in Opole Silesia, Zylberberg commented: "The militia is very weak, poorly armed and on an extremely low moral level. The deputy president of Zabrze Trąbalski (an old PPS activist in Opole) stated that there is more trouble with it than use. The militiamen take part in robberies and are often in secret conspiracy with 'looters' etc."[138]

Although not the official view, a directive issued by the Provincial Settlement Committee in Katowice in July 1945 illustrates a lack of understanding of local conditions: "Neither a German nor a Pole related to or connected with Germans, nor a friend to or favorable towards Germans—can even a day longer be head of a village. Even meritorious Poles connected with Germans can under no condition be heads"—which if strictly enforced eliminated nearly everyone in Opole Silesia. In fact settlers from Central Poland filled most positions of authority. Even at the lowest level, the communal national councils, natives in Opole Silesia held only 10 to 15 percent of seats.[139]

Nevertheless, during the first two years following the war, some Silesians held high profile positions. Deputy Governor Jerzy Ziętek as a native of Opole Silesia played a significant role. He succeeded in gathering veterans of the Polish Silesian Uprisings around him and in luring back numerous prewar civil servants.[140] At the end of 1946 three deputy governors were Silesians as was the chairman of the WRN. Silesians also held nine county executive offices and thirty-four offices of municipal presidents and deputy presidents. In mining and industry 2,994 Silesian workers advanced to executive positions. In the provincial administration at the turn of 1946, an impressive 44 percent were Silesians compared with 14.8 percent from the Dąbrowa region and 15.1 percent from the *kresy*.

But the lack of acceptance of the communist system by members of ZPwN and the supposed "uncertain origin" of many of the Silesians in the most prominent positions weighed heavily against them. They lost all importance as the PPR consolidated its political dominance. By 1949 only one Silesian served as *starosta* and only 26 out of 146 as communal heads. The authorities also did not appreciate the significance of numerous local cultural organizations and associations, such as choruses, which led to their collapse. Taken together these developments turned Silesians from being subjects into objects and were a factor in the departure of many for Germany.[141]

De-Germanization

The authorities sought not only to expel the Germans but also to remove all traces of Germanness from these "ancient Slavic" lands. Officials perceived any manifestation of German culture as an indication of pro-German sentiments and, as in prewar Polish Upper Silesia, connected use of the German language with membership in the German nation.[142]

Already on 29 January 1945 Zawadzki ordered the destruction of all German inscriptions, signs, notices, names, and newspapers; the prohibition of the use of German; and the return of Polish names for towns, squares, streets, parks, and so forth. The Organizational Department of the MAP followed on 16 March 1945 ordering the provincial authorities to supervise the removal of all German inscriptions.[143]

The native population, however, did not necessarily welcome this. The sociologist Ossowski observed that, outside of the realm of religion (sermons, confession, hymns), whether a Silesian used Polish, the local dialect, or German had no ideological significance. Even members of the prewar Polish national movement in Germany spoke the local dialect laced with German expressions, and the younger generation educated under Nazi rule often spoke no Polish at all. In addition, de-Germanization struck at elements of the regional identities of many of the natives. Re-Polonization accepted only part of the heritage from their past of living with Germans and discredited the rest.[144]

The Polonization of the very names of autochthons early on became part of the process of de-Germanization. A Polish- or Slavic-sounding name widely sufficed as evidence of a Polish identity. The Polish press and the authorities believed that those subjected to compulsory Germanization should enthusiastically embrace their previously persecuted Polishness.[145] De-Germanization required the removal of the "ugly stench" of German given names, as an article in the *Dziennik Zachodni* put it on 22 March 1945. The Silesian PZZ regarded the Polonization of names as one of its basic tasks.[146]

Even veterans of the Silesian Uprisings and members of the ZPwN had changed their names under German rule, Germanizing them to avoid persecution or simply to obtain better treatment at the hands of the authorities. Children born during the war received German names even in Polish families. But German names did not necessarily originate in the Nazi period, and first names might have been part of a family tradition that existed for generations. First names conferred at baptism also symbolized an individual's religion. The natives might well regard their names, even if German, as "theirs," to which they had emotional ties. The interference of the authorities could seem no more acceptable than Germanization.[147]

The initial efforts at Polonizing the Recovered Lands came with the expectation of imminent international recognition of the Oder-Neisse border. The Potsdam Conference disappointed Polish officials and had the effect of increasing the importance of Polonization of the borderlands through expulsion, nationality verification, and de-Germanization.

[7]
After the Potsdam Conference

ALTHOUGH THE POTSDAM Conference recognized only a provisional Polish-German border, PPR General Secretary Gomułka declared in *Głos Ludu* on 5 August 1945, "an act of great historic significance and of historic justice was performed. The greatest powers of the world approved Poland's return to the ancient Piast lands." But it came with obligations: "We can and must settle there millions of Poles—workers, peasants, engineers, artisans, the working intelligentsia and in general people of all trades, both those from Poland as well as those from abroad who will return to their own home, to Poland."[1] The Germans had to be removed to provide "living space" for the Polish settlers and repatriates. The expectation that the Western Allies would oppose the Oder-Neisse border also dictated the elimination of everything German from public life. Gomułka did not mention the autochthons, for whom the "ancient Piast lands" were truly a homeland. They took on greater importance as the authorities sought to demonstrate the Polish character of these lands.

"Voluntary" Departure

Although the Big Three approved the transfer of Germans, they requested a suspension pending a report of the Allied Control Council. But both Poland and Czechoslovakia persisted in expelling Germans. Soviet propaganda portrayed the Western Allies as pro-German in thwarting the wishes of the people, and the Soviet zone continued to accept expellees from Poland.[2]

Many Germans left Poland more or less voluntarily. On 17 April 1945 the governor of Gdańsk Province authorized issuing Germans permits to leave the country and receive free transportation to the border. On 15 September 1945 the American *chargé d'affaires* in Warsaw cited a report of the U.S. Group of the Allied Control Council that Germans were leaving at an average rate of 2,000 per day.³

Food shortages and the lack of security favored departure. On 19 October 1945 the plenipotentiary of Lower Silesia reported that the availability of provisions worsened daily and that without assistance it would not be possible to feed the population. Even potatoes were in short supply because of requisitions by the Soviet and Polish military.⁴ The shortages continued into the following year. In the early spring of 1946 the caloric consumption per capita was 1,500 to 2,000, mainly in the form of flour products. In July 1946 the United Nations Relief and Rehabilitation Administration (UNRRA) indicated that the production and stock of food fell substantially below prewar levels.⁵ Furthermore, the internal "civil war" over Poland's future prevented economic and political stabilization for several years after the war.⁶

For *Volksdeutsche* and German citizens measures that varied from place to place made the situation worse. After release from detention, some suffered the loss of their homes, exclusion from the state social welfare system, the denial of schooling for their children, and similar measures. Pensions and disability payments to German citizens ceased. The anti-German campaign; the difficulties and abuses of the rehabilitation and verification processes; disregard for their security; and, in some cases, a desire to unite with family members in Germany led a growing number to conclude that a better life awaited them on the other side of the Oder. Thus, massive numbers of Mazurs were applying for permits to leave, 30 percent with provisional certification of Polish origin, according to a report of an inspector from the Office of the Plenipotentiary of Mazuria on 26 October 1945.⁷

After Potsdam expulsions were typically organized locally. In a memorandum on 17 October 1945, Governor Zawadzki stated, "The removal of Germans out of the territory of Poland should be carried out by *starostowie* on their own."⁸ Some expellees were of Polish nationality, as confirmed by the Polish Military Mission in Berlin, accredited by the Allied Control Council as Poland's political representative. They returned to Poland, as did individuals from Pleszew, Jarocin County, and Józef and Gertruda Matysiak, whom the Nowy Tomyśl PUBP expelled despite their having filed a declaration of loyalty in August 1945 and applied for rehabilitation. But others chose to leave rather than apply for rehabilitation. One of the largest voluntary departures (about 5,500 individuals), which occurred in Turek County 20–24 November 1945, included *Volksdeutsche* in categories II–IV.⁹

On 29 September 1945 Poznań Governor Feliks Widy-Wirski ordered the "immediate resettlement" of *Volksdeutsche* in all categories who freely requested to leave Poland as well as those in category I or who declared membership in the German nation.¹⁰ On 24 October 1945 Widy-Wirski clarified that this order included *Volksdeutsche* who previously declared their loyalty to the Polish nation along with those who did not make a declaration of loyalty or did not apply for rehabilitation before the deadline. Nevertheless, he cautioned that those in categories II, III, and IV "who want to be rehabilitated and remain in Poland are *not* to be subjected to compulsory resettlement." Then on 5 December 1945 he directed officials to stop issuing departure permits to *Volksdeutsche* in those categories. As he explained to the District Court in Poznań on 19 December 1945, too many *Volksdeutsche* of Polish origin, constituting a significant portion of the 700,000 individuals in the province who applied to leave in 1945, were leaving to avoid forced labor.[11]

In the chaos attending expulsion, officials often ignored instructions. Admonished at a meeting at 11 P.M. on 20 September 1945 in Sopot not to include in any expulsion individuals who had submitted declarations of loyalty or Germans who possessed exemptions from the UB, officials often did not pay attention to these exceptions during an operation that lasted all night until 9 A.M.[12]

In November 1945 the Tczew County *starosta* ordered the expulsion of some 1,500 *Volksdeutsche* who supposedly wanted to leave for Germany. But at the collection point those who proved that they had applied for rehabilitation were allowed to return to their homes, which they found ransacked and destroyed. The *starosta* defended his action citing growing insecurity manifested by attacks on citizens, shots fired at night, escapes from detention camps, and pro-German graffiti, according to a report of the Gdańsk governor on 5 February 1946.[13]

On 20 November 1945 the Allied Control Council issued a plan providing for the resettlement of the estimated 3,500,000 Germans still in Poland tentatively beginning in December 1945—it did not begin until mid-January 1946—and to be completed by August 1946. On 22 November 1945 the MAP directed officials to concentrate on the "repatriation" of Germans as quickly as possible and on 14 December 1945 permitted local administrative offices to issue certificates to Germans requesting to leave if approved by the appropriate security official. By December 1945 593,400 individuals left Poland more or less "voluntarily" following the Potsdam conference.[14]

Problems with the Verification Process

The provisional nature of the border enhanced the importance of the verification of natives of the Recovered Lands as Polish. Governor Zawadzki, who initially spoke of recognizing those inhabitants of Opole Silesia who "unquestionably belong to the Polish nationality," by October 1945 saw the need for a flexible approach: "No paragraphs and no directives clearly reveal who should be regarded as a Pole and who as a German—in such cases the Polish conscience must decide."[15] In Gdańsk Province the plenipotentiary emphasized in November 1945 the need to retain the highest number of verified Poles possible to impress the Western Allies at the future peace conference and therefore recommended verification even in doubtful cases, to be corrected later.[16]

At first, part of the rural population did not understand the purpose or significance of the verification process. On 24 October 1945 Zawadzki noted that inspectors in Opole Silesia found, "The operation of the verification of Poles was not publicized everywhere in an appropriate manner, as a result of which many individuals having the conditions for verification did not apply."[17] A special commission operating in Prudnik County reported in January 1946 that the majority of the people saw it "as a declaration to join some party unknown to them."[18] In August 1946 the Strzelce PUIiP reported that the local population hesitated to sign a declaration of loyalty because of rumors—blamed on hostile propaganda—that signing would result in being sent to Siberia or resettled elsewhere in Poland and all others would be expelled to Germany. To remain in their homeland some declared themselves to be Silesian.[19]

Some autochthons took their Polishness for granted, saw no need for proof, and regarded the requirement as discrimination because repatriates and settlers did not have to undergo verification. Activists in the ZPwN and those whom the Nazis had persecuted particularly resented and felt humiliated by the process, especially the requirement to declare loyalty to Poland. In one village six veterans of the Silesian Uprisings refused to apply to protest their mistreatment during the verification campaign, yet they strongly resisted expulsion.[20] An article in the PSL *Gazeta Ludowa* in January 1946 concerning the Złotów region reported, "Most annoying is the matter of Polish citizenship. Not surprisingly, when given a two-month provisional certificate of citizenship Rev. Paszko, who spent the whole war in a concentration camp, said with bitterness, 'Not you [certify] us, but rather we can certify you as Poles.'"[21] Others simply refused to apply for verification for more pragmatic reasons: high fees, excessive delays in ruling on the applications, and corruption that resulted in numerous defective decisions.[22]

Local concerns often clashed directly with instructions from higher authorities. The overwhelming predominance of women, children, and the elderly in the Recovered Lands; the dire state of health of many of them; and the appalling lack of food, housing, and other necessities inclined some local officials to remove as many as possible without reference to nationality. Moreover, the material interests strongly influenced official decisions. Delegates of the PZZ

District Board in Katowice claimed that in the field "applications for verification make their way unread into the wastebasket, thrown there with one hand by the head of a hamlet or village, who with the other hand takes appropriate remuneration for assigning the farm to someone else." Local commissions often turned down applications of women whose husbands had not yet returned from the war and applications of the elderly. In this way, at first 60 to 80 percent of applications were rejected. When a provincial commission reviewed applications in Koźle County in November 1945, 90 percent were approved.[23]

Zawadzki reacted sharply to abuses in a directive on 24 October 1945: "Verification commissions—especially communal ... do not observe the [required] participation of the local Polish population in the verification commissions, or consider applications for verification from the perspective of egotistical goals and personal material gains." Furthermore, in "executing the great task of cleansing the Recovered Lands of Germans, these displacements are often undertaken without prior appropriate affirmation whether among the Germans designated for resettlement there are individuals fulfilling criteria for verification." In the resettlement camps "there are Poles who speak Polish fluently and openly admit that they are of Polish nationality." Unauthorized individuals on their own authority included people in the camps whose application for verification had not yet been ruled on and even ones to whom the *starosta* had issued certificates of Polish nationality.[24]

The governor therefore extended the deadline for filing for verification to 30 November 1945. "The guiding principle ... should be ... the unconditional procurement of the Polish population of Opole Silesia for Poland and the Polish nation."[25] As he told the WRN on 2 November 1945, "We must do this so that ... we can confirm before the world and the whole nation that not for nothing did we all along say that these lands are inhabited by Poles."[26]

Nevertheless, some local officials continued to act contrary to provincial directives. With the inhabitants of Kuźnica Ligocka, Niemodlin County, persistently refusing to apply for verification although the majority spoke Polish, the director of the local PUR in November 1945 ordered that they be sent to the Łambinowice camp.[27] Military and civilian personnel ousted the inhabitants at dawn "in a brutal manner," beating them and taking their clothes, watches, rings, and other valuables, according to testimony of a witness at a trial of camp guards in 1957. Forced to walk the twelve kilometers to the camp, they sang the Polish hymn "Pod Twoją obronę" (Under Your Protection).[28] The county PUR defended their displacement as necessary to provide residences quickly for Polish repatriates.[29] The deputy *starosta* told a PPR-MBP commission in February 1946 that it was meant to frighten others into applying for verification.

On 22 February 1946, the commission reported:

> Relations in the county are full of weeds [*bardzo zachwaszczone*]: all the positions in the state administration are mostly occupied by inhabitants of the [Dąbrowa] mining region, who treated and partly still continue to treat the native Polish population as Germans.
> ... Very common are cases in which the farms of verified Poles are inhabited by repatriates who deprive the natives of all rights and in a merciless way force them to work as their farmhands.
> In the southern part of the county, in Fryland Commune there is not a single farm where there are not two farmers—a native and a repatriate. It happened that, for the purposes of plunder, for the purposes of taking over and settling in villages not yet destroyed and looted, Polish villages—Ligota Kuźnica [Kuźnica Ligocka] and Ligota Tułowiecka, were resettled, their inhabitants deposited in the camp in Łambinowice.
> Terrible lawlessness rules in the whole county. People already lost the feeling of wrong and justice. No crime is cause for surprise. The militia and often Security [agents] rape and plunder the population. It has come to it that people flee in panic at the sight of the militia.[30]

Similar developments occurred in Głubczyce County, Silesia, where the PUIiP reported on 31 December 1945 that settlers from the Dąbrowa Basin in large part engaged in looting. "A regional division, distrust and a lack of understanding" marked the relations among the inhabitants.[31]

The Mazurian plenipotentiary also reacted to abuses. On 22 October 1945 he instructed *starostowie* to review departing Germans because some local officials, for personal gain, destroyed the certificates of Polish origin of Mazurs and Warmiaks and expelled them. Doubtful cases were to be investigated together with a nationality committee.[32]

Following a tour of several counties of Gdańsk Province, Provincial Verification Commission member Mirosław Dybowski reported on 6 April 1946 that, thanks to the *starosta,* the verification process proceeded properly in Sztum County, but the situation in Kwidzyn and Malbork Counties was "scandalous" with very few verified. The murder of two local prewar Polish activists at the beginning of 1946 by security officers and a Soviet soldier had a negative impact on the course of verification in Malbork County, with four verified individuals departing illegally for Germany.[33]

Even worse was the situation in Kwidzyn County. On 17 January 1946 the county commission denied verification to thirty-seven applicants, according to Dybowski's report on 24 May 1946: "The decisive factor in the commission was an official of the Kwidzyn UB Markieta Henryk, who 'officiated' with a pistol lying on the table, thereby terrorizing all of the members." A "typical scandalous example" of the expropriation of the more prosperous farms was the case of the Regenbrecht family, one of the first to be verified. Nevertheless, the father was arrested and killed in an accident as he was being transported to prison. His wife and three children were transferred to state property for forced labor while an UB associate took over the family's farm of twenty hectares, sharing the property and livestock with his collaborators. Yet according to witnesses Regenbrecht had demonstrated his Polishness both before and during the war. Not surprisingly, few autochthons in the county had been verified. Dybowski also listed several families "of indisputably Polish autochthons" who had been expelled. In the end, he asked to be relieved of his membership in the commission because of the resistance he encountered in trying to undo the wrongs committed and the personal threats made against him.[34]

Lawless behavior of local officials forced Poznań Governor Widy-Wirski to refine his instructions. At a conference of *starostowie* on 3 November 1945 he expressed satisfaction with the progress in the "resettlement" of Germans and urged its continuation "especially in Lubusz Land."[35] But on 5 December 1945 he admonished: "It is not permitted to resettle Poles with German citizenship for the purpose of taking over their farm, trading company, industrial enterprise, etc. Confirmed abuses will be severely punished."[36] Malfeasance by "the organs of security and order" prompted the governor to complain to the WUBP on 31 December 1945 for:

> mostly not appreciating the fact that in the territory of Lubusz Land an indigenously Polish population resides, which despite a weak, and sometimes very faint knowledge of the Polish language, nevertheless is doubtless of Polish nationality.... Yet, despite appearances and obvious influences of German culture, it constitutes from an internal feeling a biologically indigenous Polish element.

The governor warned of harmful consequences when expellees presented documents in Germany attesting to their Polish nationality. As long as members of the Polish minority of prewar Germany did not belong to the Nazi party or its organizations, "they should be treated as an element suitable, with time after careful observation, for incorporation in Polish society." He called for the next conference of directors of PUBP to decide on a procedure allowing for "an objective evaluation of the national membership of the displaced."[37] Because of the mutability of national identity, no such procedure existed.

Settlers and repatriates arriving in the Recovered Lands accused German citizens of Polish origin of being servants of the Nazis, traitors, spies, and covert Nazis. The Western Pomerania KW PPS reported on 12 September 1945 that this ignorance of the situation of Poles in Germany deeply depressed the autochthons in Złotów County and hindered Polonization to an unprecedented degree. Worse, a significant portion of the newcomers justified robbery and looting in patriotic terms. In a number of cases, officials, including the director of the Housing Commission, evicted ZPwN members from their homes, looted their property, and sent them to forced labor camps.[38]

A conference of county officials in October 1946 confirmed that abuses occurred in Złotów, Człuchów, and Bytów Counties. "The incoming population regarded themselves as conquerors and not as liberators. The element that settled in these lands was to a high degree demoralized, and the security authorities did not rise to the occasion." The former commandant of the labor camp in Złotów did not respect the decisions of the verification commission and instead made his own decisions as to the citizenship of individuals and whether to free them. Meanwhile their homes were thoroughly plundered. As a result, the native population remained passive and flocked to the opposition PSL.[39]

On 28 November 1945 the plenipotentiary of the Bytów District attributed the mistreatment to arrogance and a lack of understanding as well as a nationality policy that saw everything in black and white. Security functionaries harassed autochthons at every turn. Disillusioned and embittered, many applied for permission to leave. Directives to support autochthons and above all not to expel children of Polish origin often came too late and were not always followed.[40]

Security officials proved particularly hostile to the natives. A memorandum on 25 October 1945 of the UBP in Karb, Bytom County, described the "pro-German sentiment of the Silesian population":

> Speaking with the Silesian population, all are great Poles, did a lot for Poland, only now in the streets and even in stores one hears more German speech than Polish, only when one calls attention [to this], then she cannot express herself in Polish, because I [illegible—am ashamed?] in front of neighbors, that she is already a great Pole, and under the Germans she was again a great German. The Silesian nation, these are predominately false and unctuous people, and they never saw and never heard, they deny because they do not want to hand over these great Nazi rogues. German prisoners who are delivered to the mines often walk through Karb, then in windows, on balconies, in gates and on the street we see how Silesians greet them with what satisfaction for these people. They would give everything, so also they would spare no bread and sausage nor also tobacco; it sometimes goes to such an extent that bread, sausage, snuff simply pours down on these prisoners like hail, so that sometimes it [becomes] necessary to use weapons to disperse these people, who have pretensions to become Poles. The local youth hardly know Polish at all and do not want to go to Polish language courses. More than one has asked why he should learn the Polish language. There are also among them people who truly deserve the respect of a good Pole.[41]

The verification process itself became a flash point between autochthons and newcomers. When Zawadzki invalidated decisions made by commissions that lacked representatives of the local population, settlers in some communities took offense and refused to participate in the commissions because, according to a report of the Provincial Verification Commission in November 1945, they regarded themselves as "100-percent Poles and as such should constitute the majority in the verification commissions."[42] Some complained about natives dominating the local commissions and ignoring objections to verification raised by security personnel. Local officials, mostly newcomers, often saw themselves as performing an act of historical justice in siding with repatriates and settlers against autochthons, whom they regarded as Germans.[43]

Property Disputes

Property disputes in the borderlands played a central role in the relations among social groups and between them and the Polish authorities.[44] Conflicts over national identity served as a surrogate for a struggle over property. On 24 October 1945 Governor Zawadzki prescribed, "A certificate of verification will serve as a certificate of ownership of an occupied farm for verified native Polish families." Where the PUR settled newcomers on farmsteads inhabited by individuals subsequently verified as Poles, Zawadzki ruled that the PUR should assign the newcomers farms elsewhere. Newcomers were to remain in sole possession of farms that were abandoned. If the owners returned and were verified as Poles, the PUR was to assign them another formerly German farm.[45]

In Mazuria the provincial authorities tried to resolve property disputes by ruling on 17 November 1945 that settlers who occupied a farm before 1 September 1945 should not be removed and the native owner, if verified as Polish, should receive another property of equal value. But it became a common practice—for the proverbial money and vodka—for settlers to receive certificates antedating their occupation prior to 1 September 1945.[46]

Concerned about the shortage of housing in Gdańsk for newcomers, the settlement inspector on 17 November 1945 proposed halting the verification process and frightening those verified as Poles into emigrating by announcing that they might be resettled elsewhere to promote their assimilation.[47]

The governor of Gdańsk Province on 13 April 1946 sought to resolve disputes based on the alacrity of verification. Even if a newcomer occupied a farm since April 1945 and invested his own capital, an autochthon who had identified himself as Polish and quickly sought verification should repossess his farm but compensate the displaced newcomer with equipment and grain. If, however, the owner of an abandoned farm assigned to a newcomer sought verification only after considerable delay, then the PUR should allocate the autochthon a different farm.[48]

The link between Polish identity and property rights cast suspicion on claims of Polish origins. On 31 December 1945 the Sztum District plenipotentiary asserted that "many germans [sic] bearing Polish names and trying to speak Polish" expected a change in the political situation, and only when it did not come did they file for verification as Poles. "Despite the pretense of Polishness, this element does not have anything in common with Poles and should not be admitted to Polish society, all the more because the desire to acquire the rights of a Polish citizen is dictated by personal interest, namely to recover its farm, which meanwhile was given to a repatriate or settler."[49]

In 1946 the ownership of 24,000 farms in the Recovered Lands, more than half of them in the Opole region and a quarter in Olsztyn Province, was disputed. With autochthons discouraged from pursuing their rights, the number of farms taken from them was probably even higher.[50]

On 25 June 1946, the Olsztyn governor reported that the settlers who wanted to take over the farms of Mazurs threatened them "with burning down their farms and even murdering them if they do not leave with the Germans."[51] The most important cause of property disputes was that many settlers had "a particular view of the private property of the local Polish population and a determined attitude toward this population—as a German population," according to the report for May 1946 of the Olsztyn Provincial Settlement Department. This resulted in a number of autochthons returning their provisional certificates of Polishness and applying for departure to Germany, stating that "they are going there to wait out the current situation and to return when it calms down. One senses that unconsciously they long for the legal relations that dominated in German times." Rulings in favor of local inhabitants often did not end the disputes. The decisions of the Provincial Appeal Commission were not carried out, although the Settlement Department recommended an investigation and disciplinary measures against those responsible. Even court decisions were not enforced.[52]

Olsztyn Province saw its largest population growth of the postwar period in 1946, increasing the demand for property.[53] Already on 1 June 1946 settlers and repatriates constituted 57.9 percent of the population and outnumbered Mazurs and Warmiaks by more than three to one, according to the Provincial Settlement Department. The desperate condition of many repatriates pressured officials to accommodate them. On 8 June 1946 the Braniewo County *starosta* reported, "A mass of repatriates from beyond the Bug [River] flowed into the territory of the county, 50 percent of them a weak element—that means, they do not possess any provisions, livestock; widows with children and so on."[54]

Meanwhile, natives of the Recovered Lands were returning from Germany, 152,478 between the end of August 1946 and the end of May 1947. They included individuals who returned simply to liquidate their property and leave again for Germany, prompting some settlers to accuse the authorities "of supporting Germanness."[55] Petitions to the municipal court in Bytom for the return of property increased from 838 in 1945 to 1,020 by the end of November 1946. Although in most cases the court issued orders for the return of property once the former owners were verified as Polish, this did not always occur.[56]

A delay in preparation of a decree on land ownership increased tension and uncertainty. Therefore, on 15 July 1946 the MZO categorically prohibited the placement of newcomers on the property of the local population that obtained or applied for Polish citizenship; property disputes were to be resolved only after completion of the verification process.[57]

By then, however, newcomers had long occupied many farms. A court decision to return property left those who invested their efforts and capital feeling wronged. On 11 August 1946 thirty-seven settlers in Butowo, Kwidzyn County, protested against the verification of a "german" [sic] as Polish and a court order to return the farm assigned to one of the settlers in May 1945. The protesters claimed that they had witnesses ready to testify that the owner had maltreated Poles who worked for him during the war. They bitterly complained that they "came to the ancient Polish lands at the call of our Government" and now were being thrown out and the land returned to the Germans: "For our five-year slavery and torment in which the best sons of the Fatherland perished—this is the repayment."[58]

Finally, on 14 October 1946 Warsaw published the decree on land ownership. Newcomers who received abandoned property prior to the publication of the decree retained possession of the farm, and the former owner verified as Polish had a right to another property as compensation. A verified native owner who remained on his property from the end of the war retained possession, with any newcomer settled on the property to be compensated elsewhere—in essence, the same arrangements that Zawadzki ordered for Silesia in October 1945.[59]

Implementation of the decree, however, posed multiple problems, and disputes over property continued to enflame intergroup relations, especially in Mazuria where there were instances of settlers murdering those who repossessed their farms. At the end of 1946, there were still 1,218 disputed farms in Olsztyn Province. In Opole Silesia newcomers were resettled from about 8,000 disputed farms by the end of March 1947; an additional 2,897 autochthons applied for the return of their property in the years 1947–1948. In 2,399 cases considered, about half recovered their farms. By the end of 1948, 87 percent of cases were decided. Nevertheless, some disputes in Opole Silesia as well as in Mazuria remained unresolved until 1956.[60]

Local officials interested in winning over people useful to them, which generally meant the settlers with whom they had more in common, resisted the decree, which they saw as favoring autochthons and thereby disrupting the settlement of the Recovered Lands. To overcome an "inadequate understanding and erroneous interpretation" of the decree, the MZO on 19 April 1947 "absolutely" prohibited the confiscation of the property of autochthons even if they had not yet submitted to verification. The directive defined "abandoned" property, specifying that the owner's absence "should have the character of some durability." If the authorities incarcerated an autochthon or otherwise limited his freedom of movement, "then the absence caused by this type of actions is not regarded as abandonment of the property."[61]

But because many settlers who occupied what was considered "formerly German property" invested much into it, on 24 April 1947 the KRN Settlement and Repatriation Commission agreed that a settler who occupied a farm for a longer period of time should be recognized as the owner and the native given another farm. The Olsztyn KW PPS took the same view. In practice the local authorities continued to favor settlers in disputes.[62]

Disputes also arose over movable property. The Presidium of the Toruń Municipal National Council (*Miejska Rada Narodowa* or MRN) reported on 24 May 1947 that repatriates, former concentration camp prisoners, and individuals dispossessed of their homes and belongings and deported by the Nazis received furnishings from *Volksdeutsche* homes.

> If today these properties are to be returned to rehabilitated *Volksdeutsche,* then Poles for a second time and quite a few who were burnt out in Warsaw, for a third time will be deprived of property and that is property allocated to them as formerly German property.... As a result of the repossession of property by rehabilitated *Volksdeutsche,* many a repatriated family and many an ideological-political prisoner will remain in a home with bare walls, without beds, wardrobes, chairs, tables, and the like.

With some 600 cases for rehabilitation before the district court, the MRN petitioned the Pomeranian WRN to intervene with the president of Poland to rule that property allocated to Poles not be returned to the rehabilitated.[63]

Local officials encumbered the return of property. On 25 July 1947 the Łódź Main UL required that *Volksdeutsche* prove that ownership of the disputed property predated the war or, if acquired during the war, that it was not simply by right of registration on the DVL. Also, a court had to specify the property to be returned. In addition, the property of category III and IV *Volksdeutsche* with irrevocable rights under the Nazis was to be regarded as abandoned

German property, and only the district office of liquidation, a court, or a civil suit could decide that the property be returned.⁶⁴

Disputes over property kept controversies over verification alive. Repatriates in Rudna, Lower Silesia, feared that after two years of restoring the farms they were allocated, the farms would be returned to their former "German" owners verified as Poles. In a letter on 27 May 1947 they claimed that the owners were former Nazis and denied wanting to be Poles despite their Polish names.⁶⁵

As of July 1947 an estimated 2,300 settler families occupied disputed property in Opole Silesia alone. Vacillation in administrative decisions created uncertainty about the fruits of one's labor, stirred violent reactions, contributed to the departure of autochthons and settlers, and deepened the frustration of repatriates and their aversion to invest labor into land that might be taken from them.⁶⁶

Nevertheless, the number of property disputes reportedly declined: in Silesia from 2,236 on 1 October 1947 to 818 just a month later and to 559 on 15 November 1947; in Olsztyn Province from 2,210 on 15 September 1947 to 811 on 15 November 1947. But in Mrągowo County in September 1947, settlers, almost half of them PPR members, with the support of their local party organizations, which used expropriated land to build patronage networks, resisted surrendering farms in more than 500 of 600 cases decided by the courts. In addition, decisions regarding the property of the large number of Mazurs who refused to apply for verification were suspended. Settlers who occupied their property awaited their expulsion as Germans.⁶⁷

Challenges to Re-Polonization: The Kashubs

If national consciousness "must include the sense of a historical community and the perception of cultural uniqueness which provides a given population with a particular identity, both in their own eyes and in the eyes of those outside the population," the cultural identity and historical experience of many natives of the Recovered Lands posed a considerable challenge to "re-Polonization."⁶⁸ The authorities expected quick success and had no understanding of the difficulties that the process faced. They opposed manifestations of a separate ethnic or regional identity, whereas activists often regarded its affirmation as a means of winning loyalty to Poland.

The Kashubs manifested differences that aroused official suspicions. In Sztum and Lębork Counties conflicts frequently occurred because of the cultural affinities of Kashubs with local Germans, which separated them from Polish newcomers. In a report on 5 October 1945 the Lębork plenipotentiary belittled the value of the local MO, 75 percent of which consisted of Kashubs, because they spoke perfect German, had relations with Germans, and therefore showed too much understanding, supposedly often against the interests of the state.[69]

Kashubian activists sought to hold a congress emphasizing the unity of all Kashubs to save those who had been Germanized from expulsion. Officials, however, saw the congress as a threat to their authority and their conception of an ethnically homogeneous state and therefore forced a postponement of the meeting. A special envoy sent by the MIiP in December 1945 commented favorably about the Kashubs in general but saw the bilingualism of their publication *Zrzesz Kaszebsko* (Kashubian Union) as worse than useless in a "nationally uniform" state. On 7 January 1946, the director of the MAP Political Department warned in a secret memo of the potential danger of the planned congress. He advised minimizing its significance, not committing the government to anything (especially with regard to filling local positions), and emphasizing the martyrdom of the Kashubs during the war and their organic unity with the rest of the Polish nation.[70]

These fears proved overblown. When the Kashubs finally held their congress on 12–13 January 1946, it declared:

> The congress remembers the Germanized Kashubian lands of Gdańsk, Łebsko-Słupsk, and Bytów. The congress recognizes them as its brothers and asks that the Government of the Republic separate them together with their families from true Germans on the basis of descent and make it possible for all those who did not commit hostile acts toward the Polish nation to return to Polishness.[71]

Nevertheless, officials remained suspicious. Following the congress, an official of the Gdańsk WUIiP wrote, "We have to be vigilant so that this movement does not outstrip our intentions, and it looks like it will. The principles that the leaders of this movement propagate are correct, but insincere. They want to create a springboard. Most of all they are fighting for a union [of Kashubs]." The authorities later noted the influence of the PSL among some members of the Kashubian elite connected with the *Zrzesz Kaszebsko* and accused them of national separatism.[72]

On 29 April 1946 Provincial Verification Commission member Dybowski reported that only a small number of Kashubs had undergone the verification process, which he found particularly regrettable in the "old Kashubian coastal settlement" of Łeba. Moreover, the property of most of the verified had been plundered or confiscated. In predominantly Kashubian Cewice he found verified autochthons living in one room with repatriates whom the PUR located there. He called for an inquiry into the detention of the former mayor of Cewice and the expulsion of his family.[73] The PUR director in Bytów expressed the view of some officials by publicly declaring that he "will throw [all Kashubs] from Bytów County out of Poland head first."[74]

Volksdeutsche

Immediately following the Potsdam Conference, Czechoslovak President Beneš signed a decree stripping Germans of citizenship prior to their expulsion. Only those who actively opposed the occupation or suffered Nazi persecution could have their citizenship reinstated. On the same day the Ministry of Interior exempted Slavs who registered for German citizenship "under the threat of denunciation or particular circumstances deemed exceptional." Most of the nationally indifferent who sought to regain citizenship languished in prison while their past was scrutinized for signs of behavior marking them as German. Special commissions created by local authorities under a decree on 27 October 1945 could still punish those who regained citizenship and other Czechs for offenses against national honor, including unsuccessfully attempting to be recognized as German.[75] As in Poland, implementation of these decrees by local officials was, however, confused and random.

Poland already provided for the rehabilitation of *Volksdeutsche* by the law of 6 May 1945, but disputes over its application continued in the late summer and fall of 1945. An amendment to the law on 24 August 1945 sought to lessen the controversy by ruling that the Nazi authorities had coerced all inhabitants of Upper Silesia and Pomerania Province within its prewar borders (i.e., including counties incorporated in Gdańsk Province) into registering on the DVL, making it possible to obtain a permanent certificate of Polish citizenship based solely on a declaration of loyalty.[76]

The amendment did not include Poznań Province, which meant seeking rehabilitation through the courts and the publication of the names of applicants. On 20 August 1945 the Poznań KW PPR sent a memo to its subordinate committees calling on them to "thoroughly superintend" the rehabilitation process, investigating and revealing crimes committed by those seeking rehabilitation and mobilizing the local population to protest.[77]

In a report for September 1945, the Nowy Tomyśl County *starosta* claimed that rehabilitation prompted "ever more indignation in Polish society." Convinced that registration on the DVL was voluntary, the local population called for an amendment requiring the detention of all *Volksdeutsche*. When in September 1945 a wave of protest meetings swept over Poland because of the prosecution in the British zone of Germany of forty-eight Poles involved in a brawl and the death sentence of several of them, the meetings in Poznań Province, initiated by the KW PPR and implemented mainly through the efforts of the WUIiP and the local PZZ, targeted above all the "lenient" treatment of *Volksdeutsche*. Whereas other PZZ provincial branches sought the quickest possible positive rehabilitation of applicants, the Poznań Province PZZ initially favored a complete cleansing of foreign influence.[78]

On 23 September 1945 rallies took place in sixty-five locations in the province, demanding the abrogation of rehabilitations already approved and a halt to the process as well as the confinement of all *Volksdeutsche* and the requirement that they wear the letter "N" (for *"Niemiec,"* "German" in Polish, just as Poles wore the letter "P" under Hitler). In Nowy Tomyśl County protest meetings took place in all large centers and passed similar resolutions on 25 September 1945.[79] On 22 November 1945, however, the MAP forbade the residential segregation of Germans and the requirement of an armband or patch indicating nationality. Still, on 14 January 1946 the Presidium of the Poznań WRN sent a request to the Presidium of the KRN to lift this prohibition.[80]

The first rehabilitation hearing before a court in Poznań Province took place on 1 October 1945. On 9 October 1945 the PPR KW and allied parties called on the population to participate actively in the rehabilitation hearings: every Pole, male and female, had the obligation of providing concrete details of guilt or exoneration to the authorities. The population responded. Denunciations of *Volksdeutsche* constituted a large part of the documents at the hearings. Even residents of smaller towns became involved. The Sieraków national council on 9 October 1945 decided to send a representative to the Międzychód County seat to copy applications for rehabilitation so that inhabitants could provide information about negative behavior during the occupation. When many rehabilitation hearings resulted in positive rulings, the public complained. On 9 November 1945 even the UW requested an explanation from the prosecutor of the Special Criminal Court.[81]

Opposition to rehabilitation was particularly acute in Kępno County, which on 1 October 1943 had far more *Volksdeutsche* than any other county in Poznań Province, though a much higher proportion (40 percent) in category III. Already on 12 May 1945 the PRN sent the chairman of the KRN a letter demanding a prohibition of rehabilitation for *Volksdeutsche* and *Leistungspolen*. Even those who proved their loyalty should be subject to special restrictions for five and a half years, just as Poles were during the occupation.[82]

Political violence also affected developments in Kępno County. On orders of the Polish underground, Franciszek Olszówka (pseudonym "Otto")—a category III *Volksdeutscher* and Wehrmacht deserter—led a group that assassinated the PUBP commandant and his assistant in October 1945 because of their treatment of prisoners from the anticommunist resistance. Following the attack, some thirty innocent people were arrested and seven summarily executed. In retaliation on the night of 22 November 1945, Otto led an attack on the Kępno PUBP that resulted in the deaths of seven, including the wife of an officer and her two children who happened to be at the headquarters.[83] Security officials reacted by arresting about 300 individuals, according to a PSL interpellation in the KRN on 28 April 1946. Some were released, others were killed, their bodies found in fields and in the street and later in a county garden where they were buried.[84]

Głos Wielkopolski on 3 November 1945 attempted to link the underground in Ostrów and Kępno Counties with *Volksdeutsche*.[85] This plus the violence in Kępno apparently alarmed some inhabitants. The *starosta* informed the governor on 21 December 1945 that a growing number of Poles on farms formerly owned by category I and II *Volksdeutsche* received death threats, resulting in massive numbers abandoning their farms and requesting to remain in Kępno. The *starosta* sought permission to set up a labor camp for suspects, the assignment of units of the Internal Security Corps to the county, and an increase in the budget of the MO and UB.[86]

As the number of repatriates from the east rapidly increased, public opinion in Poznań Province pressured local officials to remove additional category III and IV *Volksdeutsche* from their properties, contrary to regulations. This seemed less offensive than not to provide farms to Polish repatriates or agricultural laborers from Central Poland, who often arrived without any means of support. Yet some properties came into the hands of inappropriate individuals, sometimes because they threatened local officials with violence.[87]

Because of a belief that material considerations most frequently motivated registration on the DVL, nothing outraged the population in Poznań Province more than the return of property to rehabilitated *Volksdeutsche*. Calls came for prosecutors and judges to decide more frequently on partial rehabilitations with confiscation of property. In April 1946 the press warmly greeted the appeal by the prosecutor of the Special Criminal Court of a decision of the magistrate's court in Międzychód, in which he argued that signing the DVL allowed the applicant to keep and farm sixty-two hectares during the occupation and that confiscating the property would be an appropriate punishment.[88]

One of the most publicized rehabilitation cases took place before the magistrate's court in Oborniki. A scathing article published on 4 December 1945 suggested that the rehabilitation of the Wieczorek family, whose son had volunteered for the Wehrmacht, resulted from connections with the local authorities. The PPR County Committee backed the sole witness against the family. But an investigation revealed that those critical of the rehabilitation simply hoped to take over the sequestered property, illustrating a common problem: those who testified against rehabilitation frequently had their eye on the property of the *Volksdeutsche*.[89]

According to the report for 1945 of Poznań Province, 28,500 *Volksdeutsche* in categories III (19,500) and IV (9,000) filed declarations of loyalty as did about 18,000 *Leistungspolen*. A press report indicates that as of 24 February 1946 the magistrate's courts ruled on 1,916 of 8,304 applications for rehabilitation in the province, rehabilitating 1,100 individuals (57.4 percent). The prosecutor appealed in 344 (31.3 percent) of these cases.[90]

In Upper Silesia the amendment of August 1945 allowing rehabilitation of *Volksdeutsche* in categories III and IV by a simple administrative decision evoked a negative reaction among newcomers. The Bytom PUIiP reported on 7 September 1945 that a significant percent objected that not all those in categories III and IV deserved to enjoy the full benefits of Polish citizenship.[91]

After the chairman of a district court told newcomers at a meeting on 7 September 1945 in Pszczyna County that local courts approve more than 90 percent of applications for rehabilitation of category II *Volksdeutsche* and that therefore the courts must return their property to them, representatives of 400 families sent a memorandum to the highest central authorities. Threatened with removal from the property they occupied, they objected that they received no compensation for the half year of repairing devastated farm buildings, obtaining equipment, and preparing the harvest: "Again we have to go wandering about." They claimed that the courts approved rehabilitation of those in category II because no one dared to make accusations and judges did not want to sentence individuals to camps for an unspecified term as required by the law. The memorandum predicted that the category II *Volksdeutsche* would sooner or later again declare themselves to be German. Meanwhile, the newcomers from the east who lost everything "because they did not want to renounce their nationality for the sake of property" faced an uncertain future.[92] The Silesian PUR Provincial Office reported on 6 October 1945, "The issue of the resettlement of repatriates already once settled belongs without doubt to the most searing issues in the territory of this department's activity."[93]

Some local officials in Upper Silesia ignored or misinterpreted the directives. The Tarnowskie Góry *starosta* sent category II *Volksdeutsche* to a camp in Lasowice, apparently without assessing the possibility of their rehabilitation. Following their expulsion, he reported on 8 October 1945 that some returned and so far 218 were again put in the camp.

> These are for the most part women with children, in every case the least harmful element since all of them, adults as well as children, speak Polish.
>
> Their main guilt is that their husbands or fathers were members of German organizations and so far have not returned whether from military service or they escaped from the German army.[94]

Rev. Gloeh claimed that Mazurs in Działdowo, mainly women and children, were taken from their homes and housed in barracks in Narzym under deplorable conditions. "According to cruel Polish laws they must seek civil rehabilitation in court." Deprived of their property, they did not even have the means to pay the fee to apply for rehabilitation. Newcomers did everything to hinder the process of rehabilitation and were assisted in this by the local authorities, who sought to delay certification, waiting for the deadline of 1 September 1945 to pass. According to Gloeh, when a court granted rehabilitation to a Mazur, he had to use force to repossess his home. Some Mazurs who approached Gloeh wanted to apply for rehabilitation, but witnesses to their loyal behavior during the war were afraid to testify because newcomers threatened them with beatings and death.

Gloeh found the young judge at a court hearing to be objective and fair whereas the prosecutor from the UBP was half-educated. The prosecutor opposed rehabilitation in one case in which, in Gloeh's view, it was rightly granted. In another case in which a woman seeking rehabilitation was rightly denied because of evidence that she was German, the prosecutor demanded a new hearing and rehabilitation because the woman was Catholic.[95]

In his report Gloeh focused specifically on Mazurian self-identification and observed that Mazurs in general and in particular in Działdowo County "are not properly nationally conscious." He accused the Roman Catholic clergy of trying to "return" Mazurs to the Catholic faith using the "Jesuitical slogan" that only a Catholic is a Pole. He claimed that many Mazurs who converted were disappointed in not regaining their civil rights and remaining in detention. He also reported that Catholic clergy on its own authority took over a church in Narzym, Protestant since the Reformation.[96]

But even for Rev. Gloeh, the situation was not entirely unambiguous. Mazurs who refused to register on the DVL were liable to be persecuted and punished, and the majority gave in or signed voluntarily. Some, however, tried harder than necessary to please the Germans. Nevertheless, he proposed, "Extend an amnesty to Mazurian *Volksdeutsche,* except those whose activity hostile to Polishness is proven."[97]

Others in Działdowo disagreed. The *starosta* reported on 5 September 1945 that the PRN complained that the rehabilitation process of category II *Volksdeutsche* was "very perfunctory and lenient."[98] On 14 September 1945 it unanimously required Mazurs regardless of DVL category to perform agricultural labor in neighboring villages, reasoning that, "despite filing a declaration of loyalty to the Democratic Polish State, they did not yet receive Polish citizenship." But the root causes lay elsewhere: "These citizens had it good during the occupation, and today they again [arrogantly] raise their heads because they signed a declaration [of loyalty] and insolently demand their property. This we cannot tolerate."[99]

In the following months the *starosta* repeatedly reported on the antagonism toward Protestants and the appropriation of their churches and buildings despite his prohibitions. For example, in Płośnica Catholics took over the Protestant church and removed all tombstones and crosses in the graveyard. In a report on 3 January 1946, he attributed "this manifestation of mutual racial hatred" "above all to the indelible memory of the martyrology of society in Działdowo County," where the Nazis organized "a camp of persecution," "and the death of Polish martyrs for the Polish cause." But he also claimed that the majority of the Protestants were Germans who did not even apply for rehabilitation. In a report on 3 March 1946 he blamed an increase in antagonism on the plenipotentiary of the Consistory of the Evangelical-Augsburg Church Rev. Lodwich, who strongly defended local Protestants as innocent victims of the Nazis even though the courts rejected many of their applications for rehabilitation. The *starosta* called for a radical solution of the "burning question" of a Mazurian identity:

> [Poles] who remember the German injustices they experienced cannot forget those who today constitute this regional branch of Polish society. On every side one also hears voices demanding setting the matter straight, that is, form out of this branch of Polish society either Poles or germans [sic]. Because this regionalism too painfully wounds the heart of a Pole who himself lived through or witnessed the six-year martyrology of the Polish nation.[100]

In Biała County dissatisfaction also reigned with what many regarded as the overly lenient treatment of category III and IV *Volksdeutsche*. At meetings the public demanded the isolation of category II and III *Volksdeutsche*, for example, by wearing a yellow armband with a black "V." Schools refused to accept the children of *Volksdeutsche*. The *starosta* himself asserted that Poles had not spared any sacrifice, from exile and loss of property to persecution and death, not to betray their nationality, whereas the *Volksdeutsche* took advantage of their misfortune, appropriating Polish property and enjoying privileges.[101]

In Żywiec County the children of *Volksdeutsche* were also prevented from attending school. In industrial regions with high unemployment, rehabilitated *Volksdeutsche* were seen as competition for scarce jobs. In rural areas confiscated property and farms were not returned to the rehabilitated. Although in principle intended for repatriates from the east, local people took over most farms, often in collusion with the local authorities.[102]

The Cracow governor saw the rehabilitation of undesirable elements as a main cause of dissatisfaction and therefore directed *starostowie* to use all means at their disposal to encourage the filing of accusations against those who during the occupation engaged in inimical activity. By the end of 1945 the Biała *starosta* received 98 denunciations. Significantly, in Wilamowice, with three-quarters of its inhabitants on the DVL, there were no denunciations.[103]

The possibility of rehabilitation did not deter local officials from expelling as many *Volksdeutsche* as possible in the second half of 1945 without regard to their category. If *Volksdeutsche* were too young, old, or feeble to be exploited as laborers, officials pushed for expulsion, pointing to the shortage of provisions and housing. In getting rid of such "weaker" elements, some officials cited the MAP directive of December 1945 authorizing permits for Germans to leave.[104] Although this applied only to Germans, they used it as a basis for expelling *Volksdeutsche,* some of whom spoke no German; some returned to Poland illegally or entered camps in Germany for those awaiting official repatriation. A representative of the Łódź WUBP Health Department reported that the majority of detainees in the Sikawa internment camp for transport to Germany in January 1946 did not express a strong desire to leave the country and in many cases begged with tears in their eyes to remain in the camp.[105] On 14 February 1946 the Łódź governor requested that the MAP issue regulations concerning the basis for providing *Volksdeutsche* with certificates allowing them to leave, "which would prevent arbitrariness in taking care of these matters on the part of the administrative authorities and put an end to all possible abuses and oversights."[106]

As the organized "resettlement" of Germans approved at the Potsdam Conference began in mid-January 1946, the Pomeranian UW directed on 17 January 1946 that those in category II of the DVL who had not yet applied for rehabilitation be treated as Germans. By the spring of 1946 many of those in categories I and II who had not fled were expelled. In Kępno County, where a majority of *Volksdeutsche* during the occupation were in categories I and II, on 1 March 1946 those in category III constituted more than two-thirds of the remaining *Volksdeutsche*.[107]

But concern about the restoration of the economy and the population losses during the war prompted Warsaw to limit the departure of elements not unquestionably German. On 21 February 1946 the MAP informed the Poznań governor that *Leistungspolen* and individuals in categories III and IV later removed from the list did not have to make a declaration of loyalty. On 20 March 1946 the PRM ruled that *Leistungspolen* who declared their loyalty to Poland possessed full rights of citizenship if during the occupation they demonstrated Polish national distinctiveness, their names did not appear on the DVL, and they did not personally seek the status of *Leistungspolen*.[108]

Nevertheless, a decree on 22 February 1946 allowed for harsh penalties in case of a less-than-complete rehabilitation, including a suspension of civil and public rights for up to five years, a fine of 500 to 2 million złoty, and full or partial confiscation of property. A complete denial or a failure to apply for rehabilitation before the deadline resulted in a permanent loss of civil and public rights and detention for an indefinite period. Individuals who failed to report that someone voluntarily registered on the DVL faced a sentence of up to five years of imprisonment.[109]

In the first months of 1946 the Cracow governor thought he detected a decline in interest in the protracted rehabilitation process. In Olkusz County some even thought that local *Volksdeutsche* should be treated more leniently than migrants, mainly from Upper and Lower Silesia, who allegedly took a pro-German stance and held lucrative positions during the occupation and presumably fled east to avoid detection. Resentment over rehabilitation, however, persisted in Biała County.[110]

Wilamowice remained the center of the conflict. The model farm of a rehabilitated *Volksdeutsche* aroused so much envy that he chose resettlement at the beginning of 1946.[111] After provincial internal security units drove some rehabilitated individuals from their farms despite an order of the minister of agriculture and agrarian reforms to halt the expropriation of property, the matter came before the RM on 25 April 1946. Ultimately, on 19 September 1946 the RM accepted the minister of justice's view that, although the population of Wilamowice did not behave very well during the occupation, the removal of rehabilitated individuals was illegal and their property should be returned.[112]

In Działdowo a conflict over rehabilitation arose between local administrative and security officials. Although the PUBP received only a small number of objections to *Volksdeutsche* in categories III and IV with provisional certificates of Polish citizenship, when they began to receive irrevocable certificates on 1 March 1946, the PUBP immediately intervened, claiming that it had to investigate the accusations it received. The *starosta* complained that this could have been done earlier and that the intervention undermined his authority and demonstrated a lack of professionalism in the ranks of the security office.[113]

The debate over the culpability of *Volksdeutsche* also continued in Upper Silesia. In a letter to Bishop Adamski on 23 March 1946 Rev. Franciszek Kuboszek contradicted his view that locals registered on the DVL *en masse* to "mask" their Polishness. He claimed that pro-German feelings grew in Rybnik and Pszczyna Counties before the war and at its start. Only the German defeat at Stalingrad prompted a decline in support for the German government. "As a Silesian it pains me all the more but does not close my eyes to reality. One cannot make everyone on the DVL into a German, but similarly one cannot make everyone on the list into a Pole." "Justice demands greater screening to defend all Polish blood, but also to separate out the German element."[114]

Others called for greater leniency. A project of the Legal Commission of the Silesian Institute dated 23 March 1946 proposed the repeal of all special measures, relying instead on the prewar criminal code to prosecute category I *Volksdeutsche,* and favored offering category II *Volksdeutsche* the possibility of rehabilitation. "The joy as a result of liberation and the establishment of our state power allow for an amnesty in relation to individuals who only because of their low intellectual level or insufficient civic consciousness let themselves be persuaded to deny their Polish nationality." The Presidium of the Silesian WRN went even further on 23 March 1946: "If it is a question of individuals registered in nationality category I, one should note that there are among them many worthwhile individuals, who against their will were put on the list, in light of which they should have the possibility of clearing themselves."[115]

In a long memorandum to the MAP on 29 April 1946 Rev. Karol Katula, pastor of an Evangelical-Augsburg parish in Łódź, called for a general amnesty for all *Volksdeutsche* who were not resolute Germans and against whom no one raised detrimental objections. He rejected all justifications for registering on the DVL, including "masking oneself," which he believed caused great moral harm. Yet application of the letter of the law was not always just and useful. He decried the abuse of *Volksdeutsche* who before the war had been upright Polish citizens. Contrary to Polish interests, society and the state approached the problem without distinguishing between those who were really guilty and those who simply made a mistake. The punishment affected many who did not deserve it, not for their behavior before the war or during the occupation, people who erred but did not deserve absolute condemnation, especially because those applying the punishment were not up to the task, and the opportunity to enrich themselves appealed to their worst instincts.

The state required proof of coercion, which Rev. Katula argued existed not just in Silesia but also in other regions, where it applied primarily to citizens of German origin, particularly following orders in 1942 to arrest those not yet on the DVL. In his view, more important than an individual's registration on the DVL was the individual's persona before the war, his preservation of his national distinctiveness, and his general stance during the occupation. Treating registration on the DVL simply as a crime did not take into account that the losses in the war required the retention in Poland of as many citizens as possible.

Although Katula agreed that not a single German should remain in Poland, he cited Zawadzki's principle of not surrendering a single Polish soul. In Silesia this applied to autochthons, who largely did not have Polish national consciousness. It should apply elsewhere to Polonized Germans, some of whom regarded themselves as Poles and Poland as their fatherland for generations and raised their children in Polish. The Nazis interrupted this Polonization and won back many for Germanness. But many either did not register or registered without conviction, some to save their lives, others to save their property. Many had nothing in common with Germanness, sometimes large families speaking Polish who could increase Poland's diminished numbers.

Because of mistreatment, many autochthons from Silesia and Mazuria as well as Polonized individuals of German origin left, forming organizations of expelled Poles, according to Katula. Faced with the rigorous application of rehabilitation, many did not even apply, and some withdrew their applications, very often not at all because of German convictions. Should not the remaining be saved for Poland? Because of errors, even the most rigorous application of verification and rehabilitation would not remove all Germans. The state could revise rehabilitation and verification and the law on revocation of citizenship. This would cause Poland less harm than removing those who identified as Polish and felt wronged in being expelled.[116]

A concise census on 14 February 1946 found that there were 222,971 residents of "Old Poland" whose applications (presumably nearly all for rehabilitation) were still in process: 44.0 percent resided in Silesia, 20.1 percent in Gdańsk Province, and 12.6 percent in Poznań Province.[117] As the number of rehabilitated *Volksdeutsche* rose, the restoration of appropriated property became increasingly problematic. On 15 April 1946, a Gdańsk Provincial PUR inspector requested specific instructions whether a farm in Wejherowo should remain in the hands of a rehabilitated native or a repatriate. If the rehabilitated category II *Volksdeutsche* retained the property, the repatriate would have to be resettled again after taking out a loan and investing his own funds in rebuilding a property that the PUR assigned to him, rendering it all worthless. The uncertainty had an economically disastrous effect on farms with two owners, neither of whom was doing the spring planting. Until the situation was clarified, the inspector proposed suspending settlement in the area "because this work is fruitless. Today settle—tomorrow resettle. This is unbecoming work for such an important agency as the State Repatriation Office." Not knowing how many property owners in category II would be rehabilitated, he declined to say how many more repatriates the area could absorb.[118]

He also questioned the rehabilitation of Kashubs. Where they predominated, he claimed that they occupied most of the fifty formerly German farms in the area, leaving only destroyed farms for repatriates, who declined to occupy them because of the hostility of locals and the lack of assistance from the local authorities, recruited from among the natives. Death threats prompted sixty families to give up the farms assigned to them. The inspector blamed German machinations seeking to prevent Poles from settling the area and to demonstrate that the Kashubian land was solely for Kashubs, a Kashub being someone other than a Pole. Although he favored re-Polonizing elements long Germanized, he argued that conditions had to be created for "the education of this element in the Polish spirit" and the prevention of German activity threatening the area. Future resettlement, as he saw it, depended on the resolution of the status of the Kashubs, whom he likened to Mazurs and Silesians.[119]

On 19 April 1946 the Economic Committee of the RM finally set the norms for workers of German nationality and unrehabilitated *Volksdeutsche* in categories I and II and in category III with irrevocable membership in the German state: a sixty-hour workweek and a 25 percent deduction from pay for "the reconstruction of the country and social services."[120] Reluctant to lose cheap labor, directors of labor camps opposed rehabilitation and the expulsion of those denied rehabilitation. A "war" broke out in the first half of 1946 between the Gronowo labor camp and the Katowice District Board of Prisoner Labor over where to register prisoners. Corruption often marked the assignment of *Volksdeutsche*. In December 1946 a case came to light of a 500 złoty bribe paid for assigning a nineteen-year-old female to a farmer in Lwówek, Poznań Province. When a family member not on the DVL tried to secure her freedom, he was arrested.[121]

Volksdeutsche worked in industry and agriculture, women often as unpaid domestics in the homes of militia, security, and military officers.[122] Regulations called for close cooperation of administrative, local self-government, and security organs in assigning *Volksdeutsche* to forced labor, but in reality security officials gradually assumed control.

The Return of Displaced Persons

Between the spring and fall of 1945 900,000 refugees and Displaced Persons—forced laborers and prisoners of war—returned to Poland from occupied Germany. But a hard core resisted repatriation to a communist-dominated Poland. In March 1946 UNRRA was caring for at least 450,000 non-Jewish Poles. In December 1946 there were still 250,000 ethnic Poles in the refugee camps.[123]

Polish officials pressured them to return by denying their families permission to leave Poland. Those who sought to return dealt mainly with the Polish Military Mission in Berlin. According to a report of the British authorities in occupied Germany on 13 April 1946, the head of the mission, former plenipotentiary of Mazuria Jakub Prawin, complained that a high proportion of those seeking to return were *Volksdeutsche*: "He prefers, of course, to have racial Poles," presumably meaning autochthons.[124] Until Warsaw defined the criteria of Polishness, the mission used knowledge of Polish or "at least a Polish folk dialect" as the basic requirement. According to a report in April 1946 on the mission's activities, "After confirming that the Kashub, Mazur, Silesian, and

Pomeranian is suited for work in the rebuilding of a great Democratic Polish State, and during the war did not commit any crimes against the Polish Nation," the mission granted permission to return but left the final determination of nationality to local verification commissions. In the summer of 1946 some 300 persons a day, mainly former German soldiers, were applying for repatriation at the missions in Berlin and Leipzig.[125]

As time passed, Polish officials scrutinized refugees with increasing suspicion. As the head of a refugee camp in Denmark told a local Danish newspaper in August 1946, Poles who previously only had to express the wish to return home now had to explain why they had not returned sooner. A returnee from the camp commented, "My mother escaped having to explain why she had not already returned to Poland. She died half a year later, whereas I, two years old and unable to account for my patriotism, was granted a permit of entry."[126]

The return of Wehrmacht veterans raised other issues. The massive number of prewar Polish citizens from the incorporated lands who served in the Wehrmacht fostered the stereotype of the Upper Silesian/Kashubian renegade in the rest of Poland. Claims that service was coerced and that the ethnically Polish veterans were victims of the war sought to lessen the shame, which still persists. But neither victimization nor active collaboration with the Germans accurately characterized the majority of cases. Most simply adapted to the situation and sought to ensure their own survival and that of their families, even at the price of far-reaching moral and political compromises.[127]

Polish military authorities focused on Wehrmacht veterans in POW camps in the west already in April 1945 when the head of the Military Judiciary asked the MAP for an expedited decision on the implementation of the degree on rehabilitation to clarify the status of prisoners of war of Polish nationality in DVL categories III and IV.[128]

At the end of August 1945 a special provincial commission in Upper Silesia interviewed thirty-two POWs, freeing thirty. On 20 December 1945 the Presidium of the WRN together with representatives of the administrative and security organs and of the coal industry, which used POWs in the mines, created a Qualification-Control Commission with the authority to free Silesians in categories III and IV (and possibly II) who spoke Polish after thoroughly examining their service records, including whether they had volunteered for service and the qualifications and behavior of the immediate family. Membership in a Nazi organization or a prewar German organization and attendance at a German school disqualified a prisoner from consideration. Those from other areas came under very stringent examination. The commission began its work on 14 January 1946. During the year, it interrogated 9,483 POWs, freed 7,842, designated 1,113 for expulsion, and turned over 528 cases to the public prosecutor for further investigation. With the transfer of POWs from camps throughout Poland to camps and mines in Silesia, the work of a reorganized Qualification-Control Commission continued in 1947 and 1948 with a notably smaller percentage of POWs released each year and a higher percentage expelled. In the third quarter of 1948 the commission also began to examine the cases of prisoners transferred from POW camps in France and Great Britain.[129]

At the turn of 1945–1946 veterans of the Polish Armed Forces in the west loyal to the government-in-exile began to return from Great Britain, some 10,000 in all, 70 percent of them Silesians conscripted into the Wehrmacht who then deserted on the western front or were recruited from POW camps. At the same time more than 10,000 soldiers from General Władysław Anders's 2nd Corps returned to Poland from Italy, about 70 percent of whom served in the Wehrmacht according to the MON. Some were captured at the battle of Monte Cassino and changed sides. A total of 105,000 Polish Army veterans returned to Poland, but only 310 from the 85,000 who left the Soviet Union with Anders.[130]

On 30 March 1946 the Chorzów municipal authorities warned that delays in the rehabilitation of veterans from abroad and *Volksdeutsche* in category II might have unpredictable consequences. They could not get work and not infrequently had nothing to live on. The growth in poverty increased prostitution, spreading venereal disease to an unprecedented degree. At the current rate, the rehabilitation process would take five years to complete. "It is not surprising that many [category] twos known as Poles voluntarily apply for departure to Germany, with the hope of finding better living conditions there."[131] The Tarnowskie Góry *starosta* thought it abnormal for veterans with two or more years of service at the front with the Polish Armed Forces who were placed in DVL category II without requesting it and who returned convinced that as Poles they would receive the rights of citizens were instead told that they were Germans and must be rehabilitated: "Rationally, this is a difficult double summersault."[132]

In urging veterans in Great Britain to return to Poland, the Warsaw government assured those in DVL categories III and IV automatic rehabilitation and those in categories I and II rehabilitation through the courts. Returnees, however, frequently claimed that the Polish Military Mission informed them that donning the uniform of an ally and fighting the German enemy sufficed for rehabilitation.[133] In Działdowo County recently returned Polish Armed Forces veterans, who accounted for most of the several thousand individuals who had not signed declarations of loyalty, gave the same explanation, according to the *starosta* on 4 May 1946. He urgently requested a ruling on the matter because of the absolutely final deadline for rehabilitation of 9 May

1946, one year after the end of the war. Earlier he reported that he investigated each late application and imposed sanctions on those who dismissed the importance of the question of nationality, which he attributed to illiterates or semi-illiterates as well as to individuals who discounted the importance of all official announcements. But by early July 1946 he lost patience with *Volksdeutsche* who continued to delay the process "because in many cases they apparently possess a German soul, and so I am currently turning to rigorous methods."[134]

Out of concern that the Polish Armed Forces veterans included "agents of Anders sent for special spying and propaganda assignments," the MON dictated that "uncertain or suspect individuals" come under the surveillance of security organs.[135] The son of a veteran who returned in 1947 with 300 others claims that they were taunted with wanting to return with Anders on a white horse and that after returning his father had to report repeatedly to the Pszczyna PUBP for questioning. The official suspicion persisted: when the son was interned under martial law in 1981, he was accused of being influenced by the followers of Anders.[136]

Questions concerning returnees arose repeatedly. On 21 August 1946 an official in Grodzisk wrote to the Nowy Tomyśl County *starosta* asking in which DVL category to consider "Rassendeutsche," individuals of Polish nationality whom the Nazis subjected to a "racial examination" against their will and resettled to Germany. Did they need to undergo "rehabilitation" before being recognized as Polish citizens?[137] On 8 October 1947 the Poznań UW asked the MAP for a ruling on category III and IV *Volksdeutsche* of Polish nationality who now requested permission to return. In the years 1946–1950 various administrative offices in Poznań Province received 200 to 300 such requests. In each case the final decision lay with the MAP.[138]

The Ministry of Recovered Lands and "Voluntary" Departure

A decree on 13 November 1945 created the Ministry of Recovered Lands (MZO). The assumption of its leadership by PPR First Secretary Gomułka indicated its importance to the regime. It dealt a blow to the political opposition by diminishing the influence of the MAP led by PSL activist Władysław Kiernik, who until then had jurisdiction over the Recovered Lands.[139]

The decree establishing the MZO made no explicit reference to the autochthons among its goals.[140] Concerned about the lack of an overall policy regarding autochthons, the PZZ sent a memorandum to the MZO already on 27 November 1945 urging, "The autochthonous population should be the core and basis of Polish life developing in the Recovered Lands."[141] Nevertheless, the resolutions of the first PPR congress in December 1945 concerning the Recovered Lands made no mention of the autochthons.[142]

Gomułka referred to autochthons in a speech before the KRN on 31 December 1945 in listing the main tasks confronting the MZO: "organization of the repatriation of the Germans to their country, re-Polonization of the Pole-autochthons, resettlement of Polish population." But expulsion took priority: "In the first place we should put emphasis on the question of transfer, that is, of the repatriation of Germans to their country. The problem is the most urgent for a variety of reasons. The basic reason is the building of a national state."[143]

At the same KRN session, a PSL deputy called attention to the tragic plight of autochthons as victims of looters and murderers and reproached Gomułka for not mentioning their problems. Another member of the opposition proposed that the political conflict in Central Poland not be allowed to spill over to the western lands, discrediting state policy in the eyes of the autochthons. Gomułka sharply attacked this proposal. The Recovered Lands played too large a role in the struggle of the PPR for hegemony. The PSL also competed for influence among autochthons. Its *Gazeta Ludowa* in December 1945 asserted the necessity of involving the local population in the verification process and rejected categorically a decisive role in the process for settlers from Central Poland. In fact the PSL succeeded to some degree in overcoming the indifference of the local population and its avoidance of any contact with Polish elements, for example, in Mazuria, whose inhabitants were otherwise largely impervious to "re-Polonization."[144]

Official data indicate that after the Potsdam Conference, 90,000 individuals were expelled from Upper Silesia in 1945: 19,000 from prewar Polish Silesia and 71,000 from Opole Silesia. In addition, 29,000 left of their own accord. Together with those expelled in June and July, 150,000 individuals left Upper Silesia in 1945. They comprised innumerable Upper Silesians of uncertain nationality, ethnically Polish German citizens, and *Volksdeutsche* as well as Germans, this despite the efforts of resettlement commissions, which in many cases freed victims of hasty expulsions from transit camps, where they often accounted for more than half of those interned.[145]

"Voluntary departure" systematically intensified in 1946. In addition, a tendency arose among those certified as Polish, particularly women on their own with children living in difficult material circumstances, to seek reunification with family members in Germany. Unorganized groups of individuals arrived on their own at transit points. Others tried to leave illegally. In May 1946 the authorities intercepted 7,308 individuals seeking to cross the Oder-Neisse border without permission, 32.6 percent of them allegedly Polish. In 1946–1947 the Frontier Defense Force in the region of Szczecin claimed to have intercepted 1,565 Poles seeking to leave for Germany and 1,575 Poles as well as 969 Germans seeking to cross the border in the opposite direction.[146]

Alleged violations of the principle not to include "one drop of Polish blood" forced the MZO on 15 January 1946 to order the establishment of special verification commissions at transit points to conduct summary proceedings concerning claims of Polish origin.[147] The ministry also made government plenipotentiaries personally responsible for a strict temporary prohibition of the expulsion of Germans from Opole Silesia, Lubusz Land, Pomerania, and the District of Mazuria because of the large percentage of autochthonous population and its incomplete verification.[148] In response the Silesian governor on 7 February 1946 called a halt to all local decisions concerning further expulsions and prohibited the issuing of permits to leave the country.[149]

Chaotic conditions at many transit points, however, prevented effective screening. On 23 January 1946 a counselor of the Western Pomerania District WS-P and representative of the Szczecin Plenipotentiary for matters related to the Gumieńce transit point reported that many thousands were being loaded onto transports every day causing serious difficulties that threatened Polish interests. One of the "grievous" matters raised in his report concerned the expellees, "among whom are found alleged and native-born Poles as well as various 'Volksdeutsche.' The whole of this multi-thousand mass of 'German' repatriates is completely unsorted and therefore include a wide variety of people."

> The most painful matter is that of Poles formerly German citizens, resettled compulsorily together with Germans. The cause of this is first of all the fact of insufficient preparation of the appropriate Polish functionaries, who lack orientation to nationality relations in the former Reich and because of this regard every resident of the former Reich as a German.
>
> The second cause is greed: a citizen reaching the recovered lands from the depths of the country, especially when he is in uniform and armed, and likes a farm occupied by a Pole, formerly a citizen of the Reich, employs threats and repression against him, as a result of which the threatened individual abandons the farm and departs together with the German population to the Reich.
>
> The third cause of the departure of Poles . . . is insufficient national consciousness and discouragement with the current temporary conditions predominant in the recovered lands, which in the mind of a former citizen of the Reich is a normal phenomenon in Poland.

He also reported, "In Berlin a Union of Poles resettled from Poland to the Reich has allegedly been formed."[150]

The Polish government feared exposure of the faulty "resettlement" procedures. A memorandum at a meeting of Silesian *starostowie* on 21 February 1946 stated:

TABLE 7.1 National Identities in the Recovered Lands, 14 February 1946

Recovered Lands	Poles	In Process	Germans	Others	Total
Białystok	33,059	831	2,136	443	36,469
Olsztyn	247,616	4,612	98,466	1,134	351,828
Gdańsk	224,450	9,127	91,803	1,852	327,232
Szczecin	405,411	5,933	473,954	7,269	892,567
Poznań	242,022	5,412	24,558	1,022	273,014
Wrocław	681,671	9,215	1,239,309	10,954	1,941,149
Silesia	890,484	159,330	14,5731	4,328	1,199,873
Total	2,724,713	194,460	2,075,957	27,002	5,022,132

Data source: Stefan Szulc, ed., *Powszechny sumaryczny spis ludności z dn. 14.II. 1946 r.* (Warsaw: Nakładem Głównego Urzędu Statystycznego, 1947), xvi, http://www.scribd.com/doc/36839158/Powszechny-Sumaryczny-Spis-Ludno%C5%9Bci-z-dn-14-II-1946-roku-1. The number in process in Silesia appears greatly overstated and probably includes individuals yet to apply.

Top secret instructions must set up preventive measures so that the displaced do not take abroad papers "compromising" and disparaging our work, such as provisional certificates of Polishness, decisions of a rehabilitation court, favorable opinions often issued to Germans by some offices, national councils, and parties. All notes, jottings, etc. In a word, the displaced must be subject to a detailed personal search from this particular angle.[151]

In a report for February 1946, an official of the Silesian UW claimed that the verification process was reaching completion.[152] A concise census on 14 February 1946 indicating the number of residents of the Recovered Lands still in process along with the nationality of residents, presumably based partly on the results of the process, belied that claim.[153]

Those in process in Opole Silesia represented 82.0 percent of the total in the Recovered Lands and constituted 13.3 percent of the population of Opole Silesia compared with 0.9 percent in process in the rest of the Recovered Lands. The numerous difficulties that verification and rehabilitation encountered required the central government to become more directly involved.

[8]

The Central Government and Nationality Verification

TROUBLED BY THE lack of uniformity in the verification process and concerned about retaining as many natives of Polish origin in the Recovered Lands as possible, the PZZ sent a memorandum to the MZO in January 1946 calling for a comprehensive approach to their problems. For the PZZ, they constituted "one of the strongest arguments justifying the right of the Polish nation to these lands." Their presence "creates the most advantageous conditions for maintaining the continuity of social, economic, and cultural life."

Yet "as a result of ignorance of the western problems and aversion to all traces of Germanness, Polish society often treats the population of the Recovered Lands as germans [sic]. What most misleads Polish opinion is the fact that the autochthons possess—which is of course understandable—citizenship of the German Reich" warranting their expulsion, "often also due to ordinary abuse of authority for personal goals," diminishing "the biological strength of the Polish nation."

"The Polish Nation having won the territorial war must also win the nationality struggle." The memorandum invoked the slogan "do not waste even one drop of Polish blood" to promote the widest possible return of the Polish autochthonous population "forcibly evacuated or evacuating voluntarily together with the retreating German army"—initially taken as evidence of pro-German sentiments.

The memorandum portrayed the Germanization of the autochthons as "a history of Polish martyrdom." Differences in the level of Germanization, however, dictated that the problem should not be resolved "in a mechanical way." Like the DVL in regard to German Polish citizens, the PZZ distinguished four classes of Polish German citizens, ranging from those who demonstrated their Polish national consciousness to "germans [sic] of Polish origin, although actively involved in the national-socialist movement, nevertheless providing proof that they took part in the national-socialist movement not out of ideological motives, but only out of opportunistic ones with the goal of more easily preserving their national distinctiveness."

The memorandum recognized that such a nationality policy posed dangers and required a long-term policy, lasting at least two generations. But the PZZ assumed responsibility for advocating this policy and, "as the leading social organization in western matters," proposed to carry out the verification process. Finally, the PZZ urgently called for uniform regulations governing verification to prevent abuse and assure the native Polish residents with a clear basis for obtaining political rights.[1]

Early in 1946, Dr. Zygmunt Izdebski, chairman of the PZZ in Silesia, published the most important statement of the principles of verification, "a new theory of nationality" based on the historical experience of Upper Silesia. Denying the usefulness of either objective criteria (language, religion, race, origins) or subjective criteria (self-identification), he advocated turning to "that which Americans call 'behavior'" in deciding an individual's nationality—without noting that the Nazis did the same. Even an individual who "is not yet nationally discerning enough" indicated "in which direction his discernment is developing and what basis it has for the future in his psychic attributes, way of life, of speaking, of educating children and so forth." In practice this meant "not the principle of determining who can be regarded as a Pole, but the principle of who cannot be verified as a Pole because of definite characteristics of Germanness," such as membership in the Nazi party or its allied organizations and explicit identification with the German nation. Although he foresaw the possibility of making exceptions, e.g., for some members of the Nazi party, he opposed Polonizing Germans, even those of Polish ancestry, if their behavior exhibited solidarity with the German nation and hostility toward the local Polish element.[2] He, however, strongly advocated the strict Polonization of the "population with an uncertain national consciousness." Its expulsion, he argued in reports to the authorities, would merely strengthen "the biological potential of Germany."[3] Thus, the continuing national conflict with Germany dictated their verification as Poles, irrespective of their wishes.

Officials, however, often interpreted the behavior of autochthons differently than their advocates. The authorities regarded the resistance of many Upper Silesians to giving up their traditional ways of life, including the use of the German language, even after qualifying for Polish citizenship, as examples of German arrogance. A report of the Silesian UW for January 1946 referred to them as "a dangerous element, which in many cases is beginning to raise its snout [łeb]."[4]

Moreover, the central authorities focused on the expulsion of Germans rather than on the verification process. At a session of the KRN Legal and Statutory Commission in mid-February 1945, the representative of the MZO Edward Qirini, who had been connected with the *Delegatura,* opposed the premature passage "of some general law concerning the granting of citizenship" prior to the removal of the Germans, averting the danger of their obtaining Polish citizenship.[5]

International Pressure, the Referendum, and Autochthons

On 5 March 1946 Winston Churchill's famous "Iron Curtain" speech decrying a situation he helped create raised the specter of a rollback of the Polish-German frontier, deepening the feeling of uncertainty and disorientation in the Recovered Lands and increasing the pressure on the Polish authorities to expel the remaining Germans and re-Polonize the autochthons. In addition, international and domestic pressure to hold elections that the PPR feared it would lose led to a decision to hold a referendum as proof of popular support for the government.[6]

During a discussion of the criteria for verification as a Pole, Gomułka publicly stated in March 1946 that "even those who over the years succumbed to Germanization should be restored to Poland."[7] On 20 March 1946 the MZO declared that the expulsion of even one person of Polish nationality solely for not yet having obtained administrative confirmation of membership in the Polish nation "would be in flagrant contradiction with a well understood Polish *raison d'état.*"[8] Mazurian Governor Robel saw this as a fundamental change in policy, stating on 6 April 1946 that it permitted officials "to search out Polishness everywhere that it might seem greatly problematical—even simply impossible." He instructed officials to examine all natives, registering those who were undoubtedly German for "repatriation" while exempting the rest whether they applied for recognition of their Polish origins or not, whether they wished to remain in Poland or not, as long as a verification commission found that they had a connection with the Polish nation, marking a return to his predecessor Prawin's policy.[9]

None of this undid the Gordian knot of distinguishing between Germans and those natives who were largely indifferent to nationality or who sought verification as Poles to keep their farms, avoid confinement in camps, or simply remain where they had "always" been and not face the uncertainty and poverty in a destroyed Germany. Bilingualism facilitated a decision to stay while uncertainty about the permanence of the border discouraged unambiguous declarations of Polish nationality. Although there was a feeling of separation between nationally conscious Germans and nationally indifferent inhabitants, society at the local level sought to persevere and maintain its former ties.[10]

Discussion of a referendum generated reports that the government could not count on the support of autochthons. On 1 March 1946 the Bytom PUIiP estimated that about 60 percent of the county's population was hostile toward the Polish State and could be expected not to vote. Of the remaining 40 percent, even among those who for some reason belonged to the PPR or its allied parties, if they voted, they would not vote with the so-called Democratic Bloc led by the PPR, which in all probability would get only 10 to 15 percent of the vote. According to the report, not infrequently one could hear criticism of a referendum, such as a statement in German overheard in a streetcar in reference to the food shortage: "Those damn Poles distribute [ration] cards, for which you have to pay, but you cannot buy grub; they think that we will vote for them—we prefer Free Germany to lousy Poland." The report also cited communities where verification supposedly recognized predominantly pro-German elements as Polish.

The report claimed that the difficult economic situation, the dissolute security organs, and the marauding Red Army inclined the overwhelming majority of Polish society to blame the Polish government for these "anomalies." Even with an improved material situation, hostile pro-German propaganda would find arguments to persuade the autochthonous masses that only German autonomy would satisfy them.[11]

On 6 April 1946, after nearly a year of Polish administration of the Recovered Lands, the MZO issued a detailed directive concerning nationality verification. Article three stated, "Persons will be recognized as having Polish nationality who file the appropriate application and prove their Polish origin or show connections with the Polish Nation and in addition submit a declaration of loyalty to the Polish Nation and State." Documents such as birth or marriage certificates, Polish kin, or even a Polish-sounding surname could prove one's Polish origins. Behavior would demonstrate "connections with the Polish Nation," as Dr. Izdebski advocated, evidence of the influence of the PZZ. An autobiography submitted with the application might note membership in a Polish organization or participation in the Polish national movement; "an internal attitude and language"—cultivation of Polish customs in the family, or ties with Polish folk culture or the life of Poles; or "an external attitude during the period of German rule, manifesting solidarity with Poles while exposing oneself to personal danger."[12] If possible, the applicant was to name two individuals known locally who could verify the applicant's claims. By relying on an evaluation of past behavior, the process placed decisive power in the hands of officials. (Marcin Kula notes that a Polish law of 7 September

2007 also empowers a bureaucrat to decide on the certification of residents of a post-Soviet state as Poles.)[13]

The MZO directive excluded those "who in their inveterate and notorious behavior demonstrated complete association with the German nation or their hostile attitude toward Polishness." Because of the widespread pressure to join the Nazi party during the occupation, mere party membership did not in principle prevent recognition as a member of the Polish nation; rather, one's party activities indicated the extent of one's ties to the German nation. If an individual came under these exclusions, the Polishness of family members depended on their concretely demonstrating a lack of solidarity with that individual.[14]

Theoretically, the MZO directive settled the controversy over the verification of former Nazi party members and indicated an evolution in nationality policy. Initially, superficial characteristics, such as Nazi party membership, seemed to define national loyalties, particularly for those from areas that had not been part of the Reich, and underestimated the pressures on German citizens to join the party. By taking into account other aspects of an individual's behavior, the central authorities broadened exclusive criteria that ignored local conditions. In Opole Silesia several thousand former party members claiming that they risked losing their jobs if they did not join the party were verified as Poles, many of them prior to Zawadzki's order of 25 October 1945 reserving such decisions for the Provincial WS-P.[15]

The MZO directed provincial officials evaluating an applicant to seek the opinion of the PUBP and of a verification commission, which was to include representatives of the administration, political parties, and the PZZ as well as three to five "Polish activists" from the local population.[16] In practice they generally consisted of local officials, social and party activists, and those connected with them, who, in the view of one historian, judged applicants not so much on "Polishness" as on acceptance of the communist-dominated authorities.[17]

Nationality verification was soon linked with the referendum. On 27 April 1946 the KRN voted unanimously for a referendum, set for 30 June 1946, with three propositions: abolition of the Senate, land reform and nationalization of basic industries, and the Oder-Neisse border.[18] The next day, 28 April 1946, the KRN unanimously passed the "Law Concerning Citizenship of the Polish State of Individuals of Polish Nationality Residing in the Territory of the Recovered Lands," which granted Polish citizenship to permanent residents of the territory before 1 January 1945 who proved their Polish nationality to the satisfaction of a verification commission, obtained confirmation from the appropriate administrative authority, and signed a declaration of loyalty.[19] In introducing the legislation, PPR Deputy Włodzimierz Sokorski stated,

We understand that the pressure of Germanization could not but leave traces, that the people of whom we speak, retaining their language and old traditions often have a Germanized way of thinking, a weak feeling of a link with Poland, but at the same time a strong feeling of separation from the German nation, of a regional consciousness, Silesian, Mazurian or Warmian.[20]

It sufficed that they were not Germans. Connecting the law with the referendum, Sokorski pointed out that granting citizenship to "autochthons" had "colossal political significance," allowing them an "open and clear" expression of their views in elections and a referendum, which "will decide the matter of the Recovered Lands in our national conscience."[21]

On 4 May 1946 the MZO issued a directive emphasizing the importance for the referendum of quick and proper nationality verification and asserting that the participation in the referendum of as many "autochthons" as possible "is in the interest of the Polish State."[22] In Gdańsk Province the report for May 1946 cited efforts to verify a maximum number of autochthons. To ensure that they would vote "yes" on all three questions, the authorities planned to distribute relief funds among them.[23] In Silesia the UW warned that the Moravian population along the border with Czechoslovakia wanted to vote against the new border and therefore should be verified only after the referendum.[24] Meanwhile, the PPR and its allies launched a frenzied all-out campaign in favor of "Three Times Yes." The campaign included such nationalist slogans as "Yes is the mark of your Polishness"; "Three Times Yes does not appeal to the Germans"; "You are a Pole, say yes."[25] The Olesno County PUIiP, however, reported on 15 June 1946 that the campaign increased hostility to Polishness among the autochthons.[26]

At the end of May 1946 Mikołajczyk and the PSL recommended voting against the abolition of the senate to prevent the Democratic Bloc from exploiting a positive vote on all three questions as an expression of confidence in its rule.[27] The supposed threat that a "no" in the referendum would bring about a reversal of the border actually heartened some inhabitants of the Recovered Lands. A mood of uncertainty marked much of the population. British Vice Consul Joseph Walters noted in May 1946, "The feeling that Stettin [Szczecin] will not remain Polish or that the port will be internationalized is firmly rooted in most minds and would appear to be the cause of the apparent indifference to any long term policy for the development of the town."[28] The MIiP received a report from Prudnik in June 1946 that "German propaganda is in action, especially whispered. One hears here and there, *The Germans are coming, they will hang those who vote for the border.*"[29]

Although the PZZ opposed extending the political conflict to the Recovered Lands, in March 1946 it decided to support the Democratic Bloc. In June 1946 the PZZ Directorate issued a handbill, printed in 50,000 copies, that called on "repatriates and settlers" to vote "yes" on the question concerning the western border. Significantly, it addressed the autochthons by their local identities:

> Silesians, Mazurs, Warmiaks, Kashubs, Poles of the lands of Lubusz and Złotów. For whole centuries of German captivity, you relentlessly pursued the return of our common Fatherland—Poland. Today—Your dream is fulfilled. Thanks to Your persistent struggle for Polishness during the period of captivity, thanks to the correct policy of Polish democracy You and Your lands, on which you have lived since your ancestors, returned forever to Poland. We know that from the side of irresponsible elements, attempting to distort the correct policy of the Government, you often still encounter injustice. The Polish Government and Polish democracy will not allow you to be wronged.

With the referendum, "You will reveal to the country and the world Your national consciousness, Your political maturity." "The Polish Western Union, heir to the heroic tradition of the Union of Poles in Germany, summons You: to massive participation in the Referendum to answer 'YES' to all three questions."[30]

About a week before the vote Gomułka referred to autochthons as "the living proof of the Polishness of the Recovered Lands" in an interview with the Workers' Press Agency. He favorably noted their class origins as workers and peasants, whereas the local nobility proved less resistant and was completely Germanized. He underlined the equality of autochthons with Poles from Poland's prewar territory. Admitting that the local authorities had made mistakes, he promised, "We will not tolerate the mistreatment of autochthon-Poles."[31]

On 26 June 1946 the Democratic Bloc, together with numerous trade unions and organizations, including the PZZ and the Union of Veterans of the Silesian Uprisings, issued a proclamation calling on Poles to vote "yes" on all three propositions. "The third question concerns lands which returned to the Motherland . . . They preserve such a border with Germany, which makes any assault on Polish lands on the part of our eternal foe impossible." The proclamation maintained that the three questions constituted one whole. Therefore "whoever would vote 'no' once writes off the unity of the nation contrary to Polish *raison d'état*. Every 'no' of a Pole is a 'yes' for German retaliatory aspirations, is a 'yes' for the protectors of Germany."[32]

Following the referendum on 30 June 1946, the chief commissioner delayed announcement of the results until 11 July 1946, raising doubts about their validity. Despite the lack of complete, reliable data, one can conclude that the referendum constituted a disastrous defeat for the PPR. No more than 26.9 percent voted "three times yes," and at least a third voted "three times no." In the Recovered Lands a substantial majority voted with the PSL on the first question, but also a significant minority voted against the border—in a few counties of Silesia even a majority did so.[33]

On 6 July 1946 Gomułka explained to party activists in Warsaw the numerous cases of *"nein"* written on the ballot in Gothic script as acts of "a verified Pole—an autochthon in Silesia or Mazuria proves that we did not yet manage to awaken in him the Polish national spirit, that he did not yet get rid of the patina of Germanness, which was imposed on him through hundreds of years." They were not traitors in his view. Others came to a harsher conclusion. On 26 July 1946 the Presidium of the ZG PZZ under its chairman Wacław Barcikowski, who was also vice president of the KRN, declared those who voted "no" to be traitors and "de facto allies of Germany." It called for greater vigilance in the expulsion of Germans, blamed the difficulties encountered in the verification process on the maltreatment of autochthons by "some authorities," and urged the government to take decisive steps to ensure the welfare of autochthons.[34]

The referendum results exacerbated local divisions. The director of the Olesno PUIiP felt vindicated. In a report on 5 July 1946 he criticized the *starosta*, who allegedly favored natives over newcomers, whereas the "three times no" votes demonstrated the scandalous nature of the verification process. The director claimed that when no one wanted to apply for verification, the "Germanophile" *starosta* threatened them with expulsion and detention, turning Germans into Poles. Repatriates and settlers were happy that the natives voted "no," which should convince Governor Zawadzki and the *starosta* to stop favoring natives. With satisfaction, the director added that the "genuine" Poles on the election commission "did their Polish work," and so the authorities could claim that 70 percent voted "three times yes."[35]

For his part, the Olesno *starosta* expelled a local priest, verified as Polish but suspected of responsibility for the distribution of a handbill in his parish church urging people to vote "three times no." On the day of his expulsion, parishioners demonstrated in protest and shouted antigovernment slogans. The PUIiP reported on 19 July 1946 that "good local Poles" and even political parties called for cancelling the expulsion. The PUIiP objected that it had not been informed beforehand but agreed with the expulsion, claiming that the priest had been secretive and "confined himself solely to the natives."[36] Officials failed to take into account the strong ties of Silesians to their Catholic faith, and the expulsion of a priest or transfer to a parish solely of settlers was bound to lead to conflict.[37]

Not all of the negative votes in the borderlands came from former German citizens. Presumably, some repatriates from the *kresy* voted "no" to protest against the loss of their homeland or even to support a reversal of the changes in Poland's western and eastern borders. "No" votes did not necessarily indicate a preference for Germany over Poland. By voting "no," autochthons protested their treatment since the end of the war or against communist and Soviet domination. The falsification of the results could only increase their alienation from the government and possibly even from Poland. As Józef Czaplicki, a leading figure in the MBP, later stated, "Society itself understood after the referendum that nobody will hand over power voluntarily."[38] In 1970 Witold Kula observed that the results of the referendum were known in advance and its propositions camouflaged the basic question: "Are you for the seizure of all power by the communists?"[39]

Implementation of the MZO Directive

The war and its immediate aftermath left many of the inhabitants of the Recovered Lands destitute, often unable even to afford ration cards for vital food supplies, which had a profoundly negative influence on opting for Poland. Postwar conditions prevented quick and effective assistance to those in need. On the initiative of the PZZ and the Union of Peasant Self-Help, a conference in Warsaw on 20 December 1945 attended by representatives of the MZO, academic institutions, political parties, and other social organizations agreed to the rapid provision of assistance for the population of Polish origin. Both PZZ Chairman Barcikowski and the deputy minister of labor and social welfare affirmed the right of verified autochthons to social assistance. Provincial authorities concurred. But a meeting of Polish activists in Opole in August 1946 confirmed a lack of sufficient financial resources to provide comprehensive assistance. In addition, the hostility of the newcomers and of many local officials prevented impoverished autochthons from receiving material support.[40]

Only in the second half of 1946, with the approach of the first postwar parliamentary elections set for January 1947, did the authorities, political parties, and social organizations begin to address the catastrophic conditions in which some natives lived. Assistance also came from abroad. By that time, massive numbers of autochthons had already left for the West.[41]

Following the MZO directive on nationality verification, citing its "insufficient clarity," the Gdańsk governor on 13 April 1946 issued criteria for verification that gave self-identification a greater role. Insisting that the process simply sought to identify Poles, he directed that questions of loyalty be left to the courts. He denied that any judicial, security, or administrative official had the right to overturn a verification decision, which depended on "consciousness of the declared and proven origins" of the individual: "Often superficially

Germanized individuals, no longer able to speak Polish adequately, show far more attachment to Polishness than individuals who speak the mother tongue fluently." But those who held a leading position in the Nazi party or other important Nazi organizations were not to be verified as Poles. Finally, he emphasized the need to bring an end to all abuses, such as treating verified Poles as Germans and confiscating their property.[42] Despite verification or rehabilitation, the native population frequently came under attack, including violence at the hands of security agencies as well as of the newcomers, according to a report of the Gdańsk UW on 23 April 1946 that attributed this hostility toward autochthons to their poor pronunciation of Polish or complete ignorance of the language.[43]

In a report for May 1946, the Gdańsk UW also blamed Germans awaiting expulsion for "conducting destructive work among autochthons."[44] Officials commonly blamed Germans for complications in the verification process. In Wrocław Province a wave of applications for verification aroused the suspicion of the chief delegate of the MZO, who suggested on 19 April 1946 that Germans, especially the intelligentsia, were playing for time to remain in the region to lead a fascist movement and, if they succeeded in slipping through the verification process, to organize a conspiracy. "German insolence goes so far that people are applying who, aside from a barbaric attitude toward Poland, have nothing in common with it."[45] More likely, local residents sought to avoid expropriation of their property and expulsion. Some genuinely despaired at leaving their homeland to the point of committing suicide.[46]

Zawadzki responded to the MZO directive on 17 April 1946 with guidelines for drawing up lists of Germans designated for expulsion. Only those who claimed to be German or were verified as German were liable for expulsion. Those claiming to be Polish could reapply for verification and were not to be "repatriated." Care was to be taken not to break up families. A German spouse of a Pole who wished to remain in Poland had to commit in writing to maintain loyalty to the Polish nation and state and to raise the children in a Polish spirit. A member of the Polish nation wishing to leave for Germany with a German spouse was to be persuaded to give up this intention voluntarily,

> even at the cost of breaking the family union and kinship with the side leaving for Germany.
> In the case of children of a mixed marriage, they are to stay with the Polish side remaining in Poland.
> One should regard a person of Polish origin or displaying a link with the Polish Nation as a person belonging to the Polish Nation. Considering the undeveloped consciousness of Polish origin in many cases, one should pay attention to the sound of the name, often distorted by germans [sic], as well as kinship ties with Poles.[47]

The emphasis on behavior, however, meant that applications "require very scrupulous research," resulting in about 1,800 cases still to be considered as of June 1946, according to the Silesian UW.[48]

The simultaneous pressure on local officials to retain autochthons and expel as many Germans as quickly as possible resulted in a certain dissonance. Thus, the Gdańsk UW complained in July 1946 that the expulsion restarted on 10 May 1946 was not proceeding fast enough and, at the same time, directed officials to ensure that only Germans leave, not individuals with the right to verification.[49]

The MZO initially set 30 June 1946 as the deadline for submitting applications for verification and 31 July for the completion of the whole process. On 10 July 1946 the Silesian UW optimistically reported that verification in the region of Opole had "in principle" been completed in June and the signing of declarations of loyalty and the issuing of permanent certificates of Polish citizenship had begun.[50] But a large number of those considered eligible for verification did not apply by the deadline, and therefore the MZO postponed the deadline until the end of September 1946, with the WS-P taking over the tasks of the already disbanded verification commissions.

Meanwhile, many male heads-of-household, oftentimes the sole breadwinners, had not yet returned to Poland. Women awaiting their return often declined to apply for verification of their nationality, fearing loss of the right to leave for Germany should their husbands decide to stay there. The question of their verification arose with increasing frequency in 1946. On 19 October 1946 the MZO directed that women could apply for verification regardless of the whereabouts of their husbands. In the case of a supposedly ethnically mixed marriage, which in practice in Opole Silesia regularly resulted in a denial of verification, the MZO ruled that if a husband present in the country did not have proof of Polish origin, the authorities were to consider his political past, his fluency in Polish, his attitude toward the Polish state and nation, the level of national consciousness of his wife, and the certainty that their children would be raised in a Polish spirit: "We cannot allow that a Pole emigrates from Poland to Germany simply because we do not allow a German husband to reside in Poland."[51]

In Szczecin Province the governor on 10 August 1946 questioned the view of a Polish historian that 80 percent of the population of Western Pomerania was of Slavic origin and opposed the re-Polonization of those who fled:

> The above-mentioned 80 percent no longer felt any link with Polishness, on the contrary, showed its adherence to Germanness, proven by the fact that despite the collapse of the Third Reich—this population decided to abandon their residences and farms and leave the terrain in which they grew up and were raised rather than stay in place and try to obtain Polish citizenship.

Only 905 individuals in the province had applied for Polish citizenship or signed a declaration of loyalty, of which the verification commission approved 489 and rejected 62, with 354 pending cases to be resolved by 1 August 1946. That, the governor stated, would bring an end to the question of the autochthonous population of the province.[52]

There were, however, problems at the local level of Szczecin Province. On 6 July 1946 the MZO informed the MBP that autochthons, including the verified, continued to be detained in the labor camp in Złotów.[53] After the Złotów PZZ District reported that, besides a large number local Polish autochthons, 90 percent of those detained in the POW camp in Złotów consisted of Germanized Poles, whose release it could not obtain despite appeals to the appropriate authorities, the director of the PZZ in Szczecin requested on 18 July 1946 that the ZG PZZ in Poznań intervene in Warsaw: "In our view the scandalous situation in Złotów County is all the more sad if one takes into account that before the war Złotów County was the mainstay of 'Militant Polonia in Germany.'"[54] Barbara Zakrzewska of Złotów later wrote to the PZZ:

> In August [1946] I was taken to the labor camp in Złotów. Officers of the local Security Office came to me and ordered me to go with them immediately.... I was taken on the basis that I am a "Reichsdeutsche." Like many other residents of this place, I left a furnished home, which together with all property was handed over to settlers.[55]

On 1 August 1946 the Szczecin Provincial WS-P questioned the *starosta* in Dębno whether repatriation was being carried out in keeping with provincial directives after a German citizen of Polish origin reported that an official gave her, "as a hostile element," three days to leave her home.[56]

The Gdańsk Committee to Assist the Verified reported on 16 September 1946 that even those recognized as Poles suffered maltreatment:

> In fact they particularly were and unfortunately still are objects of constant and massive abuse on the part of dishonest lower state functionaries as well as of people out of ill-will or ignorance, chasing after looting the property and belongings of the verified. Lawlessly resettled beyond the Oder, thrown out of homes and farmsteads, notoriously falsely accused before the UB of cooperation with the Germans, all types of violence including murder out of a desire for gain are unfortunately still the order of the day. Frightened, abused, treated as Germans, pushed by looters, they are fleeing in massive numbers beyond the Oder.[57]

Skepticism on the part of officials about the motivation of German citizens claiming to be Polish increased the likelihood that their applications would be denied. Contrary to directives, the verification commissions in Brzeg, Namysłów, and Syców Counties in Wrocław Province did not include autochthons, and their members were hostile toward the autochthons, many of whom were

Protestants. Of 11,832 applications for verification in the province by the end of August 1946, less than half (5,537) were approved. Furthermore, verification could be revoked followed by expulsion, which discouraged others from even applying. Officials estimated that more than 8,000 individuals in Lower Silesia qualified for verification had not applied by the end of 1946.[58]

When on 2 November 1946 the MZO identified thirty-one counties where the continued expulsion of autochthons not yet verified was particularly prevalent, they included Brzeg, Namysłów, and Syców Counties. The MZO ordered special county commissions that included Polish citizens from among the "autochthonous population" to check the lists of designated expellees prior to expulsion to ensure that they do not include "Polish autochthons" who had not yet filed for verification and did not possess formal evidence of membership in the Polish nation. Significantly, the ministry assigned an MZO delegate to oversee the execution of these instructions in three regions: Silesia, Western Pomerania, and Eastern Pomerania.[59]

In September 1946 the expulsion or voluntary departure of a majority of the autochthons of Polish origin in Wrocław Province prompted an interpellation in the KRN addressed to Gomułka, asking what was being done to bring the situation under control, but the minister of Recovered Lands did not respond. On 24 October 1946, however, the Wrocław UW prohibited the removal from their homes and the expulsion of those autochthons with applications for verification still pending. In a report for January 1947 it noted that the UB and MO had the practice of settling disputes in favor of newcomers, probably over property, which negatively affected the verification process.[60]

Obstacles to Verification: Mazuria

The hostility of newcomers toward the native population of Mazuria prompted Olsztyn Governor Robel to issue a warning on 22 June 1946:

> The Government of National Unity will combat with complete severity all lawlessness, theft, robberies, violence, murders, and all abuses, especially in cases if they are directed by whomever against the Polish autochthonous population.
>
> The Polish native population, no matter whether it is already verified or not yet, is guaranteed the right to a peaceful existence in the land of its forefathers and because of its difficult situation is under the protection of the state authorities. This population commends itself also to particular fraternal protection of that part of the incoming society from other sections of the country which is conscious of its historic mission for the Polish nation and state.

Those who harmed the native population faced punishment, including the death penalty. Local officials were reminded of their duty to report all crimes.[61]

Because some local officials, particularly those recruited from among settlers, hindered autochthons from certifying their Polishness and pressured Mazurs and Warmiaks to leave, on 28 June 1946 the governor directed *starostowie* to educate officials "that Polish *raison d'état* demands that we not lose one drop of our blood and that a sympathetic and loyal approach to Mazurs and Warmiaks, drawing them into social work, and care on the part of the commune will speed up the process of re-Polonization." The governor ordered *starostowie* to warn officials that the smallest deviation from directives would result in their removal. The goal was to increase the number of officials of local origin and remove inappropriate ones from Central Poland.[62]

At the end of June 1946 about 34,000 autochthons in Olsztyn Province still had not yet sought verification, 16,000 of them in Mrągowo County and 7,000 in Szczytno County. In August 1946 PZZ activists blamed the indiscriminate treatment of the autochthons as Germans. The activists and the provincial authorities attributed the failure of Polonization to the poor material conditions of the autochthons, the lack of enforcement at the local level of directives concerning property disputes, and the desire of autochthons to reunite with their families in Germany.[63]

In mid-1946 the PZZ estimated that two thirds of the autochthons of Olsztyn Province, half of them already verified, wanted to leave. On 20 July 1946 the governor complained to MZO Deputy Minister Wolski that organized gangs of looters of all kinds, including security organs and especially the MO, undermined the efforts of the administration and rendered it powerless. A Mazur explained her departure for Germany: "We were so tired of life amidst the robber-gangs that we preferred to leave the homeland."[64] In Szczytno *Starosta* Późny, one of the few officials of Mazurian origin in an executive position, on 13 March 1946 ascribed the refusal of many autochthons to undergo verification to the plundering by looters from Central Poland. "Ragged and hungry, although admitting that they are of Polish origin, they do not want to declare themselves [Polish] and prefer rather to leave their ancestral lands and go beyond the Oder in the belief that there they will find better living conditions and protection from robbery."[65] Other Mazurian activists also saw it as a rational, calculated economic choice.[66]

At the beginning of July 1946 the Mrągowo County Settlement Office described the mood as one of "'expectancy.'" "Complete discouragement and dissatisfaction is visible here, and what is worse there is no belief in the permanence of current conditions in the Recovered Lands," for which the report blamed letters from Germany with statements such as "this state of affairs will not last long" or "we are doing well." As a consequence, when the verification commission held some twenty meetings in June 1946, "the results were 99.99% negative." Only about a dozen Mazurs were verified as Polish out of 18,000

German citizens. "In discussions with them, they admit that they are Mazurian, but rather German ones. They do not want to declare their Polish nationality at all. Their sole aspiration and dream is to depart for Germany as soon as possible." In this situation, the report urged their "repatriation" as quickly as possible before they engaged in activities harmful to the state and its citizens.[67]

In Nidzica County the *starosta* reported in July 1946 that the Mazurs in one community aggressively insisted, "They will never sign the declaration, that they are Germans, and no power can compel them to do so. They will force their way on foot beyond the Oder and prefer to die, but they don't want to stay here."[68] After touring the county, a Special Verification Commission reported in the latter half of July 1946 that 75 percent of Mazurs had departed from Poland, including some who had declared themselves to be Polish, which it attributed to (1) the lack of security: "The Mazurian population lives in incessant fear"; (2) former POWs, the husbands of many Mazurs with children remained in the West; (3) "inadequate material assistance and closer warm relations with the Mazurian population"; and (4) a complete lack of consciousness-raising activity among the Mazurs. As a result, "the best element" was in Germany, leaving mainly elderly men, women, and children, many of them awaiting the return of relatives, and therefore a certain percent had not decided to sign a declaration of loyalty.[69] The Mazurian pastor in Nidzica claimed that the aggressiveness of the Catholic Church also "contributed to the emigration of many Mazurs."[70]

The combined efforts of the local PZZ section and the administrative authorities to pressure individuals to apply for verification yielded only meager results. When verification of nationality formally ended in September 1946, Olsztyn Province had the largest number of autochthons still refusing to submit to the process. As of 15 October 1946 69,470 residents were verified as Poles, but 33,869 remained unverified, nearly half of them in Mrągowo County. Nevertheless, the authorities did not want to countenance their departure for Germany.[71]

According to a memorandum on 26 October 1946 of the secretariat of the Olsztyn KW PPR,

> A lack of the most fundamental interest in the problem of liquidating the disputes as well as observed religious fanaticism as manifested by the strata of the repatriates in relation to the Protestant Mazurs leads to an ever clearer gulf between the local Polish population and the population from outside the area. Effect: passive resistance to the conferring of Polish citizenship, declarations of a desire to resettle beyond the Oder and recently a very serious signal, "3X no" in the People's Referendum.

In 1984 former Olsztyn Deputy Governor Wilamowski stated that in 1945, "The authorities thought that the Mazurian people would beg on their knees to be granted Polish citizenship," and therefore officials undertook no long-term educational effort to ensure the success of the verification process. "Many Mazurs feared that if they sign a declaration of Polishness, then in a still unstable situation, that they can be suspected of betraying Germanness and with the possible return of the lands to Germany bear specific consequences."[72]

Obstacles to Verification: Silesia

In Silesia relations between the autochthons and newcomers also hindered the verification process. In an article published on 10 June 1946 the writer Kazimierz Brandys indicated that natives saw the repatriates with their different accents or even language, customs, and lifestyles as a foreign "Ukrainian" element and those from Central Poland as "looters." At the third session of the Research Council, 16–19 June 1946, Stefan Golachowski of the Silesian Institute complained that the natives treated settlers and repatriates as "unwelcome newcomers, thieves." Local farmers allegedly preferred to hire Germans, even from another county, rather than landless repatriates looking for work, who as a result regarded the natives as Germans. According to the PUR in Kluczbork in November 1945, "People come to the local office almost every day, that natives say to them, you Polish thieves, what did you come here for, this land belongs to us, not to Poles."[73] On the other side, a native recalled her disappointment at being treated as a German:

> I almost could not believe that those are Poles. After all, we knew Poles so well who came to work for farmers. After all, not so long ago we said good-bye to them with tears in our eyes. They promised that they will write, that they will not forget. One even said that Silesia will be Polish and that Mama now lived to see Poland. Now I understand—we belong to the Germans and probably we all must suffer for the guilt of the guilty. This is collective responsibility.[74]

Of the 6,500 autochthons in Silesia who did not apply for verification of their nationality by 30 October 1946, the UW reported that some 4,000 resided in Kluczbork County, where as in Mazuria the large number of Protestant inhabitants was probably a factor.[75] In a memorandum to the PZZ Directorate in Katowice on 14 July 1946, the chairman of the Kluczbork PZZ Circle Reverend Klus (apparently, a Protestant minister) pleaded that expulsion not include the at least 3,000 people in the county who spoke Polish, prayed in

Polish in church, and maintained Polish customs yet did not apply for citizenship by the 1 July 1946 deadline because no one fostered their national consciousness. On the contrary, newcomers who illegally occupied local farms assured the owners that they were German. An acquiescent people, they only needed to be approached properly. Unfortunately, the local administration did not always fulfill its obligations. It lacked people familiar with Silesian conditions and most often did not have the necessary patience and understanding required for successful re-Polonization. But Klus remained confident that all autochthons would apply for citizenship if only appropriate officials would take the matter in hand.[76]

Blaming above all German propaganda, the county office confirmed on 30 August 1946 that about 3,000 autochthons did not file for verification and instead applied in massive numbers to depart for Germany. It accused local officials who maintained personal relations with Germans of having a highly negative influence. Only at the end did the report acknowledge one of the more significant sources of dissatisfaction: the decision that the date of occupation of a farm determined whether it belonged to an autochthon or to a newcomer. But the report recommended that the County WS-P use extraordinary means to halt the departure of the local population in the belief that its attitude mostly did not represent its true national feeling. In September 1946 a provincial inspector reported that the mayor of Kluczbork interned several hundred individuals whose Polish nationality had been verified; that their property was plundered and occupied by newcomers; that seven locals were murdered during robberies, including a veteran Polish activist; and that a well-known Polish activist was expelled to Germany.[77]

In light of such reports, Governor Zawadzki appointed a commission to visit transit points and various places in the province to examine thoroughly individuals designated for expulsion and their desire to remain in Poland. The Provincial Control Commission visited Kluczbork County for a week in mid-September 1946, meeting with local officials and autochthons. It concluded that the County Verification Commission should reexamine some individuals or simply remove them from the list of designated expellees. The *starosta* and the director of the County WS-P cited the Protestant religion of some as an important source of difficulties. Other sources were typical: looting, injustice, and so forth. Although nearly all of the natives were divested of their property unlawfully, it proved difficult to return the property.

The Control Commission regarded the Polishness of the county's local population as dormant but if awakened capable of serving Poland well. Additionally, the commission confirmed that looters from prewar Poland took everything of value at the very beginning of Polish administration of the area. The local people, it was said, welcomed settlers and especially the repatriates with open arms, seeing their suffering and misery, but these newcomers often repaid the locals with the dispossession of their property. As a result about 4,000 inhabitants of Polish origin in the county did not apply for verification and wanted to leave for Germany. The commission found contact with this population painful: "It speaks beautiful Polish, in the old robust language of the region," but it was distrustful, bitter that it was regarded as German and outraged by the insults previously unknown in Opole Silesia, especially those hurled at women.[78]

In this situation the commission decided to hold meetings in five communes to convince the population to apply for Polish citizenship. In some communes it found mainly women, many of whom wanted to join their husbands in Germany who did not intend to return because of reports, which the commission regarded as anti-Polish propaganda, that as German military veterans and members of the Nazi party or other German organizations they faced detention in special camps where they would perish. In one commune the women complained that they had not been paid for their work and had no clothes or shoes, especially for their children. Some told the commission they were not of Polish origin, as one man explained in beautiful Polish. People from various villages had no confidence in the return of their property following verification—a man fighting to repossess his property and his son were even murdered, and the perpetrators had not yet been caught. Some claimed that they wanted to be part of Poland, but the thievery with impunity had to stop and conditions had to improve.[79]

The commission also visited a transit camp in Lower Silesia with 1,700 individuals awaiting expulsion, 80 percent of them from Silesia, more than half of them of Polish origin. A significant number tried to cross the border on their own but were turned back. The commission interviewed 220, questioning the expulsion of about thirty, of whom perhaps ten returned home. The arrival of railway wagons ready for loading prevented further interviews.

Most were women leaving to join their husbands in Germany. They found employment in Germany; in some cases they received a house or a farm in compensation as former German political prisoners of Polish origin. Economic considerations played a major role in all cases. The women often explained that they could not even provide their children with the most basic nourishment. Some women had no more than the clothes on their backs or a small bundle because looters took everything they had. "Repeatedly, the images of extreme poverty met among the departing were terrible. The lack of means of livelihood often decided for departure." They also complained of being treated as Germans or "krauts." The departure of war invalids of the German army caused the commission less concern: in Germany they would receive a disability pension whereas in Poland they could become an unnecessary burden.

As a train left the transit point on the evening of 28 August 1946, those in "wagons Nos. 33 and 36 sang popular songs in Polish, a flawless Polish, and one had the impression that these were not deportees leaving for Germany, but some kind of excursion of Polish youths setting out to conquer the world. This was a sad impression after over two days of hard labor [interviewing detainees]." Nevertheless, the Silesian Provincial Control Commission concluded that the overwhelming majority

> already did not constitute an element of full value [for Poland] because . . . they are already living only for the moment of departure. This element has already decided on departing, nothing other than painful memories any longer connects it with the land, which was torn away by the power of injustice or force of law. It fears indigence, it fears neighbors, it fears conditions and flees all of this, all the more that it mostly lost everything and has relatives and acquaintances in Germany, children or parents assuring it of living conditions in the immediate future. Material considerations and entangled blood relations no doubt have their effects, and in conversations one often meets the view that the Germans made a mistake in turning Poles into Germans and therefore Poland should not repeat this error.[80]

An MZO inspector present at the departure of a transport of 2,000 on 31 December 1946 lamented,

> 70 percent despite their undoubtedly Polish origins feel like Germans and none of them wanted to remain in Poland. . . . I got the impression that these people are lost for Poland, and currently even decidedly hostile. . . . I agree that the local administrative officials, like the Militia, commune heads, village chairmen, in large part contributed to the loss for Poland of many of these people by robbing them, beatings, rapes, etc.[81]

The Voluntary Departure of Autochthons

The rising tide of already verified individuals seeking permission to leave for Germany posed one of the biggest problems faced by the authorities. The resumption of postal service with the west in 1946 enabled family members to establish contact. But one historian attributes the applications to leave Poland mainly to the hostility of newcomers, their rejection of the natives' claims to a Polish identity, and accusations of collaboration with the Germans.[82]

On 24 July 1946 the Bytom PUIiP reported that in the previous three weeks the WS-P received an increasing number of requests for permission to leave for Germany, on average about fifty per day, mostly from women with husbands in Germany who had recently contacted them, women already verified as Poles with certificates of Polish citizenship. In principle such requests were granted only if the husband was German; the wives would lose all rights of citizenship and never be allowed to return to Poland. In some cases verified individuals fled to Germany on their own, whole families leaving behind even furnished homes.[83]

The head of the Silesian WUBP reported to the MBP on 10 August 1946 that the remaining German citizens, including some verified as Poles, were impatient to depart for Germany. The verified did not pick up their certificates of Polish citizenship, claiming that they could not afford the fee, though it was only 25 złoty. He blamed German propaganda for the rumor that the peace conference would reinstate the 1939 Polish-German border, which raised fears of reprisals. But some in Lubliniec and Rybnik Counties sought to evade expulsion, even by sleeping in fields, according to the head of public security.[84]

In reports to the MZO for the months of August and September 1946, Silesian Deputy Governor Ziętek noted that those seeking to return their certificates of Polish nationality and leave voluntarily for Germany attributed their decisions to the lack of employment and of the means to support themselves. For both Silesians and Mazurs who recalled the good times under German rule, a comparison of conditions before and after the war, however unfair, did not inspire identification with the Polish state.[85]

At the session of the Silesian WRN 30 September–1 October 1946, Zawadzki expressed his outrage at the frequent attempts of women with children to join husbands in Germany: "A Polish-Silesian woman should instead break off with this husband, all the more that instead of returning to her and the children, he is waiting in Germany for the moment of revenge, when the German hordes might again invade the Polish lands with fire and sword." But he added, "The Polish state will find the means to make it possible for these women to survive the difficult times, provide their children with schooling and civic education."[86]

Reports on the deportation from Sztum, Gdańsk Province, in early August 1946 indicate that it included rehabilitated and verified individuals who returned their certificates. Many had family members in Germany, but rumors that the verified were to be resettled in eastern Poland also allegedly influenced then.[87]

Officials at transit points were supposed to prevent the departure of autochthons, but conditions at transit points and the large number designated for expulsion often made thorough investigations impossible. The Gdańsk PUR provincial inspector reported on 27 November 1946 that out of two transports totaling 3,520 expellees at the transit point in Gdańsk-Narwik, a verification commission recognized thirty individuals as Poles and withdrew their expulsion orders. At the Zielona Góra transit point in the second half of December, former detainees in the Potulice labor camp included many individuals who had Polish surnames and spoke Polish and sixteen children between the ages of four to twelve whose parents remained in the camp, which they claimed had no verification commission, according to a report on 31 December 1946.[88]

An article in the Polish press in November 1946 expressed the fear that in former East Prussia alone Poland "lost" 66,000 "valuable citizens," reflecting a belief in their essential Polishness.[89] The alarming increase in voluntary departures, including of those already in possession of certificates of Polish citizenship, the bitter failure of the PPR and its allies to gain the support of autochthons in the referendum, and the continued focus of international attention on the question of the Polish-German border—all this called for renewed efforts to win the autochthons over for Poland. On 18 August 1946 a meeting of representatives of nationally conscious Polish Silesians took place in Opole. In addition to affirming the line of the PPR, as if in exchange as one historian suggests, its resolutions spoke to the real concerns of the population of the region, including ones of special interest to autochthons such as increased social assistance, the return of Silesians from the Soviet Union, the restitution of property administratively instead of through the courts, more participation in government, and greater access to schooling.[90] Others could have added to this list of grievances.

Re-Polonization and De-Germanization

Verification did not complete the re-Polonization of autochthons. An article published in 1946 called on the population of Silesia to take advantage of a decree on 10 November 1945 that simplified procedures for changing non-Polish-sounding surnames and given names. The author claimed when more than 100,000 residents of Polish Silesia initiated the "restoration" of their Polish surnames before 1939, "the vast majority of interested parties absolutely did not realize that their surnames, their original, beautiful-sounding, frequently old Polish surnames, were deliberately converted in the spirit of German pronunciation and orthography for the convenience of the German occupier." "One needs to bring about once and for all the disappearance of the ignorance concerning the national character of given names." Every civil registry ought to have a list of Polish and Slavic names and one of German names to aid parents in choosing a child's name.[91]

Governor Zawadzki saw regional differences in personal names as an obstacle to the full integration. On 16 April 1946 he directed civil registries to begin the Polonization of given names and surnames and included a list of names generally accepted in Poland and a list of Slavic names, though the latter were not widely used in Silesia before the war.[92] On 20 May 1946 he forbade registry officials from issuing birth certificates with a German first name, which "in today's times hampers coexistence in Polish society."[93]

Nevertheless, the Polonization of names proceeded slowly. The high cost acted as a deterrent even though officials could exempt individuals from paying all or part of the required fee. The delay in granting Polish citizenship to former citizens of the Reich also deterred progress. The large number of women whose husbands had not yet returned refused to change their names in the absence of the head of the household. On 23 May 1946 the Silesian Provincial Legal Department asked the MZO for a clarification on the legality of a wife changing her surname on her own. The governor also ordered the preparation of a decree allowing divorce for individuals of Polish nationality whose spouse was not verified as Polish.[94]

Prominent linguistic, geographic, historical, and regional specialists joined in the Polonization campaign. The Commission for the Determination of Names of Places and Physiographic Objects created in 1946 undertook the Polonization of the names of more than 32,000 towns, villages, mountains, rivers, and other topographical features, resurrecting former Polish or Slavic names or reconstructing them based on documentary evidence. In a few cases, it simply Polonized the German name or invented a new one. The results were published in a two-volume dictionary in 1951. In December 1946, the MZO prohibited the public use of the old names. But the Polonization or re-Polonization in keeping with the "Polish Western Idea" did not appeal to all inhabitants of the Polish-German borderlands.[95]

The place names used by Polish-speaking autochthons usually did not prevail. Germans transformed "Kostrzyn" and "Legnica" into "Küstrin" and "Liegnitz," which Slavic-speaking locals made "Kistrzyn" and "Lignica," but officials mandated a return to the original names. A notable exception was the acceptance of "Nysa" used in the Upper Silesian dialect rather than "Nisa" found in ancient sources.[96]

In Mazuria in 1946 the Polish administration reintroduced almost all the place names used in the Polish-Mazurian language, many of which the Nazis changed in 1938. But the authorities also pursued political goals in giving towns new names to honor purported "pioneers for Polishness": Sensburg became Mrągowo after Pastor Krzysztof Celestyn Mrongowiusz (1764–1855) instead of the old Polish-Mazurian name of Żądzbork, Lötzen became Giżycko after Pastor Gustaw Gizewiusz (1810–1848) instead of Lec, and Rastenburg became Kętrzyn after Wojciech Kętrzyński (1838–1918) instead of Rastembork.[97]

In the spring of 1946 an alleged increase in the use of the German language by autochthons with certificates of Polish citizenship prompted fears that the existing practices allowed Germans to pass for Poles. On 29 May 1946 the PPS organ *Robotnik* reported that when questioned about speaking German, autochthons responded "arrogantly that after all they already got citizenship and can therefore speak any language they want." According to the press at the beginning of June 1946, the Gliwice MRN confirmed that even parents verified as Polish were teaching their children German.[98]

A secret directive of the MZO on 30 May 1946 calling for the complete elimination of all traces of German culture and for repressive measures against those who used German in public added to the tension between autochthons and newcomers. Those accused of using German came before local nationality commissions, and their personal data were handed over to the local UBP. In Upper Silesia Committees for the Struggle against Germanness, which functioned in every county office of the UB and MO, were often used to settle personal disputes or simply to obtain the property of autochthons. A denunciation of someone as favorable toward Germanness sufficed for confiscation of property and detention in a camp to await verification or expulsion.[99]

In the struggle against the remnants of German influence, the PZZ took on attributes of the security police. District and local PZZ circles were responsible for gathering information on Poles who after 1919 belonged to German organizations, who voted with Germans, or whose names appeared on the DVL. PZZ members were to report mothers using German with their children in their homes or adults using German with each other or reading German books. "Every family with weakened national consciousness must receive a guardian from the PZZ, who will intervene in matters of the use of the German language in colloquial speech."

Surveillance by PZZ circles also encompassed industrial enterprises, noting support for former German citizens and *Volksdeutsche*. The circles were to promote the material improvement of workers who took part in the struggle against German influence and the material disadvantage of those who supported Germans or German influence. PZZ circles were to submit monthly reports to the district PZZ, which in turn was to submit a monthly report to central headquarters.[100]

The Silesian UW reported that in June 1946 the PZZ led the way in the energetic de-Germanization of Gliwice and the preparations for expulsion of Germans by appealing to the MRN to order the immediate removal of all signs in German and the prohibition of the German language. On 10 November 1946 the Katowice County court fined a restaurant owner for using beer coasters with German inscriptions 3,000 złoty or twenty days in jail.[101] Nevertheless, late in 1946 press reports indicated that the problem of the removal of all German inscriptions remained. It required time and often considerable expense to replace, for example, the printing of packaging or forms. Safety required the continued posting of regulations in German in factories and mines.[102]

James F. Byrnes's Speech

Churchill's "Iron Curtain" speech and other statements by Western leaders fed doubts about the permanence of the Oder-Neisse border. On 6 September 1946 U.S. Secretary of State James F. Byrnes questioned it explicitly in a speech on U.S. policy toward Germany, pointing out that the Soviet Union transferred areas of eastern Germany to Poland prior to the Potsdam agreement and emphasizing that it made clear "the heads of government did not agree to support at the peace settlement the cession of any particular area." The territory ceded to Poland "must be determined when the final settlement is agreed upon."[103]

The communist authorities panicked. They saw the Oder-Neisse border as one of their most important links to society. In response they organized a giant political campaign portraying the statements by Western leaders as an attack on Polish independence and, with the approach of parliamentary elections, as evidence that the pro-Western opposition led by Mikołajczyk threatened the interests of the nation.[104]

American Ambassador Arthur Bliss Lane claimed that Byrnes's speech united the Polish population in defense of the Recovered Lands.[105] There, however, it caused local officials great concern. In Silesia they reported rumors, attributed to Germans and "reactionary elements," of an imminent war between America, allied with Germany, and Russia and the return of the Germans. Allegedly, verified autochthons increasingly expressed pro-German and anti-Polish feelings, speaking German both publicly and at home. Leaflets called for throwing out the "Polish thieves"; ones in German even advocated accumulating arms and murdering Poles. Numerous swastikas appeared on walls. Parents refused to send their children to Polish schools. A significant portion of verified autochthons signed up for departure to Germany, and a massive number of others simply fled across the "green border"—i.e., illegally. Out of fear of German reprisals, verified autochthons proved reluctant to sign declarations of loyalty. One official reported that more than 200 "germans" (sic) in various communities simply did not pick up their loyalty declarations. Even when in early November 1946 the Opole PUIiP reported that anticipation of a change in the international geopolitical situation and the loss of the Recovered Lands declined among autochthons thanks to the efforts of officials and the massive return of repatriates from occupied Germany, the movement of Soviet troops still fed rumors of imminent war.[106]

Persistent reports of the existence of a German underground resistance, the so-called werewolves, reinforced doubts among officials in Silesia about the loyalty of autochthons. On 21 September 1946 the Prudnik PUIiP informed the WUIiP that it declined to put up posters showing a well-armed werewolf in a German uniform with a Swastika over the slogan "Be vigilant—Werewolves are active" because it would give heart to the putatively Polish local population, "which—one has to take this into account—in the majority is on the side of Germany rather than of Poland."[107] At the end of September 1946 commenting on a report of German partisans in Silesia, an employee of the MZO Department of Inspection asserted that its activity "is supported by a certain part of the verified *autochthons* and can be especially threatening in the region of Opole."[108]

In Lubusz Land the speeches of Churchill and Byrnes "contributed greatly to lifting the spirit of the German population. The matter of a revision of the western border therefore occupies the minds of Germans more than ever," according to the governor's report for September 1946. Did this include German citizens of Polish origin? The organized expulsion of Germans from Poznań Province that began in October 1946 focused above all on Lubusz Land. Meanwhile, verification took place mainly in the counties with the largest native population and quite strictly, granting citizenship in practice only to those individuals whose Polishness was universally accepted. The aversion of some officials to local residents resulted in part of the allegedly Polish population not submitting to the process. At the same time, individuals of German nationality applied, which heightened the vigilance of the already cautious commissions, in effect increasing the number of denials. Although ultimately the authorities verified 8,500 inhabitants of the region as Poles, by November 1946 fears on the part of its inhabitants concerning their future fate prevented half of them from applying for verification.[109]

The Olsztyn governor informed Wolski on 15 October 1946 that Byrnes's speech resulted in a certain "expectation and excitement" among autochthons as evident in a commune in Olsztyn County where up to 90 percent of the Warmian children of parents verified as Polish were not enrolled in school. He feared that this might turn dangerous, especially because the natives had been robbed of all belongings and often continued to be abused by the security organs and therefore lacked any confidence in the administrative authorities and "gladly give ear to destructive propaganda." Mainly out of concern for surviving the coming winter without provisions, clothing, and medical care, verified and unverified autochthons applied for permission to depart for Germany.[110]

Particularly in Warmia and Mazuria the native population came to regard sending their children to Polish schools as a form of treason and of resignation of the hope of departing for Germany. The difficult material circumstances of many parents proved another hindrance. A shortage of teachers of local origin complicated the situation. Many of the teachers from outside of the province, like other newcomers, lacked understanding and respect for local traditions and the native dialect. The history and values taught in the schools clashed with what the native youths heard at home. Teachers were enlisted in the battle against the use of German, including during recess, and had the obligation of reporting children who spoke German outside of school.[111]

In Szczecin Province a conference of Złotów, Człuchów, and Bytów County officials projected a positive image, asserting that "the question of the autochthons already has a healthy character," according to notes dated 27 October 1946. Supposedly, verification commissions significantly lowered tensions by issuing provisional certificates of Polish citizenship, giving autochthons the basis for some feeling of Polishness respected by the administrative authorities, settlers, and repatriates. From 28 August 1945 to 30 September 1946 (the deadline for verification), 24,615 autochthons were verified as Polish. Officials claimed that the local administration and UB were fulfilling their tasks and dealing with autochthons with full understanding, and the work of the PZZ was developing very positively, with the goal of liquidating the differences between the autochthons and settlers and creating a unified society.

But even officials at the conference noted that relations among the residents were not yet normal, only that there was less tension. Indeed, disputes continued, which were "a tacit conflict over better land, better livestock and houses." Autochthons continued to regard newcomers as "intruders" who engaged in little constructive work, if not just looting. For their part, repatriates and settlers had doubts, especially about those autochthons who did not speak Polish well or at all, seeing them as Germans and an undesirable element. Instances of autochthons losing their farms as purported Germans and then being certified as Poles while their farms were handed over to settlers and repatriates deepened the antagonism and lack of trust. The director of the UL denied any responsibility for these disputes, saying that his office did not deal with the legality of ownership and that autochthons who lost property and were subsequently verified should appeal to the courts. Nevertheless, officials at the conference optimistically concluded that, thanks to the attitude of the administrative and security authorities, the question of autochthons would be justly resolved. The list of counties where the expulsion of autochthons who had not filed for verification was particularly prevalent issued by the MZO on 2 November 1946 also included Złotów and Człuchów Counties.[112]

The Congress of Autochthons

Following Byrnes's speech, the PZZ together with the PPR organized a series of regional assemblies of autochthon representatives. A memo apparently from the Bureau of the KRN Presidium to PZZ Chairman Barcikowski on 12 September 1946—less than a week after Byrnes's speech—anticipated that the assemblies would culminate in a congress of autochthons in Warsaw. In the face of "international attacks of reaction" on the border of Poland, the Presidium of the ZG PZZ on 16 September 1946 endorsed the organization of a congress in Warsaw under the slogan "Recovered Lands—Recovered People." Its goals were:

> 1. A demonstration of the historical and living Polishness of the Recovered Lands.
> 2. A manifestation by Poles-autochthons from the Recovered Lands of a strong will toward solid work on rebuilding the Recovered Lands and their Polonization.
> 3. Involvement of the autochthonous population in the area of Polish social life and its organization in the ranks of the PZZ. 4. A summation of the achievements and results of the re-Polonization operation in the Recovered Lands.[113]

Regional assemblies of delegates followed in Szczecin, Babimost, Gdańsk, Olsztyn, and Sztum, with the Congress of Autochthons in Warsaw taking place on 9–10 November 1946. The press claimed that the assemblies expressed the desire of autochthons to unite completely with the Polish nation, leveling inter-sectional differences, and to support the government and "people's democracy." At the same time, the assemblies supposedly gave autochthons the opportunity to mobilize, articulate their demands, and overcome the barrier between them and the authorities.[114]

The Congress Bureau that met in Warsaw on 21 October 1946 brought together members of the ZG PZZ and the ZPwN. They emphasized the need to oppose the "unjust" and "exaggerated" picture of Polish-speaking German soldiers. At the same time they stressed the need to convince autochthons that they had not only the right but also the obligation to participate actively in Polish political life, suggesting a political motive in connection with the coming parliamentary elections.[115]

Every effort was made to control the proceedings of the Congress. The Congress Bureau decided on the list of speakers and membership of the Congress Presidium. PZZ Districts received the "themes and guidelines for the speeches of delegate-autochthons," with instructions to report any changes in speakers or speeches and to submit in advance of the names of discussants "with an indication of what they will speak about and what proposals they will put forward." The day before the Congress, the Presidium of the ZG PZZ, without the participation of a single autochthon, prepared the resolution to be voted by the Congress. Admission to the Congress required a pass. The presence of 100 security personnel, not counting any covert agents, ensured tight control.[116]

County officials along with local offices of the PZZ and the MIiP organized the delegations to be sent off to Warsaw with an enthusiastic demonstration.

But in Opole Silesia rumors spread that participants would be sent deep into the Soviet Union, never to return. In fact some individuals resigned as delegates. Ultimately, some 2,500 traveled to Warsaw. Arranging transportation, room, and board imposed a heavy burden on the organizers, who received assistance from the PUR and the MON, which even provided 130 German prisoners to perform the physical labor.[117]

At the end of October 1946 the press quoted a speech by Bierut defending autochthons at a conference of chairmen of WRNs:

> Many of us have German passports, German culture, German habits, often a completely Germanized psyche and attitude as well as, flowing from this, a secret aversion—or even hostility to the Polish State, to Polish culture, but nevertheless these are people with Polish names, of unquestionable Polish origin, which many of them begin to realize only now for the first time in their lives. Among these autochthons there are also not a few Polish patriots.[118]

On the eve of the Congress, MZO data indicated that 819,443 autochthons had been verified as Polish but that 60,799 had not yet declared for Polish citizenship—more than half of them (33,879) in Olsztyn Province.[119] The Congress was to crown the process of Polonization, eliminating distinctions that threatened the homogeneity of the nation-state. As *Robotnik* stated the day before the opening, "The Congress in Warsaw will conclude all the assemblies. This will be the last assembly of Poles-autochthons, there cannot be any more because the concept of Pole-autochthon will disappear, the concept of a Pole with full civil authority, of the proprietor of the Recovered Lands will remain."[120] But a document for internal use, "The General Conception of the Congress," limited this "civil authority":

> The assembly of autochthons cannot be an occasion for the presentation of their concerns in the Recovered Lands, but of state and national interests. Let us leave the complex of interests of particular social groups in the Recovered Lands for the matter of the common interests of the whole of society in the Recovered Lands, which, among others, the autochthons represent.[121]

The PPR and its allies also had in mind the approach of parliamentary elections in January 1947. A document in the archive of the Ministry of Internal Affairs (*Ministerstwo Spraw Wewnętrznych* or MSW) states, "The Congress should manifest a positive relationship of the autochthonous population to a specific Poland, today's Poland, democratic Poland"—i.e., one governed by the PPR-led Democratic Bloc. Earlier the PZZ activist Izdebski had proposed binding autochthons to the socio-political system by satisfying their needs. Polish communists demanded support of the government without giving voice to grievances.[122]

Minister of Recovered Lands Gomułka's keynote address at the Congress, widely reprinted and commented on, highlighted the autochthons as proof of the "historical and living" Polishness of the territory east of the Oder-Neisse border.[123] Recounting the supposed achievements of the government, he admitted that in the first period after the war Polish autochthons "*at times* suffered various injustices," including at the hands of "uninformed people with the *best* of intentions." Other leading officials similarly downplayed the negative. PZZ Chairman Barcikowski spoke of the errors that "could have *here and there* harmed Poles of the Recovered Lands."[124]

Gomułka proposed facilitating the verification of all Polish autochthons. Late applicants had only to give credible reasons for not applying sooner, but fear, anxiety, and an aversion to state policies were not acceptable reasons. He understood prewar activists who regarded verification "as an insult to their national dignity" but argued that their objections hindered re-Polonization. He also recognized:

> Harmonious, fraternal coexistence of Poles-autochthons with Poles-settlers still leaves much to be desired. The harmful separation between them did not yet disappear, a separation that should be liquidated as quickly as possible. The Pole-autochthon sometimes still looks at the Pole-settler as at an intruder, as at an unnecessary newcomer, and the settler looks at the autochthon as at a disguised enemy, as at a German who tries to hide under the name of a Pole. Yet, both one and the other are Poles.[125]

He called the unification of all Poles in one, integrated nation-state one of the most important tasks of the Polish nation.[126]

In contrast, the speeches of autochthons focused on specific grievances and proposals. Some spoke of the indignity that re-Polonization imposed on Polish activists who did not need to prove their Polishness because they possessed "a centuries-old diploma of Polishness." What was needed was true equality of rights of all social groups. Less demoralized than others, autochthons should serve as the basis of a new society in the Recovered Lands. They should receive proportional representation in local national councils and the KRN.[127]

Several autochthons criticized the introduction of political conflict into the Recovered Lands. The audience applauded when Silesian Deputy Governor Arkadiusz Bożek called for keeping the "premature" political struggle out of the territory. Dr. Zygmunt Moczyński from the Gdańsk region warned against politicizing autochthons:

> Poles-autochthons do not know the tradition of internal conflict in Poland. They should be given time to get their bearings and assimilate these traditions in their own life. The decision should be left to their individual conviction. A certificate of Polish citizenship cannot be exclusively a membership card of this or another political party, but decisive should be the stance and positive contribution in all manifestations of national life in the Recovered Lands.

A speaker from Opole Silesia asserted, "Stirring political passions leads to causing further harm in these lands. In the terrain of the western lands there should not exist any political conflict."[128]

These appeals clashed with the goal of uniting autochthons behind the PPR. Gomułka called on the delegates to "build and solidify" a "Democratic Poland" "together with the government" and "the democratic camp," i.e., not the PSL led by Mikołajczyk. In fact Mikołajczyk's letter to the Congress was not read during the proceedings. When *Chłopski Sztandar* published it several days later, censorship deleted the editorial comment that it was not read at the Congress for political reasons. When Chairman of the PSL Main Council and Minister of Public Administration Kiernik wanted to give an unscheduled speech, only the applause of the delegates forced Barcikowski to agree. In contrast to other officials, he explicitly cited the wrongs done to the autochthons, remarks that the delegates warmly supported. Again, censorship precluded the printing of a commentary on Kiernik's speech.[129]

A conference of activist autochthons and PPR members of the PZZ on 10 November 1946 assessing the Congress made the gulf between their views explicit. PPR member Dubiel rejected the demand for wider participation of autochthons in national councils because they did not understand "the current reality." Kliszko argued that the Recovered Lands had greater significance for the country as a whole than the question of autochthons. PPR members openly attacked the PSL, accusing it of policies that would lead to Poland's loss of the western lands. The autochthons reacted strongly against these views, criticizing the political pressure put on autochthons and the lack of precise guidelines laid out at the Congress for work among autochthons. They complained that not everyone was allowed to speak at the Congress and that Mazurs had no delegates at the Congress. When Professor Bronisław Bukowski representing the Gdańsk region suggested the creation of a Council of Autochthons under the ZG PZZ, Barcikowski closed the discussion, saying that "the question of autochthons was taken care by the Congress" and that the monthly conferences of the ZG would address the remaining "difficulties."[130]

The Progress of Verification

According to the local offices of the MIiP in Gdańsk Pomerania, the very fact that the Congress took place made a positive impression on autochthons, but a report on 25 November 1946 of the Gdańsk Provincial Verification Commission on the reaction of Kashubian delegates was decidedly negative. Written by Moczyński, it complained of the tardiness of government officials—the premier and vice premier arrived more than an hour late—the disorganization of the Congress (*polnische Wirtschaft?*), the absence of government officials at the sessions, the lack of a Mazurian delegation, and the media's omission of speeches by delegates from the provinces despite extensive coverage of those by officials. That the delegates were not invited for even "the most modest tea reception with government officials" also made a bad impression. Moczyński repeated his warning about politicization: "Involving the autochthonous population in party life should ensue very delicately, without giving the impression of any sort of coercion, because this fact reminds them too much of the Nazi regime."[131]

The governor of Szczecin Province claimed in his report for November 1946 that autochthons who attended the Congress were greatly pleased and filled with hope by the proposals voted at the Congress. But his report for December 1946 noted that there were very few additional applications for verification. As a preventive measure, he ordered the creation of county consultative commissions with the task of excluding individuals of Polish origin from expulsion. Already fifteen had been excluded, of whom eight spoke Polish quite well and had been verified as Poles.[132]

The Congress as well as the earlier Szczecin regional assembly referred to the Slovincians, who survived only in the Lake Łebsko area in Słupsk County and distinguished themselves from the surrounding Germans solely by tradition, customs, and Slavic given names. In response the Szczecin governor appointed Docent Dr. Feliks Zabrocki of the University of Poznań as an expert to investigate and ordered the creation of a special committee to remind the Slovincians of their origins and "nationality," providing them with material assistance and moral support, and to conduct verification among them.[133]

The PZZ intensively sought to keep Slovincians in Poland, though they were not of Polish origin but at best descendants of Kashubs who for centuries had no contact with a Polish state. They, however, had a role in proving the Polish and Slavic origins of Western Pomerania. In 1945 no one spoke the local Slavic dialect beyond a few words and phrases. Few spoke Polish, some had a command of Kashubian, but they did not feel any connection with either Poles or Kashubs. Protestant and highly Germanized, they regarded themselves not as Slavs, Kashubs, or even Slovincians.[134] An article published in May 1946 referred to them as the "Mohicans of Western Pomerania." In September 1947 a group of Mazurs, Protestant like the Slovincians, came to the area to "awaken" their Polishness with an unrealistic description of the prosperity, peace, and the rule of law in Mazuria under Polish administration.[135]

Initially, the Slovincians showed some readiness to stay, but the difficult living conditions, which they blamed on the settlers who robbed and insulted them; the hostility directed toward them as Protestants; the abuses of local officials; and the loss of hope in the reversal of the change in borders soon altered their desire not to abandon their homeland. An MZO inspector investigating charges of maltreatment reported on 3 May 1948 that starvation reigned among them. Traditionally, they engaged in fishing, but 50 percent of their catch went to the Red Army and 30 percent of the remainder to the Polish authorities. Their fishing equipment was confiscated as German property and the practice of their religion hindered.[136]

As a result, even the older Slovincians who immediately after the war eagerly recalled Slovincian words and phrases began to resist and, like the Germanized younger generation, to declare they were German and wanted to leave for Germany. A contemporary commentator characterized their situation as "a choice between hell and just any means of getting out of that hell." A local verification commission declared several dozen families who claimed to be of Kashubian origin to be German, and they therefore gradually left their homeland. The typical Slovincian village of Kluki (Slovincian: Kláhi) had an estimated 680 inhabitants of Slovincian origin before the war, 418 in 1947, and 234 (53 families) in 1948. Of these, 29 families were verified, and the rest refused to submit to the process.[137] According to Piotr Madajczyk, few of the Kashubs and Slovincians of Pomerania had any Polish national consciousness, and their tenuous ties to the hallmarks of the Polish national identity required accommodation if they were to become Polish citizens. Inflexibility in defining the Polish identity prevented the authorities from winning the loyalty of the Slovincians. Promoting Polonization by repressive means only contributed to a decision to leave Poland.[138]

Alarmed by the large number of still unverified "Polish autochthons," the PZZ Nationality Commission at the conference of delegates on 4–5 December 1946 together with ZPwN activists proposed that the central government investigate their Polish origins and preemptively verify them.[139] In a statement published in 1947, PZZ General Secretary Pilichowski argued for "the restoration to Poland of each son who in part lost Polish national consciousness or was incorporated in the German nation against his will as a result of the perfidious German nationality policy and the systematic Germanization campaign."[140]

Yet the cultural and linguistic Germanization of the Slavic-speaking population during the centuries of German rule seems a more natural process than the Polonization fostered by the Polish authorities and the PZZ. Germanization was synonymous with an intense modernization of eastern Germany and represented a means of social advancement.[141] The PZZ oversimplified the process of winning the loyalty of resistant autochthons. As the Wrocław WUIiP noted in December 1946:

> One of the most urgent and so far unregulated problems of the Recovered Lands is the matter of a proper stance of the settlers to the autochthons. . . . Despite the

influence of Germanness on the language and frequently on the way of thinking of the autochthonous population, Polish society of the Recovered Lands must create such an atmosphere in which these people will have the feeling of being citizens of the Polish state with full rights.[142]

Meanwhile, skepticism over the Polishness of autochthons persisted. In November and December 1946 the press carried reports that individuals arrested as members of "terrorist gangs" included verified Silesians.[143] The Bytom Municipal Settlement Department claimed on 2 December 1946 that a rumor about a return to the German border of 1914—allegedly evidence of the existence of an underground German organization—found a sympathetic hearing among most of the native population.[144]

The Bytom PUIiP on 9 December 1946 attributed an increasing use of German by local inhabitants, even in the corridors of state offices and workplaces, to the probable existence of a "reactionary" German underground. Attendance at Polish language classes for young and old fell to the point that many had to be cancelled. Youths at local bars under the influence of alcohol parodied the Polish national anthem, and natives occasionally sang German songs at celebrations in their homes. Significantly, the report noted that no more than 10 percent of the autochthons, who constituted 85 percent of the county's inhabitants, were expected to vote for the PPR-dominated bloc in the parliamentary election in January 1947.[145] This may have concerned the authorities more at this point than anything else, with the use of German seen primarily as a symptom of hostility toward the government.

In principle, security officials could arrest all members of Nazi organizations, including underage members of the Hitler Youth, but in practice interned anyone regarded as German.[146] According to the German Silesian Görlich, the security organs together with the MO and the Voluntary Reserve of the Civic Militia carried out massive arrests among autochthonous youths in 1946–1947 on suspicion of Nazism regardless of whether they came from families positively disposed toward Poland or not. "As a personal witness of these incidents and as a witness of the methods of the Gestapo, I can only confirm that they differed from each other in almost nothing." He vividly recalled the reaction of a veteran of the Silesian Uprisings on seeing his maltreated son: "I am ashamed that I fought for Poland." Told they were Poles during this abuse, an increasing number began to speak German. People who before the war were punished for speaking Polish the MO now punished for speaking German.[147]

Despite a series of measures undertaken by the central and provincial Polish authorities in 1946, issues surrounding the status of autochthons remained far from resolved at the end of the year. Their treatment at the hands of local officials often negated the benevolent intentions of higher officials. The

Congress of Autochthons had little apparent success in changing attitudes. At the same time, the results of the referendum and questions raised about the Polish-German border by statesmen in the West increased the urgency of resolving these issues.

Forced expulsion to Germany reached its greatest intensity in 1946, encompassing 1,668,379 individuals, women with children and the elderly constituting the largest group.[148] There is no way of knowing how many would have chosen to remain had the authorities pursued different nationality policies and avoided the abuses that alienated so many inhabitants of the Recovered Lands.

Jews in the Recovered Lands

Following the liberation of the Groß-Rosen and outlying concentration camps in Lower Silesia, surviving Jews began to establish Jewish committees, political organizations, cooperatives, schools, and cultural associations already in 1945. They were joined by Jewish repatriates, who constituted 11.4 percent (c. 173,000) of the migrants from the Soviet Union, more than two-thirds of whom were resettled in the Recovered Lands. On 1 January 1946 18,219 Jews were registered with Jewish committees in the province. Incomplete data indicate that in the first half of 1946 the authorities steered 82,305 Jewish repatriates to forty-two locations in Lower Silesia. Jewish refugees also arrived from the West.[149]

As repatriates temporarily saturated Lower Silesia, the authorities settled 28,324 Jews in Szczecin and its environs, which unlike Lower Silesia had no well-established Jewish community.[150] In June 1946 the Szczecin governor claimed that Jews resisted dispersal out of "a desire to prevent an assimilation of the Jewish population with the Polish population, a desire to maintain their national distinctiveness."[151] Some 15,000 Jews resettled in the Łódź region and 12,000 in Upper Silesia, where industry could absorb all qualified workers. But most Jews preferred to form cooperatives where they could speak Yiddish and be among their own rather than to feel isolated in large Polish factories. For the Jews who lived in the many *shtetls* of eastern Poland, the loss of their homeland and the destruction of interpersonal bonds gave new importance to a Jewish national identity. This together with the antisemitism encountered in postwar Poland contributed to a desire for a Jewish state where Jews could live together in security.[152]

Jews with German citizenship posed a dilemma for the Polish authorities. Before Hitler came to power, the territory of the "Recovered Lands" had a significant concentration of Jews. The Jewish community of Breslau (Wrocław) was the second largest in Germany. The Holocaust, however, devastated this population, and few survived in the territory that came under Polish administration. They generally identified with German culture. In Katowice Province even Jews who knew Polish usually spoke German.[153]

A Committee of the Jewish Organization of the City of Szczecin sought to bring together Jewish citizens of the city and promote their cultural and economic interests. But, according to notes dated 22 October 1945, the director of the Municipal Department of General Administration secretly learned that the committee regarded itself as the representative exclusively of Jewish German citizens who resided in Szczecin before the war. When the Jewish Organization in Warsaw requested that the committee provide assistance to Jewish Polish citizens in need, the chairman allegedly stated, "We do not want anything to do with eastern Jews; we do not yet know what's going to happen with Szczecin, we do not want to compromise ourselves by cooperating with Polish citizens."[154]

Not all officials understood that the new Poland would include Jews. Initially, their treatment was not regulated, and consequently local officials in most cases treated them as Germans, resulting in the loss of their property and expulsion.[155] In Łódź officials distributed registration cards in two colors: white for the Polish population and yellow for those of German, Jewish, and Gypsy (Roma) nationality. The director of the MAP Political Department reacted sharply on 14 June 1945, ordering an immediate withdrawal of the yellow cards and demanding to know who was responsible for issuing them.[156]

On 6 May 1945 the Katowice Provincial Jewish Committee raised with the MAP the issue of the fate of German spouses of Jews who also suffered persecution under the Nazis, but nevertheless the authorities were treating those from Opole Silesia as Germans based on their citizenship. The committee requested a decree indicating that individuals persecuted by the Nazi authorities because of their origin and their immediate family should be treated as loyal citizens with the full rights of citizenship, with the Central Committee of Polish Jews and provincial Jewish committees empowered to issue certificates to individuals whom the decree would bring under the protection of the law.[157]

The initial MAP decree on 20 June 1945 concerning certification of Polish nationality made no allusion to Jewish German citizens. But then, as if as an afterthought, on 10 July 1945 the MAP extended the certification to victims of Nazi persecution specifically because of their nationality and their spouses, which above all meant Jews and Germans who suffered for refusing to divorce a Jewish spouse. Later decrees concerning verification also included this group.[158] Nevertheless, the overwhelming majority of German Jews was expelled.[159]

For many Jewish repatriates from the Soviet Union, Poland served as merely a way station for emigration further west or to Palestine. A well-organized Zionist underground arranged illegal departures during the last phase of the war, often facilitated by the authorities. On 25 October 1945 the Gdańsk WUIiP noted that the most recent transport of expellees to Germany included twelve wagons of Jews, reportedly Polish Jews from Kielce and other Polish towns. Seeking instructions, a local official reported that the departing Jews all had their papers in order, issued by the Soviet command for travel to places outside of Europe.[160] A train arriving at the Polish-German border on 18 May 1946 proved to have only fifty-six genuine refugees among more than 2,000 passengers; the rest were Polish Jews heading for the American zone and thence to Palestine. From July 1945 through June 1946 some 50,000 Jews left Poland illegally.[161]

The Central Committee of Polish Jews delineated the reasons for Jewish emigration in a memorandum for an Anglo-American Committee in January 1946. "The basic reason for the emigration trend is the fact that many Jews . . . cannot live in the places that are the cemeteries of their families, relatives, and friends. . . . They prefer to start anew in a completely different surrounding." Secondly, "The Jews who were alone after the slaughter have some family abroad, mostly in Palestine. . . . These lonely Jews want to join them after the horrible shock." Thirdly, "the tragedy of the Jewish people" strengthened "the inclination to create a national home in Palestine." "A large part of the Jews, especially the young, want to tie their lot to the development and the future of Palestine. Their deep ideological motivations are one of the main reasons for emigration." Finally, the memorandum referred to violence directed at Jews, including murder. "We strongly emphasize, however, that manifestations of antisemitism are not the main reason for the desire to emigrate."[162]

The situation changed drastically with the deadliest pogrom of the postwar period, in Kielce on 4 July 1946, just days after the referendum and before the announcement of its falsified results. Within a few hours thirty-six Jews, most living in a house in the town center, were shot or beaten to death by townspeople, security forces, and workers from a nearby factory. The overall toll may have been as high as forty-two dead or more counting related incidents. Antisemitism, particularly the myth of Jewish ritual murder; the actions of security forces; and the initial passivity of the local authorities—all played a role in the tragedy.[163]

The Kielce pogrom triggered the so-called "Great Exodus." In the next six months some 70,000 Jews left Poland, i.e., c. 30 percent of the total, based on an informal agreement between Zionist activists and the Frontier Defense Force to allow Jewish emigrants to pass. The Ministry of Foreign Affairs

(*Ministerstwo Spraw Zagranicznych* or MSZ) brought a halt to these illegal departures in February 1947. At that time 52,000 Jews remained in Lower Silesia. Jews continued to leave illegally but far fewer than earlier. Instead, emigration continued by legal means. In 1947 the MSZ issued 7,470 emigration passports. In the fall of 1947 the authorities recognized the right of Jews, in contrast to other Polish citizens, "to voluntary and legal emigration" but regarded "all attempts at fomenting an artificial mass emigration movement as harmful." The slower rate of emigration allowed the remaining Jewish communities in the Recovered Lands to achieve some provisional stability.[164]

[9]

The Rehabilitation of *Volksdeutsche* in 1946

THE RESULTS OF the referendum raised concerns about the loyalty of *Volksdeutsche*. Those who voted "no" on the third question were tarred as "spiritually *Volksdeutsche*." *Wola Ludu* suggested that 80 percent of the inhabitants of a village in Poznań Province voted "three times no" because of a significant number of former *Volksdeutsche* and German inhabitants.[1] That a large portion of the population in Żabiny and Lidzbark in Działdowo County voted "no" on the third question concerning the border the *starosta* saw as evidence of the presence of a large German element. On 5 August 1946 he reiterated his suspicion that many *Volksdeutsche* voted "no" on the third question.[2]

By mid-1946 a significant number of *Volksdeutsche* had left Poland. But a continuing shortage of skilled labor disinclined officials from permitting others to leave. Also, officials recognized that the examination of applicants for departure had been superficial, sometimes allowing the resettlement of *Volksdeutsche* in categories III and IV.[3]

As of 31 July 1946 the courts ruled on less than a third of the 223,331 applications for rehabilitation they received, according to the Ministry of Justice. More than half of the applications came before the Appellate Court in Katowice. The courts ruled positively in nearly two-thirds of the cases, denied 18.1 percent, and settled 16.3 percent by other means. Prosecutors filed objections in 2,937 (6.2 percent) of the positive rulings, which by 1 August 1946 resulted in confirmation of the positive rulings in 740 cases and of the objections of the prosecutor in 263.[4]

A decree on 28 June 1946 "Concerning Criminal Responsibility for the Betrayal of Nationality during the War 1939–1945," which initially applied only to Silesia, addressed a deficiency in the law of 6 May 1945 that treated *Volksdeutsche* as criminals subject to repression, expropriation, and even internment in camps until their rehabilitation, which could take months or even years, particularly for those in category II. Henceforth, the betrayal of one's Polish nationality, i.e., a voluntary declaration of German nationality, constituted a criminal offense whether it resulted in registration on the DVL or not. Furthermore, whereas previously the law provided for indefinite "isolation" of those denied rehabilitation, the decree set the sentence at up to ten years in "places of internment," which in practice—contrary to the law—meant labor camps. The decree, however, exempted individuals who acted in the interest of the Polish state, on orders of an underground resistance, or to avoid punishment or persecution—an exemption widely claimed in Silesia. In addition, it exempted those who persistently demonstrated their membership in the German nation prior to 1 September 1939, who were therefore subject to expulsion as Germans, but which had the unforeseen consequence of *Volksdeutsche* claiming German nationality to avoid prosecution.[5]

At the conference of PZZ delegates on 4–5 December 1946, Judge Z. Terlecki purported that the courts closely scrutinized claims to an exemption:

> It is obvious that while not demanding heroism, the State does not accept just any attitude of a citizen toward civil obligations and hence the stipulation in the decree that the threat of persecution alone does not suffice. The court in every concrete case considers both if the persecution was truly a grave attack on the conditions of life of the citizen and the situation, if the threatened citizen could without particular difficulty avoid persecution (e.g., without difficulty leave or give up the house or shop without loss of life).[6]

Despite the decree, difficulties persisted. On 30 July 1946 the Rybnik *starosta* reported the improper removal of 268 individuals to a transit point for expulsion.

> To resettle Germans from Upper Silesia is not as easy to do as it is to say. According to the directive of the governor of Silesia-Dąbrowa, all Germans, among whom we count those who in their behavior always showed their German national distinctiveness, are subject to resettlement. But on the other hand it was stated that it is not permitted to resettle Poles classified in German nationality groups I, II, III, and IV. In this case finding the border between a German and a Pole is difficult, all the more so since everyone from the local population speaks Polish as well as German.
>
> Communal National Councils listed Germans for resettlement without regard to their membership in nationality groups.... Yet at the last moment we were informed that we are allowed to resettle only German citizens in group I and the unrehabilitated in group II.
>
> ... Nevertheless, the county is constantly turned to by individuals, mostly married women, with children—Poles who married German citizens, who want to leave for Germany, but whom the commissions recognized as Poles and [therefore] could not leave.[7]

On 24 August 1946 the Silesian WS-P instructed local officials to exempt *Volksdeutsche* in categories III and IV from expulsion. The rare exception required a detailed account of the accusations against the individual. Those who had succumbed to Germanization to a high degree and wished to leave Poland were subject to a thorough investigation of the extent to which they were Germans or lost ties with the Polish nation. The same applied to category II *Volksdeutsche* who had been rehabilitated or filed for rehabilitation and wanted to leave.

The instructions also allowed Polish women who married Germans "in the abnormal conditions of war" to file for divorce and guaranteed their right to seek employment and, if unable to work, to receive special assistance. The membership of a dead husband or family member in a Nazi organization could not serve as the basis for expulsion. Furthermore, "Difficult material circumstances in which a family of doubtless Polish origin temporarily finds itself cannot constitute a reason for abandoning the borders of the State" nor did "just the desire of the applicant to depart."[8] The restrictions on expulsion and departure along with greater leniency in rehabilitation and verification stressed retaining in Poland anyone not clearly German.

The Cracow WUBP reported on 1 July 1946, "More and more frequently one hears the complaint that 'Germans again are beginning to throw their weight around,'" noting that the population of Biała County was outraged that category II *Volksdeutsche* were returning from labor camps to their property and allegedly engaging in speculation. In Biała textile workers resented that category II and III *Volksdeutsche* working in neighboring Bielsko received better provisions.[9] The persistent hostility toward rehabilitated *Volksdeutsche* persuaded some to claim German origins and demand to be resettled immediately. In September 1946 *Volksdeutsche* in categories III and IV who declined to apply for rehabilitation were voluntarily leaving for Germany, and positively verified individuals in Silesia were returning certificates of Polish citizenship.[10]

Prior to expulsion *Volksdeutsche* had to be stripped of Polish citizenship. A decree on 13 September 1946 (effective 8 November 1946) accomplished this for those over the age of eighteen whose "behavior exhibited German national distinctiveness." A declaration of membership in the German nation or of German origin during the war did not in itself constitute evidence of "German national distinctiveness": one might have acted under pressure to safeguard one's property or one's life. Therefore the decree did not automatically apply to all *Volksdeutsche*. Also, the citizenship of a child over the age of thirteen was not subject to revocation if the child expressed a desire to remain a Polish citizen and in behavior "exhibits membership in Polish society."[11]

In drafting the decree, the RM stated that it applied only to those eighteen years old or older because "exhibiting national distinctiveness can only be taken into account when someone is aware of his own acts," despite the exception for children over thirteen. It did not specify what constituted "German national distinctiveness" because "all definitions would here be dangerous."[12] In any case, *Volksdeutsche* were expelled prior to the decree, some 600,000 by October 1946.[13]

The decrees of 28 June and 13 September 1946 formed the basis for a new policy toward the *Volksdeutsche*. The MBP justified the change in a memorandum on 14 January 1947. Previous measures merely isolated *Volksdeutsche* in camps because of the difficulty immediately after the war of assessing their guilt and imposing appropriate penalties, resulting in an "unfair and unjust" legal situation. Some in categories III and IV were worse than those in category II. Some in categories III and IV applied for a higher category and were denied, whereas some in category II were registered without their consent or under the threat of force. The guilt of each individual had to be investigated and the appropriate punishment imposed based on the degree of culpability or, if there were no evidence of guilt, set free.[14]

The decree of 13 September 1946 did not simplify the rehabilitation process. The organs of public security had to carry out a thorough investigation of the past of each *Volksdeutsche* to check if "their behavior exhibited German national distinctiveness." A decision to deprive someone of citizenship required the consent of the local national council. *Volksdeutsche* who had not "exhibited German national distinctiveness" before 1939 were to be punished for their betrayal. With the lack of precision in what constituted "national distinctiveness," extraneous considerations often played a large role. For example, the Poznań governor on 31 October 1946 appealed to the Main Directorate of the PUR to look into the possibility of expelling *Volksdeutsche* incapable of work as well as Polish citizens of German nationality cared for in social institutions, burdening budgets to the detriment of resources available for the care of Poles.[15]

In October 1946, before the decree was published, a rumor in Łódź that the new decree would ease the rehabilitation of *Volksdeutsche* in categories III and IV prompted "great indignation," according to a report of the County and Municipal Departments of Information and Propaganda. The population loudly protested against any concession in the rehabilitation of Germans at a time when they were supposedly plotting revenge, as demonstrated by letters received by Poles in three villages threatening that expelled Germans would soon repossess the farms they were settled on and cut off their heads.[16]

Rehabilitation in Poznań Province

In Wartheland, unlike in most of the incorporated lands, the Nazi authorities generally did not coerce inhabitants to register on the DVL. The widespread conviction in Poznań Province that registration had been voluntary fueled a particularly strong hostility toward the rehabilitation of *Volksdeutsche*.

In early 1946 *Volksdeutsche* increasingly sought permission to leave Poland, as officials in Puszczykowo, Poznań County, reported on 18 February 1946. In some cases even *Volksdeutsche* who applied for rehabilitation left for Germany without waiting for the court's decision. On 1 March 1946 Governor Widy-Wirski cited the hostile attitude toward *Volksdeutsche* along with the complexity of the rehabilitation process and above all the fear of sanctions as the main reasons for their departure.[17]

Confiscation of property had wide support as the appropriate punishment for *Volksdeutsche*. At the Poznań WRN in early January 1946, Widy-Wirski criticized offering *Volksdeutsche* "rehabilitation and reconstruction of property when registration on the DVL had as its goal the preservation of property." On 4 September 1946 the WRN urged that partial rehabilitations more frequently include "confiscation of the assets of *Volksdeutsche*."[18] On 26 July 1946 the Provincial UZ complained to the Ministry of Agriculture and Agrarian Reforms that land reform expropriated holdings "even if just several hectares more than 100 hectares," "displacing from residence and home poles [sic] possessing fields, who even served the Polish nation during the occupation," while leaving "nearly all *Volksdeutsche* from categories III and IV of the DVL on the land," which offended "the national feelings of Polish society."[19]

Resentment of more prosperous *Volksdeutsche* probably played a role. On 6 April 1946 the director of the Międzychód County MO Investigative Department reported that while searching the home of a *Volksdeutsche* denounced by a neighbor, he requisitioned a significant amount of food and other goods: "Summing up the above, I come to the conclusion that such a VD . . . is prospering in our Democratic Poland much better than those Poles who survived the Gehenna of life in the fascist concentration camps as well as those Poles who fought for freedom and the liberation of our Fatherland from under the Teutonic yoke."[20]

Discrimination against rehabilitated *Volksdeutsche* induced the Poznań UW to intervene on 27 March 1946, ordering *starostowie* to instruct their subordinates to treat rehabilitated *Volksdeutsche* as possessing the full rights of citizenship and specially warning that mistreatment in Pomerania and Silesia, such as denying certificates of citizenship and ration cards and obstructing the return of sequestered property, undermined confidence in the government and encumbered rebuilding the country. On 31 July 1946 the governor reminded officials that the rehabilitated had all the rights of citizenship, but with little effect.[21]

A proclamation by Governor Widy-Wirski on 10 April 1946 that in Kępno County, unlike the rest of the province, DVL registration had been coerced caused the most controversy.²² Therefore Polish citizens in DVL categories III and IV in Kępno County, where they were especially numerous, could seek rehabilitation administratively and recover full rights of citizenship following a declaration of loyalty. Furthermore, on 18 May 1946 Widy-Wirski ordered local officials preparing lists for expulsion to exempt individuals registered in categories II, III, and IV who submitted a declaration of loyalty and applied for rehabilitation, including those who registered on the DVL voluntarily but maintained their Polish distinctiveness.²³

In Wartheland Gauleiter Greiser allowed the Polish spouse of a mixed marriage to be registered on the DVL on the condition that the couple agreed to raise their children in a German spirit.²⁴ Similarly, in April 1946 the governor directed that lists for expulsion not include ethnically mixed families who desired to remain in Poland and had not applied for citizenship but were raising their children "in a Polish spirit, using the Polish language in everyday activities, maintaining Polish customs and traditions, etc., and whose attitude toward the Polish Nation and State was and is positive." They were to apply for Polish citizenship, and the governor prohibited depriving them of their property; any abuses were to be reported to his office.²⁵

Nevertheless, fierce opposition to rehabilitation continued in Kępno County. In the hope that the governor would soon be overruled, on 19 July 1946 the PUBP requested that the *starosta* halt the rehabilitation process and proposed the expulsion of most *Volksdeutsche*. It also sabotaged the rehabilitation process by denying access to indispensable DVL documents, as the *starosta* complained to the provincial authorities on 5 August 1946; the WUBP defended the PUBP as simply reflecting popular objections to rehabilitation by administrative decision.²⁶

Moreover, a wave of petitions flowed to the governor from the WRN, the PPR and PPS, and organizations in Kępno County demanding no exceptional treatment for the county. The PRN also wrote to the PRM in July 1946 calling for a reversal of the governor's ruling; a review of all rehabilitations already granted; an immediate halt to the restitution of property; replacement of judicial personnel; and the extension of the requirement of rehabilitation to those whose applications to the DVL were rejected. The letter politicized the issue by charging that "former VDs occupy important state and social positions and promote the fastest possible rehabilitation of their partisans" and "cultivate discreet negative propaganda" in the county against to the Government of National Unity.²⁷

The results of the referendum in Kępno County added political fuel to the controversy. The first proposal, opposed by the PSL, drew a "yes" from only 38.1 percent of voters, and the third question concerning the Recovered Lands received the lowest rate of approval in the whole province, 76.5 percent. In reaction, *Wola Ludu* on 16 August 1946 endorsed resettling rehabilitated *Volksdeutsche* in eastern Poland. But MZO Deputy Minister Dubiel feared it would cause panic, especially among autochthons.[28]

Following a decision of the second secretary of the Poznań KW PPR and the WUIiP Director Zbigniew Kulczycki, the WUIiP on 24 August 1946 instructed county offices to organize mass protest meetings in conjunction with the PZZ and other organizations to demand an end to rehabilitations and the restitution of property. The directive included resolutions for the assemblies to approve and send to the president of the KRN, the premier, the minister of justice, and the WUIiP.[29] The WRN unanimously passed the same resolutions.[30]

As a result, 974 well-attended and lively protest rallies took place in September 1946, according to Kulczycki's report to the MIiP on 11 November 1946. The resolutions asserted that compulsory registration on the DVL did not exist in Wartheland and that returning property to "traitors" violated "feelings of morality and social justice." They demanded the extension to the province of the decree concerning criminal liability for denial of Polish nationality applied in Silesia.[31] The RM supposedly calmed the public when on 19 September 1946 it extended the decree beyond Silesia.[32]

With the settlement of more than 2,500 newcomers in Kępno County, many of them demobilized soldiers and war invalids who would be deprived of a means of livelihood if *Volksdeutsche* repossessed their property, the Kępno MRN passed resolutions that blocked the restitution of property and created settlement commissions to persuade *Volksdeutsche* to relinquish their property. It also recommended that the rules against overcrowding in dwellings not apply to *Volksdeutsche*. On 22 September 1946 the County Union of Peasant Self-Help called for revocation of Widy-Wirski's proclamation; proposed that "in matters of the VD not the courts decide, only society"; and voted to send a delegation to Warsaw to present a petition to President Bierut.[33] He responded on 22 October 1946 by appointing a commission to examine the *Volksdeutsche* issue in the former Wartheland and to recommend policy changes.[34]

The commission's report on 15 November 1946 charged the WUIiP with committing a political error in initiating an action directed against a binding law and, "instead of trying to pacify relations within the territory, called the proverbial wolf from the forest" by organizing mass protest meetings. The commission rejected expulsion of all *Volksdeutsche,* which "would only amplify the biological potential of the enemy with great damage to our nation, which already sustained terrible biological devastation."[35]

The commission maintained that Kępno County was an exception in Wartheland to the more restrictive DVL than in Pomerania and Silesia. As the county closest to Silesia with a large number of Silesians among its residents, the Nazis designated its population for Germanization just as in Silesia.

> The problem of whether the occupier engaged in coerced registration on the German nationality list in Poznań Province is very difficult, almost impossible to solve. Universal coercion in the strict sense of the word, and therefore through the application of force existed at no time during the occupation. Nevertheless, by means of terror and causing panic, an atmosphere was created conducive to declaring membership in the German nation by individuals of weak character, and especially individuals of unformed national consciousness, most of whom are found in the border areas of Wielkopolska. Not uncommon, however, was the phenomenon of individual coercion, without doubt having influence in creating a general atmosphere.[36]

Following Himmler's 1942 order to send individuals of German origin who did not register on the DVL to concentration camps, 20 percent of the population of Kępno County was removed and the rest applied to the DVL in massive numbers, apparently motivated primarily by a desire to save their property at any price. Shortly before the departure of German troops, 87 percent of the county's population was in the DVL.

The commission did not consider registration a reflection of national consciousness, which it regarded as "immature" among a significant portion of inhabitants. They thought they were changing citizenship, not declaring a change in nationality. The commission also cited the government-in-exile's alleged recommendation to remain "at any price" in their land and "the excessively compromising attitude of certain social authorities, with Bishop Adamski in the lead." The commission faulted the prewar Polish government for introducing inappropriate elements from other parts of Poland into the western lands instead of recruiting local elements for state positions, a charge that would be made against the postwar Polish authorities.[37]

According to the commission, almost all *Volksdeutsche* were removed from their property immediately after the departure of the Germans, and the PUR directed trustees and repatriates to occupy farms as abandoned German property: 1,969 owned by *Volksdeutsche* in categories I and II; 1,261 by those in categories III and IV. Contrary to the law, nearly all category III and IV *Volksdeutsche* in Kępno and Szamotuły Counties were deprived of their farms. Rehabilitation brought the property disputes to a head. The courts did not enforce their decisions, and the Provincial UZ halted the restitution of property in deference to public opinion. Very often the farms housed both the family of the owner and that of a repatriate. In many cases, however, officials of the UZ and UB or their family members occupied these farms.

The commission reported that, in the view of the ZG PZZ, rehabilitated

Volksdeutsche ought to regain their property, particularly in the borderlands of Wielkopolska, where the inhabitants generally identified their fatherland with their property. Otherwise, they might identify with the Germans, strengthening the German nation and mirroring Nazi policy toward Poles by depriving them of their property. In addition, the PZZ believed that, especially in a period of rebuilding, the continuity of ownership had to be maintained. This view differed significantly from that expressed earlier by the local PZZ organization.[38]

Nevertheless, the commission did not regard rehabilitated *Volksdeutsche* as entirely blameless, nor did it accept *a priori* the return of their property. Once again resettling repatriates who had already cultivated farmland and invested in livestock and equipment would expose them to additional losses, this time to the advantage of former *Volksdeutsche,* creating an atmosphere of anger and bitterness resulting in a new wave of protests.[39]

Therefore the commission advocated maintaining the current state of property possession. The removal of those occupying the thousands of *Volksdeutsche* farms would require the use of force, resulting in turmoil. It could also offend the patriotic feelings of Poles who returned from deportation or survived the occupation without signing the DVL. The law should allow for exceptions, depending on the method of expropriation, the identity of the person in possession of the property, and the motives and behavior of the individuals who registered on the DVL. At the same time, the commission called on the PUR to halt the settlement of repatriates in the province and remove those who had not yet received farms or other means of employment. To allay disputes and relieve tension, the commission recommended that *Volksdeutsche* be compensated with property in eastern or central Poland and not in concentrated groups.[40]

The commission reported the results of rehabilitation cases ruled on by magistrate's courts in Poznań Province from the beginning in October 1945 through June 1946 (table 9.1).

By the end of 1945 19,500 *Volksdeutsche* in category III and 9,000 in category IV in Poznań Province filed declarations of loyalty. In Kępno County 9,992 *Volksdeutsche*—well over half of them in category III—applied to the courts for rehabilitation by 23 October 1946. In addition, a large number in categories III and IV were rehabilitated administratively following the governor's proclamation of 10 April 1946. Yet, as of 23 October 1946 there were 54,390 *Volksdeutsche* in Poznań Province: 4,057 in category I; 21,184 in category II; 21,131 in category III; and 8,018 in category IV. On 21 January 1947 they numbered 49,737, 20 percent in Kępno County. Evidently, the status of a large number of the province's *Volksdeutsche* had yet to be decided. In all of Poland the magistrate's courts ruled on fewer than a third of the applications for rehabilitation by 31 July 1946.

TABLE 9.1 Rehabilitation in Poznań Province, June 1946

DVL Category	Full Rehab.	%	Partial Rehab.	%	Rehab. Denied	%	Total Cases
II	800	42.5	207	11.0	877	46.5	1,884
III with irrevocable citizenship	256	62.3	49	12.0	106	25.8	411
III with revocable citizenship	1,409	63.7	305	13.8	499	22.5	2,213
IV	1,189	63.7	256	13.7	422	22.6	1,867
Total	3,654	57.3	817	12.8	1,904	29.9	6,375

Data source: Krzysztof Stryjkowski, *Położenie osób wpisanych w Wielkopolsce na niemiecką listę narodowościową w latach 1945–1950* (Poznań: Instytut Historii UAM, 2004), 434. Stryjkowski claims that the commission overstated the number of VDs in category III with irrevocable German citizenship.

Significantly, the rate of full or partial rehabilitations granted was about 10 percent higher than in Poznań Province, and the courts of the province accounted for nearly 15 percent of all denials of rehabilitation.[41]

Because of the ruling that mere inclusion in the DVL did not constitute a crime, on 27 November 1946 the governor ordered the release of detained *Volksdeutsche* except those whose Polish citizenship had been revoked or whom a court had sentenced to forced labor, which probably increased the demand for the return of property. Some security agencies and units of the Polish army ignored the order and continued to intern *Volksdeutsche* prompting the MBP to prohibit such practices on 7 March 1947, an order also not universally heeded.[42]

The events in Kępno County reverberated at the conference of PZZ delegates on 4–5 December 1946. A member of the ZG PZZ defended its acceptance of rehabilitation.

> National consciousness in Poland was not everywhere at the same level. It was especially low in Działdowo, Kępno, and Ostrów Counties, all of Upper Silesia, part of Pomerania. The consequences of these deficiencies had to show up during the recent occupation. So also the laws are very often applied rather flexibly there because it would be difficult to apply to them similarly as in territories where national consciousness was resolute. They have to be treated liberally, and the PZZ must take them under its wing.

Others at the meeting made distinctions among *Volksdeutsche*, identifying those in categories I and II as Germans and those in categories III and IV as Poles.[43]

Bishop Adamski on Re-Polonization of the Borderlands

The treatment of *Volksdeutsche* in Silesia prompted Bishop Adamski to prepare a long memorandum dated 8 January 1947, charging that local officials frequently strayed far from the government's decision not to punish or expel citizens of Polish nationality who did not commit crimes against Polishness. He claimed that the expellees formed "Associations of Poles Resettled from Poland" in Germany so that they would not be regarded as Germans and the Polish authorities would reverse their unjustified expulsion. He complained that whereas many inhabitants of Mazuria and Gdańsk Province received Polish citizenship even though they did not speak Polish and efforts were directed at bringing back Mazurs who fled voluntarily with the Nazis and took an active part in the Nazi movement before the war, "in Silesia Poles are being resettled who speak Polish well . . . and who now not only they themselves declare that they are Poles but also cite the opinion of competent individuals guaranteeing that they are and remain Poles."[44]

The bishop's particular concern, however, was the expulsion of six clerics. Citing three of the cases, he argued for the essential Polishness of the clerics despite their DVL categories. He also questioned the integrity of the director of the Provincial WS-P overseeing the expulsions, in part based on unconfirmed reports that he had worked for the Germans during the war. Adamski concluded that officials often acted out of material considerations rather than excessive patriotic zeal as was initially maintained. Nevertheless, he recognized the difficulties faced by the government.

> The Polish authorities and courts are opposed to similar abuses. Yet higher instances are often helpless in the face of false accusations, facts passed over in silence or wrongly interpreted, falsified protocols or protocols taken down in a consciously biased manner and presented by unconscientious officials. The higher authorities must rely on this research as long as it is not demonstrated that the official was guilty of abuse. And this is difficult to prove. The defendants often do not even get to speak. They are resettled without waiting for a hearing or the court's decision. Documents that speak to their advantage are destroyed. A defense is simply made impossible, resulting in their imprisonment. In this manner damage is done to Poland, often depriving her of valuable people needed for rebuilding the country.[45]

Bishop Adamski sent his memorandum to President Bierut on 13 January 1947. In a cover letter he referred to inconsistencies in the assessment of the Polishness of expellees: "Some Polish authorities are guided by very extreme laxity, others again apply undue severity." He also charged that some officials expel individuals who applied for rehabilitation or verification before a court's decision. "Frequently there lies in this a material interest of outside individuals, for whom one deprives a Pole of his fatherland, property, and civil dignity. These facts naturally compromise Poland abroad, scaring away other Poles from returning to the country."[46] Adamski sent a similar letter to Minister of Public Security Radkiewicz on 15 January 1947. Both Bierut and Radkiewicz ordered investigations, resulting in a directive to the MBP Department of Prisons prohibiting expulsion of anyone whose German nationality was not conclusively determined.[47]

[10]
A Year of Crucial Changes

EFFORTS AT POLONIZING the autochthons intensified following the Congress of Autochthons. At the same time, pressure increased on them to support the Democratic Bloc in the parliamentary election on 19 January 1947. The conference of PZZ and ZPwN activists on 4–5 December 1946 reflected this duality: the ZG PZZ co-opted eight prewar autochthon-activists, including Karol Małłek; and the PZZ accepted a detailed list of proposals outlined at the Congress but at the price of a resolution calling on autochthons to vote for the Democratic Bloc.

The agreement was supposed to result in the rapid re-Polonization of autochthons and in their achievement of a position in the state appropriate to their numbers and significance. At the same time the autochthon-activists gave up not so much their opposition as their neutrality in the political struggle, an acknowledgment of the political balance of power rather than an indication of their political preferences. To prevent a repeat of the defeat in the referendum, the PPR and its allies were waging a campaign of terror against anyone who gave the impression of opposing the Democratic Bloc.[1]

In a letter sent abroad intercepted by the MBP, a correspondent in Zabrze, Silesia, wrote, "Again we are living in fear concerning our future. Two transports again departed. Now it is said that in January we must vote for Russia or else we will be resettled. What do they think of us in the Reich? There is much talk of war. But we rather prefer to die in a war than continue this slavish existence."[2] Among autochthons the PPR faced not only opposition but also indifference. The actual results of the election were not as important to the PPR, which did not intend to relinquish power, as a show of enthusiasm for the Democratic Bloc, and this was sorely lacking among autochthons. Despite threats some autochthons in fact refused to sign voter registration rolls.

The Democratic Bloc concentrated its efforts on Silesia. As with the referendum, propaganda harped on the German threat. But even many Silesians with an unambiguous Polish orientation turned away from participation in political life and in particular from the PPR. They were influenced by the Catholic Church and allegations of participation in the PPR of anti-Polish former members of the German Communist Party or of various Nazi organizations as well as the failure of the government to arrange compensation for the loss of property under the Nazis suffered by prewar Polish activists or pensions for disabled veterans of the uprisings.[3]

Nevertheless, the falsified election returns enabled the PPR to solidify its hold on power. The authorities claimed that the Democratic Bloc did exceptionally well in the Recovered Lands. Several native activists also "won" election to the parliament, including Bożek, Dubiel, and Paweł Nantke-Namirski from Silesia and Jan Baczewski from Szczecin Province.[4]

Still, the attitude of officials toward autochthons remained an issue. On 20 February 1947 the MZO sent a memorandum to governors concerning the failure of local officials to provide "equal treatment of the autochthonous population with the settlers from Central Poland." Officials were to persuade settlers that "a verified Pole-autochthon is a citizen with full rights whose Polishness cannot be called into question and his personal freedom, life and property receive full protection and care within the framework of the legally binding order in Poland." The memorandum enumerated specific abuses: arbitrary changes in the affirmation of one's Polish nationality, disregard of the rights of those with a provisional certificate of verification, the denial to verified autochthons of a full allocation of assistance from charitable and other sources, and the refusal to give the widest possible consideration to autochthons in filling positions.[5]

The Settlement Commission of the Research Council also had concerns about intergroup relations in the Recovered Lands. A resolution passed at its session 21–26 April 1947 criticized the indulgence of the cultural and moral transgressions of settlers instead of an absolute condemnation. To promote social unity in every community, the council called for activating self-government as soon as possible by creating communal national councils. It also recommended support for economic, professional, cultural, athletic, and social organizations that included people of a variety of origins but that could play a positive role only if membership were voluntary. In particular, the council recommended paying attention to parish life and religious associations. In addition, the authorities should promote the culture of the local population: "One should demand respect of the migrant population for the customs and traditions of the local population." Furthermore, the council recommended promoting the social advancement of the local population by creating conditions for the emergence of an intellectual stratum. To mitigate disputes between natives and settlers, the council urged the quickest possible granting of ownership rights and the liquidation of the occupation of farms by more than one family.⁶ Following the fraudulent parliamentary victory of the PPR, recommendations that basically called for greater democracy at the local level, respect for regional cultural differences, and the creation of a foundation for a civil society could not sway the authorities.

Meanwhile, the Council of Foreign Ministers meeting in Moscow from 10 March to 24 April 1947 gave rise to rumors in Szczecin Province that the peace conference would award the territory to Germany and Poles would have to leave. A report of the WUBP blamed the PSL for spreading a version that the Moscow conference would fail and lead to an armed intervention of the Anglo-Saxon powers resulting in the border of Poland reaching beyond Kiev and in the return of the Recovered Lands to Germany.⁷

Warsaw tried to paper over the problems that existed at the local level. On 5 June 1947 the MZO sharply criticized the local administration's treatment of the population "settled for centuries" in the western territories. As if a mere semantic change would make a difference, the MZO prohibited the use of such terms as "autochthon," "verified," or "former citizen of the Reich" in reference to natives recognized as Polish: they were to be referred to simply as "Poles."⁸ But the continued use of these terms by officials, including Warsaw, suggests that integration long remained incomplete. Ambiguous regulations concerning the status of autochthons and the provisional character of their initial certification as Poles established a basis for their unequal treatment.

Applications for Permission to Leave Poland

The parliamentary election confirmed the durability of the existing political and socioeconomic system in Poland, another reason for autochthons to turn away from their homeland. A report from Silesia for March 1947 noted an increase in autochthons applying to leave Poland, including a significant percent of verified individuals and even ones with Polish citizenship, which they freely surrendered in favor of membership in the German nation. In Poznań Province in 1947 every county received a hundred or more requests for permission to leave from unrehabilitated *Volksdeutsche* or those still in the process of rehabilitation.⁹

A conference of the heads of Silesian socio-political departments on 23–24 June 1947 addressed the frequent requests from individuals claiming to be Germans though verified as Poles and often in possession of Polish citizenship. Such individuals could not be resettled to Germany, but their nationality had to be reverified, and they were to be placed in the Gliwice labor camp pending resolution of the question.¹⁰

Those seeking to leave were often seen simply as Germans who slipped through the verification process, not as nationally indifferent or ambivalent. A memorandum of the ZG PZZ on 28 January 1947 claimed that there were at least 77,000 "fabricated" Poles in Opole Silesia alone: "The proper separation of Poles from Germans will still have to be conducted. Possibly, it will take long, even the lifespan of one generation."[11] But Grzegorz Strauchold estimates that ultimately only 2,300 certificates of Polish nationality were invalidated in Opole Silesia.[12]

As earlier, women sought to join their husbands in Germany. On 31 January 1947 a woman in Bytów verified in August 1945 applied to the Szczecin UW for the revocation of her verification and permission to reunite with her husband. But on 14 March 1947 the MZO directed that instead she receive material assistance in providing for her children, which would "certainly change her intention to leave for Germany and encourage her husband to return to Poland." The *starosta* was to handle all such cases similarly, appealing to the UW only in exceptional circumstances.[13]

The Silesian UW, which on 15 July 1947 reported a massive increase in applications for resettlement in recent months, similarly claimed that a majority of the women would agree to apply for Polish citizenship, divorce their husbands, and remain in Poland if they received the means to support themselves. Along with women significantly Germanized, they included Polish women whose families had a reputation as good Poles but complained that they and their children were treated as *Reichsdeutsche;* that they lost their homes, property, and means for support; that as unskilled individuals or individuals with small children they could not find work; and that social assistance was inadequate and demoralizing. Others seeking permission to leave included verified or rehabilitated individuals who turned against Poland because their property was confiscated and individuals with family members in Germany who did not want to return to Poland.[14]

In the first half of the summer of 1947 the PUR in Szczecin Province counted some 1,500 "wild repatriates," i.e., individuals choosing to leave on their own; it sent 180 individuals back to their places of residence, mostly autochthons from Olsztyn Province with Polish citizenship pretending to be German.[15]

Complications in the Verification Process

The continued absence of heads of households delayed the completion of the verification process. By February 1947 the Ministry of Recovered Lands received 18,743 formal petitions from Olsztyn Province alone, requesting intervention on behalf of a family member who did not return after the war,

13,739 for the return of individuals from the Soviet Union. As late as 1948 official reports claimed that there were more than 60,000 Mazurs and Warmiaks in the Soviet Union.[16]

In a report for January 1947, the Gdańsk governor noted that applications for verification continued to arrive from autochthons in Germany at the same time as requests for permission to leave Poland from individuals already verified.[17] Some officials feared that the late repatriates from Germany included Germans who were returning only to sell their property. In February 1947 the Silesian provincial authorities complained that knowledge of "a few words of Polish" could not be the basis for repatriation because "our Germans from the Opole region mostly know the Polish language, if poorly." Responding to such concerns, in March 1947 Warsaw directed the Polish Mission in Berlin to require all applicants for repatriation to provide a detailed explanation of their presence in Germany and appropriate documentation. In doubtful cases, the mission was to seek the views of the local authorities where the applicants last resided and require the applicants to name individuals who could vouch for them.[18] Still, at the end of May 1947 the Szczecin WUBP complained that the Polish Mission approved the return of many Germans expelled in 1946 simply because they were born in the Recovered Lands.[19]

Some officials favored verifying anyone not clearly German, and others, particularly security officials, opposed verifying anyone not clearly Polish. In September 1947 an MZO representative in Gdańsk overseeing the return of natives who fled to Denmark in 1945 reported "serious friction" between an MBP representative and a member of the Provincial Verification Commission who along with an official with the Polish legation in Denmark allegedly gave a higher priority to the return of the greatest possible number of residents of the Recovered Lands than to their Polish character. Publicly, the MZO representative also touted the number of returnees in this case, directing that the press be informed that 906 returned but not that they included sixty Germans refused reentry.[20]

Expulsions of autochthons of Polish origin continued in 1947. The MZO Department of Inspection, which investigated transit points in Wrocław and Oleśnica, reported on 2 June 1947 that special control commissions did not exist everywhere as directed. In one case the required list of Germans was lacking, and the official in charge was ignorant of directives concerning autochthons. The report went to the heart of the matter: "The greatest difficulty in asserting whether a given individual is of Polish origin or not is the lack, or even the impossibility of creating, an objective criterion that would differentiate a German from an autochthon." Furthermore, the decisions of verification commissions and officials vary widely. "For some the fact of having a Polish name is enough, and for the authorities to acknowledge the

Polishness of others, knowledge of the Polish language and, say, one witness confirming the applicant's Polish origins is not enough." "Especially dangerous is the fact that at times individuals already verified are suddenly deprived of their certification of Polish nationality because of a denunciation that the autochthon speaks German at home or has postal contact with Germany and therefore is a German, not a Pole." This deters many autochthons who "prefer to leave as Germans bearing their Polishness in secret rather than as spurned to whom the right to Polishness was denied and to whom is pinned the mark of treason in the eyes of their fellow Germans." In addition, "the unregulated matters of property" prevent an autochthon deprived of his property from applying for verification: "In practice the greatest number of denunciations is inspired or directed by the current Polish occupants, who in case the autochthon is verified would have to return this property."[21]

On 15 July 1947 the Silesian UW reported other complications involving mixed marriages, members of Nazi organizations, individuals who opted for German citizenship in the interwar period, participants in the Silesian Uprisings, officials of the Silesian plebiscite, and family and property ties. In addition, new applications for verification in the Opole region, mainly from individuals recently returned from abroad, including a significant number of suspected Germans, overwhelmed officials. On 6 June 1947 the MZO directed that proceedings be accelerated. But the Silesian UW received about 800 applications for verification monthly. About 500 cases awaited its decision, and it sought additional documentation from county offices in more than 2,000 cases. The UW blamed the legal complexity of the decree excluding Germans from Polish society but above all a lack of qualified personnel in the security organs and county offices.[22]

The Opole County Office admitted in a report on 12 August 1947 that it could not cope because of a shortage of personnel in the WS-P. The county issued 360 provisional certificates of Polish nationality in July 1947 while 636 individuals returned to Poland that month, resulting in about 3,000 undecided cases. Meanwhile, the office of security called for the revocation and expulsion of numerous verified individuals. In the last quarter of 1947 repatriation even intensified with 12,457 individuals returning from abroad.[23]

On 6 October 1947 the Silesian WUBP complained that the Repatriation Mission recognized many returning Germans as Poles, who did not know Polish and spoke German among themselves, which hindered isolating autochthons from the German language. Full of self-confidence, they settled on the property they abandoned, causing disputes.[24] The arrival of German women with repatriates prompted the Katowice *starosta* on 4 October 1947 to instruct mayors and village heads to register the wife of a Pole with information on her background along with a brief characterization of the family background of the Polish repatriate.²⁵

The Olsztyn Provincial WS-P reported on 1 April 1947 that a third of all autochthons in the province had still not had their Polish nationality verified: 38,859 unverified as opposed to 76,001 verified. In Mrągowo County the unverified (16,180) outnumbered the verified (8,316) nearly two to one.²⁶ In August 1947 out of 119,436 Mazurs and Warmiaks, 35,029 had not yet applied for verification.²⁷

As the expulsion of Germans entered its last phase, the Olsztyn governor on 15 September 1947 cited recent "reprehensible violations and shortcomings," including the expulsion of autochthons. He ordered that, under threat of the "most severe consequences," "repatriation" encompass solely individuals on a list of Germans drawn up by a commission that included "representatives of the local Polish population." If individuals of Polish origin were evicted from their homes and then removed from the transports for expulsion, *starostowie* were immediately to order the return of their homes and goods without delay and to bring those responsible for their eviction before the courts. *Starostowie* also were to brief commune heads on their obligations: recently a commune head wanted the farm of a native with Polish citizenship and therefore arranged for his expulsion. "That is a crime of the worst kind, and the harshest sentence imposed in a summary fashion awaits the commune head and his partners."²⁸

On 19 September 1947 the deputy director of the Olsztyn provincial PUR reported that in Reszel County the verification commission at the transit point excluded more than 250 individuals of Polish origin from among 1,700 individuals designated for expulsion. But on 30 September 1947 a report on the commission in Braniewo stated that it found no natives of Polish origin on the list of Germans to be "repatriated," although it noted that the list included individuals with Polish surnames who declared their nationality to be German. The commission, however, removed a mother of Polish origin married to a German along with her two daughters from a transport. They spoke Polish but had not applied for verification. Seeing how many Germans were leaving and knowing from letters that "hunger reigns" in Germany, the mother now expressed the wish to remain in Poland and receive Polish citizenship, illustrating the ambivalence of many autochthons.²⁹

The chief delegate of the MZO for Repatriation reported on 15 September 1947 that an inspector at the transit point in Wrocław-Psie Pole questioned the differentiation of Poles from Germans. He proposed, on one hand, that county officials more closely examine "the souls of autochthons" who admit to being Polish only when threatened with confiscation of their goods but still speak

German at home without at all trying to learn Polish. On the other hand, he lamented, there were autochthons stripped of everything and discouraged who did not seek Polish citizenship for lack of certainty that they would be treated fairly in Poland.[30]

With reports of an imminent end to expulsion, the effort to complete the resettlement of Germans and the verification process illustrated the tension between the two. In Lubusz Land the Provincial Regional Branch instructed officials to speed up the granting of citizenship to permanent residents and noted in a report to the MZO on 15 July 1947 that a number of autochthons whose verification was in process were withdrawn from expulsion at the Zielona Góra transit point, speculating that the MO sent autochthons to the transit point regardless of the type of certificate they held. But on 31 July 1947, citing a MZO directive on 7 July 1947 clearly stating that an application for citizenship should not prevent expulsion, the Regional Branch complained that the verification commission at the transit point was too hasty in leaving behind Germans whom *starostowie* had designated for resettlement. As an example, it pointed out that only two of fourteen autochthons returned to Gorzów Wielkopolski County obtained recognition as citizens.[31]

Complications in the Rehabilitation Process

As with autochthons, the higher Polish authorities sought to restrict the resettlement of Polish *Volksdeutsche*. Thus, on 9 April 1947 the Poznań governor ordered *starostowie* not to include *Volksdeutsche* of Polish nationality (except those deprived of Polish citizenship) in what was intended to be the last phase of the resettlement of Germans. At the same time, the authorities sought to accelerate the rehabilitation process. In June 1947, prosecutors in Poznań Province transferred to the administrative authorities cases in greater numbers in which proceedings "concerning the criminal liability for rejection of nationality during the war" were discontinued.[32]

The PZZ also focused on the fate of *Volksdeutsche*, e.g., the Mazurs in Działdowo County, very few of whom were rehabilitated in 1946 or made the required declaration of loyalty. Following a discussion of the Nationality Commission at the conference of PZZ delegates in December 1946, the PZZ Warsaw District sent the governor a memorandum on 26 February 1947 requesting intervention because of reports that Mazurs were not being rehabilitated and were being expelled as Germans.[33]

In other regions where DVL registration was less than voluntary, the overwhelming majority of *Volksdeutsche* successfully completed the rehabilitation process. A report on 28 February 1947 indicated that in Gdańsk Province 97.4

percent of the 182,551 cases concerned category III and IV *Volksdeutsche,* which were dealt with administratively with only 0.9 percent denied rehabilitation; the remaining 2.6 percent concerned those in category II or those who registered voluntarily, which required judicial proceedings that denied 8.8 percent of the applications for rehabilitation. In Pomerania, of the 289,148 permanent certificates of membership in the Polish nation issued to *Volksdeutsche,* the governor reported on 16 April 1947 that just over 1 percent were issued in the seven counties that were part of Wartheland, where registration was voluntary and required rehabilitation by a court.[34]

The process of rehabilitation, however, encountered a particular complication in dealing with Polish former citizens of the Free City of Danzig, most of whom were registered in category III of the DVL but had never been Polish citizens. As a result, the processes of rehabilitation and verification were typically intermingled. This apparently raised barriers for applicants. As of 28 February 1947 two-thirds of the denials of verification in the province of Gdańsk came at the hands of the Gdańsk Municipal Verification Commission, whose rate of denial was nearly double that of the province as a whole (13.5 percent versus 6.9 percent).[35] A Pole from Gdańsk later recalled,

> Those who before the war belonged to Polish organizations, maintained Polish traditions, language and culture, sent their children to Polish schools, were simply Poles, also had to undergo the procedure. A handful was saved. The majority paid for opting for the [Polish] Republic with exile. It is that much harder to understand and justify the wrong that they suffered from their own.[36]

Warsaw addressed the issue with a decree on 22 October 1947: permanent residents of the Free City of Danzig before 1 September 1939 who proved their Polish nationality before a verification commission, obtained confirmation of their Polish nationality from the appropriate administrative authorities, and filed a declaration of loyalty to the Polish Nation and State had the right to Polish citizenship.[37] Nevertheless, many of the verified chose exile. In addition to those who left illegally, in 1948 793 petitioned to return their Polish documents and to emigrate to Germany, of whom 58.1 percent received permission to leave.[38]

Hostility toward *Volksdeutsche,* even those who successfully completed the rehabilitation process, persisted among officials. Local security officials continued to mistreat *Volksdeutsche,* arbitrarily detaining them and subjecting them to forced labor irrespective of their DVL category. The frequency of these actions led the MBP to issue a directive on 7 March 1947 strictly forbidding such abuses and threatening severe punishment for misconduct on the part of officials. The status of *Volksdeutsche* also remained an issue among the population. On 3 March 1947 the Biała *starosta* reported that in general the inhabitants could not accept that *Volksdeutsche* went unpunished and enjoyed the same rights as others.³⁹

Reports from many counties in Poznań Province indicate that the organized expulsions of 1947 included individuals with certificates of membership in the Polish nation and Polish citizenship. On 3 May 1947 the governor stated that this violated his orders, could undermine the repatriation of Poles long resident in Germany, and provided fodder for unpleasant foreign propaganda. On 21 May 1947 the head of repatriation for the province threatened severe punishment of those responsible. On 27 May 1947 the authorities pulled 226 *Volksdeutsche* in categories III and IV from a transport prepared for expulsion to Germany.⁴⁰

In Kępno County officials gave the dispute over the property of rehabilitated *Volksdeutsche* no rest. At a meeting of the PRN on 31 March 1947, a councilor claimed that category III and IV *Volksdeutsche* owned 1,130 of the 3,130 *Volksdeutsche* farms in the county and that restitution would ruin the economy and cause immeasurable harm to Poles—repatriates, demobilized soldiers, etc.—to whom they were allocated. He also demanded the removal of *Volksdeutsche* from all state, self-governing, and even private offices along with Poles who obstruct the development of "Democratic" Poland. Another councilor pointed out that these individuals applied to be accepted in the German nation, not in category III or IV, and therefore they should not be treated with greater leniency than other *Volksdeutsche*. The council unanimously petitioned the WRN to request the repeal of the extension beyond Silesia of the decree of 28 June 1946 denying criminal responsibility for the mere inclusion in the DVL. One could not displace military settlers and repatriates after a year's work to return property to rehabilitated *Volksdeutsche*. For the sake of social justice and mollification of the Polish population, the resolution called for a law mandating the transfer to Poles of property still in the hands of rehabilitated *Volksdeutsche* and their resettlement to devastated areas.⁴¹

The PZZ opposed these proposals. On 16 May 1947 the Presidium of the Poznań District Directorate passed a resolution condemning the expulsion of any *Volksdeutsche* of Polish origin and endorsing the restoration of property to the rehabilitated. The ZG advocated acceptance of judicial decisions concerning rehabilitation and linked the situation in Kępno County to the character of several communities that gravitated toward Lower Silesia as well as to the Protestant religion of their inhabitants. A population with weak consciousness due to geographic and historical circumstances should not be treated the same as one in a purely Polish environment that registered on the DVL out of ordinary opportunism.

Fundamental for us is the language of a mother with a child, which survived with this population as a Silesian dialect. The Polish Western Union is of the opinion that educational efforts among the children and youths open the way for the future of this population which preserved the primordial Polishness of this land through several centuries of captivity. For this reason the PZZ sees no reason to treat this population differently than the population of the Recovered Lands. We have lost too much blood during the last war to now send children speaking Polish beyond the Oder.

A representative of the ZG also met with the chairman of the PRN and argued that the confiscation of the property of category III and IV *Volksdeutsche* had no legal basis.[42]

On 9 June 1947 the MAP sent a report to the UW stating that the Kępno resolutions "do not find justification in legally binding laws and introduce a division of the population into two categories—they create an abnormal and harmful situation from the point of view of the general interests of the state." At the same time, the MZO ordered the UW to intervene with the WRN to invalidate its resolution concerning the issue. Meanwhile, on 9 June 1947 the Kępno PRN once again passed a resolution opposing the restitution of property to *Volksdeutsche*.[43]

Despite the governor's pressure, the WRN on 17 June 1947 criticized the restitution of property to *Volksdeutsche*. Various councilors advocated even harsher measures. Ultimately, it passed a resolution supporting the demand of the Kępno PRN for an annulment of the governor's decree that DVL registration in the county had been coerced. In addition, the councilors called on the RM and the Council of State to revise the law so that no *Volksdeutsche* had the right to own property.[44]

Consequently, a special inter-ministerial commission returning property to rehabilitated *Volksdeutsche* halted its activity on 20 June 1947 after restoring 248 farms that had been in the hands of trustees or communal governments, less than 10 percent of the occupied farms. A commission member claimed on 11 July 1947 that local officials frequently refused to sign papers certifying delivery of the property or execute the ruling. Some repatriates vandalized the property they were entrusted with. Although generally peaceful, the process encountered demonstrations and active resistance in some communities. In Nowa Wieś Książęca a crowd of about 300, some of them armed with pitchforks and other farm tools, did not allow restitution to take place, shouting that it was only the first phase of a planned removal of all Poles from the community. Even the PPR and PPS county organizations sharply opposed the restitutions. At a conference of PPR activists in Kępno County on 7 September 1947, a member stated, "Guilty Germans of two generations [should] be in prison because they are already taking heart within the territory of Kępno and are saying that the Germans will soon kick out the PPRs." A report sent to the KW PPR alleged that rehabilitated *Volksdeutsche* drove settlers out of farms behaving "with true Teutonic arrogance, beating upright and honest Polish citizens."[45]

Partial restitution succeeded only by assuring the erstwhile tenants a third of the livestock and harvest and maintenance of their families in compensation. With a deadline of 1 November 1947, the process went forward in a dilatory fashion as indicated by the numerous requests and complaints by rehabilitated *Volksdeutsche*. Those in one village petitioned the MAP for the return of their property on 29 February 1948: "In signing the unfortunate application for the so-called 'Volksliste,' we did not do this for the purpose of rejecting Polishness or harming Polish interests but—in accord with the recommendation of Silesian Bishop Adamski—to save Polish lives and property."[46]

Although the opposition only succeeded in delaying restitution, the unrest continued for some time. Between 22 October and 7 November 1948 an operational group of the 10th regiment of the Internal Security Corps interviewed inhabitants and searched for arms in the farms and homes of former *Volksdeutsche*, in part because of rumored ties between numerous *Volksdeutsche* and the underground. Meanwhile, the Poznań KW PPR prepared and carried out a propaganda campaign critical of the restitution of property. Krzysztof Stryjkowski concludes that if, as in Pomerania and Silesia, rehabilitation by the administrative offices had been allowed throughout Poznań Province, the support of the WRN for the opposition in Kępno County suggests that the turmoil would have spread to the rest of the province.[47]

Disputes over property confiscated from *Volksdeutsche* also continued in Silesia in 1947. The Rybnik *starosta* reported that property had not been returned in 915 cases despite the lack of a ruling of forfeiture.[48] On 29 December 1947 a MAP inspector reported that in all of Silesia 3,602 *Volksdeutsche* had not yet had their property returned and 816 were forced to share their property with other individuals.[49]

The complex rules governing the revocation of Polish citizenship also hampered resolving the issue of *Volksdeutsche*. On 10 June 1947 Łódź Province held a conference of representatives of all levels of administrative and security agencies, spelling out the factors to be considered. Security officials had to gather testimony from witnesses and documents, especially excerpts from applications to the DVL.[50]

Expulsion began in Łódź Province at the end of August 1947, but because the local authorities did not always observe the required criteria and made a series of fundamental errors, the Provincial WS-P on 7 October 1947 reminded *starostowie* of their obligation to oversee the process, specifically that the revocation of citizenship and expulsion not divide families. Security organs played the main role. By October 1947, they recommended the revocation of the citizenship of 14,247 *Volksdeutsche* in Łódź Province, whereas local administrative officials, who could oppose these decisions, disagreed in only 177 cases (1,029 cases were still pending and 405 others were on appeal).[51]

But the situation in the former Wartheland varied. On 17 December 1947 the Kościan County *starosta* reported that "to make up for the wrong committed during the occupation, [*Volksdeutsche*] are trying to move closer to the form of the current political system as well as to Polish society itself." Perhaps similar behavior on the part of the remaining *Volksdeutsche* in Turek County—a large number left in November 1945—inclined the Turek *starosta* to conclude on the same date that the rehabilitation hearings showed Polish society no longer demanded retaliation for the denial of nationality, only the punishment of criminal activity that caused serious harm to a Polish citizen or was markedly hostile to the Polish Nation and State:

> For the good of law and order and the removal of all the causes of various disputes, the restoration of all rights to former *Volksdeutsche* is advisable, in so far as they submit or submitted a declaration of loyalty and condemn their acts threatening the good of the Polish Nation and State committed during the period of occupation. Therefore the property of former *Volksdeutsche* ought to be returned to them. . . . The punishment for deviation from the Polish Nation and State ought to be pardoned by means of an amnesty.[52]

Re-Polonization and de-Germanization

The persistence of behavior among autochthons and *Volksdeutsche* that the authorities and newcomers to the borderlands regarded as German, above all use of the German language, raised suspicions about the integrity of the verification and rehabilitation processes. Indifference to nationality or language use, common in the borderlands, did not fit the traditional concept of a Pole. On 10 April 1947 the minister of justice in consultation with other relevant ministers ordered officials to investigate "behavior indicating German national distinctiveness, especially the use of the German language, participation in any German organizations, the attitude toward Polish society."[53] A memorandum of the MBP on 17 April 1947 justified revocation of Polish citizenship in several specific cases on grounds that included speaking German at home and in public and regularly reading German books.[54]

The conference of Silesian socio-political departments on 23–24 June 1947 addressed an alleged increase in the public use of German despite the expulsion of many Germans. Officials regarded it as a deliberate act of provocation and "a demonstration of aversion to the Polish Nation" (a reference to a 1932 presidential decree concerning punishment for such behavior). Therefore the conference called for a resumption of verification to rectify errors, administratively revoking certificates of Polish nationality or citizenship of individuals not of Polish origin and expelling them. At the same time, officials were warned against acting arbitrarily since individuals of undoubted Polish origin occasionally used German. They should be punished or deterred by means such as cutting off their supply of gas. *Starostowie* were to organize conferences of activists to mobilize society around this issue.[55]

Prompted by the reports of the Silesian WS-P, on 24 June 1947 the MZO directed officials in the Recovered Lands, particularly security organs, to pay attention to the public use of German, which "must be regarded as a proof of German nationality."[56] In Opole Silesia in 1947 officials stopped issuing certificates of membership in the Polish nation to non-Polish spouses in ethnically mixed marriages and required them to learn Polish within a specified period of time or face expulsion.[57]

The use of German did not seem to diminish. On 15 July 1947 the Silesian UW reported that the return to the use of German "is assuming significant proportions. In the towns of Bytom, Gliwice, Zabrze, Opole, and others, the German language has officially come out into the streets. Numerous verified priests carry out unsupervised ceremonies in the German language. One hears German songs during dances and outings."[58]

On 2 August 1947 First Secretary of the Silesian KW PPR Edward Ochab directed local party committees to mobilize activists to unmask the supposedly substantial number of Germans who passed for Poles. "We must ascertain and put on the record individuals who use the *german* language publicly or privately, and eliminate them as germans from Polish society—that is, expel them." Citizens also had a duty to

> take an interest in signs of sympathy for germans and the spirit of families and individuals remaining under the influence of the german underground. This sympathy is expressed by using the german language, reading german books in public places, tending the graves of german soldiers, retaining german inscriptions in private homes, on pictures, decorative rugs, kitchen dishes.

Opening the door to extensive denunciations, the directive asserted, "Every citizen has not only the right but above all the duty to react immediately. One has the duty to detain a person speaking in german in a public place and conduct him to the nearest station of the Civic Militia or Public Security." The campaign was supposed to reach every Polish home and every citizen.[59]

On 11 August 1947 Zawadzki followed Ochab's lead but invoked the MZO directive of 24 June 1947 in instructing the Provincial MO Command and the WUBP to take an active part in the final removal of Germans from the province. He also appealed to all parties, organizations, and local officials to alert the population to deal with anyone speaking German in public as Ochab directed. "The use of the German language is clear proof of German nationality."[60]

On 12 August 1947 the Opole County Office reported on the difficulty of eliminating the public use of German despite severe penalties, alleging that in some places the use of German was more common than at any time under the Polish administration. Many youths who returned from abroad did not know Polish or felt more comfortable using German. They did not always behave in a loyal fashion; often they were simply hostile. Older, verified individuals, including ones holding executive positions, exhibited similar attitudes, e.g., a technical director at a factory who in an argument with a worker shouted that the territory would return to Germany; that despite being verified as a Pole, he did not want to be one; and that he would continue to use German. Because of the increase in the use of German, mainly at dances at restaurants organized by youth organizations, which shielded members from harsher penalties, the authorities restricted such events.[61]

On 19 August 1947 Zawadzki signaled the start of a campaign to eliminate the last vestiges of German culture with a directive to *starostowie* and municipal presidents, ordering them to hold meetings of their employees and local officials and brief them. Offices were absolutely forbidden to use German, except with Germans designated for expulsion and skilled Germans staying temporarily in Poland. Every office employee was to react immediately to manifestations of Germanness by Polish citizens, check their identity papers, and refer them to the WS-P to have their citizenship checked. Anyone speaking German in the street was to be delivered to the nearest MO station.

The directive, however, cautioned that only *starostowie* and municipal presidents could decide on the means of dealing with those accused of German behavior. These included a reprimand with a warning; a transfer to a worse place of work or dwelling; revocation of economic privileges entitling the person to concessions, enterprises, and local trade; a fine of up to 30,000 złoty; and detention in the labor camp in Gliwice during an investigation. In addition, officials were to hold conferences with registry employees absolutely forbidding them to record German first names or to perform marriages prior to changing German names. Stressing the importance of the matter, the governor instructed officials to report by the fifth of every month on their efforts and the results.[62]

In a similar directive to thirty-four institutions, parties, trade unions, and associations on 19 August 1947, Zawadzki provided specific guidelines concerning the liquidation of German inscriptions, including those in private homes on pictures, decorations, dishes, and the like. He lamented that "Polish families tolerate German inscriptions on the tombstones of their close relatives." In addition, he called for reporting individuals corresponding with relatives or acquaintances in Germany or meeting with individuals returning from or leaving for Germany, with special attention devoted to individuals returning as repatriates, who allegedly were often previously expelled Germans. Concerning Polonization of names, he proposed:

> With regard to individuals not displaying especially ill will, but acting not in keeping with the name of a Pole because of a lack of consciousness or out of habit rather than German conviction, one should undertake to raise their consciousness, emphasizing that their behavior discredits the dignity of a Pole and that in case of further instances, sanctions will be applied.

Finally, the governor called for these actions to be executed without publicity but nevertheless bring concrete results with active members of the organizations reaching every Polish home and again requested reports on the actions undertaken.[63]

On 9 September 1947 Zawadzki enlisted school inspectors and directors in the campaign. When few reports came in, the Silesian Board of Education on 6 October 1947 called on them to impress upon all teachers the necessity of increasing vigilance. They should admonish the parents of children with German names to change their names or risk revocation of citizenship and urge repatriates and local youths to liquidate objects from the period of German rule such as pictures, publications, drawings, and books and all German inscriptions, whether at home or in public places. The Board of Education requested a monthly report on the operation.[64]

On 19 September 1947 at a conference of representatives of industry and trade in Katowice, the governor suggested how Germans had passed as Poles. "Only now have incidents such as the falsification of the *Volksliste*, false testimony during rehabilitation and verification, the leniency of the authorities, bribery, false information of intermediary elements such as lawyers and the like come out into the open." At first these Germans were unobtrusive.

> Currently, as a result of the actions of the Anglo-Saxon friends of Germany, the Marshall Plan, and the policies of Schumacher and the like, they have taken heart and are amplifying their activity. On the other hand, hesitant individuals, who were verified and rehabilitated, are beginning to waver both with regard to their Polishness and to the position they should take in the currently complicated Polish-German political relations.

Later in his speech Zawadzki also referred to "the wrongs inflicted on Silesians after the ... liberation from under German occupation, the antagonism between autochthons and repatriates"—a realistic appraisal of the disaffection of many nationally ambivalent Silesians.[65]

Whereas Zawadzki emphasized the struggle against manifestations of Germanness, the Silesian PZZ chairman Dr. Izdebski in his speech took into account the ambivalence of many autochthons, focusing on how to "cement the population of the Recovered Lands into a uniform whole with regard to nationality. German injustices to this population should be redressed and recognition expressed for constancy in Polish convictions during the period of German rule. This population should be appointed to positions occupied till now by Germans or compromised people."[66]

Governor Zawadzki also spoke before several social organizations, including a gathering of five youth organizations, at which a resolution prepared in advance read in part, "We will guard the purity of Polish speech and stamp out from the soul of youths all poison of Germanism implanted by violence and terror"—seemingly targeting the macaronic local Slavic dialect with its admixture of Germanisms.[67]

At a conference for Silesian socio-political directors on 23–24 September 1947, the head of the Provincial Political Department paid special attention to the Polonization of first and last names, ordering the mobilization of officials at all levels against German personal names. He saw the departure of what was presumed to be the last transport of Germans from Silesia as an occasion for renewing the campaign against the use of German. He recommended that by 30 September 1947, "all German inscriptions, all traces of Germanness, German ashtrays, beer coasters, landmark signs, restaurant checks in German, inscriptions on roadside chapels and crosses be removed." But he made a notable exception: German Jews who did not know Polish could speak German in public, "nevertheless, in a way that they did not call attention to themselves. But Polish Jews should not dare to use the German language, and they should be brought to account."[68]

German Names

At the beginning of July 1947, a national council in Katowice County estimated that up to 75 percent of children born after 1939 had "purely German" first names "(and such which previously one did not encounter in Upper Silesia)" and about 20 percent had "purely 'Nordic' or rather Nazi" names. It called for simplifying the procedure for Polonizing names. The press made similar proposals, and provincial officials discussed lowering the cost. The

Koźle *starosta* resorted to more forceful means on 18 August 1947, ordering the dismissal of any local employee who refused to Polonize his name.[69]

On 2 September 1947 Zawadzki abolished fees connected with Polonizing names and instructed the Bureau of Records of Population Movement and Civil Registry to Polonize the German names of Polish citizens who apply to the bureau, "making every effort to induce them to start the proceedings and in cases of resistance . . . to report it to the *starosta*." In 1948 the MZO agreed: "Municipal and communal executives and even individual chairs of village councils have the right in their official capacity to influence citizens with German-sounding names to file petitions for a change of these names."[70]

Zawadzki also solicited the support of Opole Apostolic Administrator Kominek on 28 August 1947 and Bishop Adamski on 3 September 1947. To the latter he complained that only a small portion of the native population had taken advantage of a decree facilitating the change of non-Polish names. "What is worse, instances still occur today of Polish parents often at christenings proposing purely German names for their newborns, like Kurt, Horst, Edeltruda, Hildegarda, Ingeborga, and the like." The governor called on the Church to join the campaign, requesting that the bishop direct the clergy to explain the issue in sermons as soon as possible and that the bishop order the clergy not to accept German names at christenings and marriages. If Adamski found his requests feasible, Zawadzki boldly asked that the bishop send him copies of the directives to the clergy.[71] On 29 December 1947 Adamski countered somewhat defensively that parents decided on German names despite the influence of the clergy. Moreover, he disagreed that one can identify every name as either German or Polish and noted that some supposedly German names were common elsewhere in Poland.[72]

Social, political, and professional organizations joined in the campaign against German names. Workers' assemblies addressed the issue, and "German" names were culled from factory personnel lists. Chairman Ziętek of the Union of Veterans of the Silesian Uprisings called on members to participate in the campaign. Activists were to make sure that all members Polonized their names as soon as possible "because Silesian insurgents should be a shining example in this area as well." County sections of the Union were to submit a list of those members who did not comply by 6 December 1947.[73] Later, in protest, the well-known Polish film director Kazimierz Kutz changed his name from Kuc, the Polonized family name forced on his father, a veteran of the Silesian Uprisings, in interwar Polish Silesia.[74]

Dissatisfied with the progress of the effort, Zawadzki directed *starostowie* and municipal presidents on 14 October 1947 to brief their subordinates personally and make clear to their employees that "re-Polonization" of names is "one of the most important tasks of society and our administration." The wider citizenry would not recognize the importance of the issue as long as employees in state and local offices had German names or a surname with a "corrupted spelling." As in other cases, the governor wanted a progress report: by 8 November 1947 how many officials had German names and by 15 November 1947 the names of those who did not apply to Polonize their names.[75]

In the fall of 1947 the authorities requested that Professor Stanisław Rospond of the Linguistics Department of the Silesian Institute check the list of acceptable names, including ones about which they had doubts, such as Edward, Rajmund, Robert, and August. Based on his recommendations, in December 1947 Zawadzki distributed four lists: recommended names most common in Poland, names used in Poland that may be used on request, Slavic names, and prohibited names widely used in Germany. Although Rospond did not think it necessary to eliminate the spelling of surnames in the Silesian dialect (e.g., Nowok instead of Nowak), the head of the Administrative-Legal Department questioned this "nomenclatural separatism" and in an internal memo stated that nothing now stood in the way of changing a Silesian name to its grammatically correct form.

Zawadzki explained the importance of the issue in his December 1947 directive:

> By Polonizing given names and surnames all ties should be and must be broken that can and could even if only ostensibly indicate a connection of a given Pole with the hated invader.... The Polish citizen ... has to document by his Polonized given name or surname not only before the Polish Nation but before the whole world that he absolutely fully feels himself to be a fragment of his Nation ... not only for himself but also for his progeny and our future generations because a Polish surname will pass from generation to generation for eternity.

At a meeting of the WRN on 27 January 1948, Zawadzki turned to the problem of the names of children with absent fathers:

> A situation cannot exist in which hundreds of thousands of children attending Polish schools bear German names. Because I know one thing, ... the population here is mixed ... This child going to school grows up and lives and works as a neighbor of the boy or girl from beyond the Bug [River], from abroad—how many misunderstandings because of this? Personal tragedies due to German names. After all, the conflicts between us and the Germans in the nearest future will not ease but probably only intensify, and we Poles have reason to hate all things German.[76]

The Rybnik *starosta* claimed in his report for 1947 that Polonizing first names met no great resistance, and the same was true of correcting surnames. But changing surnames encountered numerous obstacles. It meant renouncing one's ancestors. If property were involved, one had to change all documents. Individuals widely known as good Poles who did not buckle under German pressure refused to change their German surnames, pointing out that a surname alone did not make a Pole. The civic control commissions frequently heard the complaint that pressure was exerted on ordinary people to change their names while individuals in official circles bore German names, which did not prevent them from being good Poles and working for the good of Democratic Poland.[77]

Officially voluntary, the Polonization of names came with various forms of pressure, such as officials refusing to issue certificates needed to obtain a pension or provisional citizenship. At a conference in Gliwice County on 2 March 1948, a county official explained, "We are not going to apply pressure because that misses the point. Not by means of harassment but by means of approaching this element with words, reason, and heart." As he explained, "Someone comes to take care of some matter, so one says to him, 'This will be taken care of, but you have a German given name and it will be better if you change it because you don't need it to be happy.'"[78]

Zawadzki claimed tangible success in the struggle against the remnants of Germanness in the last quarter of 1947. The German language, books, brochures, and periodicals supposedly disappeared. Civic control commissions were formed in every community, and teachers played an important role. Applications to Polonize surnames came from 15,474 families (39,316 individuals); to correct the "contaminated" spelling of their surnames from 8,365 families (17,164 individuals); and to Polonize their given names from 24,000 families (42,928 individuals).[79]

But the de-Germanization campaign itself may have alienated many autochthons. Zawadzki's call for "severe anti-German measures" and the campaign against all things German prompted the local activist Paweł Dubiel to write to Gomułka in July 1947: "I fear that these measures, undertaken as a reaction to the results of the referendum . . . with the conspicuous attitude of settlers and the local authorities toward the autochthonous population, can easily change from anti-German measures to measures directed in their severity against the autochthonous population."[80] For Silesians attached to various aspects of their traditional ways, the coerced elimination of German culture and habits not only widened the gulf between them and the authorities but also confirmed newcomers in the conviction that autochthons were simply covert Germans, which often did more to alienate them from Poland than official actions.[81]

The End of Organized Mass Expulsion

The British officially informed Warsaw on 26 July 1947 that they would not accept the last 50,000 Germans that the Polish government wanted to expel; in the following months they accepted only a few special transports. In October 1947 the Soviet authorities suddenly decided that mass resettlement to their zone would end in November 1947.[82] On 16 October 1947 the MZO deputy minister recommended that governors complete the "evacuation" of all Germans to transit points by 1 November 1947 excluding the "so far unverified Polish native population." On 24 October 1947 the MAP called a halt to the revocation of Polish citizenship of *Volksdeutsche*.[83]

In mid-December 1947 a MAP official reported that there were still almost 13,970 "Germans" (nearly all *Volksdeutsche*) in Łódź, of whom some 9,000 manifested "German national distinctiveness" and c. 500 claimed to be German to avoid punishment for denial of their Polish nationality. A Łódź administrative official blamed security officers, who gave *Volksdeutsche* the alternatives of serving ten years in prison or declaring German nationality.[84] No doubt some considered themselves German before the war, but unless they manifested "German national distinctiveness," they were seen as simply seeking to escape punishment, as the Pomeranian UW asserted on 20 December 1947 concerning 4,202 *Volksdeutsche*.[85] They may well have preferred expulsion to prosecution and persuaded county officials to revoke their citizenship, as the MAP reported on 14 June 1948.[86]

The MAP official estimated that 65 percent of the "Germans" of Łódź were female and 17 percent were children. Because they had no way of making a living or had family members in Germany, 98 percent wanted to leave; only 2 percent wanted to stay because of their children or strong emotional ties to their homeland. He did not regard them "as a useful element but as a burden both now and in the future. In principle therefore this element should absolutely be gotten rid of." If this were not possible, the state should limit its financial support to a minimum and carefully select those capable of work, sending them to state and private farms, not necessarily based on a court decision but in the interest of the state.[87]

The imminent halt to mass resettlement also focused attention on autochthons who refused to file for verification of their nationality. In Olsztyn Province they numbered more than 30,000. Following a conference with MZO Deputy Minister Dubiel on 30 October 1947, the governor ordered the compiling of a final list of Germans to be expelled, including those previously excluded from "repatriation" "who in their behavior show they are fully bound up with the German nation." He specified that an individual's Polish surname did not always indicate membership in the Polish nation, especially in the north of the province. Women with children who applied for departure because their husbands refused to return were also to be included in the list. However, presumably out of concern over demographic losses, he directed that women with more than two or three children remain in Poland and that *starostowie* provide for them and assist them in bringing their husbands home. Requests of the elderly without family in Poland to join relatives in Germany were also to be considered in drawing up the lists.

Still, the governor warned of strict accountability for any personal or material consideration in the expulsion of a member of the "native Polish population" on whose property a "settler or repatriate" resided, who made false accusations to obtain the property, "as already happened in many cases." In drawing up the lists for expulsion, the governor recommended choosing as advisors "at least two more enlightened citizens from among the local Polish population." In addition, three-person verification commissions consisting of "individuals very familiar with the question of the local population of Polish origin" were to draw up lists of autochthons who had not yet filed for verification but whose Polishness was not in doubt. These were to be excluded from "repatriation." In the two counties with the most unverified natives, Mrągowo and Szczytno, a provincial verification commission was to draw up the lists.[88] Despite the safeguards, all this constituted a shift away from the goal of re-Polonizing all of the autochthons of Olsztyn Province.

The re-Polonization of the autochthons of Olsztyn Province encountered other complications. On 25 December 1947 the director of the Provincial WS-P reported that 771 verified individuals surrendered their Polish citizenship. Moreover, he noted that more than 350,000 natives remained outside of Poland, 200,000 of them in Germany, mainly as a result of evacuation during the last phase of the war. Allegedly, the American and British authorities created obstacles for some who wanted to return home. In addition, although the Soviet authorities had indicated that by the end of the year they would repatriate the 80,000 deported for forced labor in the Soviet Union, only a few individuals—the sick, those unable to work—returned. They claimed that the remainder were forced to sign contracts to stay for another five years. The director concluded his report with the laconic comment, "In this connection it should be stressed that the question of divided families has a very negative effect on the re-Polonization of the local population."[89]

Assessments of the Situation in Silesia

With the largest concentration of autochthons, Silesia saw the most vigorous campaign of de-Germanization and re-Polonization in the Recovered Lands in 1947. Yet, as the organized mass resettlement of the German population neared its conclusion, troubling signs of German influence and incomplete re-Polonization persisted. A MAP memorandum, probably written in September 1947, addressed why Silesia was "not yet fully cleansed of Germans." Like

Zawadzki, the memorandum blamed primarily German machinations along with falsifications during verification and rehabilitation. Individuals behaving in a German manner had to be isolated, "especially from society not suitably sophisticated nationally," in the Gliwice transit camp and their nationality reassessed. If their family was Polish and a lack of consciousness or many years in a German milieu explained their behavior rather than ill will or German convictions, depriving them of Polish citizenship seemed inappropriate. Therefore, they underwent re-Polonization, including a course in the Polish language and education in the Polish spirit.[90]

In the last months of 1947 nationality control commissions examined the cases of individuals previously verified as Polish in four Silesian counties and reversed 1,062 decisions; 14,650 cases remained to be reviewed, according to the Silesian UW. Contrary to the law, the commissions revoked citizenship without the approval of local officials. Zawadzki, however, saw the removal of the remaining Germans as more important than the disquiet caused by questioning the validity of previous verification rulings.[91]

The end of organized mass resettlement also raised questions about the 76,000 individuals who, according to a memorandum of the UW apparently written in October 1947, declared themselves to be German following the decree of 28 June 1946 concerning criminal liability for denial of Polish nationality. Of these 16,000 left for Germany, although a significant portion was attempting to return to Poland through Polish consular offices. By 15 May 1947 proceedings stripped 3,227 of their Polish citizenship, but district courts quashed 55 percent of the rulings because offices of public security did not provide adequate documentation, contributing to a backlog of 6,513 cases, which was expected to rise with applications from abroad. In addition, the administration regarded 50,000 of those who declared German nationality as undoubtedly Poles who gravitated toward Germany solely because of the difficult economic situation.[92]

The director of the PZZ Silesian Office of Nationality also saw the problem as essentially an economic one, according to the report on 29 December 1947 of a MAP inspector investigating the German presence in Silesia. The director believed that manifestations of Germanness would disappear if the local population were assured of a minimum standard of living. The same Silesian population that in 1942 demonstratively spoke Polish in the streets of Katowice now, because of an inadequately developed national consciousness, tried to show its Germanness and eagerly spoke German in protest against material shortages.[93]

The MAP inspector reported that procedures concerning the citizenship of 11,360 individuals had not yet been completed and that 90 to 95 percent did not want to leave Poland. Since resettlement to Germany had officially ended, he recommended the transfer of at least some to other provinces, which would have an educational benefit because of the large number with "insufficiently crystallized national consciousness." He indicated that Zawadzki favored detention in labor camps of those hostile toward the Polish state or demonstrative in their German national distinctiveness and the dispersal of others in the eastern provinces. The governor believed that Polonization of the German population was possible but would require a long-term operation and the mobilization of the whole of Polish society.[94]

Material considerations lay at the root of the "serious and urgent problem" of Polish women married to Germans who stayed in Germany, according to Zawadzki's report for the last quarter of 1947. (Doubtless, many of these supposedly interethnic marriages were between two nationally indifferent or ambivalent individuals whose individual postwar circumstances dictated their official national identities.) But he did not want to agree to the loss of 88,225 individuals of Polish nationality. Most the women lived in very difficult economic circumstances. As proof of the effectiveness of material assistance, Zawadzki cited the mothers of several dozen children placed in schools and institutions of the Workers' Association of the Friends of Children who gave up the idea of leaving for Germany. The province, however, lacked the necessary funds.[95] The MAP inspector proposed easing the termination of the marriage in such cases, possibly by amending the law concerning marriages concluded during the war. Like Zawadzki, he did not doubt that re-Polonization with the active support of society would yield positive results.[96]

With criminal proceedings in progress against 1,356 for betraying their Polish nationality, the director of the Provincial WS-P believed that many claimed German nationality to avoid punishment, but *starostowie* cited only six such cases. Furthermore, the MAP inspector did not find that a "return of Germanness" had taken on massive proportions, perhaps because of severe administrative penalties. In addition, he credited widespread social action, for example, by the Silesian PZZ during the "III Week of the Silesian Lands" 1–8 December 1947 under the slogan of "The struggle against the remnants of Germanness" by "unmasking survivors of Germanness hiding under a mask of Polishness," liquidating German inscriptions, and so forth.[97] According to the inspector, the chairman of the WRN similarly asserted that in principle a German problem did not exist in Upper Silesia and dismissed the supposed manifestations of Germanness as mere provocations by elements attempting to maintain the nationalist ferment and prevent stabilization. Considerable antagonism existed between the natives and individuals from the Dąbrowa Basin because the latter regarded the natives as Germans. The chairman believed that the elimination of the antagonism would no doubt result in the liquidation of the German question.

The inspector noted that Deputy Governor Ziętek saw no point in revoking Polish citizenship because resettlement had ended. Ziętek also believed long-term efforts at re-Polonization could resolve the problem. He now opposed the Polonization of names of veterans of the Silesian Uprisings and their families attached to the names under which they fought against the Germans and were later persecuted. What was needed was a widespread operation to raise national consciousness.[98] Silesian PZZ Chairman Izdebski confirmed that as of January 1948 re-Polonization had not yet achieved the goal of all verified autochthons possessing consciousness of a Polish identity.[99]

Like previous foreign and domestic political developments, an ideological shift within the international communist movement influenced the direction of nationality policies. In September 1947 a meeting of communist parties in Szklarska Poręba—significantly, in Poland's Recovered Lands—resulted in the creation of the Communist Information Bureau (Cominform) with Moscow asserting greater control over individual parties and stepping back from supporting their nationalist policies.[100] Subservience to Moscow, described as "proletarian internationalism," became the touchstone of orthodoxy. This led to the expulsion of the Yugoslav communist party from the Cominform on 28 June 1948. In Poland it divided supporters of socialism of the Soviet variety from its opponents, marking the turn from one phase of Stalinism in which terror was directed against the opponents of PPR to another with terror directed against particular social groups and opponents within the PPR.[101]

Although the program of re-Polonization did not formally end, signs appeared of its subordination to new ideological goals. Whereas in June 1947 the ZG PZZ showed great concern over the meager results of re-Polonization, in December 1947 the PZZ general congress emphasized "the ideological education of society . . . according to the principles of people's democracy." A memorandum of the Ministry of Education on 10 December 1947 reminded officials that the task of teaching about Poland and the contemporary world "should be entrusted exclusively to teachers who combine the appropriate scholarly and didactic preparation with an active stance in social life with the proper political orientation."[102]

Ukrainians in the Recovered Lands

A mass resettlement from southeastern Poland of population labeled as Ukrainian complicated the Polonization of the Recovered Lands in 1947. Ironically, the resettlement was a consequence of the failure of efforts to unite all Ukrainians in an ethnically homogeneous state. Since its first congress in

Vienna in 1929, the Organization of Ukrainian Nationalists (*Orhanizatsiya Ukrains'kykh Natsionalistiv* or OUN) saw this as the only means of ensuring the independence and development of the territory then divided between Poland and the Soviet Union.[103]

In 1939 the Nazi-Soviet partitioning of Poland united the Ukrainian lands within the Soviet Union, but the OUN saw the German invasion of the Soviet Union in 1941 as a better opportunity to realize its goal. Like the Polish-German borderlands, the Ukrainian-Polish borderland was ethnically diverse with many inhabitants lacking a clear national identity. The German occupation polarized them along national lines. As Kersten notes, "When people were killed because they were Poles, Jews, or Ukrainians, or on the contrary, Polishness or Ukrainianness protected against death or persecution, national identity surpassed other systems of reference."[104] In 1943 OUN partisans formed the Ukrainian Insurgent Army (*Ukrains'ka Povstans'ka Armiya* or UPA) to oppose Polish, Soviet, and German domination. With the expectation of Polish postwar territorial claims to eastern Galicia and Volhynia, by February 1943 the OUN began to eliminate the Polish minority. The UPA together with local Ukrainians killed at least 40,000 Poles in Volhynia in the spring and summer of 1943. Polish self-defense units and partisans retaliated against the UPA and Ukrainian civilians. In the spring of 1944 the AK and UPA engaged in a conflict over eastern Galicia. In all, the victims of the ensuing massacres, often very cruel, totaled more than 80,000 Poles and more than 20,000 Ukrainians.[105]

The secret agreements of the PKWN with the Soviet Union on 27 July 1944 to shift the border westward and with Soviet Ukraine on 9 September 1944 to exchange population were supposed to unite all Ukrainians in a homogeneous Soviet Ukraine.[106] Along with Ukrainians, the border shift placed Hutsuls and many Boikos "homogenized" as Ukrainians within Soviet Ukraine, and the exchange of population and deportation to Soviet Ukraine included most Lemkos and Boikos.[107] As with the *Volksdeutsche,* the Polish authorities most often relied on a document issued by the Nazis—here a "U" on a German ID—as proof of nationality. They specifically excluded religious denomination in determining nationality, unlike some officials in relation to Protestant autochthons.[108] Thus, Roman Catholic Poles who passed as Ukrainian to avoid Nazi persecution were liable to be deported after the war.

Although late in 1944 some inhabitants left southeastern Poland for Soviet Ukraine voluntarily, many proved reluctant to abandon their ancestral lands and accept Soviet rule. Early in 1945 the Polish government began to exert pressure and soon—together with the Soviet NKVD—force, attacking Ukrainian villages, which set off a new round of reprisals. The violence prompted many to choose "repatriation," which the OUN and UPA sought to prevent through sabotage and assassination. In April 1946 Polish military and security forces began an operation to complete the expulsion, loading whole villages onto convoys headed for Soviet Ukraine. On 2 August 1946 government forces reported that 482,107 Ukrainians were sent to Soviet Ukraine.[109]

Nevertheless, a large number successfully eluded deportation. With the Soviet Union not accepting further "repatriates," Deputy Chief of Staff General Stefan Mossor suggested "resettling these people by individual family and dispersing them throughout the entire area of the Recovered Lands."[110] The assassination of Deputy Minister of National Defense General Świerczewski on 28 March 1946, probably by the UPA, provided the pretext. The next day the PPR Politburo voted to "resettle ukrainians [sic] and mixed families at a rapid rate to the recovered areas (above all northern Prussia) not forming concentrated groups and no closer than 100 km. to the border."[111] Operation Vistula *(Wisła)* encompassed all individuals identified as Ukrainian, including loyal communists and opponents of UPA, "to resolve the Ukrainian problem in Poland once and for all," as stated in the initial plan for the operation.[112] Forced assimilation would maintain the goal of an ethnically homogeneous Polish state.

Alleged collaboration with the UPA resulted in summary executions of at least 173. Others, including members of the Ukrainian intelligentsia, Eastern Rite and Orthodox clergymen, and mostly peasants not connected with the UPA were sent to the Jaworzno concentration camp. From 5 May 1947 through January 1948 more than 5,000 individuals at one time or another were held in the camp, and 161 died due to brutal treatment and conditions there. The most reliable statistics on deportees indicate that by 15 August 1947 140,660 individuals were resettled in Olsztyn (55,089), Szczecin (48,465), Wrocław (21,235), Poznań (8,042), Gdańsk (6,838), and Białystok (991) Provinces. Additional deportations came as late as the spring of 1950 and even later as individuals previously deported returned to their homes.[113]

The MZO on 10 November 1947 ordered provincial authorities to spare no effort in fostering assimilation and not even to refer to the deportees as "Ukrainian." Members of the intelligentsia were to be isolated far from others and deportees forbidden to change their place of residence even within the same county. Above all, PUBP officers were to see to it that deportees did not leave the Recovered Lands. All forms of sociocultural activity were banned. As a rule no deportee could be elected even to the lowest office. When a village in Koszalin County elected a Ukrainian chair of the village council, the head of the commune was told to "correct" the situation. For their part, deportees turned to every institution seeking permission to return to their homeland. The famous Lemko naïve artist Nikifor returned to his native Krynica three times before he was allowed to stay. As an alternative, 1,164 chose to leave for the Soviet Union in 1948, according to the PUR.[114]

Government propaganda demonizing Ukrainians and exaggerating Polish losses in Volhynia threatened intergroup relations within the Recovered Lands, which included refugees from Volhynia. In general, the deportees encountered a hostile reception. They had relatively better relations with the other groups treated with suspicion, autochthons and Germans. Characteristically, the Olsztyn governor reported secret links between deportees and unverified autochthons and blamed foreign contacts and propaganda for unrest among them, resistance to intensive labor, and the spread of rumors of war.[115]

The resettlement of a population with different customs and traditions, including dress, and a different language added to the ethnic diversity of the Recovered Lands. The fraudulent parliamentary election consolidating the communist party's grip on power and the change in the ideological emphasis made 1947 a crucial year for the ruling communist party. But of greater significance for Polish nationality policies was the end of mass expulsions to Germany, which forced a reconsideration of policies toward unverified autochthons and unrehabilitated *Volksdeutsche,* marking a turning point in these policies.

[11]

Nationality Policies Following the End of Mass Expulsion

THE END OF mass expulsion made the verification of the remaining German citizens a priority for the authorities. Although individual and group departures from Poland continued to occur, on 22 March 1948 the MZO required that an applicant submit a permit from the British or Soviet authorities to settle in their zone of Germany to the MSZ, which alone had the right to approve departure.[1]

Officials often relied on a concept of Polish identity that clashed with local traditions. The Kashubs, whom the local authorities regarded with suspicion and relied on propaganda and coercion to force them to declare an unambiguous Polish identity—contrary to their tradition—turned away from Poland, some opting for a German identity. Thus, on 17 March 1948 the Szczecin Provincial WS-P reported that the results of Polonization had been meager. Acts of outright hatred of Kashubs continued to occur despite numerous warnings. On 10 July 1948 the deputy director of the Provincial WS-P charged the MO commanding officer in Wałcz County with criminal responsibility for asserting that all autochthons were Germans and that he planned to search their homes,

> and where even one religious picture with a German inscription is found in the homes of autochthons, then in consultation with the head of the PUBP, . . . he will lock up the autochthons in such camps that they will never get out. This speech of the commanding officer . . . was received by the immigrant population with great satisfaction, whereas the autochthonous population felt it as an unfounded threat and omen of harassment and provocation of unjustified repression.[2]

The *starosta* of Ostróda, Olsztyn Province, showed more sympathy for the autochthons and proved more psychologically adept at dealing with them. He reported on 17 January 1948 that a verification campaign resulted in 200 signing declarations of loyalty to Poland and on 19 February 1948 that the campaign was coming to a close after another 447 signed declarations of loyalty. He spoke with the autochthons individually at great length to persuade them. At first the autochthon would state, "I was a German, and I will remain a German." Then the *starosta* would call them together and inform them that because they claim to be German their pay would be lowered to what Germans were paid and they would lose all social benefits as well as their homes because a German should not live better than a Mazur. As a result, some signed declarations of loyalty immediately, others several days later.[3]

At the same time, the Ostróda *starosta* emphasized his "embarrassment" over the "cordiality" of these people, who attributed their reluctance to apply for verification to the plundering and violence immediately after the war, the breakup of families, and the fear that they would continue to be slandered and treated as second-class citizens. They spoke of their poverty with no hope in the near future. Widespread rumors suggested East Prussia would sooner or later be German again, but for the *starosta*,

> The greatest obstacle in the area of re-Polonization of this population is . . . the immigrant population, which uses all means for the local population to be "German," because even today there exist a number of possibilities of exploiting the autochthon. Some want to remove them (the Mazurs), because they still have some modest meager possessions, for example, furniture, machines, contentious issues over land and cattle; others would want them to stay because they have cheap labor and a good worker whom they will pay as much as they want or not pay.

The *starosta* was convinced that the natives of the county included no Germans, "only pure-blooded Mazurs" or progeny of mixed marriages. The verification commission, in which a Catholic who found it difficult to believe that a Germanized Protestant was a Mazur represented the autochthons, was a complete failure. Unfamiliar with local conditions, it accepted his opinion and designated individuals for expulsion, and everyone from a settler to a county employee made money on the autochthon's furniture. The *starosta* demurred: "I am verifying everyone to break up the solidarity of the mass of autochthons, whereas it is up to the administration and the Security Service to find destructive and harmful German elements."[4]

On 27 February 1948 the Olsztyn governor called for pressure on the unverified autochthons, including the threat of expulsion. Szczytno *starosta* Późny responded on 15 March 1948 that about 400 of the 4,850 unverified autochthons in the county sought permission to depart for Germany. The rest, who did not intend to leave, refused to admit to being of Polish origin, all the more so because their treatment by newcomers, especially in rural areas, confirmed their conviction that they were Germans.

Późny attributed the persistent antagonism between the two groups to past wrongs and unresolved conflicts over farm ownership. Criminal elements also continued to prey upon the local population. Autochthons unable to make a living did not feel tied to society and stood apart from social and economic life. In addition, Późny referred to the significant influence of German propaganda, including reports of an approaching war and the return of the Germans, which called for "perseverance," not risking retribution when the Germans returned. Późny suspected religious gatherings in private homes of spreading this propaganda. He held a series of meetings with county officials, security personnel, representatives of political parties, and other leaders to caution them against any inappropriate behavior that could alienate the local population.[5]

As part of the governor's campaign, officials organized meetings in villages inhabited by the unverified. Speakers included autochthons returned from Germany who described the difficult conditions that prevailed there. But the campaign also faced opposition. In the spring of 1948 the MZO reported instances of armed individuals who "by means of beatings and threats tried to force those wanting to verify [their nationality] to change their decision." In Szczytno County it even came to "organized resistance to verification."[6] In this situation on 19 April 1948 the Olsztyn KW PPR considered the idea of simply granting Polish citizenship to all recognized as Mazurs, something Mazurian activists advocated when the territory first came under Polish administration and the PZZ proposed in December 1946.[7]

The Evangelical-Augsburg Church also sought to persuade the unverified to opt for Poland. But at a conference in Olsztyn on 9 March 1948, pastors of the Mazuria Diocese concluded that they did not have sufficient influence to mold the population in the Polish spirit. Those who tried to persuade Mazurs to accept Polish citizenship faced massive protests.[8]

A resumption of expulsion provided an opportunity to get rid of troublesome autochthons. On 26 June 1948 the Olsztyn governor ordered that the first transport should include "those unverified whose attitude and behavior hamper or render verification and re-Polonization impossible as well as a certain percent of those unverified who possess farms and who do not want to submit to verification despite several summonses."[9] Dispossession of unverified autochthons went forward, even amid bureaucratic bungling. On 28 July 1948 a provincial inspector reported that in Nidzica County about a thousand individuals were yet to be entered into the register of those granted certificates of membership in the Polish nation and summonses to register were sent to people verified long ago. He also reported that seven individuals warned to accept Polish citizenship or be dispossessed of their farms and sent to work on a state farm refused, claiming that they were Germans, "and even before the arrival of the commission were packed and ready for the road." They spoke Polish well "but for reasons unknown are unyielding and want to go beyond the Oder."[10] On 31 August 1948 the Olsztyn governor again called for expelling "the harmful element from among the unverified native population," which gave *starostowie* considerable leeway.[11]

The verification campaign in Olsztyn Province produced limited results: whereas on 20 November 1947 there were 21,650 unverified autochthons, at the start of 1949 there were still 16,686, with 12,395 in Mrągowo County and 4,186 in Szczytno County. Moreover, the decrease came in part through expulsion. The resistance of the unverified prompted the governor to issue a memorandum on 21 October 1948 limiting their rights.[12]

Other evidence also suggests a loosening of controls that prevented autochthons from emigrating. From 1 January 1948 verification commissions no longer officiated at transit points for expulsion. On 16 September 1948 the Wrocław UW of Inspection stated that at the final inspection of documents at transit points, if an individual had a Polish name, he was asked if he was of Polish origin, and as a rule the answer was negative, and so far in 1948 only one Pole was exempted from expulsion.[13] Inadequate supervision on the part of commissions for "repatriation" in Słupsk and Koszalin Counties resulted in the chief inspector for repatriation removing nine Mazurs and a *Volksdeutsche* with her two children from the transit point in Stargard, according to an MZO inspector on 18 July 1948.[14]

Meanwhile, Moscow's "proletarian internationalism" affected the communist leadership in Poland. On 3 June 1948 at a plenary meeting of the KC PPR, Gomułka, who criticized the creation of the Cominform and did not unequivocally support Moscow in its dispute with Yugoslavia, defended his nationalist policies. He did not attend a plenary meeting on 6 and 7 July 1948, when the agenda included the condemnation of the Yugoslav Communist Party, the planned fusion of the PPR and the PPS, and a resolution to drive out capitalist elements, i.e., to collectivize agriculture. Nor did Minister of Recovered Lands Gomułka attend the opening of the Recovered Lands Exhibition in Wrocław on 21 July 1948.[15] A plenary meeting of the KC PPR from 31 August to 3 September 1948 removed him from the post of general secretary of the party and replaced him with Bierut, who read a report titled "On Rightist and Nationalist Deviation in the Leadership of the Party and Ways to Overcome it." On 20 December 1948 the government announced the abolition of the MZO, and a law disbanded it on 11 January 1949. Also in December 1948, the PPR absorbed the PPS, forming the Polish United Workers' Party (*Polska Zjednoczona Partia Robotnicza* or PZPR). On 20 January 1949 Gomułka resigned as vice premier, and Zawadzki replaced him. A plenary meeting of the KC PZPR in November 1949 elected Soviet Marshal Rokossovsky a member while removing Gomułka and Kliszko.[16]

The changes caused anxiety in rural areas over the future introduction of Soviet-style collective farms, as reported to the PPR leadership on 18 September 1948. Kashubs persistently urged not planting more than four hectares because that would be all that they would be allowed to keep. Rumors of an imminent war spread. In Łódź Province it was said that the Anglo-Saxon states would not allow collectivization. Apparently as a result of fear of air raids, stores in a community in Katowice County ran out of black paper to cover windows. Instances occurred in Gdańsk Province of farmers demanding dollars or other currency for their products. Germans increased their activity according to a report from Katowice. Pro-German signs appeared, and the German language was used more frequently in public. Newspaper articles attacking Poland sent from Germany were widely distributed.[17]

The condemnation of the "rightist and nationalist deviation" had repercussions on nationality policies. In July 1948 the Research Council was disbanded. The PZZ continued the ideological shift begun in 1947 as it came under greater control of the party. A meeting of the Presidium of the Chief Council and the ZG on 20 May 1948 stated that the greatest current threat was "the rebuilding of German revisionism by Anglo-Saxon imperialism" to undermine the right of Poland to its western and northern lands.[18] The shift did not protect the PZZ from the criticism. At a meeting of the Propaganda Department of the Wrocław KW PPR on 9 September 1948, one member asserted, "The Polish Western Union is ossifying in its activity in the German sector, not approaching this problem in a wider context, not taking into account the role of American-English imperialism. This conceals in it the danger eating away at the PZZ on the ground of nationalism."[19]

A meeting of the PZZ Silesian District on 31 October 1948 continued to de-emphasize re-Polonization. Although General Secretary Pilichowski admitted that there were still autochthons who lacked a crystallized Polish national consciousness, he no longer saw their incorporation into the Polish nation as the most important achievement of the PZZ. Instead, their "mobilization" and their alleged positive attitude toward "People's Poland" superseded it. The worker and peasant character of the autochthonous population, previously regarded as facilitating the preservation of Polishness, now allegedly facilitated the building of socialism. *Trybuna Robotnicza* reported on the meeting with the headline "The Polish Western Union Based on the Masses of the Population in the Rural and Urban Areas Joins in the Struggle for the Implementation of the Socialist System in Poland."[20]

Following the liquidation of the MZO in January 1949, a secret report identified the autochthons outside of Poland and the unverified in Olsztyn

Province as issues requiring special attention, along with the large farms owned by autochthons, reflecting the ideological shift toward collectivization. The report also called for the centralization of re-Polonization efforts, signaling greater control by the party, and specifically criticized the PZZ for not actively engaging the mostly passive autochthons in social and political life by organizing local groups such as choruses and other amateur activities and cultivating folk customs—something the Research Council advocated in April 1947. The report, however, cautioned, "Soundly understood regionalism has a positive influence on the deepening of the social bond; of course there can be no question of separatisms," i.e., strict ideological supervision was required. The report also recognized the need to resolve religious issues, particularly among Protestants in Olsztyn Province who lacked sufficient Polish clerics or relied on their old German prayer books and German-language services. But addressing cultural and educational problems would not suffice. "Difficult financial conditions, the lack of clothes, malnutrition, the improper attitude of certain representatives of local authority embitter the autochthons and dispose them negatively toward the Polish State and Nation."[21]

Polish estimates spoke of 170,000 to 200,000 autochthons outside of Poland in 1948, mostly in Germany.[22] Moreover, the number of autochthons verified as Poles requesting permission to leave continued to increase. In Olsztyn Province in April 1948 nearly 36,000 verified women with underage children in difficult material circumstances were awaiting the return of husbands with a right to Polish citizenship. At the end of 1948 the MZO sent to the MSZ 4,000 petitions from verified families for the repatriation of family members in Soviet, British, and French prison camps and several thousand petitions for the return of autochthons in the Soviet Union. At the same time, 30,000 verified women sought permission to join their husbands in the West.[23] In addition, in 1948 26,686 autochthons had not yet submitted to verification, prompting the authorities to begin to verify them administratively as activists had proposed, though in a more brutal form, reflecting the increasing Stalinization of Poland.[24]

Re-Polonization also fell woefully short of the ideal. In January 1949 the PZZ claimed that 20 percent of the more than 13,000 autochthons in the city of Gdańsk over the age of fourteen knew practically no Polish at all, and in addition a large portion spoke Polish poorly at best and most could not read or write the language. Official data for 1949 indicate that of the 2,769 autochthons in Wrocław, 774 spoke poor Polish, 966 mediocre Polish, and only 1,029 were fluent.[25]

The Szczecin governor reported that in the first quarter of 1949 the German language continued to serve publicly as the vernacular of the autochthonous population, a significant portion of which could speak Polish only to a limited degree, hindering social contact with Polish newcomers.[26] The Opole County WS-P reported on 19 March 1949 that the use of the German language was "a mass phenomenon."[27] In May 1949 the authorities fined sixty-five individuals in Koźle for speaking German, fourteen in Niemodlin.[28] A report on 20 September 1949 noted the persistent use of German among workers at plants in Upper Silesia despite pressure from factory directors.[29]

Letters written to correspondents outside of Poland intercepted by the MBP and quoted in a report to the minister on 7 December 1948 gave voice to the discontent of some of the residents of the Recovered Lands. A woman in Opole wrote,

> You have to understand that this provisional citizenship only serves the current strategic and political situation. We as well as the Poles say that we are Poles for 25 złoty. A notary public must authenticate this great citizenship, which costs 1,500 złoty. It is therefore clear that whoever does not sign up for this great citizenship will be thrown out. But even if we were to sign for this great citizenship, even so we will remain those stupid Silesians and honorary arses. For us there is only dirty work, which Poles do not want to do. They take the cream off the top, leaving for us only soup.[30]

Polish Jews could leave Poland voluntarily at this time. Based on sociological research in late 1947 and early 1948, Irena Hurwic-Nowakowska argues that the surviving Jews in Poland had a strong feeling of injustice that led to a search for radical solutions, and the majority saw it in the creation of a sovereign Jewish nation-state. This came about with the declaration of Israeli independence on 14 May 1948 with automatic citizenship for all Jews. According to the Polish Consulate General in Jerusalem, the emigration of many Polish Jews changed from a desire to flee Poland to a desire to live in Israel.[31]

Meanwhile, the Jewish identity increasingly came under attack. Officials scrapped a planned Jewish exhibit shortly before the opening of the Recovered Lands Exhibition for overemphasizing the separateness of the Jewish community.[32] Alleged manifestations of Jewish nationalism and separatism were deemed a "rightist and nationalist deviation."[33] The "unification" of the PPR and PPS in the PZPR provided the model for the liquidation of autonomous Jewish institutions. By 1950 the impressive infrastructure that the Jewish community built in the years 1945–1947—cooperatives, stores, a ballet school in Wrocław, educational institutions, nurseries, and kibbutzim created in 1946 as transit centers for emigration—ceased to exist.[34]

A census of registered Jews in the spring of 1949 found 43,135 in Lower Silesia, but a report from the province in March 1949 indicated that applications to the Jewish committee for certificates needed for passports became a mass phenomenon.[35] The MZO issued 6,795 emigration passports in 1948 but only 1,485 emigration passports to Israel by September 1949.[36] Then in early

TABLE 11.1 Re-Polonization of the Recovered Lands, 1946–1948 (in % of 1939 population)

Recovered Lands	14 II 1946	31 VII 1946	31 XII 1946	31 V 1947	31 XII 1947	30 VI 1948	31 XII 1948
Białystok	27.2	35.8	40.1	42.6	44.1	47.9	51.1
Olsztyn	26.9	34.4	41.2	48.3	55.1	57.5	59.0
Gdańsk	32.3	39.7	48.7	52.7	57.7	61.1	60.9
Szczecin	23.0	35.6	41.5	46.6	49.5	53.0	52.4
Poznań	37.4	49.7	51.8	54.7	57.9	60.1	60.8
Wrocław	22.6	35.1	45.5	51.4	56.8	60.2	60.2
Silesia	69.2	77.1	86.9	87.6	82.3	83.9	84.8
Total	33.1	44.2	52.0	56.6	59.5	62.4	62.7

Data source: [Patrycy Dziurzyński], "Spis ludności na Ziemiach Odzyskanych z dnia 31 grudnia 1948," *Polska Ludowa* 6 (1967): 193.

September 1949 the MAP announced procedures for emigration to Israel valid until 31 August 1950, which Jews interpreted as permission to emigrate to Israel. The goal, however, was the assimilation of the Jewish population and its institutions into communist society, according to Franciszek Mazur, an alternate member of the Politburo of the KC PZPR and director of its Organizational Department. Those who did not fit in—"Zionist and religious activists, as well as private entrepreneurs"—would be allowed to emigrate. By the beginning of 1950 there were about 30,000 Jews left in Lower Silesia.[37]

The MZO measured the progress of the "re-Polonization" of the Recovered Lands by the percentage of the total population of the formerly German territory on 17 May 1939 that the "Polish" population (including "those individuals undoubtedly of Polish origin who have not yet formally established their Polish nationality") constituted on a series of dates, as if a single Polish identity encompassed the wide cultural and historical differences among Silesians, Kashubs, repatriates, settlers from Central Poland, and so forth.[38]

Noteworthy is the rapid "re-Polonization" of Silesia but also its significant decline in the second half of 1947 (by 81,008 individuals), which in part may have resulted from the departure of autochthons.

The prewar geographic origin of this "Polish" population (except of children under the age of four) on 31 December 1948 is shown in table 11.2.

Autochthons constituted a far larger portion of the Polish population of Opole Silesia than in any other part of the Recovered Lands—many in Olsztyn Province had already left. (The MZO reported that on 1 April 1948 85.3 percent of the 1,017,086 verified autochthons resided in Silesia.)[39] Settlers from Central Poland dominated everywhere else, less so in Wrocław Province and Poznań Province (Lubusz Land), where repatriates from the USSR formed a third of the population. The authorities largely ignored this variegated landscape as

TABLE 11.2 Prewar Origin of the "Polish" Population in the Recovered Lands, 31 December 1948

Recovered Lands	Children under 4	%	Autoch- thons	%	Repatriates from USSR	%	Other Repa- triates	%	Settlers	%	Total "Polish" Pop.
Białystok	6,533	10.3	3,233	5.1	5,471	8.6	964	1.5	47,517	74.6	63,718
Olsztyn	50,615	9.2	95,523	17.3	106,391	19.2	4,763	0.9	295,678	53.5	552,970
Gdańsk	46,186	10.5	46,290	10.5	61,566	14.0	13,170	3.0	271,895	62.0	439,107
Szczecin	101,028	10.8	17,920	1.9	210,985	22.5	46,983	5.0	560,147	59.8	937,063
Poznań	47,065	11.7	9,362	2.3	138,121	34.4	14,565	3.6	192,549	47.9	401,662
Wrocław	189,626	10.3	18,554	1.0	594,872	32.3	126,129	6.8	915,035	49.6	1,844,216
Silesia	83,034	6.5	744,948	57.9	214,512	16.7	28,175	2.2	216,310	16.8	1,286,979
Total	524,087	9.5	935,830	16.9	1,331,918	24.1	234,749	4.2	2,499,131	45.2	5,525,715

Data source: [Patrycy Dziurzyński], "Spis ludności na Ziemiach Odzyskanych z dnia 31 grudnia 1948," *Polska Ludowa* 6 (1967): 198.

they pressed everyone into a single national mold. They saw de-Germanization as a primary means for achieving this goal.

De-Germanization, 1948

The removal of all traces of Germanness in the Recovered Lands remained incomplete at the end of 1947. Following a tour of the Recovered Lands by MZO officials, on 26 April 1948 Deputy Minister Dubiel ordered an immediate intensification of de-Germanization, particularly in four areas: "1) Driving out the German language 2) Removal of the remaining German inscriptions 3) Polonization of first names and surnames 4) Eradication of all manifestations and remnants of Nazi and Germanizing ideology."[40]

On the first point, Dubiel called for attention to be paid to pupils using German in schools, warning their parents that this could cast doubt on their Polish origins, a not so veiled threat of dispossession and expulsion. On the second point, he above all prohibited officials from using German printed forms. German inscriptions should be removed not only from public buildings, which was already mostly accomplished, but also from private buildings and in gates and staircases as well as from commercial establishments, including small items such as ashtrays and beer coasters, and from churches, cemeteries, roadside chapels, and crosses, except objects of eminent historical value.[41]

To encourage the Polonization of names, on 10 January 1948 the MZO waived fees for such changes and the requirement of their publication. In Silesia Zawadzki issued a special memorandum on 14 March 1948 facilitating the Polonization of names.[42] Dubiel urged officials to remind the public of the concession regarding fees and to exert "even a certain pressure." This applied exclusively to Polish citizens native to the Recovered Lands, not to settlers from Central Poland with German names, which some autochthons regarded as discrimination.[43]

In the spring of 1948 Zawadzki perceived an intensification of pro-German sentiments in an increase of applications to depart for Germany; the popularity of German hit songs, radio, and books; a decline in the number of requests for name changes; the continued existence of German inscriptions in cemeteries; a rise in correspondence with Germans; and the use of German in churches.[44] Continuing his de-Germanization campaign, Zawadzki on 23 April 1948 ordered the creation of county classification commissions for the purpose of "cleansing the territory of German books." On 13 May 1948 Zawadzki ordered the mobilization of control commissions to carry out inspections and impose heavy fines on shopkeepers and managers who did not remove the German inscriptions on scales, cash registers, and other equipment that "stand in stores where they can be seen and offend the feelings of Polish clients."[45]

Following a directive on 22 July 1948 concerning the removal of German inscriptions from tombstones, the Silesian UW notified *starostowie* and municipal presidents of the format of the Central Directory of the Coal Industry in Katowice for the replacement of German inscriptions on the tombstones of former German prisoners with Polish inscriptions, including the Polonization of German names (for example, "Jan" instead of "Hans"), which it claimed did not violate the 1929 Geneva Convention concerning the treatment of prisoners of war, but directed officials to do this without provoking hostile propaganda.[46]

The Silesian Provincial WS-P also found fault with members of the clergy. On 16 November 1948, it submitted to the Katowice Board of Education a list of seventy-four priests who allegedly had not mastered Polish, used German, or spoke a dialect corrupted with Germanisms, undermining the goal of promoting correct Polish and thereby harming the political interest of the state. A second list named 157 priests who supposedly ignored directives to liquidate the remnants of Germanness in the province, particularly by not Polonizing their names. "The attitude and behavior of these priests has a demoralizing effect on society and all the more on youths." The department requested that the Board of Education deprive them of the right to teach religion or other subjects in the schools.[47]

International and Domestic Developments and the Autochthons, 1949

International developments in the late 1940s reinforced the ideological shift from nationalism to internationalism and justified a deviation from the goal of an ethnically homogeneous Poland. Late in 1948 Poland, like other members of the Soviet Bloc, began to accept refugees from the Greek civil war as the Greek communists faced defeat. By 1950 they numbered more than 12,000 and were settled primarily in the Recovered Lands. Although they were brought to Poland under the laws of political asylum, the authorities initially kept their arrival secret, concealing this break with the much-touted goal of creating a Polish nation-state. The refugees increased the heterogeneity of the area to a greater extent than Warsaw expected as they included Macedonians as well as Greeks.[48]

Other developments directly affected the autochthons. The establishment of the FRG in May 1949 with its Basic Law (Grundgesetz), which in article 116 recognized as German citizens whoever held German citizenship within the German borders of 1937, his or her spouse, and their descendants, intensified the force of attraction of West Germany and would continue to do so throughout the existence of the Polish People's Republic.[49] The FRG also constituted a source of hostile propaganda, in particular questioning the permanence of the Oder-Neisse border.

In contrast, the GDR founded in October 1949 suppressed revisionist demands and on 6 July 1950 signed an agreement recognizing the Oder-Neisse border. Nevertheless, thousands of expellees in the GDR moved close to the border in the 1940s and 1950s to be able to return to their homeland quickly.[50] In Poland the creation of the GDR drew a mixed response. In the Opole region it caused great agitation, especially among autochthons, including railway workers, who began to apply in massive numbers for Polish citizenship, possibly to avoid expulsion to the GDR.[51]

The existence of a "fraternal" German state forced the Polish authorities to alter their anti-German stance. On 16 November 1949 the Szczecin governor referred to Polish administrators of state farms who exploited Germans as chauvinists.[52] A report on 3 December 1949 for the KC labeled only those Germans hostile to Poland and the Soviet Union as "Hakatists," a historic term for anti-Polish Germans derived from the initials of the founders of the Ostmarken-Verein in Poznań in 1894.[53] Moreover, the Politburo of the KC PZPR in 1950 specifically directed that the material and cultural situation of German workers be brought up to the standards of Polish workers. It also ruled that those Germans wishing to leave for Germany, particularly those from divided families, should be assisted in doing so.[54] In effect, the Polish authorities, supposedly temporarily, recognized the existence of a German minority, however small, and granted it the rights of a national minority, breaking with its commitment to a purely Polish Poland.[55]

The presence of a German minority in Poland, however, raised concerns about its effect on autochthons, particularly those resisting verification. In areas with a significant German minority, such as the Zielona Góra region, ethnically mixed marriages posed a threat of "infiltration of Polish society by alien elements," according to a report in 1949. Interethnic relations that resulted in offspring often forced the authorities to lift prohibitions on mixed marriages. In January 1949 800 petitions for permission to marry awaited the government's decision.[56]

When on 24 November 1949 the Olsztyn governor sought Germans positively inclined toward socialism to distribute newspapers from the GDR, the Bartoszyce *starosta* warned that this would endanger the "re-Polonization" of unverified autochthons.[57] A report on 30 November 1949 concerning German miners in Lower Silesia expressed concern about a small group of verified autochthons who preferred the company of Germans, with whom they found it easier to communicate. The report warned, "The possible formation of a 'German minority' would have a pernicious influence on the mostly still wavering autochthonous element in the Recovered Lands."[58] Acknowledging a German minority, nationality policy still insisted on the Polonization of autochthons.

At the same time official policies gave greater recognition to the diversity of the autochthonous population, shifting away from an insistence on its ethnic homogeneity. On 1 July 1949 MAP data recognized 150,000 Kashubs in Poland along with Belarusians, Slovaks, Czechs, Lithuanians, Roma, and Russians as "a population stressing its distinctiveness."[59] Similarly, in December 1949 the Ministry of Culture and Art proposed the creation of ten regional artistic groups in the Recovered Lands to foster local folk culture.[60] In contrast to the earlier emphasis on Mazuria's historic ties to Poland, the Institute of Culture and Arts established in Olsztyn in 1950 collected the folksongs of Warmia and Mazuria that documented the distinctiveness of the population.[61]

In the fall of 1948 the authorities initiated another policy change with the collectivization of agriculture as part of the class struggle, which radically transformed the public image of the independent farmer. Previously, the new political system was supposed to improve the lot of all farmers; now only the poorest—so called "working farmers"—were to benefit. The rest were labeled as "kulaks," i.e., capitalists exploiting others.[62]

The new policy caused consternation among autochthons not yet dispossessed of their farms, 25 to 30 percent of whom the authorities regarded as "kulaks."[63] Even Mazurs with small and medium-size holdings were so labeled, introducing the class conflict into Mazurian villages and significantly affecting many self-sufficient Mazurian farmers. Ethnic differences turned a class conflict into a national one.[64] Silesian farmers with a relatively prosperous model farm were also stigmatized as "rural exploiters and kulaks."[65] In Szczecin Province collectivization resulted in the Kashubs losing nearly all of their farms. Alienated, they rarely participated in political and cultural life. Although their isolation existed from the beginning, the chasm that now opened up between the autochthonous population and Polish society did not change in the following years. In Opole Silesia officials noted that the arrest of former ZPwN activists, rumors of an imminent war with a readjustment of borders, and the expulsion of some autochthons contributed to their isolation.[66]

Even aspects of re-Polonization that seemed successful ran into difficulties. At a session of the Silesian WRN on 27 January 1949, Zawadzki's successor as governor reported that 275,790 individuals in the province had applied for changes in their given names, their surnames, and the spelling of their surnames. But evidence suggests that many of the changes applied for were never officially implemented. The large number of applications simply overwhelmed the bureaucracy at all levels. The destruction during the war of birth and marriage certificates posed additional complications.[67]

Forms of resistance continued. Some couples from Zabrze County, Opole Silesia, chose to get married in Katowice County because the former required a prior Polonization of names, unlike the latter. In Opole County some individuals pressured to change their names reacted by returning their provisional certificates of Polish citizenship and demanding to be resettled to Germany. An inhabitant of Radzionków, Silesia, refused to change his name from Zejer because in 1936 he had changed it from Secher on orders of the Polish authorities. When relatives of the deceased ignored orders to remove German inscriptions from tombstones, the authorities simply removed the offending tombstones. Yet the de-Germanization of cemeteries remained incomplete in Silesia in the spring of 1949.[68]

The intensity of the campaign to Polonize names, however, diminished, in keeping with the shift away from nationalism. At a meeting on 23 March 1949 directors of Upper Silesian administrative-legal departments were told that a dozen popular names, such as Artur, Hubert, Maksym, and Robert, no longer had to be changed. A subsequent meeting in November 1949 recommended a halt to all administrative pressure to Polonize names.[69]

Some autochthons still resisted applying for permanent Polish citizenship even as the repressive measures intensified. The Silesian WUBP reported on 4 November 1949 that although all but a small percentage of autochthons employed by the state railways had applied, those employed in industry where directors did not demand evidence of permanent citizenship were not applying. In one community in Opole County, leaflets appeared urging people not to seek permanent citizenship. The WUBP, however, blamed primarily radio broadcasts from West Germany and the BBC as well as newspapers sent from the West. Informants reported that some people felt terrorized and under extreme pressure to apply for citizenship, including the threat of arrest and even, according to one person, "martyrdom." Another claimed that those who wanted to leave for Germany were being arrested as spies. According to informants, a desire to leave for Germany and a fear of being regarded by Germans as traitors fed the resistance to acquiring permanent Polish citizenship.[70]

Married women, most of them impoverished, with husbands who stayed in Germany after being freed from POW camps, constituted the largest group seeking to leave Poland in 1949. At a briefing of local officials in Silesia on 27 June 1949, an official of the Provincial WS-P stated that Polish women must remain in Poland and could not be resettled at their own request. He maintained that the public interest, and not the interest of an individual, dictated whether they could leave Poland.[71]

The right of natives of the Recovered Lands to obtain German citizenship under the Basic Law of the FRG spurred these requests. When some *starostowie* in Szczecin Province raised questions concerning the "repatriation" of autochthons, the Provincial WS-P on 11 September 1949 reaffirmed its opposition:

> The local population, which despite a weakly developed national consciousness nevertheless fulfills the conditions for obtaining Polish citizenship and uniting with the population of the rest of Poland. The Provincial Office does not intend to change its stance in the matter of granting permission to leave for Germany to individuals already verified and belonging to the native Polish population (Mazurs, Warmiaks, Slovincians, and Silesians).

The directive instructed officials to establish as soon as possible *"the fundamental class profile"* of the population on the basis of *"concrete data, illustrating its social origins, its social standing, its ownership of property in the past and currently, and most urgently, its economic and vital needs."* Only Germans and individuals properly deprived of citizenship were subject to resettlement. The population of Polish origin, verified and not yet verified, which because of its social standing (the worker and peasant stratum—i.e., the non-kulaks) could count on increased assistance, was to be convinced that resettlement to Germany was out of the question. Permission to leave applied above all to nationally mixed divided families, deprived of the main breadwinner and therefore living in exceptionally difficult material circumstances. But the UW ordered that in principle applications even from divided families not be considered if their verification as Polish raised no doubts.[72]

To address the situation, the WS-P proposed informing verified individuals that their family members abroad could apply to a Polish consulate for permission to return to Poland even if previously denied. On the basis of an MAP memo, the department authorized local officials to issue certificates indicating that family members of individuals abroad were verified or rehabilitated or in the process. But local officials could not certify the nationality of those abroad. At the same time the department directed that county officials pay special attention to the welfare of those returning to Poland and their families, providing employment and appropriate material conditions. Nevertheless, the department recognized that, because of individual circumstances, an application for permission to leave for Germany could be considered, which required a detailed report in cooperation with public security officials. Only in exceptional cases would a properly documented request be forwarded to the MAP to reverse a decision concerning citizenship.[73]

In Gdańsk Province the governor reported that about 60 percent of the 2,959 German citizens and 1,504 *Volksdeutsche* whose Polish citizenship had not yet been revoked applied for emigration to Germany in the third quarter of 1949. Moreover, he noted a rise in the number of applications on the part of autochthons (543 applications involving 1,141 individuals) for permission to join family members in Germany. As in Szczecin Province, the authorities advised that family members abroad should instead apply to return home— only 143 had returned to Poland in the previous nine months. Meanwhile, natives reportedly received unsolicited entry "permits" for the FRG from "Anglo-Saxon officials" in Warsaw.[74]

A memorandum of the MAP Political Department on 22 October 1949 recognized that "the especially difficult to resolve problem of divided families" prompted individuals to renounce Polish citizenship to obtain permission to leave for Germany. Family members abroad approved for repatriation were increasingly reluctant to file the appropriate application, for which the memorandum blamed a number of factors: hostile German propaganda and "reactionary Polish spheres"; the lengthy procedure of repatriation as well as the frequently unrealistic and unfriendly attitude of Polish consular offices; fear of material difficulties in Poland because of a lack of knowledge of the Polish language as well as fear of the possible consequences of behavior widely considered improper (the overwhelming majority served in the Wehrmacht as draftees); gainful employment and housing in Germany; possession of a plot of land following the division of Junker latifundia in East Germany; the right to a disability or retirement pension in Germany; and physical disability or illness requiring constant medical attention. In addition, Polish consular offices and security authorities in Poland rejected some applications for repatriation.[75]

Based on the assumption that Polish interests lay in *"the reuniting of divided families by drawing the main breadwinner home,"* the Political Department called for *"the revival of the repatriation movement to Poland."* To this end, it recommended increasing the immediate economic assistance to repatriates from among the native population and directing to Poland (not Germany) individuals released from Soviet POW camps who expressed a desire to be reunited with their families. It also proposed a clarification of repatriation procedures. Reflecting "proletarian internationalism," the Political Department recommended that "workers and peasants who are not burdened with evidence of political activity especially hostile to Poland and its allies" be allowed to return to Poland even if they did not speak Polish.[76] In fact the authorities regularly denied the applications of members of the intelligentsia or bourgeoisie as undesirable.[77]

In many of the 28,900 divided families in four provinces (Silesia: 22,000; Olsztyn: 5,000; Gdańsk: 1,600; Białystok: 300), supposedly "the wives are of Polish origin and the husbands are ethnic Germans." But most probably had similar backgrounds: the wife in Poland was rehabilitated or verified as Polish, whereas her husband in Germany had not yet applied. The MAP Political Department anticipated that only 5,600 to 7,200 of those qualified would seek "repatriation, and only if the existing unfavorable atmosphere were overcome, especially by improving the material situation of the divided families." Nevertheless, if the breadwinner did not want to return to Poland, the Political Department suggested *"not granting families permission to depart,"* confirming the priority given to supposed *raison d'état* over the interests of the individual or family.

An appendix to the memorandum indicated that the MAP Political Department received 5,500 applications for permission to reunite with family members in Germany, most of which had not yet been examined. There were 14,800 repatriations to Poland in 1948 and 2,852 in 1949 as of 31 July.[78] This left the overwhelming majority of cases unresolved.

Olsztyn Province and the "Great Verification"

Despite past conflicts, some Mazurs gradually integrated into society as the provincial authorities and some local officials, including a number of Mazurian activists, addressed the problems faced by the autochthons. But the effect of the political changes in 1948–1949 on nationality policies quickly drove Mazurs and the government apart, more adversely affecting their adaptation than the tragic first postwar years. The emphasis on internationalism and class struggle, which overshadowed the task of winning the loyalty of autochthons for Poland, found its clearest expression in Olsztyn Province, where in August 1948 Mieczysław Moczar, formerly head of the Łódź WUBP, took over as governor. Accused of "rightist and nationalist deviation" as a supporter of Gomułka, he saved himself through self-criticism.[79] He would implement "proletarian internationalism" in his new post.

To solve the problem of unverified autochthons and yet retain as many as possible, Moczar initiated repressive measures in the so-called "Great Verification." As he told the WRN on 8 January 1949, "We desire with all our strength not to lose a single Pole, but we must be very severe in relation to those who are carrying on pro-Nazi propaganda," i.e., defending the interests of the autochthons or resisting verification.[80]

Throughout the Recovered Lands, the political changes resulted in the elimination of representatives of the local population from official positions as scapegoats for the failures of nationality policies, further undermining confidence in the authorities. In particular, Moczar regarded Mazurian activists as German agents and class enemies who incited the Mazurian peasantry against the Polish state and its social system. Thus, he removed Szczytno *starosta* Późny, who opposed the use of coercion in the verification process.[81] Shortly after Moczar became governor, Gustaw Leyding, director of the Provincial WS-P, Division of Public Security, was arrested along with Jan Lippert, chairman of the Szczytno PRN, on the absurd charges that they hindered the verification process and facilitated the departure of autochthons to Germany. Also arrested was Emil Leyk as well as Fryderyk Leyk, accused of being a nationalist and of having cooperated with the prewar *sanacja* regime. The Mazurian People's University, which Karol Małłek directed, came under political surveillance, and he had to accept official intervention in its pedagogical program. In 1950 he was removed as director. Deputy Governor Wilamowski resigned in mid-1949, supposedly in reaction to Moczar's dogmatic stance against religion.[82] In Silesia Bożek lost influence over the question of the autochthons despite his loyalty to the government, and other Silesian activists suffered repression.[83]

On 25 January 1949 the Olsztyn PZPR Provincial Executive Committee authorized Moczar and the head of the WUBP to undertake a sharper course of action toward those refusing verification. The administration mobilized the local cadre—communal officials, teachers, party members, and social activists together with the militia and security forces—to target more than 20,000 autochthons with various forms of pressure, not always stopping short of physical force, according to Karol Małłek.[84]

Moczar also alleged that the relief work of the Friends Service Council served mainly unverified Mazurs and Germans. They may well have been the neediest, and in any case the charge contradicted the nondiscriminatory principles and practices of the relief organization.[85] The Polish government soon closed down the relief work of all international agencies as the "Great Verification" brought Poland unwanted attention. On 30 March 1949 the International Committee of the Red Cross (ICRC) informed the MAP of an increasing number of complaints, mainly from Mazuria, of German citizens being forced to request Polish citizenship. The ICRC argued that forced declarations should not prevent individuals from going to Germany, which otherwise would often mean the permanent division of families. It raised the "tragic problem" of women who in 1945 applied for Polish citizenship assuming that their husbands died in the war but then learned that their husbands imprisoned in the Soviet Union were "repatriated" to Germany, and the women wanted to join them.[86]

To disabuse those resisting verification of any hope of leaving Poland, Moczar put off indefinitely a resettlement transport planned for January 1949 and ordered the dissemination of a rumor that the operation had ended. Superficially, Moczar made progress. A report on 1 April 1949 indicated that nearly 19,000 natives had been verified in the previous three months, mostly in Mrągowo and Szczytno Counties. The statistics for 1 July 1949, however, show an increase of some 2,200 in the number of unverified. A simultaneous decrease in the number of Germans during a period when there were no mass expulsions suggests the fluidity and ambiguity of the categories of "autochthon" and "German." In a letter to the KC PZPR on 28 November 1949, the first secretary of the Olsztyn KW stated that 3,472 unverified Mazurs and Warmiaks included about 1,500 Germans.[87] In a report on 16 November 1949 Moczar himself claimed that only 75 percent of the unverified had "the possibility of being verified."[88] With some 3,000 autochthons still unverified in mid-1950, the authorities considered expulsion as a possible alternative.[89]

At a conference in Mazuria on 13 June 1949, Minister of Public Administration Ochab defended the verification campaign: "Certain specialists proclaimed all Mazurs as Germans. They did not understand and did not want to understand that this Mazurian people, for long centuries remaining under German occupation, kept a Polish heart and soul, national customs in the specific Mazurian form."[90]

A resolution of the executive of the Olsztyn KW PZPR on 6 July 1949 criticized past nationality policies for retarding the involvement "of the poor peasantry, agricultural and urban workers of local origin in the class struggle against capitalists, the rural rich and speculators." It also addressed the very real issue of poverty among the natives, particularly those families whose breadwinners were in POW camps, by proposing the formation of cooperatives for the production of handicrafts and food products, such as jams and juices. In fact the authorities received countless requests from Warmian and Mazurian women for permission to join their husbands abroad. Whereas immediately after the war, permission was often granted as a way of getting rid of "weaker elements," now a resolution recommended "renewing" efforts to "repatriate" Warmiaks and Mazurs from Germany, POW camps, and the Soviet Union and to provide them with work.

In addition, the resolution called attention to "the activity of elements hostile to Poland and its democratic system, seeking to deepen differences of nationality," and advised heightened class vigilance. These "elements" included

> covert members of the Gestapo and SS, agents of Saxon imperialism, . . . collaborationists and traitors to the Polish Nation who fled from Central Poland, . . . a certain part of the Catholic clergy who . . . seek to spread hatred of the Evangelical Mazurian population according to the medieval maxim that "A Pole is a Catholic, but an Evangelical is a kraut," [and] . . . the rural rich who seek to exploit the poverty of the local population to acquire for themselves a cheap labor force.[91]

The resolution also proposed Polonization courses and the education of settlers about the history of the region, particularly the supposed resistance of the native population to foreign rule and the class oppression of Prussian landowners.[92]

Moczar, noting on 16 August 1949 that some officials remained hostile toward the autochthons because they speak German, ordered that a weak knowledge of Polish not serve as a basis for invalidating verification of Polish nationality. He regarded hostility toward Polishness as often merely a ploy to provoke expulsion to Germany and recommended punishment and compulsory attendance in a literacy course: forced "re-Polonization" replaced forced "resettlement." Revocation or denial of verification applied only to undoubted Germans or undesirable elements, especially the elderly, sick, and retired with no family in Poland and with next of kin in Germany. Others could obtain documentation for family members in Germany to seek repatriation to their homeland. Thus, on 13 May 1950 the Olsztyn *starosta* notified a commune that since Anna Longowska possessed a certificate confirming her Polish nationality, she should be informed that her efforts at "repatriation" to Germany were in vain and that she had the right to pursue the "repatriation" of family members from Germany.[93]

When the Szczytno *starosta* who replaced Późny informed autochthons who returned certificates of provisional membership in the Polish nation that they could bring their family members in Germany to Poland, it had no effect. Although he blamed letters and press articles for hostility to the Polish state and nation, he recognized that the crucial role of impoverishment: "They are mainly the elderly and children, who cannot work, whereas the autochthons who have their own farms and a labor force are well off economically and satisfied with the current system"—contrary to the assumptions of "proletarian internationalism."

The "Great Verification" achieved little in the way of the actual re-Polonization of the population. On 19 November 1949 the Organizational Department of the Olsztyn KW PZPR noted that the majority of the population in the rural areas spoke German or Ukrainian. The autochthons awaited the return of the German authorities, which hindered the work of the party. It accused the Evangelical clergy of supporting a continuation of this situation on orders of the Evangelical Church in West Germany.[94]

Moczar defended his policies at a meeting of the Education Commission of the KW PZPR on 14 January 1950:

> It is mistake to approach the problem of the autochthons solely with regard to the material needs of these 118,000 autochthons. We have to engage in an intense political and class struggle. After all, among this number of autochthons there are former exploiters as well as members of the SS and the Nazi party, and therefore we must be vigilant and conduct a class struggle.[95]

The secretary of the Olsztyn KW PZPR explained the failure of past policies in similar terms in July 1950:

> Immediately after liberation, as a result of insufficiently combated nationalist feelings among the resettled population and distortions of the party line by various elements of the state apparatus, numerous hostile and injurious incidents in relation to the autochthonous population occurred. These distortions arose on the foundation of the Gomułkian rightist-nationalist deviation. Instead of grounding the process of integrating the autochthonous population with the Polish nation on the basis of class differentiation, isolating the class enemy and encompassing the most persecuted and exploited elements with special protection—the administrative authorities, and at times also the party organizations, treated the autochthons as a homogeneous mass.... The enemy zeroed in on these errors and distortions, sowing distrust and hostility toward the authorities of People's Poland.[96]

The prevailing ideology also cast suspicion on Mazurs because of their contacts with the West. On 4 July 1950 the Presidium of the Nidzica National Council accused them of engaging in espionage and revisionist activities "under the influence of the new imperialist war."[97]

To settle the continued disputes over property in Olsztyn Province, the MAP on 30 July 1949 ordered the creation of provincial and county commissions. The Provincial Settlement Department opposed restoring farms to autochthons in a letter to the ministry on 21 March 1950, describing the social and economic harm this allegedly causes. Of 322 property disputes the provincial commission settled 200 in 1947, 83 in Mrągowo County. By 1 April 1950 it examined another 90 cases, and 60 were in process. In September 1950, 102 disputes were not yet settled. In addition, at the start of 1950, 1,288 Mazurs in Olsztyn Province were demanding the return of 462 farms in the formerly East Prussian counties in Białystok Province with little chance of success.[98] Altogether some 6,000 suits over property were initiated in Olsztyn Province, presumably with negative effects on relations between autochthons and newcomers.[99]

By the end of 1950 117,000 autochthons in the province had received Polish citizenship, and Warsaw treated the problem as solved, even cutting financial support for re-Polonization. But the use of force and repression during the "Great Verification" strengthened the aversion of Mazurs to Polish officialdom and their existing situation, and they generally continued to regard themselves as Germans.[100]

Volksdeutsche

On 1 January 1948 Łódź Province had the highest percentage of Germans in Poland. With the end of mass resettlement to Germany, the Provincial WS-P sought to minimize their number when on 23 January 1948 it ordered the registration of Germans and on 9 February 1948 of all Polish citizens who were included in the DVL or had declared German origins or membership in the German nation. Officials were instructed:

> Claiming membership in the German nationality or German origin during the war is not in itself evidence of German national distinctiveness. Care should be taken in filling out registration cards for such individuals so as not to include in the records so-called "Volksdeutsche." The decisive moment is the clear declaration of the party that he is and feels himself to be German.[101]

The Łódź WS-P also made a distinction between a decidedly German population and a population of German origin partly assimilated and in very many cases completely Polonized, particularly in urban areas, as a result of marriages with Poles. Supposedly, the Nazis recruited *Volksdeutsche* from this latter population, which denied its Polish nationality in significant numbers, influenced by propaganda, coercion, or financial reward. Of those in DVL categories III and IV, 5,542 Polish citizens in the province declared loyalty to the Polish nation and state.[102]

On 6 March 1948 the Office of the MZO Chief Delegate for the Repatriation of the German Population reported that the cases of some 35,000 *Volksdeutsche* had not yet been examined.[103] In addition, *Volksdeutsche* continued to return to Poland. Some fled in 1945, and others were expelled or left voluntarily later. In a report for February 1948 the Poznań Provincial WS-P noted "a large influx of applications of former *Volksdeutsche* residing in Germany. . . . These are mainly individuals who left family in Poland. As a reason for returning, the applicants mostly cite the difficult food situation in Germany." In the second quarter of 1948 the Poznań authorities received 106 such applications.[104]

The end of mass expulsions forced a reconsideration of what to do with the remaining Germans. On 1 April 1948 representatives of the MSZ, MAP, MBP, and MZO discussed limiting the number awaiting expulsion by expanding the right of *Volksdeutsche* deprived of citizenship to appeal the decision.[105]

The MAP drafted instructions in May 1948 declaring that the re-Polonization of those who "came under direct influence of Germanness should be the fundamental task of our nationality policy." All political, social, educational, and cultural organizations as well as special re-Polonization commissions at the local level were to participate. The plan focused especially on long-term activities, above all those related to the upbringing of the younger generation, particularly the children of mixed marriages in which the mother was of German origin "because the influence of German mothers can be harmful." If the mother was Polish and raised the children "in the Polish spirit," the authorities should facilitate their staying in Poland; if a German woman wanted to marry a Polish citizen, the authorities should not object as long as the groom-to-be was not a person of known German sympathies or a former *Volksdeutsche* "hostile to today's [political] reality"; if a Polish woman was married to a German who was abroad, she should be helped in raising the children "in a Polish spirit" even if Polish courts could not grant a divorce.

The instructions also stressed the importance of *starostowie* once more thoroughly investigating all cases of abrogation of Polish citizenship to make sure that the individuals involved were truly of German nationality. Officials were also to ensure that rehabilitated *Volksdeutsche* enjoy the same rights as other citizens, though they should not be employed in government offices in positions of particular trust.[106]

In late May 1948 an Inter-Ministerial Commission for *Volksdeutsche* Affairs was formed to investigate the revocation of Polish citizenship of those "who in their behavior did not show German national distinctiveness," Polish women married to Germans who did not consent to the loss of citizenship, and children of mixed marriages. It was also to check if internment camps held *Volksdeutsche* children of Polish origin.[107]

The last mass expulsion, though not on the scale of previous years, began in Poznań Province in the spring of 1948. The expellees consisted mainly of *Volksdeutsche* of German nationality, but also ones of Polish nationality whose Polish citizenship had been revoked.[108]

On 20 June 1948 the Regional Branch in Lubusz Land reported that category III *Volksdeutsche* were applying for "repatriation" to Germany, where they had no family, explaining, "What am I going to do here since I must be a rented servant?" "I prefer to leave though with regret and also expect that there I will not be regarded as a German." Their circumstances varied. Often parents decided to leave but children were opposed. The youths mostly did not speak German well—they spoke Polish among themselves. Mainly, the uncertainty of the situation and the unregulated relations with society motivated a decision to leave. In some cases the *Volksdeutsche* complained of being exploited at their workplace but refused to give details about unpaid wages for fear of repercussions if they were sent back. In some cases the children wanted to leave, explaining that it was difficult for them to start an independent life in Poland. Asked if she would marry a German in Germany, a girl answered yes, that she was growing old in Poland and would not be able to marry a Polish boy because some registry officials refused to allow such marriages as punishment for abandoning their nationality. In another case, two families asked for assistance to settle elsewhere in the Recovered Lands because their farms were taken over long ago, and they feared for their treatment as former *Volksdeutsche*.[109]

Deficiencies marked resettlement. Most of those approved for resettlement, especially *Volksdeutsche*, had no documentation or material on file, and therefore the commission relied solely on the word of the individual. Not all members of the commission took part in decisions, and some local officials refused to cooperate. An official of Międzyrzecz County did not know the law and ignored one woman's the right to citizenship gained through marriage. The Regional Branch had to intervene to prevent her expulsion—and recommended that proceedings be undertaken against the county official for abuse of power. It also intervened to prevent the expulsion of two other women with no family in Germany—one wanted to leave because she did not want to remain in detention.[110]

The PZZ entered into disputes over *Volksdeutsche*. On 22 April 1948 Izdebski of the Silesian PZZ complained: "Defense lawyers hamper the courts and other institutions, especially the Polish Western Union, in the battle against Germanness. Lawyers frequently undertake the defense, aware that they are defending people who deserve to be excluded from Polish society." He proposed that the pro-German element be resettled in eastern Poland if it could not be expelled.[111] On 31 August 1948 the PZZ General Secretariat sent the MAP a list of mostly rehabilitated former members in Bielsko of the prewar *Jungdeutsche Partei*, a self-identified Nazi party, objecting that this allowed a German minority to remain in Poland.[112] In addition, the Presidium of the ZG PZZ alleged on 7 July 1948 that former *Volksdeutsche* "assumed influential political and economic positions and in a completely obvious way support Germans."[113] The PZZ was not yet fully attuned to the new ideological reality, which would ultimately cost the organization its existence.

In Łódź Province the governor noted in a report for September 1948 "a certain discontent" in society in connection with the rehabilitation of *Volksdeutsche,* especially in places with a large number of Germans. He characterized the rehabilitated as often "fairly unruly and in some cases even haughty," manifesting an unwillingness to work, talking among themselves mainly in German, and raising children "in a German spirit," which he attributed to persistent "whispered propaganda and rumors of a third [world] war."[114]

In Turek County, where earlier the *starosta* recommended an amnesty for repentant *Volksdeutsche,* the county office on 9 September 1948 requested that the PUBP monitor *Volksdeutsche,* particularly where they lived in groups with the possibility of contact with each other. Allegedly, they received letters from Germany concerning the return of *Volksdeutsche* who had been expelled.[115]

The 1946 decree excluding individuals of German nationality from Polish society was to expire on 31 December 1948. On 14 October 1948 the Poznań governor requested an extension from the MAP because of the slow progress of offices of public security in filing requests for the revocation of Polish citizenship. For example, the Poznań municipal president received eighty-five such requests, whereas a German organization listed 4,000 Polish citizens of German nationality within the city. The WUBP promised to speed up the process but would not be able to finish it by the deadline and therefore also requested an extension. In fact the deadline was extended twice, first to the end of 1949 and then to the end of 1950.[116]

Volksdeutsche in Forced Labor Camps, 1948–1949

When visiting labor and detention camps, the Inter-Ministerial Commission for *Volksdeutsche* Affairs frequently found that camp records did not include information about the citizenship of detainees. It interviewed 19,450 and found 3,009 (15.5 percent) qualified to remain in Poland, including 481 whose Polish citizenship had been revoked, mainly individuals from mixed Polish-German families, predominately with weak national consciousness who identified themselves as "of local origin" (*tutejszy*) or "Protestant" (*ewangelik*), according to a report of the MAP Political Department on 31 January 1949. "The suitability for work of these individuals was good, mainly because of their physical value," which in the new ideological atmosphere favored a reinstatement of their citizenship. A small percentage consisted of non-Polish women married to Poles but who raised their children "in a Polish spirit." Others included 33 individuals from the Recovered Lands who claimed to be of Polish origin and spoke Polish well and 184 whose detention had no legal basis, 128 of them children.[117]

In interviewing detainees, the commission examined their knowledge of Polish, their wishes with regard to citizenship, their family situation—the commission attached special importance to families with a large number of children—their profession, and their activities before and during the war. Some had been detained for more than three years, exceeding the punishment for denial of Polish nationality, and therefore the commission recommended their release.

The commission urged measures ensuring that public security officials and *starostowie* immediately execute its decisions. Where prosecutors classified former *Volksdeutsche* as Germans without an investigation and passed on the cases to security organs to revoke their citizenship, prosecutors were to examine the facts of each case with great care and not rely solely on the testimony of an interested party as to the individual's "German national distinctiveness" or other unfounded opinion.[118]

On 8 October 1948 the Inter-Ministerial Commission reported that the *Volksdeutsche* of Pomerania were "known for [their] generally very hostile attitude toward Polishness and especially towards today's reality."[119] It recommended that 177 out of 3,979 deprived of Polish citizenship renew their applications for citizenship and that the authorities withdraw the motion to revoke the citizenship of 507 out of 2,384. These included individuals of Polish origin or individuals who belonged to families who identified themselves as Polish. Most spoke Polish well and were well thought of in their local communities.

The commission also ordered the immediate release of 76 prisoners in the Potulice camp, mainly orphaned children, who spoke Polish well and in many cases identified themselves as Poles, and elderly individuals, many of whom spoke Polish poorly but whose family members who regarded themselves as Poles had agreed to take them in. The commission found that the camp held more than 3,500 children, 800 of them of Polish origin who would be released with their families. Of the remaining children who were German, those kept together in the camp tended to develop a hostile attitude toward Polishness, whereas those outside the camp, working mainly with farmers, identified themselves as Poles.

The commission faulted the camp administration for its lack of basic information about prisoners. In addition, some 6,000 *Volksdeutsche* under the camp's jurisdiction in need of investigation worked outside the camp. The commission also criticized the courts for failing to notify the camp administration of decisions overturning the revocation of the citizenship of detainees. In many other cases the courts denied Polish citizenship to individuals who were clearly of Polish nationality or were of German origin but who felt Polish or had family members who were Polish. The commission requested the intervention of the Ministry of Justice to ensure that they receive Polish citizenship.[120]

In connection with the planned liquidation of the Leszno-Gronowo labor camp, an Inter-Ministerial Commission created in January 1949 investigated the cases of almost 3,500 detainees by mid-February 1949. It ruled negatively on 2,500 of the cases, recommending accelerated revocation of Polish citizenship and resettlement to Germany, but ordered the reopening of 219 cases of individuals already deprived of Polish citizenship and the immediate release of two others. An Inter-Ministerial Commission again visited the Gronowo camp in June 1949. Of 303 detainees interviewed, it ordered the withdrawal of the proposed revocation of citizenship of forty-four, a reconsideration of the cases of six, and the release of six from the camp.[121]

Questions about detainees in camps for Germans persisted, leading the chairman of the RM to appoint a commission to inspect the camps. In a report on 16 August 1949 the commission complained about the slow pace in executing the recommendations of the Inter-Ministerial Commission. As a result some individuals, including solitary children, remained in the camps without a legal basis, most of them since 1945–1946.[122] The delays as well as the recommendations of inter-ministerial commissions to release some *Volksdeutsche* illustrate the hostility of security officials toward *Volksdeutsche*, which often simply reflected the views of society.

Although laws granted rehabilitated *Volksdeutsche* equal rights, they could not guarantee equal treatment, even from officials, particularly at the local level. The enduring antagonism toward *Volksdeutsche* constituted the main obstacle to their integration.

Property disputes remained a primary source of conflict. In 1948 13,237 *Volksdeutsche* had not yet had their property returned to them and remained on 3,192 farms on which newcomers were settled. In Działdowo County the ownership of 32 farms was still being disputed in April 1949.[123] At the end of 1949 the Ministry of Agriculture and Agrarian Reforms had not yet ruled on eighty applications for the return of properties taken in 1945 in Poznań Province, although it had promised two years earlier to issue a decree regulating the matter. In the first quarter of 1950, when a pharmacist in Cekowo, Kalisz County, pursued the return of his drug store on the recommendation of the UL, the local population reacted with anger, and the communal government appealed to the *starosta* and the PZPR County Committee. Pharmacists also objected: *Volksdeutsche* should reimburse those who took over stores for their investment and the price they paid to acquire the property.[124]

Meeting on 4–5 May 1949, representatives of the MAP, MSZ, MBP, and the Ministry of Justice decided to allow the return from abroad of a Polish husband, even if a *Volksdeutscher*, with a German wife and their family under certain conditions. The authorities attached importance to whether the children spoke Polish and took into account the profession of the applicant, e.g., facilitating the return of a miner. The final decision lay with the MBP. But on 9 June 1949 the Poznań Provincial WS-P reported that, contrary to regulations, security organs continued to divide families, especially in cases of mixed Polish-German marriages.[125]

On 9 September 1949 the Poznań UW sent *starostowie* a query concerning the *Volksdeutsche* within their jurisdictions. The responses provide snapshots of the *Volksdeutsche* at the end of the 1940s in the former Wartheland, where rehabilitation caused the most controversy.

In Września and Kalisz Counties the overwhelming majority consisted of individuals in DVL category II who resided in the same villages before the war. In Września County they were mostly complete families from among the rural poor and middle- and small-sized farmers. Having lived there for many years, even from birth, they were in large measure Polonized, integrated with the Polish population, without any observable strong national antagonism. Other *Volksdeutsche* came from various places and largely belonged to divided families and for that reason wanted to leave for Germany.[126] On 19 July 1949, however, the Września *starosta* characterized the attitude of 412 *Volksdeutsche* in three communities formerly in Konin County as "arrogant," with "Germanic hatred in relation to Poles," which he attributed to "close contact with individuals residing in the German Reich [FRG]," where anti-Polish propaganda was being spread.[127]

In Kalisz County *Volksdeutsche* were employed by farmers, on state farms, or sporadically as agricultural workers, mostly women with children whose husbands resided in Germany. In general they viewed the current system and Poland negatively and wanted to leave Poland. Some would stay in Poland but for their material circumstances.[128]

In Kępno County, where in 1949 the *starosta* claimed that 93 percent of the population had registered on the DVL, the revocation of Polish citizenship was still in progress, and some *Volksdeutsche,* mainly from category II, sought full rehabilitation. The state confiscated the property of 100 to 150 families in category II. Most had farms of fifteen hectares or more, and now they worked mainly on their former farms under the current owner or lessee, fueling their discontent. At the end of August 1950 4,538 rehabilitated *Volksdeutsche* resided in Kępno County along with 1,470 unrehabilitated *Volksdeutsche*. Most of the rehabilitated must have been in categories III and IV; hence, about half of the 10,753 category III and IV *Volksdeutsche* in Kępno County in 1943 left the county and probably the country as well.[129]

Meanwhile, the PZZ fell victim to the ideological shift. The resolution at a joint meeting of the PZZ and the Maritime League on 9 October 1949 included Stalinist-style self-criticism of each organization, in the case of the PZZ, that it wrongly isolated the native population from the realities of Polish political life, i.e., it did not rally the population for the party and the building of socialism. The resolution also signaled its imminent demise: "The PZZ completed the fundamental tasks, which justified its reactivation after the war. The lands on the Oder, Baltic, and Lusatian Neisse were populated and developed. The Polish native population of these lands works on an equal basis with the rest of society, joining in trend of the building of the foundation of socialism." The PZZ lost its usefulness to the party except as a scapegoat for failed policies. On the supposition that the integration of what was now more commonly referred to as the "Western Lands" had been achieved, the PZZ officially merged with the Maritime League in April 1950, which in fact marked its liquidation and an end of an era.[130]

[12]

The Status of Autochthons at the End of 1949

AS NATIONALITY VERIFICATION approached its completion in 1949, with the authorities in some cases simply recognizing as Poles those who had not yet submitted to the process, the MO Chief Command reported their distribution in 1948 and 1949 as shown in table 12.1. Nevertheless, the authorities perceived pro-German sentiments among a significant portion of autochthons.[1] This prompted the highest central authorities to examine the problem.

In December 1949 a report prepared for the KC PZPR surveyed the situation of autochthons (and in part that of *Volksdeutsche*) in Silesia, Olsztyn, Gdańsk, and Wrocław Provinces.[2] The report as well as reports filed with the KC in November and December 1949 concerning Szczecin Province reflected the ideology of the late 1940s but nevertheless highlighted many of the failings of Warsaw's nationality policies and of their implementation at the local level as well as other sources of the alienation of the autochthons, providing an insight into why so many sought to leave their homeland.[3]

The reports documented the material hardship among autochthons. Opole Silesia had hundreds of deteriorating homes in need of restoration. Rural areas had a standard of living higher than before the war, but that of industrial workers was significantly worse. The very difficult circumstances of the 22,000 women, mostly with children, whose husbands did not return and the denial of pensions to those eligible under German law constituted the region's burning issues. Yet the natives showed greater discipline than the newcomers, resulting in a lower crime rate than in prewar Poland.[4]

In Olsztyn Province government assistance fell woefully short. The Ministry of Construction provided only 6 million złoty as opposed to the 870 million złoty required for the reconstruction of the 15,598 autochthon farmsteads in need of repair. Although the Ministry of Agriculture and Agrarian Reforms extended significant assistance for the purchase of cows in October 1949, it did not suffice; nor did the credits for the creation of four cooperatives. Still, the report recommended the creation of cooperatives as additional sources of

TABLE 12.1 Verified Autochthons in the Recovered Lands, 1948–1949

Provinces	Total Verified 1948	Total Verified 1949	In Process
Silesia	850,000	850,000	8,600
Gdańsk	25,000	37,750	126
Szczecin	24,000	19,000	140
Poznań	6,318	9,400	14
Wrocław	15,000	18,000	300
Olsztyn	67,000	107,000	7,500
Białystok	5,000	1,900	40
Total	992,318	1,043,050	16,720

Data source: Bernadetta Nitschke, *Wysiedlenie ludności niemieckiej z Polski w latach 1945–1949* (Zielona Góra: Wyższa Szkoła Pedagogiczna im. Tadeusza Kotarbińskiego, 1999), 110.

income, particularly in rural areas inhabited by impoverished Mazurs and Warmiaks, especially Mazurs evacuated during the war from counties incorporated into Białystok Province.

In rural Mazuria the autochthons consisted mostly of owners of small and midsize farms. A lack of equipment and livestock prevented the 26.4 percent who owned larger farms from working all of their land, inclining them to give up land above fifteen hectares in return for material assistance. As in Silesia, families of local origin whose breadwinner was in Germany or in a POW camp in the Soviet Union needed considerable support from the state. The problem specific to the region was the very large number of autochthons not yet verified as Polish.[5]

The report on Gdańsk Province focused on the 150,000 Kashubian farmers residing in territory that had been part of prewar Poland and the 3,000 autochthonous Kashubs in Lębork (Gdańsk Province) and Bytów (Szczecin Province) Counties. Other autochthons included 12,000 Warmiaks; 40,000 residents, mainly workers, of Gdańsk, Sopot, and Gdańsk County; and up to 100,000 Kociewiaks, who spoke a dialect of Polish and resided in an area south of Gdańsk. Despite the ethnic diversity of the population, the KW PZPR addressed issues of class conflict rather than re-Polonization with specific proposals such as "Liquidate lease-holders-exploiters and introduce cooperative forms of development" and "Reconstruct 300 community wells with the goal of limiting the capitalist exploitation by owners of wells in Kashubian villages." The report branded the weak and not very numerous Kashubian intelligentsia of clergy, officials, and a small group in the free professions as kulaks.[6]

The Szczecin governor's report of 16 November 1949 claimed that about 3,000 Polish autochthonous families (21,248 individuals) resided in the province: just over half of them in Złotów County, nearly half of the rest in Bytów and Słupsk Counties, and a large number in Człuchów County, all just west of the prewar Polish-German border.[7] A report on 3 December 1949 assessed the work of those relatively few employed on state farms mostly positively, although some often simulated illness to avoid work, which the report linked to contact with correspondents in West Germany. It, however, noted hostility toward cooperatives, explaining that the autochthons "have an inborn and deeply rooted desire to enrich themselves and have little [class] consciousness." In addition, autochthons followed the lead of parliamentary deputy Baczewski from Dębno, Chojna County, a large landowner who allegedly engaged in hostile activity. This marked the autochthons as equivalent to kulaks. Yet the report allowed that they fulfilled all obligations required by officials and were the best payers of taxes. Their children went to school, spoke correct Polish, and took an active part in youth organizations—hardly evidence of oppositional activity.[8]

Wroclaw Province reported the smallest number of autochthons of the five provinces: 15,835. About two-thirds resided in rural areas: 43.0 percent were landless and 28.6 percent small holders. Among the urban population 43.9 percent were hirelings. Yet the report cited no particular material hardships. Moreover, it claimed that a substantial majority of autochthons received their farms back and those whose farms suffered destruction during the war received substitutes. Only in Namysłów and Wałbrzych Counties did the late return of autochthons to Poland delay the restitution of farms. In urban areas the pay of autochthonous workers allegedly was in keeping with collective agreements and their housing frequently better than that of newcomers because a portion owned their homes. In Wałbrzych some autochthons owned three to four tenements, an ominous observation in light of the reported expropriation of twenty-two bakeries and painters' workshops in Lubań and Świdnica Counties.[9]

Autochthons in Public Offices and Administration

The participation of autochthons in administration fell far short of their proportions in the population. In Opole Silesia in fourteen counties and six independently administered municipalities, only two autochthons served as chairmen of national councils. Of thirteen *starostowie,* only one was an autochthon, and none were to be found among twelve deputy *starostowie.* Of 212 bureau directors, scarcely fourteen were autochthons. In Opole County, where the autochthons made up 90.9 percent of the population, only one bureau director out of twenty was an autochthon. Similarly, in Racibórz

County, where autochthons constituted 97.5 percent of the population, only one autochthon served among sixteen bureau directors. Even in rural areas, a mere thirty-six autochthons served among the 142 communal heads. Participation in the administration of cooperatives was also minimal. They fared somewhat better in industry, especially mining, where presumably skills and experience mattered. At Bytom's five mines, three autochthons served as deputy mine directors and one as personnel director.[10]

In contrast, the railways, which employed about 10,000 autochthons, had only nine autochthons in executive positions, and about a third of the autochthons were employed only on a seasonal basis. Autochthons with training were not treated as professionals and did not receive positions appropriate to their skills. Nor did they have proportional representation in the leadership of the Trade Union of Railway Employees—in some locals, they did not have a single representative among the leaders. The report for the KC criticized the railway authorities for their lack of coordination with the KC PZPR and the governor's office and the failure to educate railway employees. "All this created a feeling of inferiority among them and became one of the causes of the declaration of some autochthons of their membership in the German nation and refusal of about 8,600 autochthons to undertake efforts to obtain certificates of Polish citizenship." Therefore, the KW PZPR and the governor initiated educational efforts as a result of which 9,432 autochthons filed declarations of loyalty.[11]

Autochthons had minimal representation in the ranks of Silesian security forces, which the report attributed to a negative attitude toward security organs because of old prejudices against German police and resentment from the first period after the war.[12] The persistent regional hostilities between Silesians and individuals from the Dąbrowa Basin, who held many of the positions in the administration and security organs, found no place in the report.[13]

Not surprisingly, the situation in Olsztyn Province looked even worse. Of 4,189 persons employed in offices, state institutions, self-government, and cooperatives, ninety-seven autochthons held executive positions. National councils at all levels had only 185 autochthon members, 5 percent of the total, though verified autochthons constituted 22 percent of the population.[14]

The report on Gdańsk Province claimed a significant improvement, with Kashubs filling a high proportion of positions in the state apparatus as well as in the economy, state administration and self-government, and social and party organizations. For example, in Morski County twelve out of fourteen chairmen of national councils, ten out of twelve communal heads, 129 out of 132 chairmen of village councils, and 70 percent of the staff of the administration of self-government were Kashubs.[15] But Morski County was part of prewar Poland and therefore not typical of the situation of autochthons.

Intergroup Relations and the Clergy

The authorities attached importance to the social integration of autochthons and newcomers in the Recovered Lands. The report for the KC found their relations to be rather poor in Silesia. It pointed to autochthon resentment over their criminal treatment at the hands of newcomers immediately after the war but at the same time blamed hostile German propaganda, the clergy, and oppositional classes for exploiting the underrepresentation of autochthons in executive positions and their persistent poor treatment by administrative personnel. Also, newcomers with increasing frequency referred to the natives as "krauts." Repatriates regarded themselves as a better category of Poles and at every opportunity paraded their superiority and dominance. Reserved and humiliated, the autochthons frequently suffered maltreatment as newcomers exploited these traits, fostering the isolation of the autochthons.

The clergy supposedly contributed to this isolation by in some instances holding separate services for autochthons—e.g., in Wołczyn, Kluczbork County. Moreover, the report alleged that the vast majority of priests in Silesia were consciously and decidedly hostile to People's Poland and that priests verified as Polish had deeply absorbed the German spirit and consoled the local population by hearing confessions in German and urging perseverance.[16]

In Olsztyn Province conflicts with Ukrainians complicated intergroup relations.[17] In rural areas most autochthons spoke German. As elsewhere, the report blamed the hostility on outside influences but recognized the role "of the bureaucratized portion of administrative and self-government employees as well as teachers, who relate to the local population in an unfriendly or straightforwardly hostile manner, setting in this way an example for other groups of incoming population." The report also cited the "improper proceedings of the commission preparing nationality lists," which resorted to threats and beatings.[18]

As in Silesia, the clergy in Olsztyn Province came in for blame. Allegedly, the Evangelical clergy openly spread hostile propaganda against the Soviet Union, as a pastor in Mrągowo County did when in recent sermons he spoke of people worrying "that their sons are not returning from the Soviet Union, where they are tortured." Furthermore, the clergy supposedly followed the guidelines of the Evangelical ecclesiastical authorities in West Germany. The autochthonous population practiced its religion in tightly closed circles, praying and singing in German. In addition, some of the Catholic clergy purportedly spread hatred of the Evangelical Mazurs in keeping with "the medieval maxim that 'A Pole is a Catholic, and an Evangelical [*ewangelik*] is a kraut.'"[19]

The reports concerning Szczecin Province emphasized the numerous contacts between autochthons and the remaining Germans.[20] The report of 16 November 1949 asserted that the autochthons in Bytów and Słupsk Counties were distancing themselves from social and political life and the fewer than 200 in Sławno County developed social contacts with Germans rather than with Polish newcomers. Although those in Złotów County were more integrated socially, the governor doubted the wisdom of granting them citizenship, even though they fulfilled their civil obligations in a disciplined manner. The authorities identified those who relinquished Polish citizenship, as in Słupsk County, and claimed to be victims of persecution in letters to officials and organizations in West Germany as a source of hostile propaganda.

A report on 3 December 1949 concerning Germans in Szczecin Province accused two Evangelical pastors of spreading propaganda among their parishioners, including many autochthons and *Volksdeutsche,* by sharing information from newspapers they received from West Germany, mostly concerning imminent war and revision of the borders. The propaganda intensified following the creation of the GDR, raising doubts about the future among autochthons. In Wolin County some wanted to move east out of fear of war and the destruction of the port.[21] The report on autochthons on 3 December 1949 noted that several in Bytów County wanted to leave for Germany and cited their close contact with the clergy as a factor in their opposition to the Soviet Union and the "current [political] reality."[22]

In Gdańsk Province the report for the KC also saw an "especially strong mobilization of reactionary clergy." But with a decline in popular participation in church-sponsored events, the report belittled the clergy's efforts. Furthermore, a loss in strength of "the enemy" brought about "a mobilization on our side of a portion of the previously wavering and hesitating elements in the community of Kashubian activists, the intelligentsia of Kashubian origin," including some clerics of local origin.[23] On 26 November 1949, however, the party cell at the Gdańsk shipyard reported a conflict between Kashubs and workers from Central Poland, "consciously fomented by the enemy."[24]

In Wrocław Province relations between autochthons and newcomers in industrial centers were not bad, but in the countryside friction was common. Settlers in Wałbrzych County harassed natives in hope of seizing their farms, the sole reference to the widespread conflicts over property in any of the reports.[25]

Foreign Influences

The December 1949 report for the KC reflected the propensity to blame the alienation of autochthons on foreign influence, even postulating the existence of an active German underground organization in Olsztyn Province and partly in Silesia.[26] In the latter it purportedly consisted of Germans who slipped through the verification process, hostile elements, particularly from a class point of view—shopkeepers, industrialists, but also a certain number of war invalids, including a large number of former German military officers, who saw a revision of the border as a means of obtaining a pension. Supposedly, assistance—propaganda, personnel, and weapons—from across the border greatly strengthened this organization. Allegedly, Koźle on the Oder River had a markedly anti-Polish atmosphere and served as a link in the chain of hostile propaganda, fortified from outside by crews arriving on barges. Autochthons filled the majority of executive positions at the port, which had about 2,000 employees. The report urged the removal to other counties or even expulsion of those known to have been barge owners (i.e., kulaks) or active members of the Nazi party.[27]

With more than 30,000 autochthons from Silesia registered with the ICRC in Hamburg and a growing frequency of local contacts with representatives of the German Red Cross in Warsaw, the authorities called for greater control over the activities of these organizations. In addition to requests for permission to leave Poland from wives with husbands in West Germany, requests from women whose husbands died in the war and who wished to obtain a pension as war widows—a previously unnoted phenomenon—increased significantly. (Article 116 of the FRG Basic Law played an unacknowledged role in this development.) Assurances that the Polish state would provide a widow or orphan pension proved ineffective.

Allegedly, the vast majority of autochthons corresponded with individuals in Germany—about 85,000 individuals from the Opole region were then abroad. Even individuals who had no one abroad supposedly received letters from West Germany thanks to an organized operation of massive proportions. It exploited to the maximum the speeches of Pope Pius XII and the formation of a government in Bonn in September 1949, intensifying the feeling of transience and war psychosis, which found expression in an almost complete withdrawal from community activity, increased absences from school and re-Polonization courses, and wider use of the German language. But the creation of the GDR purportedly had a positive influence on the mood of the population, removing the enemy's principle trump card of questioning the validity of the Oder-Neisse border.[28]

Some autochthons in Szczecin Province, mainly workers who had no relatives in West Germany and did not correspond with anyone there, had a positive attitude toward the "current reality," lived in harmony with Poles, and quickly acclimatized. In contrast, the hostility of other autochthons allegedly derived to a great extent from correspondence from West Germany. They did not socialize with Poles and maintained constant contact with Germans, *Volksdeutsche,* and Poles repatriated from Germany. In Wolin and Myślibórz Counties Germans in contact with autochthons spread hostile propaganda. Although other inimical activity was not especially evident, the report on autochthons of 3 December 1949 expressed concern that foreign intelligence could exploit the not very friendly stance of the majority of autochthons toward the "current reality."[29]

To remedy the situation, the report called for consciousness-raising among autochthons, attracting them to social life, especially to mass organizations, the working class to party organizations; increasing their participation in administration and local government; and searching out positively inclined autochthons for political training to begin systematic work among autochthons "under the control of the party." Determined enemies should be isolated from other autochthons, preventing them from carrying out hostile activities.[30]

With regard to Gdańsk Province, the report for the KC noted not only intense correspondence between autochthons and those, frequently their close relatives, resettled mostly to West Germany. It also noted the significance of Kashubs in America, equal in number to those in the homeland.[31]

Participation in the PZPR and Allied Organizations

According to the report for the KC, membership of autochthons in the party matched their proportions in the population in the industrial areas of Silesia, and they engaged in considerable activity in the party's big industrial organizations. But in rural areas the autochthons typically remained passive, almost completely lacking in social initiative. Altogether natives constituted only 40 percent of the party members in the region. Moreover, they experienced the same unequal treatment in the party as elsewhere: only two out of thirteen first secretaries of PZPR county committees were autochthons. In the party-affiliated Union of Polish Youths (*Związek Młodzieży Polskiej* or ZMP), only two autochthons served in its county administration, and autochthons constituted only 12 percent of county committee members. Among 30,000 volunteer firemen, there was not a single autochthon officer.[32]

The situation in Olsztyn Province was even more dismal. Whereas in Silesia the party had some 33,500 autochthon-members, in Olsztyn Province it had only 583, with four members in county committees and four members in the KW.[33]

The report on autochthons in Szczecin Province found that, as in rural areas of Silesia, the majority of autochthons remained politically passive. Some belonged to the PZPR and the allied Peasant Party, but they hardly participated in political life. At meetings and mass rallies they did not speak up—"it is often difficult to get a word out of them—in conversation they for the most part alter their opinion and nod their heads to show that they are in agreement with the position of the government and the party."[34]

The report on Gdańsk Province characterized party membership as especially low in areas inhabited by Kashubs that were part of prewar Poland. In Morski, Kartuzy, and Kościerzyna Counties with a population of 200,000 (mostly Kashubs), the party had 5,400 members and candidates (2.7 percent compared with nearly 5 percent of Poland's total population in the party), of whom barely 830 resided in rural areas. Few from the Kashubian intelligentsia belonged to the party, and membership in other parties and the ZMP was also weak. Elsewhere in the province the party was still weaker.[35]

Yet guidelines concerning autochthons sketched at the first provincial conference of the party allegedly had a positive echo among the Kashubian masses. In addition, the following session of the WRN passed a widely promoted resolution concerning protection of Kashubian folk art. To increase the party's influence among Kashubs, the authorities organized various activities, such as thirty-six mass meetings supposedly attended by 40,000 Kashubian farmers on 22 July. According to the report, the party achieved some growth in rural areas by establishing sixteen rural and five farmer-fishermen groups of candidates and accepting 346 candidates, including some of Kashubian origin. Distribution of the press increased, even of a Gdańsk newspaper that did not at all address Kashubian concerns.

But the main deficiencies continued: the weakness and insufficient coverage of the party organization, especially in rural areas; the thin cadre of Kashubian origin; and weak influence in the community, where again the report noted the strong influence of "reactionary clergy." The transfer of Chojnice County, "an active endek [i.e., nationalist] center of the Kashubian movement," to Pomerania Province hindered the introduction of a uniform, correct party line in Kashubian affairs. The lack of a precise, clear party line as well as ignorance of the Kashubian problem among party activists resulted in a series of errors: some party activists relied on "garbage from the ideological kitchen of young Kashubianness" or came under the influence of the concept of "'stupid Kashubs.'"[36]

Criticism included the charge that initially the authorities "flirted with the Kashubian movement," sacrificing the "class approach and revolutionary vigilance." The Congress of Kashubs called by *Zrzesz Kaszebsko*—which the report characterized as decidedly "endek"—took place with the participation of many representatives of the government, who allowed the passage of openly hostile resolutions later published in *Zrzesz Kaszebsko*. This policy then took an incorrect direction, with only one Kashub holding an executive position in the party.

The report cited specific examples of discrimination against Kashubian *Volksdeutsche:* those in DVL category III were not accepted in officer schools, which enabled "the enemy" to spread hostile slogans reminiscent of those concerning Kashubs in prewar Poland. The enemy also exploited the looting of the local population "brutally carried out by elements of the petty bourgeoisie." Furthermore, clear violations of the party line continued. The personnel department in Warsaw of a state enterprise carried out a massive investigation solely of workers in Starogard in category III, and the MO Main Headquarters dismissed individuals because of marriages to category III *Volksdeutsche*.[37]

Youths and Education

The last section of the report for the KC addressed the important topic of youths and their education, crucial for re-Polonization and integration of autochthons. In Silesia, among 140,000 autochthonous youths, just over 30 percent belonged to the ZMP. In contrast, Catholic youth organizations and church associations were very active. Maturing youths, burdened with having been in the Hitler Youth or under Nazi influence, had little opportunity for social advancement. They found relatively more opportunities in industry or as teachers, but the low salaries of teachers made it difficult to attract them. The limited opportunities bred discontent, favorable grounds for enemy propaganda, with German nationalist elements exploiting the situation to incite youths to excesses.

Yet nearly all schools lacked a sufficient quantity of teaching materials. There was also a shortage of teachers: the Opole region needed 290 more, and a high percentage of teachers lacked sufficient education, with a considerable portion fully unprepared for the political education of the local population and inactive in socio political work. Despite these deficiencies, the report again accused the clergy of hindering re-Polonization and opposing the efforts of the state. In particular, 80 percent of the clergy allegedly betrayed their mother tongue by mixing in German phrases and preaching sermons translated directly from German texts.[38]

The situation in Gdańsk Province looked even worse. Among 40,000 autochthonous youths, the ZMP counted only 3,500 Kashubian members. Its county administration did not include a single Kashub. As in Silesia, the report blamed the influence of "reactionary clergy": in Morski County there were twelve "clerical" organizations encompassing a significant number of Kashubian youths.

Similarly, access to education and social advancement favored newcomers over Kashubs, whose cultural level was allegedly very low. Hostile gossip, "A school won't accept a Kashub anyway because he goes to church," prompted a widespread propaganda campaign by the party, which recruited 280 sons of Kashubian workers and farmers for various educational institutions. Nevertheless, the number of elementary schools did not suffice. In this situation the provincial party organization set itself a long list of specific tasks to further the education and re-Polonization of Kashubs and autochthons.[39]

In Olsztyn Province some of the 20,000 mostly poor and rural autochthonous youths worked on a state farm. In addition, the ranks of Service for Poland—a paramilitary youth organization to promote development—consisted mostly of autochthons, and state farm administrators exploited it, demanding more intensive labor than from qualified agricultural workers, which often resulted in dissatisfaction among the youths, at times expressed in statements indicating a still strong German nationalism.[40]

This section of the report on Olsztyn Province mainly touted the attendance of autochthonous children, youths, and adults at various levels of education and re-Polonization classes as well as the measures taken to achieve this. Deficiencies received much less attention in the report than on Silesia and Gdańsk Province. They were, however, apparent in the stated goal of ensuring elementary schooling for all autochthonous children and in the assertions that "already in April the majority of youths" in Mrągowo, Pisz, and Szczytno Counties were in schools; they received "the most essential clothing, textbooks, and school supplies," but "a severe shortage" of clothing and footwear threatened attendance in winter, and a lack of sufficient textbooks and school aids constituted another "burning issue." Moreover, the statistics on attendance in general education middle schools indicate an acute lack of equality of opportunity for autochthons, who constituted only 10 percent of the pupils in the primary grades and only 2.7 percent of those in the more advanced schools.[41]

Thus, the reports to the PZPR admitted a wide range of failings of the government's nationality policies. The impact on autochthons soon became evident as a new opportunity arose to leave Poland.

[13]

The Last Phase of Nationality Verification and Rehabilitation

AN AGREEMENT REACHED between Poland and the GDR on 2 January 1950 allowing resettlement to the GDR marked a milestone in the postwar migration to Germany. *Aktion Link* lasted from February 1950 to March 1951, encompassing 76,000 individuals, and led to further less numerous departures in the years 1952–1954. The Polish authorities treated it as a resumption of expulsions to Germany, but much of the resettlement after 1950, labeled as family unification, differed from the previous forced migration.[1]

Warsaw did not see the agreement as a license for indiscriminate expulsion. On 4 February 1950 the MAP instructed governors that individuals should not be stripped of their Polish citizenship on the day of departure but in advance to allow for appeals. Olsztyn Governor Moczar, however, directed *starostowie* on 11 February 1950 to include autochthons resisting verification in the resettlement.[2]

Preparations evoked rumors in Olsztyn Province of the imminent "repatriation" of all Warmiaks and Mazurs without exception, according to Moczar's report on 25 March 1950. A "psychosis of departure" embraced the population, which in many cases stopped spring planting and even here and there abandoned farms, packing up belongings, slaughtering the livestock, and moving to the nearest state farm or town to await the expected departure. Therefore Moczar called off the resettlement and requested the MAP to cancel all transports from the province until after the spring planting to discourage those who plowed and sowed fields from leaving.[3]

Because of the massive number of autochthons with Polish citizenship applying for permission to leave Poland, on 12 July 1950 the Presidium of the Olsztyn WRN (chaired by Moczar, it replaced the office of governor) instructed the presidia of county national councils (which replaced *starostowie*) not even to accept applications for departure from "the population of local origin," which the PRM believed conveyed the impression that they could renounce Polish citizenship and leave for Germany. Local national councils should explain that their departure was out of the question and they should instead seek the return of family members to Poland. But in keeping with the new ideology, the memorandum allowed that applications could be considered from those "alien to us from a class point of view" (*klasowo nam obcej*). The memorandum warned against treating this as an opportunity to get rid of the needy. Rather, it was indispensable to extend assistance to autochthons: "Often the fundamental cause giving rise to the desire to renounce Polish citizenship and depart for Germany is precisely this lack of care."[4]

A Wide-Ranging Resolution

A mass departure of "the population of local origin" threatened Poland's claims to the Recovered Lands, where the population density was still 30 percent lower than before the war.[5] The Politburo of the KC PZPR addressed the issue with a wide-ranging resolution, "Concerning the Tasks of Work among the Autochthonous Population and the Struggle against the Distortions of the Party Line in This Field."[6] It approved the resolution in principle on 4 July 1950 but demanded that it highlight "the political deviations of the political line," mobilize for "a battle against political deviations," and point out the many centuries of German persecution. Recognizing the failure of past policies and practices in Opole, Mazuria, and Warmia, the resolution paid homage to the reigning ideology, with its emphasis on "class differences" and references to "imperialist agents."[7]

Although the resolution admitted, "The attitude toward this [autochthonous] population and the work among it, burdened with an array of distortions and errors, requires a breakthrough," the party supposedly played a positive role: "Thanks to the work of our party, the process of strengthening national consciousness among the autochthons and uniting them with People's Poland constantly moves forward, but is still impeded by a number of factors. These factors have so far not been overcome by the party with sufficient persistence and consistency." Liberation from German rule provided an opportunity. "Nevertheless, as a result of a centuries-long campaign of Germanization and the particular chain of circumstances after liberation, which was accompanied by a massive resettlement operation of Poles, especially from beyond the Bug [River], disruptions occurred which inhibited the processes of the growth of national and social consciousness among the autochthons."[8]

These "disruptions" included "the rampant nationalistic attitudes among some of the settlers and the flagrant distortions of the party line by various links in the state apparatus," specifically "numerous instances of unfriendly, and even hostile and harmful attitudes toward the autochthonous population, reprehensible facts of discrimination, which brought about various types of antagonism between the autochthonous population and the resettled population." Of course, outside forces were also blamed:

> As a result of the low level of political consciousness, the not yet effaced influence of Germanization and isolation of the autochthonous population, it became the object of penetration—especially by Western Germany—of imperialist agents, who preyed upon the difficulties of the postwar period as well as on the excesses of nationalistic elements to sow confusion and hinder the rebuilding of People's Poland, especially in the Recovered Lands.

Ideology also colored a condemnation of the traditional leaders of the autochthons, to whom the party actually gave too little authority.

> Instead of basing the process of consolidation of the autochthonous population with the Polish nation on class diversity, on isolating the class enemy and surrounding with special protection the most disadvantaged and exploited elements among autochthons, the administrative authorities, and at times party organizations as well, treated autochthons as one united mass and rather sought support in the old cadre, often demoralized local ringleaders of the endek-sanacja type, and did not make efforts to propose a new cadre of social activists among autochthons in the struggle to instill the ideology of People's Poland.[9]

Significantly, the Politburo invoked regional and ethnic identities, obligating all levels of the party to "combat unconditionally all hostile or unfriendly manifestations in relation to Silesians, Kashubs, Mazurs, and Warmiaks"; and provincial committees to include them in national councils and their presidia as well as in administration. Inspired by Soviet Stakhanovites, the resolution proposed the popularization of the names of leading autochthons in productivity, rationalization, and inventions. It also called on the MON and MBP to select young autochthon-workers for officers' schools and the Ministry of Labor and Social Welfare to accelerate the consideration of applications for certificates entitling autochthons to pensions based on participation in the war (in the underground and in the West?) and to reconsider decisions denying pensions to *Volksdeutsche* or German army veterans.

The Politburo proposed to discuss with the GDR the return of breadwinners to Poland on a case-by-case basis and, if the breadwinner intended to remain in Germany, "in justified cases—to facilitate departure" from Poland. The resolution recommended increased economic assistance to "working autochthonous farmers" (i.e., not kulaks); social welfare measures for widows, orphans, and families without breadwinners; and improved medical care for poor families.[10]

Official recognition of regional identities did not mean a retreat from Polonization despite past failures. The Politburo proposed a network of Polish language courses to include all autochthonous youths, courses emphasizing the historic membership of autochthons in the Polish nation and their potential for development in People's Poland, and additional courses for adults in Polish language at all levels together with political education. The authorities were to collect information on autochthonous children attending elementary schools and provide poor children with material assistance, such as books and if possible footwear. County budgets were to include an appropriate number of scholarships for poor children of local origin attending secondary schools, especially those studying to be teachers. Provincial committees were to recruit autochthonous youths for professional schools as well as for preparatory courses for higher education. Regional artistic, dance, choral, and similar groups were to be fostered with the goal of their performances bringing about close relations between autochthons and the resettled population. "The whole cultural-educational work should be directed towards a deepening of national and social consciousness of the local population and its complete unification with People's Poland."[11]

Organizing autochthonous youths in the ZMP and strengthening and expanding Service for Poland were to receive special attention. To mobilize and integrate the youths, the resolution proposed sports, summer camps in various regions, and mass sightseeing excursions in the central provinces, including extensive meetings with working-class youths.[12]

The threat posed by "outside forces" obligated the security services to "rely on anti-fascist elements found in the mass organizations with the goal of building a propaganda network and strengthening the struggle against hostile agitation." The Voluntary Reserve of the Civic Militia was to replenish its ranks with autochthonous youths. Severe punishment of discrimination against autochthons would serve as a warning for others. Short courses organized for the MO and security agents had "the goal of overcoming the existing resistance and aversion to autochthons, as well as the goal of bringing the organs of the people's authorities closer to the people."[13]

The Politburo sought to increase the number of autochthons in the party apparatus and to expand the network of party organizations, particularly in villages. "Devote a lot of attention in training to the matter of overcoming the ideological legacy of nationalism, both German and Polish." Courses for activists had to include more autochthons. The party line was to be implemented in a way that would serve as examples of vigilance and harmonious coexistence with the working people of the Recovered Lands. Party cells were to initiate a campaign explaining the resolution among autochthons, the press, national councils, and organizations.[14]

On 15 August 1950 the PRM directed the chairmen of the presidia of WRN to formulate plans at their next meeting for implementing full equality for autochthons, "deepening their national and social consciousness," "increasing vigilance with regard to agents of the enemy" in the upbringing and education of youths, and focusing attention on the problem of "the autochthonous population." But the efforts of the authorities to win this population for Poland and communism had very limited success. Although the number of members of local origin in national councils increased and in 1952 several activists were elected to parliament, this veiled the problem rather than addressing it substantially.[15] After years of ill treatment and discrimination, it is difficult to imagine what measures might have won over disaffected autochthons in light of the resources and ideology of the Polish government. In any case, nothing muffled the desire of massive numbers of them to leave Poland in the 1950s under the guise of family reunification.

Volksdeutsche and the End to Rehabilitation

The unresolved issues related to *Volksdeutsche* played a major role in the German question at the local level. *Volksdeutsche* constituted a majority of the prisoners detained in camps. Many rehabilitated *Volksdeutsche* failed to regain their property and therefore sought to leave the country. Moreover, in the first half of 1950 there were still 80,000 unrehabilitated *Volksdeutsche*.[16]

On 20 July 1950 the government passed a law abolishing all sanctions and restrictions on those citizens who during the war declared their nationality to be German, formally discontinuing the process of rehabilitation. An amnesty freed those convicted, ordered an end to prosecutions, pardoned individuals, and in some cases even returned their property. Proceedings to revoke Polish citizenship and expel individuals who expressed a desire to remain in Poland ended. Excluded from the legislation were those convicted of Nazi crimes and members of the Nazi party and affiliated organizations. On 15 August 1950 the PRM confirmed the return of all public and private rights to those registered in the DVL, but the stigma persisted.[17]

Relations with the GDR, the cessation of mass expulsions, and practical considerations by now outweighed the betrayal of nationality, and the authorities minimized its importance. On 26 March 1950 at a national conference of PZPR members involved in administrating justice, Judge Cieśluk of Poznań pointed out that those found guilty were usually deprived of freedom for a couple of weeks at the price of several witnesses missing work and judicial employees spending time on the paperwork. Another speaker noted the quandary that judges faced with DVL registration as usually the sole evidence without reference to any mitigating circumstances, such as that many *Volksdeutsche* raised their children in a Polish spirit.[18]

By this time several thousand criminal prosecutions for betrayal of Polish nationality took place in Poznań Province alone. The District Court in Kalisz exonerated nearly 40 percent of the individuals involved, the District Court in Poznań almost 30 percent. The Kalisz Court also discontinued proceedings in nearly 16 percent of cases and the Poznań Court in almost 47 percent because the accused had already left Poland or been expelled. A clear majority of those found guilty received sentences of one to six months' imprisonment, with many receiving only two weeks. The sentences became lighter over the years, suggesting the declining significance of the crime.[19]

The new approach to the DVL caused some confusion. The Presidium of the Łódź WRN on 4 August 1950 explained to officials that it did not exclude the revocation of citizenship of those who manifested German national distinctiveness. The memorandum cautioned officials in revoking Polish citizenship not to "commit those errors and shortcomings that occurred in 1947." When a second stage of "repatriation" began on 1 August 1950, county and municipal officials received a quota with instructions to proceed "very judiciously," giving priority to those seeking family reunification, but not to include the "rehabilitated."[20]

On 24 August 1950 the PRM ordered an end to the revocation of citizenship and expulsion of *Volksdeutsche*. On 18 September 1950 provincial authorities received specific instructions not to expel or punish citizens claiming to be German who "in their behavior or work contributed to the reconstruction of People's Poland." Officials were also to examine the documents of *Volksdeutsche* on the lists for departure and ask directly if they wished to remain in Poland with full rights of citizenship, with three exceptions: (1) those who belonged to the Nazi party or the German police, held responsible positions in Nazi organizations, or acted with particular hostility toward Poles during the occupation; (2) those of an "alien class," such as wealthy merchants and owners of factories or farms of more than twenty hectares; and (3) those who expressed a resolute desire to leave for Germany. Revocation was to be completed prior to the expiration of the 1946 decree on 31 December 1950 but with an opportunity to appeal. If the breadwinner was in Germany, the authorities were to assist *Volksdeutsche* unable to support their children to unite with family members in Germany.[21]

Even at this point not all local authorities strictly followed the directives from Warsaw. In Poznań Province the authorities allowed the departure of some of Polish nationality who wanted to leave, largely because of family ties, and revoked the citizenship of 14,617 *Volksdeutsche* from 20 July 1950 to 11 April 1951; only eighty-three appealed the revocation and were withdrawn from a resettlement transport. Instances of dividing families also occurred, even by expelling an individual of Polish nationality and leaving German family members in Poland, mostly because of decisions by security organs. In a petition on 14 September 1950, F. Klapczyński, newly freed from the Jaworzno camp and sent to a transit point for resettlement, wrote, "The real feeling of a Pole awoke in me, and I was sorry to leave my native Fatherland. With regret for temporarily going astray [registering on the DVL], I decided to remain in beloved People's Poland and by my family." The chief delegate for repatriation had to intervene to allow him to stay in Poland.[22] In a report for October 1950 the MBP stated,

> In the most recent transports one could notice that most of the repatriates spoke only Polish and the children did not speak German at all. When asked if they are glad to be going to Germany, they answer that no one asked them if they want to go or not, but a judgment was issued and summoned us to leave, and anyway what are we to do, there is no life for us since the house and the little land that we had was taken from us, and we don't want to be farmhands here.[23]

As the deadline of 31 December 1950 approached and 45,000 *Volksdeutsche* remained on departure lists, the PRM ruled that unless they belonged to one of the three groups noted above, those who were of Polish nationality before the war were to remain in Poland, even women with children whose breadwinner was in Germany.[24]

On 18 July 1951, almost a year after the passage of the law abolishing all sanctions and restrictions on *Volksdeutsche*, the PRM directed provincial authorities to examine decisions regarding the revocation of citizenship, resettlement, and property of *Volksdeutsche* still in Poland. In Poznań Province a large number of the approximately 7,000 cases that commissions reviewed involved individuals who rejected a reversal of the revocation of Polish citizenship and insisted on leaving for Germany. An inhabitant of Bronisławki, Czarnków County, wrote: "I am returning the letter to the Presidium of the Provincial National Council.... I feel that I am a German and request departure to Germany GDR, and I cannot accept Polish citizenship. Therefore I request the granting of German citizenship ... to me and my children." On 13 August 1951 the Presidium of the Poznań WRN repealed earlier rulings revoking Polish citizenship but confirmed the *de facto* status of confiscated property, which benefited only *Volksdeutsche* who still possessed property or had partial use of it. Of the 70,000 to 80,000 *Volksdeutsche* in Poznań Province at the end of the war, many thousands were expelled or resettled. Some 21,000 were rehabilitated (70 percent of those who applied), and presumably most stayed in the province. In April 1951 at least 28,000 former *Volksdeutsche*, mostly from categories III and IV, remained in the province, including 7,296 whose Polish citizenship had been revoked.[25]

In the rest of the incorporated lands nearly all category III and IV *Volksdeutsche,* who numbered 1,772,500 in January 1944, were rehabilitated by administrative fiat.[26] One can assume that the overwhelming majority remained in Poland. According to a government document, as of 3 May 1951 there were 14,405 *Volksdeutsche* in all of Poland whose Polish citizenship had been revoked.[27] Many of them faced hardship. The Office of the RM reported on 12 July 1951 that most of those in Bydgoszcz Province lived on state farms, where they were subject to discrimination.[28]

Those with Polish citizenship also encountered difficulties. As late as 27 October 1954 the Presidium of the Poznań WRN reminded county officials that former *Volksdeutsche* as well as autochthons had the right to vote and be elected.[29] Most Poles had a hard time not believing that even those in the incorporated lands who were coerced could have somehow avoided registering and were less "Polish" for not doing so. Those who suffered during the war for being Polish sought compensation, and the property of *Volksdeutsche,* like that of Germans, autochthons, and Jews, could satisfy that demand. In Piotr Madajczyk's view, the hostility toward Germans and autochthons as well as toward Jews had a largely material basis, i.e., property that was taken over or might be. Germans and autochthons had to be removed or forced to leave to appropriate their property, and returning autochthons and Jews as well as rehabilitated *Volksdeutsche* represented a threat to those who took over their property.[30]

Discrimination, the presence of family members in Germany, and the attraction of a higher standard of living in the FRG inclined many *Volksdeutsche* to leave Poland when it became possible later in the 1950s. Notes of the Nationality Commission and Department of Propaganda in Koszalin from March 1958 indicate that those awaiting permission to leave included the entire families of ethnically mixed marriages, individuals of local origin, former *Volksdeutsche,* and individuals of German origin with Polish citizenship, many of them recruited by state farms in the years 1950–1954.[31] Polish citizens who were German citizens before 1920 might well have minimized the significance of being registered as German again during the war and Polish again after the war—before choosing, as some did, to be German again.

The Census of December 1950 and the Citizenship Law of January 1951

The census of 3 December 1950 ascertained the prewar residences of the inhabitants of the Recovered Lands within the reorganized provincial borders of 28 June 1950.

TABLE 13.1 Prewar Residences of the Inhabitants of the Recovered Lands, 3 December 1950

Recovered Lands	Natives		Settlers		Repatriates		Others		Totals	
	1,000s	%	1,000s	%	1,000s	%	1,000s	%	1,000s	%
Białystok	4.8	6.8	56.7	80.4	8.3	11.7	0.8	1.1	70.6	100
Olsztyn	111.3	18.2	352.1	57.7	137.3	22.5	9.5	1.6	610.2	100
Gdańsk	57.4	11.6	334.9	66.8	97.8	19.5	10.7	2.1	500.8	100
Koszalin	49.5	9.5	333.3	64.4	126.0	24.3	9.6	1.8	518.4	100
Szczecin	16.7	3.2	344.1	65.0	160.5	30.3	8.0	1.5	529.3	100
Poznań	2.9	5.8	30.4	61.6	15.5	31.5	0.5	1.1	49.3	100
Zielona Góra	18.1	3.2	290.4	51.8	244.7	43.7	7.4	1.3	560.6	100
Wrocław	97.5	5.7	901.8	53.1	677.7	39.9	21.9	1.3	1,698.9	100
Opole	437.7	54.1	158.1	19.5	188.3	23.3	25.4	3.1	809.5	100
Katowice	369.1	62.7	114.7	19.5	93.6	15.9	11.2	1.9	588.6	100
Totals	1,165.0	19.6	2,916.5	49.1	1,749.7	29.5	105.0	1.8	5,936.2	100

Source: Leszek Kosiński, "Pochodzenie terytorialne ludności ziem zachonich w 1950 r.," *Dokumentacja Geograficzna* 5, part 2 (1960): 6–8, 12. Although the published data of the census indicated 1.07 million "natives" out of a population of 5.6 million, these figures are based on a detailed analysis of the census data.

Significantly, the census did not ask about nationality or mother tongue. Therefore in table 13.1 "natives" includes both Polish autochthons and non-Polish natives. "Others" refers to those whose origins were unknown or who did not fit into the other categories. "Repatriates" includes migrants from the Soviet Union and other countries and re-emigrants, who resided abroad before the war.

The "natives" of Opole and Katowice, which together mostly coincided with the former province of Silesia, comprised 69.3 percent of the total number of "natives." Other provinces also illustrated the unequal distribution of the groups in question: the overwhelming dominance of settlers in Bialystok and the high percentage of repatriates and re-emigrants in Wrocław and Zielona Góra, which together nearly coincide with the former Wrocław Province and Lubusz Land. The uneven distribution was even more pronounced at the county level. In Silesia the "natives" constituted 70 percent of the population or higher in Tarnowskie Góry (94.4 percent), Lubliniec (80.0 percent), Strzelce (77.5 percent), urban and rural Racibórz (76.6 percent), Olesno (74.5 percent), rural Gliwice (72.8 percent), urban and rural Opole (71.3 percent), and Koźle (70.0 percent) Counties. Further west, "natives" made up a much smaller portion of the county population: Kluczbork (21.2 percent), Niemodlin (20.4 percent), and Glubczyce (16.3 percent). Generally, the percentage of "natives" was higher in rural areas than in urban centers, much higher in the western counties.[32]

To a lesser extent the uneven distribution of "natives" also marked Olsztyn Province, where they formed an above-average portion of the population in

Mrągowo (52.9 percent), urban and rural Olsztyn (34.6 percent), Szczytno (28.7 percent), and Reszel (20.2 percent) Counties. In addition, "natives" formed a significant portion of the population in counties along the prewar border with a tradition of a connection with Polishness: Sztum (34.3 percent) in Gdańsk Province and Złotów (27.1 percent) and Bytów (22.2 percent) in Koszalin Province (formerly in Szczecin Province). Similar concentrations occurred among the settlers, repatriates from the Soviet Union, and re-emigrants.[33]

The lack of integration into Polish society and the communal ties among autochthons, including with those who emigrated, affected even those who did not originally intend to leave or who were materially well off. Their lack of connection with newcomers led many of them to assert, "If everyone in my village leaves, then I will leave," revealing their identification with the local community as well as fatalism that departure was inevitable.[34] In fact research in the Opole region found that a significantly higher percentage of autochthons emigrated in counties where they constituted a minority dispersed among newcomers than in counties with a majority of autochthons residing in close-knit communities.[35] For those who remained in Silesia perhaps the most important factor was their attachment to their communities and "private fatherland," their place of birth, as well as a sense of collective origin, an adherence to a particular set of cultural orientations and customs.[36]

Leszek Belzyt estimates that of the 1,037,000 former German citizens recognized as Polish by the formal end of nationality verification in mid-1949, at most about 200,000 could be considered nationally conscious Poles in 1950. About a third consisted of nationally conscious Germans who underwent verification solely to remain in their homeland. Most of the rest had a primarily Kashubian, Mazurian, or regional identity and regarded nationality as a matter of expediency.[37] Piotr Madajczyk estimates that at least 77,000 individuals were mistakenly verified as Poles. In addition to Germans who passed as Poles, the fluidity of national identity among the nationally indifferent or ambivalent meant that many verified as Polish or awaiting verification gravitated toward Germany mainly because of conflicts with newcomers and the rejection of Polish policies and the political system.[38] The nationalist assumption underlying verification of a durable national identity as a source of loyalty proved deeply flawed as many of the verified and their descendants chose to leave for Germany between 1950 and 1989 or to identify themselves as members of the German minority in Poland after 1989.

On 8 January 1951 a law severed the link between nationality and citizenship. Article 3 stated: "The appropriate authority may recognize as Polish citizens individuals who do not fulfill the requirements of the previous article [i.e., verified as of Polish nationality] but nevertheless reside in Poland at least since 9 May 1945."[39] This allowed the authorities to impose Polish citizenship on autochthons who refused verification of their nationality—some 102,000 at the beginning of the 1950s—and even on Germans, who prior to the law did not even possess official IDs.[40]

Nevertheless, the PRM on 7 April 1951 explicitly permitted Polish citizens from among the "autochthonous population and former *Volksdeutsche*" who were living in exceptionally difficult material circumstances to apply to join immediate family members in the GDR.[41] Some local officials, however, misinterpreted the directive. On 29 June 1951 the Poznań Provincial authorities sharply rebuked the Presidium of the Turek PRN for misleading former *Volksdeutsche* about the grounds for departure.[42] Between May and September 1951, of 11,200 applications considered, only 15 percent were approved. Of some 2,000 from September until the beginning of November 1951, 186 were accepted. Germans wishing to reunite with their families in Poland faced even greater odds: of 932 applications by November 1951, only two were approved.[43]

Meanwhile, some autochthons persisted in their resistance. The Opole KW PZPR reported that a commune in Niemodlin County inhabited solely by autochthons deliberately boycotted a meeting about the National Plebiscite for Peace initiated by Warsaw in May 1951 and refused to endorse it, saying that they were Germans and wanted to go to West Germany and that signing would make them Poles. A worker in Kędzierzyn responded to calls in the press for every Pole to support the plebiscite by saying it "doesn't concern us because we are Silesians and have only a temporary certificate of Polish citizenship."[44]

Officials continued to promote integration and re-Polonization. They rejected a proposal for a separate educational program for native children, which may in part account for a relatively large 6 percent of native youths who avoided obligatory school attendance in the 1951–1952 school year.[45] Those in school had difficulty learning the language and continued to speak either German or a regional dialect. Autochthons educated before 1945 in German schools could obtain recognition of their diplomas only after they passed examinations in the Polish language and in the history and geography of Poland.[46] But at a consistory of the Evangelical Church held in Szczytno on 1 August 1951, Pastor Jerzy Sachs, one of the first pastors to come to Mazuria after the war and a grandson of prewar Bishop Bursche, declared that a further re-Polonization of the Mazurs was unrealistic.[47]

In connection with 1951 Polish citizenship law, individuals had to file forms and provide photos for personal IDs. Anticipating difficulties, the authorities prepared a propaganda campaign as well as sanctions to enforce these procedures. But as of 12 May 1952, 114,000 natives in Opole, Olsztyn, and Katowice Provinces declared their nationality to be German, refused to fill out the forms, or refused to sign them, according to the MO Central Bureau.[48] By February 1955, their number approached 180,000, not including underage children.[49]

Many had already obtained documents of German nationality through various channels—the British and American embassies and the FRG—based on Article 116 of the FRG Basic Law concerning German citizenship. In Mrągowo County 63 percent of Mazurs possessed such documents.[50] In Szczytno County 46 percent had them and were "sitting on their suitcases."[51] According to one estimate, probably more than 200,000 Polish citizens or over 20 percent of autochthons risked serious conflict with the Stalinist government by in effect holding dual citizenship.[52]

Consternation and even panic marked the response of the authorities. They blamed weak political work among autochthons and increased activity of hostile elements, supposedly including former members of the Nazi party, Wehrmacht officers, Nazi administrative officials, kulaks, and the clergy. "Open agitation and propaganda carried on by these elements succeeded in seducing the middle and small-holding autochthonous peasantry, and even party members and officials of national councils."[53] In her diary on 26 June 1952 Dąbrowska relates how the panic among officials "gave birth, like a mountain to a mouse, to the idea of writers going to convince these resistant autochthons of the benefits of belonging to Poland. What a pitiful comedy, one wants to cry bloody tears over this infinite political stupidity."[54]

A government informer reported a conversation with the chairman of a cooperative in Wałcz on 26 May 1952, illuminating the origins of resistance. Labeled a "resolute opponent of the system of People's Poland and implacable agrarian," the chairman claimed that four-fifths of the native population hated the government for burdening farmers by implementing rapid collectivization. They expected a different Poland than the one that came in 1945, when some three-fourths of detainees in camps for Germans were Poles on the pretext of cooperation with the Germans while the MO and PPRs robbed them of their goods.[55]

On 4 June 1952 the Secretariat of the KC PZPR passed a resolution recommending repressive measures, including resettlement to southeastern Poland of those "alien from a class point of view" who by their hostile activity affected their milieu and of those priests who had an especially harmful influence. Individuals who did not accept a change in citizenship were to receive provisional certificates of identity. A Special Central Commission, including representatives of the MBP, the Public Prosecutor General's Office, and the KC PZPR, was to oversee the selection of people for resettlement. In Olsztyn Province eleven families were earmarked, with preparatory steps taken for an additional thirty, and fines were levied on 191 individuals. In Opole Province eleven families were also designated for resettlement, four persons fined, and two imprisoned for one year each.[56] The resettlement, however, never took place.

On 6 June 1952 the PRM retreated, explicitly ordering that recognition of persons of German nationality as Polish citizens occur only at their request.[57] Still, the authorities resorted to repression, from psychological to physical violence and imprisonment. The basic method, however, was individual conversations to persuade the resistant to accede. The effort began in the largest concentrations of resistance in June 1952 with meetings at factories and in rural communities. At one such meeting on 22 August 1952, attended by a representative of the Olsztyn KW PZPR, the employees of a workshop in Mrągowo County were forced to sign the required forms, having been threatened even with violence. "After the end of the meeting, there were still several [female] autochthons, who crying pleaded for the return of the forms they were forced to sign, saying that if not, they will commit suicide."[58] On 9 November 1952 the Silesia KW PZPR reported to the KC on the resistance, including that of individuals previously recognized as Poles: "They state that even if they have to go to jail, they will not accept Polish citizenship." Nevertheless, this second, more repressive effort achieved some superficial success as 60,000 retreated from earlier declarations of German nationality or citizenship. But the authorities most often allowed those stubbornly holding to German nationality to leave. A new development also occurred when some autochthons in Olsztyn Province turned to the diplomatic mission of the GDR to request passports.[59]

A census taken in connection with an election on 1 January 1952 found that the number of natives in the Recovered Lands declined since the 1950 census by some 82,000. In Lower Silesia official statistics indicate that the number of "persons of local origin" in the province declined from 17,236 in mid-1948 to 10,294 in 1952. From 1 February 1952 to December 1954, 10,425 individuals left Poland for the GDR as a result of additional agreements with Poland, 46.6 percent of them autochthons and 7.4 percent former *Volksdeutsche*. More members of divided families resided in the FRG, but the authorities feared a massive increase in applications if they allowed more than a select few of the 20,000 autochthons who by the fall of 1953 applied to emigrate there.[60]

In 1955 a change in the international situation, symbolized by the Soviet leader Nikita Khrushchev receiving FRG Chancellor Konrad Adenauer in Moscow in September, contributed to a reassessment of nationality policies. In November the Secretariat of the KC PZPR issued a letter to provincial committees touting significant progress in strengthening the national consciousness of autochthons and integrating them into the nation. "Nevertheless, . . . serious deficiencies and negligence exist, resulting above all from excessively slow and inadequate realization of the Resolution of the KC PZPR of 1950." The letter proceeded to list some of the same problems identified in the resolution and called on the local authorities to remedy them. Concerning the problem of divided families, it allowed for somewhat wider grounds for granting permission to leave Poland.[61]

In December 1955 the Polish Red Cross and the FRG reached an agreement, which went beyond what the Polish side termed "family reunification." Applications immediately poured in, and lines formed outside passport bureaus. Appeals to Polish patriotism did nothing to stanch the flood. But identifying all the applicants as Germans wrongly verified as Poles after the war would be misleading. Among those wishing to leave were veterans of the Polish Silesian Uprisings and activists in ZPwN, Roman Catholic clergymen (presumably verified as Poles since German clergy were generally expelled earlier), and former prisoners of Nazi concentration camps.[62]

Still, the Polish authorities sought to exploit the hostility toward *Volksdeutsche* to maintain their hold on power. When riots and demonstrations broke out in Poznań in June 1956, the authorities spread the word among the troops mobilized to pacify the situation that *Volksdeutsche* had stirred up the unrest.[63]

The political changes that followed, culminating in Gomułka's return to power in October 1956, brought a further liberalization in emigration but also raised questions about the local population of the borderlands. In November the Opole KW PZPR recognized the existence of a German minority. A group of Silesian activists, however, denied the presence of blocks of Germans in Upper Silesia, "only people disappointed with the social and economic conditions prevalent in Silesia," and proposed steps for achieving equal rights for Silesians. The Mazurian village of Leszno illustrates the ambiguity: in the 1920 plebiscite 98 percent of its inhabitants voted for Poland; in the 1950s the whole village declared a desire to leave for the FRG.[64] The easing of emigration encouraged those wishing to leave to declare their nationality to be German. No doubt many, but not all, were German or had developed a German national consciousness. Considerations other than nationality entered into the complex motives to leave one's homeland.[65] On the basis of their German or Mazurian origins, ten Evangelical pastors left for the FRG, including the son of Karol Małłek, Pastor Ryszard Małłek, who joined his uncle Edward Małłek, who had earlier emigrated to Germany.[66]

The widespread agitation for reform prompted the Secretariat of the KC PZPR in April 1957 to extend eligibility for departure to "advocates of revisionism, consciously stirring up departure tendencies among the Polish autochthonous population." According to the MSW, the 70,000 autochthons seeking to leave Poland included about 10,000 individuals recognized as Polish citizens who frequently stressed their German nationality, 259 of them classified as "advocates of revisionism." "Family reunification" provided the occasion to get rid of them.⁶⁷

Broadened criteria for departure, decentralization of the decisions, and improvement in the procedures and organization of resettlement significantly increased the rate of departure. In the first half of 1957 nearly 57,000 left, almost triple the number that left in 1956. Paradoxically but not surprisingly, as the number of departures grew, so did the number of applications, overwhelming the authorities, who strove to stem the tide in 1958, eventually by simply refusing to accept additional applications. With the last transports in the first weeks of 1959, total departures since the agreement in December 1955 exceeded 275,000, including 20 percent of the remaining autochthons in the Recovered Lands and 70 percent of the "recognized" Germans in Poland. In February 1959 the Secretariat of the KC declared that except for 3,000 GDR citizens, the remaining autochthonous population was Polish. This had no more validity than the assertion in 1983 of FRG Foreign Ministry *Staatsminister* Alois Mertes that c. 1.1 million Germans still lived in Poland, an estimate based on the total native population of the Recovered Lands in the 1950 census.⁶⁸

By 1959 the less numerous autochthons in Olsztyn Province emigrated at more than twice the rate of those in Silesia, and twice as many in Olsztyn Province refused to accept a denial of their applications to leave Poland as in Katowice Province.⁶⁹ In a letter to the MSW on 25 June 1957 a bishop of the Evangelical-Augsburg Church detailed the reasons for the departure of the Mazurs, which in part applied to other autochthons. First, he noted the wrongs suffered during and after the war. "Mazurs cannot forget this." Next he referred to the economic situation, with many losing their farms to newcomers and often working for them. News of a completely different standard of living in the FRG and even the GDR provided a further incentive. "Denominational wrongs"—the loss of churches and other church property—"played no small role" in turning Mazurs against Poland. The still repeated watchword *"Poland is Catholic, and a Pole is a Catholic"* led the Catholic population to treat Mazurs as Germans and to discriminate against them. Finally, he saw the lack of law and order in Poland, in such sharp contrast to what the Mazurs knew under German rule, as "a very important factor prompting departure."⁷⁰

The mass departures of the 1950s did not eliminate the issue. In the following decade autochthons formed the largest group seeking to depart for the FRG. Of approximately 70,000 autochthons in Olsztyn Province, about 5,000 sought permission to leave. Significantly, the majority were relatively well off materially but nevertheless were prepared to relinquish their property. Many were elderly farmers who had a right to a high pension in the FRG. A large number of others were seeking to avoid military service. Some applied just in case restrictions on emigration eased so as not to have regrets later. But they

TABLE 13.2 Leading National-Ethnic Identities in Poland, 2011

National-Ethnic ID	As Sole ID (1,000s)	% of ID	Dual ID (1,000s)	% of ID	Total (1,000s)	% of Total Population
Silesian	376	44.4	471	55.6	847	2.2
Kashubian	16	6.9	217	93.1	233	0.6
German	45	30.4	103	69.6	148	0.4
Polish	36,522	97.7	872	2.3	37,394	97.1

Data source: Główny Urząd Statystyczny, "Przynależność narodowo-etniczna ludności—NSP 2011," http://stat.gov.pl/obszary-tematyczne/ludnosc/narodowy-spis-powszechny-ludnosci-i-mieszkan-2011/przynaleznosc-narodowo-etniczna-ludnosci-nsp-2011,16,1.html.

also included the families of activists who had fought for the Polishness of the area and seemingly integrated elements such as teachers, administrative employees, and national council members of various levels, signaling the failure of nationality policies even to prevent a renunciation of Polishness.[71]

Edward Małłek later wrote that he took a pro-Polish stance because he thought the interests of Mazurs could best be achieved in a Polish state. Disappointed in this hope, he declared that Poland had no right to Mazuria. In the birthplace of the Małłek family in Brodowo, Działdowo County, a monument in memory of his brother Karol bears the epitaph, "He fought for the Polishness [*Polskość*] of this land." Edward would correct this to say that Karol risked his life fighting for the right of Mazurs to their homeland.[72]

Too late for most Mazurs, free manifestations of regional and even national identities became possible after 1989. Apparently, no Mazurs identified themselves as such when in 2011 the Polish census for the first time allowed inhabitants to indicate one or two national-ethnic identities. The most numerous after Polish were Silesian, Kashubian, and German.

Despite the folly of definitively categorizing the nationally indifferent or ambivalent inhabitants of the borderlands as either Polish or German and forcibly "re-Polonizing" those supposedly of Polish origin, the postwar nationality policies superficially succeeded in that 94.8 percent of the population of Poland declared Polish as their sole national-ethnic identity. But this success was achieved in part through the unnecessary expulsion, more or less forced departure, and alienation of many individuals who could have been loyal citizens contributing to Poland's reconstruction had these policies and their implementation been different.

Conclusion

Between 1939 and 1951 two different regimes pursued the ethnic homogenization of the Polish-German borderlands by officially recognizing selected inhabitants as belonging to the titular nation, removing others through more or less forced migration or execution and repopulating the area with individuals of the desired ethnicity. The criteria varied, and inconsistency marked their implementation under both regimes. Superficially, the Nazis took a more nuanced approach by classifying Germans based on their supposed degree of Germanness. The Polish authorities sought to enforce a strict dichotomy of Poles and Germans. Neither regime succeeded in ethnically homogenizing the borderlands during six years of occupation, illustrating the difficulty if not the impossibility of creating and maintaining an ethnically homogeneous nation-state, even in the age of "the apogee of nationalism."[1]

The Nazi goal of a Greater German Reich with "living space" for the "fragments" of the German nation scattered throughout central and eastern Europe ultimately fell victim to Germany's defeat in war. The Polish communist effort had a more lasting impact, but the illusion that the inhabitants of the borderlands constituted an integral part of the Polish nation depended on the communists' monopoly of power.

Under both regimes material and political considerations often overrode the officially declared bases for decisions regarding nationality. Regional and local authorities executed the policies according to their own lights. The task in any case frequently overwhelmed officials, resulting in arbitrary decisions. By attaching serious, even life-threatening consequences to the officially ascribed nationality of the inhabitants, the authorities gave it an overriding importance, reducing an individual's complex identity to a single trait.

Similar efforts at ethnic homogenization occurred elsewhere in Europe in this period, e.g., in Czechoslovakia. But the contested sovereignty over the Polish-German borderlands gave developments a special character. As in other borderlands, the identities of many of the inhabitants included traits that did not match those of the national identity that the authorities sought to impose. Historical experiences and cultural developments that differed from those of the reigning nation fostered regional identities often more deeply rooted than any national identity and bred ambivalence and indifference to national identity. Despite decades of efforts to inculcate Polish national consciousness in the peasantry of Austrian and Russian Poland prior to World War I, Jan Molenda concludes that the patriotism of even its socio-political elite was more closely associated with its "private fatherland" (*Heimat, mała ojczyzna*) than with an "ideological fatherland."[2] The Polish-German borderlands illustrate that the emotive power of the personally experienced "private fatherland" can override acceptance of a particular "ideological fatherland" and that a national identity is not immutable."[3]

The prevalent view of national identity in the mid-twentieth century might be characterized as primordial, i.e., that it dates back in time immemorial. This falsified history, denying the multiethnic past of a state identified with a particular nation. It maintained that national identity belonged to the essence of an individual, an attribute of the soul, a fundamental characteristic of a human being, setting an individual off from members of other nations. Therefore the essence of a national identity remained even if forced de-nationalization and assimilation distorted its external uniformity. With a biological basis, it passed from generation to generation. Some primordialists, however, required the external ethnic characteristics of a national identity, such as language or religion, before recognizing an individual as a fellow national.

Such views were common both east and west, and Nazi and Polish officials applied them in deciding the nationality of residents of the borderlands. Some officials initially recognized as members of the ruling nation virtually all residents who did not manifestly identify with the enemy. An emphasis on "objective" links to "race" or ethnicity, however, posed difficulties, particularly in light of the wide range of ethnic traits exhibited by inhabitants of the borderlands. Ultimately, both the Nazis and Polish officials took the behavior of the individual into account, which in practice meant giving wide latitude to the local authorities to decide the matter.[4]

Like other countries occupied by Germany, Poland had to deal with alleged collaborators, specifically Polish citizens whom the Nazis recognized as *Volksdeutsche*. They were widely viewed as traitors to the Polish nation who ought to be expelled or otherwise punished. Variations in the implementation of Nazi nationality policies from one region to another as well as over the course of the war caused difficulties in determining who among the *Volksdeutsche* sought or accepted their status voluntarily. Issues concerning their motivation as well as their perceptions of the dangers posed by a refusal to seek or accept the status of *Volksdeutsche* clouded any judgments. The Nazis further complicated the question in the incorporated lands by placing *Volksdeutsche* in four categories with different rights and privileges.

To regain their civil rights after the war, *Volksdeutsche* underwent a process of rehabilitation. Officials unwittingly lent legitimacy to the categories to which the Nazis assigned *Volksdeutsche*, with those in categories I and II generally regarded as Germans and those in categories III and IV as Poles. Disputes centered on the question of whether DVL registration had been coerced. In any case, *Volksdeutsche* suffered legal (and illegal) consequences in the immediate postwar years along with the infamy of being branded as "traitors to the nation": "*Volksdeutsche*" continues to carry a pejorative connotation.[5]

Registration on the DVL and the processes of nationality verification and rehabilitation were based on typically nationalist assumptions that everyone has a national identity, at least a dormant one, which is stable and palpable and indicates where his or her primary loyalty lies. These false assumptions undermined the goal of these procedures from the outset, particularly among the many inhabitants of the Polish-German borderlands indifferent to or at least ambivalent concerning their national identity.[6] The authorities and the public did not recognize that "the essence of the nation is not tangible. It is psychological, a matter of attitude rather than of fact."[7] When they were forced to choose between a Polish and a German identity, the contingent nature of the nationality meant that for many of the inhabitants the treatment they encountered and social, economic, and political conditions had a decisive influence on which nationality they claimed, even if only temporarily.

The Nazi authorities regarded regional identities in the borderlands as inclined toward Germanness or as culturally German even when individuals spoke a Slavic language. Although initially some of the Polish authorities accepted Slavic-speaking inhabitants of the Recovered Lands as essentially Polish, a more rigid concept of the Polish identity gradually took hold as the communist authorities sought to create a monolithic society over which they could exercise a monopoly of power. They did not respect the culture and traditions of the very population whose presence supposedly justified possession of the borderlands. The autochthons had to adapt to the culture of the newcomers, not vice versa, as is usual with immigrants.[8] Only after the achievement of that monopoly of power and an ideological shift in the international communist movement did this change.

The imposition of a Polish national identity based on an anti-German paradigm clashed with the existing links of the inhabitants with Germans. In certain respects, the autochthons had more in common with Germans in their midst than with newcomers arriving from the territory of prewar Poland, whose culture they found alien. The authorities, however, treated elements of

German culture as evidence of opting for German nationality. The struggle to eliminate these elements had contrary effects. The prohibition of the German language prompted many Warmiaks and Mazurs to switch to the use of German. In Silesia sympathy for Germany and German culture increased even among those who could not speak German and had no ties to Germany.[9]

Isolation of the autochthons served to preserve their values and traditions. Unjustified detention in labor camps, the shock of being robbed by Polish looters, and the treatment that autochthons received at the hands of security officials and newcomers contributed greatly to the development of anti-Polish feelings.[10] Disputes over property played an important role in their alienation from the state. Moreover, in the first contact with a Polish administration, natives encountered a new socio-political system dominated by communist officials and an ideology hostile to religion, which played a significant role in their lives and constituted an important element of their identity. For many Catholicism and its extensive rituals were Polishness. They looked for a different Poland than one that fought against the Church. They were not so much rejecting Poland as "this Poland."[11]

The chaos and violence of the immediate postwar years prompted an unknown but substantial number of inhabitants of the Polish-German borderlands who did not necessarily think of themselves as German to leave Poland more or less willingly. Many of them yearned for the old prewar order and agreed with the German woman who wrote to a correspondent, "We want to go to Germany because our homeland has become for us a foreign country."[12] The national indifference or ambivalence common in the borderlands made national identity contingent, facilitating passing as Poles or Germans as an assessment of the situation required.

Wilamowski, who fought for Mazurian interests in a tolerant Poland, stated in August 1956 that the main cause for the mass departure of Mazurs for the West during the political thaw in Poland in the mid-1950s was the lack of understanding and sensitivity of the Polish settlers, who often acted as if they were the new masters in relation to the Mazurs. The Mazurs in turn equated their new neighbors with the stereotypes of the "Pollacken" and the "polnische Wirtschaft" of German propaganda.[13] The "primitiveness" of the Polish newcomers in clothes, customs, and agrarian technology regularly caused a shock. The alienation process intensified and led to mass emigration of the local population that finally stopped only in the 1980s.[14]

Burski blamed the prewar Polish government for the Germanization of the Mazurs of Działdowo in his speech before the KRN on 2 January 1945.[15] But already at the end of July 1946, a journalist writing in the Polish Socialist *Robotnik* claimed that the 700-year preservation of Polishness in Mazuria had been destroyed in just one year.[16] Later a young autochthon writing to the press characterized the impact of the nationality policies: "What the Germans did not manage to Germanize in 700 years, People's Poland re-Germanized in four years."[17]

Diverse factors prompted many autochthons and *Volksdeutsche* to leave their homeland prior to 1950. From 1950 to 1958 the 350,000 who emigrated to one of the two German states included well over 100,000 autochthons, according to the Polish authorities.[18] Today, it is a commonplace among Poles that primarily economic opportunities offered by the West German "Economic Miracle" lured inhabitants of the Recovered Lands, whereas a significant portion of the German public believes that they were simply victims of "ethnic cleansing." In ignoring the postwar situation in the borderlands, these views oversimplify the complex of weighty reasons underlying a decision to abandon one's homeland, particularly for an overwhelmingly rural population.

The Allied powers, Western and Eastern, supported the goal of creating an ethnically homogeneous Poland and therefore also bear some responsibility for the consequences of the attempt.[19] They advocated the expulsions as a means of avoiding future conflicts. The elimination of ethnic minorities suited Polish communists in justifying the loss of eastern Poland to the Soviet Union and creating "living space" for its Polish refugees. The annexation of the Recovered Lands, expulsion of the Germans, and re-Polonization of the autochthons had enthusiasts in Poland across the political spectrum, including the Catholic Church with its identification of Polishness with Catholicism, casting doubt on the Polishness of non-Catholics. The supporters of these policies also share in the responsibility for the manner in which these goals were pursued even if they would have preferred that it were done "in an orderly and humane manner." (Is it ever possible to drive people from their homes in this manner?)[20] Shared nationalist values won the hegemony of Polish communists "a modicum of consent," facilitating the achievement of a monopoly of power that lasted for nearly a half of a century.[21] But the process also contributed to the undoing of that monopoly by validating the question of who is a "genuine" Pole, a question that still divides Poland today.[22]

Defenders of the expulsion of the Germans, past and present, assert the impossibility of Poles and Germans living peacefully under the same sovereign roof following the brutal German occupation.[23] The violence against innocent Germans immediately following the retreat of the German military and the deep hostility toward the rehabilitation of *Volksdeutsche*, particularly in Poznań Province, seem to prove that. But the Polish authorities sought to exploit this hostility rather than to dampen it. Nevertheless, mass lynching and acts of revenge did not occur at the moment when Polish settlers came into contact with Germans in the Recovered Lands as happened in Czechoslovakia. Mutual hatred and distrust did not make living side by side and even engaging in limited forms of cooperation impossible.[24]

Intermarriage between Germans and Poles and other instances of interethnic amity indicate that the rejection of coexistence was not universal. Different nationality policies could have multiplied such cases. Polish authorities could have taken cognizance of the wide differences among prewar Poland's Germans, further fragmented by the German conquest of Poland, by allowing those Germans who opposed the Nazi regime to stay in Poland.[25] Just as the Nazi regime retained Poles in the incorporated lands as forced laborers, a substantial number of Germans were exempted from expulsion because of their importance to economic development and long remained in Poland, though initially under slave-like conditions, which were alleviated in the late 1940s.

Among the theoretical considerations of nationalism, Ernest Renan's celebrated lecture "Qu'est-ce qu'une nation?" delivered in 1882 still seems relevant in this case. He famously argued, "Forgetting . . . is a crucial factor in the creation of a nation. . . . No French citizen knows whether he is a Burgundian, an Alan, a Taifale, or a Visigoth, yet every French citizen has to have forgotten the massacre of Saint Bartholomew, or the massacres that took place in the Midi in the thirteenth century."[26] The passage of centuries facilitated this amnesia. But in the lands incorporated into the Reich, Polish citizens of German nationality were barely a generation removed from being German citizens. In the Recovered Lands far too many inhabitants knew that they were Mazurs, Kashubs, or Silesians. Following the German occupation, too few Poles were ready to forget that Mazurs generally supported the Nazis and that Silesians and others served in the Wehrmacht and accepted or at least did not risk rejecting the status of *Volksdeutsche*. Direct personal experiences branded all this into the memory of Polish society.

Renan rejected ethnicity or race as the basis for constituting a nation. "The truth is that there is no pure race and that to make politics depend upon ethnographic analysis is to surrender to a chimera"[27]—a chimera that entranced not only the advocates of *Ostforschung* and the *Polska myśl zachodnia* but also the statesmen of the Big Three who approved the mass movement of populations based on ethnographic considerations. Prescient about the future ideological conflict between *Ostforschung* and *Polska myśl zachodnia,* Renan asked, "Can you be sure that the Germans, who have raised the banner of ethnography so high, will not see the Slavs in their turn analyze the names of villages in Saxony and Lusatia, search for any traces of the Wiltzes or of the Obotrites, and demand recompense for the massacres and wholesale enslavements that the Ottos inflicted upon their ancestors?" He foresaw where such thinking would lead: "One does not have the right to go through the world fingering people's skulls, and taking them by the throat saying: 'You are of our blood; you belong to us!'"[28]

Renan also rejected language as a basis for a nation and warned of the consequences of relying on it.

> Such exaggerations enclose one within a specific culture, considered national; one limits oneself, one hems oneself in. One leaves the heady air that one breathes in the vast field of humanity in order to enclose oneself in a conventicle with one's compatriots. Nothing could be worse for the mind; nothing could be more disturbing for civilization. Let us not abandon the fundamental principle that man is a reasonable and moral being, before he is cooped up in such and such a language, before he is a member of such and such a race, before he belongs to such and such a culture.[29]

To some extent these consequences found fulfillment in the Polish People's Republic.[30]

If one rejects such supposedly "objective" factors as ethnic origin or language in the formation of a nation, what remains?

> A nation is a soul, a spiritual principle. Two things, which in truth are but one, constitute this soul or spiritual principle. One lies in the past, one in the present. One is the possession in common of a rich legacy of memories; the other is present-day consent, the desire to live together, the will to perpetuate the value of the heritage that one has received in an undivided form.[31]

Most of the autochthons of the Recovered Lands and the Polish newcomers lacked "the possession in common of a rich legacy of memories." The Polish authorities sought to impose their own selected "rich legacy of memories," including that of the medieval Piast past, and deny that of the autochthons. The lack of democracy negated the possibility of a "present-day consent . . . to live together."

The results demonstrate the validity of Renan's well-known dictum: "A nation's existence is, if you will pardon the metaphor, a daily plebiscite."[32] *Volksdeutsche* who voluntarily registered on the DVL engaged in this plebiscite as did those *Volksdeutsche* and autochthons who left Poland more or less willingly after the war or who underwent rehabilitation or verification of their nationality. Poles who rejected verified autochthons and rehabilitated *Volksdeutsche* as full and equal citizens engaged in a plebiscite to exclude them from the nation. Since 1990 the inhabitants of the Recovered Lands have increasingly honored the German past of the territory.[33] Had the Polish government honored this "legacy of memories" of the autochthons, it might have more successfully won their consent to be part of a Polish nation shorn of strict ethnic requirements.

In the 1990s the Kashubian activist Cezary Olbracht-Prondzyński explained that although he did not feel that he was of Kashubian nationality, he was a Kashub in the sense that he was at home in his ancestral homeland.[34] In 1994 a history student of Kashubian origin at the University of Gdańsk serving as a guide for a tour of the Kashubian region confirmed the existence of a separate identity when he referred to newcomers who bought vacation homes in the area as "people from Poland."[35] In 1998 the sociologist and Kashubian activist Brunon Synak wrote that the Kashubs of Poland have a double ethnic identity: national (Polish) and regional (Kashubian).[36]

A half century after Ossowski's investigations, sociological research in the same Silesian village found that German national sentiment suffused the regional bonds of the local society and that institutions and associations manifesting German national sentiments swamped those of a Polish character in Opole Silesia. Yet Polish remains the dominant language of all religious rites in the village, which play an important role in local traditions. Ossowski found that Polish national activists ("great Poles") stood out as exceptions in the local population, and the more recent research found no "great Germans," illustrating the continuity of the supremacy of the regional identity over any national identity, which depends on changing circumstances. Indeed, the circumstances of the postwar period played a role in the massive departure for Germany of local inhabitants, including "great Poles" and their descendants.[37]

Currently, legislation in Poland exempts national minorities from requirements that parties must fulfill to elect representatives to parliament, which has enabled the German minority to elect a representative to parliament on a regular basis. Silesians are free to form their own ethnic organizations. The Movement for the Autonomy of Silesia founded in January 1990 with a membership in 2012 of 7,000 has as its main goal the autonomy of historic Upper Silesia within a Poland of autonomous regions.[38] Late in 2013, however, the Supreme Court repealed the registration of the Association of Individuals of Silesian Nationality, denying the existence of a Silesian nation and asserting that the association's statute violates the constitution because the goal of autonomy weakens Poland's unity.[39] The dilemma of combining unity with pluralism remains.

Nevertheless, all this demonstrates that ethnic homogeneity is not a necessary ingredient in the loyalty of citizens. What different circumstances might have persuaded more autochthons and their descendants to remain in Poland after 1945 and to define their identity as a subgroup within the broader nation, not in opposition to it? Officially recognizing the regional identities of autochthons, i.e., as Silesians and Mazurs, instead of insisting on an ethnically homogeneous Polish identity, might have eventually won more of them for Poland.[40] The creation of a province of Mazuria as the pro-Polish Mazurian activists advocated and of an autonomous province of Silesia without the Dąbrowa Basin accompanied by elections allowing local leaders to hold positions of regional authority are examples of what might have made a difference.

The widespread preference for ethnic homogeneity frequently results in violations of democracy and individual rights, whereas ethnic diversity can contribute to the further development of democracy.[41] Research on the eve of

Poland's entry into the European Union in 2004 found a somewhat higher percentage of inhabitants of the Recovered Lands who feel equally European and Polish (30 percent) and lower percentage who feel exclusively Polish than the inhabitants of other regions of Poland, and those who identified as equally European and Polish were more committed to democracy and somewhat more tolerant than those identified as exclusively Polish.[42]

Hannah Arendt argues:

> The reason why highly developed political communities, such as the ancient city-states or modern nation-states, so often insist on ethnic homogeneity is that they hope to eliminate as far as possible those natural and always present differences and differentiations which by themselves arouse dumb hatred, mistrust, and discrimination because they indicate all too clearly those spheres where men cannot act and change at will, i.e., the limitations of the human artifice. The "alien" is a frightening symbol of the fact of difference as such, of individuality as such, and indicates those realms in which man cannot change and cannot act and in which, therefore, he has a distinct tendency to destroy.[43]

Variety is of the essence of humanity. By eliminating or destroying this variety, states deprive themselves of potentially loyal and valuable citizens, as happened in the Polish-German borderlands and elsewhere during World War II and its immediate aftermath as well as in the decades that followed.

ABBREVIATIONS

NOTES

ACKNOWLEDGMENTS

INDEX

Abbreviations

AAN	Archiwum Akt Nowych (Archive of Contemporary Documents)
AK	Armia Krajowa (Home Army)
DPSR	Documents on Polish-Soviet Relations 1939–1945
DVL	Deutsche Volksliste (German Nationality List)
DzURP	Dziennik Ustaw Rzeczypospolitej Polskiej (Register of Laws of the Polish Republic)
FRG	Federal Republic of Germany
FRUS	Foreign Relations of the United States. Diplomatic Papers
GDR	German Democratic Republic
KC	Komitet Centralny (Central Committee)
KPP	Komunistyczna Partia Polski (Communist Party of Poland)
KRN	Krajowa Rada Narodowa (National Council of the Homeland)
KW	Komitet Wojewódzki (Provincial Committee)
MAP	Ministerstwo Administracji Publicznej (Ministry of Public Administration)
MBP	Ministerstwo Bezpieczeństwa Publicznego (Ministry of Public Security)
MIiP	Ministerstwo Informacji i Propagandy (Ministry of Information and Propaganda)
MO	Milicja Obywatelska (Civic Militia)
MON	Ministerstwo Obrony Narodowej (Ministry of National Defense)
MRN	Miejska Rada Narodowa (Municipal National Council)
MSW	Ministerstwo Spraw Wewnętrznych (Ministry of Internal Affairs)
MSZ	Ministerstwo Spraw Zagranicznych (Ministry of Foreign Affairs)
MZO	Ministerstwo Ziem Odzyskanych (Ministry of Recovered Lands)
NKVD	Narodnyj Komissariat Vnutrennych Del (People's Commissariat of Internal Affairs)
NSDAP	Nationalsozialistische Deutsche Arbeiterpartei (National Socialist German Workers' Party, the Nazi Party)

OPKN	Okręgowy Polski Komitet Narodowościowy (District Polish Nationality Committee
OUN	Orhanizatsiya Ukrains'kykh Natsionalistiv (Organization of Ukrainian Nationalists
PKWN	Polski Komitet Wyzwolenia Narodowego (Polish Committee of National Liberation
PPR	Polska Partia Robotnicza (Polish Workers' Party)
PPS	Polska Partia Socjalistyczna (Polish Socialist Party)
PRM	Prezydium Rady Ministrów (Presidium of the Council of Ministers)
PRN	Powiatowa Rada Narodowa (County National Council)
PSL	Polskie Stronnictwo Ludowe (Polish Peasant Party)
PUBP	Powiatowy Urząd Bezpieczeństwa Publicznego (County Office of Public Security)
PUIiP	Powiatowy Urząd Informacji i Propagandy (County Office of Information and Propaganda)
PUR	Państwowy Urząd Repatriacyjny (State Repatriation Office)
PZPR	Polska Zjednoczona Partia Robotnicza (Polish United Workers' Party)
PZZ	Polski Związek Zachodni (Polish Western Union)
RM	Rada Ministrów (Council of Ministers [Warsaw])
SA	Sturm-Abteilung (Storm Troops, paramilitary of the NSDAP)
SS	Schutzstaffel (Defense Squadron, NSDAP internal security)
UB	Urząd Bezpieczeństwa (Office of Security)
UBP	Urząd Bezpieczeństwa Publicznego (Office of Public Security)
UL	Urząd Likwidacyjny (Office of Liquidation)
UNRRA	United Nations Relief and Rehabilitation Administration
UPA	Ukrains'ka Povstans'ka Armiya (Ukrainian Insurgent Army)
UW	Urząd Wojewódzki (Provincial Office)
UZ	Urząd Ziemski (Land Office)
VD	Volksdeutsche, Volksdeutscher (Ethnic German)
WRN	Wojewódzka Rada Narodowa (Provincial National Council)
WS-P	Wydział Społeczno-Polityczny (Socio-Political Department)
WUBP	Wojewódzki Urząd Bezpieczeństwa Publicznego (Provincial Office of Public Security)
WUIiP	Wojewódzki Urząd Informacji i Propagandy (Provincial Office of Information and Propaganda)
ZG	Zarząd Główny (Main Directorate)
ZPP	Związek Patriotów Polskich (Union of Polish Patriots)
ZPwN	Związek Polaków w Niemczech (Union of Poles in Germany)

Notes

Introduction

1. Biray Kolluoğlu, "Excesses of Nationalism: Greco-Turkish Population Exchange," *Nations and Nationalism* 19, no. 3 (2013): 532.
2. Geoff Eley cites Germany and Italy, "A Disorder of Peoples: The Uncertain Ground of Reconstruction in 1945," in *The Disentanglement of Populations: Migration, Expulsion and Displacement in Postwar Europe, 1944-9,* ed. Jessica Reinish and Elizabeth White (Basingstoke: Palgrave Macmillan, 2011), 299-300.
3. Ernest Gellner defines nationalism as "primarily a political principle, which holds that the political and the national unit should be congruent," *Nations and Nationalism* (Ithaca: Cornell University Press, 1983), 1.
4. Geoff Eley, "Crossing East and West: Convergence and Interdependence in the History of the Left in Europe," (lecture, King's College, University of London, UK, 9 Feb. 2004); Eley, "Europe in Motion: Refugees, Displacement, and the Remaking of National Space, 1939-73" (lecture, American Historical Association annual meeting, Chicago, IL, 6 Jan. 2012). *Past and Present* 218, suppl. 8 (2013) focuses on transnationalism in this period.
5. Peter Gatrell, "Introduction: World Wars and Population Displacement in Europe in the Twentieth Century," *Contemporary European History* 16, no. 4 (2007): 415-426; Gatrell, "Displacing and Re-Placing Population in the Two World Wars: Armenia and Poland Compared," ibid., 511-527; A. Dirk Moses, "Partitions and Peoples: Forced Population Movement and the Construction of Nations in India/Pakistan, Palestine, and Europe, 1945-71," (lecture, American Historical Association annual meeting, Chicago, IL, 6 Jan. 2012).
6. 406 Parl. Deb., H. C. (5th ser.) (1944) 1483, 1484.
7. Mark Kramer questions the efficacy of avoiding conflict by separating ethnic groups, "Introduction," in *Redrawing Nations: Ethnic Cleansing in East-Central Europe, 1944-1948,* ed. Philipp Ther and Ana Siljak (Lanham, MD: Rowman & Littlefield Publishers, Inc., 2001), 9-10; as does Ther, "A Century of Forced Migration: The Origins and Consequences of 'Ethnic Cleansing,'" ibid., 62-63.

8. Rita Chin and Heide Fehrenbach suggest that "the historical processes of racialization and ethnicization across postwar Europe" overcome the East-West divide, "Introduction: What's Race Got to Do with It? Postwar German History in Context," in *After the Nazi Racial State: Difference and Democracy in Germany and Europe*, ed. Chin, Fehrenbach, and Geoff Eley (Ann Arbor: University of Michigan Press, 2009), 28; Tony Judt asserts, "The history of the two halves of post-war Europe cannot be told in isolation from one another," *Postwar: A History of Europe since 1945* (New York: Penguin Press, 2005), 5.

9. John Connelly, "Nazis and Slavs: From Racial Theory to Racist Practice," *Central European History* 32, no. 1 (Winter 1999): 32; Chad Bryant, "Either German or Czech: Fixing Nationality in Bohemia and Moravia, 1939–1946," *Slavic Review* 61, no. 4 (Winter 2002): 683.

10. Marcin Król, "Długie trwanie a PRL, *Res Publica Nowa*, no. 3 (Mar. 1993): 39. Milada Anna Vachudová and Tim Snyder similarly suggest that Poland, Hungary, and the Czech Republic benefit from ethnic homogeneity, "Are Transitions Transitory? Two Types of Political Change in Eastern Europe since 1989," *East European Politics and Societies* 11, no. 1 (Dec. 1996): 1–35.

11. Maria Dąbrowska, *Dzienniki*, vol. 3, *1945–1950*, ed. Tadeusz Drewnowski (Warsaw: Cztelnik, 1988), 137–138. Alfred-Maurice de Zayas similarly lacks a sense of proportion in equating the German victims of expulsion with "the Polish officers in the Katyn Forest, or the gypsies liquidated by Nazi hit squads, or the Jews murdered at Auschwitz," *A Terrible Revenge: The Ethnic Cleansing of the East European Germans, 1944–1950* (New York: St. Martin's Press, 1994), 145.

12. Anthony D. Smith, *Nationalism in the Twentieth Century* (New York: New York University Press, 1979), 2–4; on "Volk" and race, see 69–74; Christian Giordano, "The Comeback of the National State: Ethnic Discourse in East Central Europe," in *Ethnicity, Nation, Culture: Central and East European Perspectives*, ed. Bálint Balla and Anton Sterbling (Hamburg: Krämer, 1998), 105.

13. Teresa Torańska, *"Them:" Stalin's Polish Puppets* (New York: Harper & Row, 1987). According to prosecutors, a suspect arrested in a plot to bomb the Polish parliament said that the people running the country were "not true Poles," Chris Borowski, Wojciech Zurawski, and Marcin Goettig, "Bumbling Bomb Plot Exposes Poland's Dark Side," *Reuters*, 23 Nov. 2012, http://www.reuters.com/article/2012/11/23/us-poland-attack-plot-idUSBRE8AM0KX20121123. On 4 Dec. 2011, celebrated in Poland as Miners' Day, Polish television showed the leader of the main Polish opposition party Jarosław Kaczyński with a Silesian family wishing them "God speed" (*Szczęść Boże*) and adding that this is what one says in parts "of that genuine Poland" (*tej prawdziwej Polski*). Marcin Kula brought this incident to my attention. According to the sociologist Rafal Pankowski, what unites all of the extremist groups in Poland is the pursuit of a "mono-ethnic society," Anna Maciol, "Right-Wing Extremism: Fears as Far Right Gains Fresh Foothold in Poland," *Deutsche Welle*, 24 Dec. 2011, http://www.dw-world.de/dw/article/0,,15613796,00.html.

14. Rogers Brubaker, *Nationalism Reframed: Nationhood and the National Question in the New Europe* (Cambridge: Cambridge University Press, 1996), 21; Geoff Eley, "The Trouble with 'Race': Migrancy, Cultural Difference, and the Remaking of Europe," in *After the Nazi Racial State*, ed. Chin, Fehrenbach, and Eley, 175.

15. For Hans Kohn nationalism is "a state of mind, in which the supreme loyalty of an individual is felt to be due the nation-state," *Nationalism: Its Meaning and History,* rev. ed. (Princeton: D. Van Nostrand Company, Inc., 1965), 9; for Brubaker "nationality is not a fixed, given, indelible objectively ascertainable property; and even subjective, self-identified nationality is variable across time and context of elicitation," *Nationalism Reframed,* 56n1; Siniša Malešević questions the existence of a durable, continuous, stable, and monolithic entity called "national identity," "The Chimera of National Identity, *Nations and Nationalism* 17, no. 2 (2011): 272–290.
16. Padraic Kenney, "After the Blank Spots Are Filled: Recent Perspectives on Modern Poland," *Journal of Modern History* 79 (Mar. 2007): 161; Andrew Demshuk, "Ethnic Cleansing and Its Legacies in Twentieth-Century East Central Europe," *European History Quarterly* 43, no. 2 (2013): 333.
17. The most relevant is James E. Bjork, *Neither German nor Pole: Catholicism and National Indifference in a Central European Borderland* (Ann Arbor: The University of Michigan Press, 2008). Tara Zahra lists other studies, "Imagined Noncommunities: National Indifference as a Category of Analysis," *Slavic Review* 69, no. 1 (Spring 2010): 94n2. "Sites of Indifference to Nationhood" is the theme of the *Austrian History Yearbook* 43 (2012).
18. Brubaker warns of this illusion but still finds use of the terminology necessary, *Nationalism Reframed,* 56, 56n1, 62, 62n10.
19. Jan Penrose distinguishes "homeland" defined by the state from "homeland" derived from culture and territory, "Nations, States and Homelands: Territory and Territoriality in Nationalist Thought," *Nations and Nationalism* 8 (July 2002): 277–297; decades after the exchange of population under the Treaty of Lausanne, the inhabitants of Anatolia distinguish between "exchangees" and "immigrants," Kolluoğlu, "Excesses," 542.
20. Maren Röger, *Flucht, Vertreibung und Umsiedlung. Mediale Erinnerungen und Debatten in Deutschland und Polen seit 1989* (Marburg: Herder-Institut, 2011); Stefan Troebst, ed., *Vertreibungsdiskurs und europäische Erinnerungskultur: Deutsch-polnische Initiativen zur Institutionalisierung. Eine Dokumentation* (Osnabrück: fibre Verlag, 2006); Zbigniew Mazur, *Centrum przeciwko wypędzeniom ,1999–2005* (Poznań: Instytut Zachodni, 2006); Agnieszka Łada, *Debata publiczna na temat powstania Centrum przeciw Wypędzeniom w prasie polskiej i niemieckiej* (Wrocław: Oficyna Wydawnicza "Atut"; Wroclawskie Wydawnictwo "Oswiatowe," 2006).
21. R. M. Douglas, *Orderly and Humane: The Expulsion of the Germans after the Second World War* (New Haven: Yale University Press, 2012).
22. Włodzimierz Borodziej and Hans Lemberg, eds., *Niemcy w Polsce 1945–1950: wybór dokumentów* (hereafter cited as *Niemcy*), 4 vols. (Warsaw: Neriton, 2000–2001), vol. 4 ed. Daniel Boćkowski; Włodzimierz Borodziej and Hans Lemberg, eds., *Die Deutschen östlich von Oder und Neiße, 1945–1950: Dokumente aus polnischen Archiven* (hereafter cited as *Die Deutschen*), 4 vols. (Marburg: Verlag Herder-Institut, 2000–2004).
23. Eley, "A Disorder of Peoples," 291, and the list in 307n1; on the value of studies of this period, see 295–296.

24. Marek Romaniuk, *Podzwonne okupacji: Deutsche Volksliste w Bydgoszczy (1945–1950)* (Bydgoszcz: Agencja ARTPRESS, 1993); Krzysztof Stryjkowski, *Położenie osób wpisanych w Wielkopolsce na niemiecką listę narodowościową w latach 1945–1950* (Poznań: Instytut Historii UAM, 2004); Leszek Olejnik, *Zdrajcy narodu? Losy Volksdeutschów w Polsce po II wojnie światowej* (Warsaw: Wydawnictwo Trio, 2006); Grzegorz Strauchold, *Autochtoni, Polscy, Niemieccy, czy . . . od nacjonalizmu do komunizmu (1945–1949)* (Toruń: Wydawnictwo Adam Marszałek, 2001).
25. Stryjkowski, *Położenie*, 12; Czesław Łuczak, *Pod niemieckim jarzmem (Kraj Warty 1939–1945)* (Poznań: PSO Sp. z o.o., 1996), 57; Gerhard Wolf, *Ideologie und Herrschaftsrationalität: Nationalsozialistische Germanisierungspolitik in Polen* (Hamburg: Hamburger Edition HIS, 2012).
26. Chin and Fehrenbach, "Introduction: What's Race Got to Do with It?," 26

1. The Disputed Polish-German Borderlands

1. Karin Friedrich, *The Other Prussia: Royal Prussia, Poland and Liberty, 1569–1772* (New York: Cambridge University Press, 2000), 217; Peter Brock, "Polish Nationalism," in *Nationalism in Eastern Europe*, ed. Peter F. Sugar and Ivo J. Lederer (Seattle: University of Washington Press, 1969), 311.
2. Repr. in Manfred Kridl, Władysław Malinowski, Józef Wittlin, eds. *Polska myśl demokratyczna w ciągu wieków: antologia* (Warsaw: Ludowa Spółdzielnia Wydawnicza, 1986), 113; see also John D. Stanley, "Joachim Lelewel (1786–1861)," in *Nation and History: Polish Historians from the Enlightenment to the Second World War*, ed. Peter Brock, Stanley, and Piotr Wróbel (Toronto: University of Toronto Press, 2006), 67; etymologically the Polish word for citizen, *obywatel*, suggests a resident or inhabitant, Sławomir Łodziński, "Polish Citizenship—Ethnic Boundaries and Issue of Citizenship in Polish Society," in *Ethnicity, Nation, Culture: Central and East European Perspectives*, ed. Bálint Balla and Anton Sterbling (Hamburg: Krämer, 1998), 152.
3. Elie Kedourie, *Nationalism,* 4th rev. ed. (Oxford: Blackwell, 1993), 1.
4. Thomas Spira, ed., *Nationalism and Ethnicity Terminologies: An Encyclopedia Dictionary and Research Guide* (Gulf Breeze, FL: Academic International Press, 1999), 416–417; the quote is on 416; see also Oren Yiftachel, "The Homeland and Nationalism," in *The Encyclopedia of Nationalism*, vol. 1, *Fundamental Themes,* ed. Alexander Motyl (San Diego, CA: Academic, 2001), 364; Derek Heater, *National Self-Determination: Woodrow Wilson and His Legacy* (New York: St. Martin's Press, 1994), 3–27. Hannah Arendt sees the Declaration of the Rights of Man of the French Revolution as a turning point that in practice made human rights dependent on national rights, *The Origins of Totalitarianism* (New York: Harcourt Brace Jovanovich, 1973), 290–292, 299.
5. John Stuart Mill, *Considerations on Representative Government* (Hazleton, PA: Pennsylvania State University Electronic Classics Series, http://www2.hn.psu.edu/faculty/jmanis/jsmill/considerations.pdf, 2004), 197, 199.
6. Kedourie, *Nationalism*, xvi.

7. Brock, "Polish Nationalism," 315–316; Piotr S. Wandycz, *The Lands of Partitioned Poland, 1795–1918* (Seattle: University of Washington Press, 1974), 239–259; Jarosław Hrycak, *Historia Ukrainy 1772–1999: narodziny nowoczesnego narodu* (Lublin: Instytut Europy Środkowo-Wschodniej, 2000), 67; Virgil Krapauskas, *Nationalism and Historiography: The Case of Nineteenth-Century Lithuanian Historicism* (Boulder: East European Monographs, 2000).
8. Michał Bobrzyński, *Dzieje Polski w zarysie* (Warsaw: Nakład Geberthnera i Wolffa, 1879), 450; see also Philip Pajakowski, "Michał Bobrzyński," in *Nation and History*, ed. Brock, Stanley, and Wróbel, 152.
9. Repr. in Krzysztof Dunin-Wąsowicz, ed., *Przegląd Społeczny 1886–1887* (Wrocław: Zakład imienia Ossolińskich, Wydawnictwo Polskiej Akademii Nauk, 1955), 64 (emphasis in original); the author was the ethnographer Adam Zakrzewski, but it presumably had Wysłouch's approval; see Peter Brock, "List do redakcji roczników dziejów ruchu ludowego," *Roczniki dziejów ruchu ludowego* 20 (1980): 403.
10. Brock, "Polish Nationalism," 339–346.
11. Aviel Roshwald, *Ethnic Nationalism and the Fall of Empires: Central Europe, Russia, and the Middle East, 1914–1923* (London: Routledge, 2001), 68.
12. Wojciech Wrzesiński, "Polska: kraina przejściowa, pomost czy obszar narodowy," in *Do niepodległości 1918, 1944/45, 1989: wizje, drogi, spełnienie*, ed. Wrzesiński (Warsaw: Wydawnictwo Sejmowe, 1998), 21; Leszek Kołakowski, *Main Currents of Marxism: Its Origins, Growth and Dissolution*, vol. 2, *The Goldern Age* (Oxford: Oxford University Press, 1978), 208, 213–214; Timothy Snyder, *Nationalism, Marxism, and Modern Central Europe: A Biography of Kazimierz Kelles-Krauz (1872–1905)* (Cambridge, MA: Ukrainian Research Institute, Harvard University, 1997), xii, 205, 208, 248–249.
13. Walentyna Najdus, *Ignacy Daszyński, 1866–1936* (Warsaw: Czytelnik, 1988), 382, 390.
14. Aleksander Łuczak and Józef Ryszard Szaflik, eds. *Druga Rzeczpospolita: wybór dokumentów* (Warsaw: Ludowa Spółdzielna Wydawnicza, 1988), 19–22.
15. Roman Wapiński, *Narodowa Demokracja, 1893–1939: ze studiów nad dziejami myśli nacjonalistycznej* (Wrocław: Zakład Narodowy im. Ossolińskich—Wydawnictwo, 1980), 170; Grzegorz Strauchold, *Myśl zachodnia i jej realizacja w Polsce Ludowej w latach 1945–1957* (Toruń: Wydawnictwo Adam Marszałek, 2003), 11–12.
16. Roman Dmowski, *Problems of Central and Eastern Europe* (London: privately printed, 1917), 73.
17. Ibid., 17, 20, 76.
18. Wapiński, *Narodowa Demokracja*, 172.
19. Heater, *National Self-Determination*, 14, 24, 29–30, 206.
20. Thomas D. Musgrave, *Self-Determination and National Minorities* (Oxford: Clarendon Press, 1997), 24, 26; E. J. Hobsbawm, *Nations and Nationalism since 1780: Programme, Myth, Reality*, 2nd ed. (Cambridge: Cambridge University Press, 1992), 21–22, 97–100.
21. Max Broesike, "Die Polen im westlichen Preussen 1905," *Zeitschrift des Königlich Preussischen Statistichen Landesamts* 48 (1908): 264; Broesike, "Einiges über

Deutsche und Polen nach der Volkszählung von 1910," *Zeitschrift des Königlich Preussischen Statistischen Landesamtes* 52 (1912): 87; Józef Buzek, *Historya polityki narodowościowej rządu pruskego wobec Polaków od traktatów wiedeńskich do ustaw wyjątkowych z r. 1908* (Lwów: Nakład Księgarni H. Altenberga, 1909), 62, 152–170, 189–210, 309–316, 382–406, 454–513.

22. Roshwald, *Ethnic Nationalism*, 160–161, 252n11.
23. Heater, *National Self-Determination*, 38, 71–76, 79, 99, 103.
24. Ibid., 121, 135.
25. Arendt, *Origins*, 272–275; Michael Burleigh, *The Third Reich: A New History* (New York: Hill and Wang, 2000), 46–48; Heater, *National Self-Determination*, 121, 129–130, 138–139. On the propaganda, see Rudolf Jaworski, "Deutsch-Polnische Feindbilder 1919–1932," *Internationale Schulbuchforschung* 6, no. 2 (1984): 140–156. Poland also used the Polish diaspora as a foreign policy tool, Marcin Kula, "Obywatel kraju i świata," *Ethos* 87–88 (July–Dec. 2009): 61.
26. Christian Raitz von Frentz, *A Lesson Forgotten: Minority Protection under the League of Nations. The Case of the German Minority in Poland, 1920–1934* (New York: St. Martin's Press, 1999), 1–2, 10, 25–27, 240, 245; the quote is on 245.
27. Quoted in Hans Lemberg, "'Ethnische Säuberung': Ein Mittel zur Lösung von Nationalitätenproblem?," *Aus Politik und Zeitgeschichte* B46 (1992): 28.
28. Biray Kolluoğlu, "Excesses of Nationalism: Greco-Turkish Population Exchange," *Nations and Nationalism* 19, no. 3 (2013): 533, 535, 539; Norman M. Naimark, *Fires of Hatred: Ethnic Cleansing in Twentieth-Century Europe* (Cambridge, MA: Harvard University Press, 2001), 13, 53–56; Stefan Wolff, "Can Forced Population Transfers Resolve Self-Determination Conflicts? A European Perspective," *Journal of Contemporary European Studies* 12, no. 1 (Apr. 2004): 15. Jannis Panagiotidis argues that in an age of national self-determination and collective rights of minorities, the treaty still made sense, but not in the post–World War II era with its recognition of individual human and civil rights, "Machen hohe Zäune gute Nachbarn? 90 Jahre Vertrag von Lausanne," *Religion & Gesellschaft in Ost und West* 41, no. 6 (2013): 24. Because religion determined nationality, the inhabitants of some Muslim villages still speak Byzantine Greek, Neil Trevithick, "Turkish Mountains Where They Still Speak Ancient Greek," *BBC from Our Correspondent*, 18 Feb. 2010, http://news.bbc.co.uk/2/hi/programmes/from_our_own_correspondent/8520668.stm.
29. Alfons Krysiński, "Tendencje rozwojowe ludności Polski pod względem narodowościowym i wyznaniowym w dobie powojennej," *Sprawy Narodowościowe* 5, no. 1 (Jan.–Apr. 1931): 60.
30. R. M. Douglas, *Orderly and Humane: The Expulsion of the Germans after the Second World War* (New Haven: Yale University Press, 2012), 18.
31. "Nationality follows language" was the shibboleth of the *Deutscher Ostmarken-Verein*, which advocated the Germanization of Prussian Poland, John J. Kulczycki, *School Strikes in Prussian Poland, 1901–1907: The Struggle over Bilingual Education* (Boulder: East European Monographs, 1981), 34–35. On linking language and nationality, see Benedict Anderson, *Imagined Communities: Reflections on the Origin and Spread of Nationalism* (London: Verso, 1991), 71–75.
32. Heater, *National Self-Determination*, 209–210.

33. Ernest Renan, "What Is a Nation?," repr. in *Becoming National: A Reader,* ed. Geoff Eley and Grigor Suny (New York: Oxford University Press, 1996), 53.
34. Ingo Eser, "Niemcy na Górnym Śląsku," in *Niemcy,* ed. Włodzimierz Borodziej and Hans Lemberg, vol. 2, *Polska Centralna. Województwo śląskie,* ed. Eser and Jerzy Kochanowski (Warsaw: Wydawnictwo NERITON, 2000), 295–298.
35. Eugeniusz Kłosek, *"Swoi" i "obcy" na Górnym Śląsku od 1945 roku. Środowisko miejskie* (Wrocław: Wydawnictwo Uniwersytetu Wrocławskiego, 1994), 19–21; Bernard Linek, "Górnoślązacy a nacjonalizm na początku XX wieku," *CzasyPismo: o historii Górnego Śląska* 1, no. 1: 21; Danuta Berlińska, "Identität and natonale Identification der Schlesier in der Region Oppeln nach 1989," in *Die Grenzen der Nationen: Identitätenwandel in Oberschlesien in der Neuzeit,* ed. Kai Struve and Philipp Ther (Marburg: Verlag Herder-Institut, 2002), 278, 280–284.
36. James E. Bjork, *Neither German nor Pole: Catholicism and National Indifference in a Central European Borderland* (Ann Arbor: University of Michigan Press, 2008), 196–198, 203, 212–213, 216–217, 234–240.
37. Ibid., 1–4, 244–257; the quote is on 4.
38. Quoted in Raitz von Frentz, *A Lesson Forgotten,* 81.
39. Bernard Linek, "'De-Germanization' and 'Re-Polonization' in Upper Silesia, 1945–1950," in *Redrawing Nations: Ethnic Cleansing in East-Central Europe, 1944–1948,* ed. Philipp Ther and Ana Siljak (Lanham, MD: Rowman & Littlefield Publishers, Inc., 2001), 123. Rogers Brubaker discusses Poland's nationalizing efforts but not Germany's, *Nationalism Reframed: Nationhood and the National Question in the New Europe* (Cambridge: Cambridge University Press, 1996), 86–93, 107–134.
40. Bjork, *Neither German nor Pole,* 264–266; Linek, "'De-Germanization,'" 122.
41. Danuta Berlińska, *Mniejszość niemiecka na Śląsku Opolskim w poszukiwaniu tożsamości* (Opole: Stowarzyszenie Instytut Śląski, Państwowy Instytut Naukowy—Instytut Śląski w Opolu, 1999), 104–105; Tomasz Kamusella and Petr Kacir, "Upper Silesia 1918–1945," in *The Politics of Ethnicity in Central Europe,* ed. Karl Cordell (New York: St. Martin's Press, 2000), 99, 102; Eser, "Niemcy," 302.
42. Quoted in Stanisław Ossowski, "Zagadnienia więzi regionalnej i więzi narodowej na Śląsku Opolskim," in *O ojczyźnie i narodzie* (Warsaw: Państwowe Wydawnictwo Naukowe, 1984), 116.
43. Andrzcj Michalczyk, "Migrationsprozesse und gesellschatliche Integration in polnischen Teil des Industriereviers 1922–1939," summarized in "Region—Industrie—Zuwanderung. Oberschlesische Gesellschaftsgeschichte im 20. Jahrhundert. 27.11/2009–28.11.2009, Kattowitz/Katowice," ed. Gregor Ploch, in: H-Soz-u-Kult, 25.01.10, http://hsozkult.geschichte.hu-berlin.de/tagungsberichte/id=2966.
44. Emil Szramek, "Śląsk jako problem socjologiczny," *Roczniki Towarzystwa Przyjaciół Nauk na Śląsku* 4 (1932/33 [1934]): 44, 47; the quote is on 44.
45. Barbara Kalinowska-Wójcik, "Austausch der Eliten am Beispiel der Stadt Kattowitz nach 1922," summarized in "Region—Industrie—Zuwanderung," ed. Ploch; Bernard Linek, *Polityka antyniemiecka na Górnym Śląsku w latach 1945–1950* (Opole: Stowarzyszenie Instytut Śląski, Państwowy Instytut Naukowy, Instytut Śląski w Opolu, 2000), 30–33; Krzysztof Stryjkowski, *Położenie osób*

wpisanych w Wielkopolsce na niemiecką listę narodowościową w latach 1945–1950 (Poznań: Instytut Historii UAM, 2004), 30.
46. Richard Blanke, *Polish-Speaking Germans? Language and National Identity among the Masurians since 1871* (Cologne: Böhlau Verlag, 2001), 14–15, 20, 41–42.
47. Andreas Kossert, *Preußen, Deutsche oder Polen?: die Masuren im Spannungsfeld des ethnischen Nationalismus 1870–1956* (Wiesbaden: Harrassowitz Verlag, 2001), 22–31, 70, 81–83, 86, 123 134–135.
48. Ibid., 116, 118; the quote is on 118.
49. Heater, *National Self-Determination*, 209; Raitz von Frentz, *A Lesson Forgotten*, 23; Blanke, *Polish-Speaking Germans?*, 127, 187.
50. Archiwum Akt Nowych (hereafter cited as AAN), Ambasada Rzeczypospolitej Polskiej w Berlinie 1840, fols. 68–69.
51. Blanke, *Polish-Speaking Germans?*, 195, 252; Claudia Kraft, "Who Is a Pole, and Who Is a German? The Province of Olsztyn in 1945," in *Redrawing Nations*, ed. Ther and Siljak, 107–108; Kossert, *Preußen*, 5–6, 157–160, 162–165.
52. Kossert, *Preußen*, 177, 180–181; the quote is on 177; Andrzej Sakson, *Mazurzy— społeczność pogranicza* (Poznań: Instytut Zachodni, 1990), 53.
53. Kossert, *Preußen*, 168–170, 185–190; Claudia Kraft, "Wojewodschaft Allenstein," in *Die Deutschen*, ed. Włodzimierz Borodziej and Hans Lemberg, vol. 1, *Zentrale Behörden. Wojewodschaft Allenstein*, ed. Borodziej and Kraft (Marburg: Verlag Herder-Institut, 2000), 438, 442, 422n26, 443, 433n27.
54. Kossert, *Preußen*, 230–243.
55. Ibid., 205–207; Sakson, *Mazurzy*, 58–59.
56. Kossert, *Preußen*, 208–212; Sakson, *Mazurzy*, 60–63; on the influence of the rightwing National Democrats and the link between the Polish nation and the Catholic Church in Pomerania, see Ryszard Michalski, *Systemy wartości na łamach polskiej prasy pomorskiej w latach 1870–1939 oraz 1945–1980* (Toruń: Uniwersytet Mikołaja Kopernika, 1998), 18–23.
57. Thomas Lekan, "German Landscape: Local Promotion of the Heimat Abroad," in *Heimat Abroad: The Boundaries of Germanness*, ed. K. Molly O'Donnell, Renate Bridenthal, and Nancy Reagin (Ann Arbor: University of Michigan Press, 2005), 153–155.
58. Rogers Brubaker, *Citizenship and Nationhood in France and Germany* (Cambridge, MA: Harvard University Press, 1992), 5. Paul Robert Magocsi maps the Germanic settlement, *Historical Atlas of Central Europe*, rev. ed. (Seattle: University of Washington Press, 2002), 105; Marek Zybura gives an overview, "Deutsche Migration nach Polen in vergangenen Jahrhunderten—wirtschaftliche, soziale und politische Auswirkungen in Polen" (lecture, Fachseminar, "Migration— Motor der europäischen Integration? Deutsche und polnische Erfahrungen in Geschichte und Gegenwart," Berlin, Germany, 28 Oct. 2011), 1–13, http://www.bpb.de/files/K4V8L8.pdf.
59. On the following, see Geoff Eley, "Empire, Ideology, and the East: Thoughts on Nazism's Spatial Imaginary," in *Heimat, Region and Empire: Spatial Identities under National Socialism*, ed. Claus-Christian W. Szejnmann and Maiken Umbach (Basingstoke: Palgrave Macmillan, 2012), 252–275.
60. Brubaker, *Citizenship and Nationhood*, 116–119.

61. Nancy R. Reagin, "German Brigadoon? Domesticity and Metropolitan Perceptions of Auslandsdeutschen in Southwest Africa and Eastern Europe," in *Heimat Abroad,* ed O'Donnell, Bridenthal, and Reagin, 248-255.
62. Jörg Hackmann, "Deutsche Ostforschung und Geschictswissenschaft," in *Deutsche Ostforschung und polnische Westforschung im Spannungsfeld von Wissenschaft und Politik. Disziplinen in Vergleich,* ed. Jan M. Piskorski, Hackmann, and Rudolf Jaworski (Osnabrück and Poznań: fibre Verlag, PTPN, 2002), 29-31.
63. Carsten Klingemann, "Ostforschung und Soziologie während des Nationalsozialismus," ibid., 163.
64. Michael Burleigh, *Germany Turns Eastwards: A Study of* Ostforschung *in the Third Reich* (Cambridge: Cambridge University Press, 1988), 29.
65. Michael Fahlbusch, "Deutsche Ostforschung und Geographie seit 1918," in *Deutsche Ostforschung,* ed. Piskorski, Hackmann, and Jaworski, 225-226.
66. Wilhelm Fielitz, "Deutsche Ostforschung und Volkskunde am Beispiel volkskundlicher Forschung in Wolhynien," ibid., 261, 270-271, 275-276.
67. Fahlbusch, "Deutsche Ostforschung," 226-228, 230.
68. Bronisław Kortus, "Der polnische Westgedanke und die Geographie," in *Deutsche Ostforschung,* ed. Piskorski, Hackmann, and Jaworski, 250; Werner Clever, *Germanen, Slawen und Deutsche in Ostmittel- und Osteuropa: (2. Jh. v. Chr.—16. Jh.): zur Darstellung ihrer Beziehungsgeschichte in Schulgeschichtsbüchern der nationalsozialistischen Zeit* (Dortmund: Forschungsstelle Ostmitteleuropa, 2000).
69. Quoted in Kossert, *Preußen,* 197.
70. Burleigh, *Germany Turns Eastwards,* 28, 31, 61, 138-139; Kamusella and Kacir, "Upper Silesia 1918-1945," 99; Fahlbusch, "Deutsche Ostforschung," 237.
71. Norbert Götz, "German-Speaking People and German Heritage: Nazi Germany and the Problem of Volksgemeinschaft," in *Heimat Abroad,* ed. O'Donnell, Bridenthal, and Reagin, 58-60, 62, 64-65; Reagin, "German Brigadoon?," 259. Howard Sargent notes that "competing biological and cultural definitions of Germanness continue to influence citizenship law," "Diasporic Citizens: Germans Abroad in the Framing of German Citizenship Law," ibid., 17.
72. Fielitz, "Deutsche Ostforschung und Volkskunde," 278-280.
73. Quoted in Hackmann, "Deutsche Ostforschung und Geschictswissenschaft," 42.
74. Marek Prawda, "Der polnische Westgedanke und die Soziologie," in *Deutsche Ostforschung,* ed. Piskorski, Hackmann, and Jaworski, 205.
75. Adam S. Labuda, "Polnische Kunstgeschichtsschreibung und die 'Wiedergewonnenen Gebiete,'" ibid., 141-142; Kortus, "Der polnische Westgedanke," 240.
76. Zofia Kurnatowska and Stanisław Kurnatowski, "Der Einfluss nationalistischer Ideen auf die mitteleuropäische Urgeschichtsforschung," in *Deutsche Ostforschung,* ed. Piskorski, Hackmann, and Jaworski, 98-99.
77. Kortus, "Der polnische Westgedanke," 241-242.
78. Ibid., 243-249.
79. Quoted in Peter Brock, "Florjan Cenôva and the Kashub Question," in *Folk Cultures and Little Peoples: Aspects of National Awakening in East Central Europe* (Boulder: East European Quarterly, 1992), 77, 102n37.

80. Tadeusz Lewaszkiewicz, "Der polnische Westgedanke und die Sprachwissenschaft," in *Deutsche Ostforschung,* ed. Piskorski, Hackmann, and Jaworski, 105–107; the quote in German translation is on 105.
81. Ibid., 108–109; the quote in German translation is on 109.
82. Strauchold, *Myśl zachodnia,* 15, 20, 22.
83. Kortus, "Der polnische Westgedanke," 253–255.
84. Grzegorz Strauchold, *Autochtoni, Polscy, Niemieccy, czy . . . od nacjonalizmu do komunizmu (1945-1949)* (Toruń: Wydawnictwo Adam Marszałek, 2001), 17, 17n34, 23–24; Wojciech Wrzesiński, *Polski ruch narodowy w Niemczech w latach 1922-1939,* 2nd rev. ed. (Wrocław: Zakład Narodowy imienia Ossolińskich—Wydawnictwo, 1993), 272.
85. Repr. in Strauchold, *Autochtoni,* 201–203.

2. The German Occupation of Poland

1. Geoffrey Roberts, "Research Note: Stalin, the Pact with Nazi Germany, and the Origins of Postwar Soviet Diplomatic Historiography," *Journal of Cold War Studies* 4, no. 4 (2002): 97. Those who call it a "nonaggression pact" inadvertently confirm the Nazi-Soviet claim to its pacific nature.
2. Raymond Sontag and James Stuart Beddie, eds., *Nazi-Soviet Relations, 1939-1941: documents from the Archives of the German Foreign Office as Released by the Dept. of State* (New York: Didier, 1948), 102–103; Włodzimerz Borodziej begins with this treaty, "Wstęp: sprawa polska i przemieszczenia ludności w czasie II wojny światowej," in *Niemcy,* ed. Borodziej and Hans Lemberg, vol. 1, *Władze i instytucje centralne. Województwo olsztyńskie,* ed. Borodziej and Claudia Kraft (Warsaw: Wydawnictwo NERITON, 2000), 37–105.
3. 351 Parl. Deb., H. C. (5th ser.) (1939) 1855.
4. Jochen Böhler, *Auftakt zum Vernichtungskrieg: die Wehrmacht in Polen 1939* (Frankfurt am Main: Fischer Taschenbuch Verlag, 2006).
5. Quoted in Edward B. Westermann, "Shaping the Police Soldier as an Instrument for Annihilation," in *The Impact of Nazism: New Perspectives on the Third Reich and Its Legacy,* ed. Alan E. Steinweis and Daniel E. Rogers (Lincoln: University of Nebraska Press, 2003), 139–140; Winfried Baumgart, "Zur Ansprache Hitlers vor den Führen der Wehrmacht am 22 August 1939," *Vierteljahrshefte für Zeitgeschichte* 16 (April 1968): 120–149.
6. Quoted in Michael Burleigh, *The Third Reich: A New History* (New York: Hill and Wang, 2000), 439, 434, respectively. For John Connelly Polish resistance, which blocked the German goal of *Lebensraum,* rather than racism explains the treatment of the Poles, "Nazis and Slavs: From Racial Theory to Racist Practice," *Central European History* 32, no. 1 (Winter 1999): 20–22
7. Quoted in Martin Broszat, *Nationalsozialistische Polenpolitik 1939-1945* (Frankfort: Fischer-Bucherei, 1965), 178n36. See also Czesław Łuczak, *Polska i Polacy w drugiej wojnie światowej* (Poznań: Uniwersytet im. Adama Mickiewicza w Poznaniu, 1993), 92.
8. "Gesetz über die Wiedervereinigung der Freien Stadt Danzig mit dem Deutschen Reich, 1.9.1939," in *Dokumente und Materialien zur ostmitteleuropäischen Geschichte,*

Themenmodul: "Deutsche Besatzungspolitik in Polen 1939–1945," ed. Markus Roth (Herder-Institut, 2012), http://www.herder-institut.de/resolve/qid/986.html; "Erlaß des Führers und Reichskanzlers über die Gliederung der Verwaltung der Ostgebiete," ibid.

9. Łuczak, *Polska i Polacy,* 93–95; maps following 96; Witold Sienkiewicz, Grzegorz Hryciuk, eds. *Wysiedlenia, wypędzenia i ucieczki 1939–1959: Atlas ziem Polski* (Warsaw: Demart, 2008), 24–25.
10. Michael Burleigh, *Germany Turns Eastwards: A Study of Ostforschung in the Third Reich* (Cambridge: Cambridge University Press, 1988), 158–159.
11. Stefan Wolff, *The German Question since 1919: An Analysis with Key Documents* (Westport, CT: Praeger, 2003), 47, 49; Valdis O. Lumans, "A Reassessment of *Volksdeutsche* and Jews in the Volhynia-Galicia-Narew Resettlement," in *Impact of Nazism,* ed. Steinweis and Rogers, 82–83; Michael Burleigh and Wolfgang Wipperman, *The Racial State: Germany 1933–1945* (Cambridge: Cambridge University Press, 1991), 306.
12. Doris L. Bergen, "The 'Volksdeutschen' of Eastern Europe, World War II, and the Holocaust: Constructed Ethnicity, Real Genocide," in *Germany and Eastern Europe: Cultural Identities and Cultural Differences,* ed. Keith Bullivant, Geoffrey Giles, and Walter Pape, *Yearbook of European Studies* 13 (Amsterdam: Rodopi, 1999), 70–71; Bergen, "The *Volksdeutsche* of Eastern Europe and the Collapse of the Nazi Empire, 1944–1945," in *Impact of Nazism,* ed. Steinweis and Rogers, 102–104.
13. "Reichstagsrede Adolf Hitlers," in "Deutsche Besatzungspolitik," ed. Roth, http://www.herder-institut.de/resolve/qid/997.html.
14. "Erlaß des Führers und Reichskanzlers zur Festigung deutschen Volkstums," ibid.
15. Quoted in Michael Thad Allen, "The Business of Genocide," in *Forced and Slave Labor in Nazi-Dominated Europe: Symposium Presentations* (Washington, DC: Center for Advanced Holocaust Studies, United States Holocaust Memorial Museum, 2004), 13.
16. Wolff, *German Question,* 12; Götz Aly, *"Final Solution": Nazi Population Policy and the Murder of the European Jews* (London: Arnold, 1999), 5, 19, 150; Czesław Łuczak, *Pod niemieckim jarzmem (Kraj Warty 1939–1945)* (Poznań: PSO Sp. z o.o., 1996), 71.
17. Lumans, "Reassessment," 82–83, 86–87; Łuczak, *Polska i Polacy,* 146.
18. Broszat, *Nationalsozialistische Polenpolitik,* 85–87.
19. At a secret meeting of Wartheland Nazi leaders, 20 Mar. 1943, quoted in Łuczak, *Pod niemieckim jarzmem,* 15.
20. Ibid., 15–16, 19–22, 33–39; Stanisław Jankowiak, "Niemcy w Wielkopolsce i na Ziemi Lubuskiej w latach 1945–1950," in *Niemcy,* ed. Włodzimierz Borodziej and Hans Lemberg, vol. 3, *Województwa poznańskie i szczecińskie,* ed. Jankowiak and Katrin Steffen (Warsaw: Wydawnictwo NERITON, 2001), 17–21.
21. Łuczak, *Pod niemieckim jarzmem,* 42–48; Lumans, "Reassessment," 94–96; Gerhard Wolf, *Ideologie und Herrschaftsrationalität: Nationalsozialistische Germanisierungspolitik in Polen* (Hamburg: Hamburger Edition HIS, 2012), 355–358.
22. Broszat, *Nationalsozialistische Polenpolitik,* 89–90; the quote is on 90.

23. Ibid., 89; Czesław Łuczak, ed., *Położenie ludności polskiej w tzw. Kraju Warty w okresie hiterowskiej okupacji. Wybór źródeł* (Poznań: Instytut Zachodni, 1990), 157–158; Łuczak, *Pod niemieckim jarzmem*, 56. Maria Rutowska states that 364,665 Wartheland Poles were deported to the *Generalgouvernement*, and another 109,548 were forced to move elsewhere within the incorporated territory from Dec.1939 to 15 Mar. 1941, *Wysiedlenia ludności polskiej z Kraju Warty do Generalnego Gubernatorstwa 1939–1941* (Poznań: Instytut Zachodni, 2003), 37.
24. Franciszek Kubiczek, ed., *Historia Polski w liczbach: ludność, terytorium* (Warsaw: Główny Urząd Statystyczny, 1993), 196.
25. Letter, 17 Mar. 1941, Łuczak, *Położenie*, 141–142; Stanisława Bartkiewicz, "U Niemców," in *Wysiedlenie i poniewierka, 1939–1945: Wspomnienia Polaków wysiedlonych przez okupanta hitlerowskiego z ziem Polskich "wcielonych" do Rzeszy*, ed. Ryszard Dyliński, Marian Flejsierowicz, Stanisław Kubiak (Poznań: Wydawnictwo Poznańskie, 1974), 52–60.
26. Quoted in Broszat, *Nationalsozialistische Polenpolitik*, 87–88.
27. R. M. Douglas, *Orderly and Humane: The Expulsion of the Germans after the Second World War* (New Haven: Yale University Press, 2012), 49–50, 53–54.
28. Stanisław Jankowiak, "Wojewodschaft Posen," in *Die Deutschen*, ed. Włodzimierz Borodziej and Hans Lemberg, vol. 3, *Wojewodschaft Posen. Wojewodschaft Stettin (Hinterpommern)*, ed. Jankowiak and Katrin Steffen (Marburg: Verlag Herder-Institut, 2004), 21; Wolf, *Ideologie*, 326.
29. *Die Nürnberger Gesetze vom 15. September 1935*, http://www.dhm.de/lemo/html/dokumente/nuernbergergesetze. Stanford University President David Starr Jordan's 1902 racial epistle "Blood of a Nation" originated the notion of the eugenics movement that blood was the carrier of human conditions, Edwin Black, "The Horrifying American Roots of Nazi Eugenics," *San Francisco Chronicle*, 25 Nov. 2003, repr. in *History News Network*, http://hnn.us/articles/1796.html.
30. Chad Bryant, "Either German or Czech: Fixing Nationality in Bohemia and Moravia, 1939–1946," *Slavic Review* 61, no. 4 (Winter 2002): 686–691; the quotes are on 690.
31. Wolf, *Ideologie*, 177–178.
32. Quoted in Aly, *Final Solution*, 100n3. On the Ruhr Poles, see John J. Kulczycki, *The Polish Coal Miners' Union and the German Labor Movement in the Ruhr, 1902–1934: National and Social Solidarity* (Oxford, New York: Berg, 1997).
33. Connelly, "Nazis and Slavs," 17.
34. Regina Mühlhäuser, "Between Extermination and Germanization: Children of German Men in the 'Occupied Eastern Territories,' 1942–1945," in *Children of World War II: The Hidden Enemy Legacy*, ed. Kjersti Ericsson and Eva Simonsen (Oxford: Berg Publishers, 2005), 175.
35. Quoted in Burleigh, *Third Reich*, 449, and in Aly, *Final Solution*, 88 and 89.
36. Carsten Klingemann, "Ostforschung und Soziologie während des Nationalsozialismus," in *Deutsche Ostforschung und polnische Westforschung im Spannungsfeld von Wissenschaft und Politik. Disziplinen in Vergleich*, ed. Jan M. Piskorski, Jörg Hackmann, and Rudolf Jaworski (Osnabrück and Poznań: fibre Verlag, PTPN, 2002), 201; Connelly, "Nazis and Slavs," 16, 33.

37. "Runderlaß des Reichsministers des Innern, betr.: Erwerb der deutschen Staatsangehörigkeit in den in das Deutsche Reich eingegliederten Ostgebieten," in "Deutsche Besatzungspolitik," ed. Roth, http://www.herder-institut.de/resolve/qid/999.html.
38. Wolf, *Ideologie*, 183–184, 188, 267–273; the quotes are on 271 (emphasis in original).
39. Ibid., 188–189, 277; the quotes are on 277.
40. Ibid., 189, 301, 305–306, 309, 313.
41. "Der Reichsführer SS, Erlaß für die Überprüfung und Aussonderung der Bevölkerung in den eingegliederten Ostgebieten," in "Deutsche Besatzungspolitik," ed. Roth, http://www.herder-institut.de/resolve/qid/1002.html.
42. Broszat, *Nationalsozialistische Polenpolitik*, 118–119; Bergen, "*Volksdeutsche* of Eastern Europe," 105; Wolf, *Ideologie*, 376–377.
43. Broszat, *Nationalsozialistische Polenpolitik*, 119; Wolf, *Ideologie*, 379–381; Himmler's decree, 9 Feb.1942, repr. in *Trials of War Criminals before the Nuernberg Military Tribunals under Control Council Law no. 10: Nuernberg Oct. 1946–April 1949*, 15 vols. (Washington, DC: U.S. Government Printing Office, 1949–1953), vol. 4, "*The Einsatzgruppen Case.*" "*The RuSHA Case*" (1950), 721–727. Roman numerals were used for DVL categories during and after the war.
44. Himmler, 9 Feb. 1942, repr. in *Trials*, 4:723.
45. Broszat, *Nationalsozialistische Polenpolitik*, 119; see also Burleigh, *Third Reich*, 449–450.
46. Wolf, *Ideologie*, 405–408; the quote is on 407.
47. Doris L. Bergen, "The Nazi Concept of 'Volksdeutsche' and the Exacerbation of Anti-Semitism in Eastern Europe, 1939–45," *Journal of Contemporary History* 29 (1994): 575.
48. Himmler, 16 Feb. 1942, repr. in *Trials*, 4:728–733; Stryjkowski, *Położenie*, 24–25, 33; Bergen, "*Volksdeutsche* of Eastern Europe," 104–105; Tomasz Kamusella and Petr Kacir, "Upper Silesia 1918–1945," in *The Politics of Ethnicity in Central Europe*, ed. Karl Cordell (New York: St. Martin's Press, 2000), 109, 130n5.
49. Himmler, 9 Feb. 1942, repr. in *Trials*, 4:724; Broszat, *Nationalsozialistische Polenpolitik*, 124; Wolf, *Ideologie*, 471; Leszek Olejnik, *Zdrajcy narodu? Losy Volksdeutschów w Polsce po II wojnie światowej* (Warsaw: Wydawnictwo Trio, 2006), 38.
50. Quoted in Jan Grabowski and Zbigniew R. Grabowski, "Germans in the Eyes of the Gestapo: The Ciechanów District," *Contemporary European History* 13, no. 1 (2004): 38.
51. Ryszard Kaczmarek, *Polacy w Wehrmachcie* (Cracow: Wydawnictwo Literackie, 210), 95, 97.
52. Bryant, "Either German or Czech," 691–696.
53. Wolf, *Ideologie*, 266; Broszat, *Nationalsozialistische Polenpolitik*, 120.
54. Wolf, *Ideologie*, 381–382, 488; Łuczak, *Pod niemieckim jarzmem*, 58.
55. Wolf, *Ideologie*, 170–176.
56. Ibid., 169–176, 275–277; the quotes are on 275 (emphasis in original); Jankowiak, "Niemcy w Wielkopolsce," 21; see also Broszat, *Nationalsozialistische Polenpolitik*, 115–116; Greiser's notes of 6 Sept. 1940 concerning Germanization, excerpt, Łuczak, *Położenie*, 171–173.

57. Łuczak, *Położenie*, 354–357, 358–361.
58. Wolf, *Ideologie*, 383–386.
59. Ibid., 409–410.
60. Reproductions, ibid., 186–187, 318–319.
61. Ibid., 473, 478; the quote is on 473. Stryjkowski states that 7.1 percent of 45,000 Poles in Wolsztyn County were found suitable for re-Germanization, *Położenie*, 26.
62. Report, 1 Nov. 1944, Łuczak, *Położenie*, 158–160.
63. Wolf, *Ideologie*, 475–477; Włodzimierz Borodziej and Hans Lemberg, eds., *Niemcy*, vol. 2, *Polska Centralna. Województwo śląskie*, ed. Ingo Eser and Jerzy Kochanowski (Warsaw: Wydawnictwo NERITON, 2000), 95n1; Stryjkowski, *Położenie*, 28. For a report, 12 Nov. 1943, of two Poles who refused the status, see Łuczak, *Położenie*, 370.
64. Łuczak, *Pod niemieckim jarzmem*, 61–60; Jankowiak, "Niemcy w Wielkopolsce," 21–22, 39; Stryjkowski, *Położenie*, 44.
65. Wolf, *Ideologie*, 165–166.
66. Reproductions, http://upload.wikimedia.org/wikipedia/commons/7/70/Fingerabdruck%2C_german_identity_card.JPG and http://pl.wikipedia.org/w/index.php?title=Plik:Fingerabdruck,_german_identity_card,_second_page.JPG&filetimestamp=20061226123329 (emphasis mine).
67. Kamusella and Kacir, "Upper Silesia," 106; Tomasz Kamusella, *Schlonzsko: Horní Slezsko, Oberschlesien, Górny Śląsk: Esej o regionie i jego mieszkańcach* (Elbląg: Elbląska Oficyna Wydawnicza, 2001), 51.
68. Łuczak, *Polska i Polacy*, 147; Ingo Eser, "Niemcy na Górnym Śląsku," in *Niemcy*, ed. Borodziej and Lemberg, 2:306–307.
69. Jerzy Myszor, *Stosunki Kościół—państwo okupacyjne w diecezji katowickiej 1939–1945* (Katowice: Księgania św. Jacka, 2010), 41, 46–47, 54, 55n161 41; Myszor, "Adamski Stanisław," in *Słownik biograficzny katolickiego duchowienstwa Ślaskiego XIX i XX wieku*, ed. Mieczysław Pater (Katowice: Księgarnia św.Jacka, 1996), 10. Andrzej Grajewski cites the Curia recommending registration as Germans on 15 May 1940, *Wygnanie. Diecezja katowicka w czasach stalinowskich*, 3rd rev. ed. (Katowice: Księgarnia św. Jacka; Gość niedzielny, 2002), 34–35; Wolf does not mention Adamski in connection with the "palcówka," *Ideologie*, 278.
70. Wolf, *Ideologie*, 279–280.
71. Ibid., 280–281; the quote is on 281.
72. Kaczmarek, *Polacy w Wehrmachcie*, 301–307, 360–361.
73. Wolf, *Ideologie*, 281–284, the quotes are on 281.
74. Broszat, *Nationalsozialistische Polenpolitik*, 121, 123, 198n32; Wolf, *Ideologie*, 387–388.
75. Wolf, *Ideologie*, 411, 456–457; the quotes are on 411, 457; Kaczmarek, *Polacy w Wehrmachcie*, 98; Łuczak, *Polska i Polacy*, 148.
76. Wolf, *Ideologie*, 460–461.
77. Łuczak, *Polska i Polacy*, 148; Wolf, *Ideologie*, 389–392.
78. Stryjkowski, *Położenie*, 72–75.
79. Quoted in Grajewski, *Wygnanie*, 35. See also Kazimierz Popiołek, *Historia Śląska od pradziejów do 1945 roku* (Katowice: Wydawnictwo "Śląsk," 1972), 484.
80. Myszor, *Stosunki Kościół*, 48, 51–52; the quote is on 51.

81. Ibid., 51.
82. Bernadetta Nitschke reports as fact that Adamski consulted with Sikorski through his representatives, *Wysiedlenie ludności niemieckiej z Polski w latach 1945-1949* (Zielona Góra: Wyższa Szkoła Pedagogiczna im. Tadeusza Kotarbińskiego, 1999), 114-115; the quote is on 115.
83. Myszor, *Stosunki Kościoł*, 52-53; the quote is on 53.
84. Olejnik, *Zdrajcy narodu?*, 31; Eser, "Niemcy," 307-308.
85. Borodziej and Lemberg, *Niemcy,* 3:146n8; Kaczmarek, *Polacy w Wehrmachcie*, 73-77.
86. The prewar leader of Polish Silesia Wojciech Korfanty assessed the national indifference of its inhabitants at about 30 percent; in the first months of the war, Himmler at 36 percent, Łuczak, *Polska i Polacy,* 147.
87. Quoted in Stryjkowski, *Położenie,* 157n267.
88. Quoted in Wolf, *Ideologie,* 166-167 (emphasis in original).
89. Ibid., 284-286; the quote is on 285.
90. Ibid., 329-331, 449; the quotes are on 329, 331.
91. Ibid., 332, 336-338.
92. Ibid., 393-395, 402.
93. Quoted ibid., 396
94. Ibid., 414-416, 420-421.
95. Quoted in Douglas, *Orderly and Humane,* 59.
96. Quoted in Nitschke, *Wysiedlenie,* 113 (emphasis in original).
97. Kaczmarek, *Polacy w Wehrmachcie,* 58-59.
98. Olejnik, *Zdrajcy narodu?,* 38; Broszat, *Nationalsozialistische Polenpolitik,* 39, 55; Łuczak, *Polska i Polacy,* 153-154.
99. Andreas Kossert, *Preußen, Deutsche oder Polen?: die Masuren im Spannungsfeld des ethnischen Nationalismus 1870-1956* (Wiesbaden: Harrassowitz Verlag, 2001), 289-290, 295-296, 296n30.
100. Ibid., 290-292; the quote is on 291.
101. Quoted in Andrzej Sakson, *Mazurzy—społeczność pogranicza* (Poznań: Instytut Zachodni, 1990), 58.
102. Kossert, *Preußen,* 293, 298-299.
103. Olejnik, *Zdrajcy narodu?,* 27. Łuczak estimates that it included 1.9 million "Poles" from the incorporated lands, *Polska i Polacy,* 160.
104. Stryjkowski, *Położenie,* 32.
105. Quoted in Jerzy Kochanowski, "Kto ty jesteś? Niemiec mały!," *Polityka,* no. 36 (6 May 2003), http://archiwum.polityka.pl/art/kto-ty-jestes-niemiec-maly,380566.html.
106. Stryjkowski, *Położenie,* 50-52; the quote is on 50.
107. Ibid., 50, 52-54; the quote is on 50.
108. Jerzy Kochanowski, "Losy Niemców w Polsce Centralnej w latach 1945-1950. Na przykładzie województw łódzkiego, warszawskiego i krakowskiego (powiat Biała)," in *Niemcy,* ed. Borodziej and Lemberg, 2:24-25, 35; the quote is in Klingemann, "Ostforschung," 202. Olejnik cites estimates as high as 150,000, *Zdrajcy narodu?,* 45-47.
109. Stanisław Drygas, *Czas zaprzeszły. Wspomnienia 1890-1944* (Warsaw: Czytelnik, 1970), 443-446.

110. Quoted in Edmund Dmitrów, *Niemcy i okupacja hitlerowska w oczach Polaków. Poglądy i opinie z lat 1945–1948* (Warsaw: Czytelnik, 1987), 148.
111. Kochanowski, "Losy Niemców," 18–19, 19n32; East German scholars accepted the accusation, e.g., Felix Heinrich Gentzen, "Rola niemieckiego Związku Marchii Wschodnich (Ostmarkenverein) w tworzeniu V kolumny niemieckiego imperializmu w Polsce i przygotowaniu II wojny Światowej," *Przegląd Zachodni* 15, no. 3 (May–June 1959): 56–75. Christian Raitz von Frentz disputes it without referring to Polish sources, *A Lesson Forgotten: Minority Protection under the League of Nations. The Case of the German Minority in Poland, 1920–1934* (New York: St. Martin's Press, 1999), 251–254. For a recent study, see Grzegorz Bębnik, ed., *Koniec pokoju, początek wojny. Niemieckie działania dywersyjne w kampanii polskiej 1939 r. Wybrane aspekty* (Katowice: Instytut Pamięci Narodowej, 2011).
112. Burleigh, *Germany Turns Eastwards*, 181–182; Doris L. Bergen, "Instrumentalization of Volksdeutschen in German Propaganda in 1939: Replacing/Erasing Poles, Jews, and Other Victims," *German Studies Review* 31, no. 3 (2008): 455–457, 461; Douglas, *Orderly and Humane*, 45; Halik Kochanski, *The Eagle Unbowed: Poland and the Poles in the Second World War* (Cambridge, MA: Harvard University Press, 2012), 69–70, 76. On the controversy over "Bloody Sunday," see Markus Krzoska, "Der 'Bromberger Blutsonntag' 1939. Kontroversen und Forschungsergebnisse," *Vierteljahrshefte für Zeitgeschichte* 60, no. 2 (2012): 237–248.
113. Kaczmarek, *Polacy w Wehrmachcie*, 99; Douglas, *Orderly and Humane*, 45.
114. Bergen, "Instrumentalization of Volksdeutschen," 448.
115. Michael Mann, *The Dark Side of Democracy: Explaining Ethnic Cleansing* (Cambridge: Cambridge University Press, 2005), 223–228.
116. Ingo Eser and Witold Stankowski, "Wojewodschaften Pommerellen und Danzig (Westpreussen)," in *Die Deutschen*, ed. Włodzimierz Borodziej and Hans Lemberg, vol. 4, *Wojewodschaften Pommerellen und Danzig (Westpreussen). Wojewodschaft Breslau (Niederschlesien)*, ed. Eser, Stankowski, Claudia Kraft, and Stanisław Jankowiak (Marburg: Verlag Herder-Institut, 2004), 27–30, 30n141; Thomas Urban, *Deutsche in Polen: Geschichte und Gegenwart einer Minderheit* (Munich: Verlag C. H. Beck, 1993), 22; Borodziej, "Wstęp," 41.
117. Grabowski and. Grabowski, "Germans in the Eyes of the Gestapo," 31.
118. Doris L. Bergen, "*Volksdeutsche* of Eastern Europe," 104–106.
119. Wolf, *Ideologie*, 472.
120. Broszat, *Nationalsozialistische Polenpolitik*, 126; Kaczmarek, *Polacy w Wehrmachcie*, 301; Stryjkowski, *Położenie*, 31. The British and the Polish government-in-exile encouraged desertion and enlistment in forces fighting the Germans, Kochanski, *Eagle Unbowed*, 230, 273, 475, 558.
121. Stryjkowski, *Położenie*, 582.
122. Kaczmarek, *Polacy w Wehrmachcie*, 173–177, 317.
123. Ibid., 9, 11, 16, 299–300.
124. Quoted in Wojciech Wrzesiński, "Naród niemiecki w polskiej myśli politycznej lat II wojny światowej, in *Polska—Polacy—mniejszości narodowe* (Wrocław: Zakład Narodowy imienia Ossolińskich—Wydawnictwo, 1992), 100.
125. Kazimierz Przybysz, ed., *Wizje Polski: Programy polityczne lat wojny i okupacji 1939–1944* (Warsaw: Dom Wydawniczy i Handlowy "ELIPSA," 1992), 268.

126. Stryjkowski, *Położenie*, 68–72; Łuczak, *Polska i Polacy*, 152–153
127. Stryjkowski, *Położenie*, 78–81. Agnieszka Haska found little discussion of the DVL in the underground press, "Discourse of Treason in Occupied Poland," *East European Politics & Societies* 25, no. 3 (2011), 535.
128. Stryjkowski, *Położenie*, 82–87; the quotes are on 86–87.
129. Repr. ibid., 93–95.
130. Borodziej and Lemberg, *Niemcy*, 1: 109–110.
131. Quoted in Piotr Madajczyk, *Niemcy polscy: 1944–1989* (Warsaw: Oficyna Naukowa, 2001), 17.
132. Quoted in Piotr Madajczyk, *Przyłączenie Śląska Opolskiego do Polski, 1945–1948* (Warsaw: Instytut Studiów Politycznych PAN, 1996), 240. See *Dziennik Ustaw Rzeczypospolitej Polskiej* (hereafter cited as DzURP), no. 4, Entry 16, 1944, http://dziennikustaw.gov.pl/DU/1944/s/4/16.
133. Łuczak, *Polska i Polacy*, 145–146. About a third of all inhabitants of Nazi-occupied Poland were at some point forced from their homes, Philipp Ther, "A Century of Forced Migration: the Origins and Consequences of 'Ethnic Cleansing,'" in *Redrawing Nations: Ethnic Cleansing in East-Central Europe, 1944–1948*, ed. Ther and Ana Siljak (Lanham, MD: Rowman & Littlefield Publishers, Inc., 2001), 66n33; Krystyna Kersten estimates that nearly half the population of postwar Poland was more or less radically and permanently torn from its environment during the war, "Nowy model terytorialny Polski a kształtowanie postaw ludności w pierwszych latach władzy ludowej (1944–1948)," *Dzieje Najnowsze* 6, no. 2 (1974): 26; Jan T. Gross states that the Germans deported 2.5 million, *Revolution from Abroad: The Soviet Conquest of Poland's Western Ukraine and Western Belorussia*, rev. ed. (Princeton: Princeton University Press, 2002), 228.
134. Paul Robert Magocsi, *Historical Atlas of Central Europe*, rev. ed. (Seattle: University of Washington Press, 2002), 193.

3. The Creation of a New Poland

1. Edmund Dmitrów, *Niemcy i okupacja hitlerowska w oczach Polaków. Poglądy i opinie z lat 1945–1948* (Warsaw: Czytelnik, 1987), 279.
2. Detlef Brandes, *Großbritannien und seine osteuropäischen Alliierten 1939–1943: die Regierungen Polens, der Tschechoslowakei und Jugoslawiens im Londoner Exil vom Kriegsausbruch bis zur Konferenz von Teheran* (Munich: R. Olderbourg Verlag, 1988), 61–62; Bronisław Pasierb, "Polskie i alianckie koncepcje granicy zachodniej RP w latach 1939–1945: Element bezpieczeństwa Europy czy rekompensata?," in *Przełomy w historii: XVI Powszechny Zjazd Historyków Polskich; Wrocław 15—18 września 1999 roku*, ed. Krzysztof Ruchniewicz, Jakub Tyszkiewicz, and Wojciech Wrzesiński, Pamiętnik II, pt. 2: 336–337.
3. Brandes, *Großbritannien*, 107.
4. Detlef Brandes, *Der Weg zur Vertreibung 1938–1945: Pläne und Entscheidunger zum "Transfer" der Deutschen aus der Tschechoslowakei und aus Polen* (Munich: R. Oldenbourg Verlag, 2001), 419–420.
5. Quoted ibid., 103, 159. Eduard Beneš also cites the German precedent, "The Organization of Postwar Europe," *Foreign Affairs* 20, no. 2 (Jan. 1942): 237–238.

6. 114 Parl. Deb., H. L. (5th ser.) (1939) 1565. On the advice of the president of a group of Russian émigrés, the Supreme Council of the Allied powers in December 1919 drew a provisional Polish-Soviet border based on the prewar administrative division between the Russian-ruled Kingdom of Poland and the rest of the Russia. The 1921 Treaty of Riga gave Poland considerable territory east of the line, but most of the territory Russia gained in the partitioning of Poland remained under Soviet control as did a large Polish ethnic minority. Nevertheless, the so-called Curzon Line gained acceptance as a supposedly legitimate "ethnographic" boundary, Piotr S. Wandycz, "The Polish Question," in *The Treaty of Versailles: A Reassessment after 75 Years*, ed. Manfred F. Boemeke, Gerald D. Feldman, and Elisabeth Glaser (Washington, DC.: German Historical Institute and Cambridge University Press, 1998), 330–332. On the acceptance of the Line, see Sarah Meiklejohn Terry, *Poland's Place in Europe: General Sikorski and the Origin of the Oder-Neisse Line, 1939–1945* (Princeton: Princeton University Press, 1983), 282.
7. *Foreign Relations of the United States. Diplomatic Papers* (hereafter cited as FRUS), *1939*, vol. 1, *General* (Washington, DC: U.S. Government Printing Office, 1956), 492–493.
8. Piotr S. Wandycz, *The United States and Poland* (Cambridge, MA: Harvard University Press, 1980), 247, 252.
9. Quoted in Włodzimierz T. Kowalski, *Walka dyplomatyczna o miejsce Polski w Europie (1939–1945)*, 2nd rev. ed. (Warsaw: Książka i Wiedza, 1967), 67.
10. General Sikorski Historical Institute, *Documents on Polish-Soviet Relations 1939–1945* (hereafter cited as DPSR), vol. 1, *1939–1943* (London: Heinemann, 1961), 116, 141–142.
11. James MacGregor Burns, *Roosevelt: The Soldier of Freedom* (New York: Harcourt Brace Jovanovich, Inc., 1970), 128–131, 185; quote is on 130.
12. Brandes, *Weg*, 106.
13. Quoted in A. F. Noskova, "Migration of the Germans after the Second World War: Political and Psychological Aspects," in *Forced Migration in Central and Eastern Europe, 1939–1950*, ed. Alfred J. Rieber (London: FRANK CASS, 2000), 98.
14. Brandes, *Weg*, 423.
15. Quoted in Terry, *Poland's Place*, 128.
16. DPSR, 1:264–265.
17. Brandes, *Weg*, 402.
18. Brandes, *Großbritannien*, 406; Brandes, *Weg*, 215–217.
19. Memorandum, FRUS, *1943*, vol. 3, *The British Commonwealth, Eastern Europe, the Far East* (Washington, DC: U.S. Government Printing Office, 1963), 15.
20. Jan Rychlík, Thomas D. Marzik, and Miroslav Bielik, eds., *R. W. Seton-Watson and His Relations with the Czechs and Slovaks: documents/dokumenty, 1906–1951* (Prague: Ústav T. G. Masaryka; Martin: Matica Slovenská, 1995), 622. R. M. Douglas regards Beneš as the prime mover of the expulsion, *Orderly and Humane: the Expulsion of the Germans after the Second World War* (New Haven: Yale University Press, 2012), 16–38.
21. Philipp Ther, "A Century of Forced Migration: The Origins and Consequences of 'Ethnic Cleansing,'" in *Redrawing Nations: Ethnic Cleansing in East-Central Europe, 1944–1948*, ed. Ther and Ana Siljak (Lanham, MD: Rowman & Littlefield

Publishers, Inc., 2001), 53; Jerzy Lukowski, *The Partitions of Poland: 1772, 1793, 1795* (London: Longman, 1999), 15.
22. Quoted in Douglas, *Orderly and Humane,* 32–33.
23. DPSR, 1:523–534, 606; Christian Lowe, "War-Time Allies Hushed Up Katyn Massacre of Poles: documents," 11 Sept. 2012, http://www.reuters.com/article/2012/09/11/us-usa-poland-katyn-idUSBRE88A0O020120911.
24. Kowalski, *Walka dyplomatyczna,* 262.
25. DPSR, vol. 2, *1943–45* (London: Heinemann, 1967), 49, 63; the quote is on 63.
26. FRUS, *The Conferences at Cairo and Tehran 1943* (Washington, DC: U.S. Government Printing Office, 1961), 512; Winston S. Churchill, *The Second World War,* vol. 5, *Closing the Ring* (Boston: Houghton Mifflin, 1951), 361–362.
27. FRUS, *Tehran,* 594.
28. Quoted in Wandycz, *United States and Poland,* 276.
29. Michael Charlton exemplifies this view, *Footsteps from the Finland Station: Five Landmarks in the Collapse of Communism* (New Brunswick, NJ: Transaction Publishers, 1992), 82.
30. Yuri Slezkine, "The USSR as a Communal Apartment, or How a Socialist State Promoted Ethnic Particularism," *Slavic Review* 53 (Summer 1994): 416.
31. Francine Hirsch, "Toward an Empire of Nations: Border-Making and the Formation of Soviet National Identities," *Russian Review* 59 (Apr. 2002): 202–204; Terry Martin, "The Origins of Soviet Ethnic Cleansing," *The Journal of Modern History* 70 (Dec. 1998): 826.
32. Terry Martin, *The Affirmative Action Empire: Nations and Nationalism in the Soviet Union, 1923–1939* (Ithaca: Cornell University Press, 2001), 442–451, 461.
33. Francine Hirsch, "The Soviet Union as a Work-in-Progress: Ethnographers and the Category *Nationality* in the 1926, 1937, and 1939 Censuses," *Slavic Review* 56 (Summer 1997): 258n22.
34. Francine Hirsch, "Race without the Practice of Racial Politics," *Slavic Review* 61 (Spring 2002): 38–39.
35. Slezkine, "USSR as a Communal Apartment," 444.
36. Rasma Karklins, *Ethnic Relations in the USSR: The Perspective from Below* (Boston: Unwin Hyman, 1986), 43.
37. Timothy Snyder, *Bloodlands: Europe between Hitler and Stalin* (New York: Basic Books, 2010), 89, 96–99, 103–104, 109.
38. Quoted in Michał Gnatowski, "Radziecka polityka na ziemiach północno-wshodnich Rzeczypospolitej (wrzesień-grudzień 1939 r.)," *Dzieje Najnowsze* 29 (1997): 34.
39. Telegram, German ambassador to the German Ministry for Foreign Affairs, DPSR, 1:51
40. Bernard Linek and Karl Martin Born, "Polish and Czech Silesia under Communist Rule: A Comparison," in *The Politics of Ethnicity in Central Europe,* ed. Karl Cordell (London: Macmillan Press; New York: St. Martin's Press, 2000), 136.
41. Henryk Cimek, *Komuniści, Polska, Stalin, 1918–1939* (Białystok: Krajowa Agencja Wydawnicza, 1990), 8–12, 14–18.
42. Jan B. de Weydenthal, *The Communists of Poland: an Historical Outline,* rev. ed. (Stanford: Hoover Institution Press, 1986), 26; R. V. Burks estimates that in 1931

about half the party's members were Jewish, *The Dynamics of Communism in Eastern Europe* (Princeton: Princeton University Press, 1961), 160.
43. Cimek, *Komuniści*, 67, 71–77, 80. Until 1935 the Czechoslovak Communist Party similarly advocated national self-determination for minorities, Douglas, *Orderly and Humane*, 26–27.
44. Jan Jachymek and Waldemar Paruch, *More than Independence: Polish Political Thought 1918–1939* (Lublin: Maria Curie-Skłodowska University Press, 2003), 328.
45. Cimek, *Komuniści*, 90, 95, 98–99, 101–103, 108–111.
46. Snyder, *Bloodlands*, 90, 94.
47. Cimek, *Komuniści*, 112–116, 123, 130; the quote is on 130.
48. Krystyna Kersten, "Polska—państwo narodowe. Dylematy i rzeczywistość," in *Narody. Jak powstawały i jak wybijały się na niepodległość*, ed. Marcin Kula (Warsaw: Państwowe Wydawnictwo Naukowe, 1989), 473.
49. Alfred Lampe, "Zagadnienie," repr. in *Zeszyty Historyczne* 26 (1973), 195–200 (emphasis in original); Piotr Wandycz dates it to 1942, "Przystanki do niepodległości: bilans, strat i dokonań," in *Do niepodległości 1918, 1944 / 45, 1989: wizje, drogi, spełnienie*, ed. Wojciech Wrzesiński (Warsaw: Wydawnictwo Sejmowe, 1998), 321.
50. In Polish *nacjonalizm* is defined as a negative version of an otherwise positive national ideology, Adam Łopatka et al., eds., *Słownik wiedzy obywatelskiej* (Warsaw: Państwowe Wydawnictwo Naukowe, 1970), 259–260.
51. Quoted in Mirosław Dymarski, *Ziemie postulowane (ziemie nowe) w prognozach i działaniach polskiego ruchu oporu 1939–1945* (Wrocław: Wydawnictwo Uniwersytetu Wrocławskiego, 1997), 111.
52. Quoted ibid., 112.
53. Krystyna Kersten, "The Polish-Ukrainian Conflict under Communist Rule," *Acta Poloniae Historica* 73 (1996): 139.
54. Kazimierz Przybysz, ed., *Wizje Polski: Programy polityczne lat wojny i okupacji 1939–1944* (Warsaw: Dom Wydawniczy i Handlowy "ELIPSA," 1992), 228–229.
55. Ibid., 268, 292, 318.
56. Jan Czerniakiewicz, *Repatriacja ludności polskiej z ZSRR 1944–1948* (Warsaw: Państwowe Wydawnictwo Naukowe, 1987), 179.
57. Quoted in Mieczysław Jaworski, *Na Piastowskim szlaku. Działalność Ministerstwa Ziem Odzyskanych w latach 1945–1948* (Warsaw: Wydawnictwo Ministerstwa Obrony Narodowej, 1973), 41.
58. DPSR, 2: 132–133; the quotes are on 133; FRUS, *1944*, vol. 3, *The British Commonwealth and Europe* (Washington, DC: U.S. Government Printing Office, 1965), 1218–1220.
59. DPSR, 2:169, 182, 186.
60. Stanisław Grabski, *Pamiętniki*, vol. 2 (Warsaw: Czytelnik, 1989), 463–468; see also DPSR, 2:754.
61. Antony Polonsky and Bolesław Drukier, eds., *The Beginnings of Communist Rule in Poland* (Boston: Routledge & Kegan Paul, 1980), 20–21.
62. Ibid., 21–23.
63. Wiesław Skrzydło, ed., *Manifest Polskiego Komitetu Wyzwolenia Narodwego* (Lublin: Wydawnictwo Lubelskie, 1984), 41–43

64. Eugeniusz Misiło, ed., *Repatriacja czy deportacja: Przesiedlenie Ukraińców z Polski do USSR 1944–1946*, vol. 1, *Dokumenty 1944–1945* (Warsaw: Oficyna Wydawnicza "Archiwum Ukraińskie," 1996), 17–18.
65. DPSR, 2:316–318; the quote is on 318.
66. Ibid., 405–415.
67. Quoted in Michael Fleming, *Communism, Nationalism and Ethnicity, 1944–50* (London: Routledge, 2010), 29–30.
68. Brandes, *Weg*, 361–363; the quote is on 361.
69. DPSR, 2: 437, 455, 468–469, 471, 476, 478.
70. Quoted in Krystyna Kersten, *Narodziny systemu władzy, Polska 1943–1948* (Poznań: SAWW, 1990), 104.
71. Grabski, *Pamiętniki*, 2:476
72. George F. Kennan, *Memoirs: 1925–1950* (Boston: Little, Brown and Company, 1967), 213–214; the quote is on 214.
73. Brandes, *Weg*, 366, 368–370.
74. FRUS, *The Conferences at Malta and Yalta 1945* (Washington, DC: U.S. Government Printing Office, 1955), 233, 230, 510.
75. Ibid., 974
76. DPSR, 2:521, 533.
77. 408 Parl. Deb., H. C. (5th ser.) (1945) 1267, 1278–1279.
78. Quoted in Winston S. Churchill, *The Second World War*, vol. 6, *Triumph and Tragedy* (Boston: Houghton Mifflin, 1953), 489.
79. See the communiqué, DPSR, 2:616–618.
80. FRUS, *The Conference of Berlin (The Potsdam Conference)*, 2 vols. (Washington, DC: U.S. Government Printing Office, 1960), 1:757–777; the quotes are on 758, 760.
81. Ibid., 761. A Piast prince invited the Teutonic Knights into the area to assist in repelling the attacks of the pagan Prussians, a Baltic, not a Slavic, people.
82. Ibid., 762. There is no mention of the key role of Catherine the Great in the partitioning of Poland.
83. Ibid., 762, 766.
84. Ibid., 2:208–213, 216–221.
85. Brandes, *Weg*, 408–409.
86. FRUS, *Berlin*, 2:1140–1141.
87. Ibid., 357, 480, 1151. Grabski credited Stalin and Molotov with Poland receiving "fully that what we sought," repr. in Stanisław Kirkor, "Listy Stanisława Grabskiego (1941–1949)," *Zeszyty Historyczne* 19 (1971): 70.
88. Stanisław Jankowiak, "Terminologia w stosunkach polsko-niemieckich," *Sprawy Narodowościowe* 6, no. 2 (1997): 286–290; Jankowiak, "'Cleansing' Poland of Germans: The Province of Pomerania, 1945–1949," in *Redrawing Nations*, Ther and Siljak, 87.
89. Krystyna Kersten, "Przymusowe przemieszczenia ludności—próba typologii," in *Utracona ojczyzna: Przymusowe wysiedlenia, deportacje i przesiedlenia jako wspólne doświadczenie*, ed. Hubert Orłowski and Andrzej Sakson (Poznań: Instytut Zachodni, 1997), 21–22.
90. Anthony H. Richmond, "Sociological Theories of International Migration: The Case of Refugees," *Current Sociology* 36, no. 2 (1988): 17, 21; Rogers Brubaker

expresses a similar view: "Yet the centrality of war and, more generally, violence does not mean that postimperial ethnic unmixing can be neatly subsumed under the rubric of 'forced migration.' That rubric is in fact too narrow and misleading." *Nationalism Reframed: Nationhood and the National Question in the New Europe* (Cambridge: Cambridge University Press, 1996), 168.

91. Gerard Labuda, "Geneza przysłowia: 'Jak świat światem, nie będzie Niemiec Polakowi bratem,'" *Historia* 8 (1968): 17–32; Beata Katarzyna Cholewa, "The Migration of Germans from Lower Silesia after World War II," *Polish Western Affairs* 31, nos. 1–2 (1990): 54.

92. Philipp Ther, *Deutsche und polnische Vertriebene: Gesellschaft und Vertriebenenpolitik in der SBZ/DDR und in Polen 1945–1956* (Göttingen: Vandenhoeck & Ruprecht, 1998), 33–35; Piotr Madajczyk, *Przyłączenie Śląska Opolskiego do Polski, 1945–1948* (Warsaw: Instytut Studiów Politycznych PAN, 1996), 9, 42; Krystyna Kersten, "Nowy model terytorialny Polski a kształtowanie postaw ludności w pierwszych latach władzy ludowej (1944–1948)," *Dzieje Najnowsze* 6, no. 2 (1974): 26.

93. Fleming, *Communism*, 82.

94. Tony Judt, *Postwar: A History of Europe since 1945* (New York: Penguin Press, 2005), 41–42.

95. Krzysztof Stryjkowski, *Położenie osób wpisanych w Wielkopolsce na niemiecką listę narodowościową w latach 1945–1950* (Poznań: Instytut Historii UAM, 2004), 116.

96. Excerpt, Włodzimierz Borodziej and Hans Lemberg, eds., *Niemcy*, vol. 2, *Polska Centralna. Województwo śląskie*, ed. Ingo Eser and Jerzy Kochanowski (Warsaw: Wydawnictwo NERITON, 2000), 209–213; Jerzy Kochanowski, "Losy Niemców w Polsce Centralnej w latach 1945–1950. Na przykładzie województw łódzkiego, warszawskiego i krakowskiego (powiat Biała)," ibid., 39–41.

97. Doris L. Bergen, "The *Volksdeutsche* of Eastern Europe and the Collapse of the Nazi Empire, 1944–1945," in *The Impact of Nazism: New Perspectives on the Third Reich and Its Legacy*, ed. Alan E. Steinweis and Daniel E. Rogers (Lincoln: University of Nebraska Press, 2003), 117.

98. Krzysztof Kosiński, Marcin Kula, Paweł Sowiński, "Trzy pokolenia," in *Polska-Niemcy-Europa: Księga Jubileuszowa z okazji siedemdziesiątej rocznicy urodzin Profesora Jerzego Holzera*, ed. Katarzyna Karaskiewicz (Warsaw: Oficyna Wydawnicza RYTM, 2000), 292.

99. Włodzimierz Borodziej and Hans Lemberg, eds., *Niemcy*, vol. 3, *Województwa poznańskie i szczecińskie*, ed. Stanisław Jankowiak and Steffen (Warsaw: Wydawnictwo NERITON, 2001), 63–64n1–2.

4. The Recovered Lands and Their Inhabitants

1. Marcin Kula questions all such uses of history, including that of the Piast dynasty, *Krótki raport o użytkowaniu historii* (Warsaw: Wydawnictwo Naukowe PWN, 2004), 384–385; Irena Grzesiuk-Olszewska, *Polska rzeźba pomnikowa w latach 1945–1995* (Warsaw: Wydawnictwo NERITON, 1995), 35–36.
2. A young Polish historian at the International Congress of Historical Sciences,

Montreal, 1995, admitted that he used the term as a matter of habit without being conscious of its political implications.

3. Henryk Samsonowicz, "W garderobie teatru historii," *Gazeta Wyborcza* (*Świąteczna*), 30 Dec. 2005, http://wyborcza.pl/1,75248,3090583.html. Wojciech Roszkowski calls the Polishness of the Recovered Lands a myth, *Do horyzontu i z powrotem: eseje o historii i współczesności* (Cracow: Wydawnictwo ZNAK, 2000), 52–53; Antoni Furdal sees it as factual: "Without doubt the greatest event of our history a thousand years ago was the integration of Slavic tribes on the Oder, Warta, and Vistula in one ethnic conglomerate." *Polska oda do radości: język i kultura narodowa we wspólnej Europie* (Wrocław: Zakład Narodowy imienia Ossolińskich—Wydawnictwo, 2000), 51; Władysław Czapliński and Tadeusz Ładogórski, eds., identify Piast Poland with contemporary Poland cartographically, *The Historical Atlas of Poland* (Warsaw: Państwowe Przedsiębiorstwo Wydawnictw Kartograficznych, 1986), 54.

4. Piotr Madajczyk, "Experience and Memory: The Second World War in Poland," in *Experience and Memory: The Second World War in Europe*, ed. Jörg Echternkamp and Stefan Martens (New York: Berghahn Books, 2010), 72.

5. Katrin Steffen, "Ucieczka, wypędzenie i przymusowe wysiedlenie Niemców z województwa szczecińskiego w latach 1945–1950," in *Niemcy*, ed. Włodzimierz Borodziej and Hans Lemberg, vol. 3, *Województwa poznańskie i szczecińskie*, ed. Stanisław Jankowiak and Steffen (Warsaw: Wydawnictwo NERITON, 2001), 203. On administrative divisions, see Aleksander Kochański, *Polska 1944–1991. Informator historyczny*, vol. 1 (Warsaw: Wydawnictwo Sejmowe, 1996), 8–15.

6. Ingo Eser, "Pomorze Gdańskie do wybuchu I wojny światowej," in *Niemcy*, ed. Daniel Boćkowski, vol. 4, *Pomorze Gdańskie i Dolny Śląsk*, ed. Eser, Witold Stankowski, Claudia Kraft, and Stanisław Jankowiak (Warsaw: Wydawnictwo NERITON, 2001), 9, 9n21, 11.

7. Claudia Kraft, "Wojewodschaft Allenstein," in *Die Deutschen*, ed. Włodzimierz Borodziej and Hans Lemberg, vol. 1, *Zentrale Behörden. Wojewodschaft Allenstein*, ed. Borodziej and Kraft (Marburg: Verlag Herder-Institut, 2000), 434n2, 448, 448n44.

8. Jörg Hackmann, Rudolf Jaworski, Jan M. Piskorski, "Vorwort," in *Deutsche Ostforschung und polnische Westforschung im Spannungsfeld von Wissenschaft und Politik. Disziplinen in Vergleich*, ed. Piskorski, Hackmann, and Jaworski (Osnabrück and Poznań: fibre Verlag, PTPN, 2002), 7.

9. Rudolf Jaworski, "Deutsche Ostforschung und polnische Westforschung in ihren historisch-politischen Bezügen," ibid., 15, 17; Zofia Kurnatowska and Stanisław Kurnatowski, "Der Einfluss nationalistischer Ideen auf die mitteleuropäische Urgeschichtsforschung," ibid., 99–100.

10. Jaworski, "Deutsche Ostforschung," 17–18.

11. Excerpt repr. in Grzegorz Strauchold, *Autochtoni, Polscy, Niemieccy, czy . . . od nacjonalizmu do komunizmu (1945–1949)* (Toruń: Wydawnictwo Adam Marszałek, 2001), 204; on the date of the memorandum, see 24, 203.

12. Repr. ibid., 205–206.

13. Ibid., 23–24; the quote is on 24n6.

14. Aleksander Kochański, ed., *Dokumenty do dziejów PRL*, Part 1: *Protokół obrad KC PPR w maju 1945 roku* (Warsaw: Instytut Studiów Politycznych PAN, 1992), 37–38.
15. Ibid., 11, 27. Krystyna Kersten confirms Gomułka's claim, "Forced Migration and the Transformation of Polish Society in the Postwar Period," in *Redrawing Nations: Ethnic Cleansing in East-Central Europe, 1944–1948*, ed. Philipp Ther and Ana Siljak (Lanham, MD: Rowman & Littlefield Publishers, Inc., 2001), 80.
16. Wacław Długoborski, "Polen—Zwischen zwei Besatzungsdiktatoren," in *Kriegsende in Europe: Von Beginn des deutschen Machtzerfalls bis zur Stabilisierung der Nachkriegsordnung 1944–1948*, ed. Ulrich Herbert and Axel Schildt (Essen: Klartext, 1998), 135; Wojciech Wrzesiński, "The Problem of the Indigenous Polish Population in the Territories Postulated by Poland during World War II," *Polish Western Affairs*, nos. 1–2 (1990): 4; Tomasz Szarota, *Niemcy i Polacy: wzajemne postrzeganie i stereotypy* (Warsaw: Wydawnictwo Naukowe PWN, 1996), 150–153, 180n29.
17. Excerpts repr. in Stanisław Kirkor, "Listy Stanisława Grabskiego (1941–1949)," *Zeszyty Historyczne* 19 (1971): 69, 71. On 3 Aug. 1945, Grabski wrote, "There are houses, workshops, factories, farms, schools, administrative positions ready for people in the western territories. But if decent people hold back from occupying them—then they will be taken by scoundrels and ignoramuses, and the first to push their way in everywhere will be Jews," ibid., 70.
18. Krzysztof Stryjkowski, *Położenie osób wpisanych w Wielkopolsce na niemiecką listę narodowościową w latach 1945–1950* (Poznań: Instytut Historii UAM, 2004), 402–403; Markus Krzoska, *Für ein Polen an Oder und Ostsee: Zygmunt Wojciechowski (1900–1955) als Historiker und Publizist* (Osnabrück: fibre Verlag, 2003), 332–334; Włodzimierz Borodziej and Artur Hajnicz, "Raport końcowy: Warszawa, 7 grudnia 1996 r.," in *Kompleks wypędzenia*, ed. Borodziej and Hajnicz (Cracow: Wydawnictwo ZNAK, 1998), 413–414 .
19. See the memorandum of the pro-Polish Mazurian activists discussed below. On 18 Feb. 2000 at a meeting in Opole of former members of the ZPwN, Prof. Antoni Marek stated, "At least 25 generations of Silesians suffered for Poland, prayed for it, persevered for it, bore for it the greatest sacrifices and humiliations," quoted in Adam Roszel, "Śląsk chciał być polski," *Dziennik Związkowy*, 23–25 June 2000, 22; Andrzej Paczkowski speaks of "Poles who had outlasted centuries of German presence" in the western territories, *The Spring Will Be Ours: Poland and the Poles from Occupation to Freedom* (University Park, PA: Pennsylvania State University Press, 2003), 147.
20. Jerzy Marczewski, ed., *Związek Polaków w Niemczech w latach 1922–1982* (Warsaw: Wydawnictwo Polonia, 1987).
21. Czesław Osękowski, *Społeczeństwo Polski zachodniej i północnej w latach 1945–1956: procesy integracji i dezintegracji* (Zielona Góra: Wyższa Szkoła Pedagogiczna im. Tadeusza Kotarbińskiego, 1994), 108; Długoborski, "Polen—Zwischen zwei Besatzungsdiktatoren," 135.
22. Quoted in Wrzesiński, "Problem," 14.
23. *O Ziemie Polskie na Zachodzie* (Poznań: Oddział Propagandy Gł. Zarządu Polit. Wychowawczego W.P., n.d [1945]), 41.

24. Mirosław Dymarski, *Ziemie postulowane (ziemie nowe) w prognozach i działaniach polskiego ruchu oporu 1939–1945* (Wrocław: Wydawnictwo Uniwersytetu Wrocławskiego, 1997) 174–175; the quote is on 175.
25. Bronisław Kortus, "Der polnische Westgedanke und die Geographie," in *Deutsche Ostforschung*, ed. Piskorski, Hackmann, and Jaworski, 258.
26. At a PZZ Silesian District Extraordinary Congress of Delegates, 19 Aug. 1945, Bytom, excerpt, Włodzimierz Borodziej and Hans Lemberg, eds., *Niemcy*, vol. 2, *Polska Centralna. Województwo śląskie*, ed. Ingo Eser and Jerzy Kochanowski (Warsaw: Wydawnictwo NERITON, 2000), 384–385, 385n6. Anna Wolff-Powęska quotes a slightly different version, "Rola Polskiego Związku Zachodniego w zagospodarowaniu Ziem Zachodnich," *Przegląd Zachodni* 26, no. 4 (1970): 433.
27. Osękowski, *Społeczeństwo*, 95–96.
28. Jan Misztal exemplifies this view, *Weryfikacja narodowościowa na Ziemiach Odzyskanych* (Warsaw: Państwowe Wydawnictwo Naukowe, 1990), 5, 73.
29. Krzysztof Karwat, *Ten przeklęty Śląsk* (Katowice: Towarzystwo Zachęty Kultury, 1996), 23.
30. Grzegorz Strauchold, *Polska ludność rodzima ziem zachodnich i północnych. Opinie nie tylko publiczne lat 1944–1948* (Olsztyn: Ośrodek Badań Naukowych im. Wojciecha Kętrzyńskiego, 1995), 142.
31. Quoted in Stryjkowski, *Położenie*, 278.
32. Wrzesiński, "Problem," 9–10. Tomáš Masaryk, the first president of Czechoslovakia and the son of a Czech-German mother, in his inaugural address referred to Sudeten Germans as "immigrants and colonists," quoted in R. M. Douglas, *Orderly and Humane: The Expulsion of the Germans after the Second World War* (New Haven: Yale University Press, 2012), 9.
33. Ingo Eser, "Niemcy na Górnym Śląsku," in *Niemcy*, Borodziej and Lemberg, 2:322.
34. *O Ziemie Polskie*, 41.
35. Quoted in Strauchold, *Polska ludność*, 35.
36. Dymarski, *Ziemie postulowane*, 175.
37. Quoted in Strauchold, *Autochtoni*, 78–79.
38. Ibid., 41–42; Wrzesiński, "Problem," 4.
39. Walker Connor, *Ethnonationalism: The Quest for Understanding* (Princeton: Princeton University Press, 1994), 197.
40. Tara Zahra, "'A Human Treasure': Europe's Displaced Children between Nationalism and Internationalism," *Past and Present* 210 (2011): 335; Strauchold, *Polska ludność*, 38, 73, 96; Borodziej and Lemberg, *Niemcy*, 1:471.
41. Bożena Stelmachowska, "Polska kultura ludowa czynnikiem zespalającym Ziemie Odzyskane," *Przegląd Zachodni*, no. 12 (1946): 979.
42. Strauchold, *Polska ludność*, 38, 73, 96; Strauchold, *Autochtoni*, 41; James E. Bjork, *Neither German nor Pole: Catholicism and National Indifference in a Central European Borderland* (Ann Arbor: University of Michigan Press, 2008), 171.
43. Osękowski, *Społeczeństwo*, 65.
44. Bernard Linek, "'De-Germanization' and 'Re-Polonization' in Upper Silesia, 1945–1950," in *Redrawing Nations*, Ther and Siljak, 123–124.
45. *Upper Silesia* (London: The Polish Research Centre, 1941), 30.

46. Report, 2 May 1945, excerpt, Borodziej and Lemberg, *Niemcy,* 2:338–339.
47. Stanisław Ossowski, "Zagadnienia więzi regionalnej i więzi narodowej na Śląsku Opolskim," in *O ojczyźnie i narodzie* (Warsaw: Państwowe Wydawnictwo Naukowe, 1984), 123; Kevin Hannan takes a similar view, *Borders of Language and Identity in Teschen Silesia* (New York: Peter Lang, 1996).
48. Ossowski, "Zagadnienia," 91, 99–105, 108, 116, 119, 129–130.
49. Borodziej and Lemberg, *Niemcy,* 2:363–364.
50. Ossowski, "Zagadnienia," 103.
51. Stanisław Bieniasz, "Co dzieli, a co powinno łączyć," *Kultura,* no. 4/511 (1990): 25, 28; the quote is on 28. In 1994 after returning to Poland following his emigration to Germany in 1981, Bieniasz stated, "I am neither a one-hundred-percent German nor a one-hundred-percent Pole. I am simply a Silesian," Gabriela Łęcka, "Na razie jestem wściekły," *Polityka (Kultura),* no. 39 (24 Sept. 1994): iv.
52. Maria Szmeja, "Czy Ślązacy mogą się czuć Polakami?" in *U progu wielokulturowości. Nowe oblicza społeczeństwa polskiego,* ed. Marian Kempny, Alina Kapciak, and Sławomir Łodziński (Warsaw: Oficyna Naukowa, 1997), 190.
53. See, for example, Joachim Georg Görlich, "Autochtoni," *Kultura,* nos. 1/195–2/196 (1964): 133.
54. Strauchold, *Autochtoni,* 20n47; Kraft, "Wojewodschaft Allenstein," 438, 442, 442n26, 443, 443n27; Michael Mann, *The Dark Side of Democracy: Explaining Ethnic Cleansing* (Cambridge: Cambridge University Press, 2005), 225–227.
55. Repr. with ellipses in Tadeusz Filipowski, "Zagadnienia Prus Wschodnich w memoriałach przedłożonych Polskiemu Komitetowi Wyzwolenia Narodowego," *Komunikaty Mazursko-Warmińskie* 147 (1980): 61–68; the quote is on 64–65.
56. Ibid., 66.
57. Ibid., 67.
58. Strauchold, *Autochtoni,* 29.
59. Leszek Belzyt, *Między Polską a Niemcami. Weryfikacja narodowościowa i jej następstwa na Warmii, Mazurach i Powiślu w latach 1945–1960* (Toruń: Wydawnictwo Adam Marszałek, 1998), 44; Filipowski, "Zagadnienia," 59–60. Andreas Kossert regards the memorandum as one of the most significant documents in Mazurian history, *Preußen, Deutsche oder Polen?: die Masuren im Spannungsfeld des ethnischen Nationalismus 1870–1956* (Wiesbaden: Harrassowitz Verlag, 2001), 302–303.
60. Repr. in Filipowski, "Zagadnienia," 68–79; the quote is on 68.
61. Ibid., 74.
62. Ibid., 75, 74, respectively.
63. Ibid., 76–79; the quote is on 79.
64. Strauchold, *Autochtoni,* 30.
65. Tadeusz Baryła, ed., *Warmiacy i Mazurzy w PRL. Wybór dokumentów. Rok 1945* (Olsztyn: Ośrodek Badań Naukowych im. Wojciecha Kętrzyńskiego, 1994), 1–2; the quotes are on 2.
66. Kraft, "Wojewodschaft Allenstein," 450n51. In the fall of 1944 the *Delegatura* blamed defeat in the 1920 plebiscite on the Mazurs' Protestant religion, Borodziej and Lemberg, *Niemcy,* 1:470n1.
67. Piotr Madajczyk, *Przyłączenie Śląska Opolskiego do Polski, 1945–1948* (Warsaw: Instytut Studiów Politycznych PAN, 1996), 118; Strauchold, *Autochtoni,* 194.

When Jerzy Buzek, a Protestant born in formerly Austrian Silesia, was appointed premier in 1997, a relative in Poland of a Chicago resident told him that Poland had chosen a "German" as premier.

68. Michael Fleming, *Communism, Nationalism and Ethnicity, 1944–50* (London: Routledge, 2010), 116; Kossert, *Preußen*, 321.
69. Borodziej and Lemberg, *Niemcy*, 1:139–140.
70. Kossert, *Preußen*, 321–323; Strauchold, *Autochtoni*, 80–81.
71. Brunon Synak, "The Kashubes' Ethnic Identity: Continuity and Change," in *The Ethnic Identities of European Minorities: Theory and Case Studies*, ed. Synak (Gdańsk: Wydawnictwo Uniwersytetu Gdańskiego, 1995), 156–158.
72. Cezary Obracht-Prondzyński, "Kaszubi ziem 'dawnych' i 'nowych'—bilans z perspektywy sześćdziesięciolecia," in *Ziemie Odzyskane/Ziemie Zachodnie i Północne 1945–2005: 60 lat w granicach państwa polskiego*, ed. Andrzej Sakson (Poznań: Instytut Zachodni, 2006), 219–231.
73. John J. Kulczycki, *School Strikes in Prussian Poland, 1901–1907: The Struggle over Bilingual Education* (Boulder: East European Monographs, 1981), 142.
74. Mathias Niendorf, *Minderheiten an der Grenze: Deutsche und Polen in den Kreisen Flatow (Złotów) und Zempelburg (Sępólno Krajeńskie) 1900–1939* (Wiesbaden: Harrasssowitz Verlag, 1997), 46, 270.
75. Borodziej and Lemberg, *Niemcy*, 3:307–309, 309n2; for a similar categorization of Poles in Złotów, Człuchów, and Bytów Counties by officials, see conference notes, 27 Oct. 1946, 362.
76. Stelmachowska, "Polska kultura," 980–981; the quotes are on 981, 980, respectively. The Lower Silesian folk tradition that developed was a pale reflection of that of the expelled Germans. The melodies and lyrics of songs of the autochthons of Namysłów and Syców, with German elements deleted, were the main source of the repertory promoted by the government in Lower Silesia for decades. The effort to create an authentic regional folklore resumed in 2010, Natalia Gańko-Laska, "Dolny Śląsk się stroi. Ubiór zdobi Dolnoślązaka," *Polityka.PL Newsletter*, 15 Sept. 210, http://www.polityka.pl/spoleczenstwo/artykuly/1508050,1,dolny-slask-sie-stroi.read?utm_source=Polityka+Spoldzielnia+Pracy+List&utm_campaign=366e80a716-UA-11208742-1&utm_medium=email.
77. Anna Matysiak, *Między regionalizmem a uniwersalizmem. O poezji Erwina Kruka* (Warsaw: Wydawnictwo Naukowe Semper,1995), 10–11; Strauchold, *Autochtoni*, 40; Strauchold, *Polska ludność*, 35, 48, 50, 97; the quote is on 48n52.
78. Reproduced in Karol Jonca, ed., *Wysiedlenia Niemców i osadnictwo ludności polskiej na obszarze Krzyżowa-Świdnia (Kreisau-Schweidnitz) w latach 1945–1948: wybór dokumentów* (Wrocław: Wydawnictwo "Leopoldinum" Fundacji dla Uniwersytetu Wrocławskiego, 1997), 364.
79. Włodzimierz Borodziej and Hans Lemberg, "Einleitung," in *Die Deutschen*, ed. Borodziej and Lemberg, 1:56.
80. Eugeniusz Misiło, ed., *Repatriacja czy deportacja: Przesiedlenie Ukraińców z Polski do USSR 1944–1946*, vol. 1, *Dokumenty 1944–1945* (Warsaw: Oficyna Wydawnicza "Archiwum Ukraińskie," 1996), 10–11; Hugo Service illustrates the link in a local study, "Reinterpreting the Expulsion of Germans from Poland, 1945–9," *Journal of Contemporary History* 47, no. 3 (2012): 528–550.

81. Repr. in Stanisław Ciesielski, ed., *Przesiedlenie ludności polskiej z kresów wschodnich do Polski, 1944–1947* (Warsaw: Wydawnictwo NERITON, Instytut Historii PAN, 1999), 89–94; the quote is on 89.
82. Wolski's report, repr. ibid., 100–102; RM minutes, repr. 104.
83. Repr. ibid., 155.
84. Eser, "Niemcy," 310n91; Jan Misztal, "Przesunięcie Polski na zachód," in *Kompleks wypędzenia*, ed. Borodziej and Hajnicz, 97–99.
85. Jan Czerniakiewicz, *Repatriacja ludności polskiej z ZSRR 1944–1948* (Warsaw: Państwowe Wydawnictwo Naukowe, 1987), 12, 54, 58–59, 194, 204.
86. The words are from Maria Konopnicka's 1908 poem "*Rota*," which Feliks Nowowiejski set to music in 1910 and became a popular patriotic anthem.
87. Kazimierz Robakowski and Marek Żurowski, eds., *Materiały źródłowe do historii Polski Ludowej, Part 1: (1944–1949)* (Poznań: Uniwersytet im. Adama Mickiewicza w Poznaniu, 1982), 63–64; *Robotnik*, no. 91 (15 Apr. 1945), repr. in Dariusz Baliszewski and Andrzej Krzysztof Kunert, *Ilustrowany przewodnik po Polsce stalinowskiej: 1944–1956* (Warsaw: Wydawnictwo Naukowe PWN, 1999), 256.
88. Misztal, "Przesunięcie," 99.
89. Kochański, *Protokół*, 11.
90. Repr. in Mieczysław Jaworski, *Na Piastowskim szlaku. Działalność Ministerstwa Ziem Odzyskanych w latach 1945–1948* (Warsaw: Wydawnictwo Ministerstwa Obrony Narodowej, 1973), 275.
91. Hugo Service, *Germans to Poles: Communism, Nationalism and Ethnic Cleansing after the Second World War* (Cambridge: Cambridge University Press, 2013), 144.
92. Douglas sees the diversity among *Volksdeutsche* as the greatest obstacle to the success of the Nazi resettlement program, *Orderly and Humane*, 55.
93. Strauchold, *Autochtoni*, 103.
94. Quoted in Jakub Tyszkiewicz, *Sto wielkich dni Wrocławia: wystawa Ziem Odzyskanych we Wrocławiu a propaganda ziem zachodnich i północnych w latach 1945–1948* (Wrocław: Wydawnictwo Arboretum, 1997), 45n88.
95. Hannah Arendt noted in 1951 that refugees and Displaced Persons "develop a fierce, violent group consciousness and . . . clamor for rights as—and only as—Poles or Jews or Germans, etc.," *The Origins of Totalitarianism* (New York: Harcourt Brace Jovanovich, 1973), 292.
96. Madajczyk, *Przyłączenie*, 179; Belzyt, *Między Polską a Niemcami*, 66.
97. Eser, "Niemcy," 317–318; Ossowski, "Zagadnienia," 110.
98. Eugeniusz Kłosek, *"Swoi" i "obcy" na Górnym Śląsku od 1945 roku. Środowisko miejskie* (Wrocław: Wydawnictwo Uniwersytetu Wrocławskiego, 1994), 32–35, 40.
99. Bieniasz, "Co dzieli," 24–26, 28–29.
100. Görlich, "Autochtoni," 134.
101. Piotr Wróblewski, "Regional and National Bonds in the Opole District of Silesia: Gielczyn Fifty Years Later," in *Ethnicity, Nation, Culture: Central and East European Perspectives*, ed. Bálint Balla and Anton Sterbling (Hamburg: Krämer, 1998), 202.
102. Quoted in Jacek Ruszczewski, "Nacjonalizm, szowinizm, czy syndrom odwetu i odpowiedzialności zbiorowej? (Konflikty międzygrupowe na przykładzie Śląska Opolskiego w latach 1945–1949)," in *Fenomen nowoczesnego nacjonalizmu w*

Europie Środkowej, ed. Bernard Linek, Jörg Lüer, and Kai Struve (Opole: Wydawnictwo Instytut Śląski, 1997), 115.
103. Quoted in Kłosek, "Swoi," 41. The term "gorol" (a deformation of "góral" or highlander) originally applied to newcomers from Austrian Galicia, regarded as primitive and poor, and came to be applied to all Polish newcomers, ibid., 55–56.
104. Barbara Törnquist Plewa, *The Wheel of Polish Fortune: Myths in Polish Collective Consciousness during the First Years of Solidarity* (Lund, Sweden: Lund University, 1992), 31–37, 115–128; Ossowski, "Zagadnienia," 124; Bieniasz, "Co dzieli," 28–29.
105. Excerpt, Borodziej and Lemberg, *Niemcy*, 2:417–418.
106. Kłosek, "Swoi," 6, 11, 15, 104, 114, 124–127. In Sept. 2012 Archbishop Wiktor Skworc of Katowice criticized the division between "true" and "foreign" Silesians, *Donosy*, no. 5410 (3 Sept. 2012), http://oldwww.fuw.edu.pl/donosy/.

5. The Prologue to Polonizing Identities

1. Quoted in Włodzimierz Borodziej and Hans Lemberg, eds., *Die Deutschen*, vol. 4, *Wojewodschaften Pommerellen und Danzig (Westpreussen). Wojewodschaft Breslau (Niederschlesien)*, ed. Ingo Eser, Witold Stankowski, Claudia Kraft, and Stanisław Jankowiak (Marburg: Verlag Herder-Institut, 2004), 93n3.
2. Quoted in Krzysztof Stryjkowski, *Położenie osób wpisanych w Wielkopolsce na niemiecką listę narodowościową w latach 1945-1950* (Poznań: Instytut Historii UAM, 2004), 111.
3. Marcin Zaremba, *Wielka trwoga. Polska 1944-1947. Ludowa reakcja na kryzys* (Cracow: Wydawnictwo Znak, Instytut Studiów Politycznych Polskiej Akademii Nauk, 2012), 158.
4. Tadeusz Baryła, ed., *Warmiacy i Mazurzy w PRL. Wybór dokumentów. Rok 1945* (Olsztyn: Ośrodek Badań Naukowych im. Wojciecha Kętrzyńskiego, 1994), 9.
5. American GIs also sought revenge, Seth A. Givens, "Liberating the Germans: The US Army and Looting in Germany during the Second World War," *War in History* 21, no.1 (2014): 33–54; for a comparison with the Red Army, see 34, 42, 45–46.
6. Quoted in Stryjkowski, *Położenie*, 102.
7. Quoted in Baryła, *Warmiacy*, 6n2; Leszek Belzyt, *Między Polską a Niemcami. Weryfikacja narodowościowa i jej następstwa na Warmii, Mazurach i Powiślu w latach 1945-1960* (Toruń: Wydawnictwo Adam Marszałek, 1998), 52–53.
8. Beata Halicka differentiates the levels of Red Army violence by time and place and opposes a one-sided portrayal of Soviet soldiers, *Polens Wilder Westen: erzwungene Migration und de kuturelle Aneignung des Oderraums 1945-1948* (Paderborn: Ferdinand Schöningh, 2013), 91–93.
9. Anna Magierska, *Ziemie zachodnie i pólnocne w 1945 roku. Ksztaltowanie się podstaw polityki integracyjnej państwa polskiego* (Warsaw: Książka i Wiedza, 1978), 131–132.
10. Excerpt, Włodzimierz Borodziej and Hans Lemberg, eds., *Niemcy*, vol. 3, *Województwa poznańskie i szczecińskie*, ed. Stanisław Jankowiak and Katrin Steffen (Warsaw: Wydawnictwo NERITON, 2001), 58–60; the quote is on 58.
11. Baryła, *Warmiacy*, 7.

12. Piotr Madajczyk, *Przyłączenie Śląska Opolskiego do Polski, 1945–1948* (Warsaw: Instytut Studiów Politycznych PAN, 1996), 91; Andreas Kossert, *Preußen, Deutsche oder Polen?: die Masuren im Spannungsfeld des ethnischen Nationalismus 1870–1956* (Wiesbaden: Harrassowitz Verlag, 2001), 307.
13. Norman Naimark, *The Russians in Germany: A History of the Soviet Zone of Occupation, 1945–1949* (Cambridge, MA: Harvard University Press, 1995), 74–75; Hugo Service, *Germans to Poles: Communism, Nationalism and Ethnic Cleansing after the Second World War* (Cambridge: Cambridge University Press, 2013), 72–74.
14. Krzysztof Karwat, *Ten przeklęty Śląsk* (Katowice: Towarzystwo Zachęty Kultury, 1996), 19–26; Halicka, *Polens Wilder Westen*, 86; Dorota Wodecka, "Modlitwa za Ruskich," *Gazeta Wyborcza*, 24 June 2008, http://ofiaromwojny.republika.pl/teksty2/0757.htm.
15. Excerpt, Włodzimierz Borodziej and Hans Lemberg, eds., *Niemcy*, vol. 1, *Władze i instytucje centralne. Województwo olsztyńskie*, ed. Borodziej and Claudia Kraft (Warsaw: Wydawnictwo NERITON, 2000), 419–421; the quotes are on 420.
16. Excerpt, ibid., 3:281.
17. Quoted in Milovan Djilas, *Conversations with Stalin* (New York: Harcourt, Brace & World, Inc., 1962), 95; see also, 110–111. For analogous behavior of American soldiers, see Givens, "Liberating the Germans," 40–41, 48; Mary Louise Roberts. *What Soldiers Do: Sex and the American GI in World War II France* (Chicago: University of Chicago Press, 2013).
18. Excerpt repinted in Włodzimierz Borodziej and Hans Lemberg, eds., *Niemcy*, vol. 2, *Polska Centralna. Województwo śląskie*, ed. Ingo Eser and Jerzy Kochanowski (Warsaw: Wydawnictwo NERITON, 2000), 340.
19. Quoted in Baryła, *Warmiacy*, 6n2.
20. Ibid., 4–6.
21. Belzyt, *Między Polską a Niemcami*, 53–54; the quote is on 53.
22. Excerpt, Borodziej and Lemberg, *Niemcy*, 2:334.
23. Aleksander Kochański, ed., *Dokumenty do dziejów PRL*, Part 1: *Protokół obrad KC PPR w maju 1945 roku* (Warsaw: Instytut Studiów Politycznych PAN, 1992), 17–18, 20, 33–34, 42.
24. Repr. in Jan Misztal, *Weryfikacja narodowościowa na Ziemiach Odzyskanych* (Warsaw: Państwowe Wydawnictwo Naukowe, 1990), 123–124n90.
25. Excerpt, Borodziej and Lemberg, *Niemcy*, 3:347–348; the quotes are on 347; see also 348n1.
26. Reproduced in Karol Jonca, ed., *Wysiedlenia Niemców i osadnictwo ludności polskiej na obszarze Krzyżowa-Świdnia (Kreisau-Schweidnitz) w latach 1945–1948: wybór dokumentów* (Wrocław: Wydawnictwo "Leopoldinum" Fundacja dla Uniwersytetu Wrocławskiego, 1997), 484.
27. Tatiana Cariewskaja et al., eds., *Teczka specjalna J. W. Stalina: raporty NKWD z Polski 1944–1946* (Warsaw: Oficyna Wydawnicza RYTM, 1998), 547. As chairman of the KRN, Bierut was titular head of state and was referred to as chairman or president.
28. Borodziej and Lemberg, *Niemcy*, 3:61–62. The order specified "males of German nationality," but this could be taken to mean German citizens. Claudia Kraft

states that no distinctions were made concerning nationality, "Wojewodschaft Breslau (Niederschlesien). Das Jahr 1945," in *Die Deutschen*, Borodziej und Lemberg, 4:364.
29. Borodziej and Lemberg, *Die Deutschen*, 4:93n3; Theodor Schieder, ed., *Dokumentation der Vertreibung der Deutschen aus Ost-Mitteleuropa*, vol . 1, *Die Vertreibung der deutschen Bevölkerung aus den Gebieten östlich der Oder-Neiße* (Munich: Deutscher Taschenbuch, 1984), Part 1, 79E; Stryjkowski, *Położenie*, 148.
30. Ingo Eser and Witold Stankowski, "Wojewodschaften Pommerellen und Danzig (Westpreussen)," in *Die Deutschen*, Borodziej and Lemberg, 4:34–35, 50.
31. Stryjkowski, *Położenie*, 155 157; the quote is on 156.
32. Andrzej Sakson, *Stosunki narodowościowe na Warmii i Mazurach 1945–1997* (Poznań: Instytut Zachodni, 1998), 27; Belzyt, *Między Polską a Niemcami*, 37, 51.
33. Antoni Dudek and Andrzej Paczkowski, "Poland," in *A Handbook of the Communist Security Apparatus in East Central Europe 1944–1989*, ed. Krzysztof Persak and Łukasz Kamiński (Warsaw: Institute of National Remembrance, 2005), 222; Mieczysław Jaworski, *Na Piastowskim szlaku. Działalność Ministerstwa Ziem Odzyskanych w latach 1945–1948* (Warsaw: Wydawnictwo Ministerstwa Obrony Narodowej, 1973), 173. Łukasz Kamiński, "Książki nienapisane," *Tygodnik Powszechny*, 15 Dec. 2009, http://tygodnik.onet.pl/35,0,38162,artykul.html, states that the fate of miners deported to the Soviet Union is not yet fully clarified.
34. Witold Sienkiewicz and Grzegorz Hryciuk, eds. *Wysiedlenia, wypędzenia i ucieczki 1939–1959. Atlas ziem Polski* (Warsaw: Demart, 2008), 176; Schieder puts the total at 218,000 deportees, 62,000 from Silesia, *Dokumentation*, 83E.
35. Copy, Cariewskaja, *Teczka*, 548–551.
36. Ingo Eser, "Niemcy na Górnym Śląsku," in *Niemcy*, Borodziej and Lemberg, 2:310–311.
37. Excerpt, ibid., 421.
38. Tomasz Kamusella and Terry Sullivan, "The Germans of Upper Silesia: The Struggle for Recognition," in *Ethnicity and Democratization in the New Europe*, ed. Karl Cordell (London: Routledge, 1999), 172.
39. Bogusław Kopka, *Obozy pracy w Polsce 1944–1950. Przewodnik encyklopedyczny* (Warsaw: Niezależna Oficyna Wydawnicza NOWA, Ośrodek Karta, 2002), 174.
40. Madajczyk, *Przyłączenie*, 237.
41. Stryjkowski, *Położenie*, 130–131, 132n143.
42. Jan Misztal, "Przesunięcie Polski na zachód," in *Kompleks wypędzenia*, ed. Włodzimierz Borodziej and Artur Hajnicz (Cracow: Wydawnictwo ZNAK, 1998), 88–93.
43. Madajczyk, *Przyłączenie*, 245.
44. Michael Mann, *The Dark Side of Democracy: Explaining Ethnic Cleansing* (Cambridge: Cambridge University Press, 2005), 224–228.
45. Chad Bryant, "Either German or Czech: Fixing Nationality in Bohemia and Moravia, 1939–1946," *Slavic Review* 61, no. 4 (Winter 2002): 697. Eagle Glassheim, "The Mechanics of Ethnic Cleansing: The Expulsion of Germans from Czechoslovakia, 1945–1947," in *Redrawing Nations: Ethnic Cleansing in East-Central Europe, 1944–1948*, ed. Philipp Ther and Ana Siljak (Lanham, MD: Rowman & Littlefield Publishers, Inc., 2001), 200, 205–208, 214–215, sees the emphasis on

German collective guilt, the advocacy of "cleansing" the Germans by Czech leaders, particularly communists, and a diffusion of authority at the local level without central directives as explanations for the unprecedented Czech violence.

46. Zenon Romanow, *Ludność niemiecka na ziemiach zachodnich i północnych w latach 1945–1947* (Słupsk: Wyższa Szkoła Pedagogiczna w Słupsku, 1992), 43–44.
47. Cariewskaja, *Teczka*, 251–252. Beria gave 20 Apr. 1945 as the date when the Commander-in-Chief ordered a change in the Red Army's relations with Germans.
48. Kochański, *Protokół*, 12.
49. Romanow, *Ludność*, 9–15; the number includes German citizens of Polish origin forced to evacuate, 15; Theodor Schieder puts the number of returnees at 1,250,000, *The Expulsion of the German Population from the Territories East of the Oder-Neisse Line* (Bonn: Federal Ministry for Expellees, Refugees and War Victims, 1956), 62.
50. Stanisław Jankowiak, "Niemcy w Wielkopolsce i na Ziemi Lubuskiej w latach 1945–1950," in *Niemcy*, ed. Borodziej and Lemberg, 3:33–34; Włodzimerz Borodziej, "Wstęp: sprawa polska i przemieszczenia ludności w czasie II wojny światowej," ibid., 1:60.
51. Romanow, *Ludność*, 16–19.
52. Borodziej and Lemberg, *Niemcy*, 1:144–146, 147; 3:70–71.
53. Excerpts, ibid., 2:377–378; the quote is on 378.
54. Schieder, *Expulsion*, 120. Service cites an estimate of 300,000 to 400,000, *Germans to Poles*, 97.
55. Stryjkowski, *Położenie*, 259–260.
56. Borodziej and Lemberg, *Niemcy*, 3:101–102.
57. Quoted in Edmund Dmitrów, *Niemcy i okupacja hitlerowska w oczach Polaków. Poglądy i opinie z lat 1945–1948* (Warsaw: Czytelnik, 1987), 267. Kopka maps the distribution of 206 various types of camps, *Obozy*.
58. Zenon Romanow, "Polityka władz polskich wobec ludności niemieckiej na Pomorzu Zachodnim w latach 1945-1958," in *Pomorze—trudna ojczyzna? Kształtowanie się nowej tożsamości 1945–1995*, ed. Andrzej Sakson (Poznań: Instytut Zachodni, 1996), 208–210.
59. Stryjkowski, *Położenie*, 145, 158, 160–162, 345–346; the quotes are on 161, 158, 145, respectively.
60. Ibid., 116, 122, 127; the quote is on 116.
61. Borodzicj and Lemberg, *Niemcy*, 3:61–62, 62n11.
62. Stryjkowski, *Położenie*, 148, 167–168; the quotes are on 148, 168.
63. Borodziej and Lemberg, *Niemcy*, 2:333
64. Misztal, "Przesunięcie," 95–96, 110. Czechs gave a higher priority to expulsion than to retribution through forced labor, Benjamin Frommer, "To Prosecute or to Expel? Czechoslovak Retribution and the 'Transfer' of Sudeten Germans," in *Redrawing Nations*, ed. Ther and Siljak, 234.
65. Baryła, *Warmiacy*, 7–8.
66. Ibid., 10; 14n17.
67. Borodziej and Lemberg, *Niemcy*, 2:366; Silesian Control Commission report, 8 Oct., 1946, excerpt, ibid., 441–443.

68. Madajczyk, *Przyłączenie*, 273.
69. Borodziej, "Wstęp," 83, 85–86.
70. Stryjkowski, *Położenie*, 171; Madajczyk, *Przyłączenie*, 243, 249; the quote is on 249.
71. Memo, Borodziej and Lemberg, *Niemcy*, 1:485–486.
72. Ibid., 2:77–78, 78n1.
73. Adam Dziurok, *Obóz pracy w Świętochłowicach w 1945. Dokumenty, zeznania, relacje, listy* (Warsaw: Instytut Pamięci Narodowej, Komisja Ścigania Zbrodni przeciwko Narodowi Polskiemu, 2002), 78, 83–100; Associated Press, "Israel Won't Extradite Polish Jew Accused of Post-WWII genocide," *Haaretz.com*, 7 July 2005, http://www.haaretz.com/print-edition/news/israel-won-t-extradite-polish-jew-accused-of-post-wwii-genocide-1.163208; BBC report, 7 July 2005, http://news.bbc.co.uk/2/hi/europe/4659985.stm.
74. Madajczyk, *Przyłączenie*, 267; Czesław Osękowski puts the number at more than 8,000, *Społeczeństwo Polski zachodniej i północnej w latach 1945–1956: procesy integracji i dezintegracji* (Zielona Góra: Wyższa Szkoła Pedagogiczna im. Tadeusza Kotarbińskiego, 1994), 83, 85, 86; Gerhard Gnauck states c. 5,000, of whom c. 1,500 died in the camp, "Wie Lamsdorf zur 'Hölle' für Deutsche wurde," *Die Welt*, 16 Jan. 2014, http://www.welt.de/geschichte/zweiter-weltkrieg/article123906298/Wie-Lamsdorf-zur-Hoelle-fuer-Deutsche-wurde.html.
75. Excerpt, Borodziej and Lemberg, *Niemcy*, 2:405–406; the quote is on 405; Borodziej, "Wstęp," 87.
76. Stryjkowski, *Położenie*, 212, 217–218, 220–227; the quote is on 217.
77. Belzyt, *Między Polską a Niemcami*, 77–78; Eser and Stankowski, "Wojewodschaften," 55.
78. Reports, 21 and 28 May 1946, Daniel Boćkowski, ed., *Niemcy*, vol. 4, *Pomorze Gdańskie i Dolny Śląsk*, ed. Ingo Eser, Witold Stankowski, Claudia Kraft, and Stanisław Jankowiak (Warsaw: Wydawnictwo NERITON, 2001), 129–130, 133–135.
79. Belzyt, *Między Polską a Niemcami*, 141–142.
80. Madajczyk, *Przyłączenie*, 243, 253–254; Eser and Stankowski, "Wojewodschaften," 45–46.
81. Eugeniusz Kłosek, *"Swoi" i "obcy" na Górnym Śląsku od 1945 roku. Środowisko miejskie* (Wrocław: Wydawnictwo Uniwersytetu Wrocławskiego, 1994), 32–35.
82. Stanisław Ossowski, "Zagadnienia więzi regionalnej i więzi narodowej na Śląsku Opolskim," in *O ojczyźnie i narodzie* (Warsaw: Państwowe Wydawnictwo Naukowe, 1984), 120.
83. Quoted in Borodziej, "Wstęp," 89.
84. Zaremba, *Wielka trwoga*, 295–296; Eser, "Niemcy," 316; Piotr Madajczyk, *Niemcy polscy: 1944–1989* (Warsaw: Oficyna Naukowa, 2001), 58–59.
85. Jan Tomasz Gross, *Polish Society under German Occupation: The Generalgovernement, 1939–1944* (Princeton: Princeton University Press, 1979), 166; Czesław Miłosz, *The Captive Mind* (New York: Vintage Books, 1981), 28; Kazimierz Wyka, "Gospodarka wyłączona," in *Życie na niby: Pamiętnik po klęsce*, ed. Henryk Markiewicz and Marta Wyka (Cracow-Warsaw: Wydawnictwo Literackie, 1984), 138–175. Dmitrów notes the importance of Wyka's conclusion concerning demoralization, *Niemcy*, 153.

86. Belzyt, *Między Polską a Niemcami*, 56; Claudia Kraft, "Who Is a Pole, and Who Is a German? The Province of Olsztyn in 1945," in *Redrawing Nations,* ed. Ther and Siljak, 114. Jan Tomasz Gross notes the linguistic parallel between *"mienie pożydowskie"* (formerly Jewish property) and *"mienie poniemieckie"* (formerly German property) but not the context of postwar violence, *Fear: Anti-Semitism in Poland after Auschwitz: An Essay in Historical Interpretation* (New York: Random House, 2006), 248.
87. Belzyt, *Między Polską a Niemcami,* 56; Leszek Belzyt, "Zum Verfahren der national Verifikation in den Gebieten des ehemaligen Ostpreussen 1945-1950," *Jahrbuch für die Geschichte Mittel- und Ostdeutschlands* 39 (1990): 253.
88. Misztal, "Przesunięcie," 99-101.
89. Excerpt, Boćkowski, *Niemcy,* 50-51.
90. Quoted in Belzyt, *Między Polską a Niemcami,* 57.
91. Claudia Kraft, "Wojewodschaft Allenstein," in *Die Deutschen,* ed. Włodzimierz Borodziej and Hans Lemberg, vol. 1, *Zentrale Behörden. Wojewodschaft Allenstein,* ed. Borodziej and Kraft (Marburg: Verlag Herder-Institut, 2000), 459-460.
92. Report, 10 Sept. 1945, Baryła, *Warmiacy,* 74.
93. Quoted in Misztal, *Weryfikacja,* 96.
94. Excerpt, Borodziej and Lemberg, *Niemcy,* 1:462-463.
95. Quoted in Belzyt, *Między Polską a Niemcami,* 57.
96. Misztal, *Weryfikacja,* 96-97; Belzyt, *Między Polską a Niemcami,* 122.
97. Wiesław Skrzydło, ed., *Manifest Polskiego Komitetu Wyzwolenia Narodwego* (Lublin: Wydawnictwo Lubelskie, 1984), 43.
98. DzURP, No. 4, Entry 17, 6 Sept. 1944, 18-21, http://dziennikustaw.gov.pl/DU/1944/s/4/17; Andrzej Korbonski, *Politics of Socialist Agriculture in Poland: 1945-1960* (New York: Columbia University Press, 1965), 75-76.
99. DzURP, No. 17, Entry 97, 7 May 1945, 126-130, http://dziennikustaw.gov.pl/DU/1945/s/17/97.
100. Misztal, *Weryfikacja,* 98-99; Misztal, "Przesunięcie," 99; Stryjkowski, *Położenie,* 485.
101. Report of a Silesian Control Commission, 8 Oct. 1946, excerpt, Borodziej and Lemberg, *Niemcy,* 2:439-440.
102. Baryła, *Warmiacy,* 39-40.
103. Borodziej and Lemberg, *Niemcy,* 2:358.
104. Misztal, *Weryfikacja,* 122.
105. Katrin Steffen, "Ucieczka, wypędzenie i przymusowe wysiedlenie Niemców z województwa szczecińskiego w latach 1945-1950," in *Niemcy,* Borodziej and Lemberg, 3:223-225.
106. Reproduced in Jonca, *Wysiedlenia,* 392.
107. Liah Greenfeld, *Nationalism: Five Roads to Modernity* (Cambridge, MA: Harvard University Press, 1992), 490.

6. The Initial Polish Government Nationality Measures

1. Jerzy Kochanowski, "Losy Niemców w Polsce Centralnej w latach 1945-1950. Na przykładzie województw łódzkiego, warszawskiego i krakowskiego (powiat Biała)," in *Niemcy,* ed., Włodzimierz Borodziej and Hans Lemberg, vol. 2, *Polska*

Centralna. Województwo śląskie, ed. Ingo Eser and Kochanowski (Warsaw: Wydawnictwo NERITON, 2000), 21; Edmund Dmitrów, Niemcy i okupacja hitlerowska w oczach Polaków. Poglądy i opinie z lat 1945–1948 (Warsaw: Czytelnik, 1987), 147; Czesław Osękowski, Społeczeństwo Polski zachodniej i północnej w latach 1945–1956: Procesy integracji i dezintegracji (Zielona Góra: Wyższa Szkoła Pedagogiczna im. Tadeusza Kotarbińskiego, 1994), 99.

2. Ingo Eser and Witold Stankowski, "Wojewodschaften Pommerellen und Danzig (Westpreussen)," in Die Deutschen, ed. Włodzimierz Borodziej and Hans Lemberg, vol. 4, Wojewodschaften Pommerellen und Danzig (Westpreussen). Wojewodschaft Beslau (Niederschlesien), ed. Eser, Stankowski, Claudia Kraft, and Stanisław Jankowiak (Marburg: Verlag Herder-Institut, 2004), 38, 49–50; Osękowski, Społeczeństwo, 101.

3. Krzysztof Stryjkowski, Położenie osób wpisanych w Wielkopolsce na niemiecką listę narodowościową w latach 1945–1950 (Poznań: Instytut Historii UAM, 2004), 553–554, 556.

4. Eugeniusz Kłosek takes this view, "Swoi" i "obcy" na Górnym Śląsku od 1945 roku. Środowisko miejskie (Wrocław: Wydawnictwo Uniwersytetu Wrocławskiego, 1994), 42.

5. Stryjkowski, Położenie, 10n4, 419; the quote is on 10n4.

6. Borodziej and Lemberg, Niemcy, 2:231–232; the quote is on 231.

7. Tadeusz Baryła, ed., Warmiacy i Mazurzy w PRL. Wybór dokumentów. Rok 1945 (Olsztyn: Ośrodek Badań Naukowych im. Wojciecha Kętrzyńskiego, 1994), 6–7; the quote is on 6.

8. Andrzej Sakson, Mazurzy–społeczność pogranicza (Poznań: Instytut Zachodni, 1990), 113.

9. Protocol, excerpt, Włodzimerz Borodziej and Hans Lemberg, eds., Niemcy, vol. 1, Władze i instytucje centralne. Województwo olsztyńskie, ed. Borodziej and Claudia Kraft (Warsaw: Wydawnictwo NERITON, 2000), 118.

10. DzURP, no. 7, Entry 30, 10 Mar. 1945, 39–41, http://dziennikustaw.gov.pl/DU/1945/s/7/30.

11. Baryła, Warmiacy, 9–14; the quotes are on 10, 12, respectively.

12. Excerpt, Borodziej and Lemberg, Niemcy, 2:338.

13. DzURP, no. 17, Entry 96, 7 May 1945, 123–126, http://dziennikustaw.gov.pl/DU/1945/s/17/96; Włodzimierz Borodziej, "Wstęp: sprawa polska i przemieszczenia ludności w czasie II wojny światowej," in Niemcy, ed. Borodziej and Hans Lemberg, 1:99.

14. Borodziej, "Wstęp," 59; report, 15 Nov. 1946, excerpt Włodzimierz Borodziej and Hans Lemberg, eds., Niemcy, vol. 3, Województwa poznańskie i szczecińskie, ed. Stanisław Jankowiak and Katrin Steffen (Warsaw: Wydawnictwo NERITON, 2001), 132.

15. DzURP, no. 55, Entry 307, 30 Oct. 1945, 506–507, http://dziennikustaw.gov.pl/DU/1945/s/55/307.

16. Ingo Eser, "Niemcy na Górnym Śląsku," in Niemcy, ed. Borodziej and Lemberg, 2:324–325, 325n198.

17. DzURP, no. 21, Entry 128, 11 June 1945, Attachment no. 1, 164, http://dziennikustaw.gov.pl/DU/1945/s/21/128.

18. Ibid., no. 25, Entry 150, 1945, http://dziennikustaw.gov.pl/DU/1945/s/25/150.
19. Kochanowski, "Losy Niemców," 62–63.
20. Borodziej and Lemberg, *Niemcy*, 2:263.
21. Ibid., 159–160.
22. Stryjkowski, *Położenie*, 570–571; the quote is on 571.
23. Report, 15 Nov. 1946, excerpt, Borodziej and Lemberg, *Niemcy*, 3:137–138; Stryjkowski, *Położenie*, 572.
24. Kochanowski, "Losy Niemców," 42–43.
25. Eser and Stankowski, "Wojewodschaften," 51.
26. Reproduced in Stryjkowski, *Położenie*, 446. The governor recognized some cases of coercion in 1942–1945, e.g., individuals with German-sounding surnames, 420–421.
27. Ibid., 417–418, 439, 556; the quote is on 417–418.
28. Chad Bryant, "Either German or Czech: Fixing Nationality in Bohemia and Moravia, 1939–1946," *Slavic Review* 61, no. 4 (Winter 2002): 698; David Gerlach, "Beyond Expulsion: The Emergence of 'Unwanted Elements' in the Postwar Czech Borderlands, 1945–1950," *East European Politics and Societies* 24, no. 2 (2010): 273.
29. Kochanowski, "Losy Niemców," 47–48; the quote is on 48. Borodziej and Lemberg name two other communities that protested, *Niemcy*, 2:80n1.
30. Reprnted in Borodziej and Lemberg, *Niemcy*, 2:79–80; the quote is on 80.
31. Excerpt, ibid., 80–81.
32. Excerpt, ibid., 85–87; report, 9 Apr. 1946, excerpt, ibid., 100; see also 93n1.
33. Adam Dziurok, *Śląskie rozrachunki. Władze komunistyczne a byli członkowie organizacji nazistowskich na Górnym Śląsku w latach 1945–1956* (Warsaw: PMK Paweł Kaczmarski, 2000), 100, 102n313.
34. Borodziej and Lemberg, *Niemcy*, 2:87.
35. *Starosta* report for 15 June to 10 July 1945, excerpts; reports, 9 Apr., 13 May 1946, ibid., 88, 100, and 102, respectively.
36. Excerpt, report, 14 August 1945, ibid., 93.
37. Excerpt, ibid., 94–95; report, 5 Nov. 1945, excerpt, ibid., 97.
38. Ibid., 365; see also 366n2.
39. Eser, "Niemcy," 322.
40. Janusz Wycisło, "Adamczyk Rudolf (1905–1980), proboszcz, prawnik, działacz społeczno-oświatowy, więzień polityczny," in *Słownik biograficzny katolickiego duchowieństwa Śląskiego XIX i XX wieku*, ed. Mieczysław Pater (Katowice: Księgarnia św. Jacka, 1996), 2.
41. Andrzej Grajewski, *Wygnanie. Diecezja katowicka w czasach stalinowskich*, 3rd rev. ed. (Katowice: Księgarnia św. Jacka; Gość niedzielny, 2002), 40–43.
42. Peter Raina, ed., *Kościół w PRL. Dokumenty*, vol. 1, *1945–1959* (Poznań: W drodze, 1994), 142–143; the quote is on 142.
43. Excerpt, Borodziej and Lemberg, *Niemcy*, 2:383–384.
44. Ibid., 379.
45. Kochanowski, "Losy Niemców," 48–50, 49n131; Eser, "Niemcy," 324–325, 325n198.
46. Report for 15 May to June 15, 1945, excerpt, Borodziej and Lemberg, *Niemcy*, 2:85.
47. Ibid., 89.

48. Ibid., 83–84; the quote is on 83; Bernadetta Nitschke, *Wysiedlenie ludności niemieckiej z Polski w latach 1945–1949* (Zielona Góra: Wyższa Szkoła Pedagogiczna im. Tadeusza Kotarbińskiego, 1999), 117.
49. Stryjkowski, *Położenie*, 179–182.
50. Report for 15 May to 15 June 1945, Borodziej and Lemberg, *Niemcy*, 2:85; Stanisław Jankowiak, "Niemcy w Wielkopolsce i na Ziemi Lubuskiej w latach 1945–1950," ibid., 3:42; Stryjkowski, *Położenie*, 424, 427; the quote is on 424.
51. Report, 19 July 1945, excerpt, Borodziej and Lemberg, *Niemcy*, 2:88; report, 15 Nov. 1946, excerpt, ibid., 3:131–145.
52. Protocol, 15 June 1945, excerpt, ibid., 65.
53. Report, 15 Nov. 1946, excerpt, ibid., 135–136.
54. Stryjkowski, *Położenie*, 345, 349.
55. Ibid., 422–423.
56. Kochanowski, "Losy Niemców," 53–58.
57. Jankowiak, "Niemcy w Wielkopolsce," 33.
58. Stryjkowski, *Położenie*, 11n7.
59. Nitschke, *Wysiedlenie*, 102.
60. Hugo Service attributes the failure of "ethnic screening" to "a crude nationalist outlook which sought to distil complex cultural identities and collective self-understandings into simplistic national categories" but also does not question its goal, "Sifting Poles from Germans? Ethnic Cleansing and Ethnic Screening in Upper Silesia, 1945–1949," *Slavonic and East European Review* 88, no. 4 (October 2010): 655.
61. Piotr Madajczyk, *Przyłączenie Śląska Opolskiego do Polski, 1945–1948* (Warsaw: Instytut Studiów Politycznych PAN, 1996), 195.
62. Stanisław Bieniasz, "Co dzieli, a co powinno łączyć," *Kultura* 511, no. 4 (1990): 28.
63. Borodziej and Lemberg, *Niemcy*, 3:290–291.
64. Quoted in Jan Misztal, *Weryfikacja narodowościowa na Ziemiach Odzyskanych* (Warsaw: Państwowe Wydawnictwo Naukowe, 1990), 93.
65. Piotr Madajczyk, *Niemcy polscy 1944–1989* (Warsaw: Oficyna Naukowa, 2001), 45–47.
66. Grzegorz Strauchold, *Autochtoni, Polscy, Niemieccy, czy . . . od nacjonalizmu do komunizmu (1945–1949)* (Toruń: Wydawnictwo Adam Marszałek, 2001), 26.
67. "Nowa sytuacja—nowe zadania," *Tribuna Wolności*, 28 Feb. 1945, no. 72, cited ibid., 34–35.
68. Baryła, *Warmiacy*, 4–6; Osękowski, *Społeczeństwo*, 90; Grzegorz Strauchold, *Polska ludność rodzima ziem zachodnich i północnych. Opinie nie tylko publiczne lat 1944–1948* (Olsztyn: Ośrodek Badań Naukowych im. Wojciecha Kętrzyńskiego, 1995), 17, 19, 34; Zenon Romanow, "Kształtowanie się polityki władz polskich wobec ludności rodzimej ziem zachodnich i północnych w latach 1945–1946," unpublished paper [1996?], 1–2.
69. Strauchold, *Autochtoni*, 37, 45.
70. Quoted in Romanow, "Kształtowanie się," 3.
71. Ibid.; Misztal, *Weryfikacja*, 192–193, 201; the quote is on 201.
72. Wojciech Wrzesiński, "Proces zasiedlania województwa olsztyńskiego w latach 1945–1949," in *Problemy rozwoju gospodarczego i demograficznego Ziem*

Zachodnich w latach 1945–1958, ed. Bohdan Gruchman and Janusz Ziólkowski (Poznań: Instytut Zachodni, 1960), 177.
73. Baryła, *Warmiacy,* 36.
74. Quoted in Leszek Belzyt, *Między Polską a Niemcami. Weryfikacja narodowościowa i jej następstwa na Warmii, Mazurach i Powiślu w latach 1945–1960* (Toruń: Wydawnictwo Adam Marszałek, 1998), 83.
75. Baryła, *Warmiacy,* 37–38; Wrzesiński quotes a similarly worded directive issued on 27 June 1945, "Proces zasiedlenia," 179n14.
76. Baryła,*Warmiacy,* 39–42; see also the directive, 16 June 1945, Borodziej and Lemberg, *Niemcy,* 1:429–430.
77. Borodziej and Lemberg, *Niemcy,* 3:62–63; the quote is on 63.
78. Jankowiak, "Niemcy w Wielkopolsce," 33, 35–37; report of the Poznań governor, 1 Mar. 1946, Borodziej and Lemberg, *Niemcy,* 3:102; Strauchold, *Autochtoni,* 51.
79. Excerpt, Daniel Boćkowski, ed., *Niemcy,* vol. 4, *Pomorze Gdańskie i Dolny Śląsk,* ed. Ingo Eser, Witold Stankowski, Claudia Kraft, and Stanisław Jankowiak (Warsaw: Wydawnictwo NERITON, 2001), 264; see also 265n3.
80. Stanisław Jankowiak, "Wojewodschaft Breslau (Niederschlesien). Die Jahre 1946–1950," in *Die Deutschen,* Borodziej and Lemberg, 4:428.
81. Baryła, *Warmiacy,* 28.
82. Ibid., 42–44; the quote is on 42.
83. Borodziej, "Wstęp," 86; excerpt, Borodziej and Lemberg, *Niemcy,* 2:360.
84. Misztal, *Weryfikacja,* 285, 288–290; the quote is on 288.
85. Stanisław Ossowski, "Zagadnienia więzi regionalnej i więzi narodowej na Śląsku Opolskim," in *O ojczyźnie i narodzie* (Warsaw: Państwowe Wydawnictwo Naukowe, 1984), 85, 116, 130.
86. Quoted in Misztal, *Weryfikacja,* 205–206; Philipp Ther, *Deutsche und polnische Vertriebene: Gesellschaft und Vertriebenenpolitik in der SBZ/DDR und in Polen 1945–1956* (Göttingen: Vandenhoeck & Ruprecht, 1998), 308; for other examples of a lack of hostility toward Germans, see Madajczyk, *Przyłączenie,* 58; Dmitrów, *Niemcy,* 304–305.
87. Strauchold, *Polska ludność,* 54.
88. Boćkowski, *Niemcy,* 73.
89. Ossowski, "Zagadnienia," 131.
90. Boćkowski, *Niemcy,* 60–62, 74. Lębork County became part of Gdańsk Province on 7 July 1945, Aleksander Kochański, *Polska 1944–1991. Informator historyczny,* vol. 1 (Warsaw: Wydawnictwo Sejmowe, 1996), 9.
91. Osękowski, *Społeczeństwo,* 92.
92. Misztal, *Weryfikacja,* 201–202; Service, "Sifting," 659.
93. Eser, "Niemcy," 323–324.
94. Minutes, Borodziej and Lemberg, *Niemcy,* 2:380.
95. Excerpt, ibid., 373.
96. Ibid., 381, 349, respectively.
97. Madajczyk, *Przyłączenie,* 195; Strauchold, *Autochtoni,* 53.
98. Misztal, *Weryfikacja,* 291–293, 296–297, 334; excerpt, Borodziej and Lemberg, *Niemcy,* 2:389–390.
99. Benjamin Frommer, "To Prosecute or to Expel? Czechoslovak Retribution and

the 'Transfer' of Sudeten Germans," in *Redrawing Nations: Ethnic Cleansing in East-Central Europe, 1944–1948*, ed. Philipp Ther and Ana Siljak (Lanham, MD: Rowman & Littlefield Publishers, Inc., 2001), 225–226, 230–231; Ossowski, "Zagadnienia," 85, 110, 112.
100. Baryła, *Warmiacy*, 46.
101. Ibid., 50, 52; the quote is on 52.
102. Michał Lengowski, *Na Warmii i w Westfalii. Wspomnienia*, ed. Janusz Jasiński (Warsaw: Instytut Wydawniczy Pax, 1972), 195–198; the quotes are on 197–198.
103. Władysław Gębik, *Pod warmińskim niebem. (O Michale Lengowskim)* (Warsaw: Ludowa Spółdzielnia Wydawnicza, 1974), 123. He also noted the lack of influence of locals in important matters, 132.
104. Leszek Belzyt, "Zum Verfahren der national Verifikation in den Gebieten des ehemaligen Ostpreussen 1945–1950," *Jahrbuch für die Geschichte Mittel- und Ostdeutschlands* 39 (1990): 266–268; excerpt, Borodziej and Lemberg, *Niemcy*, 1:436–438; see also 438n3, 466n3.
105. Quoted in Mieczysław Jaworski, *Na Piastowskim szlaku. Działalność Ministerstwa Ziem Odzyskanych w latach 1945–1948* (Warsaw: Wydawnictwo Ministerstwa Obrony Narodowej, 1973), 183.
106. Excerpts repr. in Strauchold, *Autochtoni*, 208–211.
107. Ibid., 45–46, 55, 73n90; the quote is on 73n90.
108. Zenon Romanow, *Ludność niemiecka na ziemiach zachodnich i północnych w latach 1945–1947* (Słupsk: Wyższa Szkoła Pedagogiczna w Słupsku, 1992), 46.
109. Jerzy Myszor, "Adamski Stanisław," in *Słownik biograficzny*, Pater, 9–10; Strauchold, *Autochtoni*, 15n21.
110. Claudia Kraft, "Wojewodschaft Breslau (Niederschlesien). Das Jahr 1945," in *Die Deutschen*, Borodziej und Lemberg, 4:388–390; Johannes Kaps, ed., *The Tragedy of Silesia, 1945–46: A Documentary Account with a Special Survey of the Archdiocese of Breslau* (Munich: Christ Unterwegs, 1952/53), 70.
111. Reproduced in Karol Jonca, ed., *Wysiedlenia Niemców i osadnictwo ludności polskiej na obszarze Krzyżowa-Świdnia (Kreisau-Schweidnitz) w latach 1945–1948: wybór dokumentów* (Wrocław: Wydawnictwo "Leopoldinum" Fundacji dla Uniwersytetu Wrocławskiego, 1997), 116, 118.
112. Madajczyk, *Przyłączenie*, 225–226; Bernard Linek, *Polityka antyniemiecka na Górnym Śląsku w latach 1945–1950* (Opole: Stowarzyszenie Instytut Śląski, Państwowy Instytut Naukowy, Instytut Śląski w Opolu, 2000), 293–297.
113. See Hans-Jürgen Karp, "Kardinal Hlond und das schwierige deutsch-polnische Verhältnis. Zu den Anfragen von Franz Scholz," *Zeitschrift für die Geschichte und Altertumskunde Ermlands* 45 (1989): 153.
114. Baryła, *Warmiacy*, 50–51, 51n1, 53, 56n5; Józef Pater, "Milik Karol, pseudo. Karol Bargieł (1892–1976), proboszcz, katecheta, infułat, administrator apostolski Dolnego Śląska, działacz oświatowy, redaktor," in *Słownik biograficzny*, Pater, 279. James E. Bjork notes that of seventeen bishops and five apostolic administrators in 1946, nine apparently were born within fifty miles of Poznań and five within fifty miles of Gliwice, private correspondence, 13 Mar. 2012. This suggests an overwhelming concern with the German threat and the Recovered Lands.

115. Maria Dąbrowska on 22 Nov. 1948 noted propaganda citing historic Catholic churches and cemeteries as evidence of the "immemorial Polishness of the area," *Dzienniki,* vol. 2, *1933–1945,* ed. Tadeusz Drewnowski (Warsaw: Cztelnik, 1988), 180.
116. Michael Fleming, *Communism, Nationalism and Ethnicity, 1944–50* (London: Routledge, 2010), 105, 123.
117. Ibid., 109.
118. Borodziej and Lemberg, *Niemcy,* 1:334n2.
119. Wiesław Kozub-Ciembroniewicz and Jacek M. Majchrowski, *Najnowsza historia polityczna Polski: wybór źródeł,* vol. 4, *1945–1948* (Cracow: Wydawnictwa "Księgarni Akademickiej," 1993), 167–170; the quote is on 167. Interestingly, the letter refers to settlers but not to autochthons.
120. Strauchold, *Autochtoni,* 194n121.
121. AAN, KC PZPR 237/VIII-119, fol. 35.
122. Baryła, *Warmiacy,* 57–58, 58n1, 79, 83n18; the quote is on 58n1.
123. Ibid., 74–83.
124. Ibid., 76, 79.
125. Ibid., 51–2. Currently, Warmia-Mazuria Province comprises all except Kwidzyn, Malbork, and Sztum.
126. Ibid., 52–53.
127. DzURP, no. 28, Entry 177, 28 June 1946, 329, http://dziennikustaw.gov.pl/DU/1946/s/28/177
128. Baryła, *Warmiacy,* 53–55; the quotes are on 54–55.
129. Ibid., 79–81.
130. Antoni Dudek and Andrzej Paczkowski, "Poland," in *A Handbook of the Communist Security Apparatus in East Central Europe 1944–1989,* ed. Krzysztof Persak and Łukasz Kamiński (Warsaw: Institute of National Remembrance, 2005), 242. See also Krzysztof Szwagrzyk, ed., *Aparat bezpieczeństwa w Polsce: kadra kierownicza* (Warsaw: Instytut Pamięci Narodowiej. Komisja Ścigania Zbrodni przeciwko Narodowi Polskiemu, 2005), 71–72.
131. Baryła, *Warmiacy,* 78; concerning Soviet advisors to the MBP and the MAP with the approval of Bierut and Osóbka-Morawski, see Beria to Stalin and Molotov, 1 Mar. 1945, Tatiana Cariewskaja et al., eds., *Teczka specjalna J. W. Stalina: raporty NKWD z Polski 1944–1946* (Warsaw: Oficyna Wydawnicza RYTM, 1998), 196. A "*sowietnik*" was assigned to each county and province; they were removed from the county level in 1947, Łukasz Kamiński, "Aparat Bezpieczeństwa i zbrodnie komunizmu," in *PRL od lipca 44 do grudnia 70,* ed. Krzysztof Persak and Paweł Machcewicz (Warsaw: Bellona, 2010), 243.
132. Baryła, *Warmiacy,* 81.
133. Belzyt, *Między Polską a Niemcami,* 59–60; Sakson, *Mazurzy,* 97.
134. Strauchold, *Autochtoni,* 85; Richard Blanke, *Polish-Speaking Germans? Language and National Identity among the Masurians since 1871* (Cologne: Böhlau Verlag, 2001), 298.
135. Report, 2 May 1945, excerpt, Borodziej and Lemberg, *Niemcy,* 2:338.
136. Madajczyk, *Przyłączenie,* 124–126.

137. Fleming, *Communism*, 161n20. See also Andrzej Paczkowski, "Żydzi w UB," in *Komunizm: Ideologia, system, ludzie,* ed. Tomasz Szarota (Warsaw: Wydawnictwo NERITON, 2001), 192–204. Jews filled 37.1 percent of executive positions in MBP 1944–1954 and 13.7 percent of positions as heads or deputy heads of WUBP; they constituted 14.6 percent of the security cadre in Silesia, Szwagrzyk, *Aparat bezpieczeństwa,* 59, 63–64. Jews held ten of sixty-five executive positions in the Silesian WUBP, Dudek and Paczkowski, "Poland," 241.
138. Excerpt, Borodziej and Lemberg, *Niemcy,* 2:339–340.
139. Madajczyk, *Przyłączenie,* 113–114, 119; the quote is on 114.
140. Franciszek Jonderko and Bernard Linek, "Austausch der Eliten in der Wojewodschaft Schlesien 1945–1950," summarized in "Region—Industrie—Zuwanderung. Oberschlesische Gesellschaftsgeschichte im 20. Jahrhundert. 27.11.2009–28.11.2009, Kattowitz/Katowice," ed. Gregor Ploch, in: H-Soz-u-Kult, 25.01.10, http://hsozkult.geschichte.hu-berlin.de/tagungsberichte/id=2966.
141. Danuta Berlińska, *Mniejszość niemiecka na Śląsku Opolskim w poszukiwaniu tożsamości* (Opole: Stowarzyszenie Instytut Śląski, Państwowy Instytut Naukowy—Institut Śląski w Opolu), 118, 118n52; Kłosek, "Swoi," 42–43. Bieniasz argues that those who advanced did so as communists, not as Upper Silesians, and had to represent exclusively the Polish elements in Upper Silesian consciousness, "Co dzieli," 29.
142. Matthias Kneip, *Die deutsche Sprache in Oberschlesien: Untersuchungen zur politischen Rolle der deutschen Sprache als Minderheitensprache in den Jahren 1921–1998,* 2nd ed. (Dormund: Forschungsstelle Ostmitteleuropa, 2000), 48–49. Kneip ignores the goal of cultural homogenization in stating that the Nazi ban on Polish explains but does not justify the ban on German, "Die politische Rolle der deutschen Sprache in Oberschlesien 1945–1998," in *Oberschlesische Dialoge: Kulturräume im Blickfeld von Wissenschaft und Literatur,* ed. Ante Johanning and Franz Steinfort (Frankfurt: Peter Lang, 2000), 231.
143. Excerpt repr. in Kneip, "Politische Rolle," 237; Linek, *Polityka,* 236.
144. Ossowski, "Zagadnienia," 104–107; Maria Szmeja, "Dlaczego Ślązacy z Opolszczyzny nie chcą być Polakami?" in *Mniejszości narodowe,* ed. Zbigniew Kurcz (Wrocław: Wydawnictwo Uniwersytetu Wrocławskiego, 1997), 113; Service, "Sifting," 676–677.
145. Strauchold, *Polska ludność,* 128.
146. Quoted in Linek, *Polityka antyniemiecka,* 225.
147. Ibid., 223–228.

7. After the Potsdam Conference

1. Władysław Gomułka, *On the German Problem. Articles and Speeches* (Warsaw: Książka i Wiedza Publishers, 1969), 30, 37.
2. FRUS, *1945,* vol. 2, *General: Political and Economic Matters* (Washington, DC: U.S. Government Printing Office, 1967), 1266, 1276–1277, 1279, 1318–1319; Alfred M. De Zayas, *Nemesis at Potsdam: The Expulsion of the Germans from the East,* 3rd rev. ed. (Lincoln: University of Nebraska Press, 1989), 94–96, 118; Arthur Bliss

Lane, *I Saw Poland Betrayed: An American Ambassador Reports to the American People* (Boston: Western Islands, 1965), 122–123.

3. Bernadetta Nitschke, *Wysiedlenie ludności niemieckiej z Polski w latach 1945–1949* (Zielona Góra: Wyższa Szkoła Pedagogiczna im. Tadeusza Kotarbińskiego, 1999), 136; Leszek Belzyt, *Między Polską a Niemcami. Weryfikacja narodowościowa i jej następstwa na Warmii, Mazurach i Powiślu w latach 1945–1960* (Toruń: Wydawnictwo Adam Marszałek, 1998), 77; FRUS, *1945*, 2:1277.

4. Reproduced in Karol Jonca, ed., *Wysiedlenia Niemców i osadnictwo ludności polskiej na obszarze Krzyżowa-Świdnia (Kreisau-Schweidnitz) w latach 1945–1948: wybór dokumentów* (Wrocław: Wydawnictwo "Leopoldinum" Fundacji dla Uniwersytetu Wrocławskiego, 1997), 408, 410.

5. Krystyna Kersten, *Narodziny systemu władzy, Polska 1943–1948* (Poznań: SAWW, 1990), 149; Michael Fleming, *Communism, Nationalism and Ethnicity, 1944–50* (London: Routledge, 2010), 57. UNRRA's mission in Poland was the most expensive single-country program in Europe targeted to stem typhus and cholera epidemics and alleviate mass starvation, Jessica Reinisch, "'Auntie UNRRA' at the Crossroads," *Past and Present* 218, suppl. 8 (2013), 73, 75.

6. Anita J. Prażmowska, *Civil War in Poland, 1942–1948* (New York: Palgrave Macmillan, 2004). Maria Turlejska characterizes the "civil war" as one-sided communist terror, *Te pokolenia żałobami czarne... Skazani na śmierć i ich sędziowie* (Warsaw: Niezależna Oficyna Wydawnicza, 1990) 64–71.

7. Włodzimierz Borodziej, "Wstęp: sprawa polska i przemieszczenia ludności w czasie II wojny światowej," in *Niemcy*, ed. Borodziej and Hans Lemberg, vol. 1, *Władze i instytucje centralne. Województwo olsztyńskie*, ed. Borodziej and Claudia Kraft (Warsaw: Wydawnictwo NERITON, 2000), 92–93; protokol, Tadeusz Baryła, ed., *Warmiacy i Mazurzy w PRL. Wybor dokumentów. Rok 1945* (Olsztyn: Ośrodek Badań Naukowych im. Wojciecha Kętrzyńskiego, 1994), 93–94.

8. Quoted in Ingo Eser, "Niemcy na Górnym Śląsku," in *Niemcy*, ed. Włodzimierz Borodziej and Hans Lemberg, vol. 2, *Polska Centralna. Województwo śląskie*, ed. Eser and Jerzy Kochanowski (Warsaw: Wydawnictwo NERITON, 2000), 320.

9. Krzysztof Stryjkowski, *Położenie osób wpisanych w Wielkopolsce na niemiecką listę narodowościową w latach 1945–1950* (Poznań: Instytut Historii UAM, 2004), 267, 272, 278.

10. Report, Poznań governor, 1 Mar. 1946, Włodzimierz Borodziej and Hans Lemberg, eds., *Niemcy*, vol. 3, *Województwa poznańskie i szczecińskie*, ed. Stanisław Jankowiak and Katrin Steffen (Warsaw: Wydawnictwo NERITON, 2001), 102; Stryjkowski, *Położenie*, 275.

11. Borodziej and Lemberg, *Niemcy*, 3:87, 92–93; see also 93n1; the quote is on 87 (emphasis in original); Stryjkowski, *Położenie*, 277, 288–290.

12. Daniel Boćkowski, ed., *Niemcy*, vol. 4, *Pomorze Gdańskie i Dolny Śląsk*, ed. Ingo Eser, Witold Stankowski, Claudia Kraft, and Stanisław Jankowiak (Warsaw: Wydawnictwo NERITON, 2001), 89.

13. Repr. in Leszek Olejnik, *Zdrajcy narodu? Losy Volksdeutschów w Polsce po II wojnie światowej* (Warsaw: Wydawnictwo Trio, 2006), 240–241.

14. FRUS, *1945*, 2: 1316–1317; memo, Łódź governor, 14 Feb. 1946, Borodziej and Lemberg, *Niemcy*, 2:153–154; Nitschke, *Wysiedlenie*, 162.
15. Quoted in Eser, "Niemcy," 324.
16. Leszek Belzyt, *Między Polską a Niemcami*, 77.
17. Repr. in Jan Misztal, *Weryfikacja narodowościowa na Ziemiach Odzyskanych* (Warsaw: Państwowe Wydawnictwo Naukowe, 1990), 346–351; the quote is on 346.
18. Quoted ibid., 226.
19. Sept. 1946, excerpt, Borodziej and Lemberg, *Niemcy*, 2:436.
20. Bernard Linek, "Realizacja idei polskiego państwa narodowego na Górnym Śląsku po II wojnie światowej," *Sprawy Narodowościowe*, nos. 12–13 (1998): 24; Grzegorz Strauchold, *Polska ludność rodzima ziem zachodnich i północnych. Opinie nie tylko publiczne lat 1944–1948* (Olsztyn: Ośrodek Badań Naukowych im. Wojciecha Kętrzyńskiego, 1995), 26, 77; Misztal, *Weryfikacja*, 226–227.
21. Quoted in Grzegorz Strauchold, *Autochtoni, Polscy, Niemieccy, czy . . . od nacjonalizmu do komunizmu (1945–1949)* (Toruń: Wydawnictwo Adam Marszałek, 2001), 61n48.
22. Bernard Linek, *Polityka antyniemiecka na Górnym Śląsku w latach 1945–1950* (Opole: Stowarzyszenie Instytut Śląski, Państwowy Instytut Naukowy, Instytut Śląski w Opolu, 2000), 234; Eser, "Niemcy," 326–327.
23. Misztal, *Weryfikacja*, 249–251, 261, 325; the quote is on 261.
24. Repr. ibid., 346–351; the quotes are on 346, 347, and 347, respectively.
25. Repr. ibid., 350.
26. Quoted in Mieczysław Jaworski, *Na Piastowskim szlaku. Działalność Ministerstwa Ziem Odzyskanych w latach 1945–1948* (Warsaw: Wydawnictwo Ministerstwa Obrony Narodowej, 1973), 164.
27. Borodziej and Lemberg, *Niemcy*, 2:406n4; Eser, "Niemcy," 326.
28. Jacek Ruszczewski dates the expulsion of some 400, including women, children, and the elderly, to the end of Aug. 1945, "Nacjonalizm, szowinizm, czy syndrom odwetu i odpowiedzialności zbiorowej? (Konflikty międzygrupowe na przykładzie Śląska Opolskiego w latach 1945–1949)," in *Fenomen nowoczesnego nacjonalizmu w Europie Środkowej*, ed. Bernard Linek, Jörg Lüer, and Kai Struve (Opole: Wydawnictwo Instytut Śląski, 1997), 118.
29. Borodziej and Lemberg, *Niemcy*, 2:406n6.
30. Excerpt, ibid., 404–405.
31. Excerpt, ibid., 399–400; the quote is on 400.
32. Baryła, *Warmiacy*, 92.
33. Belzyt, *Między Polską a Niemcami*, 77–78; the quote is on 78; Ingo Eser and Witold Stankowski, "Wojewodschaften Pommerellen und Danzig (Westpreussen)," in *Die Deutschen*, ed. Włodzimierz Borodziej and Hans Lemberg, vol. 4, *Wojewodschaften Pommerellen und Danzig (Westpreussen). Wojewodschaft Beslau (Niederschlesien)*, ed. Eser, Stankowski, Claudia Kraft, and Stanisław Jankowiak (Marburg: Verlag Herder-Institut, 2004), 55.
34. Boćkowski, *Niemcy*, 130–133; the quote is on 131.
35. Stryjkowski, *Położenie*, 289.
36. Borodziej and Lemberg, *Niemcy*, 3:92.

37. Ibid., 94–95.
38. Ibid., 307–309. The ZPwN in Złotów had about 1,500 members and included Rev. Bolesław Domański, who led the ZPwN 1931–1939, ibid., 309n2.
39. Notes of a MZO Department of Inspection official, 27 Oct. 1946, ibid., 361–362.
40. Katrin Steffen, "Ucieczka, wypędzenie i przymusowe wysiedlenie Niemców z województwa szczecińskiego w latach 1945-1950," in *Niemcy*, Borodziej and Lemberg, 3:261.
41. Borodziej and Lemberg, *Niemcy*, 2:393–394.
42. Quoted in Misztal, *Weryfikacja*, 205.
43. Strauchold, *Autochtoni*, 111.
44. Christopher Lash focuses on disputes between repatriates and settlers in Zielona Góra, where autochthons were largely absent, "'Conflict Over Property': Lodging in Times of Displacement, Poland 1944-1946, the Case of Zielona Góra," *Europe-Asia Studies* 65, no. 10 (2013): 1991–92. Property disputes embittered intergroup relations in Anatolia following the Treaty of Lausanne, Biray Kolluoğlu, "Excesses of Nationalism: Greco-Turkish Population Exchange," *Nations and Nationalism* 19, no. 3 (2013): 541–542.
45. Repr. in Misztal, *Weryfikacja*, 346–351; the quote is on 349. Zawadzki recommended a similar procedure on 28 Aug. 1945, Strauchold, *Autochtoni*, 109.
46. Borodziej and Lemberg, *Niemcy*, 1:474n1; Strauchold, *Autochtoni*, 111–112.
47. Report, excerpt Boćkowski, *Niemcy*, 101.
48. Report, Gdańsk UW, excerpt, ibid., 128.
49. Ibid., 115.
50. Borodziej, "Wstęp," 75, 102; Jaworski, *Na Piastowskim szlaku*, 177; Zenon Romanow, *Ludność niemiecka na ziemiach zachodnich i północnych w latach 1945-1947* (Słupsk: Wyższa Szkoła Pedagogiczna w Słupsku, 1992), 47.
51. Quoted in Misztal, *Weryfikacja*, 222.
52. Excerpt, Borodziej and Lemberg, *Niemcy*, 1:473–474.
53. Andreas Kossert, *Preußen, Deutsche oder Polen? Die Masuren im Spannungsfeld des ethnischen Nationalismus 1870–1956* (Wiesbaden: Harrassowitz Verlag, 2001), 309.
54. Borodziej and Lemberg, *Niemcy*, 1:476–477.
55. Misztal, *Weryfikacja*, 185. Strauchold cites 110,057 returnees in 1946–1948, *Autochtoni*, 58.
56. Report, Settlement Department, Bytom Municipal Government, 2 Dec. 1946, excerpt, Borodziej and Lemberg, *Niemcy*, 2:450, 452.
57. Strauchold, *Autochtoni*, 113.
58. Boćkowski, *Niemcy*, 143.
59. DzURP, no. 49, Entry 279, 14 Oct. 1946, 513–518, http://dziennikustaw.gov.pl/DU/1946/s/49/279.
60. Borodziej and Lemberg, *Niemcy*, 1:474n1; Strauchold, *Autochtoni*, 109n245.
61. Quoted in Strauchold, *Autochtoni*, 169–170, 170n18.
62. Jaworski, *Na Piastowskim szlaku*, 178.
63. Boćkowski, *Niemcy*, 166–167; the quote is on 166.
64. Stryjkowski, *Położenie*, 497
65. Boćkowski, *Niemcy*, 400.

66. Strauchold, *Autochtoni*, 170–171, 170n19.
67. Jaworski, *Na Piastowskim szlaku*, 178–179; Leszek Belzyt, "Zum Verfahren der national Verifikation in den Gebieten des ehemaligen Ostpreussen 1945–1950," *Jahrbuch für die Geschichte Mittel- und Ostdeutschlands* 39 (1990): 261; Jerzy Kochanowski, "Gathering Poles into Poland: Forced Migration from Poland's Former Eastern Territories," in *Redrawing Nations: Ethnic Cleansing in East-Central Europe, 1944–1948*, ed. Philipp Ther and Ana Siljak (Lanham, MD: Rowman & Littlefield Publishers, Inc., 2001), 147–148; Strauchold, *Autochtoni*, 171.
68. Barbara Törnquist Plewa, *The Wheel of Polish Fortune: Myths in Polish Collective Consciousness during the First Years of Solidarity* (Lund, Sweden: Lund University, 1992), 18.
69. Brunon Synak, "Kaszubi w nowych warunkach ustrojowych," in *U progu wielokulturowości. Nowe oblicza społeczeństwa polskiego*, ed. Marian Kempny, Alina Kapciak, and Sławomir Łodziński (Warsaw: Oficyna Naukowa, 1997), 203; Piotr Madajczyk, *Niemcy polscy 1944–1989* (Warsaw: Oficyna Naukowa, 2001), 20; excerpt, Boćkowski, *Niemcy*, 91.
70. Strauchold, *Autochtoni*, 88–90; the quote is on 89.
71. Quoted in Madajczyk, *Niemcy*, 40.
72. Strauchold, *Autochtoni*, 88–90 and 88n165; the quote is on 88n165.
73. Borodziej and Lemberg, *Die Deutschen*, 4:210–213; the inhabitants of Łeba included Slovincians, 212n12. On Cewice, see Cezary Obracht-Prondzyński, "Kaszubi ziem 'dawnych' i 'nowych'—bilans z perspektywy sześćdziesięciolecia," in *Ziemie Odzyskane/Ziemie Zachodnie i Północne 1945–2005: 60 lat w granicach państwa polskiego*, ed. Andrzej Sakson (Poznań: Instytut Zachodni, 2006), 225.
74. Memo, Gdańsk Provincial Verification Commission, 22 July 1946, Steffen, "Ucieczka," 261–262; the quote is on 262.
75. Benjamin Frommer, *National Cleansing: Retribution against Nazi Collaborators in Postwar Czechoslovakia* (Cambridge: Cambridge University Press, 2005), 200–201; Chad Bryant, "Either German or Czech: Fixing Nationality in Bohemia and Moravia, 1939–1946," *Slavic Review* 61, no. 4 (Winter 2002): 698–700; the quote is on 698; Benjamin Frommer, "To Prosecute or to Expel? Czechoslovak Retribution and the 'Transfer' of Sudeten Germans," in *Redrawing Nations*, ed. Ther and Siljak, 222, 225–227.
76. DzURP, no.34, Entry 203, 19 Sept. 1945, 274, http://dziennikustaw.gov.pl/DU/1945/s/34/203.
77. Stanisław Jankowiak, "Niemcy w Wielkopolsce i na Ziemi Lubuskiej w latach 1945–1950," in *Niemcy*, ed. Borodziej and Lemberg, 3:41.
78. Stryjkowski, *Położenie*, 521–522, 547. On the events in Germany, see Edmund Dmitrów, *Niemcy i okupacja hitlerowska w oczach Polaków. Poglądy i opinie z lat 1945–1948* (Warsaw: Czytelnik, 1987), 228–230, 356n29.
79. Borodziej and Lemberg, *Niemcy*, 3:127n1; *starosta* report, 4 Oct. 1945, excerpt ibid., 85. In Czechoslovakia Germans were commonly forced to wear the letter *N*, Eagle Glassheim, "National Mythologies and Ethnic Cleansing: The Expulsion of Czechoslovak Germans in 1945," *Central European History* 33, no. 4 (2000): 479.
80. Stryjkowski, *Położenie*, 505–506.
81. Ibid., 432–433.

82. Ibid., 43, 527–528, 528n92.
83. Małgorzata Pośpiech provided this information. See her novel inspired in part by incidents in Kępno, *Miasteczko* (Toruń: Wydawnictwo Adam Marszałek, 2014).
84. Repr. in Romuald Turkowski, ed., *Opozycja parlamentarna w Krajowej Radzie Narodowej i Sejmie Ustawodawczym 1945–1947* (Warsaw: Wydawnictwo Sejmowe, 1997), 70–73.
85. Stryjkowski, *Położenie*, 566.
86. Borodziej and Lemberg, *Niemcy*, 3:93.
87. Report, 15 Nov. 1946, excerpt, ibid., 134–135.
88. Stryjkowski, *Położenie*, 522, 525–526.
89. Ibid., 436–438.
90. Ibid., 43, 428, 433.
91. Borodziej and Lemberg, *Niemcy*, 2:386.
92. Ibid., 394–395; 395n3, 4; 396n5; the quotes are on 394, 395, respectively.
93. Ibid., 390.
94. Report, 8 Oct. 1945, ibid., 391.
95. Baryła, *Warmiacy*, 76–78; the quote is on 76.
96. Ibid., 74–83; the quotes are on 75.
97. Ibid., 76–77, 81; the quote is on 81.
98. Excerpt, Borodziej and Lemberg, *Niemcy*, 2:239.
99. Quoted in Andrzej Sakson, *Mazurzy—społeczność pogranicza* (Poznań: Instytut Zachodni, 1990), 112.
100. Excerpts, Borodziej and Lemberg, *Niemcy*, 2: 240, 242–246; the quotes are on 244 and 246, respectively.
101. Excerpts, reports, 1 Sept., 10 Oct., 1 Oct. 1945, respectively, ibid., 94–96.
102. Jerzy Kochanowski, "Losy Niemców w Polsce Centralnej w latach 1945–1950. Na przykładzie województw łódzkiego, warszawskiego i krakowskiego (powiat Biała)," in *Niemcy*, ed., Borodziej and Lemberg, 2:50.
103. Reports, 12 Dec. 1945, 31 Dec. 1945, 16 February 1946, 9 April 1946, excerpts, ibid., 97–100.
104. Ibid., 3:146n5, citing a memo of the Poznań governor, 29 Sept. 1945; report, Działdowo *starosta*, 4 Feb. 1946, excerpt, ibid., 2:244.
105. Kochanowski, "Losy Niemców," 58, 58n172, 58n173.
106. Borodziej and Lemberg, *Niemcy*, 2:153–154; the quote is on 153.
107. Boćkowski, *Niemcy*, 117; table, 15 Nov. 1946, Borodziej and Lemberg, *Niemcy*, 3:129.
108. Borodziej and Lemberg, *Niemcy*, 3:107n3; ibid., 1:191–192.
109. DzURP, no. 11, Entry 73, 31 Mar. 1946, 137–139, http://dziennikustaw.gov.pl/DU/1946/s/11/73.
110. Reports, 12 Jan., 11 Mar., 13 May 1946, excerpts, Borodziej and Lemberg, *Niemcy*, 2:99, 100, 102.
111. Kochanowski, "Losy Niemców," 49–50.
112. Report, 13 May 1946, excerpt, Borodziej and Lemberg, *Niemcy*, 2:102; 102–3n1.
113. Reports, 3 Jan. 1946, 3 Mar. 1946, excerpts, ibid., 243–244, 245, respectively.
114. Quoted in Andrzej Grajewski, *Wygnanie. Diecezja katowicka w czasach stalinowskich,* 3rd rev. ed. (Katowice: Księgarnia św. Jacka; Gość niedzielny, 2002), 42.

115. Quoted in Stryjkowski, *Położenie*, 413n46.
116. Repr. in Olejnik, *Zdrajcy narodu?*, 241–246.
117. Stefan Szulc, ed., *Powszechny sumaryczny spis ludności z dn. 14.II. 1946 r.* (Warsaw: Nakładem Głównego Urzędu Statystycznego, 1947), xvi, http://www.scribd.com/doc/36839158/Powszechny-Sumaryczny-Spis-Ludno%C5%9Bci-z-dn-14-II-1946-roku-1.
118. Boćkowski, *Niemcy*, 126–127; the quote is on 127.
119. Ibid.
120. Borodziej and Lemberg, *Niemcy*, 1:213–214; the quote is on 213.
121. Marek Romaniuk, *Podzwonne okupacji: Deutsche Volksliste w Bydgoszczy (1945–1950)* (Bydgoszcz: Agencja ARTPRESS, 1993), 136; Stryjkowski, *Położenie*, 229, 352–353.
122. See for example Borodziej and Lemberg, *Niemcy*, 2:252; Kochanowski, "Losy Niemców," 51n138, 53n147.
123. Gerald Daniel Cohen, *In War's Wake: Europe's Displaced Persons in the Postwar Order* (New York: Oxford University Press, 2012), 5, 18, 139; Pieter Lagrou, *The Legacy of Nazi Occupation: Patriotic Memory and National Recovery in Western Europe, 1945–1965* (Cambridge: Cambridge University Press, 2000), 81–82. See also Keith Sword with Norman Davies and Jan Ciechanowski, *The Formation of the Polish Community in Great Britain 1939–1950* (London: School of Slavonic and East European Studies, University of London, 1989), 63–64, 198.
124. Quoted in Fleming, *Communism*, 45.
125. Misztal, *Weryfikacja*, 185, 187; the quote is on 187.
126. Arne Øland, "Silences, Public and Private," in *Children of World War II: The Hidden Enemy Legacy*, ed. Kjersti Ericsson and Eva Simonsen (Oxford: Berg Publishers, 2005), 67–68; the quote is on 68.
127. See Aleksandra Klich, "Został z nich maras," *Gazeta Wyborcza*, 13 Jan. 2010, http://wyborcza.pl/1,75515,7450538,Zostal_z_nich_maras.html?utm_source=Nlt&utm_medium=Nlt&utm_campaign=961608; "W znienawidzonym mundurze. Losy Polaków przymusowo wcielonych do Wojska niemieckiego w okresie II wojny światowej," http://www.wehrmacht-polacy.pl/index.html; Ryszard Kaczmarek, *Polacy w Wehrmachcie* (Cracow: Wydawnictwo Literackie, 210), 297–299, 360–366, 373. During the 2005 Polish presidential campaign, political opponents of Premier Donald Tusk made an issue of his grandfather's service in the Wehrmacht.
128. Stryjkowski, *Położenie*, 582–583.
129. Misztal, *Weryfikacja*, 166–171.
130. Kaczmarek, *Polacy w Wehrmachcie*, 378; Stryjkowski, *Położenie*, 582; Halik Kochanski, *The Eagle Unbowed: Poland and the Poles in the Second World War* (Cambridge, MA: Harvard University Press, 2012), 475, 559.
131. Excerpt, Borodziej and Lemberg, *Niemcy*, 2:412–413; the quote is on 413.
132. Kaczmarek, *Polacy w Wehrmachcie*, 380–381; the quote is on 381.
133. Kochanski, *Eagle Unbowed*, 583–584.
134. Excerpts, Borodziej and Lemberg, *Niemcy*, 2:248, 246, 250, respectively.
135. Quoted in Stryjkowski, *Położenie*, 583.
136. Kaczmarek, *Polacy w Wehrmachcie*, 380.
137. Stryjkowski, *Położenie*, 24–25n23.

138. Ibid., 467.
139. Strauchold, *Autochtoni*, 46–47.
140. Excerpt, ibid., 211.
141. Baryła, *Warmiacy*, 116.
142. Strauchold, *Autochtoni*, 47.
143. Excerpt, Gomułka, *On the German Problem*, 70–77; the quote is on 74–75.
144. Strauchold, *Autochtoni*, 47–48, 56.
145. Eser, "Niemcy na Górnym Śląsku," 321.
146. Linek, "Realizacja," 25–26; Stryjkowski, *Położenie*, 280–281, 281n132.
147. Reproduced in Jonca, *Wysiedlenia*, 152, 154.
148. Misztal, *Weryfikacja*, 230; Czesław Osękowski, *Społeczeństwo Polski zachodniej i północnej w latach 1945-1956: Procesy integracji i dezintegracji* (Zielona Góra: Wyższa Szkoła Pedagogiczna im. Tadeusza Kotarbińskiego, 1994), 93.
149. Eser, "Niemcy," 327.
150. Borodziej and Lemberg, *Niemcy*, 3:330–332; the quotes are on 331–332.
151. Quoted in Piotr Madajczyk, *Przyłączenie Śląska Opolskiego do Polski, 1945-1948* (Warsaw: Instytut Studiów Politycznych PAN, 1996), 234.
152. Excerpt, Borodziej and Lemberg, *Niemcy*, 2:411.
153. Jan Berger states that no postwar census included questions concerning nationality or mother tongue, "Organizacja i tematyka badań statystyki ludności w okresie 1918–1990," in *Historia Polski w liczbach: ludność, terytorium*, ed. Franciszek Kubiczek (Warsaw: Główny Urząd Statystyczny, 1993), 124.

8. The Central Government and Nationality Verification

1. Repr. in Grzegorz Strauchold, *Autochtoni, Polscy, Niemieccy, czy . . . od nacjonalizmu do komunizmu (1945-1949)* (Toruń: Wydawnictwo Adam Marszałek, 2001), 220–222. Anna Wolff-Powęska quotes a version published in Mar. 1946, "Rola Polskiego Związku Zachodniego w zagospodarowaniu Ziem Zachodnich," *Przegląd Zachodni* 26, no. 4 (1970): 433; Zenon Romanow dates a similar memorandum 2 Feb. 1946, "Kształtowanie się polityki władz polskich wobec ludności rodzimej ziem zachodnich i północnych w latach 1945-1946," unpublished paper [1996?], 11.
2. Zygmunt Izdebski, "Podstawy weryfikacji ludności na Śląsku Opolskim," *Zaranie Śląskie*, nos. 1–2 (1946): 29–34; the quotes are on 30, 29, 32, respectively; Strauchold, *Autochtoni*, 57.
3. Quoted in Philipp Ther, *Deutsche und polnische Vertriebene: Gesellschaft und Vertriebenenpolitik in der SBZ / DDR und in Polen 1945-1956* (Göttingen: Vandenhoeck & Ruprecht, 1998), 318.
4. Quoted in Ingo Eser, "Niemcy na Górnym Śląsku," in *Niemcy*, ed. Włodzimierz Borodziej and Hans Lemberg, vol. 2, *Polska Centralna. Województwo śląskie*, ed. Eser and Jerzy Kochanowski (Warsaw: Wydawnictwo NERITON, 2000), 330.
5. Strauchold, *Autochtoni*, 62.
6. Andrzej Paczkowski, *Od sfałszowanego zwycięstwa do prawdziwej klęski. Szkice do portretu PRL* (Cracow: Wydawnictwo Literackie, 1999), 18–19.

7. Quoted in Strauchold, *Autochtoni,* 58.
8. Quoted in Jan Misztal, *Weryfikacja narodowościowa na Ziemiach Odzyskanych* (Warsaw: Państwowe Wydawnictwo Naukowe, 1990), 230; Czesław Osękowski, *Społeczeństwo Polski zachodniej i pólnocnej w latach 1945-1956: procesy integracji i dezintegracji* (Zielona Góra: Wyższa Szkoła Pedagogiczna im. Tadeusza Kotarbińskiego, 1994), 93.
9. Włodzimerz Borodziej and Hans Lemberg, eds., *Niemcy,* vol. 1, *Władze i instytucje centralne. Województwo olsztyńskie,* ed. Borodziej and Claudia Kraft (Warsaw: Wydawnictwo NERITON, 2000), 471.
10. Piotr Madajczyk, *Niemcy polscy: 1944-1989* (Warsaw: Oficyna Naukowa, 2001), 45.
11. Excerpt, Borodziej and Lemberg, *Niemcy,* 2:410-411.
12. Repr. in Misztal, *Weryfikacja,* 351-362; the quotes are on 351, 352. All counties of the Recovered Lands were under Polish administration by 17 July 1945, ibid., 101.
13. Marcin Kula, "Obywatel kraju i świata," *Ethos* 87-88 (July-Dec. 2009): 65-68.
14. Misztal, *Weryfikacja,* 352-353; the quote is on 352.
15. Hugo Service, "Sifting Poles from Germans? Ethnic Cleansing and Ethnic Screening in Upper Silesia, 1945-1949," *Slavonic and East European Review* 88, no. 4 (October 2010): 666-668; Misztal, *Weryfikacja,* 349.
16. Misztal, *Weryfikacja,* 355.
17. Włodzimerz Borodziej, "Wstęp: sprawa polska i przemieszczenia ludności w czasie II wojny światowej," in *Niemcy,* ed. Borodziej and Lemberg, 1:102.
18. DzURP, no. 15, Entry 104, 10 May 1946, 1989-1990, http://dziennikustaw.gov.pl/DU/1946/s/15/104
19. Ibid., Entry 106, 10 May 1946, 195, http://dziennikustaw.gov.pl/DU/1946/s/15/106.
20. Quoted in Grzegorz Strauchold, *Polska ludność rodzima ziem zachodnich i północnych. Opinie nie tylko publiczne lat 1944-1948* (Olsztyn: Ośrodek Badań Naukowych im. Wojciecha Kętrzyńskiego, 1995), 24.
21. Quoted in Strauchold, *Autochtoni,* 112.
22. Quoted in Strauchold, *Polska ludność,* 25.
23. Excerpt, Daniel Boćkowski, ed., *Niemcy,* vol. 4, *Pomorze Gdańskie i Dolny Śląsk,* ed. Ingo Eser, Witold Stankowski, Claudia Kraft, and Stanisław Jankowiak (Warsaw: Wydawnictwo NERITON, 2001), 136.
24. Piotr Madajczyk, *Przyłączenie Śląska Opolskiego do Polski, 1945-1948* (Warsaw: Instytut Studiów Politycznych PAN, 1996), 195.
25. Quoted in Krystyna Kersten, *The Establishment of Communist Rule in Poland, 1943-1948* (Berkeley: University of California Press, 1991), 271-272.
26. Strauchold, *Autochtoni,* 92.
27. Andrzej Paczkowski, ed., *Referendum z 30 czerwca 1946 r. Przebieg i wyniki* (Warsaw: Instytut Studiów Politycznych Polskiej Akademii Nauk, 1993), 10.
28. Quoted in Włodzimierz Borodziej and Hans Lemberg, eds., *Niemcy,* vol. 3, *Województwa poznańskie i szczecińskie,* ed. Stanisław Jankowiak and Katrin Steffen (Warsaw: Wydawnictwo NERITON, 2001), 349n3.
29. Quoted in Strauchold, *Autochtoni,* 130-131 (emphasis in original).
30. Repr. ibid., 226-227.
31. Quoted ibid., 130.

32. Wiesław Kozub-Ciembroniewicz and Jacek M. Majchrowski, *Najnowsza historia polityczna Polski: wybór źródeł*, vol. 4, *1945–1948* (Cracow: Wydawnictwa "Księgarni Akademickiej," 1993), 110–113; the quote is on 112.
33. Paczkowski, *Referendum*, 11–14, 97, 105.
34. Quoted in Strauchold, *Autochtoni*, 135, 134, respectively.
35. Excerpt, Borodziej and Lemberg, *Niemcy*, 2:420–421.
36. Memo, Olesno PUIiP, 19 July 1946, excerpt, ibid., 423.
37. Joachim Georg Görlich, "Autochtoni," *Kultura*, nos. 1/195–2/196 (1964): 135.
38. Quoted in Paczkowski, *Referendum*, 16.
39. Witold Kula, "Nikt nas nie kocha," in *Rozdziałki*, ed. Marcin Kula (Warsaw: Wydawnictwo TRIO, 1996), 252.
40. Strauchold, *Autochtoni*, 81–83.
41. Leszek Belzyt, "Zum Verfahren der national Verifikation in den Gebieten des ehemaligen Ostpreussen 1945–1950," *Jahrbuch für die Geschichte Mittel- und Ostdeutschlands* 39 (1990): 259; [Peter Brock], "Poland," in Roger C. Wilson, *Quaker Relief; An Account of the Relief Work of the Society of Friends 1940–1948* (London: George Allen & Unwin Ltd., 1952), 301–320; Belzyt, *Między Polską a Niemcami. Weryfikacja narodowościowa i jej następstwa na Warmii, Mazurach i Powiślu w latach 1945–1960* (Toruń: Wydawnictwo Adam Marszałek, 1998), 67.
42. Boćkowski, *Niemcy*, 125–126; the quotes are on 125.
43. Włodzimerz Borodziej and Hans Lemberg, eds., *Die Deutschen*, vol. 4, *Wojewodschaften Pommerellen und Danzig (Westpreussen). Wojewodschaft Breslau (Niederschlesien)*, ed. Ingo Eser, Witold Stankowski, Claudia Kraft, and Stanisław Jankowiak (Marburg: Verlag Herder-Institut, 2004), 208–210.
44. Excerpt, Boćkowski, *Niemcy*, 136.
45. Ibid., 349–350; the quote is on 350.
46. Stanisław Jankowiak, "Wojewodschaft Breslau (Niederschlesien). Die Jahre 1946–1950," in *Die Deutschen*, Borodziej and Lemberg, 4:417, 429.
47. Borodziej and Lemberg, *Niemcy*, 2:415.
48. Report, 10 July 1946, excerpt, ibid., 421.
49. Borodziej and Lemberg, *Die Deutschen*, 4:232.
50. Report for June 1946, excerpt, ibid., 421.
51. Misztal, *Weryfikacja*, 291–292; the quote is on 292.
52. Excerpt, Borodziej and Lemberg, *Niemcy*, 3:355–356; the quote is on 355.
53. Madajczyk, *Przyłączenie*, 242.
54. Borodziej and Lemberg, *Niemcy*, 3:353–354, 354n2; the quote is on 354n2.
55. Letter, 4 July 1947, quoted in Katrin Steffen, "Ucieczka, wypędzenie i przymusowe wysiedlenie Niemców z województwa szczecińskiego w latach 1945–1950," in *Niemcy*, Borodziej and Lemberg, 3:261.
56. Ibid., 354.
57. Quoted in Bernadetta Nitschke, *Wysiedlenie ludności niemieckiej z Polski w latach 1945–1949* (Zielona Góra: Wyższa Szkoła Pedagogiczna im. Tadeusza Kotarbińskiego, 1999), 109–110.
58. Jankowiak, "Wojewodschaft Breslau," 430–431. Borodziej and Lemberg, *Die Deutschen*, 4:374n59, states that only 16,000 of the province's 40,000 autochthons were verified by the end of 1946 and only 17,000 by the 1950s.

59. Borodziej and Lemberg, *Niemcy,* 1:250–251.
60. Strauchold, *Autochtoni,* 79; Elżbieta Kaszuba, *Między propagandą a rzeczywistością: Polska ludność Wrocławia w latach 1945-1947* (Warsaw-Wrocław: Wydawnictwo Naukowe PWN, 1997), 69, 79.
61. Repr. in Władysław Gębik, *Pod warmińskim niebem. (O Michale Lengowskim)* (Warsaw: Ludowa Spółdzielnia Wydawnicza, 1974), 125–126.
62. Repr. ibid., 127–128; the quote is on 128.
63. Misztal, *Weryfikacja,* 234–235.
64. Belzyt, "Zum Verfahren," 259, 268; quoted in Richard Blanke, *Polish-Speaking Germans? Language and National Identity among the Masurians since 1871* (Cologne: Böhlau Verlag, 2001), 293.
65. Borodziej and Lemberg, *Niemcy,* 1:466–468.
66. Jan Szczepański, "Przedmowa," in Andrzej Sakson, *Mazurzy—społeczność pogranicza* (Poznań: Instytut Zachodni, 1990), ix–x, xii–xiii.
67. Excerpt, Borodziej and Lemberg, *Niemcy,* 1:477–478.
68. Belzyt, *Między Polską a Niemcami,* 127.
69. Excerpt, Borodziej and Lemberg, *Niemcy,* 1:478–479; also governor's report, 484.
70. Quoted in Blanke, *Polish-Speaking Germans?,* 296.
71. Belzyt, *Między Polską a Niemcami,* 116, 154–159. Kraft cites an MZO estimate of 75,000 unverified autochthons in Oct. 1946, 45,000 in Olsztyn Province, "Wojewodschaft Allenstein," 466; Strauchold cites these same figures for 1 Aug. 1946, *Autochtoni,* 166n5; Misztal cites 60,789 in the Recovered Lands at the end of Sept. 1946, *Weryfikacja,* 218; Osękowski cites an MZO figure of 57,789 for Nov. 1946, *Społeczeństwo,* 95.
72. Quoted in Sakson, *Mazurzy,* 99n103, 94n80, respectively.
73. Quoted in Strauchold, *Autochtoni,* 117, 117n281.
74. Quoted in Nitschke, *Wysiedlenie,* 109.
75. Misztal, *Weryfikacja,* 219.
76. Borodziej and Lemberg, *Niemcy,* 2:422–423.
77. Excerpt, ibid., 431–433; Jan Misztal, "Przesunięcie Polski na zachód," in *Kompleks wypędzenia,* ed. Włodzimierz Borodziej and Artur Hajnicz (Cracow: Wydawnictwo ZNAK, 1998),103–105.
78. Report, 8 Oct. 1946, excerpt, Borodziej and Lemberg, *Niemcy,* 2:439–440.
79. Ibid., 441–443.
80. Ibid., 437–439; the quotes are on 438, 439, respectively.
81. Quoted in Madajczyk, *Przyłączenie,* 229.
82. Steffen, "Ucieczka," 261–262.
83. Borodziej and Lemberg, *Niemcy,* 2:424.
84. Excerpt ibid., 426, 428.
85. Strauchold, *Autochtoni,* 135; Görlich, "Autochtoni," 135.
86. Quoted in Strauchold, *Autochtoni,* 69–70, 70n81; Strauchold, *Polska ludność,* 89. The popular novel *With Fire and Sword* by Henryk Sienkiewicz is about conflict with Cossacks, not Germans.
87. Report, 12 Aug. 1946, and report, 31 Aug. 1946, excerpt, Boćkowski, *Niemcy,* 144.
88. Ibid., 148; see also the MZO commission report on Lębork, 24 Sept. 1947, 177; excerpt, Borodziej and Lemberg, *Niemcy,* 3:154.

89. Strauchold, *Autochtoni*, 68–69.
90. Madajczyk, *Przyłączenie*, 193.
91. Stanisław Wierzbiański, "Oczyśćmy imiennictwo śląskie," *Śląsko-Dąbrowski Przegląd Administracyjny*, no. 3 (1946), repr. in Strauchold, *Autochtoni*, 227–229.
92. Bernard Linek, *Polityka antyniemiecka na Górnym Śląsku w latach 1945–1950* (Opole: Stowarzyszenie Instytut Śląski, Państwowy Instytut Naukowy, Instytut Śląski w Opolu, 2000), 229–231; Linek, "Realizacja idei polskiego państwa narodowego na Górnym Śląsku po II wojnie światowej," *Sprawy Narodowościowe*, nos. 12–13 (1998): 25.
93. Quoted in Strauchold, *Autochtoni*, 87.
94. Linek, *Polityka antyniemiecka*, 231–235.
95. Tadeusz Lewaszkiewicz, "Der polnische Westgedanke und die Sprachwissenschaft," in *Deutsche Ostforschung und polnische Westforschung im Spannungsfeld von Wissenschaft und Politik. Disziplinen in Vergleich*, ed. Jan M. Piskorski, Jörg Hackmann, and Rudolf Jaworski (Osnabrück and Poznań: Fibre Verlag, PTPN, 2002), 112–115; Bronisław Kortus, "Der polnische Westgedanke und die Geographie," ibid., 257; Osękowski, *Społeczeństwo*, 33–34.
96. Gregor Thum, *Uprooted: How Breslau Became Wrocław during the Century of Expulsions* (Princeton: Princeton University Press, 2011), 250.
97. Andreas Kossert, *Preußen, Deutsche oder Polen?: die Masuren im Spannungsfeld des ethnischen Nationalismus 1870–1956* (Wiesbaden: Harrassowitz Verlag, 2001), 319–320; Blanke calls these individuals "pioneers of Polishness," *Polish-Speaking Germans?*, 45–47.
98. Quoted in Strauchold, *Autochtoni*, 92n182, 176n41; the quote is on 92n182.
99. Andrzej Grajewski, *Wygnanie. Diecezja katowicka w czasach stalinowskich*, 3rd rev. ed. (Katowice: Księgarnia św. Jacka; Gość niedzielny, 2002), 38–39.
100. Repr. in Strauchold, *Autochtoni*, 230–232; the document is undated.
101. Report, 10 July 1946, excerpt, Borodziej and Lemberg, *Niemcy*, 2:421; court order, reproduced, 451.
102. Linek, *Polityka antyniemiecka*, 240–241.
103. Quoted in James F. Byrnes, *Speaking Frankly* (New York: Harper & Brothers Publishers, 1947), 190.
104. Krystyna Kersten, "Nowy model terytorialny Polski a kształtowanie postaw ludności w pierwszych latach władzy ludowej (1944–1948)," *Dzieje Najnowsze* 6, no. 2 (1974): 27.
105. Kersten, *Establishment of Communist Rule*, 304.
106. Report, 17 Sept. 1946, Olesno PUIiP; report, 21 Sept. 1946, Bytom Municipal Office of Information, Borodziej and Lemberg, *Niemcy*, 2:433–435; report, Oct. 1946, Silesian WUBP, Wanda Chudzik, Irena Marczak, and Marek Olkuśnik, eds., *Biuletyny Informacyjne Ministerstwa Bezpieczeństwa Publicznego 1946* (Warsaw: Ministerstwo Spraw Wewnętrznych, 1996), 58, 62; report, 22 Oct. 1946, Strzelce PUIiP; reports, 24 Oct. and Nov. 1946, Opole PUIiP, excerpts, Borodziej and Lemberg, *Niemcy*, 2:444–446, 448; the quote is on 446.
107. Borodziej and Lemberg, *Niemcy*, 2:434. On unfounded reports of werewolf activity in Czechoslovakia, see Eagle Glassheim, "The Mechanics of Ethnic Cleansing: The Expulsion of Germans from Czechoslovakia, 1945–1947," in *Redrawing*

Nations: Ethnic Cleansing in East-Central Europe, 1944–1948, ed. Philipp Ther and Ana Siljak (Lanham, MD: Rowman & Littlefield Publishers, Inc., 2001), 209–210.
108. Quoted in Strauchold, *Autochtoni,* 91n180 (emphasis in original).
109. Excerpt, Borodziej and Lemberg, *Niemcy,* 3:117; Stanisław Jankowiak, "Niemcy w Wielkopolsce i na Ziemi Lubuskiej w latach 1945–1950," ibid., 38; Krzysztof Stryjkowski, *Położenie osób wpisanych w Wielkopolsce na niemiecką listę narodowościową w latach 1945–1950* (Poznań: Instytut Historii UAM, 2004), 296.
110. Borodziej and Lemberg, *Niemcy,* 1:490–491.
111. Madajczyk, *Niemcy,* 52.
112. Borodziej and Lemberg, *Niemcy,* 3:361–363; ibid., 1:250–251.
113. Strauchold, *Autochtoni,* 136, 139n53, 142–143; the quotes are on 143.
114. Ibid., 139, 139n52, 140n56. Strauchold includes the meeting in Opole on 18 Aug. 1946 in the series, though it does not fit the pattern; Władysław Rusinski lists Szczecin as the first meeting, "Autochtoni ziem odzyskanych. Stan dzisiejszy i perspektywy jutra," *Przegląd Zachodni,* no. 10 (1946): 815.
115. Strauchold, *Autochtoni,* 139–140.
116. Ibid., 146–148.
117. Ibid., 148–150.
118. Quoted ibid., 144n77.
119. Ibid., 176n40.
120. Ibid., 140, 141n60; the quote is on 141n60.
121. Quoted ibid., 143–144.
122. Madajczyk, *Przyłączenie,* 193, 193n176; the quote is on 193n176.
123. *Tribuna Robotnicza,* no. 311 (1946), quoted ibid., 55n269.
124. Strauchold, *Autochtoni,* 151 (emphases added).
125. Quoted ibid., 65, 152n108.
126. Borodziej and Lemberg, *Niemcy,* 3:366n1.
127. Silesian Deputy Governor and Chairman of the Union of Veterans of the Silesian Uprisings Ziętek and others expressed this view, Strauchold, *Autochtoni,* 153n115, 153.
128. Quoted ibid., 153n117; see also 152–153.
129. Ibid., 152, 154.
130. Ibid., 154–156.
131. Quoted in Madajczyk, *Przyłączenie,* 193–194.
132. Excerpts, Borodziej and Lemberg, *Niemcy,* 3:365–366, 368–369.
133. Steffen, "Ucieczka," 209n35, 260, 261n357; the quote is in Borodziej and Lemberg, *Niemcy,* 3:366; Strauchold, *Autochtoni,* 90, 158.
134. Madajczyk, *Niemcy,* 42; Lewaszkiewicz, "Der polnische Westgedanke," 115; Borodziej and Lemberg, *Niemcy,* 3:366n2.
135. Strauchold, *Autochtoni,* 90n176, 178, 178n51.
136. Madajczyk, *Niemcy,* 42; Steffen, "Ucieczka," 262.
137. Strauchold, *Autochtoni,* 178–179, 179nn54–56. According to Steffen, the militia expelled Slovincians from Kluki in May 1947 for settlers who took over their property, "Ucieczka," 263. There is now a Slovincian Village Museum in Kluki.
138. Madajczyk, *Niemcy,* 42; Borodziej and Lemberg, *Niemcy,* 3:366n2.
139. Misztal, *Weryfikacja,* 232; Osękowski, *Społeczeństwo,* 95–96.
140. Quoted in Strauchold, *Autochtoni,* 72.

141. Włodzimierz Stępiński, "Kilka uwag na temat stanu polskiej historiografii regionalnej XIX I XX wieku," in *O nowy model historycznych badań regionalnych*, ed. Krzysztof A. Makowski (Poznań: Instytut Zachodni, Centrum "Instytut Wielkopolski" Uniwersytetu im. Adama Mickiewicza w Poznaniu, 2007), 66.
142. Quoted in Kaszuba, *Między propagandą a rzeczywistością*, 70.
143. Strauchold, *Autochtoni*, 92.
144. Excerpt, Borodziej and Lemberg, *Niemcy*, 2:450.
145. Excerpt, ibid., 452.
146. Eser, "Niemcy," 312.
147. Görlich, "Autochtoni," 134–135.
148. Osękowski, *Społeczeństwo*, 106.
149. Edward Kołodziej, "Polityka Rządu RP w Warszawie wobec repatriacji i reemigracji obywateli polskich z ZSRR w latach 1944–1948, *Komunikaty Mazursko-Warmińskie*, 1994, nos.2–3: 331; Jan Czerniakiewicz, *Repatriacja ludności polskiej z ZSRR 1944-1948* (Warsaw: Państwowe Wydawnictwo Naukowe, 1987), 12, 54, 58–59; Bożena Szaynok, *Ludność żydowska na Dolnym Śląsku 1945–1950* (Wrocław: Wydawnictwo Uniwersytetu Wrocławskiego, 2000), 26–43, 50–52; Jan Misztal cites a total of 75,145 Jewish repatriates settled in Lower Silesia, "Osadnictwo Żydów polskich repatriantów z ZSRR na Ziemiach Zachodnich i Pólnocnych," *Przegląd Zachodni* 48, no. 2 (1992): 176.
150. Józef Adelson, "W Polsce zwanej Ludową" in *Najnowsze dzieje Żydów w Polsce w zarysie (do 1950 roku)*, ed. Jerzy Tomaszewski (Warsaw: Wydawnictwo Naukowe PWN, 1993), 395–397.
151. Quoted in Natalia Aleksiun, *Dokąd dalej? Ruch syjonistyczny w Polsce (1944–1950)* (Warsaw: Wydawnictwo TRIO, 2002), 80n132.
152. Misztal, "Osadnictwo," 178; Bożena Szaynok, "The Impact of the Holocaust on Jewish Attitudes in Postwar Poland," in *Contested Memories: Poles and Jews during the Holocaust and Its Aftermath*, ed. Joshua D. Zimmerman (New Brunswick, NJ: Rutgers University Press, 2003), 244.
153. Sebastian Siebel-Achenbach, *Lower Silesia from Nazi Germany to Communist Poland, 1942–49* (New York: St. Martin's Press, 1994), 23; Piotr Madajczyk, *Przyłączenie*, 57.
154. Borodziej and Lemberg, *Niemcy*, 3:319.
155. Boćkowski, *Niemcy*, 305n2.
156. Borodziej and Lemberg, *Niemcy*, 1:141.
157. Ibid., 2:341–343.
158. Misztal, *Weryfikacja*, 210, 152.
159. Hugo Service, *Germans to Poles: Communism, Nationalism and Ethnic Cleansing after the Second World War* (Cambridge: Cambridge University Press, 2013), 113.
160. Excerpt, Boćkowski, *Niemcy*, 96.
161. R. M. Douglas, *Orderly and Humane: The Expulsion of the Germans after the Second World War* (New Haven: Yale University Press, 2012), 158–159; Szaynok, *Ludność żydowska*, 91.
162. Quoted in Szaynok, "Impact," 241; Bożena Szaynok, "The Role of Antisemitism in Postwar Polish-Jewish Relations," in *Antisemitism and Its Opponents in Modern Poland*, ed. Robert Blobaum (Ithaca: Cornell University Press, 2005), 269.

163. Jan Tomasz Gross, *Fear: Anti-Semitism in Poland after Auschwitz: An Essay in Historical Interpretation* (New York: Random House, 2006), 81–117; Bożna Szaynok, "Kielce Pogrom (1946)," in *Antisemitism: A Historical Encyclopedia of Prejudice and Persecution,* vol. I: *A–K,* ed. Richard S. Levy (Santa Barbara, CA: ABC CLIO, 2005), 398–399; Szaynok, *Pogrom Żydów w Kielcach 4 lipca 1946* (Warsaw: Wydawnictwo Bellona, 1992).
164. Quoted in Dariusz Stola, *Kraj bez wyjścia?: migracje z Polski 1949–1989* (Warsaw: Instytut Pamięci Narodowej, Komisja Ścigania Zbrodni przeciwko Narodowi Polskiemu; Instytut Studiów Politycznych PAN, 2010), 51; Szaynok, *Ludność żydowska,* 93, 99, 103.

9. The Rehabilitation of *Volksdeutsche* in 1946

1. Krzysztof Stryjkowski, *Położenie osób wpisanych w Wielkopolsce na niemiecką listę narodowościową w latach 1945–1950* (Poznań: Instytut Historii UAM, 2004), 9, 559–560.
2. Excerpts, Włodzimerz Borodziej and Hans Lemberg, eds., *Niemcy,* vol. 2, *Polska Centralna. Województwo śląskie,* ed. Ingo Eser and Jerzy Kochanowski (Warsaw: Wydawnictwo NERITON, 2000), 250.
3. Jerzy Kochanowski, "Losy Niemców w Polsce Centralnej w latach 1945–1950. Na przykładzie województw łódzkiego, warszawskiego i krakowskiego (powiat Biała)," ibid., 59.
4. Leszek Olejnik, *Zdrajcy narodu? Losy Volksdeutschów w Polsce po II wojnie światowej* (Warsaw: Wydawnictwo Trio, 2006), 104–105.
5. DzURP, no. 41, Entry 237, 11 Sept. 1946, 447–450, http://dziennikustaw.gov.pl/DU/1946/s/41/237; Włodzimierz Borodziej and Hans Lemberg, eds., *Niemcy,* vol. 3, *Województwa poznańskie i szczecińskie,* ed. Stanisław Jankowiak and Katrin Steffen (Warsaw: Wydawnictwo NERITON, 2001), 127n2; report, 15 Nov. 1946, excerpt, 132, 134; Włodzimierz Borodziej, "Wstęp: sprawa polska i przemieszczenia ludności w czasie II wojny światowej," in *Niemcy,* ed. Borodziej and Lemberg, vol. 1, *Władze i instytucje centralne. Województwo olsztyńskie,* ed. Borodziej and Claudia Kraft (Warsaw: Wydawnictwo NERITON, 2000), 59; Ingo Eser, "Niemcy na Górnym Śląsku," in *Niemcy,* ed. Borodziej and Lemberg, 2:325–326; Kochanowski, "Losy Niemców," 48n127.
6. Repr. in Stryjkowski, *Położenie,* 628–633; the quote is on 631.
7. Excerpt, Borodziej and Lemberg, *Niemcy,* 2:424–425.
8. Ibid., 430–431.
9. Excerpt, ibid., 103; see also report, 2 Sept. 1946, excerpt, ibid., 106.
10. Stanisław Jankowiak, "Niemcy w Wielkopolsce i na Ziemi Lubuskiej w latach 1945–1950," in *Niemcy,* ed. Borodziej and Lemberg, 3:42; Stryjkowski, *Położenie,* 268, 270–271.
11. DzURP, no. 55, Entry 310, 8 Nov. 1946, 633–635, http://dziennikustaw.gov.pl/DU/1946/s/55/310; the quotes are on 633.
12. Draft decree, Borodziej and Lemberg, *Niemcy,* 1:238–239; the quotes are on 239. Grzegorz Strauchold links the decree to an intensified campaign against Germans

following the referendum, *Autochtoni, Polscy, Niemieccy, czy . . . od nacjonalizmu do komunizmu (1945–1949)* (Toruń: Wydawnictwo Adam Marszałek, 2001), 136.
13. Piotr Madajczyk, *Niemcy polscy: 1944–1989* (Warsaw: Oficyna Naukowa, 2001), 33.
14. Borodziej and Lemberg, *Niemcy*, 1:259–261.
15. Excerpt, ibid., 3:120–121.
16. Report, Nov. 1946, ibid., 2:162.
17. Stryjkowski, *Położenie*, 268; Borodziej and Lemberg, *Niemcy*, 3:102–103.
18. Quoted in Stryjkowski, *Położenie*, 486; see also 501.
19. Quoted in Agnieszka Łuczak, "Ziemiaństwo wielkopolskie w czasie reformy rolnej," *Biuletyn Instytutu Pamięci Narodowej* 1 (12) (Jan. 2002): 40; Stryjkowski, *Położenie*, 494.
20. Quoted in Stryjkowski, *Położenie*, 515.
21. Ibid., 443–444, 519; Jankowiak, "Niemcy w Wielkopolsce," 41–42, 45–46.
22. Borodziej and Lemberg, *Niemcy*, 3:107.
23. Jankowiak, "Niemcy w Wielkopolsce," 49.
24. Ibid., 43. In the Nazi Reich even Jews had much better chances of survival if married to a German; it mattered that their children were half-German, especially if not raised as Jews, Evan Burr Bukey, *Jews and Intermarriage in Nazi Austria* (Cambridge: Cambridge University Press, 2010).
25. Excerpt, Borodziej and Lemberg, *Niemcy*, 3:109.
26. Stryjkowski, *Położenie*, 529–530.
27. Quoted ibid., 531.
28. Ibid., 531–532, 531n106.
29. Ibid., 533; report, director, Poznań WUIiP, 11 Nov. 1946, Borodziej and Lemberg, *Niemcy*, 3:125; see also 112, 127n1. The author is unrelated to the director.
30. MIiP to MAP, 27 Nov. 1946, Borodziej and Lemberg, *Niemcy*, 3:149.
31. Ibid., 125–127; the quotes are on 127.
32. DzURP, no. 53, Entry 300, 21 Oct. 1946, 621, http://dziennikustaw.gov.pl/DU/1946/s/53/300.
33. Stryjkowski, *Położenie*, 535–536; the quote is on 535.
34. Borodziej and Lemberg, *Niemcy*, 3:145n1.
35. Excerpt, ibid., 139–140; the quotes are on 140; see also 146n6.
36. Quoted in Stryjkowski, *Położenie*, 610–611.
37. The quotes are ibid., 608–609, 611.
38. Report, 15 Nov. 1946, excerpt, Borodziej and Lemberg, *Niemcy*, 3:134–141; Stryjkowski, *Położenie*, 549.
39. Stryjkowski, *Położenie*, 624.
40. Report, 15 Nov. 1946, excerpt, Borodziej and Lemberg, *Niemcy*, 3:141–145.
41. Stryjkowski, *Położenie*, 428, 434–435, 619; Olejnik, *Zdrajcy narodu?*, 104.
42. Stryjkowski, *Położenie*, 380–382, 384.
43. Ibid., 549.
44. Reproduced in Karol Jonca, ed., *Wysiedlenia Niemców i osadnictwo ludności polskiej na obszarze Krzyżowa-Świdnia (Kreisau-Schweidnitz) w latach 1945–1948: wybór dokumentów* (Wrocław: Wydawnictwo "Leopoldinum" Fundacji dla Uniwersytetu Wrocławskiego, 1997), 120. No evidence indicates such "Associations of Poles Resettled from Poland" existed.

45. Ibid., 122–144.
46. Borodziej and Lemberg, *Niemcy,* 2:454.
47. Andrzej Grajewski, *Wygnanie. Diecezja katowicka w czasach stalinowskich,* 3rd rev. ed. (Katowice: Księgarnia św. Jacka; Gość niedzielny, 2002), 43–45.

10. A Year of Crucial Changes

1. Grzegorz Strauchold, *Autochtoni, Polscy, Niemieccy, czy . . . od nacjonalizmu do komunizmu (1945-1949)* (Toruń: Wydawnictwo Adam Marszałek, 2001), 160–161, 160n143.
2. Excerpts, Włodzimierz Borodziej and Hans Lemberg, eds., *Niemcy,* vol. 2, *Polska Centralna. Województwo śląskie,* ed. Ingo Eser and Jerzy Kochanowski (Warsaw: Wydawnictwo NERITON, 2000), 526.
3. Strauchold, *Autochtoni,* 161–162; Piotr Madajczyk, *Niemcy polscy: 1944-1989* (Warsaw: Oficyna Naukowa, 2001), 51.
4. Strauchold, *Autochtoni,* 163.
5. Repr. ibid., 232–234.
6. Repr. ibid., 234–235.
7. Bernadetta Gronek and Irena Marczak, eds., *Biuletyny Informacyjne Ministerstwa Bezpieczeństwa Publicznego,* vol. 1, *1947* (Warsaw: Ministerstwo Spraw Wewnętrznych, 1993), 15, 39.
8. Strauchold, *Autochtoni,* 119, 165–166.
9. Madajczyk, *Niemcy,* 51; Piotr Madajczyk, *Przyłączenie Śląska Opolskiego do Polski, 1945-1948* (Warsaw: Instytut Studiów Politycznych PAN, 1996), 213; Krzysztof Stryjkowski, *Położenie osób wpisanych w Wielkopolsce na niemiecką listę narodowościową w latach 1945-1950* (Poznań: Instytut Historii UAM, 2004), 297.
10. Protocol, excerpt, Borodziej and Lemberg, *Niemcy,* 2:467–468n1.
11. Jan Misztal, *Weryfikacja narodowościowa na Ziemiach Odzyskanych* (Warsaw: Państwowe Wydawnictwo Naukowe, 1990), 338.
12. Strauchold, *Autochtoni,* 177.
13. Memo, 13 [sic] Mar. 1947, Włodzimierz Borodziej and Hans Lemberg, eds., *Niemcy,* vol. 3, *Województwa poznańskie i szczecińskie,* ed. Stanisław Jankowiak and Katrin Steffen (Warsaw: Wydawnictwo NERITON, 2001), 388.
14. Excerpt, ibid., 2:469–470.
15. Report, Gronek and Marczak, *Biuletyny Informacyjne,* 118.
16. Leszek Belzyt, "Zum Verfahren der national Verifikation in den Gebieten des ehemaligen Ostpreussen 1945-1950," *Jahrbuch für die Geschichte Mittel- und Ostdeutschlands* 39 (1990): 261; Andrzej Sakson, *Stosunki narodowościowe na Warmii i Mazurach 1945-1997* (Poznań: Instytut Zachodni, 1998), 27; Belzyt, *Między Polską a Niemcami. Weryfikacja narodowościowa i jej następstwa na Warmii, Mazurach i Powiślu w latach 1945-1960* (Toruń: Wydawnictwo Adam Marszałek, 1998), 51.
17. Excerpt, Daniel Boćkowski, ed., *Niemcy,* vol. 4, *Pomorze Gdańskie i Dolny Śląsk,* ed. Ingo Eser, Witold Stankowski, Claudia Kraft, and Stanisław Jankowiak (Warsaw: Wydawnictwo NERITON, 2001), 154.
18. Misztal, *Weryfikacja,* 187–188; the quote is on 187.

19. Gronek and Marczak, *Biuletyny Informacyjne,* 97.
20. Report, 9 Sept. 1947, Boćkowski, *Niemcy,* 174–175, 174–175n1; Włodzimerz Borodziej and Hans Lemberg, eds., *Die Deutschen,* vol. 4, *Wojewodschaften Pommerellen und Danzig (Westpreussen). Wojewodschaft Breslau (Niederschlesien),* ed. Ingo Eser, Witold Stankowski, Claudia Kraft, and Stanisław Jankowiak (Marburg: Verlag Herder-Institut, 2004), 290–292.
21. Excerpt, Boćkowski, *Niemcy,* 403–404.
22. Excerpt, Borodziej and Lemberg, *Niemcy,* 2:469–470.
23. Excerpt, ibid., 473; report, 13 Jan. 1948, excerpt, ibid., 508; Zawadzki to MAP, 25 Jan. 1948, ibid., 510.
24. Gronek and Marczak, *Biuletyny Informacyjne,* 206.
25. Borodziej and Lemberg, *Niemcy,* 2:488–489.
26. Włodzimerz Borodziej and Hans Lemberg, eds., *Niemcy,* vol. 1, *Władze i instytucje centralne. Województwo olsztyńskie,* ed. Borodziej and Claudia Kraft (Warsaw: Wydawnictwo NERITON, 2000), 511.
27. Andrzej Sakson, *Mazurzy—społeczność pogranicza* (Poznań: Instytut Zachodni, 1990), 95.
28. Borodziej and Lemberg, *Niemcy,* 1:519–522; the quotes are on 519, 522.
29. Excerpts, ibid., 522–524; the quote is on 524.
30. Ibid., 2:188–190; the quote is on 189.
31. Excerpts, ibid., 3:165, 167.
32. Stryjkowski, *Położenie,* 296; report, 15 July 1947, excerpt, Borodziej and Lemberg, *Niemcy,* 2:469.
33. Sakson, *Mazurzy,* 113; excerpt, Borodziej and Lemberg, *Niemcy,* 2:257.
34. Borodziej and Lemberg, *Die Deutschen,* 4: 258–259; Stryjkowski, *Położenie,* 426.
35. Ingo Eser and Witold Stankowski, "Wojewodschaften Pommerellen und Danzig (Westpreussen)," in *Die Deutschen,* Borodziej and Lemberg, 4:53–54; report, ibid., 259–260.
36. Quoted in Witold Stankowski, "Pomorze Gdańskie 1918–1950," in *Niemcy,* Boćkowski, 4:37.
37. DzURP, no.65, Entry 378, 1947, 1091, http://dziennikustaw.gov.pl/DU/1947/s/65/378.
38. Belzyt, *Między Polską a Niemcami,* 141.
39. Borodziej and Lemberg, *Niemcy,* 1:273; report, ibid., 2:108.
40. Stryjkowski, *Położenie,* 302, 306.
41. Meeting minutes, repr. ibid., 634–635.
42. Ibid., 549–550; the quote is on 550.
43. Ibid., 538.
44. Ibid., 539–540.
45. Ibid., 540–542, 541n141; the quotes are on 542.
46. Stanisław Jankowiak, "Niemcy w Wielkopolsce i na Ziemi Lubuskiej w latach 1945–1950," in *Niemcy,* ed. Borodziej and Lemberg, 3:56.
47. Stryjkowski, *Położenie,* 542–544.
48. Report, 5 Jan. 1948, excerpt, Borodziej and Lemberg, *Niemcy,* 2:506–508.
49. Ibid , 499.
50. Protocol, ibid., 178–179.
51. Report, WS-P, Łódź UW, 13 Feb. 1948, excerpt, ibid., 209–213; ibid., 194–196.

52. Stryjkowski, *Położenie*, 519–20, 589; the quotes are on 589, 520, respectively.
53. DzURP, no.34, Entry 163, 1947, vol. 1, 554–556, http://dziennikustaw.gov.pl/du/1947/s/34/163/1; the quote is on 554.
54. Borodziej and Lemberg, *Niemcy*, 1:277–281.
55. Protocol, excerpt, ibid., 2:467.
56. Reproduced in Karol Jonca, ed., *Wysiedlenia Niemców i osadnictwo ludności polskiej na obszarze Krzyżowa-Świdnia (Kreisau-Schweidnitz) w latach 1945–1948: wybór dokumentów* (Wrocław: Wydawnictwo "Leopoldinum" Fundacji dla Uniwersytetu Wrocławskiego, 1997), 174.
57. Misztal, *Weryfikacja*, 293.
58. Excerpt, Borodziej and Lemberg, *Niemcy*, 2:471.
59. Quoted in Marcin Zaremba, *Komunizm, legitymizacja, nacjonalizm. Nacjonalistyczna legitymizacja władzy koumistycznej w Polsce* (Warsaw: Wydawnictwo TRIO, Instytut Studiów Politycznych Polskiej Akademii Nauk, 2001), 158–159. "German" is deliberately not capitalized in the original.
60. Borodziej and Lemberg, *Niemcy*, 2:472.
61. Excerpt, ibid., 473.
62. Ibid., 475–476.
63. Ibid., 476–478; the quotes are on 477, 478.
64. Ibid., 489–490.
65. Protocol, ibid., 479–483; the quotes are on 480, 481.
66. Ibid., 481–482; the quote is on 482.
67. Ibid., 491–492; the quote is on 492.
68. Protocol, excerpt, ibid., 483–484.
69. Bernard Linek, *Polityka antyniemiecka na Górnym Śląsku w latach 1945–1950* (Opole: Stowarzyszenie Instytut Śląski, Państwowy Instytut Naukowy, Instytut Śląski w Opolu, 2000), 319, 326–327, 340; the quote is on 319.
70. Quoted ibid., 321, 324; Borodziej and Lemberg, *Niemcy*, 2:491n1.
71. Borodziej and Lemberg, *Niemcy*, 2:478–479.
72. Archiwum Archidiecezalne w Katowicach, ARZ0004 [Duchowieństwo Generalia Personalia (1941–50)], notes of James E. Bjork.
73. Linek, *Polityka antyniemiecka*, 336–337; the quote is on 336.
74. Jerzy Skrobot, "Chłopak, który jest Ślązkiem," *Dziennik Związkowy (Kalejdoskop)*, 3 Dec. 1999, 14.
75. Borodziej and Lemberg, *Niemcy*, 2:490.
76. Linek, *Polityka antyniemiecka*, 329–332; the quotes are on 332, 330, 331, respectively.
77. Report, 5 Jan. 1948, excerpt, Borodziej and Lemberg, *Niemcy*, 2:506–508.
78. Linek, *Polityka antyniemiecka*, 326–327, 340–341; the quote is on 341.
79. Report, 13 Jan. 1948, excerpt, Borodziej and Lemberg, *Niemcy*, 2:508; Zawadzki to MAP, 25 Jan. 1948, ibid., 510.
80. Quoted in Andrzej Grajewski, *Wygnanie. Diecezja katowicka w czasach stalinowskich*, 3rd rev. ed. (Katowice: Księgarnia św. Jacka; Gość niedzielny, 2002), 39.
81. Strauchold, *Autochtoni*, 177–178.
82. Włodzimerz Borodziej, "Wstęp: sprawa polska i przemieszczenia ludności w czasie II wojny światowej," in *Niemcy*, 1:97–98.

83. Report, 13 Feb. 1948, excerpt, ibid., 2:209–213; Jerzy Kochanowski, "Losy Niemców w Polsce Centralnej w latach 1945–1950. Na przykładzie województw łódzkiego, warszawskiego i krakowskiego (powiat Biała)," ibid., 62–63. Stryjkowski, *Położenie*, 310, dates the directive to 23 Oct. 1947.
84. Borodziej and Lemberg, *Niemcy*, 2:201–203.
85. Boćkowski, *Niemcy*, 186.
86. Stryjkowski, *Położenie*, 461.
87. Borodziej and Lemberg, *Niemcy*, 2:201–203.
88. Ibid., 1:525–527; the quotes are on 525, 526.
89. Ibid., 528–530; the quote is on 530.
90. Excerpts, ibid., 2:501–503.
91. Madajczyk, *Przyłączenie*, 216–217.
92. Excerpt, Borodziej and Lemberg, *Niemcy*, 2:486–487.
93. Ibid., 500.
94. Ibid., 497–501; the quote is on 501.
95. Excerpt, ibid., 508.
96. Ibid., 497–501.
97. Ibid., 499.
98. Ibid., 500.
99. Strauchold, *Autochtoni*, 174.
100. Silvio Pons, "Stalin and the European Communists after World War Two (1943–1948)," *Past and Present* 210 (2011): 134.
101. Antoni Dudek, *Ślady PeeReLu: ludzie, wydarzenia, mechanizmy* (Cracow: Wydawnictwo ARCANA, 2000), 66.
102. Quoted in Strauchold, *Autochtoni*, 190, 187n92, respectively.
103. Timothy Snyder, "To Resolve the Ukrainian Problem Once and for All: The Ethnic Cleansing of Ukrainians in Poland, 1943–1947," *Journal of Cold War Studies* 1, no. 2 (1999): 92n7.
104. Krystyna Kersten, *Między wyzwoleniem a zniewoleniem: Polska 1944–1956* (London: Aneks, 1993), 11.
105. Igor Hałagida, *Ukraińcy na zachodnich i północnych ziemiach Polski 1947–1957* (Warsaw: Instytut Pamięci Narodowej, Komisja Ścigania Zbrodni przeciwko Narodowi Polskiemu, 2002), 25; Snyder, "To Resolve," 89–100. In Volhynia a minimum of 36,543 Polish inhabitants perished 1939–1945, primarily from Mar. to Oct. 1943, with an estimated total death toll of 50,000 to 60,000, Władysław Siemaszko, Ewa Siemaszko, *Ludobójstwo dokonane przez nacjonalistów ukraińskich na ludności polskiej Wołynia 1939–1945*. 2 vols. (Warsaw: Wydawnictwo von borowiecky, 2000), 2:1038, 1045, 1056–1057.
106. The latter agreement is repr. in Eugeniusz Misiło, ed., *Repatriacja czy deportacja: Przesiedlenie Ukraińców z Polski do USSR 1944–1946*, vol. 1, *Dokumenty 1944–1945* (Warsaw: Oficyna Wydawnicza "Archiwum Ukraińskie," 1996), 30.
107. Patrice M. Dabrowski, "Borderland Encounters in the Carpathian Mountains and Their Impact on Identity Formation," in *Shatterzone of Empires: Coexistence and Violence in the German, Habsburg, Russian, and Ottoman Borderlands,* ed. Omer Bartov and Eric D. Weitz (Bloomington, IN: Indiana University Press, 2013), 205; Orest Subtelny, "Expulsion, Resettlement, Civil Strife: The Fate of

Poland's Ukrainians, 1944–1947," in *Redrawing Nations: Ethnic Cleansing in East-Central Europe, 1944–1948,* ed. Philipp Ther and Ana Siljak (Lanham, MD: Rowman & Littlefield Publishers, Inc., 2001), 158.
108. Misiło, *Repatriacja,* 1: 74–75; Kersten, "Polish-Ukrainian Conflict," 147.
109. Snyder, "To Resolve," 104–108; Subtelny, "Expulsion," 163.
110. Quoted in Snyder, "To Resolve," 108.
111. Eugeniusz Misiło, ed., *Akcja 'Wisła': dokumenty* (Warsaw: Archiwum Ukraińskie, 1993), 65.
112. Ibid., 93.
113. Snyder, "To Resolve," 113–114; Hałagida, *Ukraińcy,* 34–37.
114. Hałagida, *Ukraińcy,* 49–53; the quotes are on 49 and 53.
115. Ibid., 68–71.

11. Nationality Policies Following the End of Mass Expulsion

1. Krzysztof Stryjkowski, *Położenie osób wpisanych w Wielkopolsce na niemiecką listę narodowościową w latach 1945–1950* (Poznań: Instytut Historii UAM, 2004), 313.
2. Katrin Steffen, "Ucieczka, wypędzenie i przymusowe wysiedlenie Niemców z województwa szczecińskiego w latach 1945–1950," in *Niemcy,* ed. Włodzimierz Borodziej and Hans Lemberg, vol. 3, *Województwa poznańskie i szczecińskie,* ed. Stanisław Jankowiak and Steffen (Warsaw: Wydawnictwo NERITON, 2001), 263, 263n373; the quote is on 263n373.
3. Excerpts, Włodzimierz Borodziej and Hans Lemberg, eds., *Niemcy,* vol. 1, *Władze i instytucje centralne. Województwo olsztyńskie,* ed. Borodziej and Claudia Kraft (Warsaw: Wydawnictwo NERITON, 2000), 532–533; the quote is on 533.
4. Report, 19 Feb. 1948, excerpts, ibid., 532–534, 534n2; the quotes are on 533, 534.
5. Ibid., 534–535.
6. Quoted in Leszek Belzyt, *Między Polską a Niemcami. Weryfikacja narodowościowa i jej następstwa na Warmii, Mazurach i Powiślu w latach 1945–1960* (Toruń: Wydawnictwo Adam Marszałek, 1998), 155–156.
7. Andrzej Sakson, *Mazurzy—społeczność pogranicza* (Poznań: Instytut Zachodni, 1990), 99.
8. Andreas Kossert, *Preußen, Deutsche oder Polen? Die Masuren im Spannungsfeld des ethnischen Nationalismus 1870–1956* (Wiesbaden: Harrassowitz Verlag, 2001), 324.
9. Borodziej and Lemberg, *Niemcy,* 1:538.
10. Ibid., 539–540; the quotes are in on 540.
11. Excerpt, ibid., 546–547.
12. Belzyt, *Między Polską a Niemcami,* 156; for conflicting data on the progress of verification among Mazurs, raising questions about the reliability of such data, see Sakson, *Mazurzy,* 103; Czesław Osękowski, *Społeczeństwo Polski zachodniej i północnej w latach 1945–1956: Procesy integracji i dezintegracji* (Zielona Góra: Wyższa Szkoła Pedagogiczna im. Tadeusza Kotarbińskiego, 1994), 97.
13. Daniel Boćkowski, ed., *Niemcy,* vol. 4, *Pomorze Gdańskie i Dolny Śląsk,* ed. Ingo Eser, Witold Stankowski, Claudia Kraft, and Stanisław Jankowiak (Warsaw: Wydawnictwo NERITON, 2001), 422.

14. Report, 18 July 1948, Borodziej and Lemberg, *Niemcy*, 3:424.
15. Antoni Dudek, *Ślady PeeReLu: ludzie, wydarzenia, mechanizmy* (Cracow: Wydawnictwo ARCANA, 2000), 66; Jakub Tyszkiewicz, *Sto wielkich dni Wrocławia: wystawa Ziem Odzyskanych we Wrocławiu a propaganda ziem zachodnich i północnych w latach 1945–1948* (Wrocław: Wydawnictwo Arboretum, 1997), 128.
16. Jakub Karpiński, *Poland since 1944: A Portrait of Years* (Boulder: Westview Press, 1994), 27–30, 34–35.
17. Bernadetta Gronek, Irena Marczak, and Marek Olkuśnik, eds., *Biuletyny Informacyjne Ministerstwa Bezpieczeństwa Publicznego*, vol. 2, *1948* (Warsaw: Ministerstwo Spraw Wewnętrznych, 1995), 161–162, 169. The *Biuletyn* was distributed exclusively among top PPR leaders.
18. Quoted in Grzegorz Strauchold, *Myśl zachodnia i jej realizacja w Polsce Ludowej w latach 1945–1957* (Toruń: Wydawnictwo Adam Marszałek, 2003), 362.
19. Quoted in Grzegorz Strauchold, *Autochtoni, Polscy, Niemieccy, czy ... od nacjonalizmu do komunizmu (1945–1949)* (Toruń: Wydawnictwo Adam Marszałek, 2001), 191, 195n126; the quote is on 195n126.
20. Ibid., 186–187, 190.
21. Excerpt repr. ibid., 237–238.
22. Włodzimierz Borodziej, "Wstęp: sprawa polska i przemieszczenia ludności w czasie II wojny światowej," in *Niemcy,* Borodziej and Lemberg, 1:103.
23. Mieczysław Jaworski, *Na Piastowskim szlaku. Działalność Ministerstwa Ziem Odzyskanych w latach 1945–1948* (Warsaw: Wydawnictwo Ministerstwa Obrony Narodowej, 1973), 185.
24. Osękowski, *Społeczeństwo*, 97.
25. Report, Włodzimierz Borodziej and Hans Lemberg, eds., *Die Deutschen*, vol. 4, *Wojewodschaften Pommerellen und Danzig (Westpreussen). Wojewodschaft Breslau (Niederschlesien)*, ed. Ingo Eser, Witold Stankowski, Claudia Kraft, and Stanisław Jankowiak (Marburg: Verlag Herder-Institut, 2004), 337; Gregor Thum, *Uprooted: How Breslau Became Wrocław during the Century of Expulsions* (Princeton: Princeton University Press, 2011), 92.
26. Steffen, "Ucieczka," 265.
27. Quoted in Hugo Service, "Sifting Poles from Germans? Ethnic Cleansing and Ethnic Screening in Upper Silesia, 1945–1949," *Slavonic and East European Review* 88, no. 4 (October 2010): 676.
28. Matthias Kneip, "Die politische Rolle der deutschen Sprache in Oberschlesien in den Jahren 1950–1990," *Berichte und Forschungen: Jahrbuch des Bundesinstituts für Ostdeutsche Kultur und Geschichte* 8 (2000): 48.
29. AAN, KC PZPR 237/VII–118, fol. 424.
30. Excerpt, Włodzimierz Borodziej and Hans Lemberg, eds., *Niemcy*, vol. 2, *Polska Centralna. Województwo śląskie*, ed. Ingo Eser and Jerzy Kochanowski (Warsaw: Wydawnictwo NERITON, 2000), 525.
31. Irena Hurwic-Nowakowska, *A Social Analysis of Postwar Polish Jewry* (Jerusalem: The Zalman Shazar Center for Jewish History, 1986), 53–54, 56; Natalia Aleksiun, *Dokąd dalej? Ruch syjonistyczny w Polsce (1944–1950)* (Warsaw: Wydawnictwo TRIO, 2002), 204.

32. Tyszkiewicz, *Sto*, 117.
33. Aleksiun, *Dokąd dalej?*, 209n146.
34. Józef Adelson, "W Polsce zwanej Ludową" in *Najnowsze dzieje Żydów w Polsce w zarysie (do 1950 roku)*, ed. Jerzy Tomaszewski (Warsaw: Wydawnictwo Naukowe PWN, 1993), 470–471, 477; "Wszyscy krawcy wyjechali: O Żydach w PRL z Natalią Aleksiun i Dariuszem Stolą rozmawia Barbara Polak," *Biuletyn Instytutu Pamięci Narodowej*, no. 11 (Nov. 2005): 9–10.
35. Bożena Szaynok, *Ludność żydowska na Dolnym Śląsku 1945–1950* (Wrocław: Wydawnictwo Uniwersytetu Wrocławskiego, 2000), 178, 193.
36. Dariusz Stola, *Kraj bez wyjścia? Migracje z Polski 1949–1989* (Warsaw: Instytut Pamięci Narodowej, Komisja Ścigania Zbrodni przeciwko Narodowi Polskiemu; Instytut Studiów Politycznych PAN, 2010), 51, 53. From Jan. 1948 to mid-Sept. 1949 14,800 individuals left Poland on MSZ documents, Albert Stankowski, "Nowe spojrzenie na statystyki dotyczące emigracji Żydów z Polski po 1944 roku," in *Studia z historii Żydów w Polsce po 1945 r.*, ed. Grzegorz Berendt et al. (Warsaw: Żydowski Institut Historyczny, 2000), 113–114.
37. Bożena Szaynok, *Poland—Israel 1944–1968: In the Shadow of the Past and of the Soviet Union* (Warsaw: Institute of National Remembrance, Commission for the Prosecution of Crimes against the Polish Nation, 2012), 180–186; the quote is on 182; Szaynok, *Ludność żydowska*, 194.
38. [Patrycy Dziurzyński], "Spis ludności na Ziemiach Odzyskanych z dnia 31 grudnia 1948," *Polska Ludowa* 6 (1967): 190.
39. Osękowski, *Społeczeństwo*, 97–98.
40. Borodziej and Lemberg, *Niemcy*, 1:314.
41. Ibid., 314–316.
42. Strauchold, *Autochtoni*, 177.
43. Borodziej and Lemberg, *Niemcy*, 1:315.
44. Piotr Madajczyk, *Przyłączenie Śląska Opolskiego do Polski, 1945–1948* (Warsaw: Instytut Studiów Politycznych PAN, 1996), 217.
45. Bernard Linek, *Polityka antyniemiecka na Górnym Śląsku w latach 1945–1950* (Opole: Stowarzyszenie Instytut Śląski, Państwowy Instytut Naukowy, Instytut Śląski w Opolu, 2000), 346, 359–361; the quotes are on 346, 359.
46. Borodziej and Lemberg, *Niemcy*, 2:515–516.
47. Ibid., 521–522; the quote is on 522.
48. Michael Fleming, "Greek 'Heroes' in the Polish People's Republic and the Geopolitics of the Cold War, 1948–1956," *Nationalities Papers* 36, no. 3 (2008): 378–380.
49. Zbigniew Czahór, "Podwójne obywatelstwo w Polsce i Niemczech," in *Polacy i Niemcy: na drodze do partnerskiego sąsiedztwa: próba bilansu dziesięciolecia 1989–1998*, ed. Dieter Bingen and Krzysztof Malinowski (Poznań: Instytut Zachodni, 2000), 503–504. See Article 116, http://www.gesetze-im-internet.de/bundesrecht/gg/gesamt.pdf, 38–39.
50. Philipp Ther, "A Century of Forced Migration: the Origins and Consequences of 'Ethnic Cleansing,'" in *Redrawing Nations: Ethnic Cleansing in East-Central Europe, 1944–1948*, ed. Ther and Ana Siljak (Lanham, MD: Rowman & Littlefield Publishers, Inc., 2001), 71n99.
51. AAN, KC PZPR 237/VII-119, fols. 66, 71, 116.

52. Borodziej and Lemberg, *Niemcy*, 3:443–445. Michael Fleming does not connect a change in policy toward Germans with the creation of the GDR, *Communism, Nationalism and Ethnicity, 1944–50* (London: Routledge, 2010), 99–100.
53. Borodziej and Lemberg, *Niemcy*, 3:446–448.
54. Ibid., 1:363–365, probably in July 1950.
55. Fleming, *Communism*, 21, argues that in 1948–1950 the focus of nationality policy shifted to integration and inclusion without noting the acceptance of a German minority.
56. AAN, MZO (1944) 1945–1949, 196/50, "Sprawozdanie z działalności MZO w okresie od 27 listopada 1945 do 21 stycznia 1949 roku," 23, notes of Marek Suszko.
57. Borodziej and Lemberg, *Niemcy*, 1:557; see also 558n1.
58. Boćkowski, *Niemcy*, 444–449; the quote is on 449.
59. Steffen, "Ucieczka," 260–261; the quote is on 261.
60. Fleming links this to the previous emphasis on a common Polish folk culture, which is at odds with developing regional cultures, *Communism*, 74.
61. Michał Lengowski, *Na Warmii i w Westfalii. Wspomnienia*, ed. Janusz Jasiński (Warsaw: Instytut Wydawniczy Pax, 1972), 198.
62. Dariusz Jarosz, *Obraz chłopa w krajowej policystyce czasopiśmienniczej 1944–1959* (Warsaw: Stowarzyszenie Redaktorów, 1994), 81; Jarosz, *Polityka władz komunistycznych w Polsce w latach 1948–1956 a chłopi* (Warsaw: Wydawnictwo—DiG, 1998), 54, 155.
63. Strauchold, *Autochtoni*, 197.
64. Kossert, *Preußen*, 314.
65. Joachim Georg Görlich, "Autochtoni," *Kultura*, nos. 1/195–2/196 (1964): 136.
66. Steffen, "Ucieczka," 263–264; Madajczyk, *Przyłączenie*, 212.
67. Linek, *Polityka antyniemiecka*, 335, 338.
68. Ibid., 339–340, 350–354, 356; Borodziej and Lemberg, *Niemcy*, 2:521n5.
69. Linek, *Polityka antyniemiecka*, 341–342.
70. Excerpts, Borodziej and Lemberg, *Niemcy*, 2:529–530; the quote is on 530.
71. Ibid., 3:388n1; protocol, excerpt, ibid., 2:528–529.
72. Ibid., 3:439–440 (emphasis in original).
73. Ibid., 440–441.
74. Report, Oct. 1949, Borodziej and Lemberg, *Die Deutschen*, 4:347–348; the quotes are on 348.
75. Borodziej and Lemberg, *Niemcy*, 1:356–359; the quotes are on 356, 357.
76. Ibid.; the quotes are on 358 (emphasis in original).
77. Jan Misztal, *Weryfikacja narodowościowa na Ziemiach Odzyskanych* (Warsaw: Państwowe Wydawnictwo Naukowe, 1990), 191.
78. Borodziej and Lemberg, *Niemcy*, 1:358–359; the quotes are on 358, 359 (emphasis in original).
79. Sakson, *Mazurzy*, 124–125; Antoni Dudek and Andrzej Paczkowski, "Poland," in *A Handbook of the Communist Security Apparatus in East Central Europe 1944–1989*, ed. Krzysztof Persak and Łukasz Kamiński (Warsaw: Institute of National Remembrance, 2005), 282.
80. Quoted in Belzyt, *Między Polską a Niemcami*, 163. According to Fleming, nationality policy after 1947 shifted from a "*hard* ethno-nationalism" (greater reliance

on coercion, often physical, and exclusion) to a *"soft* ethno-nationalism" (aimed at integration, assimilation, and inclusion), which hardly describes the nationality policy pursued in Mazuria, *Communism,* 126.
81. Borodziej and Lemberg, *Niemcy,* 1:467n1.
82. Kossert, *Preußen,* 312; Andrzej Sakson, *Stosunki narodowościowe na Warmii i Mazurach 1945-1997* (Poznań: Instytut Zachodni, 1998), 198; Sakson, *Mazurzy,* 125-127; Strauchold, *Autochtoni,* 196; Piotr Madajczyk, "Warmia, Mazury i nie tylko," *Borussia* 18/19 (1999): 383.
83. Strauchold, *Autochtoni,* 196.
84. Ibid., 168; Belzlyt, *Między Polską a Niemcami,* 163-164.
85. Borodziej and Lemberg, *Niemcy,* 1:490n2; [Peter Brock], "Poland," in Roger C. Wilson, *Quaker relief; An account of the relief work of the Society of Friends 1940-1948* (London: George Allen & Unwin Ltd., 1952), 310-311, 318; Brock, a leading participant in the relief effort, denied Moczar's charges in an interview on 22 Sept. 2005.
86. Borodziej and Lemberg, *Niemcy,* 1:346-347; the quote is on 347.
87. Belzyt, *Między Polską a Niemcami,* 163-168; Claudia Kraft, "Wojewodschaft Allenstein," in *Die Deutschen,* ed. Włodzimierz Borodziej and Hans Lemberg, vol. 1, *Zentrale Behörden. Wojewodschaft Allenstein,* ed. Borodziej and Kraft (Marburg: Verlag Herder-Institut, 2000), 475-476.
88. Excerpt, Borodziej and Lemberg, *Niemcy,* 1:555.
89. Belzyt, *Między Polską a Niemcami,* 170.
90. Quoted in Fleming, *Communism,* 73.
91. Borodziej and Lemberg, *Niemcy,* 1:549-550, 550n4.
92. Fleming, *Communism,* 73-74.
93. Borodziej and Lemberg, *Niemcy,* 1:552-553, 563.
94. Report, 1 Dec. 1949, excerpt, ibid., 556-558; the quote is on 558.
95. Quoted in Belzyt, *Między Polską a Niemcami,* 170
96. Quoted in Osękowski, *Społeczeństwo,* 124n187.
97. Quoted in Kossert, *Preußen,* 315.
98. Belzyt, *Między Polską a Niemcami,* 169-170.
99. Leszek Belzyt, "Zum Verfahren der national Verifikation in den Gebieten des ehemaligen Ostpreussen 1945-1950," *Jahrbuch für die Geschichte Mittel- und Ostdeutschlands* 39 (1990): 261.
100. Ibid., 262; Sakson, *Mazurzy,* 128-129.
101. Excerpts, Borodziej and Lemberg, *Niemcy,* 2:206-9.
102. Excerpt, ibid., 209-213.
103. Report, ibid., 1:310-312.
104. Quoted in Stryjkowski, *Położenie,* 315.
105. Notes, 2 Apr. 1948, Borodziej and Lemberg, *Niemcy,* 1:312-314.
106. Ibid., 317-320; the quotes are on 318, 319; although the fate of this draft is unknown, it illustrates the views of some in the central government.
107. Ibid., 320-321.
108. Stryjkowski, *Położenie,* 312
109. Excerpt, Borodziej and Lemberg, *Niemcy,* 3:179-180; the quotes are on 179.
110. Ibid., 180-181.

111. Stryjkowski, *Położenie*, 434, 550–551; the quote is on 434.
112. Borodziej and Lemberg, *Niemcy*, 2:516.
113. Stryjkowski, *Położenie*, 551.
114. Report, 15 Oct. 1948, excerpt, Borodziej and Lemberg, *Niemcy*, 2:221.
115. Stryjkowski, *Położenie*, 570.
116. Ibid., 470–471; Borodziej and Lemberg, *Niemcy*, 3:184–185.
117. Borodziej and Lemberg, *Niemcy*, 1:340–342; the quotes are on 341.
118. Report, 9 July 1948, ibid., 2:118–122.
119. Boćkowski, *Niemcy*, 194.
120. Ibid., 192–194; report, 5 Nov. 1948, 196.
121. Stanisław Jankowiak, "Niemcy w Wielkopolsce i na Ziemi Lubuskiej w latach 1945–1950," in *Niemcy*, ed. Borodziej and Lemberg, 3:56; Stryjkowski, *Położenie*, 469–470.
122. Borodziej and Lemberg, *Niemcy*, 1:351–352, 354.
123. Bernadetta Nitschke, *Wysiedlenie ludności niemieckiej z Polski w latach 1945–1949* (Zielona Góra: Wyższa Szkoła Pedagogiczna im. Tadeusza Kotarbińskiego, 1999), 118; Sakson, *Mazurzy*, 113.
124. Stryjkowski, *Położenie*, 500, 527.
125. Nitschke, *Wysiedlenie*, 220; Stryjkowski, *Położenie*, 308, 314.
126. Report, 8 Nov. 1949, Borodziej and Lemberg, *Niemcy*, 3:199.
127. Ibid., 191–192.
128. Report, 21 Oct. 1949, ibid., 198.
129. Report, 5 Oct. 1949, ibid., 195; Stryjkowski, *Położenie*, 43, 544.
130. Strauchold, *Myśl zachodnia*, 369–370, 362, 369–371; the quote is on 369–370; Maria Tomczak, "Ludność rodzima na Ziemiach Zachodnich i Północnych w latach 1945–1952," *Przegląd Zachodni* 55, no. 3 (July–Sept. 1999): 158.

12. The Status of Autochthons at the End of 1949

1. Maria Szmeja, "Dlaczego Ślązacy z Opolszczyzny nie chcą być Polakami?" in *Mniejszości narodowe*, ed. Zbigniew Kurcz (Wrocław: Wydawnictwo Uniwersytetu Wrocławskiego, 1997), 113; Grzegorz Strauchold, *Polska ludność rodzima ziem zachodnich i północnych. Opinie nie tylko publiczne lat 1944–1948* (Olsztyn: Ośrodek Badań Naukowych im. Wojciecha Kętrzyńskiego, 1995), 53.
2. AAN, KC PZPR, 237/VII–2618; Włodzimierz Borodziej and Hans Lemberg, eds., *Niemcy*, vol. 2, *Polska Centralna. Województwo śląskie*, ed. Ingo Eser and Jerzy Kochanowski (Warsaw: Wydawnictwo NERITON, 2000), 530–536.
3. Włodzimierz Borodziej and Hans Lemberg, eds., *Niemcy*, vol. 3, *Województwa poznańskie i szczecińskie*, ed. Stanisław Jankowiak and Katrin Steffen (Warsaw: Wydawnictwo NERITON, 2001), 443–451.
4. Ibid., 2:530–531.
5. AAN, KC PZPR 237/VII–2618, 27–30.
6. Ibid., 24–27; the quotes are on 26, 27.
7. Borodziej and Lemberg, *Niemcy*, 3:443.
8. Ibid., 448, 450–451.
9. AAN, KC PZPR 237/VII–2618, 30–31.
10. Excerpts, Borodziej and Lemberg, *Niemcy*, 2:533–534.

11. Excerpts, ibid., 534–535; the quote is on 534.
12. Excerpts, ibid., 533.
13. Gregor Ploch, "Oberschlesier in oberschlesischen Industrierevier und im Ruhrgebiet. Bildungsprozesse von Wir-Gruppen nach 1950," summarized in "Region—Industrie—Zuwanderung. Oberschlesische Gesellschaftsgeschichte im 20. Jahrhundert. 27.11.2009–28.11.2009, Kattowitz/Katowice," ed. Ploch, in: H-Soz-u-Kult, 25.01.10, http://hsozkult.geschichte.hu-berlin.de/tagungsberichte/id=2966.
14. AAN, KC PZPR 237/VII-2618, 41; Leszek Belzyt, *Między Polską a Niemcami. Weryfikacja narodowościowa i jej następstwa na Warmii, Mazurach i Powiślu w latach 1945-1960* (Toruń: Wydawnictwo Adam Marszałek, 1998), 167.
15. AAN, KC PZPR 237/VII-2618, 40.
16. Excerpts, Borodziej and Lemberg, *Niemcy*, 2:531, 533.
17. AAN, KC PZPR 237/VII-2618, 27–30.
18. Ibid., 36.
19. Ibid., 37.
20. Borodziej and Lemberg, *Niemcy*, 3:443–451.
21. Ibid., 448–449.
22. Ibid., 450–451.
23. AAN, KC PZPR 237/VII-2618, 35–36.
24. Ibid., 237/VII-119, fol. 216.
25. Ibid., 237/VII-2618, 30–31.
26. Ibid., 36.
27. Excerpts, Borodziej and Lemberg, *Niemcy*, 2:532.
28. Excerpts, ibid., 532–533.
29. Ibid., 3:448–451; the quotes are on 448.
30. Ibid., 450–451.
31. AAN, KC PZPR 237/VII-2618, 35–36.
32. Excerpts, Borodziej and Lemberg, *Niemcy*, 2: 533–534.
33. AAN, KC PZPR 237/VII-2618, 46.
34. Borodziej and Lemberg, *Niemcy*, 3:450–451.
35. AAN, KC PZPR 237/VII-2618, 44–46, 48; on party membership in 1950, see Jan B. de Weydenthal, *The Communists of Poland: An Historical Outline*, rev. ed. (Stanford, CA: Hoover Institution Press, 1986), 229; on Poland's population, see Główny Urząd Statystyczny, "Narodowy spis powszechny ludności i mieszkań," http://www.stat.gov.pl/gus/6591_PLK_HTML.htm.
36. AAN, KC PZPR 237/VII-2618, 44–46.
37. Ibid., 40–41; the quotes are on 40.
38. Excerpts, Borodziej and Lemberg, *Niemcy*, 2:535–536.
39. AAN, KC PZPR 237/VII-2618, 48–49.
40. Ibid., 49.
41. Ibid., 50–51; the quotes are on 50.

13. The Last Phase of Nationality Verification and Rehabilitation

1. Dariusz Stola, *Kraj bez wyjścia?: migracje z Polski 1949-1989* (Warsaw: Instytut Pamięci Narodowej, Komisja Ścigania Zbrodni przeciwko Narodowi Polskiemu; Instytut Studiów Politycznych PAN, 2010), 71, 73.

2. Włodzimerz Borodziej and Hans Lemberg, eds., *Niemcy*, vol. 1, *Władze i instytucje centralne. Województwo olsztyńskie*, ed. Borodziej and Claudia Kraft (Warsaw: Wydawnictwo NERITON, 2000), 361–362, 558–560.
3. Ibid., 562; see also, the Mrągowo *starosta*'s report, 20 Mar. 1950, ibid., 560–561.
4. Ibid., 564–565.
5. Stola, *Kraj bez wyjścia?*, 73–74.
6. Borodziej and Lemberg, *Niemcy*, 1:365–370; a draft of the resolution was prepared in Jan. 1950, Włodzimierz Borodziej and Hans Lemberg, eds., *Niemcy*, vol. 2, *Polska Centralna. Województwo śląskie*, ed. Ingo Eser and Jerzy Kochanowski (Warsaw: Wydawnictwo NERITON, 2000), 536n1.
7. AAN, KC PZPR, Paczka 2, vol. 9, protocol, Biuro Polityczny, 2.
8. Borodziej and Lemberg, *Niemcy*, 1:365.
9. Ibid., 366.
10. Ibid., 366–367; the original states "departure to Poland," but the context indicates this is an error.
11. Ibid., 368.
12. Ibid., 368–369.
13. Ibid., 369.
14. Ibid., 369–370.
15. Andrzej Sakson, *Stosunki narodowościowe na Warmii i Mazurach 1945–1997* (Poznań: Instytut Zachodni, 1998), 375–376; Leszek Belzyt, "Zum Verfahren der national Verifikation in den Gebieten des ehemaligen Ostpreussen 1945–1950," *Jahrbuch für die Geschichte Mittel- und Ostdeutschlands* 39 (1990): 268, concludes that the accurate description of the needs of Mazurs and Warmiaks had no consequences.
16. Włodzimerz Borodziej, "Wstęp: sprawa polska i przemieszczenia ludności w czasie II wojny światowej," in *Niemcy*, ed. Borodziej and Lemberg, 1:100.
17. DzURP, no. 29, Entry 270, 1950, 328, http://dziennikustaw.gov.pl/DU/1950/s/29/270; Sakson, *Stosunki*, 202; Jerzy Kochanowski, "Losy Niemców w Polsce Centralnej w latach 1945–1950. Na przykładzie województw łódzkiego, warszawskiego i krakowskiego (powiat Biała)," in *Niemcy*, ed., Borodziej and Lemberg, 2:70; Borodziej, "Wstęp," 100.
18. Krzysztof Stryjkowski, *Położenie osób wpisanych w Wielkopolsce na niemiecką listę narodowościową w latach 1945–1950* (Poznań: Instytut Historii UAM, 2004), 457.
19. Ibid., 454–457.
20. Borodziej and Lemberg, *Niemcy*, 2:227–228; the quotes are on 228.
21. Excerpt, ibid., 1:370–371.
22. Stryjkowski, *Położenie*, 476–477, 479; the quote is on 479.
23. Quoted in Piotr Madajczyk, *Niemcy polscy: 1944–1989* (Warsaw: Oficyna Naukowa, 2001), 37.
24. Draft, Borodziej and Lemberg, *Niemcy*, 1:373–374.
25. Stryjkowski, *Położenie*, 473, 477, 481–483, 500, 600; the quote is on 482.
26. *Trials of War Criminals before the Nuernberg Military Tribunals under Control Council Law no. 10: Nuernberg Oct. 1946–April 1949*, 15 vols. (Washington, DC: U.S. Government Printing Office, 1949–1953), vol. 4, *"The Einsatzgruppen Case." "The RuSHA Case"* (1950), 937–938.

27. Bernadetta Nitschke, *Wysiedlenie ludności niemieckiej z Polski w latach 1945–1949* (Zielona Góra: Wyższa Szkoła Pedagogiczna im. Tadeusza Kotarbińskiego, 1999), 119.
28. Report, Włodzimerz Borodziej and Hans Lemberg, eds., *Die Deutschen,* vol. 4, *Wojewodschaften Pommerellen und Danzig (Westpreussen). Wojewodschaft Breslau (Niederschlesien),* ed. Ingo Eser, Witold Stankowski, Claudia Kraft, and Stanisław Jankowiak (Marburg: Verlag Herder-Institut, 2004), 351–353.
29. Stryjkowski, *Położenie,* 458.
30. Piotr Madajczyk, *Przyłączenie Śląska Opolskiego do Polski, 1945–1948* (Warsaw: Instytut Studiów Politycznych PAN, 1996), 192, 291.
31. Repr. in Madajczyk, *Niemcy,* 193–195.
32. Leszek Kosiński, "Pochodzenie terytorialne ludności ziem zachonich w 1950 r.," *Dokumentacja Geograficzna* 5, part 2 (1960): 9.
33. Ibid., 10–13, 16–17, 34–35.
34. Quoted in Andrzej Sakson, *Mazurzy—społeczność pogranicza* (Poznań: Instytut Zachodni, 1990), 171.
35. Stola, *Kraj bez wyjścia?,* 128.
36. Stanislaw Ossowski, "Analiza socjologiczna pojęcia ojczyny," in *O ojczyźnie i narodzie* (Warsaw: Państwowe Wydawnictwo Naukowe, 1984), 26–30.
37. Leszek Belzyt, "Die deutsche Minderheit nach dem Zweiten Weltkrieg: das Problem der sogenannten Autochtonen," in *Anerkannt als Minderheit. Vergangenheit und Zukunft der Deutschen in Polen,* ed. Hans van der Meulen (Baden-Baden: Nomos Verlagsgesellschaft, 1994), 56, 58. Karl Cordell and Stefan Wolff, "Ethnic Germans in Poland and the Czech Republic: A Comparative Evaluation," *Nationalities Papers* 33, no. 2 (June 2005): 263, conclude that the expulsion of Germans from Poland was less thorough than from Czechoslovakia.
38. Madajczyk, *Niemcy,* 45; Madajczyk, *Przyłączenie,* 209.
39. DzURP, no. 4, Entry 25, 19 Jan. 1951, 21–23, http://dziennikustaw.gov.pl/DU/1951/s/4/25.
40. Borodziej, "Wstęp," 103; Czesław Osękowski, *Społeczeństwo Polski zachodniej i pólnocnej w latach 1945–1956: procesy integracji i dezintegracji* (Zielona Góra: Wyższa Szkoła Pedagogiczna im. Tadeusza Kotarbińskiego, 1994), 107.
41. Quoted in Nitschke, *Wysiedlenie,* 247; see also Beata Katarzyna Cholewa, "The Migration of Germans from Lower Silesia after World War II," *Polish Western Affairs* 31, nos. 1–2 (1990): 64.
42. Stryjkowski, *Położenie,* 323.
43. Stola, *Kraj bez wyjścia?,* 77.
44. AAN, KC PZPR 237/VII–1667, fol. 107.
45. Osękowski, *Społeczeństwo,* 124; on autochthons and schools in general, see 195–210; Madajczyk, *Przyłączenie,* 210.
46. Jan Misztal, *Weryfikacja narodowościowa na Ziemiach Odzyskanych* (Warsaw: Państwowe Wydawnictwo Naukowe, 1990), 163.
47. Andreas Kossert, *Preußen, Deutsche oder Polen?: die Masuren im Spannungsfeld des ethnischen Nationalismus 1870–1956* (Wiesbaden: Harrassowitz Verlag, 2001), 327.
48. Document, repr. in Andrzej Sakson, "Tajny plan wysiedleń ludności rodzimej (mazurskiej) z 1952 roku w świetle dokumentów Archiwum Akt Nowych w Warszawie," in *Mniejszości narodowe,* ed. Zbigniew Kurcz (Wrocław: Wydawnictwo

Uniwersytetu Wrocławskiego, 1997), 124–126; Ingo Eser, "Niemcy na Górnym Śląsku," in *Niemcy*, ed. Borodziej and Lemberg, 2:331; Leszek Belzyt, "Zur Frage des nationalen Bewußtseins der Masuren im 19. und 20. Jahrhundert (auf der Basis statistischer Angaben)," *Zeitschrift für Ostmitteleuropa-Forschung* 45, no. 1 (1996): 50.

49. Stola, *Kraj bez wyjścia?*, 106.
50. Sakson, "Tajny plan," 120–121.
51. Sakson, *Mazurzy*, 136.
52. Osękowski, *Społeczeństwo*, 118–119.
53. Quoted ibid., 120.
54. Maria Dąbrowska, *Dzienniki*, vol. 4, *1951–1957*, ed. Tadeusz Drewnowski (Warsaw: Cztelnik, 1988), 96.
55. Quoted in Nitschke, *Wysiedlenie*, 245.
56. Osękowski, *Społeczeństwo*, 121–122.
57. Cholewa, "Migration," 64n52.
58. Quoted in Osękowski, *Społeczeństwo*, 120–21n178.
59. Ibid., 119n174, 122; the quote is on 119n174.
60. Osękowski, *Społeczeństwo*, 117, 120; Stanisław Jankowiak, "Wojewodschaft Breslau (Niederschlesien). Die Jahre 1946–1950," in *Die Deutschen*, Borodziej and Lemberg, 4:431–432; the quote is on 432; Stanisław Jankowiak, *Wysiedlenie i emigracja ludności niemieckiej w polityce władz Polskich w latach 1945–1970* (Warsaw: Instytut Pamięci Narodowej, Komisja Ścigania Zbrodni przeciwko Narodowi Polskiemu), 298, 306.
61. Repr. in Madajczyk, *Niemcy*, 204.
62. Cholewa, "Migration," 74; Osękowski, *Społeczeństwo*, 124; Bernard Linek, "Realizacja idei polskiego państwa narodowego na Górnym Śląsku po II wojnie światowej," *Sprawy Narodowościowe*, nos. 12–13 (1998): 28–30.
63. Stryjkowski, *Położenie*, 596.
64. Madajczyk, *Niemcy*, 223–225, 240; the quote is on 225.
65. Stola, *Kraj bez wyjścia?*, 109.
66. Kossert, *Preußen*, 327.
67. Stola, *Kraj bez wyjścia?*, 119–120; the quote is on 119.
68. Ibid., 121, 124–126, 481; Christian Raitz von Frentz, *A Lesson Forgotten: Minority Protection under the League of Nations. The Case of the German Minority in Poland, 1920–1934* (New York: St. Martin's Press, 1999), 260.
69. Stola, *Kraj bez wyjścia?*, 126–127.
70. Quoted in Nitschke, *Wysiedlenie*, 248 (emphasis in original).
71. Jankowiak, *Wysiedlenie i emigracja*, 443; Sakson, *Stosunki*, 284.
72. Kossert, *Preußen*, 330–331. See a picture of the monument, http://pl.wikipedia.org/w/index.php?title=Plik:Brodowo_02_beax.jpg&filetimestamp=20080829210101.

Conclusion

1. E. J. Hobsbawm so titles the chapter on 1918–1950, *Nations and Nationalism since 1780: Programme, Myth, Reality*, 2nd ed. (Cambridge: Cambridge University Press, 1992), 131–162.

2. Jan Molenda, *Chłopi, naród, niepodległość: kształtowanie się postaw narodowych i obwatelskich chłopów w Galicji i Królestwie Polskim w przededniu odrodzenia Polski* (Warsaw: Wydawnictwo NERITON, Instytut Historii PAN, 1999), 349.
3. Stanislaw Ossowski distinguishes between the "private fatherland" and an "ideological fatherland" based on an "imagined" community, "Analiza socjologiczna pojęcia ojczyny," in *O ojczyźnie i narodzie* (Warsaw: Państwowe Wydawnictwo Naukowe, 1984), 26–30.
4. Krystyna Kersten, "The Transfer of German Population from Poland in 1945–1947 (on the Example of West Pomerania)," *Acta Poloniae Historica* 10 (1968): 33.
5. Krzysztof Stryjkowski, *Położenie osób wpisanych w Wielkopolsce na niemiecką listę narodowościową w latach 1945–1950* (Poznań: Instytut Historii UAM, 2004), 602.
6. Piotr Madajczyk refers to them as "labile Zwischenschicht," *Przyłączenie Śląska Opolskiego do Polski, 1945–1948* (Warsaw: Instytut Studiów Politycznych PAN, 1996), 235.
7. Walker Connor, *Ethnonationalism: The Quest for Understanding* (Princeton: Princeton University Press, 1994), 42.
8. Dariusz Stola, *Kraj bez wyjścia?: migracje z Polski 1949–1989* (Warsaw: Instytut Pamięci Narodowej, Komisja Ścigania Zbrodni przeciwko Narodowi Polskiemu; Instytut Studiów Politycznych PAN, 2010), 415n132.
9. Bernard Linek, "Realizacja idei polskiego państwa narodowego na Górnym Śląsku po II wojnie światowej," *Sprawy Narodowościowe*, nos. 12–13 (1998): 25, 31; Piotr Madajczyk, "Niemcy," in *Mniejszości narodowe w Polsce: państwo i społeczeństwo polskie a mniejszości narodowe w okresach przełomów politycznych (1944–1989)*, ed. Madajczyk (Warsaw: Instytut Studiów Politycznych Polskiej Akademii Nauk, 1998): 73; Linek, "'De-Germanization' and 'Re-Polonization' in Upper Silesia, 1945–1950," in *Redrawing Nations: Ethnic Cleansing in East-Central Europe, 1944–1948*, ed. Philipp Ther and Ana Siljak (Lanham, MD: Rowman & Littlefield Publishers, Inc., 2001), 130.
10. Piotr Madajczyk, *Niemcy polscy: 1944–1989* (Warsaw: Oficyna Naukowa, 2001), 44–45.
11. Maria Szmeja, "Dlaczego Ślązacy z Opolszczyzny nie chcą być Polakami?" in *Mniejszości narodowe*, ed. Zbigniew Kurcz (Wrocław: Wydawnictwo Uniwersytetu Wrocławskiego, 1997), 109, 113, 107; Madajczyk, *Niemcy,* 50–51.
12. Quoted in a report, 7 Dec. 1948, excerpt, Włodzimierz Borodziej and Hans Lemberg, eds., *Niemcy,* vol. 2, *Polska Centralna. Województwo śląskie*, ed. Ingo Eser and Jerzy Kochanowski (Warsaw: Wydawnictwo NERITON, 2000), 524.
13. Andreas Kossert, *Preußen, Deutsche oder Polen?: die Masuren im Spannungsfeld des ethnischen Nationalismus 1870–1956* (Wiesbaden: Harrassowitz Verlag, 2001), 331; Tomasz Szarota traces the first publication of the phrase "polnische Wirtschaft" characterizing Polish mismanagement to 1829, *Niemcy i Polacy: wzajemne postrzeganie i stereotypy* (Warsaw: Wydawnictwo Naukowe PWN, 1996), 84; Andrew Demshuk examines the impact of the stereotypes of "deutscher Ordnung" und "polnischer Wirtschaft" among expellees, *The Lost German East: Forced Migration and the Politics of Memory, 1945–1970* (Cambridge: Cambridge University Press, 2012).

14. Kossert, *Preußen*, 320–321, 331.
15. Tadeusz Baryła, ed., *Warmiacy i Mazurzy w PRL. Wybor dokumentów. Rok 1945* (Olsztyn: Ośrodek Badań Naukowych im. Wojciecha Kętrzyńskiego, 1994), 2.
16. Grzegorz Strauchold, *Polska ludność rodzima ziem zachodnich i północnych. Opinie nie tylko publiczne lat 1944–1948* (Olsztyn: Ośrodek Badań Naukowych im. Wojciecha Kętrzyńskiego, 1995), 82.
17. Quoted with approval in Joachim Georg Görlich, "Autochtoni," *Kultura*, nos. 1/195–2/196 (1964): 136.
18. Czesław Osękowski, *Społeczeństwo Polski zachodniej i północnej w latach 1945–1956: procesy integracji i dezintegracji* (Zielona Góra: Wyższa Szkoła Pedagogiczna im. Tadeusza Kotarbińskiego, 1994), 138; Stola, *Kraj bez wyjścia?*, 125.
19. Michael Fleming makes this point regarding the treatment of national minorities generally, *Communism, Nationalism and Ethnicity, 1944–50* (London: Routledge, 2010), 145.
20. Ana Siljak surveys the literature on pursuing ethnic homogeneity through forced migration and concludes that "misery, coercion, and even violence" inevitably accompany it, a cost often ignored by advocates, "Conclusion," in *Redrawing Nations*, ed. Ther and Siljak, 327–335; the quote is on 330.
21. Fleming, *Communism*, 2.
22. According to Krystyna Kersten, "Mistrust toward foreigners became a permanent fixture on the Polish stage" as a consequence of forced migration, "Forced Migration and the Transformation of Polish Society in the Postwar Period," in *Redrawing Nations*, Ther and Siljak, 84.
23. See, for example, Stryjkowski, *Położenie*, 598. On the occasion of a German award for the contribution of *Tygodnik Powszechny* to Polish-German reconciliation, the editor Jerzy Turowicz defended the expulsion, Wojciech Pięciak, "Dyskusje historyczne i ich rola w pamięci zbiorowej i stosunkach polsko-niemieckich," in *Polacy—Niemcy. Sąsiedztwo z dystansu*, ed. Anna Wolff-Powęska and Dieter Bingen (Poznań: Wydawnictwo Instytutu Zachodniego, 2004), 407.
24. Elżbieta Kaszuba, *Między propagandą a rzeczywistością: Polska ludność Wrocławia w latach 1945–1947* (Warsaw-Wrocław: Wydawnictwo Naukowe PWN, 1997), 200.
25. On German fragmentation, see Winson Chu, *The German Minority in Interwar Poland* (Cambridge: Cambridge University Press, 2012), 3–4, 255–259, 270.
26. Ernest Renan, "What Is a Nation?" repr. in *Becoming National: a Reader*, ed. Geoff Eley and Grigor Suny (New York: Oxford University Press, 1996), 45.
27. Ibid., 48.
28. Ibid., 49. The Obodrites and Wilcy were the westernmost Slavs dwelling between the Elbe and Oder Rivers. Otto I (912–973) and Otto II (955–983) expanded into Slavic territory, "Polab," in *Encyclopædia Britannica. Encyclopædia Britannica Online Academic Edition*. Encyclopædia Britannica Inc., 2011, http://www.britannica.com.proxy.cc.uic.edu/EBchecked/topic/466670/Polab; "Otto I," ibid., http://www.britannica.com.proxy.cc.uic.edu/EBchecked/topic/434895/Otto-I; "Otto II," ibid., http://www.britannica.com.proxy.cc.uic.edu/EBchecked/topic/434929/Otto-II.
29. Renan, "What Is a Nation?" 50.

30. Beata Halicka comes to a similar conclusion, *Polens Wilder Westen: erzwungene Migration und de kuturelle Aneignung des Oderraums 1945–1948* (Paderborn: Ferdinand Schöningh, 2013), 287.
31. Renan, "What Is a Nation?" 52.
32. Ibid., 53.
33. Zbigniew Mazur, *O adaptacji niemieckiego dziedzictwa kulturowego na Ziemiach Zachodnich i Północnych* (Poznań: Instytut Zachodni, 2001).
34. Quoted in Madajczyk, *Niemcy,* 41–42.
35. Personal experience during the XV Powszechny Zjazd Historyków Polskich, 19–21 Sept. 1994, Gdańsk, Poland.
36. Brunon Synak, "The Kashubes in Poland: Ethnicity in Transition," in *Ethnicity, Nation, Culture: Central and East European Perspectives,* ed. Bálint Balla and Anton Sterbling (Hamburg: Krämer, 1998), 179.
37. Piotr Wróblewski, "Regional and National Bonds in the Opole District of Silesia: Gielczyn Fifty Years Later," ibid., 197, 199, 204–206.
38. Ibid., 193–196; *Donosy* 5343 (23 Mar. 2012), http://www.fuw.edu.pl/donosy; *Donosy,* 5153 (13 Dec. 2010), http://oldwww.fuw.edu.pl/bin/donosy-pokaz?numer=2010/101213.5153; Marek S. Szczepański and Anna Śliz, "Die Bewegung für die Autonomie Schlesiens (RAŚ)," *Polen-Analysen,* no. 112 (3 July 2012): 2–8, http://www.laender-analysen.de/polen/pdf/PolenAnalysen112.pdf. In regional and local elections in the fall of 2010, the chairman of the Movement for the Autonomy of Silesia Jerzy Gorzelik was elected to the executive board of Silesia Province.
39. *Donosy,* no. 5598 (6 Dec. 2013), http://www.fuw.edu.pl/donosy.
40. Andrzej Sakson suggests this for the Mazurs, *Stosunki narodowościowe na Warmii i Mazurach 1945–1997* (Poznań: Instytut Zachodni, 1998), 103; Madajczyk disputes this possibility, *Niemcy,* 45–47.
41. Yitzhak M. Brudny and Evgeny Finkel, "Why Ukraine Is Not Russia: Hegemonic National Identity and Democracy in Russia and Ukraine," *East European Politics and Societies* 25 (2011): 813–83.
42. Clare McManus-Czubińska et al., "Understanding Dual Identities in Poland," *Political Studies* 51 (2003): 132, 135–136; see 128–133 for correlation of identity with other factors.
43. Hannah Arendt, *The Origins of Totalitarianism* (New York: Harcourt Brace Jovanovich, 1973), 302

Acknowledgments

I had the good fortune at an early stage of being a student of Piotr S. Wandycz, the late Peter Brock, and the late Witold Jakóbczyk, all masters of their specialties, and am grateful for their cordiality. From the beginning of this project, Edward Kołodziej and Marcin Kula provided encouragement, advice, and source materials. Barbara Törnquist Plewa of Lund University and Piotr J. Wróbel of the University of Toronto invited me to make presentations at their institutions. James E. Bjork gave a thorough reading to an early version of the manuscript and made invaluable suggestions. Stephen E. Wiberley Jr. and John H. Matthews of the Richard J. Daley Library of the University of Illinois at Chicago obtained materials not in the library's collection. Laura E. Hostetler, chairperson of the Department of History, gave me access to the department's physical resources in preparing the manuscript. Doris L. Bergen, Regina Bowgierd, Mark Bullock, Wojciech J. Burszta, Karl Cordell, Geoff Eley, Klaus-Peter Friedrich, Benjamin Frommer, Stanisław Jankowiak, Dariusz Jarosz, Tomasz Kamusella, Matthias Kneip, Virgil Krapauskas, Richard S. Levy, Bernard Linek, Paweł Machcewicz, Przemysław Mrówka, Jerzy Myszor, Małgorzata Pośpiech, John D. Stanley, Dariusz Stola, Krzysztof Stryjkowski, Marek Suszko, Bożena Szaynok, Jakub Tyszkiewicz, and Marcin Zaremba provided source materials or other assistance. Grzegorz Kaźmierczak resolved all computer issues. Paul Mirocha drew the maps.

Index

Adamski, Stanisław, 39, 41, 42, 115, 116, 129, 158, 212, 215–216, 228, 234, 326, 327
AK. *See* Home Army
Aktion Link, 284
alienation: of *Volksdeutsche*, 110; of autochthons, 129, 176, 201, 236, 247, 257, 273, 278, 299, 303
Allenstein, ix, 16, 45. *See also* Olsztyn
Allies (World War I), 10, 11, 12, 14. *See also* Supreme Council of the Allies (World War I)
Allies (World War II), 56, 92, 123, 304. *See also* Control Council of the Allies (World War II); Great Powers (World War II); Western Allies (World War II)
Alsace, 34
Alster, Antoni, 109
Alwernia, 114
amnesty for *Volksdeutsche*, 155, 159, 229, 268, 288
Anatolia, 12, 315, 356
Anders, Władysław, 163, 164
Anglo-Saxon powers. *See* Western Allies (World War II)
antisemitism, 201, 203
apostolic administrators, 129, 234, 351
Arendt, Hannah, 308, 316, 340
Armia Krajowa. *See* Home Army
Article 116. *See* Basic Law
Association of Productive Poles, 38, 102, 111, 152, 154, 157, 326
Atlantic Charter, 55, 57
Attlee, Clement, 66
Auschwitz, 97, 314
Auslandsdeutsche. *See* Germans abroad
Austria, viii, 8, 10, 20, 22, 56
Austrian Poland, 9, 15, 301

Austrian Silesia, 15, 26, 32, 40, 41, 339. *See also* Cieszyn
autonomy: provincial, 86, 171, 307; Silesian, 15, 85, 385; Mazurian, 81

Babimost, 194
Baczewski, Jan, 218, 275
Baltic Germans, 29, 30
Baltic Sea, viii, x, 10, 61, 272
Baltic states, 20
Barcikowski, Wacław, 175, 176, 194, 196, 197
Bardach, Juliusz, 92
Bartoszyce, x, 256
Basic Law, 250, 255, 279, 295
Belarusians, 3, 59, 63, 256
Belorussian Front, 58, 95
Belorussian Soviet Republic, viii, 62
Belzyt, Leszek, 293
Beneš, Edvard, 12, 56, 151, 329, 330
Bensch, Teodor, 129
Bergen, Doris L., 49
Beria, Lavrenty, 91, 95, 97, 344, 352
Berlińska, Danuta, 13
Berman, Jakub, 73, 109
Biała, x, 114, 115, 117, 126, 156, 158, 207, 225
Białystok, viii, x, 26, 71, 106, 127, 132, 167, 243, 252, 253, 260, 264, 274, 292
Bielitz. *See* Bielsko
Bielsko, ix, 41, 207, 267
Bieniasz, Stanisław, 80, 119, 338, 353
Bierut, Bolesław, 73, 82, 96, 110, 112, 131, 195, 211, 215, 216, 248, 342, 352
bilingualism, 11, 14, 16, 39, 77, 91, 125, 150, 170
Blanke, Richard, 17, 364
Bobrzyński, Michał, 9
Bock, Fedor von, 25
Bodzanowice, 79

Boguszyce, 93
Bohemian Crown, Lands of, 2, 13
Bohlen, Charles, 57
Boikos, 242
Bolesław III, 64
Bożek, Arkadiusz, 196, 218, 261
Bracht, Fritz, 36, 40–41
Brandt, Willy, 20
Brandys, Kazimierz, 183
Braniewo, x, 146, 223
Breslau. *See* Wrocław
British: radio, 41; Foreign Office, 53, 54; War Cabinet, 55; government, 61, 63, 64, 66, 73, 87, 161, 236, 238, 245, 328; ambassador, Moscow, 65, 66; origin, 115; zone of Germany, 151; vice consul, Stettin, 173; imperialism, 249; embassy, Warsaw, 295
Brock, Peter, 377
Brodowo, 299
Bromberg. *See* Bydgoszcz
"Bromberg Bloody Sunday," 49. *See also* Bydgoszcz
Bronisławki, 290
Bronze Age, 22
Brubaker, Rogers, 5, 315, 319, 333–334
Brzeg, x, 179, 180
Bug, viii, 23, 146, 235, 285
Bukovina, 30
Bukowski, Bronisław, 197
Bulgaria, 11
Buławski, Rajmund, 128
Burleigh, Michael, 20, 25
Bursche, Juliusz, 83, 294
Burski, Jerzy, 82, 83, 92, 121, 122, 132, 133, 303
Butowo, 147
Bydgoszcz, viii, ix, x, 47, 49, 291
Byrnes, James F., 67, 191–193, 194
Bytom, x, 77, 96, 98, 144, 147, 154, 171, 186, 200, 230, 276
Bytów, x, 84, 144, 150–151, 193, 220, 274, 275, 278, 293, 339

camps: Nazi, 28, 29, 35, 38, 40, 45, 49, 50, 83, 84, 140, 148, 156, 209, 212, 297; Polish 52, 99, 100–103, 114, 116, 118, 121, 123, 130, 139, 141–142, 144, 153, 154, 157, 161, 170, 179, 188, 190, 201, 205, 206, 207, 208, 219, 231, 240, 243, 245, 266, 268–270, 288, 290, 295, 303, 344, 345; Soviet, 96, 97, 250, 274; refugee, 157, 161, 162; transit, 157, 165, 185, 239; POW, 162–163, 179, 185, 250, 258, 260, 262, 274

capitalism, 57, 59
capitalist, 60, 248, 256, 262, 274
Carpathian Mountains, 10
Casimir the Great, 70
Catholic Church, 5, 13, 34, 41, 42, 82, 84, 88, 116, 129, 130, 131, 182, 218, 234, 303, 304, 320
Cenôva, Florjan, 23
censorship, 197
census, 11, 14, 15, 16, 18, 22, 40, 43, 79, 114, 160, 167, 251, 291–292, 296, 298, 299, 360
Central Committee: of the KPP, 59; of the PPR, 60, 73, 87, 88, 94, 97, 248; of Polish Jews, 202, 203; of the PZPR, 249, 252, 255, 262, 273, 276, 277, 278, 280, 282, 285, 295, 296, 297, 298
Central Directory of the Coal Industry, 254
Central Poland, 6, 87, 88, 89, 104, 119, 134, 153, 165, 181, 183, 213, 218, 252, 254, 263, 278
Chamberlain, Neville, 25
Chełm, 62
Chełmno, ix, 29
Chłopski Sztandar, 197
Chodzież, x, 118
Chojna, 275
Chojnice, x, 281
Chorzów, 163
Chrzanów, x, 114, 118
Churchill, Winston, 2, 11, 54, 55, 57, 62, 63, 65, 66, 170, 191, 192
Ciechanów, ix, 26, 45, 47
Cieszyn, ix, 117. *See also* Austrian Silesia
citizenship: of *Volksdeutsche*, 1, 4 33, 34, 50, 51, 69, 100, 109, 110, 111, 112, 151, 154, 155, 158, 207, 208, 209, 210, 212, 214, 224, 226, 228, 229, 237, 266, 267, 268, 269, 270, 271, 288, 289–291; laws and decrees, 4, 19, 31, 160, 172, 208, 293, 294, 321; of autochthons, 4, 94, 99, 107, 111, 121, 122, 123, 126, 127, 140, 143, 144, 147, 168, 169, 170, 173, 178, 179, 182, 183, 184, 185, 186–187, 188, 189, 190, 192, 193, 195, 196, 202, 207, 208, 215, 219, 220, 223, 224, 225, 230, 231, 232, 236, 238, 239, 241, 247, 250, 251, 255, 257, 258, 259, 262, 265, 276, 278, 284, 285, 294, 295, 296; of Poles, 5, 52, 100; of Germans, 14, 51, 52, 103, 151, 222, 255, 258, 261, 295, 296; revocable, 35, 214; of *Leistungspolen*, 111, 157; of Jews, 201, 202, 251; irrevocable, 214
Civic Committee of Poles of Opole Silesia, 93, 94
clergy: in general, 28, 140, 243; Catholic, 13, 14, 39, 42, 76, 78, 85, 115, 129, 155, 158, 175, 215, 230, 234, 254, 263, 277, 278, 281, 282, 295,

297; Protestant, 17, 83, 84, 92, 159, 182, 183, 189, 247, 250, 264, 277, 294, 297; Kashubian, 274, 278. *See also* apostolic administrators; Catholic Church; Evangelical-Augsburg Church; Prussian Union Evangelical Church
cold war, 3, 6, 72
collective guilt, 49, 68, 97, 99, 183, 344
collectivization, 248, 249, 250, 256, 295
Cominform, 241, 248
Comintern, 59, 60
Communist Information Bureau. *See* Cominform
Communist International. *See* Comintern
Communist Party of Poland, 59–60, 332
Communist Workers' Party of Poland. *See* Communist Party of Poland
concentration camp, Nazi. *See under* camps
confiscation of property: by Germans, 27, 30, 34, 35, 47; by military, 92; by Poles, 101, 106–107, 113, 118, 125, 142, 148, 149, 150, 153, 156, 157, 158, 177, 185, 190, 199, 205, 209, 212, 213, 220, 223, 227, 228, 247, 253, 256, 271, 275, 290. *See also* property
Congress of Autochthons, 193–198, 201, 217
Congress of Kashubs, 150, 281
Constantinople, Treaty of, 11
Control Council of the Allies (World War II), 37, 138, 139
Council of Foreign Ministers, 219
Council of Ministers, Homeland, 51
Council of Ministers, Polish (London), 55
Council of Ministers, Polish (Warsaw), 73, 86, 100, 110, 132, 157, 158, 161, 207, 210, 211, 227, 270, 285, 288, 289, 290, 291, 294, 296
Council of Ministers, Soviet, 96
Council of National Unity, 63, 65
Council of the Evangelical Church, 130
Cracow: municipality, viii, ix, x; province, x, 26, 39, 101, 114–115, 156, 158, 207; inhabitants of, 23, 89, 341
Crimea. *See* Yalta, conference of
criteria: national, 3, 4, 7, 98, 300, 305; ethnic, 11; of Germanness, 15, 17, 21, 32, 33, 34, 35, 37, 38, 39, 40, 41, 43, 45, 48, 119, 178, 207, 265, 303; racial, 32, 33, 37, 43; of Polishness, 76, 79, 81, 82, 94, 119, 120–123, 126, 127, 135, 141, 155, 161, 168–169, 170–173, 176, 177, 192, 196, 221–222; of Kashubianness, 125
"current reality," 197, 279, 280
Curzon, Lord, 54
Curzon Line, 56, 61, 62, 63, 64, 65, 330
Czaplicki, Józef, 176

Czarnków, x, 290
Czech lands, 2
Czechoslovak Communist Party, 332
Czechoslovakia, viii, x, 12, 31, 55, 56, 72, 97, 114, 126, 137, 151, 300, 304, 337, 357, 364, 381. *See also* Bohemia and Moravia, Protectorate of
Czech Republic, 314. *See also* Bohemia and Moravia, Protectorate of
Czechs, 2–3, 23, 31, 35, 97, 151, 256, 344
Człuchów, x, 84, 144, 193, 275, 339

Danzig, viii, ix, 26, 28, 30, 32, 50, 55, 56, 59, 70, 71, 84, 225. *See also* Danzig-West Prussia; Gdańsk
Danzig-West Prussia, ix, 26, 36, 39, 43–45, 47, 48, 49, 50. *See also* Danzig; Gdańsk
Daszyński, Ignacy, 10
Dąbrowa Basin, ix, 26, 71, 78, 103, 133–134, 142, 240, 276, 307
Dąbrowa Górnicza, x, 71
Dąbrowska, Maria, 3, 295, 352
de-Germanization, 67, 135–136, 188–190, 229–232, 233, 236, 238, 253–254, 257
Delegatura, 41, 42, 47, 48, 63, 74, 76, 128, 129, 170, 338
Democratic Bloc, 171, 173, 174, 195, 217, 218
demographic structure of the borderlands, 68, 92, 93, 119, 140
de-nationalization, 24, 61, 75, 76, 301
Denmark, 162, 221
Deutscher Ostmarken Verein, 318
deutschstämmig. *See* German origin
Dębno, x, 179, 275
Dimitrov, Georgi, 60
divided families, 127, 141, 178, 182, 185, 186, 187, 189, 220, 237, 238, 229, 238, 250, 255, 258, 259, 260, 262, 271, 273, 274, 279, 286, 289, 290, 296, 297
Djilas, Milovan, 93
Dmowski, Roman, 9, 10, 64. *See also* National Democratic Party
Domański, Bolesław, 85, 356
"Drang nach Osten," 120
Drygas, Stanisław, 48
Dubiel, Józef, 133, 197, 211, 218, 237, 253
Dubiel, Paweł, 236
Dybowski, Mirosław, 142, 143, 150
Działdowo, ix, x, 16, 17–18, 26, 45, 81, 82, 83, 92, 100, 107, 110, 111, 117, 131, 132, 133, 154, 155, 156, 158, 163, 205, 214, 224, 270, 299, 303
Dziennik Zachodni, 135

eastern border, Germany, 20
eastern border, Poland, 10, 56, 57, 60, 62, 63, 64, 65, 70, 176. *See also* Curzon Line
eastern borderlands, Poland, 6, 50, 59, 67, 70, 72, 73, 77, 87, 88, 107, 134, 175, 201, 304
eastern Germany, 1, 2, 4, 23, 66, 191, 199
East Germany. *See* German Democratic Republic
East Prussia, viii, ix, 9, 12, 16, 17, 22, 24, 26, 45–46, 49, 53, 55, 56, 61, 62, 64, 65, 66, 71, 80, 81, 82, 91, 93, 96, 100, 110, 111, 127, 131, 188, 246, 264. *See also* Mazuria; Olsztyn
Eden, Anthony, 54, 55, 56, 57, 62, 63, 64
eigensprachiger Kulturdeutsche, 21
Einsatzgruppen, 28, 49
Elbe, 22, 23, 35
Elbląg, x, 131
Eley, Geoff, 5, 313
Ełk, ix, x, 46, 127, 132
endecja. *See* National Democratic Party
endek [i.e., nationalist], 281, 286
Estonia, 28. *See also* Baltic states
"ethnic cleansing," 3, 6, 120, 304
ethnic homogeneity, 2, 3, 4, 7, 9, 52, 53, 56, 59, 61, 62, 65, 66, 67, 70, 150, 195, 241, 242, 243, 255, 256, 300, 304, 307, 308, 353, 314, 384. *See also* ethnographic considerations; national homogeneity
ethnic identity. *See under* identity
ethnographic considerations, 9, 10, 11, 19, 20, 54, 55, 57, 58, 60, 61, 84, 85, 96, 305, 330
ethno-nationalism, 376–377
eugenics, 324
European center against expulsion, 6
Evangelical-Augsburg Church, 18, 34, 83, 84, 130, 131, 156, 159, 247, 298
Evangelical Lutheran Church, 16, 82, 84, 264, 277, 294. *See also* Council of the Evangelical Church; Evangelical-Augsburg Church; Protestant *under* clergy; Prussian Union Evangelical Church
exchanges of population, 2, 11, 25, 54, 62, 86, 242, 315
expropriation. *See* confiscation of property

family reunification, 165, 286, 288, 289, 297, 298. *See also* divided families
fifth column, 27, 48, 52, 56
folk culture, 85, 171, 250, 256, 281, 339, 376
Forster, Albert, 36, 43, 44, 50, 113
France, 18, 19, 30, 163, 46, 250, 305, 316
Freikorps, 14
FRG. *See* Germany, Federal Republic of

Friends Service Council, 261
Frontier Defense Force, 165, 203

Galicia, 13, 15, 242, 341
Gazeta Ludowa, 140, 165
Gazeta Robotnicza, 105
Gdańsk: municipality, ix, x, 61, 125, 145, 194, 221, 225, 250, 274, 278, 281, 306; province, x, 71, 103, 105, 124, 125, 132, 137, 139, 140, 142, 145, 150, 151, 160, 167, 173, 176, 177, 178, 187, 196, 197, 203, 215, 221, 224, 243, 249, 252, 253, 259, 260, 273, 274, 276, 278, 280, 281, 282, 283, 292, 293. *See also* Danzig; Danzig-West Prussia
Gdańsk-Narwik, 187
GDR. *See* German Democratic Republic
Gellner, Ernest, 313
Generalgouvernement, ix, 26, 29, 30, 42, 48, 51, 91, 104, 110, 114, 324
Generalplan Ost, 21
Geneva Convention (1922), 14, 15
Geneva Convention (1929), 254
"genuine Poles," 4–5, 175, 304, 314
German Democratic Republic, 72, 259, 278, 279, 284, 286, 288, 290, 294, 296, 298, 376
Germanization, 13, 14, 16, 17, 21, 23, 24, 27, 28, 30, 31, 33, 34, 35, 36, 37, 38, 40, 41, 43–44, 45, 46, 47, 53, 56, 61, 67, 75, 76, 77, 78, 80, 82, 83, 84, 86, 87, 89, 110, 111, 119, 120, 123, 125, 128, 135, 150, 160, 168, 170, 173, 174, 177, 179, 195, 198, 199, 207, 212, 220, 246, 253, 285, 286, 303, 304, 318, 326
"German national distinctiveness," 206, 207–208, 229, 237, 240, 265, 266, 269, 289
German nationality, 32, 33, 39, 51, 52, 76, 88, 99, 107, 114, 116, 119, 121, 161, 192, 206, 208, 212, 216, 230, 231, 237, 239, 240, 265, 266, 268, 295, 296, 297, 303, 305. *See also* German origin; Germanness
Germanness, 21, 24, 31, 33, 36, 37, 39, 43, 51, 72, 73, 75, 76, 87, 90, 122, 135, 147, 159, 168, 169, 175, 178, 183, 190, 200, 231, 233, 236, 239, 240, 253, 254, 256, 267, 300, 302, 321. *See also* German nationality; German origin
German origin, 27, 32, 33, 34, 35, 36, 37, 40, 44, 45, 47, 48, 52, 68, 115, 159, 160, 207, 212, 265, 266, 269, 291. *See also* German nationality; Germanness
German Red Cross, 279
Germans abroad, 19, 20
German-Soviet Boundary and Friendship Treaty, 25
German-Soviet Nonaggression Pact, 25, 322

German spirit, 52, 210, 268, 277. *See also* Germanness
German underground resistance, 191, 192, 200, 230, 279, 364
German Upper Silesia. *See under* Upper Silesia
Germany, Federal Republic of, 20, 72, 255, 258, 259, 271, 279, 291, 295, 296, 297, 298. *See also* Basic Law
Gestapo, 49, 50, 69, 200, 263
Gębik, Władysław, 127
Gizewiusz, Gustaw, 189
Giżycko, 189
Gliwice, x, 77, 94, 124, 190, 219, 230, 231, 236, 239, 292, 351
Gloeh, Feliks, 105, 130, 131, 132, 133, 154, 155
Głos Wielkopolski, 153
Gniezno, x, 100
Gołdap, x, 131
Gomułka, Władysław, 73, 87, 94, 95, 97, 120, 137, 164, 165, 170, 174, 175, 180, 195–196, 197, 236, 248–249, 260, 297, 336
Görlich, Joachim Georg, 89, 200
Gorzów Wielkopolski, x, 71, 122, 224
Gostynin, x, 112
Gość Niedzielny, 116
"Go West," 87, 104
Grabski, Stanisław, 64, 74, 333, 336
Grabski, Władysław, 76
Great Britain. *See* British
"great Germans," 307
Great Poland, 22, 23, 24, 26, 29, 45, 73, 212, 213. *See also* province *under* Poznań; Warthegau
"great Poles," 79, 144, 307
Great Powers (World War II), 54–57, 64–66, 67, 91, 137, 305. *See also* Allies (World War II)
Great Terror, 64
"Great Verification," 260–265
Greece, 11–12, 54, 56, 255, 318
Greenfield, Liah, 108
Greiser, Arthur, 28, 29, 36, 37–38, 45, 210
Grodków, x, 101
Gromadki, 16, 17
Gronowo, 161, 269, 270
Gross, Jan Tomasz, 104, 329, 346
Groß-Rosen, 201
Grundgesetz. See Basic Law
"gypsies." *See* Roma

Halifax, Viscount, 54
Heimat. See "private fatherland"
Heim ins Reich, 27, 52, 67, 86

Heydrich, Reinhard, 28, 35
Highest Court of Examination for Nationality Questions, 33, 49
Himmler, Heinrich, 21, 27, 28, 29, 31, 32–33, 34, 36, 38, 40, 41, 44, 49, 50, 212, 327
Hitler, Adolf, 12, 25, 27, 31, 33, 36, 37, 43, 54, 56, 59, 67, 68, 78, 81, 83, 117, 127, 152, 201
Hitler Youth, 200, 282
Hlond, August Cardinal, 129, 130
Holocaust, 6, 102, 201
Home Army, 42, 73, 94, 242
homeland, 4, 6, 12, 13, 20, 21, 45, 52, 63, 67, 111, 137, 140, 175, 177, 181, 199, 201, 219, 237, 243, 255, 263, 273, 280, 293, 297, 299, 303, 304, 306, 315
Home to the Reich. *See Heim ins Reich*
House of Commons, 2, 65
House of Lords, 54
Hull, Cordell, 54
Hurwic-Nowakowska, Irena, 251
Hutsuls, 242

ICRC. *See* International Committee of the Red Cross
identity: national, 3, 4, 5, 6, 11, 12, 19, 26, 40, 50, 57, 59, 68, 75, 78, 79, 85, 90, 108, 120, 143, 145, 149, 167, 240, 242, 293, 299, 301, 302, 303, 307, 315; ethnic, 5, 6, 9, 12, 84, 149, 286, 299, 307; contingent, 5, 14, 15, 17, 31, 36, 39, 40, 42, 50, 80, 84, 108, 120, 126, 143, 155, 177, 190, 212 220, 233, 239, 240, 249, 256, 278, 285, 291, 293, 299, 301, 302, 303; Silesian, 13, 15, 40, 59, 79, 89, 140, 299, 307; regional, 14, 16, 17, 85, 90, 135, 149, 174, 286, 287, 293, 299, 301, 302, 307; Mazurian, 16, 17, 18, 21, 46, 80, 81, 83, 84, 88, 110, 111, 121, 131, 132, 155, 156, 182, 293; German, 17, 34, 245, 299; Polish, 74, 77, 89, 90, 120, 135, 146, 186, 199, 241, 245, 252, 299, 302, 307; Kashubian, 84, 293, 299, 306–307; cultural, 85, 149, 349; Jewish, 201, 251; religious, 303
"ideological fatherland," 301, 383
ideological shift, 241, 249, 250, 254, 271, 302
ideologies, revisionist, 18. *See also Ostforschung; Polska myśl zachodnia*
Ilkenau. *See* Olkusz
in-between strata, 32, 36, 40, 383. *See also* contingent *under* identity; national indifference
incorporated lands, viii, ix, 1, 26, 27, 28, 29, 30, 33, 34, 36, 37, 38, 39, 41, 43, 44, 46–47, 50, 51, 52, 88, 91, 107, 110, 111, 114, 120, 162, 208, 291, 302, 305, 324, 327

Instytut Mazurski. See Mazurian Institute
Instytut Śląski. See Silesian Institute
Instytut Zachodni. See Western Institute
Interior Ministry, Reich, 31, 32, 33, 34, 36, 39, 40, 43, 49
inter-ministerial commission, 227, 266, 268, 269, 270
Internal Security Corps, 98, 153, 228
International Committee of the Red Cross, 56, 261
internationalism, 254, 260. *See also* "proletarian internationalism"
International Statistical Congress, 10
interpellation, parliamentary, 153, 180
Israel, 102, 251–252
Izdebski, Zygmunt, 169, 171, 195, 233, 241, 267

Jagiellonian University, 21, 126
Jarocin, x, 138
Jawor, 101
Jaworzno, 96, 102, 114, 243, 290
Jews, 2, 3, 4, 21, 26, 27, 28, 29, 31, 32, 33, 35, 36, 37, 43, 45, 49, 52, 59, 89, 124, 133–134, 163, 201–204, 233, 242, 251, 252, 291, 314, 332, 336, 340, 345, 346, 353, 366, 368
Jędrychowski, Stefan, 64

Kaczmarek, Ryszard, 50
Kaczyński, Jarosław, 314
Kalisz, x, 270, 271, 289
Kartuzy, x, 281
Kashubs, 8, 20, 22, 23, 26, 28, 33, 34, 50, 59, 84, 94, 122, 125, 149–151, 160, 161, 162, 174, 197, 198, 199, 245, 249, 252, 256, 274, 276, 278, 280, 281, 282, 283, 286, 293, 299, 305–307
Katowice: municipality, viii, ix, x, 15, 22, 102, 205, 232, 239, 249, 254; county: 35, 190, 222, 233, 249, 257; diocese, 39, 42, 341; province, 86, 134, 202, 292, 294, 298; district, 141, 161, 183. *See also* Silesia, province of (post 1945)
Kattowitz. *See* Katowice
Katula, Karol, 159–160
Katyń, 56, 314
KC. *See* Central Committee
Kelles-Krauz, Kazimierz, 10
Kennan, George F., 64
Kersten, Krystyna, 60, 67, 242, 329, 336, 384
Kępno, x, 152, 153, 157, 209, 210, 211–212, 213, 214, 226–228, 271, 358
Kętrzyn, 189
Kętrzyński, Wojciech, 16, 189
Kielce, viii, ix, x, 26, 39, 203
Kielce pogrom, 203

Kiernik, Władysław, 164, 197
Kláhi. *See* Kluki
Kliszko, Zenon, 73, 197, 249
Klondike, 105
Kluczbork, x, 13, 101, 107, 183, 184, 277, 292
Kluki, 199, 365
Klus, Rev., 183–184
Koch, Erich, 45
Kociewiaks, 274
Kohn, Hans, 315
Kominek, Bolesław, 129, 234
Konev, Ivan, 93
Konin, x, 271
Korfanty, Wojciech, 327
Kostrzewski, Józef, 22
Koszalin, x, 243, 248, 291, 292, 293
Kościan, x, 99, 110, 229
Kościerzyna, x, 281
Koźle, x, 90, 141, 234, 251, 279, 292
KPP. *See* Communist Party of Poland
krauts, 48, 107, 185, 277
kresy. See eastern borderlands, Poland
KRN. *See* National Council of the Homeland
Król, Marcin, 3
Kula, Marcin, 171, 314, 334
Kula, Witold, 68–69, 176
kulaks, 58, 256, 258, 274, 275, 279, 286, 295
Kulczycki, Zbigniew, 211
Kulturarbeit, 20, 21
Kulturboden, 20
Kutz, Kazimierz, 234
Kuźnica Ligocka, 141–142
Kwidzyn, x, 131, 142, 147, 352

Lampe, Alfred, 60, 61
Lamsdorf. *See* Łambinowice
Lane, Arthur Bliss, 191
Latvia, 28. *See also* Baltic states
Lausanne, Treaty of, 11–12, 54, 315, 356
League of Nations, 11
Lebensmittel Liste, 34
Lebensraum, 25, 27, 86, 137, 300, 304, 322
Lebus, x, 71
Lec. *See* Giżycko
Lechitic, 23
Leipe. *See* Lipno
Leistungspolen. See Association of Productive Poles
Lemkos, 242, 243
Lengowski, Michał, 127
Leszno (Mazuria), 297
Leszno-Gronowo. *See* Gronowo
Leyding, Gustaw, 132, 261

Leyk, Emil, 261
Leyk, Fryderyk, 92, 132, 261
Lębork, x, 71, 84, 125, 149, 274, 350, 363
Lidzbark (Działdowo County), 205
Lidzbark (Warmia), x, 106
Ligota Kuźnica. *See* Kuźnica Ligocka
Lipno, ix, 44
Lithuania, ix, 9, 25, 58, 62. *See also* Polish-Lithuanian Commonwealth
Lithuanians, 3, 8, 9, 256
Litzmannstadt, ix, 29, 37, 38, 47, 48. *See also* Łódź
"living space." *See* Lebensraum
Lodwich, Ewald, 92, 156
Lötzen. *See* Giżycko
Lower Silesia, 13, 22, 26, 30, 38, 71, 85, 98, 123, 129, 138, 149, 158, 180, 185, 201, 204, 226, 239, 251, 252, 256, 296, 339, 366. *See also* province *under* Wrocław
Lublin, x, 24, 62
Lublin government, 64
Lubliniec, x, 292
Lubusz. *See* Lebus
Lubusz Land, 71, 122, 143, 166, 192, 224, 252, 279, 292
Lusatian culture, 22
Lusatian Neisse. *See* Oder-Neisse
Lwów, viii, 22, 63, 65, 89
Lwówek, 161
Lyck. *See* Ełk

Łambinowice, 102, 141–142
Łeba, 150, 357
Łebsko, Lake, x, 198
Łebsko-Słupsk, 150
Łódź, viii, ix, x, 26, 29, 68, 113, 117, 148, 157, 159, 201, 202, 208, 228–229, 237, 249, 260, 265, 267, 289. *See also* Litzmannstadt

Madajczyk, Piotr, 119, 120, 199, 291, 293, 383, 385
Malbork, x, 131, 142, 352
Małłek, Edward, 81, 133, 297, 299
Małłek, Karol, 18, 45, 81, 82, 92, 121, 132, 217, 261, 297, 299
Małłek, Robert, 45
Małłek, Ryszard, 297
Małłek family, 110, 299
MAP. *See* Ministry of Public Administration
Maritime League, 271, 272
marriages, ethnically mixed, 34, 37, 38, 82, 126, 177, 178, 189, 202, 206, 207, 210, 220, 222, 223, 230, 240, 246, 256, 260, 265, 266, 268, 271, 291, 305, 368

Marshall Plan, 232
Marxism, 10, 57, 68
Masaryk, Tomáš, 337
"masking oneself," 39, 41, 42, 158, 159
"masquerade." *See* "masking oneself"
Mazovia, 15, 46, 131
Mazur, Franciszek, 252
Mazur, Stanisław, 100, 111
Mazuria: autochthons, 8, 15, 16, 17, 18, 20, 21, 22, 23, 26, 32, 34, 45, 46, 76, 80, 81, 82, 83, 84, 85, 88, 92, 94, 100, 103, 105, 106, 110, 111, 121, 122, 126–128, 130, 131, 132, 133, 138, 142, 146, 149, 154, 155, 161, 173, 174, 181, 182, 183, 187, 192, 197, 198, 215, 221, 223, 224, 246, 247, 248, 256, 258, 260, 261, 262, 263, 264, 265, 274, 277, 284, 286, 294, 295, 297, 298, 299, 303, 305, 307, 338, 373, 380, 385; region: 9, 15–18, 22, 61, 70, 71, 76, 77, 80, 82, 85, 87, 94, 105, 110, 121, 125, 126–127, 130, 131, 133, 138, 142, 145, 147, 148, 160, 161, 165, 166, 170, 175, 180, 183, 189, 192, 198, 215, 247, 256, 261, 262, 274, 285, 294, 297, 299, 303, 307, 338, 352, 377; language, 16, 17, 23, 24, 45, 46, 80, 93, 189; pro-Polish activists, 17, 18, 45, 81, 82, 92, 110, 121, 122, 130, 131, 132, 133, 181, 247, 260, 261, 307, 336; separatism, 83, 131
Mazurian Institute, 81, 82
Mazurian People's University, 261
MBP. *See* Ministry of Public Security
Mertes, Alois, 298
Miastko, x, 84, 95, 107
Międzychód, x, 152, 153, 209
Międzyrzecz, x, 123, 267
MIiP. *See* Ministry of Information and Propaganda
Mikołajczyk, Stanisław, 56, 62, 63, 65, 66, 173, 191, 197
Milik, Karol, 129
Mill, John Stuart, 8
millet, 11
Miłosz, Czesław, 104
Minc, Hilary, 61
Minister of Internal Affairs, Soviet, 95, 96
Ministry of Agriculture and Agrarian Reforms, 209, 270, 274
Ministry of Construction, 274
Ministry of Culture and Art, 256
Ministry of Information and Propaganda, 83, 150, 173, 194, 197, 211
Ministry of Interior, Czechoslovak, 151
Ministry of Internal Affairs, 195, 297, 298
Ministry of Justice, 101, 113, 118, 123, 205, 269, 270

Ministry of Labor and Social Welfare, 286
Ministry of National Defense, 101, 163, 164, 195, 286
Ministry of Public Administration, 83, 98, 105, 111, 123, 125, 126, 129, 130, 131, 135, 139, 150, 152, 157, 159, 162, 164, 202, 227, 228, 237, 238, 239, 240, 252, 256, 258, 259, 260, 261, 264, 266, 267, 268, 270, 284, 352
Ministry of Public Security, 83, 101, 102, 103, 118, 141, 176, 179, 187, 208, 214, 216, 217, 221, 225, 229, 251, 266, 270, 286, 290, 295, 352
Ministry of Recovered Lands, 76, 95, 105, 106, 133, 147, 148, 164, 165, 166, 168, 170, 171, 172, 173, 176, 177, 178, 179, 180, 181, 186, 187, 189, 190, 192, 193, 195, 199, 211, 218, 219, 220, 221, 222, 223, 224, 227, 230, 231, 234, 237, 243, 245, 247, 248, 249, 250, 251, 252, 253, 265, 266, 363
minorities, 1, 2, 3, 4, 10, 11, 12, 14, 20, 24, 27, 28, 31, 36, 38, 48, 49, 54, 55, 56, 59, 60, 64, 65, 68, 120, 128, 129, 130, 143, 242, 255, 256, 267, 293, 297, 304, 307, 318, 330, 332, 376, 384
Minority Protection System, 11
minority treaties, 54
Moczar, Mieczysław, 260–263, 264, 284, 377
Moczyński, Zygmunt, 196, 197, 198
Mogilno, x, 69
Molenda, Jan, 301
Molotov, Vyacheslav, 65, 66, 67, 333
MON. *See* Ministry of National Defense
Montandon, George, 11
Monte Cassino, 163
Moravians, 173
Morski County, x, 276, 281, 282
Moscow, 54, 55, 61, 62, 63, 64, 65, 66, 219, 296
Mossor, Stefan, 243
Mrągowo, x, 181, 182, 189, 223, 238, 248, 262, 277, 283, 293, 295, 296
Mrongowiusz, Krzysztof Celestyn, 189
MSW. *See* Ministry of Internal Affairs
Muslims, 6, 12, 318
Myślibórz, x, 280
myths: German, 19; nationalist, 20; Polish, 89, 335; antisemitic, 203
MZO. *See* Ministry of Recovered Lands

Namysłów, x, 179, 180, 275, 339
Narzym, 154, 155
national consciousness, 20, 42, 76, 78, 79, 89, 93, 121, 131, 149, 155, 159, 166, 168, 169, 171, 174, 178, 184, 188, 190, 199, 212, 214, 239, 240, 241, 249, 258, 268, 285, 293, 296, 297, 301
National Council (London), 54

National Council of the Homeland, 61, 62, 72, 73, 74, 76, 83, 92, 106, 111, 116, 123, 148, 152, 153, 165, 170, 172, 175, 180, 194, 196, 211, 303
National Democratic Party, 9, 10, 64, 74, 320. *See also* Dmowski, Roman
National Democrats. *See* National Democratic Party
national homogeneity, 2, 5, 64, 75. *See also* ethnic homogeneity
national identity. *See under* identity
national indifference, 5, 32, 39, 40, 42, 50, 80, 120, 126, 151, 164, 170, 171, 220, 229, 233, 240, 242, 293, 299, 301, 302, 303, 327. *See also* in-between strata
nationalism, 3–4, 8, 16, 17, 58, 74, 77, 104, 249, 251, 254, 257, 283, 287, 300, 305, 313, 315, 376–377
nationalist assumptions, 12, 75, 119, 293, 302
"nationalist deviation," 248, 249, 251, 260, 264, 285
nationality committee, 101, 106, 121, 122, 127, 142
"nationality follows language," 12, 318
National Party. *See* National Democratic Party
national self-determination, 2, 9, 10, 11, 12, 13, 19, 57, 59, 60, 70, 318, 332
National Socialist German Workers' Party. *See* Nazi party
nation-state, 1, 10, 11, 12, 14, 16, 57, 58–59, 61, 120, 195, 196, 251, 255, 300, 308, 315
Nazi party, 17, 27, 32, 34, 90, 97, 123, 124, 125, 126, 143, 169, 172, 177, 185, 264, 267, 279, 288, 289, 295
Neisse. *See* Oder-Neisse
Nidzica, x, 92, 182, 247, 264
Niemodlin, x, 102, 141, 251, 292, 294
Nikifor, 243
Nitschke, Bernadetta, 119, 274, 327
NKVD. *See* People's Commissariat of Internal Affairs
Nowiny Opolskie, 130
Nowy Tomyśl, x, 98, 99, 113, 138, 151, 152, 164
NSDAP. *See* Nazi Party
Nysa, x, 90, 189

Oborniki, x, 68, 153
Ochab, Edward, 91, 94, 115, 123, 230, 231, 262
Oder. *See* Oder-Neisse
Oder-Neisse, viii, 13, 22, 23, 24, 53, 55, 57, 62–63, 64, 65, 66, 67, 71, 73, 91, 96, 97, 98, 107, 130, 136, 137, 138, 165, 172, 179, 181, 182, 191, 196, 227, 248, 255, 272, 279, 335, 384
Ojczyzna, 51, 74

Olbracht-Prondzyński, Cezary, 306
"Old Reich," 30, 37, 38, 41, 50
Olecko, x, 16, 131
Olesno, x, 79, 101, 173, 175, 292
Oleśnica, x, 221
Olkusz, ix, x, 41, 158
Olsztyn: municipality, viii, x, 105, 127, 194, 247, 256; province, 71, 106, 128, 146–149, 167, 180–183, 192, 195, 220, 223, 237–238, 243–244, 245–250, 252, 253, 256, 260–265, 273–274, 276, 277, 279, 280, 283, 284, 292, 294–296, 298, 363; Land Office, 93; District Nationality Committee, 101; county 127, 192, 263, 293. *See also* Allenstein
Operation Vistula, 243
Opole: municipality, viii, ix, x, 93, 125, 134, 176, 188, 230, 251, 292, 336; region, xi, 14, 22, 55, 56, 62, 66, 71, 78–79, 87, 88, 93, 94, 105, 106, 107, 120–121, 123, 124, 126, 130, 134, 139, 140, 141, 146, 147, 148, 149, 165, 166, 167, 172, 178, 185, 192, 195, 197, 202, 220, 221, 222, 230, 252, 255, 257, 273, 275, 279, 282, 285, 292, 293, 294, 296, 297, 307; county, 125, 191, 222, 231, 251, 257, 275; apostolic administration, 129, 234. *See also* German *under* Upper Silesia
Opole Silesia. *See* region *under* Opole
Oppeln. *See* Opole
Organization of Ukrainian Nationalists, 242
Ortelsburg. *See* Szczytno
Osmańczyk, Edmund, 79
Osóbka-Morawski, Edward, 74, 352
Ossowski, Stanisław, xi, 79, 88, 103, 124, 135, 307, 383
Ostforschung, 19, 20–21, 22, 71, 72, 110, 305
Ostpolitik, 20
Ostróda, x, 245, 246
Ostrów, x, 153, 214
Ottoman Empire, 11. *See also* Turkey
OUN. *See* Organization of Ukrainian Nationalists

"*palcówka*," 38, 326
Palestine, 2, 203
pan-Slavism, 58
Paris Peace Conference, 10, 22
Parliamentary election, 95, 200, 217, 218, 219, 244
patriotism, 13, 16, 20, 21, 35, 47, 58, 59, 60, 72, 74, 79, 80, 104, 115, 128, 144, 162, 195, 213, 215, 297, 301
Peasant Party, 132, 281

Penck, Albrecht, 20, 22
pénétration pacifique, 19
People's Commissariat of Internal Affairs, 58, 74, 91, 97, 242, 306
Piast: rulers, 1, 13, 22, 23, 61, 66, 70, 333, 334; territory, 13, 15, 71, 87, 129, 137, 335; ethnic homogeneity, 70
Pilichowski, Czesław, 83, 199, 249
Pisz, x, 127, 283
PKWN. *See* Polish Committee of National Liberation
plebiscites, 12, 13, 14, 16, 17, 18, 21, 39, 81, 82, 121, 222, 294, 297, 306, 338
Podolians, 8
Polish-Americans, 57, 63
Polish Armed Forces, 163, 164
Polish-Bolshevik War, 17
Polish Committee of National Liberation, 52, 62, 63, 64, 80, 82, 83, 86, 106, 242
Polish communists. *See* Communist Party of Poland; Polish United Workers' Party; Polish Workers' Party; Union of Polish Patriots
"Polish Federal Soviet Republic," 58
Polish-German border, 12, 14, 22, 24, 53, 64, 137, 187, 188, 201, 203, 275. *See also* Oder-Neisse
Polish-German borderlands, 1, 2, 3, 4, 5, 6, 17, 19, 22, 59, 67, 75, 91, 92, 95, 97, 101, 107, 119, 136, 145, 175, 189, 228, 242, 297, 299, 300, 301, 302, 303, 304, 308
Polish government-in-exile, 41, 42, 51, 52, 53, 54, 56, 58, 62, 65, 74, 82, 83, 116, 163, 212, 328
Polish-Lithuanian Commonwealth, 1, 8, 9, 18
Polish Military Mission, 138, 161, 162, 163, 221
"Polish national distinctiveness," 111, 112, 113, 157, 159, 169, 201, 210
Polish nationality, 4, 74, 94, 96, 98, 107, 119, 120, 121, 122, 123, 124, 125, 126, 128, 138, 139, 141, 143, 159, 162, 164, 170, 171, 172, 182, 184, 187, 189, 202, 206, 211, 215, 218, 220, 222, 223, 224, 225, 230, 237, 239, 240, 244, 252, 263, 265, 266, 269, 289, 290, 293. *See also* Polishness; Polish origin
Polishness, 4, 18, 34, 41, 43, 56, 61, 72, 75, 76, 78, 79, 82, 85, 94, 105, 115, 117, 119, 120, 121, 122, 123, 124, 126, 128, 130, 135, 140, 143, 146, 150, 155, 158, 161, 167, 170, 172, 173, 174, 177, 178, 181, 183, 184, 188, 189, 192, 193, 194, 196, 198, 200, 215, 218, 222, 227, 228, 232, 238, 240, 242, 249, 263, 269, 293, 299, 303, 304, 335, 352, 364. *See also* Polish nationality; Polish origin

Polish origin, 1, 4, 14, 21, 24, 37, 48, 75, 76, 77, 82, 85, 86, 87, 94, 96, 101, 103, 106, 107, 113, 119, 120, 121, 122, 123, 124, 127, 128, 138, 139, 142, 143, 144, 146, 166, 168, 170, 171, 176, 177, 178, 179, 180, 181, 185, 186, 192, 195, 198, 199, 207, 221, 222, 223, 226, 230, 238, 246, 248, 252, 253, 258, 260, 266, 268, 269, 299, 344. *See also* Polish nationality; Polishness
Polish Peasant Party, 133, 140, 144, 150, 153, 164, 165, 173, 174, 197, 210, 219
Polish Socialist Party, 10, 85, 109, 134, 143, 148, 189, 210, 227, 248, 251
Polish-Soviet border, 25, 54, 55, 59, 61, 65, 330. *See also* Curzon Line
Polish spirit, 90, 113, 122, 124, 130, 160, 177, 178, 210, 239, 247, 266, 268, 289. *See also* Polishness
Polish underground resistance, 42, 45, 48, 50, 51–52, 80, 152, 322. *See also* Home Army
Polish United Workers' Party, 248, 249, 251, 252, 255, 261, 262, 264, 270, 271, 272, 273, 274, 276, 278, 280, 281, 282, 283, 285, 286, 287, 288, 294, 295, 296, 297
Polish Western Idea. *See Polska myśl zachodnia*
Polish Western Union, 24, 72, 73, 74, 75, 79, 83, 94, 97, 110, 116, 120, 123, 125, 133, 135, 140, 152, 164, 168, 169, 171, 172, 173, 174, 175, 176, 179, 181, 182, 183, 190, 193, 194, 195, 196, 197, 198, 199, 206, 211, 212, 213, 214, 217, 220, 224, 226, 227, 233, 239, 240, 241, 247, 249, 250, 267, 271, 272
Polish Workers' Party, 51, 60, 61, 68, 73, 74, 77, 87, 94, 96, 97, 102, 109, 113, 114, 117, 120, 130, 132, 134, 137, 141, 149, 151, 152, 153, 164, 165, 170, 171, 172, 173, 174, 182, 188, 193, 195, 197, 200, 210, 211, 217, 218, 219, 227, 228, 230, 241, 243, 247, 248, 249, 250, 251, 295, 417
"Polnische Wirtschaft," 198, 303, 383
Polonization, 5, 15, 17, 18, 34, 36, 43, 44, 46, 56, 64, 75, 76, 78, 80, 81, 83, 84, 86, 87, 107, 129, 130, 131, 135, 136, 142, 149, 159, 160, 165, 169, 170, 178, 181, 184, 188, 189, 194, 195, 196, 199, 215, 217, 229, 232, 233–236, 238, 239, 240, 241, 245, 246, 247, 249, 250, 252, 253, 254, 256, 257, 263, 265, 266, 271, 274, 279, 282, 283, 287, 294, 299, 304
Polska myśl zachodnia, 19, 20, 21, 22, 23, 24, 66, 70, 71, 72, 73, 110, 189, 305
Pomerania, ix, x, 9, 18, 22, 26, 28, 35, 42, 45, 47, 48, 50, 53, 59, 61, 62, 64, 71, 84, 85, 91, 93, 96, 97, 98, 102, 107, 109, 113, 125, 143, 148, 153, 157, 166, 178, 180, 197, 198, 199, 209, 211, 214, 225, 228, 237, 269, 287, 320. *See also* province *under* Szczecin; Western Pomerania
Pomeranians, 23, 76, 122, 162
Pope Pius XII, 129, 130, 279
Posen. *See* Poznań
Potsdam, 65–67, 97, 129, 136, 137, 138, 139, 151, 157, 165, 191
Potulice, 103, 188, 269
Poznań: municipality, viii, ix, x, 24, 29, 30, 36, 38, 48, 92, 110, 118, 119, 129, 139, 179, 255, 268, 288, 297, 351; province, x, 26, 69, 71, 91, 98, 99, 100, 110, 113, 117, 118, 122, 138, 143, 151, 152, 153, 154, 157, 160, 161, 164, 167, 192, 205, 208–209, 211, 212, 213, 214, 219, 224, 226, 228, 243, 252, 253, 265, 266, 268, 270, 271, 274, 289, 290, 291, 292, 294, 304; region, 22; university, 22, 23, 198; county, 99, 118, 209; district, 107, 226, 289. *See also* Great Poland; Wartheland
Późny, Walter, 92, 101, 133, 246, 247, 261, 263
PPR. *See* Polish Workers' Party
PPS. *See* Polish Socialist Party
Prawin, Jakub, 94, 121, 122, 126, 127, 130, 132, 133, 161, 170
"private fatherland," 293, 301, 383
"proletarian internationalism," 241, 248, 260, 263
propaganda, 10, 14, 16, 17, 18, 21, 49, 58, 73, 77, 83, 93, 113, 120, 126, 132, 137, 140, 164, 171, 173, 184, 185, 187, 192, 210, 217, 226, 228, 244, 245, 247, 254, 255, 259, 261, 265, 268, 271, 277, 278, 279, 280, 282, 283, 287, 294, 295, 303, 352
property: abandoned, 82, 87, 88, 105, 106, 145, 147, 148, 153, 166, 178, 212, 222, 284; disputed, 118, 128, 145–149, 180, 181, 184, 185, 188, 193, 210, 211, 212, 213, 214, 218–219, 222, 223, 226, 227, 228, 229, 247, 264, 270, 275, 278, 288, 303, 356. *See also* confiscation of property
Protectorate of Bohemia and Moravia, ix, 31, 35; *See also* Czechoslovakia
Provisional Government of National Unity, 65, 180, 210
Provisional Government of the Polish Republic, 64, 71, 92, 100, 107, 110
Prudnik, x, 89, 126, 140, 173, 191
Prussia, 1, 8, 11, 13, 16, 17, 18, 22, 24, 26, 27, 36, 41, 45, 56, 72, 84, 110, 131, 243. *See also* East Prussia; Prussian Poland
Prussian Poland, 11, 41, 318
Prussians, xi, 16, 21, 32, 56, 79, 87, 131, 263, 333

INDEX 399

Prussian Union Evangelical Church, 18, 130, 131
Przegląd Społeczny, 9
Przegląd Zachodni, 77, 85
PSL. *See* Polish Peasant Party
PUR. *See* State Repatriation Office
PZPR. *See* Polish United Workers' Party
PZZ. *See* Polish Western Union

race, 3, 7, 9, 10, 14, 19, 20, 21, 23, 24, 25, 29, 31, 32, 33, 34, 35, 36, 37, 38, 43, 45, 48, 49, 50, 62, 69, 121, 156, 161, 164, 169, 301, 305, 306, 322, 324
Racibórz, x, 275, 292
Radkiewicz, Stanisław, 52, 216
Raitz von Frentz, Christian, 11
rape, 68, 92, 93, 95, 100, 102, 121, 142, 186
Rastembork. *See* Kętrzyn
Rastenburg. *See* Kętrzyn
Recovered Lands Exhibition, 248, 251
referendum, 170, 171, 172, 173, 174, 175, 176, 182, 188, 201, 203, 205, 210, 217, 236, 368
regional identity. *See under* identity
regionalism, 85, 132, 156, 250. *See also* separatism
Reich, Greater German, 27, 300
Reich Commission for the Consolidation of German Nationhood, 27, 29, 30, 33
Reich Interior Ministry. *See* Interior Ministry, Reich
Reichsbürger, 31. *See also* citizenship
Reichsdeutsche, 99, 110, 115, 179, 220. *See also* citizenship
Reichsgau Danzig-West Prussia. *See* Danzig-West Prussia
Reichsgau Wartheland. *See* Wartheland
Renan, Ernest, 12, 305–306
"renegades," 34, 37, 83, 85, 103, 128, 162
Research Council for Issues of the Recovered Lands, 74, 76, 77, 88, 128, 183, 218, 249, 250
Research on the East. *See* Ostforschung
Reszel, x, 223, 293
Rhineland, 18–19
Richmond, Anthony, 68
Riga, Treaty of, 330
Rippin. *See* Rypin
RKF. *See* Reich Commission for the Consolidation of German Nationhood
Robel, Zygmunt, 131, 170, 180
Robotnik, 190, 195, 301
Rogalski, Mieczysław, 80–81, 82, 83

Rokossovsky, Konstantin, 95, 97, 249
Roma, 2, 6, 30, 202, 256, 314
Romer, Eugeniusz, 22
Roosevelt, Franklin, 55, 56, 57, 62, 63, 66
Royal Prussia, 8, 84
Ruhr, 31, 81, 110
Russian Poland, 13, 15, 301, 330
Ruthenian, 8, 9
Rybnik, x, 112, 116, 158, 182, 206, 228, 235
Rypin, ix, 44

SA. *See* Sturm-Abteilung
sanacja, 83, 261, 286
Saybusch. *See* Żywiec
Schieder, Theodor, 21
Schlonsaks, 32, 40
Schumacher, Kurt, 232
Scotland, 6, 115
Selbstschutz militias. *See* "self-defense" militias
"self-defense" militias, 49
Sensburg. *See* Mrągowo
separatism, 18, 19, 83, 85, 131, 150, 235, 250, 251. *See also* regionalism
Service for Poland, 283, 287
Sichelberg. *See* Sierpc
Sierpc, ix, 35
Sikorski, Władysław, 41, 53, 55, 56, 60, 327
Silesia, ix, 9, 13, 14, 26, 48, 50, 61, 70, 77, 133, 343. *See also* Lower Silesia; Upper Silesia
Silesia, province of (post 1945), x, 71, 75, 79, 86, 87, 89, 96, 97, 100, 101, 103, 115, 116, 120, 121, 124, 125, 126, 133, 134, 135, 147, 149, 154, 159, 160, 163, 166, 167, 169, 173, 175, 178, 180, 183, 184, 185, 186, 187, 189, 190, 191, 192, 196, 205, 206, 207, 209, 211, 212, 215, 217, 218, 219, 220, 221, 222, 226, 228, 229, 230, 232, 233, 238, 239, 240, 241, 249, 252, 253, 254, 257, 258, 260, 261, 267, 273, 274, 276, 277, 279, 280, 282, 283, 292, 293, 296, 297, 298, 303, 307, 353, 385. *See also* province *under* Katowice
Silesian dialect, 13, 23, 39, 79, 88, 93, 133, 135, 189, 227, 235
Silesian Institute, 22, 158, 183, 235
Silesians, 15, 23, 50, 61, 76, 80, 85, 86, 88, 89, 90, 96, 97, 103, 116, 119, 128, 129, 133, 134, 135, 144, 158, 161, 162, 163, 173, 174, 175, 185, 187, 188, 200, 207, 212, 217, 233, 234, 236, 239, 241, 251, 252, 256, 258, 276, 286, 294, 297, 305, 307, 314, 336, 338, 341
Silesian Uprisings, 14, 40, 90, 97, 124, 126, 134, 135, 140, 174, 200, 222, 234, 241, 297, 365

Slonsaks. *See* Schlonsaks
"slonzakisch." *See* Silesian dialect
Slovaks, 256
Slovincians, 198–199, 258, 357, 365
Sławno, x, 95, 278
Słupsk, x, 84, 95, 150, 198, 248, 275, 278
Smith, Anthony, 3
Sohrau. *See* Żory
Sokorski, Włodzimierz, 172–173
Soldau. *See* Działdowo
Solidarity Trade Union, 2, 4
Sopot, 125, 139, 274
Sorbs, 23
Southeast Prussia, 26, 45, 46, 47
sowietnik, 133, 352
SS, 27, 28, 30, 34, 46, 49, 50, 96, 115, 124, 263, 264
Staatsangehörige. *See* state member
Stakhanovites, 286
Stalin, Joseph, 52, 53, 55, 56, 57, 58, 62–63, 65, 67, 93, 96, 97, 132, 133, 333
Stalingrad, 158
Stalinism, 241
Stalinist, 4, 271, 295
Stalinization, 250
state member, 31, 32, 33, 34, 37, 39, 40
State Repatriation Office, 86, 87, 89, 105, 117, 118, 141, 145, 146, 150, 154, 160, 183, 187, 195, 208, 212, 213, 220, 223, 243
Stettin. *See* Szczecin
Stoß, Veit, 21
Strauchold, Grzegorz, 220, 356, 363, 365, 367
Stryjkowski, Krzysztof, 214, 228, 326
Strzelce, x, 97, 140, 292
Sturm-Abteilung, 17, 115, 124
Sudeten Germans, 12, 337
Supreme Council of the Allies (World War I), 14, 330
Syców, x, 179, 180, 339
Synak, Brunon, 307
Szamotuły, x, 99, 212
Szczecin: municipality, viii, x, 53, 119, 173, 179, 194, 198, 201, 202, 365; province, x, 71, 84–85, 95, 166, 167, 178, 179, 193, 198, 201, 218, 219, 220, 221, 243, 245, 250, 252, 253, 255, 256, 258, 259, 273, 274, 278, 279, 280, 292, 293; region, 165. *See also* Pomerania; Western Pomerania
Szczytno, ix, x, 17, 132, 181, 238, 246, 247, 248, 261, 262, 263, 283, 293, 294, 295
Szklarska Poręba, 241
Szramek, Emil, 15

Sztum, x, 124, 131, 142, 146, 149, 187, 194, 293, 352

Ślązacki, 38
Świdnica, x, 95, 275
Świerczewski, Karol, 98, 243

Tarnowskie Góry, x, 154, 163, 292
task forces of security personnel. *See* Einsatzgruppen
Tczew, x, 139
Tehran Conference, 57, 63
Teschen. *See* Austrian Silesia; Cieszyn
Teutonic Knights, 16, 66, 82, 87, 209, 228, 333
Thorn. *See* Toruń
Toruń, ix, 44, 103, 148
transnational, 1, 2, 3, 313
Transnistria, 30
Truman, Harry, 66, 67
Turek, x, 138, 229, 268, 294
Turkey, 12, 54, 56, 62
Turks, 11, 12
Turowicz, Jerzy, 384

Ukraine, 6, 62, 70, 86, 96, 242, 243
Ukrainian Insurgent Army, 242
Ukrainian language, 264
Ukrainianness, 242
Ukrainian-Polish borderland, 242
Ukrainians, 3, 8, 9, 26, 52, 59, 63, 187, 241–244, 277
Union of Mazurs, 18, 81–83
Union of Peasant Self-Help, 176, 211
Union of Poles in Germany, 74, 78, 79, 85, 90, 92, 102, 105, 128, 134, 135, 140, 144, 174, 194, 199, 217, 257, 297, 336, 356
Union of Polish Patriots, 60, 61, 62
Union of Polish Youths, 280, 281, 282, 287
Union of Veterans of the Silesian Uprisings, 174, 234, 365
United Nations, 55
United Nations Relief and Rehabilitation Administration, 138, 167
UNRRA. *See* United Nations Relief and Rehabilitation Administration
UPA. *See* Ukrainian Insurgent Army
Upper Silesia: region, 9, 12, 13, 36, 39, 162, 165, 201, 214, 240, 251, 257, 297, 307; identity, 13, 79; German, 14, 15, 23, 38, 51, 53, 55, 70, 71, 87, 88, 89, 165, 190, 206; Polish, 14, 15, 26, 32, 34, 35, 37, 38, 39, 40, 41, 42, 44, 47, 48, 49, 50, 59, 64, 73, 79, 89, 90, 103, 109, 110, 111, 115,

116, 117, 135, 154, 158, 165, 169, 188, 189, 233, 234, 327; inhabitants, 15, 20, 32, 33, 34, 38, 30, 39, 40, 41, 42, 49, 77, 80, 96, 111, 116, 151, 162, 165, 169, 353. *See also* Silesia

Vatican, 130
Verband der Leistungspolen. *See* Association of Productive Poles
Versailles, Treaty of, 2, 11, 14, 16, 18, 19, 20, 22, 54
Vistula, viii, 22, 23, 66, 335
Volhynia, 242, 244, 322
Volhynian, 8
Volksboden, 20
Volksgemeinschaft, 19, 21, 33, 50
Voluntary Reserve of the Civil Militia, 200, 287

Wadowice, x, 114
Wałbrzych, x, 275, 278
Wałcz, x, 245, 295
Wandycz, Piotr S., 332
Wannsee Conference, 29
Warmia, 45, 61, 71, 87, 106, 127, 129, 131, 192, 256, 285
Warmiaks, 101, 105, 111, 121, 122, 127, 133, 142, 146, 174, 181, 192, 221, 223, 258, 262, 274, 284, 286, 303, 380
Warmia-Mazuria, 352
Warmian consciousness, 173
Warsaw, province of, x, 26, 100, 106, 107, 110, 111, 112, 117, 131, 132, 224
Warsaw Uprising, 51, 68, 73
Warthegau. *See* Wartheland
Wartheland, ix, 26, 27, 28–30, 33, 36–38, 39, 46, 47, 48, 110, 208, 210, 211, 225, 229, 271, 323, 324
Warthenau. *See* Zawiercie
Wasilewski, Leon, 9
Wasser-Poles, 32. *See also* inhabitants *under* Upper Silesia
Wągrowiec, x, 117
Wejherowo, x, 160
Wends, 20
werewolves. *See* German underground resistance
Western Allies (World War II), 52, 54, 55, 56, 63, 65, 97, 98, 137, 140, 219, 232, 249, 259
western border, Poland, 1, 10, 22, 52, 61, 62, 70, 72, 86, 91, 98, 174, 192. *See also* Oder-Neisse
Western Institute, 74, 77, 110, 114
western Poland, 1, 4, 20, 27

Western Pomerania, 61, 72, 84, 93, 98, 107, 125, 143, 166, 178, 180, 198. *See also* Pomerania; province *under* Szczecin
Western Powers. *See* Western Allies (World War II)
West Germany. *See* Federal Republic of Germany
West Prussia, 28, 43, 49, 50. *See also* Danzig-West Prussia
Węgorzewo, x, 106
Widy-Wirski, Feliks, 138, 143, 209, 210, 211
Wielkopolska. *See* Great Poland; province *under* Poznań
Wilamowice, 99, 114, 115, 156, 158
Wilamowski, Bohdan, 92, 183, 261, 301
Wilkowice, 115
Wilno, viii, 63
Wilson, Woodrow, 10, 11, 20
Wojciechowski, Zygmunt, 23, 24, 74
Wola Ludu, 205, 211
Wolf, Gerhard, 6, 36, 326
Wolin, x, 278, 280
Wollstein. *See* Wolsztyn
Wolski, Władysław, 86, 87, 116, 128, 181, 192
Wolsztyn, ix, 37, 326
Workers' Association of the Friends of Children, 240
Wrocław: municipality, viii, ix, x, 63, 129, 201, 221, 248, 250, 251; province, x, 71, 95, 167, 177, 179, 180, 199, 243, 248, 249, 252, 253, 273, 274, 278, 292; archdiocese, 129
Wrocław-Psie Pole, 223
Września, x, 89, 271
Wrzosek, Antoni, 22, 24
Wyka, Kazimierz, 104, 345
Wysłouch, Bolesław, 9, 317

Yalta, conference of, 64–65, 72, 86, 91
Yugoslav communist party, 241, 248
Yugoslavia, 3, 6, 93, 248

Zabrze, x, 77, 124, 134, 217, 230, 257
Zaleski, August, 54
Zawadzki, Aleksander, 75, 85, 93–94, 97, 100, 106, 107, 109, 115, 116, 120, 125, 126, 133, 135, 138, 139, 140, 141, 144, 145, 147, 159, 172, 175, 177, 184, 187, 188, 231, 232, 233, 234, 235, 236, 239, 240, 248, 253, 254, 257, 356
Zawiercie, ix, 41
Zhukov, Georgy, 95
Zichenau. *See* Ciechanów
Zielona Góra, x, 187, 224, 256, 292, 356

Ziemia Lubuska. See Lubusz Land
Ziętek, Jerzy, 134, 187, 234, 241, 365
Złotów, x, 84, 85, 96, 102, 140, 143, 144, 174, 179, 193, 275, 278, 293, 339, 356
Zmorski, Roman, 23
ZMP. *See* Union of Polish Youths
ZPP. *See* Union of Polish Patriots
ZPwN. *See* Union of Poles in Germany
Zrzesz Kaszebsko, 150, 281, 282

Zylberberg, Benjamin, 78, 93, 111, 133, 134

Żądzbork. *See* Mrągowo
Żmudzins, 8
Żołna, Szymon, 72
Żory, ix, 39
Żymierski, Michał, 98
Żywiec, ix, x, 43, 114, 117, 156